SK

S0-AEP-600

The European Discovery of America

of America

THE SOUTHERN VOYAGES
A.D. 1492-1616

OTHER BOOKS BY SAMUEL ELIOT MORISON

The Life and Letters of Harrison Gray Otis, 2 vols., 1913

The Maritime History of Massachusetts, 1921, 1941

The Oxford History of the United States, 2 vols., 1927

Builders of the Bay Colony, 1930, 1964

The Tercentennial History of Harvard University, 4 vols., 1929–36

Three Centuries of Harvard, 1936, 1963

Portuguese Voyages to America Before 1500, 1940

Admiral of the Ocean Sea: A Life of Christopher Columbus, 1942

Christopher Columbus, Mariner, 1955

History of U. S. Naval Operations in World War II, 15 vols., 1947–62

By Land and By Sea, 1953

The Intellectual Life of Colonial New England, 1956

Freedom in Contemporary Society, 1956

The Story of the "Old Colony" of New Plymouth, 1956

John Paul Jones: A Sailor's Biography, 1959

The Story of Mount Desert Island, 1960

One Boy's Boston, 1962

The Two-Ocean War, 1963

Vistas of History, 1964

Spring Tides, 1965

The Oxford History of the American People, 1965

Life of Commodore Matthew C. Perry, 1794–1858, 1967

Harrison Gray Otis, The Urbane Federalist, 1969

The European Discovery of America: The Northern Voyages A.D. 500–1600, 1971

Samuel de Champlain, Father of New France, 1972

WITH HENRY STEELE COMMAGER AND WILLIAM E. LEUCHTENBURG

The Growth of the American Republic, 2 vols., 1930, 1969

WITH MAURICIO OBREGÓN

The Caribbean as Columbus Saw It, 1964

Magellan's fleet leaving Seville.
(Painting in Naval Officer's Club, Valparaiso de Chile)

The European Discovery of America

THE SOUTHERN VOYAGES

A.D. 1492-1616

SAMUEL ELIOT MORISON

New York OXFORD UNIVERSITY PRESS 1974

To the memory of my beloved wife

Priscilla Barton Morison

1906–1973

"And o'er the hills, and far away
 Beyond their utmost purple rim,
Beyond the night, across the day,
 Through all the world she followed him."

Tennyson's "Day-Dream," The Departure, stanza IV.

Preface

This volume completes my European Discovery of America. The first volume, *The Northern Voyages*, which the Oxford University Press published in 1971, covered voyages to Canada and the northern United States to 1600; and, as a supplement, Atlantic Press brought out next year my *Samuel de Champlain, Father of New France*. Now I return to Columbus, of whom I have been an almost lifelong student, and carry the story of the Southern Voyages down to 1616 when Le Maire and Schouten discovered Cape Horn. The core of this volume, however, relates to the work of three of the greatest navigators of history, Columbus, Magellan, and Drake, and the story of their voyages is told in greater detail than those of the others, partly because of their importance, but also because we know more about them. My readers should not expect accounts of the great conquests such as Mexico, Peru, New Granada, and Brazil—or of the colonial wars such as the Franco-Spanish quarrel over Florida. In a book of this scope I have had to limit the story to voyages—to how the conquerors got here. And much of what appeared on shipbuilding and navigation in my *Northern Voyages* needs no repetition.

Pray keep in mind the vast length of these Southern Voyages compared with the Northern. The crossing of the North Atlantic from

Bristol in the west of England to St. John's, Newfoundland, is only 1940 nautical miles, and 700 miles more will take a ship to Quebec. The entire coastal voyage from New York around Florida to Galveston, Texas, is only 1887 miles. Columbus's great circle distance from Gomera, his 1492 jumping-off place in the Canaries, to San Salvador in the Bahamas, was 3116 nautical miles, whilst his shortest transatlantic crossing, from Gomera to Dominica in 1502, measures 2500 miles. But suppose your destination to have been the Strait of Magellan. First, you have a 1529-mile sail from Cadiz to São Vicente in the Cape de Verdes; then a 1616-mile ocean crossing direct to Pernambuco (Recife), just under the bulge of Brazil, and after that you must coast South America for 2062 miles to reach Montevideo, touching at Rio de Janeiro halfway. If you cross the River Plate and continue along Patagonia to the entrance of the Strait of Magellan, you would have to cover another 1254 nautical miles.* So it is no wonder that the Southern Voyages, at least those south of the Caribbean, required months rather than weeks, or that their leading problem was food. You seldom hear of food giving out on a Northern transatlantic voyage in the sixteenth century, but on Southern Voyages scurvy and starvation were commonplace; and very many, perhaps a majority of the men who set out on them, never returned.

What made them do it? I wish I knew. Was it mere adventure and glory, or lust for gold or (as they all declared) a zeal to enlarge the Kingdom of the Cross? Bernal Diaz del Castillo well said, in his *Historia Verdadera* of the conquest of Mexico, "We came here to serve God, and also to get rich." One quality all these mariners had in common with the ancient Greeks was restlessness. Just as Ulysses, returning home to Penelope after infinite pains and wanderings, had to make one last voyage; just as Alexander, after marching to northern India, regretted there were no more worlds to conquer; so these paladins of discovery never had enough. Columbus could have settled for a castle in Spain and a pension after any one of his first three voyages; but he always had to make one more. Sebastian Cabot held an honorable and

---

* These figures are for the shortest, great circle course between two points, except where I have followed modern steamship courses in Brown's Almanac, or "stepped it off" on a modern chart. The actual course sailed, owing to wind fluctuation and other causes, was always considerably longer. For the 1492 calculations, see John W. McElroy in *American Neptune*, I (1941), pp. 215–16. Columbus estimated that he had sailed 3466 nautical miles.

lucrative position in Spain, but he had to go to sea and prove himself a sailor. Drake sailed around the world, brought home (some say) a million pounds in booty, bought a country estate, and set up as an English squire; but, at the first call, off again to sea went he, and at sea he left his bones. And many other examples of this restlessness my readers will see.

Few of the sources and other writings on voyages south of the Caribbean are in English. The historians who have mainly concerned themselves with these voyages have been Spaniards, Portuguese, Brazilians, Uruguayans, Argentinians, Chileans, and Paraguayans. And so are practically all those now living. Their works, many in the form of short magazine articles, are almost never reviewed or even noticed in England or North America. Thus, most readers in English-speaking countries have never heard of such important figures as Ladrillero, Loaysa, and Sarmiento de Gamboa. The greatest of all, Columbus, Magellan, and Drake, are indeed well known; but I have contributed something new in retracing their courses at sea.

T. S. Eliot's injunction in his *East Coker*, "Old men ought to be explorers," has appealed to me; and I would add, "Young historians, too!" In the 1930s I followed Columbus across the Atlantic and around the West Indies in barquentine *Capitana* and ketch *Mary Otis*, to write *Admiral of the Ocean Sea* and *Christopher Columbus, Mariner*. In 1963 Mauricio Obregón flew me around the Caribbean, with his wife and David Crofoot as photographers, and my wife as passenger, resulting in *The Caribbean as Columbus Saw It* (1964). In preparation for the volume at hand, Obregón and James F. Nields flew me in the latter's Baron Beechcraft to cover landfalls and routes of Pinzón, Cabral, Vespucci, and Cabot along the coast of Brazil and (following Cabeza de Vaca's second stupendous walk) to Asunción, Paraguay. In May 1973 my daughter Emily Beck and my old friend John Gordon accompanied me to California, where the United States Coast Guard lent us a cutter to check up on Drake's landing. Everywhere the navies of the United States and Great Britain have afforded me assistance, as did the navies of Brazil, the Argentine, and Chile in their waters.

I cannot claim to have followed the discoverers of the River Plate under sail; but I have flown over that great inland waterway where the adaptable Spaniards rowed, towed, and kedged their *bergantinas* for thousands of miles. There is nothing like a personal visit to newly discovered lands to bring home to one the pioneers' dangers and difficulties. My admiration for them increases with time. For years I have been living with the records of heroic navigators and with the ordinary grousing, grumbling, believing but blaspheming mariner. God bless 'em all! The world will never see their like again.

Maps are still a problem. The difficulties inherent in reproducing old maps in a book of this format are still insurmountable; so in this volume I have largely substituted original maps by Vaughn Gray, for which my readers will doubtless be grateful. Fortunately there is now available a quarto edited by W. P. Cumming, R. A. Skelton, and D. B. Quinn, *The Discovery of North America* (New York: American Heritage Press, 1972), an ideal companion to my *Northern Voyages* and, to a lesser degree, to this volume. Here these three cartographical scholars have produced in color some of the most important mappemondes such as the Cantino (1502), the Vespucci (1526), the Ribero (1529), the Royal Library of the Hague (1540), and the Rotz (1542), which include parts of Florida, California, and Central and South America, and have added hundreds of black-and-white maps and illustrations. Yet even they have been unable to make the toponymy of the oldest maps legible, and for that the scholar must still resort to the old folio reproductions, and the modern *Portugaliae Monumenta Cartographica* (1960), and *Mapas Españoles de América Siglos XV–XVII* (Madrid, 1951, Duke of Alba head of the editorial board).

For want of facts from which to generalize, dialectic has played an inordinate part in the history of American discovery. "Occam's Razor," a principle of the schoolman William of Occam that in explaining obscure matters, imaginary things should never be postulated as existing,* is so frequently violated that mythical coasts and islands have become almost as substantial as New York. I am all in favor of Occam's Razor, and would rather leave something unexplained than create imaginary links in a shadowy chain. Now that my English colleague Parkinson has formulated "Parkinson's Law," I venture to add two principles which, if you will, you may call "Morison's Musings":—(1) The invention or publication of some new method of navigation does not prove that it was promptly used at sea, as the school of the late Professor E. G. R. Taylor generally assumes; and (2) No theory is valid

---

* As he put it, *Entia non sunt multiplicanda praeter necessitatem.*

that makes nonsense of what follows. To illustrate the second point: If there were any truth in the theory now favored by several English geographers, that men of Bristol discovered Newfoundland in 1480, the prudent and economical Henry VII would never have called it the "New Isle," much less rewarded John Cabot for discovering it. Whilst crackpot theories about Columbus continue to proliferate, and Portuguese historians still claim that their compatriots were first everywhere, I do not have to deal with so much nonsense here as in my *Northern Voyages*. Nobody has yet claimed that Vikings sailed through the great Strait before Magellan, but my revered master Leo Wiener insisted that Africans were in Mexico ahead of Cortés, and Professor Cyrus W. Gordon of Brandeis University has Phoenicians swarming over Brazil even before that.

A word as to dates. All to 1582 are in the Julian Calendar. The Gregorian Calendar, which we still use, went into effect that year in Spain, Portugal, Italy, France, and certain provinces of the Netherlands; but the Protestant countries stuck to the Julian for a century or more after that. Dates of round-the-world voyages are one day too early from Guam westward (as Elcano and Drake later discovered), because sailors knew no international date line. Another source of misunderstanding is the nautical day used in ships' logs, which began at noon until well into the twentieth century. That is why, for instance, the pilot Albo's dates often differ from Pigafetta's on Magellan's voyage.

Many, many people have helped me. First, as always, my wife, to whose blessed memory this volume is dedicated. Miss Antha E. Card, my devoted and efficient secretary for twenty-three years, performed numerous research tasks besides typing and retyping, checking, and compiling the index. Librarians, notably Miss Wallis of the British Museum and Mr. Trout of the Harvard Map Room, have been most helpful. Airlifts by Messrs. Obregón and Nields were indispensable. My daughter Catharine Cooper performed valuable research at the British Museum and Greenwich, and helped me with the conclusion. Her sister Emily (Mrs. Brooks Beck) accompanied me to California to study Drake. My grandson Lt. (j.g.) Samuel Loring Morison USNR, at present in the Naval Intelligence Division at Washington, looked up such essential factors as tides and phases of the moon. Among my Harvard colleagues, Professors John H. Parry and Francis M. Rogers have been very helpful, Rogers particularly so with his knowledge of navigation, of early Portuguese voyages, and of the Iberian languages. He also read and criticized the entire typescript. Professor Rogers has also been of great assistance about Spanish and Portuguese spellings and accents, which differ in the two languages. For instance, *historia*, Spanish for "history," has no accent; *história*, the Portuguese word, has. After consulting with several Spanish scholars, I decided to place no accent on short words like *Rio, Luis, Maria*, and *Bahia*, and largely to suppress the circumflex accent in Portuguese. Of foreign historians, Capitão-de-mar-e-guerra Avelina Teixeira da Mota of Lisbon, Capitão-de-mar-e-guerra Max Justo Guedes of the Brazilian Navy, Colonel Rolando Laguarda Trías of the Uruguayan Army, Captain Laurio H. Destéfani of the Argentine Navy, and Dr. Ricardo Donoso of Santiago de Chile have given me freely of their time, advice, and wisdom. Nor have I forgotten old friends like Paul and Susy Hammond who helped me to organize and conduct the Harvard Columbus Expedition.

But, alas, this preface is written under the shadow of a great grief, the loss of my beloved Priscilla, still sharing my life as we approached the end of a long literary voyage. She accompanied me almost everywhere by land, sea, and air; her sparkling account of *Our Magellan Expedition from the Distaff Side* has been privately printed for distribution among our friends. Besides her innate and wonderful qualities of beauty, wit, gaiety, and grace, and her lovely singing and speaking voice, Priscilla was an excellent critic; and almost every page of this volume prior to the chapters on Drake, I read aloud to her before grievous pain made it impossible for her to pay attention. Her favorite criticism, born of her early experience on charitable boards, was, "Sam, that sounds like the secretary reading the minutes of the last meeting!" Any passage thus castigated was summarily removed or rewritten until it satisfied her. Thus my readers, as well as myself, owe Priscilla a great debt.

"Good Hope"   S. E. Morison
Northeast Harbor, Maine
15 May 1974

Contents

The European Discovery of America

of America

THE SOUTHERN VOYAGES

A.D. 1492-1616

Christopher Columbus

The African Background

On 12 October 1492, when the little fleet of Christopher Columbus raised a Bahamian island that he named San Salvador, neither he nor anyone else guessed that this would be an historic date. Even Columbus, who regarded himself as a child of destiny, thought he had merely found an outlying island to "the Indies." Had his entire fleet been wrecked, nobody would have been the wiser, and in all probability America would not have been discovered until 1500 when Pedro Álvares Cabral, on his way to the real India, sighted a mountain near the coast of Brazil. Thus, the entire history of Europeans in America stems from Columbus's First Voyage. The Northmen's discovery of Newfoundland almost five centuries earlier proved to be dead-end. Pre-Columbian Portuguese, Welsh, Irish, English, and Venetian voyages to America are modern-made myths, phantoms which left not one footprint on the sands of time. But Columbus's First Voyage proved to be the avant-garde for thousands of hidalgos who, weary of sustaining their haughty pride in poverty, were ready to hurl themselves on the New World in search of gold and glory.

Columbus's discovery led within a year to the first permanent European colony in America, in Hispaniola; and he himself made three more voyages of discovery, as well as sparking off those of Ojeda, Juan de La Cosa, the younger Pinzón, Vespucci, both Cabots, Magellan, and countless others. Not only the northern voyages, starting with John Cabot's of 1497, which are related in my earlier volume, but all southern voyages of discovery described in this volume, and Spain's vast empire stretching from Florida to Patagonia and out to the Philippines, stem from the First Voyage of that intrepid mariner and practical dreamer Christopher Columbus, Admiral of the Ocean Sea.*

Just as these southern voyages flow from Columbus's First, of 1492, so that was an indirect result of Portuguese voyages south along the west coast of Africa and out to the Madeiras and Azores. This had been going on since about 1430, when the Infante Dom Henrique (Prince Henry the Navigator) established himself at Sagres near Cape St. Vincent "where endeth land and where beginneth sea," as the great Portuguese poet Camoëns described it. There, a natural place for ships on all north-south routes to anchor, he set up a sort of information service where shipmasters might consult the latest charts and pick up useful data about wind and currents. This was no "naval academy" or "astronomical observatory" as some of the Infante's more enthusiastic biographers have maintained, but he did encourage the bolder navigators and reward new discoveries out of his royal revenues, with such success that his nephew D. Afonso V and great-nephew D. João II, kings of Portugal, carried on the good work after his death in 1460.

It took some time before D. Henrique could persuade anyone to round Cabo de Não ** on the western bulge of Africa, because of two superstitions: that one would never get back against the prevailing northerlies, and that anyone who persisted would run into boiling hot water at the Equator. Finally Gil Eanes, a Portuguese captain, rounded this cape in 1434 and found that the reputed terrors of the southern ocean did not exist, and that with a new type of ship, the

* Since ancient times Ocean had been regarded as one and indivisible.
** In English called Cape Nun, and subject of a punning verse:

> Quem passar o Cabo de Não
> Ou voltará ou não.

> When old Cape Nun heaves into sight
> Turn back, me lad, or else—good night!

It was, apparently, the next cape after the better known Bojador.

caravel, one could beat to windward and get back. Within a few years ships had gone far enough along West Africa to trade for black slaves and gold dust, and the Portuguese had erected a fortified trading factory on Arguin Island near latitude 20° N. By 1460, when the Infante died, his caravels had passed the site of Dakar and were within hailing distance of Sierra Leone, only ten degrees above the Equator.

It is still a matter of controversy whether or not D. Henrique consciously sought India by circumnavigating Africa. The Pope did indeed grant Portugal in 1455 exclusive jurisdiction over the coast of Guinea "and past that southern shore all the way to the Indians": but did he mean the real India or only the "Hither India" of Prester John? That mythical Christian potentate was supposed to hold sway somewhere in western Asia or northern Africa. The substance behind this legend was Ethiopia; but in European imagination Prester John was a more wealthy and powerful monarch than any of their own princes. Contact with him was ardently desired in order to kindle a Christian backfire against the infidel Turk. Columbus once thought he was hot on the trail of Prester John in Cuba!

For almost a decade after Prince Henry's death the Portuguese made no great progress southward, except to settle the Cape Verde Islands. Then, in 1469, D. Afonso V gave a Lisbon merchant named Fernão Gomes the monopoly of trading with the Guinea coast, on condition that he explore a hundred leagues farther every year. And there is no doubt that by this time the crown was seeking a southern sea route to India. Gomes's vessels promptly swung around the bulge and opened up the richest part of West Africa: the Gold and Ivory Coasts and Malagueta, where a variety of pepper almost as hot as the East Indian was found. By 1474, when his monopoly expired, Fernão Gomes had sent ships clean across the Gulf of Guinea and reached the island of Fernando Po on latitude 3°30′ N, where the African coast again turns southward.

In this African exploration the Portuguese developed a type of small sailing ship that they named *caravella*, the caravel. We know little of its hull design or construction, which, combined with its lateen sail plan, enabled the caravel to sail closer to the wind and faster than any square-rigger. This capability enabled a mariner to go as far as he pleased along the African coast, with assurance that he could get back. A long reach on the starboard tack, which the Portuguese called *a volta do* *mar largo*, would take her from the Canaries or the west coast of Africa to the Azores,* where she could replenish at the port of Angra in Terceira and catch a good slant for Lisbon.

This long hitch off soundings taught the Portuguese mariners confidence and led to the development of celestial navigation—shooting the sun or the North Star with astrolabe or quadrant, applying declination and working out your latitude. Land-based European geographers already knew how to calculate latitude by observation of sun and North Star, but to introduce those methods on board ship took time. Most master mariners and pilots of that era were illiterate, and for them the application of declination to altitude was an insoluble problem. Whether or not D. Henrique held "refresher courses" for pilots in Sagres, the fact is that by 1484, when Diogo Cão discovered the mouth of the Congo, Portuguese ships carried charts with a latitude grid, and Portuguese pilots had built up such a reputation that all organizers of Spanish, English, and French voyages of discovery sought to engage one for their ships.

All, that is, except Columbus. But he himself had been trained in the Portuguese service for years before beginning his great voyage.

Enter Columbus

Christopher Columbus was born Cristoforo Colombo, in or near the city of Genoa some time between 25 August and the end of October 1451. He was son and grandson to woolen weavers who had been living in various towns of the Genoese Republic for at least three generations. His long face, tall stature, ruddy complexion, and red hair suggest a considerable share of "barbarian" rather than "Latin" blood, but do not prove anything; and he himself was conscious only of his Genoese origin. There is no more reason to doubt that Christopher Columbus was a Genoa-born Catholic, steadfast in his faith and proud of his native city, than to doubt that Abraham Lincoln was born in Hardin, Kentucky, in 1809, of British stock.

This is not to say that Columbus was an Italian in the modern sense. The people of proud Genoa, *Genova la Superba*, have always held themselves apart from (and superior to) other Italians. In the *majorat*

* See my *European Discovery of America: The Northern Voyages*, pp. 94–97, for the Portuguese discovery of the Azores.

Christopher Columbus in middle age. Courtesy Museo Giovio, Como.

or entail of his estate that Columbus executed before departing on his Third Voyage to the New World, he charged his heirs "always to work for the honor, welfare and increase of the city of Genoa," and there to maintain a house for some member of the Colombo family, "so that he can live there honorably and have foot and root in that city as a native thereof . . . *because from it I came and in it I was*

7

born." And, "being as I was born in Genoa," his executors shall accumulate a fund in the Bank of St. George at Genoa, that "noble and powerful city by the sea."

Every contemporary Spaniard or Portuguese who wrote about Columbus and his discoveries calls him Genoese. Four contemporary Genoese chroniclers claim him as a compatriot. Every early map on which his nationality is recorded describes him as Genoese or *Ligur*, a citizen of the Ligurian Republic. Nobody in his lifetime, or for three centuries after, had any doubt about his origin or birthplace.

Nevertheless, by presenting far-fetched hypotheses as proved, and innuendoes as facts, by attacking authentic documents as false, and by fabricating others, Columbus has been presented as Castilian, Catalan, Corsican, Majorcan, Portuguese, French, German, English, Irish, Greek, Armenian, Polish, and Russian. And now, American! A Scandinavian writer named Thorwald Brynidsen has "proved" that the discoverer was a native North American, a descendant of the eleventh-century Norse colony. He built himself a Viking ship, sailed her to Spain, changed his name to Colón, and set forth to rediscover Vinland!

Enough of these fantasies.

Giovanni Colombo, the Discoverer's paternal grandfather, was a weaver, his son Domenico, a master weaver; hired a house just inside the Porta dell' Olivella, the eastern gate of Genoa. About 1445 he married Susanna Fontanarossa, daughter of another local weaver. She brought Domenico a small dowry, and he obtained a respectable municipal appointment as warder of the Olivella gate. In this house, near the gate, in a quarter so rebuilt that the site cannot now be definitely fixed, Cristoforo was born in the late summer or early fall of 1451.

Thus Columbus's forty-first birthday fell during his first great voyage of discovery. Very likely he did not remember the exact date, since boys and girls then celebrated the feast day of their patron saint rather than their own birthday. On 25 June, the feast of Saint Christopher, young Cristoforo would have made a point of attending Mass with his mother, and then would have received a little pocket money and a glass of wine from his father.

The story of Saint Christopher,* familiar to every child in the Middle Ages, made Columbus's baptismal name far more significant to him than his patronymic. Christopher was a great hulk of a pagan who,

---

* Recently and regrettably demoted from saintly status by the Vatican.

hearing of Christ, went forth in search of Him. A holy hermit said, "Perhaps Our Lord will show Himself to you if you fast and pray." "Fast I cannot," said Christopher, "and how to pray I know not; ask me something easier." So the hermit said, "Knowest thou that river without a bridge which can only be crossed at great peril of drowning?" "I do," said Christopher. "Very well, do thou who art so tall and strong take up thine abode by the hither bank, and assist poor travelers to cross; that will be very agreeable to Our Lord, and mayhap He will show Himself to thee." So Christopher built himself a cabin by the river bank and, with the aid of a tree trunk as staff, carried wayfarers across on his broad shoulders.

One night the big fellow was asleep in his cabin when he heard a child's voice cry, "Christopher! come and set me across!" Out he came, staff in hand, and took the infant on his shoulders. But as he waded through the river the child's weight increased so that it became almost intolerable, and he had to call forth all his strength to avoid falling and to reach the other bank. "Well now, my little fellow," said he, "thou hast put me in great danger, for thy burden waxed so great that had I borne the whole world on my back, it could have weighed no more than thou." "Marvel not, Christopher," replied the child, "for thou hast borne upon thy back the whole world and Him who created it. I am the Christ whom thou servest in doing good; and as proof of my words, plant that staff near thy cabin, and tomorrow it shall be covered with flowers and fruit." The saint did as he was bid, and found his staff next day transformed into a beautiful date palm.

This story would certainly have gone home to the boy who became the man we know as Columbus. He conceived it his destiny to carry the word of that Holy Child across the ocean to countries steeped in heathen darkness. Many years elapsed and countless discouragements were surmounted before anyone would afford him means to take up the burden. Once assumed, it often became intolerable, and often he staggered under it; but never did he set it down until his appointed work was done.

In 1455, when Christopher was four years old, his parents removed to a house with a courtyard and garden near the Porta Sant' Andrea. His next younger brother, Bartholomew, the future *Adelantado*, was then about two years old. His youngest brother, Giacomo or Diego, seems to have been Christopher's junior by seventeen years. Christopher felt for him the affection that an older brother often does for the baby of the family. He took him on his Second Voyage, and after ascertaining the young man to be an indifferent seaman and a bad administrator, helped him to obtain holy orders and made futile efforts to procure a bishopric for him.

Domenico Colombo, the father of these three boys, was a master clothier (to use the old English term) who owned one or more looms, bought his own wool, sold the finished cloth, and taught apprentice boys their trade. As a citizen of Genoa and member of the local clothiers' gild, he had a respectable position in the middle class. A fairly vivid personality emerges from the dry records. He made promises that he was unable to fulfill, bought goods for which he could not pay, and started unprofitable sidelines such as selling cheese and wine instead of sticking to his loom. Although a poor provider for his family, Domenico must have been a popular and plausible sort of fellow to obtain property on credit and to be appointed on committees of his gild. He was the kind of father who would shut up shop when trade was poor and take the boys fishing; and the sort of wine seller who was his own best customer.

For years the records tell us nothing of the Colombos. By March 1470 Domenico had removed to nearby Savona with his family and looms. He also retailed wine; on 31 October of that year, son Cristoforo, "over 19 years of age," acknowledged a debt of 48 Genoese pounds for wines delivered to him and his father. He lived at Savona long enough to make two fast friends in the upper class:—Michele de Cuneo, who accompanied him on the Second Voyage, and Bartolomeo Fieschi, who on the Fourth Voyage shared the famous rescue voyage from Jamaica to Haiti.

Domenico died about 1496, but was not forgotten; for Christopher and his brother Bartholomew named their new capital, Santo Domingo, after the patron saint of their father.

Such are the facts that we have of the life of Christopher Columbus to the age of twenty-two, and of his family. Since this boy was father to the man of recorded history, we may assume that he was a proud and sensitive lad, faithful to his religious duties, following a hereditary calling in order to help support his parents, but eager for adventure, mystically assured of a high mission and a noble destiny.

The absence of Italian in his preserved writings, except for a stray word or phrase, is a great talking point of the *Colón Español* and *Colom Català* sects. The earliest bit of his writing that has been preserved, a postil (marginal note) dated 1481 on one of his books, is in bad Spanish mingled with Portuguese; all his letters, even those to Genoese friends and to the Bank of St. George, are in Spanish. None of the authors to whom he alludes wrote in Italian; the *Divine Comedy*, ever beautiful where Dante describes the sea, apparently he knew not.

Actually the lack of Italian in Columbus's writings is good evidence of his Genoese birth. The Genoese dialect of his day, even more than in ours (when a Genoese speaking it in a trial at Rome around 1910 had to have an Italian interpreter), was very different from Tuscan or classical Italian; possibly even more so than the Venetian and Neapolitan dialects. It was essentially a language of common speech, rarely written. A poor boy of Genoa would not have known Italian, unless he learned it at school. Christopher undoubtedly left home almost if not completely illiterate, and when he finally learned to read and write, used the Castilian language because it was that of his new associates. Many thousands of peasant Italian emigrants have done just that. Arriving in their New World home illiterate, they learn to read and write in English, Spanish, or Portuguese according to the country of their residence, and eventually forget the dialect they were brought up to speak.

A careful analysis of Columbus's writings has been made by the most eminent Spanish philologist of the last hundred years, Ramón Menéndez Pidal. The Discoverer, he reports, did not write Jewish-Spanish or Italian-Spanish, but Portuguese-Spanish. To the end of his life he wrote Castilian with Portuguese spellings, indicating that he spoke Portuguese first. During the decade he lived at Lisbon, Castilian was a widely favored language among the educated classes of Portugal into which Columbus married; even Camoëns used that language for his sonnets. So an ambitious young man would naturally have chosen the more literary and widely expanded language.

What effect if any did Christopher's residence of some twenty-two years on Genoese territory have on his future career? Genoa was certainly the place to give any active lad a hankering for sea adventure. The Ligurian Republic bathes in the sea, spreads her arms to embrace it, looks southward to a clean horizon. The *libeccio* (southwest wind) blows in fresh from the Mediterranean and gives the terraced hills above the coast sufficient moisture for tilth, vineyard, and pasture. Shipbuilding went on in little coves and harbors all along the shore. Great galleys and carracks were constantly clearing for and arriving from the Aegean, the Levant, and North Africa. Genoa cherished traditions of navigators like the Vivaldi who sought the ocean route to India by way of Africa as early as 1291, and of Malocello, one of the discoverers of the Canaries. Genoa had a noted school of mapmakers who supplied portolan charts to half the Mediterranean, and who helped the Portuguese to chart their new African possessions. One may picture young Christopher looking wistfully out on the harbor from his parents' house while he worked at a loathed trade. Here, too, he may even have conceived his grand enterprise; for the achievements of a great man are often but the fulfillment of youthful dreams.

Such speculations are for the poet or novelist, not the historian. All we now know and all we shall probably ever know of Columbus's life to the age of twenty-two is that he helped his parents at Genoa and Savona in their respectable trade of weaving woolens, and that he had little or no schooling. Yet his youth was neither so hard nor his life so bitter as to cause him to forsake allegiance to "that noble and powerful city by the sea."

Early Years at Sea

Cristoforo grew up in a community where every healthy boy went sailing whenever he could. Fishing trips, out with the evening land breeze to net sardines by the light of flaring torches and race the fleet home at dawn. Maybe a run over to Corsica and back; seeing the points of a high, jagged island shoulder up over the horizon, watching them run together into one island, and the white specks on the shore become houses. You anchor in a strange harbor where the men jabber in a weird dialect, and the girls seem so much more beautiful and outgoing than those of your home town. Most of Genoa's commerce went by sea; and it would have been natural for Domenico to send Cristoforo along the coast in a little lateen-rigged packet to sell his cloth, and buy wool, wine, and cheese. Coastwise experience is not to be despised. Whoever can cope with a sudden squall off the mountains near home is half prepared to meet a storm at sea.

In a letter to the Spanish Sovereigns written from Hispaniola in

January 1495, Columbus describes a trip across the Mediterranean on board a Genoese ship chartered by King René of Anjou for his short war with the king of Aragon. That could have happened between October 1470 and March 1472. His next recorded voyage was in a Genoese ship named *Roxana* in 1474, to help the city's trading factory on Chios defend itself against the Turks. The valuable product of Chios was the lentisk, from which they extracted gum mastic (*Pistacia lenticus*), a base for varnish; and twice on his First Voyage Columbus inaccurately designated a local tree, the gumbo limbo, as the lentisk, "which I have seen in the island of Chios." He may have made another voyage to Chios in 1475. On these trips, Christopher learned to "hand, reef and steer," to estimate distances by eye, to make sail, let go and weigh anchors properly, and other elements of seamanship. He learned seamanship the old way, the hard way, and the best way, in the school of experience. As yet illiterate, he could not navigate and thus rate an officer's billet.

Not long after returning from Chios, Columbus joined a fleet that played into the hands of destiny by casting him up on the shore of Portugal. In May 1476, Genoa organized a big convoy to protect a quantity of Chian mastic being shipped to Lisbon, England, and Flanders. One ship, named *Bechalla*, owned by Luis Centurione of Genoa and manned largely by men of Savona, took young Christopher on as foremast hand. On 13 August, off the coast of Portugal near Lagos, the convoy was suddenly attacked by a Franco-Portuguese war fleet commanded by a famous naval hero, Guillaume de Casenove. The Genoese proved no easy prey. All day the battle raged, and by nightfall seven ships, including *Bechalla*, had gone down and the surviving vessels were glad to sheer off and seek the nearest friendly port. When *Bechalla* sank, Columbus leaped into the sea, grasped a sweep that floated free, and by pushing it ahead of him and resting when exhausted (for he had been wounded in the battle), he managed to reach the shore, over six miles distant. The people of Lagos treated the survivors kindly and passed Columbus on to Lisbon, where someone of the local Genoese colony took him in and cured his wounds. His host may have been his younger brother Bartholomew, who had already established a small chart-making business in Lisbon.

Christopher was in luck to fall on his feet in Portugal. At the age of twenty-five, chance had brought him to the European center for blue-

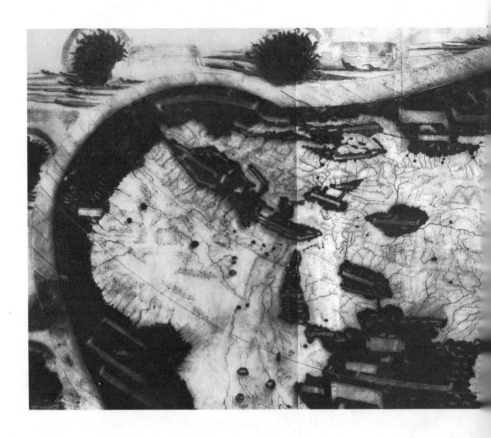

water voyaging and overseas discovery. He was among people who could teach him all he wanted to learn: Portuguese, Castilian, and Latin; mathematics and astronomy for celestial navigation. He already knew all the basic seamanship that a common sailor could pick up.

And he had plenty more on a northern voyage. His son Ferdinand wrote that among his father's notes he found a statement that in February 1477 he sailed a hundred leagues north of Iceland, to which island "which is as big as England, come the English, especially of Bristol, with their merchandise." And he adds that in this particular winter season the sea was not frozen, and the range of tides ran up to fifty feet. This statement has aroused no end of controversy. But the

Henricus Martellus Germanus world map of 1492. Courtesy Beinecke Collection, Yale University.

winter of 1476–77 was unusually mild, so that this Portuguese ship could have sailed beyond Iceland to Jan Mayen Land in latitude 70°50′ N. If, however, Columbus actually did make this voyage, did he land in Iceland and pick up data on the Northmen's explorations of the eleventh century? Son Ferdinand's statement is full of inaccuracies —the latitude he gives for Iceland is more than ten degrees out, and the spring range of tides at Reykjavik is only thirteen feet, not fifty. And even if the ship did land in Iceland, would this young mariner have attended a saga-reading party (in translation) and have heard about Vinland? Not likely. In any case, there was nothing in the Greenland-Vinland story of polar bears, walrus ivory, and white falcons to interest a young seaman already dreaming of an ocean route to the fabulous Indies of gems, spices, and precious metals.

More important to him was something he saw at Galway, going or coming: two boats drifting ashore containing "a man and a woman of extraordinary appearance," both dead. These probably were flatfaced Lapps or Finns who had escaped from a sinking ship; but Christopher and the Irish assumed that they were Chinese, "blown across." As for tides, Professor Ruddock of the University of London has a plausible explanation. She found record of a Bristol ship trading in 1481 with the friary of La Rábida where (as we shall see) Columbus became intimate. The Bristolians told the monks about the tremendous tides on the Avon, and they somehow applied this to the Arctic Ocean when Ferdinand, much later, picked up the story of the Iceland voyage.

We find Christopher at sea again in the summer of 1478 as captain of a Portuguese ship which Centurione, his former employer, had chartered to buy sugar in Madeira. This Genoese merchant provided the young captain with so little money that Funchal merchants refused to deliver, and he sailed empty-handed to his old home. Next year Christopher, at twenty-eight years a master mariner, contracted an advantageous marriage with Dona Filipa de Perestrelo e Moniz, daughter of Bartolomeu Perestrelo, hereditary captain of Porto Santo in the Madeira group, and a contemporary of the Infante D. Henrique. The young couple shortly went to live in Porto Santo where their only son, Diego (later the second admiral and viceroy), was born, and where Dona Filipa's mother placed at Christopher's disposal the charts and journals of her seagoing husband. Not long after the birth of this, their one and only child, the Columbus couple moved to Funchal, Madeira.

In 1481 D. Afonso V died and was succeeded by his son D. João "the Complete Prince." Young (aged 26), energetic, wise and learned, ruthless and ambitious, D. João II equaled any monarch of his age. Just before his accession, a long and fruitless war with Castile had been concluded by the Treaty of Alcáçovas. In this Spain recognized Portugal's exclusive rights to the African coast and islands south of the Canaries, which Spain retained. D. João, who had formerly managed the crown monopoly of the African trade, determined to build a castle or fortified trading factory on the Gold Coast, strong enough to beat off any European rival, and to keep the natives in order. A fleet of eleven vessels was fitted out at Lisbon, soldiers, stonemasons, and other artisans were engaged, and late in 1481 it set sail from Lisbon under the command of Diogo d'Azambuja. On the Gold Coast the men worked hard and well that winter, erecting a great stone castle of medieval design, complete with turrets, moat, chapel, warehouse, and market court; and a garrison was left in charge. São Jorge da Mina (St. George of the Mine), as this castle was named, upheld Portuguese sovereignty and protected her trade on the Gold Coast for centuries. The site and the ruins today are called Cape Coast Castle.

Columbus either took part in Azambuja's expedition or, more probably, made a voyage to São Jorge da Mina in 1482–83 or 1483–84, as officer of a trading expedition. West Africa deeply impressed the young mariner. In the journal of his First Voyage to America he frequently compares people and products of "The Indies" with those of Guinea; he expected to find a *mina* in Hispaniola, and his Third Voyage had particular reference to the supposed latitude of Sierra Leone. The experience of a passage to the Gold Coast and back, in company with Portuguese pilots, must greatly have improved his seamanship, although it may be doubted whether it gave him any competence in celestial navigation.

Christovão Colom, as he was called in Portugal, learned many useful things from his Portuguese shipmates, the world's finest mariners of that era: how to handle a caravel in head wind and sea, how to claw off a lee shore, what kind of sea stores to take on a long voyage and how to stow them, and what sort of trading truck is wanted by primitive people. Every voyage that he sailed under the flag of Portugal made it more likely that he would succeed in the great enterprise that was already in his brain. Above all, he learned from the Portuguese confidence that, with a good ship under him and with God's assistance, the boundaries of the known world might be indefinitely enlarged; that the Age of Discovery had only just begun. From his own experiences he had learned that the ancients did not know everything; despite their denials the Torrid Zone was habitable.

By 1484, when he returned from Guinea voyaging, Columbus was ready to make an amazing proposition to the king of Portugal.

Bibliography and Notes

THE AGE OF DISCOVERY

For books on this wide subject I can do no better than refer the reader to Wilcomb E. Washburn's pamphlet *The Age of Discovery*, published by the American Historical Association's Service Center for Teachers of History, No. 63 (1961). Two recommended background books are George H. T. Kimble, *Geography in the Middle Ages* (London, 1938) and Boies Penrose, *Travel and Discovery in the Renaissance* (Cambridge, Mass., 1952).

COLLECTIONS OF COLUMBIAN SOURCES

Martín Fernández de Navarrete, *Colección des los Viages y Descubrimientos . . . desde Fines del Siglo XV* (5 vols., Madrid, 1825–37), is the beginning of all source collections for Columbus and carries the story of southern voyages almost as far as 1600. Navarrete was a Spanish naval officer who began this work even before the Napoleonic wars. It has been reprinted, and there is a new edition in three volumes (Madrid, 1954–55), which is unreliable, as some of the documents are truncated or omitted.

At the approach of the Columbian 400th anniversary in 1892, the Italian government commissioned the classical scholar Cesare de Lollis to compile the fourteen volumes of *Raccolta di Documenti e Studi Pubblicati della R. Commissione Columbiana* (Rome, 1892–94), which includes the best texts of almost all the sources and numerous learned monographs.

S. E. Morison (ed.), *Journals and Other Documents on the Life and Voyages of Christopher Columbus* (New York, 1963), includes translations (mostly my own) of the Capitulations, the Toscanelli Letter, certain Postils, his first Letter to the Sovereigns (commonly called Letter to Santangel), narratives and documents of the other three voyages. The illustrations by Lima de Freitas in this volume are far the best of Columbus's voyages that have appeared.

City of Genoa, *Christopher Columbus, Documents and Proofs of His Genoese Origin*. English-German edition (folio, Bergamo, 1932). Facsimiles and translations of every known document bearing on his paternity and birthplace. A useful compendium, with opinions by latest historians, is in the periodical *Liguria*, XXXIX, No. 11 (Nov. 1972), special number on the *Genovesità di Colombo*. One of the most significant documents relates to Christopher's first cousin Gianetto (Johnny) Colombo. In 1496 his two brothers financed his trip to Spain to ask his cousin "D. Cristoforo de Colombo, Admiral of the King of Spain" for a job. Johnny's quest succeeded. The Admiral gave him command of a caravel on the Third Voyage to America, and entrusted him with confidential matters as well.

Benjamin F. Stevens, ed., *Chrstopher Columbus His Own Book of Privi-

leges, 1502, with translation, abundant notes, and introduction by Henry Harrisse (London, 1893).

The so-called *Pleitos de Colón,* testimony taken at various hearings conducted by the crown and by Columbus's descendants, are an indispensable source. A rather inaccurate and partial edition, by Cesáreo Fernández Duro, is printed in *Colección de Documentos Inéditos Relativos al Descubrimiento . . . de las Antiguas Posesiones Españoles de Ultramar,* 2nd series, vols. VII and VIII (Madrid, 1892–94). A better edition, *Pleitos Colombinos,* edited by Antonio Muro Orejon *et al.,* is now (1974) in the course of appearing, published at Seville by Escuela de Estudios Hispanoamericanos; only vols. I (1967) and VIII (1964) were available in time for me to use.

In addition to the above-mentioned *Colección de Documentos Inéditos . . . de Ultramar,* there are at least three compilations with similar titles that are useful for almost all southern voyages: (1) *Colección de Documentos Inéditos Para la Historia de España* (112 vols., Madrid, 1842–95); (2) Navarrete, (ed.), *Colección de los Viajes y Descubrimientos . . . desde Fines del Siglo XV* (5 vols., Madrid, 1825–37); (3) *Colección de Documentos Inéditos relativos al Descubrimiento . . . de las Antiguas Posesiones Españoles de América y Oceania,* 1st series (42 vols., Madrid, 1864–84), of which the half-title is *Colección . . . del Archivo de Indias.*

The Duquesa de Berwick y de Alba published two volumes of Columbus's Letters and other documents: *Autógrafos de Cristóbal Colón,* and *Nuevos Autógrafos de Cristóbal Colón* (Madrid, 1892 and 1902). The latter includes the best reproduction of the Admiral's holograph map of northern Hispaniola, and the *Rol,* or list, of his 1492 crew.

CONTEMPORARY HISTORIES AND BIOGRAPHIES

Contemporary historians and biographers, most of whom knew Columbus personally, are most important:—

Peter Martyr d'Anghiera, an Italian humanist at the Spanish court, wrote the earliest History of the New World, as he was the first to call it. He wrote it in Latin, by decades; first decade was published in a thin folio, *P. Martyris Angli Mediolanensis Opera* (Seville, 1511); the first three decades as *De Orbe Novo* at Alcalá in 1516; the first edition of the complete work in eight decades is of 1530. The Eden translation of the first three, called *The Decades of the Newe Worlde or West India* (1555) is reprinted in Edward Arber, *First Three English Books on America* (1885). There is a modern English translation of the whole by F. A. MacNutt (2 vols., 1912). A pirated edition of the first decade, called *Libretto de tutta la Navigatione de Re de Spagna de le Isole et Terreni Novamente Trovati,* was published in Italian at Venice in 1504; Lawrence C. Wroth edited a facsimile with introduction (Paris, 1930). Peter Martyr is pedantic but honest, informing, and occasionally amusing, as where he writes of the Chamorros: "The natives, though animated with friendly sentiments toward us, managed to steal everything they could pick up." The French translation by Paul Gaffarel,

De Orbe novo, les huit decades (Paris, 1907), is excellent. Henry R. Wagner wrote a good account of Peter Martyr for American Antiquarian Society *Proceedings*, LVI (1946), 239–81.

Gonzalo Fernández de Oviedo y Valdés witnessed Columbus's triumph at Barcelona in 1493. He spent the years 1513–47 in different parts of the Caribbean, became official chronicler of overseas Spain; in 1535 appeared his first volume, *Historia General y Natural de las Indias*, which includes an account of Columbus and his voyages. The standard edition was published by the Royal Academy of History (4 vols., Madrid, 1851–55). There is nothing about Columbus in Oviedo's *Natural Historia de las Indias* of 1526 (generally called the *Sumario*) although this was selected for translation by Richard Eden in 1555 as an appendix to his *Decades of the Newe Worlde*. Writing at a period when Columbus's privileges were being impugned by the court, Oviedo manages to be fair, although he tries to please his masters by asserting a pre-discovery by Visigothic Spain!

Bartolomé de Las Casas, *Historia de las Indias*. Son and nephew of Columbus's shipmates on the Second Voyage, he came over himself in 1500, and in 1510 was the first priest to be ordained in the New World. Out of his experience as a missionary in Cuba arose a passionate conviction that the Indians were men and brothers who should be converted and treated as fellow Christians; he devoted the rest of his life to this cause. At all times he was the Indians' apostle, protector, and friend; and at various times their advocate at court, governor on the Pearl Coast, and bishop of Chiapas in Mexico. *Indias* was mostly written between 1550 and 1563 but not printed until 1875. The best edition is the one edited by Lewis Hanke (Mexico and Buenos Aires, 1951), with Manuel Giménez Fernández. Hanke compiled a critical bibliography, *Bartolomé de Las Casas 1474–1566* (Santiago de Chile, 1954), with a good biographical introduction. Las Casas's early exposure of Spanish cruelty to the natives of America, and zeal for their welfare, has made him as unpopular among Spanish and Latin nationalists as the Northern abolitionists used to be among Southern whites; and for the same reason—he exposed a cruel but profitable system of labor. I follow Hanke in the conviction that Las Casas is fundamentally reliable. He admired Columbus, and while pulling no punches on his enslavement of Indians, used his now lost journals (which he was the first to edit) and personal knowledge, to good advantage.

Hernán Pérez de Oliva (1494–1532), a Spanish writer famous in his day, wrote an *Ystoria de Colón*, never yet printed; the only known ms. copy, in the Yale Library, is described and analyzed by Leonardo Olschki in *Hispanic American Historical Review*, XXIII (1943), 165–96. It is, he says, essentially a digest of the first decade of Peter Martyr, written after 1524, and contains nothing original.

Hernando (Ferdinand) Colón, *Historie . . . della vita e de' fatti dell' Ammiraglio D. Christoforo Colombo* (Venice, 1571). Translation of a Spanish biography (now lost) by Columbus's younger son, who accompanied him on the Fourth Voyage. Best edition of the Italian text is by R. Caddeo (2 vols., Milan, 1930). An excellent English translation by Benjamin Keen, *The Life of . . . Columbus by His Son Ferdinand*, was published by Rutgers University Press in 1959.

PREVIOUS WORKS ON COLUMBUS BY S. E. MORISON

Admiral of the Ocean Sea, a Life of Christopher Columbus (2 vols., Boston, 1942; long out of print). One-volume edition with the same title, place, and year; now in its 16th printing. This contains the text of the two-volume edition except the chapter on syphilis, some navigational data, and the notes and bibliography. The two-volume edition was well translated by Héctor R. Ratto as *Almirante de la Mar Océano* and printed in one volume (Buenos Aires, 1943).

Christopher Columbus Mariner (Boston and London, 1955). A shorter biography than the foregoing; also in paperback (Mentor books) and in many translations.

Journals and Other Documents (see above, under Sources).

The Caribbean as Columbus Saw It (Boston, 1964), with Mauricio Obregón. Liberally illustrated with photos by David L. Crofoot, Señora Obregón, and others; both this and the *Journals* contain many footnotes on fauna and flora furnished by our scientific friends; the introduction to *The Caribbean* contains a fresh account by Obregón of Columbus's navigation.

OTHER BIOGRAPHIES OF COLUMBUS

There are hundreds of these, including juveniles; most of them are trash. Here I have selected a few—besides my own! For more, see *Harvard Guide to American History* (1969), §74.

Diego Luis Molinari, *La Empresa Colombiana* (Buenos Aires, 1938) and *El Nacimiento del Nuevo Mundo 1492–1534 Historia y Cartografía* (Buenos Aires, 1941), by the distinguished professor of American history at the University of Buenos Aires, 1889–   ), together make the best biography of Columbus in Spanish, and an excellent, well-mapped continuation of the southern voyages. The first is particularly useful for pricking bubbles blown by Columbian crackpots. Henry Vignaud, *The Columbian Tradition* (Oxford, 1920) and *Le Vrai Ch. Colomb et la légende* (Paris, 1921) are useful epitomes of his several volumes, of which the most important are: *Histoire critique de la grande entreprise de Christophe Colomb* (2 vols., Paris, 1911), *Toscanelli and Columbus* (London, 1902), and *Etudes critiques sur la vie de Colomb avant ses découvertes* (Paris, 1905). Although his main object was to disprove Columbus's Oriental objective, he uncovered more hitherto concealed facts than any other researcher of the last century. Vignaud was a member of the Confederate delegation to France during the Civil War who made his peace with the Union, became a permanent secretary to the U.S. Embassy in Paris, and devoted his leisure time for almost half a century to the study of Columbus.

Good biographies which have appeared since mine and are indebted to it (as only the first-named acknowledges) are: Bjorn Landström, *Columbus* trans. from the Swedish (New York, 1966), handsomely illustrated; Armando Álvarez Pedroso, *Cristóbal Colón* (Havana, 1944), with original maps and character analysis; and Antonio Ballesteros y Beretta, *Cristóbal Colón y el Descubrimiento de América* (Barcelona and Buenos Aires, 1945), vols. IV and V of that author's *Historia de América* (a popular illustrated book; charts taken from Morison).

Marianne Mahn-Lot, *Columbus* (New York, 1961), a translation of her *Christophe Colomb* (Paris, 1960).

Enrique de Gandía, *Historia de Cristóbal Colón Análisis Crítico* (Buenos Aires, 1942), with a workmanlike, common-sense examination of Columbian problems, but little beyond First Voyage.

José Antonio Calderón Quijano, "Colón, su cronistas e historiadores en Menéndez y Pelayo" (Seville, 1957), a review of all biographies of Christopher Columbus.

The Mexican historian Edmundo O'Gorman has challenged Columbus's title of Discoverer in *La Idea del Descubrimiento de América* (Mexico, 1951) and *The Invention of Amèrica* (Bloomington, 1961). The French historian Marcel Bataillon reviewed O'Gorman in *Bulletin Hispanique*, IV, 1 (1953), 23–35, and with him wrote *Dos Concepciones de la Tarea Histórica* (Mexico, 1955). My own critique of O'Gorman's thesis is in *History and Theory*, II (1963), 292–96.

Portraits of Columbus. See John B. Thacher, *Christopher Columbus*, III (1904), 8–83, where 39 alleged portraits are illustrated. Seventy-one allegedly original portraits of Columbus were exhibited at the Chicago Exposition of 1893. They showed lean-faced, long-jowled Columbuses and fat-faced, pudgy Columbuses; blond Columbuses and swarthy, olive-tinted Columbuses; smooth-visaged Columbuses and Columbuses variously mustached, bearded, and whiskered; Columbuses garbed in all manner of costume, lay and ecclesiastical, noble and vulgar, from the Franciscan robe to the courtier's dress, and in styles ranging over three centuries. Most of them tallied in no way with the contemporary descriptions, and the jury who examined them could find no satsfactory evidence that any were authentic. The one I have selected for this book is the so-called Giovio, now in the Galeria Gioviana at Como. Originally painted for the gallery of famous men established as early as 1537 by Bishop Paolo Giovio (d. 1552) at his villa on Lake Como. A good colored reproduction is in *City of Genoa Documents*, p. 230. A very similar portrait, evidently by the same unknown artist, is in the Biblioteca Nacional, Madrid, and there exists a wood engraving of one or the other, with fancy embellishments. The Como portrait represents a chastened Columbus after his Third Voyage, wearing a vaguely monastic robe. See Armando Álvarez Padroso, "El Verdadero retrato de Cristóbal Colón," in *Studi Colombiani*, III, 25–29, and Thacher, III, 11–41. Most European authorities have come to believe that this Giovio portrait is the oldest one of the Admiral, although painted not less than 30 years after his death. The "Talleyrand" portrait of Columbus, attributed to Sebastiano del Piombo and now in the Metropolitan Museum, New York, has artisic merit but resembles in no way the contemporary descriptions. Reproduced in Thacher, III, 48.

NOTES ON SPECIFIC PAGES OF CHAPTER I

The Portuguese-African background. While some Portuguese historians, notably the brothers Cortesão, have been postulating a Portuguese pre-Columbian discovery of America (a subject dealt with in my *Northern Voyages* and in *Portuguese Voyages to America before 1500*), other Portuguese historians have been cutting the Infante D. Henrique down to size. Ironically, just as this was being done, the Salazar government erected a colossal monument to D. Henrique on the bank of the Tagus, near Lisbon. See Comandante Teixeira da Mota, "Prince Henry of Portugal," *International Hydrographic Review,* XXXIX (1962), 29–37; Thomas Oscar Marcondes de Sousa, "Aínda a suposta Escola Naval de Sagres," separate from *Revista de História* (São Paulo, 1953), pp. 1–12; and P. E. Russell, *Prince Henry the Navigator* (London, 1960). This title of Navigator for the Infante was invented by English biographers, especially R. H. Major, about a century ago, despite the fact that he never navigated any further than Ceuta. But his mother was the English princess Philippa, daughter of "old John of Gaunt, time-honored Lancaster," which makes him a sort of honorary Englishman. Nobody should make up his mind about the Infante before reading the numerous articles on him in *Congresso Internacional de História dos Descobrimentos, Actas,* especially Vol. IV (Lisbon, 1961). A. Teixeira da Mota, *Mar, Além Mar,* I (Lisbon, 1972), contains a thorough study of the discovery of Guinea, and several articles on navigation.

My esteemed colleague Professor Francis M. Rogers has published several important articles and books on the dawn of ocean navigation, viz: *Precision Astrolabe: Portuguese Navigators and Trans-Oceanic Navigation* (Lisbon, 1971); *The Quest for Eastern Christians: Travels and Rumor in the Age of Discovery* (Minneapolis, 1962); *The Vivaldi Expedition* (Cambridge, Mass., 1955); *Valentim Fernandes, Rodrigo Santaella, and the Recognition of the Antilles as Opposite India* (Lisbon, 1957); *The Travels of the Infante Dom Pedro of Portugal* (Cambridge, Mass., 1961). The notion that the Portuguese reached American territory before 1492 is based on surmise and sentiment, and nothing else.

Columbus's Birth and Early Life. See the City of Genoa *Columbus* Documents mentioned under Sources. These are enough to convince any sane person that he was born to a Christian family in Genoa, or some nearby town of the Ligurian Republic. After the "Pontevedra Documents" which had the entire Colón family living in the Genoese quarter of that Spanish town had been examined and exposed as fakes by a committee of the Real

Academia de Historia headed by the eminent Spanish historian Altolaguirre,* the equally eminent Spanish writer Salvador de Madariaga (*Christopher Columbus*, London, 1939), no longer able to argue that our hero was born in Spain, insisted on his being the Genoa-born offspring of exiled Catalonian Jews. The arguments he uses for Columbus's Jewishness are fantastic: —his mother's name was Susanna, he loved gold, he beat to windward along Hispaniola to get to Isabella—"so like a wandering Jew"—that I had a little fun with him in my review of his book in *American Historical Review*, XLV, No. 3 (April 1940), 653–55. To which Madariaga retorted in his second edition (London, 1949, pp. 407–8) by paying a compliment to me as a yachtsman, but warning the public not to accept me as a scholar. He challenges me and Armando Alvarez Pedroso (who published his excellent *Cristóbal Colón* at Havana in 1944) to "produce a solution of the incompatibility between the Genoese and Spanish documents." The solution is easy: some of the Spanish documents on which Madariaga relies are fakes, whilst the *mayorazgo* or entail of 1498, in which Columbus expresses his loyalty to Genoa and leaves several legacies there, is genuine.

Here is a story. The *mayorazgo* was first published from the Duke of Veragua's muniments, together with the royal confirmation in the Simancas archives, by Navarrete in 1825. Neither document could later be found, which led the *Colón Español* boys to denounce it as something faked up in Genoa which Navarrete was paid to print. The facts are that Navarrete did his research at Simancas before the Napoleonic wars, during which General Murat's troopers used documents from the archives as bedding for their chargers. After Wellington's victory, such as could be salvaged from the horse stalls were tossed into a big pit. Successive royal archivists were supposed to sort these out, but a century and more passed and all flinched from so laborious and unpleasant a task. It remained for the indefatigable Alice Gould of Boston to fish around in this old cavalry dump, among dried Napoleonic manure, and pull up some sheets of the original royal confirmation of the *mayorazgo*. Sensation! Alfonso XIII, pleased at this vindication of the honor of a royal naval officer, then conferred on Miss Gould a suitable decoration. See my *Journals and Documents*, p. 6 notes.

Of late years the *Colom Català* argument has been more popular in Spain. Enrique Bayerri y Bertomeu, *Colón Tal Cual Fué* (Barcelona, 1961), amusingly concludes that our hero was born on the *Isla de Génova* (since disappeared), on the Rio Ebro opposite Tortosa, Catalonia. Señor José Porter, proprietor of an excellent antiquarian bookstore in Barcelona, a center for Catalan studies, himself has written a pamphlet, *¿Fué escrita en lengua Catalana la Primera Noticia del Descubrimiento de América?* (Barcelona, 1971).

* Angel de Altolaguirre y Duvale, *Declaraciones hechas por D. Cristobal . . . acerca de su Nacionalidad* (Madrid, 1925). This pamphlet also reprints most of the contemporary accounts of the Discoverer's nationality; all without exception call him Genoese.

The latest argument, which I heard in Barcelona in 1972, is that the sources which call Columbus "Genoese" do not mean that he came from the city of Genoa but merely that he was a sailor—since all the best mariners in Europe were Genoese! Bibliography in my *Admiral of the Ocean Sea*, I, 20–23.

It remained for a supposedly authoritative work, an article by "C. R." in *Encyclopaedia Judaica Jerusalem*, V (1971), 755, to bring all the hints and innuendoes about Columbus's Jewishness together, and to give Hebrew interpretations to his famous signature. One of this ponderous article's most delicious conclusions is that Columbus "used nautical instruments perfected by Jews such as Joseph Vecinho" (*sic*). This is the José Vizinho whose latitude of the Los Islands was wrong by four and a half degrees. His instrument or his head certainly needed perfecting!

The Iceland Voyage. Alwyn A. Ruddock, "Columbus and Iceland," *Geographical Journal*, CXXXVI (1970), 176–89. Professor Ruddock also doubts that Columbus ever made this northern voyage, but his hearing the story about the dead couple in a boat at Galway, a natural port of call between Lisbon and Iceland, seems to confirm that he got at least that far north, and he may have picked up the rest of the story in Ireland. Pedro Bilbao, "Was Columbus in Canada?" in *Américas*, XVIII (July 1960), 17–28 brings Columbus to the Bay of Fundy with its high-ranging tides, in 1477!

* II *

His "Enterprise of the Indies"

Columbus's Great Idea

Columbus's "Enterprise of the Indies," *Empresa de las Indias,* as he called it, and to the furthering of which he devoted all his time and energy from about 1483 on, was simple enough. It was to discover a short sea route to the Indies * instead of thrusting along the African coast as the Portuguese were doing. He also hoped to pick up en route some island or archipelago which would be a useful staging area; but the be-all and end-all was to rediscover eastern Asia by sailing west from Europe or Africa. He expected to set up a factory or trading post, like Chios or La Mina, on some island off the Asiatic coast, where European goods could be exchanged for the fragrant and glittering wares of the Orient much more cheaply than by trans-Asia caravans with their endless middlemen and successive mark-ups.

Exactly when Columbus conceived this momentous plan, or had it planted in his brain, is still a mystery. It may have come silently, like the grace of God, or in a rush and tumult of emotional conviction, or from observing, in Lisbon, the painful effort of the Portuguese to

---

* "The Indies," as the term was then used in Europe, included China, Japan, the Ryukyus, the Spice Islands, Indonesia, Thailand, and everything between them and India proper.

approach the Orient by sailing around Africa. All educated men of western Europe knew that the world was a sphere; all observant sailors knew that its surface was curved, from seeing ships hull-down. Columbus never had to argue the rotundity of the earth. When he had learned enough Latin to read ancient and medieval cosmographers, he ascertained that Aristotle was reported to have written that you could cross the Ocean from Spain to the Indies *paucis diebus*, in comparatively few days; and Strabo recorded that certain Greeks or Romans had even tried it but returned empty-handed, "through want of resolution and scarcity of provisions." He picked up from two famous medieval books, Pierre d'Ailly's *Imago Mundi* and Pope Pius II's *Historia Rerum Ubique Gestarum*, numerous guesses about the narrowness of the Ocean; and fortunately we have his own copies of these works, amply underlined, and their margins filled with his postils. He combed the Bible and ancient literature for quotations that might apply to his enterprise, such as Psalm lxxi (or lxxii) 8, "He shall have dominion also from sea to sea, and from the river unto the ends of the earth." He cherished the prophecy in Seneca's *Medea*—"An age will come after many years when the Ocean will loose the chains of things, and a huge land lie revealed; when Tethys will disclose new worlds and Thule no more be the ultimate."

Against this passage in Columbus's own copy of Seneca his son Ferdinand wrote this proud annotation:

This prophecy was fulfilled by my father the Admiral,

in the year 1492.

The first trace we have of any outside influence on Columbus forming his great idea is the Toscanelli correspondence, his earliest known scholarly backing. Paolo dal Pozzo Toscanelli was a leading Florentine physician in an era when the best astronomers and cosmographers were apt to be medicos, since they alone acquired enough mathematics to be men of science. Toscanelli had become what nowadays is called a "pen pal" of a canon of Lisbon Cathedral named Fernão Martins, to whom he conveyed the idea that the Ocean between Spain and the Indies was much narrower than anyone else supposed. Martins passed this on to the king, D. Afonso V, who invited the Florentine to develop his views in a letter; and that Toscanelli did. Dated 25 June 1474, a copy of this "Toscanelli Letter" in Columbus's hands became his principal exhibit when arguing for a narrow Atlantic. In brief, it says

that Paul the Physician is pleased to hear that the King of Portugal is interested in finding a shorter sea route to "the land of spices" than the one his mariners are seeking via Africa. Quinsay (modern Hang-chow), capital of the Chinese province of Mangi, is about 5000 nautical miles due west of Lisbon. An alternate, and shorter, route to the Orient goes by way of Antilia * to the "noble island of Cipangu"—

* See *Northern Voyages*, pp. 97–102.

Seville in the early XVI century, by Sanchez Coelho. Courtesy Museo de América, Madrid.

Marco Polo's name for Japan, where the temples and royal palaces are roofed with massy gold. At some time not later than 1481 (Toscanelli died in May 1482), Columbus was shown a copy of this letter, became greatly excited over such exalted backing for his ideas, and wrote to Florence, asking for more. Toscanelli replied by sending a copy of his earlier letter, with a chart (long since lost) to illustrate his notion of the Ocean's width, and a covering letter praising the young mariner's "great and noble ambition to pass over to where the spices grow."

By this time Columbus had learned enough Latin to read ancient and medieval authors who speculated on the length of the land and width of the Ocean. The result of his studies was to arrive at an extraordinary perversion of the truth. The distance from the Canaries to Japan via Antilia, which Toscanelli estimated at 3000 nautical miles (and Columbus whittled down to 2400) is actually about 10,000 miles between their respective meridians, measured on latitude 28° N. Toscanelli's Canaries-to-Quinsay route of 5000 miles (reduced by Columbus to 3550) is actually about 11,766 nautical miles by air.

How did he arrive at this colossal miscalculation, upon which his great voyage of discovery was based? Through several basic errors: reducing the length of a degree of longitude by one-quarter, stretching Ptolemy's estimate of the length of the Eurasian continent (Cape St. Vincent to eastern Asia) from 180° to 225°, adding another 28° for the discoveries of Marco Polo, plus 30° for his reputed distance from the east coast of China to the east coast of Japan, and saving another nine degrees of westing by starting his Ocean crossing from the outermost Canary Island.* That left only 68 degrees of Ocean to cross before hitting Japan; still too much for Columbus. The medieval calculators used too long a degree of longitude, he argued; he proposed to cross on latitude 28° N where the degree (he thought) measured but 40 nautical miles; thus he would have only 60 × 40 or 2400 miles of open water to cover. In other words, his figures placed Japan in relation to Spain about where the West Indies actually are. That is why those islands were given the name *Las Indias* and their inhabitants called *Indios,* Japan then being reckoned as part of "The Indies." And a Nuremberg geographer named Martin Behaim in the Portuguese service compiled in 1492 a globe (a tracing from which we reproduce) that showed a close correlation with what Toscanelli had written.

TRANSOCEANIC DISTANCES IN NAUTICAL MILES

	Toscanelli	Behaim	Columbus	Actual Airline
Canaries to Cipangu (Japan)	3000	3080	2400	10,600
Canaries to Quinsay (Hangchow)	5000	4440	3550	11,766

* Columbus owned a copy (still in the Biblioteca Colombina, Seville) of the 1485 edition of Marco Polo, who placed Japan some 1500 miles east of the coast of China, thus shortening the projected ocean passage.

Columbus's calculations were illogical, but his mind never followed the rules of logic. He *knew* he could make it, and had to put the mileage low in order to attract support.

Another colossal miscalculation of his was the relative proportion of land to water on the globe. Modern measurements divide our planet's surface into 30 per cent land and 70 per cent water,* but Columbus more than reversed this figure by insisting on the medieval notion (based on 2 Esdras vi. 42, "Six parts hast Thou dried up") that water covered less than 15 per cent. Very comforting, if true!

Dealing with Princes

Columbus in 1484, subsequent to his voyage or voyages to Guinea, received a hearing from D. João II. The leading Portuguese historian of this reign, João de Barros, recorded that *Christovão Colom,* "Of Genoese nation, a man expert, eloquent and good Latinist," requested the king to "give him some vessels to go and discover the Isle Cypango by this Western Ocean." D. João referred Christopher to a newly appointed maritime advisory committee. They dismissed him politely but firmly, considering his plan "as vain, simply founded on imagination, or things like that Isle Cypango of Marco Polo." For most learned men at that era regarded *The Book of Ser Marco Polo* as pure fiction, and Cipangu-Japan as a mythical island in a class with Hy-Brasil and Antilia. They felt that the length of the proposed voyage had been fantastically underestimated.

Columbus and D. João parted friends, and were to see each other twice again. But, for the present, there was nothing for him in Lisbon. His wife Dona Filipa had already died. Brother Bartholomew, first convert to the Enterprise of the Indies, then took off for England and France, to promote it.

About the middle of 1485 Columbus and his little son Diego took passage on a merchant ship for Spain and disembarked at a sleepy little seaport called Palos de la Frontera because of its nearness to the Portuguese frontier. Although he probably chose that port to enter Spain for no better reason than having been offered free passage to it by the skipper, it turned out to be as lucky as swimming ashore at Lagos nine years earlier. When his ship rounded the promontory

* Peter J. Herring (ed.), *Deep Oceans*, p. 13. In the Northern Hemisphere the proportion is 40–60; in the Southern, 19–81.

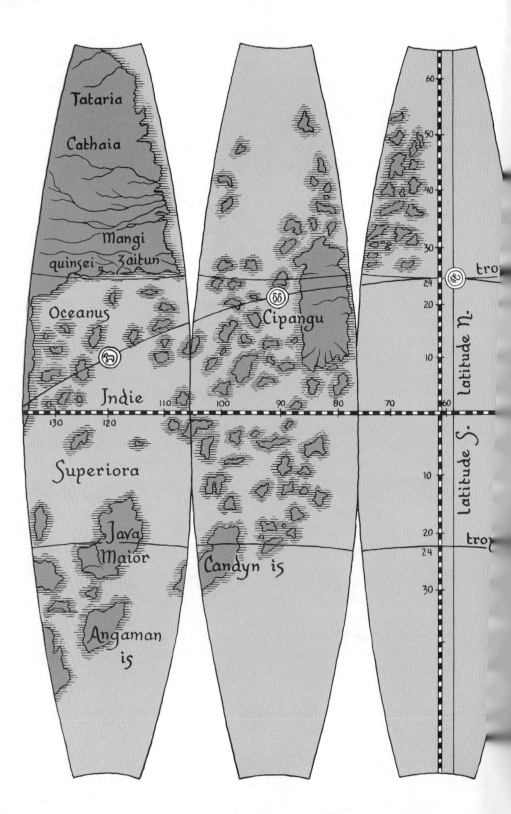

Tataria

Cathaia

Mangi

quinsei   Zaitun

Oceanus

Indie

Superiora

Java
Maior

Candyn is

Angaman
is

Cipangu

tro

tro

Latitude N.

Latitude S.

130   120   110   100   90   80   70   60

60

50

40

30

24

20

10

10

20

24

30

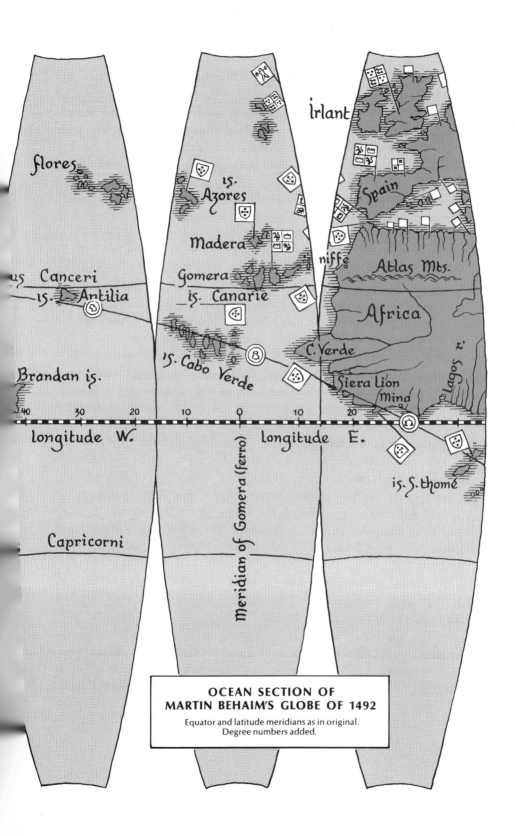

flores

Canceri

15. Antilia

Brandan is.

Capricorni

Azores

15. Azores

Madera

Gomera

is. Canarie

'is. Cabo Verde

longitude W.

Meridian of Gomera (ferro)

40   30   20   10   0   10   20

longitude E.

Irlant

Spain

niffe

Atlas Mts.

Africa

C. Verde

Siera Lion

Mina

Lagos z.

is. S. thomé

**OCEAN SECTION OF
MARTIN BEHAIM'S GLOBE OF 1492**

Equator and latitude meridians as in original.
Degree numbers added.

where the Rio Tinto joins the Saltés, Columbus noted the conspicuous buildings of La Rábida, a friary of the Franciscan order which took more interest in discovery than did any other branch of the church. Franciscan missionaries had been to China around 1320 and others were eager to return. For the present, Columbus, puzzled what to do with little Diego while he tramped about Spain seeking support, remembered that Franciscans often maintained boarding schools in connection with their friaries. Over a quarter-century later, a physician who happened to be present testified that father and son made the long, dusty walk from Palos to La Rábida, that Christopher asked for bread and a cup of water for the boy, and then got into conversation with Antonio de Marchena, a highly intelligent Franciscan who happened to be visiting. Columbus not only arranged for Diego's admission as a boarder but convinced Marchena, an astronomer of repute, that he "had something"; and Marchena gave him a letter of introduction to the Duke of Medina Sidonia. Columbus called at the ducal castle and was referred to a kinsman, the Count of Medina Celi, who owned a merchant fleet based at Puerto Santa Maria near Cadiz. This nobleman (later promoted duke) declared himself ready to provide Columbus "with three or four well equipped caravels," for he asked no more, "but felt that the Enterprise of the Indies was too great for a mere subject to take over; that the Genoese must see the Queen.

As Pierre Chaunu observes, La Rábida became a key to the Christian expansion that flowed from Columbus's voyage, as Palos and the caravels were the keys to immediate success. For Palos, a nursery of Spanish blue-water mariners, lay so close to the Portuguese frontier that an exchange of caravel designs was easy. Without La Rábida and Palos, there would have been no Voyage of Discovery, at least not in 1492.

Columbus now proceeded to the royal city of Cordova. Arriving in January 1486, he missed the Catholic Sovereigns, but tarried to await the Queen's return, and her pleasure.

In the meantime he made a pleasant connection with a pretty peasant girl. At Cordova there was a colony of Genoese, one of them an apothecary, and apothecary shops in those days were informal meeting places for physicians and amateur scientists. Columbus naturally dropped in at his compatriot's shop and there became acquainted with one Diego de Harana, who frequented it. Diego invited him to his house, where he met a twenty-year-old cousin of the Haranas, Beatriz Enriquez. She became Columbus's mistress and in 1488 bore him his second son, Ferdinand. The undoubted fact that Columbus never married Beatriz has troubled his more pious biographers, and judging from certain provisions for her in his will, it troubled his conscience too; but nobody at the time seems to have held it against him. A second marriage with a peasant's daughter would have been unsuitable for one who intended to become a nobleman and an admiral. The Harana family were pleased with the connection; at least two of them later served under Columbus, and the friendship between them and his legitimate descendants continued for two or three generations.

On May Day 1486, almost a year from the time he first set foot in Spain, Columbus was received by the Queen in the Alcazar of Cordova. *Isabel la Católica* (Isabella in English) was one of the ablest European sovereigns in an age of strong kings. She had an intuitive faculty for choosing men, and for timing. Close to Columbus in age, she had blue eyes and auburn hair resembling his, and she shared his religious mysticism. Her marriage with Ferdinand of Aragon had united all "the Spains" excepting Portugal (to whose royal family she was allied) and the remnant of the Moorish caliphate of Cordova, which she had resolved to conquer. Some spark of understanding evidently passed between Christopher and Isabella at their first meeting, and although she turned down his enterprise more than once, he found that he could count on her in the end. On this occasion she appointed a special commission under her confessor Hernando de Talavera to examine the Enterprise of the Indies and recommend whether it should be accepted or rejected.

The most unhappy period in Columbus's life extended over the next six years. He had to sustain a continual battle against prejudice, contumely, and sheer indifference. A proud, sensitive man who *knew* that his project would open fresh paths to wealth and for the advancement of Christ's kingdom, he had to endure clownish witticisms and crackpot jests by ignorant courtiers, to be treated like a beggar; even at times to suffer want. Hardest of all, he learned by experience the meaning of the phrase *cosas de España*, the endemic procrastination of Spaniards. In later years he often alluded bitterly to these experiences and contrasted the enormous wealth and power his

Isabella of Castile. Flemish school. Original in Windsor Castle. Courtesy,
Keeper of H.M. Paintings, Windsor Castle.

Ferdinand of Aragon. Flemish School. Original in Windsor Castle. Courtesy,
Keeper of H.M. Paintings, Windsor Castle.

discoveries had conferred on Spain to his own protracted efforts to obtain a fair hearing, and later to secure his just rights.

Even in our day we have known men of great strength of character who felt inspired by God in the pursuit of some ideal goal, who exasperated people who held other views, and were almost impossible to fight against. You can argue your head off against people like that, but they always come up with a fresh argument.

The Talavera commission, meeting at Salamanca around Christmastide 1486, could not agree. Its deliberations have been distorted by Washington Irving and other writers into a debate as to whether the world was round or flat. Actually, we know nothing definite about the arguments, but we may be certain that since the commission consisted of men of learning, the sphericity of the earth never came into question. At least one member, Diego de Deza, favored the Great Enterprise; and it was doubtless due to his influence, or Talavera's, that early in 1487 Columbus received a retaining fee of 12,000 maravedis a year, the pay of an able seaman, enough to support a man of his simple tastes.*

Christmas of 1487 passed without any report from the Talavera commission. So, early in 1488, Columbus wrote to D. João II of Portugal, requesting another hearing and asking for a safe-conduct from arrest for his unpaid bills in Lisbon. The King replied promptly and most cordially, urging Columbus to come immediately, and promising protection. The probable reason for this sudden and flattering change of attitude was that Bartholomew Dias, embarked on one more Portuguese attempt to reach the Indies by rounding Africa, had been gone seven months and nothing had yet been heard from him.

For want of funds, Christopher delayed leaving for Lisbon, and before he and his brother Bartholomew (who had remained there) could "do business" with the King, Dias returned. The Columbus brothers were present in December 1488 when his three caravels sailed

---

* To convey the equivalent of Spanish currency of this era, I have tried to state the gold content in U. S. coinage before we went off the gold standard. Thus, 12,000 maravedis equaled about $83 in gold of 1934. Whatever way you figure it, a maravedi was less than a cent in specie value, but its purchasing power was much greater. Twelve maravedis a day were allowed by the crown for feeding each seaman in the navy. A bushel of wheat in 1493 cost 73 maravedis. Sancho Panza's wages from Don Quixote were 26 maravedis a day and found, much better pay than that of Columbus's gromets.

proudly up the Tagus. Dias had rounded the southernmost cape of Africa—the Cape of Good Hope as the King named it—and sailed well up the east coast, when the men mutinied and forced him to turn back. But he had discovered a sea route to India. That ended D. João's interest in Columbus. Why now invest money in a doubtful West-to-the-Orient project?

Around New Year's 1489 the Columbus brothers decided on a plan of action. Christopher returned to Spain where he still hoped for support from the slow-moving Talavera commission, while Bartholomew sold his chart-making business and embarked on a long journey to persuade some other prince to support the Great Enterprise. Henry VII of England, first to be approached, turned him down flat. Bartholomew then proceeded to France, where Anne de Beaujeu, sister to King Charles VIII, befriended him and employed him to make charts for her at Fontainebleau. Through her, Bartholomew became friendly with the French king, but never obtained any real prospect of his support.

Success always seemed to be just around the corner, but in 1489 Christopher still had three years to wait before obtaining anything definite. We know very little of how he passed the time, except that he not only sold books but did purposeful reading in works on cosmography that he found in the libraries of monasteries where he received hospitality. Some of these books have been preserved in his son Ferdinand's Biblioteca Colombina at the Cathedral of Seville, and Columbus's marginal notes, especially in Pierre d'Ailly's *Imago Mundi* (3 vols., Louvain, 1480–83) and Pius II's *Historia Rerum Ubique Gestarum* (1477), are most revealing. For instance, these from Pierre d'Ailly:

> The end of the habitable earth toward the Orient and the end of the habitable earth toward the Occident are near enough, and between them is a small sea.
>
> Between the end of Spain and the beginning of India is no great width.
>
> An arm of the sea extends between India and Spain.
>
> India is near Spain.
>
> Aristotle [says] between the end of Spain and the beginning of India is a small sea navigable in a few days. . . . Esdras

[says] six parts [of the globe] are habitable and the seventh is covered with water. Observe that the blessed Ambrose and Austin and many others considered Esdras a prophet.

The end of Spain and the beginning of India are not far distant but close, and it is evident *that this sea is navigable in a few days with a fair wind.*

The Queen took notice of his return to Castile by giving him an open letter to all local officials, ordering them to feed and lodge him en route to court, which was then being held in a fortified camp outside the Moorish city of Baza, under siege by the Spanish army. There is some indication that Columbus joined the army as a volunteer while waiting for an answer.

Late in 1490 the Talavera commission issued an unfavorable report. The experts advised the Queen that the West-to-the-Orient project "rested on weak foundations"; that its attainment seemed "uncertain and impossible to any educated person"; that the proposed voyage to Asia would require three years' time, even if the ship returned, which was doubtful; that the Ocean was infinitely larger than Columbus supposed, and much of it unnavigable. And finally, God would never have allowed any uninhabited land of real value to be concealed from His people for so many centuries! But one must admit that most of the commission's arguments were sound. Suppose that no America existed, no ship of that era, however resolute her master and crew, or frugal in provision, could have made a 10,000-mile non-stop voyage from Spain to Japan. Magellan's voyage would prove that.

Apparently a complete stand-off. Columbus knew he could do it; the experts were certain he could not. It needed something as powerful as feminine intuition to break the deadlock. The Queen did give Columbus fresh hope. He could apply again, said she, when the war with the Moors was over. He waited almost another year and then decided to leave Spain and join his brother in France. Calling at the La Rábida friary near Palos to pick up son Diego, now about ten years old, he was persuaded by the prior, Father Juan Pérez, to give the Queen another chance, and he wrote to her to that effect. She replied by summoning Columbus to court and sent him some money to buy decent clothing and a mule.

Columbus always found more friends and supporters among priests than among laymen. They seemed to understand him better, since his

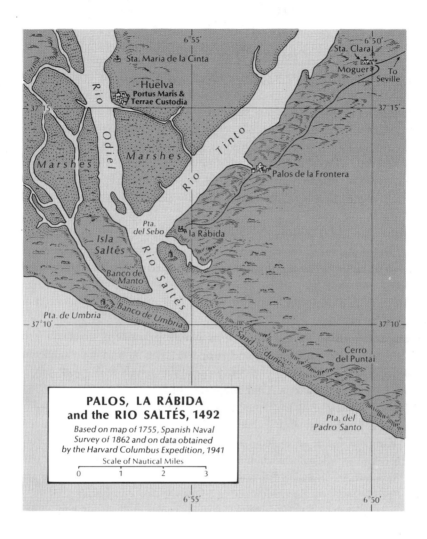

**PALOS, LA RÁBIDA
and the RIO SALTÉS, 1492**

Based on map of 1755, Spanish Naval
Survey of 1862 and on data obtained
by the Harvard Columbus Expedition, 1941

Scale of Nautical Miles

0   1   2   3

thoughts, deeds, and aspirations were permeated with religious faith. He was more particular than many clergymen in saying daily the Divine Office of the church—prime, tierce, sext, none, and compline; and seldom missed an opportunity to hear Mass. He had a fine presence and an innate dignity that impressed people of whatever estate, and although he never spoke perfect hidalgo Castilian, it was not expected that he should as Genoa-born and a former resident of Portugal.

41

Isabella Takes Him On

At about Christmastime 1491 Columbus again appeared at court, then
being held in the fortified camp of Santa Fe during the final siege of
Granada. The Royal Council reviewed the findings of a new commission. Although the exact details are not known, it seems probable that
the commission, reading the Queen's mind, recommended that Columbus be allowed to try, but the Council rejected it because of the price
he asked. For this extraordinary man, despite poverty, delay, and dis-
couragement, had actually raised his demands. In 1485 he had been
willing to sail west for Medina Celi on an expense-account basis without any particular honors or emoluments. Now he demanded not only
the title of Admiral, but also that he be made governor and viceroy of
any new lands he might discover, that both titles be hereditary in his
family, and that he and his heirs be given a 10 per cent cut on the
trade. He had suffered so many insults and outrages during his long
residence in Spain that—by San Fernando!—he would not glorify
Spain for nothing. If the Sovereigns would grant him, contingent on
his success, such rank, titles, and property that he and his issue could
hold up their heads with the Spanish nobility, well and good; but no
more bargaining. Take it, Your Majesties, or leave it.

Leave it they did, in January 1492, immediately after the fall of
Granada. Ferdinand and Isabella told him this at an audience which
the King, at least, intended to be final. Columbus saddled his mule,
packed the saddlebags with his charts and other exhibits, and started
for Seville with his faithful friend Juan Pérez, intending to take ship
for France and join Bartholomew in a fresh appeal to Charles VIII.

Just as, in Oriental bargaining, a storekeeper will often run after a
departing customer to accept his last offer, so it happened here. Luis
de Santangel, keeper of King Ferdinand's privy purse, called on the
Queen the very day that Columbus left Santa Fe and urged her to
meet Columbus's terms. The expedition, he pointed out, would not
cost as much as a week's entertainment of a foreign prince. This
Genoese asked for honors and emoluments only in the event of success; and they would be a small price to pay for the discovery of new
islands and a western route to the Indies. The Queen jumped at this,
her really last chance. She even proposed to pledge her crown jewels
for the expenses, but Santangel said that would not be necessary; he

would find the funds, and did. A messenger overtook Columbus at a
village four miles from Santa Fe, and brought him back.

Although the voyage was now decided upon in principle, there
were plenty more *cosas de España* to be endured, and it was not until
April 1492 that the contracts between Columbus and the Sovereigns,
the Capitulations as they are generally called, were signed and sealed.
Therein the Sovereigns, in consideration that Cristóbal Colón (as
Columbus was now called in Spain) is setting forth "to discover and
acquire certain islands and mainlands in the Ocean Sea," promise him
to be Admiral thereof, and Viceroy and Governor of lands that he
may discover. He shall have 10 per cent of all gold, gems, spices, or
other merchandise produced or obtained by trade within those
domains, tax free; he shall have the right to invest in one-eighth of any
ship going thither; and these offices and emoluments will be enjoyed
by his heirs and successors forever. The Sovereigns also issued to him
a brief passport in Latin, stating that they were sending him with three
caravels "toward the regions of India" (*ad partes Indie*) and three
identical letters of introduction, one to the "Grand Khan" (the
Chinese emperor) and the other two with a blank space so that the
proper title of any other prince could be inserted.

To us, accustomed to the power of Asiatic countries, it seems im-
possibly naïve for a European to expect to land somewhere on the
coast of China or Japan with fewer than one hundred men, and "take
over." But Europe was then grossly ignorant of the Far East; the
Portuguese had had no difficulty in dealing with black kings in
Africa, so why should not Columbus do the same thing in Asia?
Moreover, the establishment that Columbus had in mind was not what
we think of as a colony, but a *factoria, feitoria,* or factory, long familiar to Europeans. This was something more than a trading post; an
extension of sovereignty for commercial purposes. It might be armed,
if located in a relatively savage region like São Jorge da Mina on the
Gold Coast; or it might be a peaceful extraterritorial settlement such
as the Hanseatic League's steelyard in London and the Merchants Adventurers' factory in Amsterdam. The 1492 globe of Martin Behaim,
who shared Columbus's geographical ideas, shows an archipelago
south of Japan, corresponding to the Ryukyus. Supposing the Ocean
had been as narrow as Columbus estimated, and no American barrier,
he might have fetched up on an island like Okinawa and there set up

an entrepôt between China and the West, both for commerce and conversion. That was what eventually happened at Manila.

Preparing for the First Voyage

Practical details came next. For good reasons, it was decided to fit out the fleet and recruit the men at Palos, the same little port in the Niebla district of Andalusia, where Columbus had first set foot in Spain. There he had made friends of the Pinzón family, leading ship-owners and master mariners who had built caravels like those of nearby Portugal, and who enjoyed the confidence of local sailors. Palos, moreover, had committed some municipal misdemeanor for which the Queen conveniently fined her two well-equipped caravels. Columbus, with his friend Fray Juan Pérez, made a public appearance in the Church of St. George, Palos, on 23 May 1492, while a notary read the royal order. It so happened that a ship from Galicia, owned and captained by Juan de La Cosa, then lay in port. Columbus chartered her as his flagship, making a fleet of three.

This *Santa Maria*, the most famous of Columbus's ships, left her bones on a reef off Hispaniola, and no picture or model of her has survived; but several conjectural models have been made, and at least three full-size "replicas" have been constructed in Spain. The original *Santa Maria* was probably of about 100 tuns' burthen, which meant that her cargo capacity was 100 tuns (double hogsheads) of wine. Her rig, the conventional one for a *nao*, or ship, called for a mainmast taller than her length; the main yard, as long as the keel, spread an immense square sail (the main course), counted on to do most of the driving. Above the main course a short yard spread a tiny main topsail, The foremast, much shorter than the main, carried but one square sail. The mizzen mast, stepped on the high poop, carried a lateen sail, and under the bowsprit hung a square spritsail, which performed rather inefficiently the function of a modern jib.

Here, as near as we can state it after the careful researches of the late Alice Gould and Admiral Julio Guillén y Tato, and of the Admiral's former subordinate Juan Maria Martínez-Hidalgo, is the task organization of Columbus's First Voyage of Discovery. This little fleet with the great destiny had no official name—so at long last let us give it one:—

LA ARMADA DE INDIA, 1492.
CAPITÁN GENERAL: CRISTOBAL COLON

SANTA MARIA, *nao* (ship) of *c.* 100 tuns' burthen, *c.* 85 feet overall.
Captain: Columbus. Master and owner, Juan de La Cosa. Pilot, Peralonso Niño. *Alguacil* (marshal), Diego de Harana. *Escribano* (scribe, secretary), Rodrigo de Escobedo. Interpreter, Luis de Torres. Surgeon, Juan Sánchez. Seven petty officers, captain's steward and page, 11 able seamen, 10 *grumetes.** Total, 40.

PINTA, *caravela redonda* (square-rigged caravel) of *c.* 60 tuns, *c.* 69 feet overall.
Captain: Martín Alonso Pinzón. Owner and able seaman, Cristóbal Quintero. Master, Francisco Martín Pinzón. Pilot, Cristóbal García Sarmiento. Marshal, Juan Reynal. Surgeon, Maestro Diego. Two petty officers, 10 able seamen, 8 gromets. Total, 27.

NIÑA, caravel of *c.* 50 tuns, *c.* 55 feet overall.
Captain: Vicente Yáñez Pinzón. Master and owner, Juan Niño. Pilot, Sancho Ruiz de Gama. Surgeon, Maestre Alonso. Marshal, Diego Lorenzo. Two petty officers, 8 able seamen, 6 gromets. Total, 21.

Allowing for three more people whose names have not been found, the fleet's grand total was about 90 men and boys.

Compared with other recorded task organizations in the era of discovery, this one was exceedingly modest. Only John Cabot's and Verrazzano's single-ship expeditions were smaller.

Regarding the crew, two qualities stand out: homogeneity and good health. The only foreigners on board were Columbus, one other Genoese, one Venetian, and one Portuguese; and not one man died at sea—an extraordinary record as we shall see in comparison with later voyages. The only casualties were the men left behind in Haiti. In contrast to later Spanish voyages such as Magellan's and Loaysa's, there were no priests and few "idlers" (as sailors used to call everyone who did no physical work); each captain was allowed but one page or servant.

* "Gromets," in Elizabethan English; these were either young landsmen who had never been to sea before so not entitled to be called *marineros*, or ship's boys, or apprentice seamen.

Señor Martínez-Hidalgo's model of *Santa Maria*. Note especially, the tiny size of the topsail, foresail, and spritsail compared with that of the main course. Courtesy of Señor Martínez-Hidalgo, Maritime Museum, Barcelona.

A Spanish ship in those days had an official name, usually that of a saint, and a nickname which the sailors used; theirs for *Santa Maria* was *La Gallega*, "The Galician." One of the two caravels provided by the town of Palos took her name *Santa Clara* from a local saint, but is better known by her nickname *Niña*, so given because she belonged to the Niño family of Palos. *Niña* was Columbus's favorite. She carried him safely home from his First Voyage, took him to western Cuba and back to Spain on the Second, and made another voyage to Hispaniola. At the start she was rigged with three lateen sails like a Portuguese caravel, but in the Canaries Columbus had her rerigged

Stern view of Señor Martínez-Hidalgo's model of *Santa Maria*. The jars under the *toldilla* were to keep fish or meat fresh. Note the "round tuck" at the stern. Courtesy of Señor Martínez-Hidalgo, Maritime Museum, Barcelona.

square like her two companions, because square sails are much handier than lateen rig when running before the wind. *Pinta*, also a locally built caravel, was a little larger than *Niña*, and square-rigged from the first. Her real name we do not know; *Pinta* was probably derived from a former owner named Pinto. She was a smart sailer; the New World was first sighted from her deck, and she made first home.

All three were fastened mostly with wooden trunnels or pins such as one sees in the frames of colonial houses; iron fastenings were used only in key spots. They carried inside stone ballast. Their sides were painted gay colors above the waterline and, below it, payed with pitch to discourage barnacles and teredos (ship worms). Crosses and heraldic devices were emblazoned on the sails, and the ships carried a variety of brightly colored flags to be flown on entering and leaving port. Queen Isabella's royal ensign, quartering the castles and lions of Castile and Leon, streamed from the main truck, and on the foremast flew the banner of the expedition: a green cross on a white field with a crown on each arm—a concession to Aragon. All three vessels carried a little crude artillery, to repel pirates or other unwelcome boarders, but they were in no sense combatant ships, and carried neither soldiers nor gunners.

Columbus as a foreigner could never have recruited officers and men without the enthusiastic support of the three leading shipping families of Palos—Pinzón, Niño, and Quintero. Martín Alonso Pinzón commanded *Pinta* and took his younger brother Francisco along as master, a rank that corresponds roughly to the modern first mate. Another brother, Vicente Yáñez Pinzón, commanded *Niña*, and Vicente Yáñez became a discoverer in his own right. *Niña*'s master-owner was Juan Niño; his brother Peralonso Niño, who piloted *Santa Maria*, also became an explorer. La Cosa remained on board the flagship as master. Each vessel had a pilot, a very important rank as he was supposed to take charge of deep-sea navigation.* Each carried a surgeon. Among the "idlers" were certain specialists—Luis de Torres, a converted Jew who knew Arabic (Columbus thought that this would enable him to converse with Chinese and Japanese); Rodrigo Sánchez, the royal comptroller, whose main duty was to see that the crown got its share of any gold acquired; and Pedro Gutiérrez, formerly butler of the king's dais, who shipped as chief steward. Diego

* On Spanish ships the order of precedence was captain, pilot, *escribano* (secretary or scribe), and master.

de Harana, a cousin of Columbus's mistress, served as *alguacil,* marshal of the fleet, corresponding to the old naval rating of master-at-arms.

Almost all the enlisted men were from the Niebla or the cities of Andalusia: Seville, Cordova, and Jerez de la Frontera. Each seaman received about the equivalent of $7.00 in gold per month, the petty officers twice that, and the boys about $4.60.

It is not true that an Englishman and an Irishman were on board, but there is foundation for the jailbird tradition. Three local lads who had been sentenced to life imprisonment for helping a condemned murderer to break jail were set free in return for shipping with Columbus; they turned out to be trustworthy and sailed with him on later voyages, as did a considerable number of the others. In general, Columbus's crews were made up of sound, capable men and boys from the locality, with members of three leading families in key positions. Encouraged by an ancient pilot who was sure he had just missed the Indies on a Portuguese voyage westward forty years earlier, these *hombres* overcame a mariner's natural conservatism in the hope of winning glory, gold, and adventure. Those who survived won plenty of the first two, and all shared in one of the greatest adventures of all time—Columbus's First Voyage.

Bibliography and Notes

For this period of Columbus's life, see my *Admiral of the Ocean Sea,* I, chap. vii with notes. All Columbus's postils are in the *Raccolta,* Vol. I, part ii, 289–525, and in part iii and Supplement. Edmond Buron, *Ymago Mundi de Pierre d'Ailly* (3 vols., Paris, 1930), includes a complete reprinting of Columbus's own copy of the *Imago* and of his postils, with French translation of both on opposite pages, and learned notes and introduction. The original is reproduced by photostat in the Massachusetts Historical Society's *Americana* series.

An important recent work of over 500 pages on seven years of Columbus's life is Juan Manzano Manzano, *Cristóbal Colón, Siete Años Decisivos de Su Vida 1485–1492* (Madrid, 1964). Dr. Paolo Emilio Taviani of Rome is currently engaged in a work of the same scope, including, however, his life in Genoa, to be entitled *Cristoforo Colombo, Il Concepimento del Grande Disegno.*

Pierre Chaunu, *Séville* (see Notes to Chapter IX below), VIII, pt. i, p. 92.

Columbus's Fleet of 1492–93. No sailing ships in history have been subjected to so much research as these three, nor has any research met with less success. No blueprints, pictures, dimensions, etc., have survived. The "replicas" are educated guesses built around some rare detail that has survived; it is like reconstructing a dinosaur from one leg-bone. See my *Admiral of the Ocean Sea*, I, 149–53, 169–76. The best books by competent marine archaeologists are by the late (and much lamented) director of the marine museum at Madrid, Almirante Julio F. Guillén y Tato, *La Carabela Santa Maria, Apuntes para su Reconstitución* (Madrid, 1927); and *Columbus' Ships* (Howard I. Chapelle, ed., Barre, Mass., 1966) by the director of the Barcelona Museo Marítimo, Sr. Martínez-Hidalgo. Both are illustrated, and the second includes many details on other ships of that era.

Of the reconstructions, *Santa Maria II*, constructed for the Chicago World's Fair of 1893, sailed across to Havana under a Spanish naval crew and thence was towed to Chicago where for many years she was exhibited at Jackson Park. She burned in 1951, and only her anchor (now in the Chicago Historical Society) was saved. See Capt. Victor M. Concas y Palau, *La Nao Histórica Santa Maria* (Madrid, 1914). *Santa Maria III*, designed by Admiral Guillén for the Seville exposition of 1929, after being anchored for many years in the river opposite La Rábida, sank when under tow in 1945. Another, redesigned and built at Valencia from the same plans in 1951, somewhat modified by Señor Martínez-Hidalgo, has since been moored off the Columbus monument at Barcelona; and a copy of her, brought to the United States in a freighter, has been on public show at various American sea and river ports. The model of her, here reproduced, is in the Barcelona Museo Marítimo.

Columbus's crews. See my *Admiral of the Ocean Sea*, I, 183–99. On the basis of the original crew list printed in the late Duchess of Alba's *Nuevos Autógrafos de Colón* (1902), pp. 7–10, Alice B. Gould of Boston devoted many years to seeking out data on the men and establishing an impregnable list. Her findings appeared in the *Boletín* of the Real Academia de Historia, Madrid, between 1924 and 1944. At the time of her death, her data were incomplete, and she left the notes with the Director of the Archives of the Indies, Señor José de la Peña, to finish; his son informed me in 1972 that the work was almost done, and that this compilation, the most important piece of original Columbian research performed in the present century, only awaits a publisher. The notion that an Englishman and an Irishman were in Columbus's fleet is derived from a list printed in Navarrete, *Colección*, II, 19–20, which includes not a single real crew member.

Luis de Santangel's part. He was the *escribano de ración* (keeper of the privy purse) to King Ferdinand who advanced 1,400,000 maravedis from the funds of that portion of the Santa Hermandad, a police force which operated within the kingdom of Aragon. When Columbus's descendants adopted a motto giving all credit to Castile:

> *Por Castilla y por León*
> *Nuevo Mundo halló Colón*

some wit of Barcelona proposed to add:

> *Pero lo pagó Aragón*—But Aragon paid for it!

King Ferdinand eventually repaid Santangel's loan.

Santangel is supposed to have been a *converso*, a converted Jew; but this is denied by Francisco Martínez y Martínez, *El Descubrimiento de América y las Joyas de Doña Isabel* (1916). The fact that Columbus addressed to Santangel his Letter to the Sovereigns on his First Voyage has no significance. A mere subject could not write to the sovereign direct; it had to go to a court official who would read it at a suitable moment. (This is still the court etiquette of the Bourbons; if you wish to write to D. Juan Carlos, Franco's designated heir to the throne, you must send it to his chamberlain.) Incidentally, many editions of the Columbus Letter have a cover depicting King Ferdinand advancing victoriously into newly discovered islands; the tradition that Isabella did it all and Ferdinand merely made objections began in a later century.

Cartographical background. Carlos Sanz, *El Descubrimiento de América. Los Tres Mapas que lo Determinaron* (Madrid, 1972), brings together a pre-Columbian Ptolemy, the Henricus Martellus Germanus world map, and the Waldseemüller map of 1507, to show their relationships. E. G. Ravenstein, *Martin Behaim His Life and His Globe* (London, 1908), is still the most valuable work on this famous globe of 1492, and includes colored reproductions of the gores. Important studies of it are those of Luis Molinari in his *Historia de la Nación Argentina*, II (Buenos Aires, 1937), 448–69, G. H. Kimble in *Scottish Geographical Magazine*, XLIX (1933), 91–98, and J. S. Fonseca Hermes, "Christovam Colombo e Martim Behaim," in *Boletim Sociedade de Geografia de Lisboa* (1950), pp. 1–50. The best study of the Germanus is by A. O. Vietor in *Yale University Library Gazette*, XXXVII (1962). Significantly, Germanus places Cipangu at about 60° longitude west of the Canary Islands, just where Columbus expected to find it. R. A. Skelton's "Cartography of Columbus's First Voyage," an appendix (pp. 217–25) to the Vigneras edition (1960) of Cecil Jane's *Journal of Columbus*, is scholarly, and exceptionally well illustrated.

* III *

Columbus's First Voyage of Discovery

August-October 1492

Columbus the Man

Although there exists no contemporary portrait of Christopher Columbus, we are fortunate to have descriptions of his appearance, personality, and character from several men who knew him: his son Ferdinand who lived with him many years, Oviedo the official historian of the Indies who witnessed his triumphal return in 1493, and Bishop Las Casas, who met him in 1500 in Hispaniola, and whose father and uncle had been Columbus's shipmates. All three agree that the Admiral was more than middling tall, long-visaged, blue-eyed, with bright red hair which turned gray early; impressive in port and countenance, exuding authority, "worthy of all reverence." Usually pleasant and affable, he became irascible when crossed; and when moved to rebuke sailors, instead of culling obscenities from the choice assortment of seagoing profanity, he uttered no other oath than "By San Fernando!" and no reprimand except "May God take you!" Persistent to the point of stubbornness, and so confident of being right that Las Casas said he seemed to know the world as if it were his own chamber, Columbus believed that God willed him to discover this short route to the Indies, therefore he must succeed; anything else discovered en route should be considered a divine gift to him and to Spain. He daily read the Divine

Office like a priest, observed faithfully all church festivals, cultivated the company of ecclesiastics, headed every letter with a little cross, and often concluded with the prayer

Jesus et Maria	Jesus and Mary
Sint nobis in via	Be with us on the way.

Confident of being God's instrument, Columbus met the hardships of the sea with stoic endurance. Yet he also had a keen business sense, and planned to establish solidly his rank, titles, and fortune for generations to come. To maintain communication with the Catholic Sovereigns, he saw to it that one or both sons became pages at court, to defend his interests. It is rare that in the twentieth century we can find any descendant of a sixteenth-century discoverer, but Columbus's descendants through his son D. Diego are now numerous and include people of high rank such as the Dukes of Alba and of Veragua.

Columbus's character, tempered in the fire of adversity, did not come out pure steel. A proud and sensitive man, he never forgot the jeers of witless courtiers at his enterprise; and too often, after his triumphal return, he would say, "What a fool you were not to believe me!" Or, "I did it, despite your bad advice!" Thus he got men's backs up, and they did all they could to pull him down, or otherwise bedevil him. They succeeded only too well.

But in this bright August of 1492 his fortunes were at young flood, and that tide in his affairs carried him to a New World.

From Palos to San Salvador

The fleet was ready for sea on 2 August 1492. Every man and boy confessed his sins, received absolution, and received communion at the Church of St. George in Palos. The Captain General (as we should call Columbus at this juncture) went on board *Santa Maria* in the small hours of Friday the third, and at break of day made signal to get under way. Before the sun rose, all three vessels were floating down the Rio Tinto on the morning ebb, with sails hanging limp from their yards, the men pulling on long ash sweeps to maintain steerageway. As they swung into the Saltés and passed La Rábida close aboard, they could hear the friars chanting the ancient hymn *Iam lucis orto sidere* with its haunting refrain, *Et nunc et in perpetuum*, "Evermore and evermore."

This fleet of high promise, destined radically to affect world history, sailed parallel to a very different fleet of misery and woe. On the very same tide there dropped down the Saltés the last vessel carrying the Jews whom Ferdinand and Isabella had expelled from Spain; 2 August was their deadline; anyone who remained thereafter was to be executed unless he embraced Christianity. Thousands of pitiful refugees, carrying what few household goods they could stow in the crowded ships, were bound for the more tolerant lands of Islam, or for the Netherlands, the only Christian country which would receive them. Columbus has left no word of pity for this persecuted people; he even expressed the wish to exclude them from the lands that he discovered. But, had there been a new prophet of Israel, he might have pointed out the Columbian fleet to his wretched compatriots on that August morning, as the ships which in due time would lead the way to a new life for the Jewish exiles.

The Captain General's simple, seaman-like plan for the voyage ensured its success. He would carefully avoid the boisterous head winds, monstrous seas, and dark unbridled waters of the North Atlantic which had already baffled Portuguese would-be discoverers thrusting westward. Instead, he would run south before the northerlies prevailing off Spain and North Africa to the Canary Islands and there make, as it were, a right-angle turn. For he had observed on his African voyages that winter winds in the latitude of the Canaries blew from the east. Moreover, the mean latitude of the Canaries 28° N, he believed would cut Japan, and also pass the spot where several maps of the period located the mythical isle of Antilia, which would make a good break. Thus, he proposed to reach the Indies by the same traditional "latitude sailing" practised by northern seamen even before the invention of the compass.*

On the first leg of the voyage, Pinta's rudder jumped its gudgeons, so Columbus decided to send her into Las Palmas for repairs while Santa Maria and Niña went to Gomera, westernmost of the conquered Canary Islands. There he sent men ashore to fill water casks, buy breadstuffs and cheese, and salt down native beef. He then sailed to Las Palmas to superintend Pinta's repairs and with her returned to Gomera. By 2 September all three ships were anchored off San Sebastián, the port of Gomera. Columbus there met Doña Beatriz de Peraza y Bobadilla, widow of the former captain of the island, a beautiful lady still

* See my Northern Voyages, pp. 34, 94, 170, 479.

under thirty. He is said by a shipmate to have fallen deeply in love with her; nonetheless, he did not tarry. Additional ship's stores were quickly hoisted on board and struck below, and on 6 September 1492 the fleet weighed anchor for the last time in the Old World. It had still another island to pass, lofty Ferro, or Hierro. Owing to calms and variables, Ferro and the 12,000-foot peak of Tenerife were in sight until the ninth, but by nightfall that day every trace of land had sunk below the eastern horizon, and the three vessels were alone on an uncharted ocean. The Captain General himself gave out the course: "West; nothing to the north, nothing to the south."

How were those vessels navigated? * Celestial navigation was then in its infancy, but rough estimates of latitude could be made from the height of the North Star above the horizon and its relation to the two outer stars (the Guards) of the Little Bear, or Little Dipper. A meridian altitude of the sun, corrected by the sun's declination, for which tables had long been provided, also produced latitude. But the instruments of observation—a wood or brass quadrant and the seaman's astrolabe—were so crude, and the movement of a ship threw them off to such an extent, that most navigators took their latitude sights ashore. Columbus relied almost completely on "dead reckoning," which means plotting your course and position on a chart from the three elements of direction, time, and speed.

The direction he had from one or more compasses, which were similar to the dry-card type used in small craft until recently. His had a circular card graduated to the 32 points (N, N by E, NNE, NE by N, NE, and so on), with a lodestone under the north point. It was mounted on a pin and enclosed in a binnacle with gimbals so it could swing freely with the motion of the ship. Columbus's standard compass was mounted on the poop deck under observation of the officer of the watch. The helmsman, who steered with a heavy tiller attached directly to the rudder head, operated from the main deck below, and could see very little ahead. *Santa Maria* may have had another compass for him to steer by, but in the two caravels he was conned by the officer of the deck through a hatch, and kept his course steady by the feel of the helm. On a sailing vessel you can do that; it would be impossible in a power craft.

Time on the vessels of that day was measured by a half-hour glass

* For more details on navigation methods of that era, see my *Northern Voyages*, pp. 136–51.

which hung from a beam, so the sand could flow freely from the upper to the lower half. As soon as all the sand had come down a ship's boy turned the glass, and the officer of the deck recorded it by making a stroke on a slate. Eight glasses made a watch; the modern ship's bells were originally a means of marking the glasses. This half-hour-glass time could be corrected daily in fair weather, since local noon came when the sun bore due south. Columbus did this every week or so.

Speed long remained the most variable of these three elements. Columbus had no chip log or other method of measuring the speed of his vessels. He or the officer of the watch merely estimated it. Captain J. W. McElroy, by carefully checking Columbus's Journal of his First Voyage, ascertained that he made an average 9 per cent overestimate of distance. This did not prevent his finding the way home, because the mistake was constant, and time and course were correct. It only resulted in Columbus's placing the islands of his discovery further west than they really were.

Even after making the proper reduction for this overestimate, the speed of Columbus's vessels is surprising. Ships of that day were expected to make 3 to 5 knots in a light breeze, up to 9½ in a strong, fair gale, and at times to be capable of 12 knots. In October 1492 for five consecutive days, the Columbus fleet made an average of 142 miles per day, and the best day's run, 182 miles, averaged almost 8 knots. On the homeward passage, in February 1493, Niña and Pinta covered 198 miles one day, and at times hit it up to 11 knots. Any yachtsman today would be proud to make such records. Improvements in sailing vessels since 1492 have been more in comfort than in speed. Square-riggers of around 1500 actually could sail closer on the wind than their descendants of 1900, because they had much less standing rigging to prevent the yards' being braced sharp up; the mainmast, a stout and not very tall tree, needed much less support than the masts of later centuries.

One reason Columbus always wanted two or more vessels was to have someone to rescue survivors in case of sinking. But he made an unusual record for that era by never losing a ship at sea, unless we count the Santa Maria's grounding without loss of life. Comforts and conveniences were almost totally lacking. Cooking was done over a bed of sand in a wooden firebox protected from the wind by a hood, and tucked under the forecastle. The diet, a monotonous one of salt meat, hardtack, lentils, and beans, was washed down by red wine, and when that gave out, by water which often went bad in the casks. Only the captains had cabins with bunks; others slept where they could, in their clothes.

On 9 September 1492, the day he dropped the last land below the horizon, Columbus decided to keep a true reckoning of the course for his own use, and a false one to give out to his people so that they would not be frightened at sailing so far from land. But, owing to his overestimate of speed, the "false" reckoning was more nearly correct than the "true"!

During the first ten days (9 to 18 September), the easterly trade wind blew steadily, and the fleet made 1163 nautical miles westward. This was the honeymoon of the voyage. *Que era plazer grande el gusto de las mañanas*—"What a delight was the savor of the mornings!"—wrote Columbus in his Journal. That entry speaks to the heart of anyone who has sailed in the trades. It recalls the dawn, kindling both clouds and sails rose-color, the smell of dew drying on a wooden deck, and (a pleasure Columbus never knew) the first cup of coffee. This feeling is beautifully expressed by my old friend Dr. Frederick Fraley in his poem "The Morning Watch"—

> Wide waste of waters, dim receding stars,
> The breeeze of dawn that barely fills the sail. . . .
> Creak of the rigging, gently furrowed wave
> Under the bows that answer to the swell,
> Set sails, wet deck, breath of the salty air
> And clear resounding stroke of brazen bell.
> "Our little life is rounded with a sleep."
> Strangers and sojourners we are with Thee,
> But, we who sail the reaches of the deep
> Feel of its might, know its serenity,
> Look for the sun in measured course to keep
> Appointment with the morning watch at sea.

Succinctly is the beauty of sailing expressed in a stanza (i. 19) of Camoëns' *Lusiads:*—

> Já no largo Oceano navegavam
> As inquietas ondas apartando;
> Os ventos brandamente respiravam,
> Das naos as velas concavas inchando:
> Da branca escuma os mares se mostravam . . .

"Now in broad ocean navigating / the restless waves parting, / the winds softly blowing, / concave sails filling, / the white foam of their waves following. . . ."

Since Columbus's ships were sailing near the northern limit of the northeast trades, where the wind first strikes the water, he found a smooth sea; and the air (he remarked in his Journal), was "like April in Andalusia, the only thing wanting was to hear the song of the nightingale." But there were plenty of other birds following the ships: the little Mother Carey's chickens dabbling for plankton in the bow waves and the wake; the boatswain bird, so called (as old seamen used to say) because it carries a marlinspike in its tail; the man-of-war or frigate bird, "thou ship of the air that never furl'st thy sails," as Walt Whitman wrote; and when the fleet passed beyond the range of these birds, big Jaeger gulls gave it a call.

On 16 September the fleet first entered a field of sargassum (gulf-weed) and found that it was no hindrance to navigation. "Saw plenty weed" became an almost daily notation in Columbus's Journal. The gulfweed bothered him much less than observing a westerly variation of the compass, for in European waters the variation at this era was easterly.

Ten days out from Ferro, the fleet temporarily ran into an area of variable winds and rain. It had reached the point on Columbus's chart where the fabled island of Antilia should have been, and all hands expected to sight land. The Captain General ordered the deep-sea lead to be hove, and spliced together his two 100-fathom lines for that purpose. Naturally he found no bottom—the ocean there is about 2300 fathom deep! Ordinary seamen who, on the tenth day of the northeast trades, were beginning to wonder whether they could ever beat back home, were cheered by the change of wind. They were never bothered by fear of "falling off the edge of the world"—that is just one of the many old wives' tales about this voyage.

Only 234 miles were made good during the next five days. During this spell of moderate weather it was easy to converse from ship to ship. In the middle of one of these colloquies, a seaman of *Pinta* gave the "Land Ho!" and everyone thought he saw an island against the setting sun. Columbus fell on his knees to thank God, ordered *Gloria in Excelsis Deo* to be sung by all, and set a course for the island. But at dawn no island was visible, for none was there. A cloudbank above the western horizon, a common phenomenon at sea, had deceived all hands. Columbus refused to beat about looking for this island because, he said, "His object was to reach the Indies, and if he had delayed, it would not have made sense."

The trade wind now returned moderately, and during the six days, 26 September to 1 October, the fleet made only 382 miles. Under these circumstances the people began to mutter and grumble. Three weeks was probably more than they had ever been beyond sight of land. They were all getting on each other's nerves, as happens even nowadays on a long voyage to a known destination. Grievances, real or imaginary, were blown up; cliques were formed; fist fights had to be broken up by the alguacil, the master-at-arms. Every minute Spain grew further away, and what lay ahead? Probably nothing, except in the eye of that cursed Genoese. Let's make him turn back, or throw him overboard!

On the first day of October the wind increased, rain fell in torrents, replenishing the water casks, and in five days (2 to 6 October) the fleet made 710 miles. On the sixth, when they had passed longitude 65° W and actually lay directly north of Puerto Rico, Martín Alonso Pinzón shot his agile *Pinta* under the flagship's stern and shouted, "Alter course, sir, to southwest by west . . . Japan!" Columbus did not understand whether Martín Alonso meant that he thought they had missed Japan and should steer southwest by west for China, or that Japan lay in that direction; but he knew and Pinzón knew that the fleet had sailed more than the 2400 miles which, according to their calculations, lay between the Canaries and Japan. Naturally Columbus was uneasy, but he held to the west course magnetic, which, owing to the variation for which he did not allow, was about west by south, true.

On 7 October, when *Niña* made another false landfall, great flocks of birds passed over the ships, flying west-southwest; this was the autumn migration from eastern North America to the West Indies. Columbus decided that he had better follow Pinzón and the birds rather than his chart, and changed course accordingly that very evening. A very good guess, for this was his shortest route to the nearest land. Every night the men were heartened by seeing against the moon (full on 5 October) flocks of birds flying their way. But mutiny once more reared its ugly head. Even by Columbus's phony reckoning which he gave out, they had sailed much further west than anyone

The "White Cliffs" first sighted by Columbus. David Crofoot photo.

had expected. Enough of this nonsense, sailing west to nowhere; let the Captain General turn back or else—! Columbus, says the record, "cheered them as best he could, holding out good hope of the advantages they might gain; and he added, it was useless to complain, *since he had come to go to the Indies, and so had to continue until he found them, with the help of Our Lord.*"

How typical of Columbus's determination! Yet even he, conscious of divine guidance, could not have kept on indefinitely without the support of his captains and officers. According to one account, Martín Alonso Pinzón cheered him by shouting, *Adelante! Adelante!* which the poet Joaquin Miller translated, "Sail on! Sail on!" But, according to Oviedo, one of the earliest historians who talked with the participants, it was Columbus who persuaded the Pinzóns to sail on, with the promise that if land were not found within three days he would turn back. This promise was made on 9 October. Next day the trade wind blew fresher, sending the fleet along at 7 knots, and on the 10th the fleet made a record day's run. On the 11th the wind continued to blow hard, with a heavy following sea. Now signs of land, such as branches of trees with green leaves and even flowers, became so frequent that the people were content with their commander's decision, and the mutinous mutterings died out in keen anticipation of making a landfall in the Indies.

As the sun set under a clear horizon 11 October, the northeast trade breezed up to gale force, and the three ships tore along at 9 knots. Columbus refused to shorten sail, signaled everyone to keep a par-

The cross at the landing place, San Salvador. David Crofoot photo.

ticularly sharp watch, and offered extra rewards for first landfall in addition to the year's pay promised by the Sovereigns. That night of destiny was clear and beautiful with a late-rising moon, but the sea was the roughest of the entire passage. The men were tense and expectant, the officers testy and anxious, Columbus serene in the confidence that presently God would reveal to him the promised Indies.

At 10:00 p.m., an hour before moonrise, Columbus and a seaman, also simultaneously, thought they saw a light "like a little wax candle rising and falling." Others said they saw it too, but most did not; and after a few minutes it disappeared. Volumes have been written to explain what this light was or might have been. It may well have been a mere illusion created by over-tense watchfulness. But Mrs. Ruth Malvin, a long-time resident of San Salvador, believes it to have been a bonfire lighted by natives living on cliffs or hills on the windward side, to keep sand fleas out of their cabins; and this is the best rational explanation yet made. She had fires lighted on High Cay and other places, and when some 28 miles out to sea could see light "rising and falling" just as Columbus said.

The little light does not cause Columbus to alter his course. His ships rush on, pitching, rolling, and throwing spray, white foam at their bows and wakes reflecting the moon. *Pinta* is perhaps half a mile in the lead, *Santa Maria* on her port quarter, *Niña* on the other side. Now one, now another forges ahead. With the fourth glass of the night watch, the last sands are running out of an era that began with the dawn of history. Not since the birth of Christ has there been a night so full of meaning for the human race.

At 2:00 a.m. 12 October, Rodrigo de Triana, lookout on *Pinta*, sees something like a white cliff shining in the moonlight and sings out, *Tierra! tierra!* "Land! land!" Captain Pinzón verifies the landfall, fires a gun as agreed, and shortens sail to allow the flagship to catch up. As *Santa Maria* approaches, Columbus shouts across the rushing waters, "Señor Martín Alonso, you *did* find land! Five thousand maravedis for you as a bonus!"

Land it was this time; gray clay cliffs, white in the moonlight, on the windward side of a little island of the Bahama group. The fleet would have crashed had it held course, but these men were no fools to pile up on a lee shore. Columbus ordered sail to be shortened and the fleet to jog off and on until daylight. At dawn they made full sail, passed the southern point of the island, and sought an opening on the west coast through the barrier reef. Before noon they found it, sailed into a shallow bay, and anchored in the lee of the land, in five fathoms.

Here on a gleaming beach of white coral occurred the famous first landing of Columbus. The commander (now by general consent called Admiral) went ashore in the flagship's longboat displaying the royal standard of Castile, accompanied by the two Captains Pinzón in their boats, flying the banner of the expedition—a green crowned cross on a white field. "And, all having rendered thanks to Our Lord, kneeling on the ground, embracing it with tears of joy for the immeasurable mercy of having reached it, the Admiral rose and gave this island the name *San Salvador*"—Holy Saviour.

Bibliography and Notes

Columbus's Journal of First Voyage. For the unique *Diario* or Journal of the First Voyage there are many editions and translations, most of them bad.* There is no further excuse for using these defective sources, since the distinguished Spanish historian and bibliographer Carlos Sanz has published a facsimile of Las Casas's original manuscript in the Biblioteca Nacional, Madrid (*Diario de Colón*, Madrid, 1962), and also a printed edition following the ms. line by line, with the same title and a learned introduction. Both volumes are in his *Biblioteca Americana Vetustissima* series. With the aid of the late Professor Jeremiah D. M. Ford and of Dr. Milton Anastos, I made a fresh translation of the *Diario*, which is printed in my *Journals and Other Documents* (1963), pp. 41–179.** Cecil Jane (of *Jane's Fighting Ships* fame) compiled two important collections, *Select Documents Illustrating the Four Voyages of Columbus* (2 vols., London, Hakluyt Society, 1930–33) and *The Voyages of Christopher Columbus* (London, 1930). This last contains Jane's translation of the *Diário*. Each publication is preceded by a long, boring introduction which attempts to prove that Columbus was illiterate and had no definite objective in 1492. Professor L. A. Vigneras edited a beautifully illustrated reprint of Cecil Jane's translation of the *Diario* (*The Journal of Christopher Columbus*, New York, 1960).†

*S.E. Morison, "Texts and Translations of the Journal of Columbus's First Voyage," *Hispanic American Historical Review*, XIX (1939), 235–61; Emiliano Jos, "El Libro del Primero Viaje. Algunas Ediciones Recientes," *Revista de Indias*, X (1950), 719–51.
** Mr. J. A. Vázquez has written a very useful article, "Las Casas' Opinions in Columbus's Diary" (*Topic: A Journal of the Liberal Arts*, Washington, Penna., 1971, pp. 145–56), in which he infers the Bishop's opinions from his *abrégé* of the Journal, and prints for the first time some of his marginal notes from the ms.
† Professor Vigneras kindly pointed out some mistakes in my translation of the *Diario*, which I set forth here, in the hope that owners of my *Journals and Other Documents* will correct their copies accordingly: P. 122 (*Journal* for 16 Dec.),

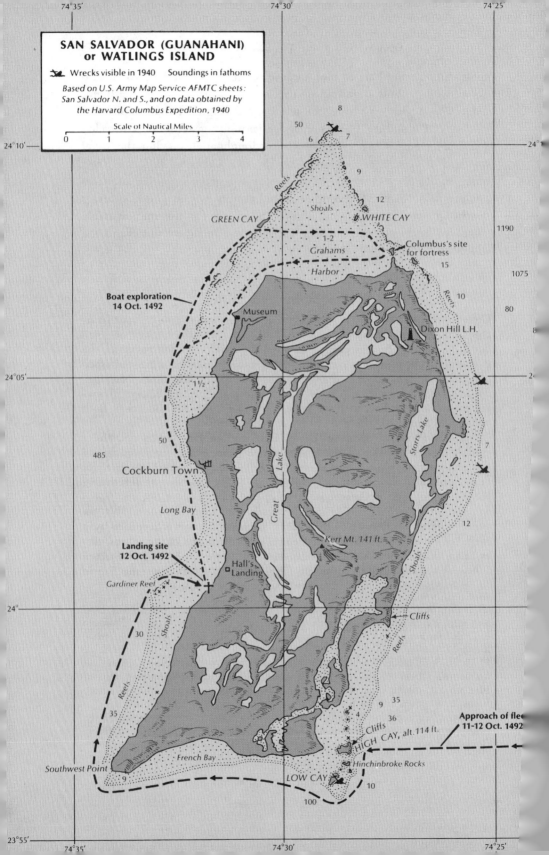

**SAN SALVADOR (GUANAHANI)
or WATLINGS ISLAND**

Wrecks visible in 1940　　Soundings in fathoms

*Based on U.S. Army Map Service AFMTC sheets:
San Salvador N. and S., and on data obtained by
the Harvard Columbus Expedition, 1940*

Scale of Nautical Miles

0　　1　　2　　3　　4

24°10'

24°

8

50

6　　7

9

12

GREEN CAY

WHITE CAY

1190

Shoals

Columbus's site
for fortress

1-2

Grahams

15

Harbor

1075

Reefs

**Boat exploration
14 Oct. 1492**

10

80

Museum

Dixon Hill L.H.

8

24°05'

1½

Storrs Lake

50

7

485

Cockburn Town

12

Long Bay

Great Lake

Kerr Mt. 141 ft.

**Landing site
12 Oct. 1492**

Shoals

Hall's
Landing

Gardiner Reef

24°

Cliffs

30

Shoals

Reefs

Reefs

35

35

4

36

**Approach of fleet
11-12 Oct. 1492**

Cliffs

HIGH CAY, alt. 114 ft.

Southwest Point

French Bay

Hinchinbroke Rocks

9

LOW CAY

10

100

23°55'

74°35'　　　　　　　　　74°30'　　　　　　　74°25'

The Landfall. Ruth G. Durlacher Wolper (now Mrs. Malvin), a long-time resident of San Salvador, in *A New Theory Identifying the Locale of Columbus's Light, Landfall and Landing* (Smithsonian Institution *Collections* Vol. 148, No. 1, Sept. 1964), tells of her experiment, having bonfires lighted on the highest cliff of the windward side, and seeing the light rise and fall when she was some 28 miles out, just as Columbus did. She also relates earlier theories of the landfall, and has a mass of information on San Salvador, and a bibliography. Captain P. Verhoog of the Dutch merchant marine challenged my (and many earlier) identifications of Guanahaní—San Salvador—as the island that the English called Watlings, in his *Guana-haní Again* (Amsterdam, 1947), and U.S. Naval Institute *Proceedings,* LXXX (1954), 1100–11. E. A. and M. C. Link supported him in a pamphlet, *A New Theory on Columbus's Voyage Through the Bahamas* (Smithsonian Institution, 1958). Another Dutch captain, Edzer Roukema, answered them in an article demolishing the Links' theory that it was Caicos: "It was San Salvador," *American Neptune,* XIX (1959), 79–113. For more references to the landfall, see my *Journals and Other Documents,* pp. 65–66. Caicos, the choice of Verhoog and the Links, has an immense lagoon, very shallow and full of coral heads; the island does not in the least correspond to Columbus's description of San Salvador; and if you backtrack with Columbus's own Journal from Baracoa in Cuba, the first sure place upon which everyone agrees, you come out at the present San Salvador and nowhere else.

One of the most amusing hoaxes of our day is the story about Columbus submitting his great enterprise to the Senate of Genoa, all of whom turned it down (in a 964-page report) as impractical, impossible, and incredible, except the junior member, none other than Leonardo da Vinci! After seeing this squib given the dignity of print in the *Congressional Record* for 28 June 1971, p. S 10, 107, I ran it to ground. Through my friend Robert Sherrod I found that it was written as a satire by Dr. Ralph S. Cooper of the Scientific Laboratory at Los Alamos, to whose dismay it was taken seriously in many quarters.

---

insert in mid-page between "leg" and "And,": "And he says all these people were stout and brave and not weak like the others which he had earlier seen, and of very sweet talk, [but] no religious doctrine." P. 125 (18 Dec.), line 8 up: insert between "honor" and "His," "A seaman who had met him en route and seen everything that the Admiral had given him, said that a man who appeared to be highly honored carried them ahead of the king." P. 145 (5 Jan.), note 2, last line: change "and" to "but", and "there" to "not". P. 151 (13 Jan.), line 7 up: between "islands." and "Of," insert: "Copper or inferior gold they call *tuob* in Hispaniola."

* IV *

The Greater Antilles

12 October 1492 – 15 March 1493

South to Cuba

The first natives encountered on Guanahaní (their own name for this island) fled to the jungle when they saw three winged monsters approaching; but curiosity proved too much for them, and when they saw strangely dressed human beings coming ashore, they approached timidly, with propitiatory gifts. Columbus, of course, had to believe that he was in the Indies, so he named these people "Indians," and Indians the native inhabitants of the Americas have become in all European languages.

These were of the Taino branch of the Arawak language group. Within the previous century they had wrested the Bahamas and most of Cuba from the more primitive Siboney. They grew corn, yams, and other roots for food; they knew how to make cassava bread, to spin and weave cotton, and to make pottery. The Spaniards observed with wonder their fine physique and almost complete nakedness, and noted with keen interest that some wore, suspended from the nose, little pendants of pure gold. The guilelessness and generosity of these children of nature—"They invite you to share anything that they possess, and show as much love as if their hearts went with it," wrote Columbus—their ignorance of money and of iron, and their nudity,

66

suggested to every educated European that these people were hold-overs from the Golden Age. Peter Martyr, the court historian, wrote that "They seem to live in that golden world of the which old writers speak so much, wherein men lived simply and innocently without enforcement of laws, without quarreling, judges and libels, content only to satisfy nature."

Columbus would much rather have encountered sophisticated Orien-tals than "noble savages," but as usual he made the best of the situation. He observed "how easy it would be to convert these people—and to make them work for us." In other words, to enslave them in return for saving their souls. Every Spaniard seems to have concluded from the tales of mariners who returned from this voyage that no white man need do a hand's turn of work in the New World; God had provided docile natives to labor for the lords of creation.

For two days Columbus explored San Salvador. It was a pretty island then, with a heavy covering of tropical hardwood; but the Admiral knew full well that, interesting as the discovery of an island inhabited by Golden Age natives might be, he must take home certain evidence of Japan or China, or plenty of gold and spices, to prove his voyage a success. The natives indicated by sign language that scores of islands lay to the west and south; it seemed to the Admiral that these must be those shown on his chart, lying south of Cipangu; and that if they did not lead him to golden Japan, they would prove to be stepping-stones to China.

So, detaining six Indians as guides, Columbus weighed anchors on the afternoon of 14 October. That day he discovered another island which he named *Santa Maria de la Concepción;* the English prosaically re-named it Rum Cay. This is still one of the prettiest Bahamian islands; hilly, well timbered, free of development blight. Today it has only about one hundred inhabitants clustered in a small village ambitiously called Port Nelson. The island has no roads, and a virgin forest covers it.

The natives here proved to be similar to those on San Salvador and were equally pleased with the Admiral's gifts of red caps, glass beads, and hawks' bells. These were little spherical bells about the diameter of a quarter-dollar or shilling, which were attached to the birds used in falconry; they had the pleasant tinkle of a miniature sleighbell, and the natives loved them. Indians would paddle out to the flagship wagging their fingers and saying, *Chuq! chuq!* meaning, "More hawks'

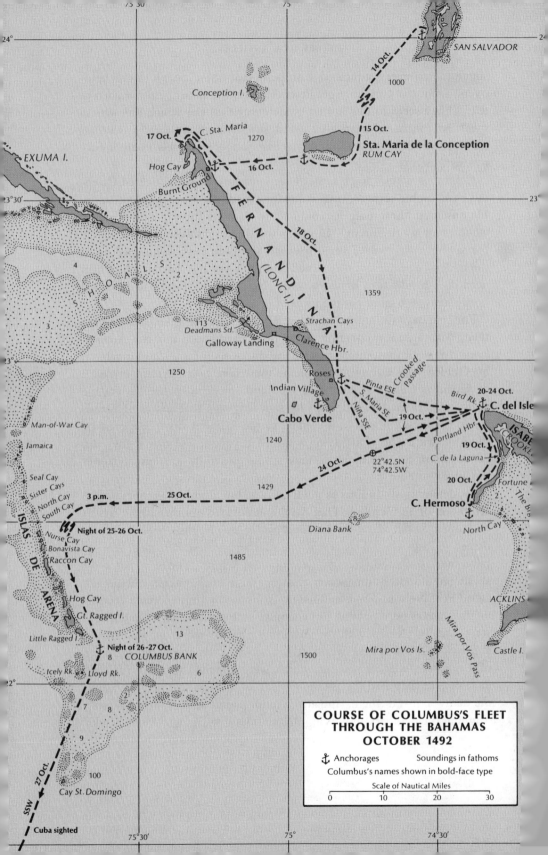

24°

75°30'   75°   24°

SAN SALVADOR

14 Oct.   1000

Conception I.

15 Oct.

17 Oct.   C. Sta. Maria   **Sta. Maria de la Conception**
                                                                        RUM CAY
                        1270

EXUMA I.   Hog Cay   16 Oct.

                        Burnt Ground

23°30'   23°

                    F
                    E
                    R
        S   N
        H   A   18 Oct.
        O   N
        A   D
        L   I   1359
    4   S   N
        2   A
                    (LONG I.)

3

                        Strachan Cays

113   Clarence Hbr.
Deadmans Sd.
Galloway Landing

23°   23°

1250   Roses   Crooked
                                                                Passage
            Indian Village   Pinta ESE   Bird Rk.   20-24 Oct.
                                        S. Maria SE   C. del Isle
                Cabo Verde   Niña SSE   19 Oct.
                                                                                ISABEL
                                                        Portland Hbr.   CROOKE

Man-of-War Cay   1240   19 Oct.
                                                        C. de la Laguna
Jamaica
                                        22°42.5N
                        24 Oct.   74°42.5W   20 Oct.   Fortune
Seal Cay   **C. Hermoso**
Sister Cays   25 Oct.   1429   The bi
North Cay   3 p.m.   North Cay   2
South Cay

        Night of 25-26 Oct.   8
ISLAS   Diana Bank
    Nurse Cay
DE   Bonavista Cay   1485
    Raccon Cay

ARENA
        Hog Cay   ACKLINS
        Gt. Ragged I.   13
Little Ragged I.   Mira por Vos Is.   Castle I.
        Night of 26-27 Oct.
        8   COLUMBUS BANK   1500   Mira por Vos Pass
Icely Rk. Lloyd Rk.   6

22°   22°
    7   8

    9

27 Oct.   100
        Cay St. Domingo

SSW

Cuba sighted

        75°30'   75°   74°30'

> ### COURSE OF COLUMBUS'S FLEET
> ### THROUGH THE BAHAMAS
> ### OCTOBER 1492
>
> ⚓ Anchorages   Soundings in fathoms
> Columbus's names shown in bold-face type
>
> Scale of Nautical Miles
> 0   10   20   30

Columbus's *Maravilloso Puerto*, Santa Maria Harbor, Long Island. David Crofoot photo.

bells, please!" Lace points, which were metal tips for the laces then used to fasten men's clothing, brass tambourine jingles, and Venetian glass beads were also favorites.

The Admiral's native guides, eager to please, kept assuring him by signs that in the next island there would be plenty of gold; but each one in succession—Long, Crooked, and Fortune—proved to be no different from San Salvador. Each was jungle-covered, inhabited by friendly natives who had no gold except for a few ornaments which they had obtained elsewhere. Where they got them he could never make out, because of the language barrier; Torres, the interpreter, found his Arabic completely useless. The Spaniards observed, and Columbus noted, the first maize or Indian corn ever seen by a European, the first hammocks, woven from native cotton, and the first yams and sweet potatoes; also, a tree that he estimated correctly would prove to be good dye-wood. But no sign of gold except on the natives' persons.

As the Admiral and his Indian guides came to understand each other better, he heard about a big island that they called *Colba* (Cuba), and made up his mind that it must be either Japan or a part of China. So to Colba he must go, and the Indians took him there by their usual canoe route, so laid out as to be the shortest possible jump over blue water.

First they sailed due west from Rum Cay to the northern end of Long Island, which they could see from the mastheads. *Fernandina,* as Columbus named Long Island, he described as very green, level, and fertile, and the natives friendly. He anchored off a village, and next day (17 October) investigated a *maravilloso puerto*—a marvelous harbor. Entering by a high bluff, he found it big enough to hold a hundred ships, "if it were deep, and clean bottom, and deep at the entrance," which unfortunately it was not. This description perfectly fits Santa Maria Harbor just east of the cape of that name. You enter it around high limestone cliffs, where there is now a small lighthouse, and it has water enough for small craft, but is much too shoal for a caravel or any other seagoing vessel.

While a shore party filled water casks from a well (one that is still used, since fresh water is scarce in the Bahamas), Columbus, in his own words, "walked among some trees, which were the most beautiful thing to see that ever I had seen, viewing as much verdure in so great a development as in the month of May in Andalusia, and all the trees were as different from ours as day from night, and so the fruits, the herbage, the rocks, and all things." This is a good example of his rapturous descriptions of scenery, flora, and natives, in which he stands out from all other discoverers and explorers of that era.

Sailing to the south end of Long Island on the 18th, Columbus decided to cross the Crooked Island Passage, now an important sea route to Cuba. Next day he ordered his ships to fan out on an easterly course so they would not miss the next island—Crooked Island, which he named *Isabela* after the Queen. Here again he writes about the scenery

Crooked Island, Portland Harbor and Bird Rock.

ecstatically, and even notes the "fair and sweet smell of flowers or trees from the land . . . sweetest in the world." As we hove-to in the lee of this land in 1940, the land breeze similarly favored us with delicious odors.

Finding much to admire but nothing to detain him at Crooked and Fortune islands, Columbus sailed back across Crooked Island Passage to the line of cays at the southeast edge of the Great Bahama Bank. On 27 October, from an anchorage off Ragged Island, the fleet made a fast sail with a fresh northeast wind to a big island which the Indians pointed out as "Colba." And on the morning of 28 October they entered a Cuban harbor easily identified as Bahia Bariay. It is marked by a beautiful mountain now called La Teta de Bariay, which Columbus said had "on its summit another peak like a pretty little mosque." He

71

had never seen so beautiful a harbor—trees all fair and green and different from ours, some with bright flowers and some heavy with fruit, and the air full of birdsong. But where was the evidence of Japan? Where were the gold-roofed temples, dragon-mouthed bronze cannon? Where were the lords and ladies in gold-stiffened brocade?

Next day the three ships sailed westward along the many-harbored coast of Oriente Province of Cuba, hoping every moment to meet a welcoming fleet of Chinese junks. They anchored in Puerto Gibara, and there remained for twelve days, except for a brief jaunt westward to Punta Cobarrubia and back.

The interpreters shipped at San Salvador assured local Indians that the strangers in the white-winged monsters were good people, with plenty of trading truck, so Columbus's Cuban relations were pleasant and peaceful. The natives told him that plenty of gold could be found at *Cubanacan* (mid-Cuba) in the interior. The Admiral, mistaking this word for *El Gran Can*, the Great Khan, sent an "embassy" up country to present his letter of introduction to the Chinese emperor; he remained in Puerto Gibara to oversee the beaching and graving of his ships. Luis de Torres the Arabic scholar took charge of this diplomatic mission, and beside him trudged Rodrigo de Jerez, a seaman who had once met a black king in Guinea and so was thought to know the proper way to address pagan royalty. They carried the diplomatic portfolio (Latin passport and royal letter of credence to the Grand Khan), strings of glass beads to buy food, and a gift suitable for royalty. The embassy tramped up the valley of the Cacoyuguin River, past fields cultivated with corn, beans, and sweet potatoes, to what they hoped would be Cambaluk, the imperial city of Cathay. Alas, it turned out to be a village of about fifty palm-thatched huts, on the site of the present town of Holguin. The two Spaniards, regarded as having come from above, were feasted by the local cacique while the populace swarmed up to kiss their feet and present simple gifts. Rodrigo the sailor loved it—he had never had it so good in Africa—but Torres, expecting a reception by mandarins in a stone-built capital of ten thousand houses, felt badly let down.

Yet, on their way back to the harbor, the embassy made a discovery which would have more far-reaching results than any possible treaty. They met "many people who were going to their villages, both women and men, with a firebrand in the hand and herbs to drink the smoke thereof, as they are accustomed." You have guessed it, reader; this was the first European contact with tobacco smokers. The Tainos used it in the form of cigars which they called *tobacos*. A walking party, such as the embassy encountered, would carry a large cigar and at every halt light it from a firebrand; everyone then took three or four "drags" of the smoke through his nostrils; after this refreshment the march resumed, small boys keeping the firebrand alight until the next stop. Not long after Spaniards settled in the New World, they tried smoking tobacco and liked it, and through them its use spread rapidly through Europe, Asia, and Africa.

Columbus, in the meantime, totted up his dead reckoning and figured that he was right where China began. He decided that Cuba was the "Province of Mangi," a name which the imaginative maps of China that he had seen located on a peninsula at the southeast corner of the Celestial Empire. The Admiral also tried to shoot the North Star with his primitive quadrant. But he picked the wrong star—Alfirk of the constellation Cepheus—which on that November evening hung directly over Polaris. Thus he found Cuba to be on latitude 42° N, that of Cape Cod! Of course he knew this to be wrong, since he had sailed across on 28° N; and in his Letter to the Sovereigns he corrected the latitude of northern Cuba to 26°, still 5 degrees too high.

Here the Admiral began to collect specimens which he hoped would convince people that he was at least on the fringe of Asia. There was a shrub which smelled something like cinnamon and so must be cinnamon; the gumbo-limbo, supposedly an Asiatic form of the gum mastic that he had seen in Chios; and a small inedible nut, now called *nogal del pais*, he identified as the big coconut mentioned by Marco Polo. Coconut palms are such a feature of the Caribbean coast today that we forget that they, like the banana, were introduced later. The men dug up some roots which Sánchez the surgeon pronounced to be Chinese rhubarb, a valuable drug imported into Europe, but it turned out to be something quite different, not even as valuable as the humble pieplant.

As yet, no gold. When the Spaniards asked for gold, the Cubans always waved them on to some other place. According to them, there was an island called Babeque where the people gathered gold on the beach by candlelight and hammered it into bars. This choice piece of misinformation brought about the first rift in the Spanish high command. Without asking the Admiral's permission, Martín Alonso Pinzón took off in *Pinta*, hoping to be the first to reach Babeque. He called at

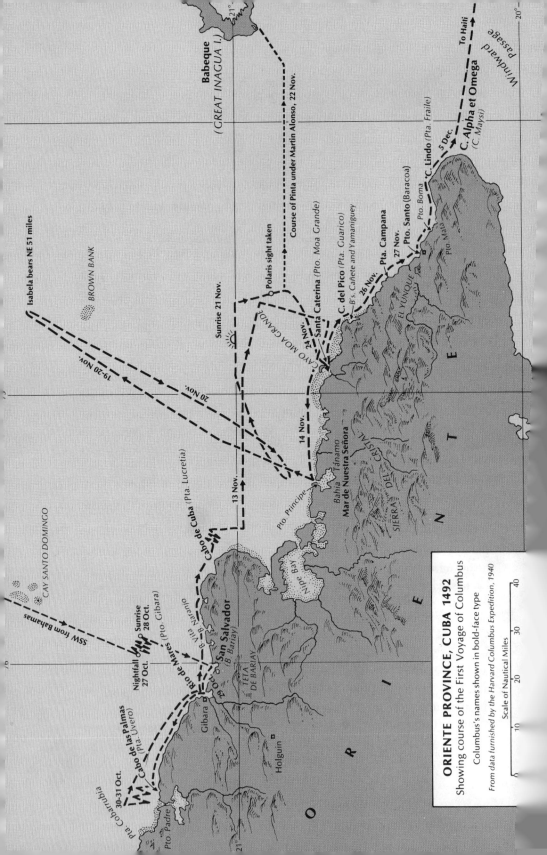

ORIENTE PROVINCE, CUBA 1492

Showing course of the First Voyage of Columbus

Columbus's names shown in bold-face type

From data furnished by the Harvard Columbus Expedition, 1940

Scale of Nautical Miles

10   20   30   40

Isabela bears NE 51 miles

BROWN BANK

Babeque
(GREAT INAGUA I.)

Course of Pinta under Martin Alonso, 22 Nov.

Polaris sight taken

Sunrise 21 Nov.

19-20 Nov.

20 Nov.

14 Nov.

13 Nov.

Santa Caterina (Pto. Moa Grande)

C. del Pico (Pta. Cuarico)

B's. Cañete and Yamaniguey

Pta. Campana

Pto. Santo (Baracoa)

26 Nov.

27 Nov.

Pto. Boma

C. Lindo (Pta. Fraile)

Pto. Mata

Pto. Mala

5 Dec.

C. Alpha et Omega
(C. Maysi)

To Haiti

Windward passage

EL YUNQUE

SIERRA DEL CRISTAL

Mar de Nuestra Señora

Bahía Tánamo

Pto. Principe

CAYO MOA GRANDE

Cabo de Cuba (Pta. Lucretia)

Nipe Bay

Vita Naranjo

B's. Bariay

San Salvador
(B. Bariay)

Río de Mares (Pto. Gibara)

Gibara

TETA DE BARIAY

Holguin

Nightfall 27 Oct.

Sunrise 28 Oct.

29 Oct.

Cabo de las Palmas (Pta. Uvero)

30-31 Oct.

Pta. Cogarrubia

Pto. Padre

SSW from Bahamas

CAY SANTO DOMINGO

CAY SANTO DOMINGO

O R I E N T E

Great Inagua Island, which lay in the general direction indicated by the Indians, and, needless to say, found no gold by candle or any other light.

The Admiral in *Santa Maria* with *Niña* sailed eastward along the superb coast of Oriente Province. Noble mountains rise directly from the sea, but every few miles there is a river whose mouth makes a good land-locked harbor. He called at Bahia Tánamo, entered its bottle-neck entrance, and within noted little wooded islands running up "like diamond points," and others flat-topped "like tables." You can see them all today. He put in at Puerto Cayo Moa, where you have to pick an opening through the breakers but then find yourself, as Columbus said, in "a lagoon in which all the ships of Spain could lie and be safe." The peculiar charm of this harbor, so calm between lofty mountains and the barrier of foaming reefs, was noted by Columbus in words that are not in the least exaggerated. He had an eye, too, for practical matters; when the men rowed him inside the river mouth, he observed on the mountain slopes pine trees which he said would make timber for the Spanish navy. The descendants of those pines, when we passed that way, were being sawed at a mill run by a mountain stream, whose distant roar Columbus heard on a Sunday in November 1492.

On he sailed, with a breeze that fortunately came from the west, noting nine little harbors, behind which leafy valleys ran up into the lofty sierra. He passed the anvil-shaped mountain El Yunque, landmark for Baracoa, a harbor which Columbus well described as round "like a little porringer." Here the Spaniards pitched their first settlement in Cuba in 1512; but Baracoa afforded no gold, and the fleet passed on as soon as the wind turned fair. At sunrise 5 December it was off Cape Maisi, easternmost point of Cuba. Identifying this as the eastern extremity of Asia, corresponding to Cape St. Vincent, the western extremity of Europe, Columbus named it Cape Alpha and Omega, where East ends and West begins. He later remarked that if you had the time and strength, you could walk from here around the back of the world, to Spain!

Hispaniola

The fleet now crossed the Windward Passage, and at nightfall arrived off the Haitian harbor of San Nicolás, so named by Columbus be-

Moustique Bay, where Columbus named Hispaniola. David Crofoot photo.

cause he entered it on 6 December, the feast day of that favorite saint of children. It is still St. Nicolas Môle. His Indian guides promised that gold would be found on this great island, the home of their ancestors, and they were right. This island saved Columbus's reputation, for had he returned home with no more "evidence" than hitherto he had obtained, people would have said, "This Genoese has found a few islands inhabited by gentle natives of the Golden Age, but as for their being the Indies—pooh!"

And what beauty! I sailed the same waters in January 1939, deck passenger on a chaloupe of the Haitian Coast Guard. The shores were lined with bayahonde and other great tropical trees which Columbus mistook for clove and nutmeg. At night the Southern Cross was poised like a great kite over the headland that Columbus named *Cabo del Estrella* (Cape of the Star); and in the northern sky the Great Bear stood up on his tail.

A fair breeze took *Santa Maria* and *Niña* into Moustique Bay, where easterly winds detained them for five days. Here the Admiral, "seeing the grandeur and beauty of this island and its resemblance to the land of Spain," named it *La Isla Española*—the Spanish Isle. His seamen captured a young and beautiful girl wearing only a golden nose plug, and brought her on board. She indicated that she would gladly stay with the boys, but the Admiral "sent her ashore very honorably," decently clad in slopchest clothing and bedecked with jingles and hawks' bells. This move proved to be good for public relations, as the damsel was a cacique's daughter. Next day nine Spaniards ashore were conducted to a big village of a thousand people and given everything they wanted—food, drink, girls, and parrots.

On 15 December *Santa Maria* and *Niña* beat up the Tortuga Channel to the mouth of Trois Rivières, a clear mountain stream that flows through a valley that Columbus well named the Valley of Paradise. Next day, when the fleet lay off a beach, some five hundred people came down accompanied by their youthful cacique, who made the Admiral a state visit. Bedecked with gold jewelry, he dined alone with the Admiral in his cabin and behaved with royal poise and dignity. Dinner over, Columbus had the cacique piped over the side in naval style and given a twenty-one-gun salute. Again the thought passed through his mind that these people were ripe for exploitation—"very cowardly," and "fit to be ordered about and made to work, to sow, and do aught else that may be needed." A wonderful opportunity, he observed, for his Sovereigns, whose subjects were not notably fond of hard work!

At sunrise 20 December the ships were off Acul Bay, the beauty of which was so striking that the Admiral ran out of adjectives describing it in his Journal; declared that all "ancient mariners" on board would bear him out. In 23 years at sea he had never seen so perfect a harbor as the one here, landlocked so completely that even in a blow one's anchor cable does not stretch taut. The high mountains part to reveal a conical peak at the head of the valley, which since 1806 has been crowned by the stone citadel of Henri Christophe, king of Haiti. Here the natives of 1492 were in an even more pristine state of innocence than elsewhere; the women, completely naked, had "very pretty bodies," and no male jealousy prevented their offering themselves freely. Moreover, these natives appeared to have plenty of gold.

During the night of 22–23 December and the following morning, about a thousand people came out in canoes to visit *Santa Maria*, and

Acul Bay. David Crofoot photo.

some five hundred more swam out, although she anchored more than three miles from the nearest shore. A messenger now arrived from Guacanagarí, the cacique of Marien (the northwestern part of Haiti), and a more important potentate than the one entertained a few days earlier. Guacanagarí sent the Admiral a magnificent belt with a solid-gold buckle, and invited him to call. He needed no second invitation, since everyone assured him that the gold mines were in that direction, the central part of the island called Cibao, which suggested Cipangu, Japan. So, before sunrise on 24 December, *Santa Maria* and *Niña* departed Acul Bay, all hands planning to spend a merry Christmas at the court of the cacique, who might even turn out to be the emperor of Japan!

Fate decreed otherwise. With a contrary wind, the two vessels were unable to cover the few miles between Acul and Guacanagarí's capital on Caracol Bay by daylight. At 11:00 p.m., when the watch was changed, *Niña* and *Santa Maria* were becalmed east of Cape Haitien, inside the Limonade Pass to the barrier reef. Everyone on board was exhausted from the previous all-night entertainment of the natives; and as the water was calm, with only a slight ground swell and no wind, a feeling of complete security—the most dangerous delusion a seaman can entertain—stole over the flagship. Even the Admiral retired to get his first sleep in forty-eight hours; the helmsman gave the big tiller to a small boy and joined the rest of the watch in slumber.

Just as midnight ushered in Christmas Day, *Santa Maria* settled on a coral reef so gently that nobody awoke with the shock. The boy helmsman, feeling the rudder ground, sang out; the Admiral came first on deck, followed by Master Juan de La Cosa and all hands. As the bow only had grounded, Columbus saw a good chance to get her off stern first, and ordered La Cosa and a boat's crew to run an anchor out astern. Instead of obeying orders, they rowed to *Niña*, which had passed well outside the reef. Captain Pinzón refused to receive them, and sent a boat of his own ship.

But an hour had been wasted, owing to La Cosa's cowardice or insubordination, and that doomed *Santa Maria*. The ground swell drove her higher and higher up the reef, and coral heads punched holes in her bottom. As the hull seemed to be filling with water, Columbus ordered abandon ship, hoping that daylight would make it easier to float her. Guacanagarí and his subjects worked hard with the Spaniards to get her off after daybreak, but it was too late. All they could salvage were the equipment, stores, and trading truck, which the Indians faithfully guarded without (so the Admiral recorded) purloining so much as a lace point.

The Admiral tried to figure out what this apparently disastrous accident meant. Presently he had it: God intended him to start a colony at that point, with *Santa Maria*'s crew. Guacanagarí begged him to do so, as he wanted help against enemies elsewhere on the island. The Spaniards fell over each other to volunteer, because signs of gold were now so plentiful that they were confident of making their fortunes. So Columbus gave orders to erect a fortified camp ashore and named it *Villa de la Navidad* (Town of the Nativity) in honor of the day of disaster, which he fondly thought God had turned to his advantage.

Navidad, first attempt by Europeans since the Northmen to establish themselves in the New World, was quickly built, largely out of *Santa Maria*'s timbers. It was probably located on the sandspit now called

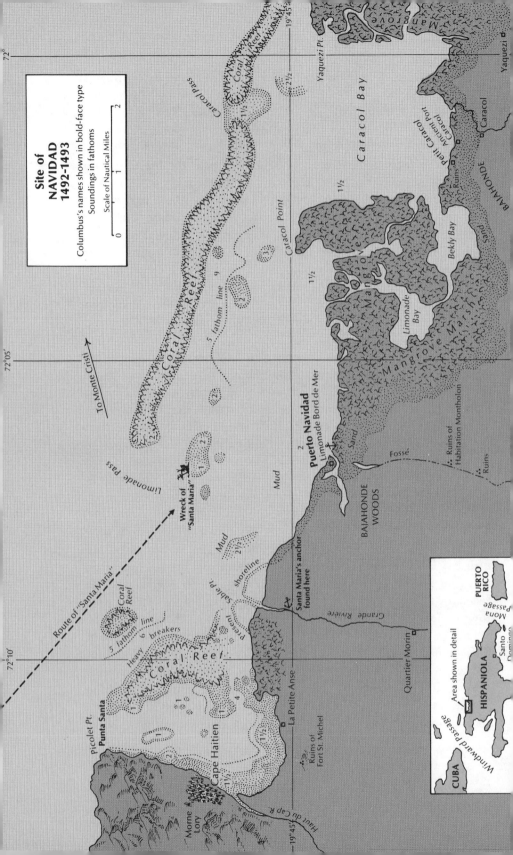

Site of
NAVIDAD
1492-1493

Columbus's names shown in bold-face type

Soundings in fathoms

Scale of Nautical Miles

0   1   2

To Monte Cristi

Coral Pass

Coral Reef

Coral Reef

5 fathom line

9

3

2

2

Caracol Point

1½

Caracol Bay

Yaquezi Pt.

2½

Yaquezi

Caracol

Ruins

Bekly Bay

Sand

Caracol Creek

Petit Caracol

Anse au Port

BAIAHONDE

Mangrove Marsh

Mangrove Marsh

1½

Limonade Bay

1½

Ruins of Habitation Montholon

Ruins

Fossé

Sand

Puerto Navidad

Limonade Bord de Mer

2

BAIAHONDE WOODS

Grande Riviere

Quartier Morin

Mud

2½

Mud

Santa Maria's anchor found here

present shoreline

Sable Pt.

Coral Reef

5 fathom line

6 breakers

Heavy breakers

Coral Reef

Limonade Pass

Wreck of "Santa Maria"

1   2

2

Route of "Santa Maria"

Picolet Pt.

Punta Santa

Cape Haitien

1½

2

1

8

1

4

1½

1

1½

La Petite Anse

Ruins of Fort St. Michel

Morne Lory

Haut du Cap R

19° 45'

72°

72° 05'

72° 10'

19° 45'

CUBA

HISPANIOLA

Area shown in detail

Windward passage

Santo Domingo

Mona passage

PUERTO RICO

Limonade Bord-de-Mer, off which there is good anchorage. Sixteen men from the flagship and five from *Niña* volunteered to stay behind, under command of Columbus's Cordovan friend Diego de Harana. The Admiral gave them a share of his provisions, most of the trading truck, and the flagship's boat. They were instructed to explore the country with a view to finding a permanent settlement, to trade for gold, and to treat the natives kindly.

Columbus was now certain that he had found the Indies.

On the day after New Year's 1493, Guacanagarí and Columbus held a farewell party. *Niña* fired cannon balls through what was left of the hull of *Santa Maria* to impress the natives, and the cacique feasted all hands. After final expressions of mutual love and esteem, the allies parted and the Admiral went on board *Niña*, to return home in her. At sunrise 4 January she set sail, and the homeward passage began.

Homeward Passage

Two days later, Columbus sighted *Pinta* sailing in a contrary direction, down-wind. Martín Alonso came on board and gave a fairly convincing account of his doings during the last three weeks. He had called at the Great Inagua, ascertained that the yarn about picking up gold by candlelight was a myth, then sailed along the coast of Hispaniola and anchored in Puerto Blanco. There a shore party penetrated the Cibao and found plently of gold. Pinzón had heard of the flagship's wreck by Indian "grapevine," and so sailed back to lend the Admiral a hand. Columbus, pleased to have company on the voyage home, decided to let bygones be bygones.

While waiting for a fair wind to double Monte Cristi peninsula, with its tent-like promontory behind which he anchored, Columbus explored by boat the lower course of the Rio Yaque del Norte and found gold nuggets as large as lentils. Even today there is gold in that river valley; the country women pan it out laboriously, and when they have enough to fill a turkey quill, they use it to pay for their shopping.

At midnight 8 January, *Niña* and *Pinta* resumed their homeward passage. Passing along the coast of Hispaniola, they looked in at *Puerto Plata* (so named by Columbus on account of silver clouds over the mountains) and anchored near the mouth of Samaná Bay. There, at a place still called *Punta de las Flechas*, the Spaniards encountered the

Monte Cristi, which Columbus compared to a great Moorish tent.

first natives who were not pleased to meet them, and who were armed with bows and arrows. These were a branch of the Tainos called Ciguayos, who in self-defense against raiding Caribs had adopted their weapons. By dint of catching one Ciguayo, treating him well and sending him ashore with an assortment of red cloth and trinkets, the rest were appeased, and a brisk if somewhat cautious trade was conducted. Also, one or two were persuaded to join the native contingent bound for Spain.

On Wednesday, 18 January, three hours before daybreak, the caravels sailed from Samaná Bay. A rough, tough voyage lay ahead. This homeward passage was a far greater test of Columbus's seamanship and ability to handle men than anything he had hitherto undertaken. With the greatest geographical discovery of all time locked in his breast, knowing that it would be of no use to anybody unless delivered, the Admiral had to fight the elements and human weakness for his survival.

The west wind with which they took off soon petered out, easterly trade winds returned, and the caravels sailed as best they could, close-hauled on the starboard tack. Modern sailing craft can sail as close to the wind as four points (45 degrees) or, if very smart racers in smooth water, even closer. *Niña* and *Pinta* would lay up to five points (56 degrees) if the sea was smooth, but under ordinary conditions could not do better than six points (67½ degrees); and *Pinta* was slow on the wind, owing to a sprung mizzenmast. This meant, in practice, that if it blew from the southeast, the caravels could steer ENE; with a due east wind the best course toward Spain of which they were capable was NNE; and if it backed to NE (as the trade wind often does), the Admiral had to bring them about on the port tack and steer ESE.

In this manner *Niña* and *Pinta* continued through January of 1493, reaching further north and edging a little closer to Spain. As they were near the northern limit of the trades, the sea was smooth, and providentially the wind held and blew them across the horse latitudes, as seamen used to call the calms between latitudes 30° and 33° N. They crossed the Sargasso Sea, having the rare and beautiful experience of sailing with a fresh wind across an undulating meadow of gulfweed, under a full moon. Boatswain birds, boobies, and the fork-tailed frigate bird were flying about; and one day the sea abounded in tunnies, which the Admiral (making the only humorous remark recorded in his writings) said he expected to end in the Duke of Cadiz's tunny factory at Cadiz. That name caused the seamen to lick their lips in anticipation of seeing again the Cadiz girls, famous through Europe for their saucy beauty and salty wit.

During this uneventful part of the voyage the Admiral took time and pains to write a report on his impressions to Ferdinand and Isabella. Of the natives he writes, "In their islands I have so far found no human monstrosities" (as everyone expected from John de Mandeville). "On the contrary . . . good looks are esteemed; nor are they blacks, as in Guinea, but with flowing hair." A glowing account of their products follows—gum mastic as in Chios, spices, cotton, aloes, slaves.

> All go naked, men and women, as their mothers bore them, except that some women cover one place only with the leaf of a plant or with a net of cotton which they make for that. Although they are well-built people of handsome stature, they are wonderfully timorous. They have no other arms than arms of canes, and they dare not make use of these. . . . After they have been reassured and have lost this fear, they are artless and so free with all they possess, that no one would believe it with-

out having seen it. Of anything they have, if you ask them for it, they never say no; rather they invite the person to share it, and show as much love as if they were giving their hearts; they are content with whatever little thing of whatever kind may be given to them. I forbade that they should be given things so worthless as pieces of broken crockery and broken glass, and ends of straps, although when they were able to get them, they thought they had the best jewel in the world; thus it was ascertained that a sailor for a strap received gold to the weight of two and half *castellanos*,* and others much more for other things which were worth much less; yea, for new *blancas*,** for them they would give all that they had, although it might be two or three castellanos' weight of gold or an *arrova* † or two of spun cotton. . . . They believe very firmly that I, with these ships and people, came from the sky . . . and this does not result from their being ignorant, for they are of a very keen intelligence and men who navigate all those seas.

He particularly admired their dugout *canoas* (here that word enters European language) "made of a single log," carrying up to seventy or eighty men. His description of the scenery and the flora are ecstatic, and not exaggerated, except that he identified very ordinary and useless plants as spices or rare drugs.

Without knowing it, Columbus had followed the best sailing directions for reaching home quickly. Had he tried to sail straight across to Spain (as he did in 1496), he would have had to beat to windward most of the way; but this long northerly leg took him up to the latitude of Bermuda into the zone of rough, strong westerlies.

On the last day of January the wind swung into the west, and four days later, when the Admiral figured by a simple "eye sight" of the North Star that he had reached the latitude of Cape St. Vincent (and actually was on that of Gibraltar), he set the course due east, 90 degrees. Owing to compass variation, this worked out as about 80 degrees true, right for picking up the Azores. The weather now turned cold and a fresh gale made up. During four days the caravels made an average run of 150 miles, and at times attained a speed of 11 knots.

When any sailing yacht the length of *Niña* and *Pinta* hits it up to

---

* $7.50 in gold.
** A copper coin worth half a maravedi, a fraction of a cent.
† A weight equivalent to 25 lbs., or 11½ kilos.

11 or 12 knots today, you have something to talk about; and these caravels were having the finest kind of sailing. They were running before a fresh gale over deep blue, white-crested water. On they sped through bright, sunny days and nights brilliant with Orion and other familiar constellations that seemed to be beckoning them home. It is hard for any sailor to be sorry for Columbus, in spite of his later misfortunes; he enjoyed such glorious sailing weather on almost every voyage. But he had some very tough experiences, and one of the worst was about to come.

The westerly gale died down by nightfall 7 February, and for two days the caravels had light variables and made little progress. On the ninth they were able to square away again eastward. Next day the pilots and captains held a ship-to-ship discussion of their position. Everyone, including Columbus, thought they were much further south than they actually were, and all except the Admiral put them on the meridian of the eastern Azores; but Columbus estimated correctly that they were almost due south of Flores, and decided to call at one of the Azores, if possible.

He very nearly didn't make it. The two caravels were sailing into an area of dirty weather in one of the coldest and most blustery winters on record—a winter in which hundreds of vessels went down, scores crashed ashore, ships lay windbound at Lisbon for months, and the harbor of Genoa froze over. The center of an area of very low pressure was passing north of the Azores with southwest to west winds of full gale strength, and the caravels had to pass through three weather fronts.

Niña, stripped down to bare poles, on 12 February scudded before the wind, laboring heavily. The wind moderated slightly next morning, then increased, and the little caravel ran into frightful seas. The elongated isobaric system brought opposite winds very close to one another, and the resulting cross seas formed dangerous pyramidical waves that broke over the caravels from stem to stern. With only her reefed main course set, and the yard slung low, *Niña* sailed in a general northeasterly direction, while the Admiral and Captain Pinzón took turns as officer of the deck, watching every wave to warn the helmsman below. One mistake by either, and she would have broached-to, rolled over and sunk, and *Pinta* could never have rescued survivors in such a sea.

The following night, 13–14 February, the two caravels lost sight of each other and never met again that side of Spain. We have no record of how *Pinta* fared, but *Niña*'s crew almost gave up hope on St. Valentine's Day. Thrice, officers and men drew lots for one to go on a pilgrimage to some famous shrine if they were saved; but the wind only blew harder. Then all made a vow "to go in procession in their shirts" to the first shrine of the Virgin they might encounter. The wind then began to abate. Columbus afterward admitted that he was as frightened as anyone. Desperate lest both ships and all hands perish, at the height of the gale he wrote on a parchment an abstract of his journal of the voyage, wrapped it in waxed cloth, headed it up in a cask, and hove it overboard in the hope that someone might pick up the true story of his discovery. The cask never was recovered but sundry faked-up versions of the Admiral's "Secrete Log Boke" are still being offered to credulous collectors.

Shortly after sunrise 15 February, land was sighted dead ahead. Columbus correctly guessed that it was one of the Azores, he dared not guess which. The wind then whipped into the east, and three days elapsed before *Niña* was able to come up to this island and anchor. The Admiral sent his boat ashore and ascertained that it was Santa Maria, southernmost of the group. He anchored near a village called Nossa Senhora dos Anjos (Our Lady of the Angels), where a little church was dedicated to the Virgin, who had appeared surrounded by angels to a local fisherman. Anjos was an answer to prayer, and the proper place for the crew to fulfill their vow made at the height of the storm.

There then took place what, in retrospect, seems really comic. Here were men bursting with the greatest piece of news in centuries, a discovery that would confer untold benefits on all Europeans; yet, how were they, and it, received? While saying their prayers in the chapel, clad only in their shirts (as a sign of penitence), half the crew was set upon by "the whole town" and thrown into jail. The Portuguese captain of the island suspected that they had been on an illicit voyage to West Africa! He even rowed out, hoping to capture Columbus and the few members of *Niña*'s crew who had stayed on board, intending to make their pilgrimage later. The Admiral refused to receive him and threatened to shoot up the town and carry off hostages if his people were not released. Before the captain could make up his mind, another storm blew up. *Niña*'s cables parted, and she was blown almost to São Miguel and back. And she did well to get back, because only three seamen and the Indians were left on board to help the Admiral and the skipper. By the time *Niña* returned, the Portuguese captain, having grilled the captured sailors and discovered no evidence of poaching on royal preserves, surrendered them and furnished the entire crew with much-needed fresh provisions.

Columbus resumed his homeward voyage on 24 February 1493. The distance to his desired landfall, Cape St. Vincent, was only 800 miles, which should have required only a week's sail in the prevailing north wind. But this piece of ocean in winter is a place where low-pressure areas hang around and make trouble for sailors, and the winter of 1493 was unusually foul. Another tempest overtook *Niña* about 250 miles from Santa Maria and stayed with her all the way, giving her an even worse beating than did the storm west of the Azores.

Two days out from Santa Maria, trouble began. The wind shifted to southeast, forcing *Niña* to change course to ENE. Next day both wind and sea made up, and for three days more they were blown off their course. On the night of 2 March the warm front of the circular storm hit *Niña*, the wind changed to southwest, and she was able to sail her course; but that same night the cold front overtook her with a violent squall which split the main course and blew the furled foresail and mizzen out of their gaskets, whipping them to ragged ribbons. Columbus did the only thing he could do, forge ahead under bare poles. *Niña* pitched and rolled frightfully in cross seas and the wind made another shift, to northwest, on 3 March. This was the backlash of the cyclone, worse than the forelash. As the dark winter afternoon waned, anxiety became intense. Columbus and the pilots knew by dead reckoning that they were driving right onto the ironbound coast of Portugal, and that only a miracle could prevent a fatal crash against the cliffs.

Shortly after six o'clock, when the sun set, the crisis came. Lightning flashed overhead, and great seas broke aboard from both sides. The wind blew so strong it "seemed to raise the caravel into the air." Fortunately, it was the night of full moon, which sent enough light through the clouds so that at seven o'clock land was sighted dead ahead, distant perhaps five miles. Columbus then performed the difficult maneuver, well known to every old-time seaman, of "clawing off" a lee shore. The coast ran north and south, the wind blew from the northwest, so they set one little square foresail that had been saved intact, wore ship in a smother of foam, and shaped a course south, parallel to the coast, with wind on the starboard quarter. No wonder *Niña* became the Admiral's favorite vessel, to stand all that beating and respond to this difficult maneuver without broaching.

When day broke on 4 March, Columbus recognized prominent Cabo da Roca that juts into the ocean from the mountains of Sintra, just north of the entrance to the Tagus. With only one square sail between him and utter destruction, the Admiral naturally elected to enter the Tagus and call at Lisbon to refit, rather than attempt to continue around Cape St. Vincent to Spain. He well knew that he was taking a great risk in placing himself in the power of D. João II, the monarch who had turned him down twice; but his first consideration was to get word of his discovery to Spain. So, after sunrise, *Niña* whipped around Cabo da Roca, passed Cascais where the fishermen were amazed to see so tiny a vessel coming in from the sea, crossed the smoking bar at the river mouth, and by nine o'clock anchored off Belém, the outer port of Lisbon.

To be safely anchored in a snug harbor after long tossing at sea gave the sailors a wonderful feeling of relief, but the Admiral and his battered crew still had plenty to worry about. *Niña* would have to be refitted before proceeding to Spain, and would the Portuguese allow it? And what had happened to *Pinta?*

The first Portuguese gesture was not assuring. Moored near *Niña* was a large warship, the name of whose master was Bartholomew Dias —not, apparently, the discoverer of the Cape of Good Hope. Dias came over in an armed boat and ordered Columbus to report on board and give an account of himself. The Admiral stood on his dignity and refused; but he showed his credentials, which satisfied both Dias and his captain. Columbus had already sent a letter to D. João II asking permission to enter Lisbon, and on 8 March a nobleman brought the answer, which not only granted his request—ordering that *Niña* be supplied with all she needed—but invited the Admiral to visit the king at his country residence. Columbus decided he had better accept, although he feared lest visiting the King of Portugal before reporting to the Queen of Castile would offend her—as indeed it did. So, selecting two or three followers and some of the healthiest of his captive Indians, Columbus landed at Lisbon and chartered a train of mules to take himself and his suite up-country. Pity the poor Indians who, after their terrible buffeting at sea, must now suffer the rigors of muleback transport along the narrow, muddy roads of Portugal! It took them two days to make the thirty-mile journey to the monastery of Santa Maria das Virtudes, where the King was then staying.

D. João II received Columbus with unexpected graciousness, but his court chronicler tells us that he was really furious with the Admiral and suspected that the new discoveries had been made in a region where Portugal had prior rights. Courtiers urged the King to have this boastful upstart discreetly assassinated, as he had recently disposed of an annoying brother-in-law. Fortunately, he refused. And the King had to admit that his Indian guests looked very different from any Africans he had ever seen or heard of. Two of them made a rough chart of the Antilles with beans, convincing the King, who smote his breast and cried out, "Why did I let slip such a wonderful chance?"

On 11 March Columbus and his suite departed, escorted by a troop of cavaliers, and made a detour to call on the Queen of Portugal at the Convent of Santo António da Castanheira. The Admiral was so sore from his muleback cruise that on reaching the Tagus he chartered a boat to take him down-river to *Niña*. During his absence she had been fitted with a new suit of sails and running rigging, and had taken on fresh provisions, wood, water, and wine. She was now ready for the last leg of the voyage, all her crew were on board, and on the following morning, 13 March, the gallant little caravel weighed anchor from Lisbon.

Strange to relate, *Pinta* was following her, not far astern. She had missed the Azores, thus escaping the worst of the tempests that swept over *Niña*, and about the end of February made Bayona near Vigo in northwest Spain. Here Martín Alonso Pinzón attempted to beat Columbus home with the great news. He sent a message across Spain to Ferdinand and Isabella at Barcelona, announcing his arrival and begging permission to come himself and tell them about the voyage. The Sovereigns sent back word that they preferred to hear the news from Columbus himself. *Pinta* then sailed from Bayona for Palos.

Niña wore ship around Cape St. Vincent at daybreak 14 March and passed the beach where Columbus had swum ashore after the sea fight seventeen years earlier. At midday 15 March she crossed the bar of the Saltés and dropped anchor off Palos. *Pinta* followed on the same tide.

The sight of *Niña* already there, snugged down as if she had been at home a month, finished Martín Alonso Pinzón. Older than Columbus, ill from the hardships of the voyage, mortified by his snub from the Sovereigns, he could bear no more. He went directly to his country house near Palos, took to his bed, and died within the month.

So ended, 224 days after it began, the greatest recorded voyage in history. Here is Columbus's final prophecy in his Letter to the Sovereigns:—

> So, since our Redeemer has given this victory to our most illustrious King and Queen, and to their famous realms, in so great a matter, for this all Christendom ought to feel joyful and make celebrations and give solemn thanks to the Holy Trinity with many solemn prayers for the great exaltation which it will have, in the turning of so many peoples to our holy faith, and afterwards for material benefits, since not only Spain but all Christians will hence have refreshment and profit.

Bibliography and Notes

Site of Navidad and of the Fatal Reef. Morison, "Route of Columbus along the North Coast of Haiti, and the Site of Navidad," American Philosophical Society *Transactions*, n.s., XXXI, Part IV (1940), 239–85. Louis Amaré, *Rapport à propos de l'emplacement de la Nativité* (Port au Prince, 1954), supports me.

While I was doing my last revision, Mr. John Frye of Virginia brought me an advance copy of his book *The Search for the Santa Maria* (New York, 1973). This is a fascinating account of the efforts of Fred Dickson, Jr., to discover and excavate the remains of Columbus's *Santa Maria* in a boat-shaped mound on an underwater coral reef in Cap Haitien Bay. His most convincing artifact brought up was a pottery shard which, subjected to the latest process of dating, the thermoluminescent, yielded the date 1475, give or take a century. Unfortunately, Mr. Dickson died in November 1972 from the effects of a diving accident incurred during this work, and the probing of this promising mound has been suspended for want of funds.

Columbus's Letter on His First Voyage. The unique original, a treasure of the New York Public Library, is a four-page black-letter folio with neither title nor colophon, printed in Barcelona probably in mid-April 1493. The leading authority on this letter is Carlos Sanz, author of *Bibliografía General de la Carta de Colón* and *El Gran Secreto de la Carta de Colón* (Madrid, 1957 and 1958) and editor of facsimiles of the first seventeen printed editions (Madrid, 1958). Nine, in Latin, were printed at Rome, Antwerp, Basle, and Paris; two in Castilian, printed at Barcelona; one in German was printed at Strasbourg; and five in Italian verse by Giuliano Dati, printed in Rome and Florence. See also the article by Francis M. Rogers on Dati's *Os Cantares das Indias* ("Songs of the Indies"), in *Actas, Congresso Internacional de História dos Descobrimentos*, IV (Lisbon, 1961), 387–440.

The document is usually called "Columbus's Letter to Santangel," since the first edition was addressed to that crown official, or to "Gabriel" or "Raphael" Sanchez or Sanxis, treasurer of the kingdom of Aragon. The Latin translation states that it was addressed to Sanchez. Actually, it is Columbus's official report on his First Voyage to Ferdinand and Isabella, transmitted to them with a covering letter, long since lost. It was then, as now, considered disrespectful to address the king or queen of Spain directly unless one were a grandee or royal official; thus Columbus sent his important reports to a friend at court, who was supposed to read them to the Sovereigns at the proper moment. Santangel was the official who helped the Queen to make up her mind and who had found the money for the voyage. The Latin translator assumed that Gabriel Sanchez, not Santangel, was the *escribano de ración* (keeper of the privy purse) referred to as the addressee.

The New York Public Library also has a copy of the first illustrated edition (Basle, 1493). The illustrations, including an ocean-going ship and an alleged Landing of Columbus (from a forty-oar Mediterranean galley!), had been used in earlier works printed in Switzerland and have nothing to do with the First Voyage. Facsimiles of this edition have frequently been printed, and every Columbus Day the phony illustrations in it reappear in the newspapers, along with fancy portraits of Columbus.

This letter is not only the earliest of all *Americana*; it is a vital document for the Admiral himself, relating what he wished important people to think about his discovery, appealing alike to their piety and their cupidity, and concealing matters that he did not care to be broadcast, such as the near mutiny of his men, the loss of his flagship, and the disloyalty of Martín Alonso Pinzón. The translation that I made for Carlos Sanz is printed in my *Journals and Other Documents*, pp. 180–89, and *Christopher Columbus, Mariner*, pp. 149–54; also as a separate pamphlet.

V

Triumph and Tragedy

March 1493-April 1494

Hour of Triumph

Columbus had already sent a copy of his official report on the voyage from Lisbon to Barcelona. Fearing lest it miscarry or be impounded by D. João II, he now sent another copy to the Sovereigns by official courier, and a third to the municipality at Cordova. Before proceeding to Seville to await the reply, he fulfilled his vows at the local church and spent two weeks with Fray Juan Pérez and other friends at La Rábida. On Palm Sunday, 31 March, he entered Seville in time to take part in the traditional ceremonies of Holy Week.

Holy Week in Seville, with its alternation of humility and pride, penance and pardon, death and victory, seemed at once a symbol and a fitting conclusion to this great adventure. The daily processions of the brotherhoods with their gorgeously bedecked statues of saints, the ancient ceremonies in the Cathedral—rending of the temple veil, knocking at the great door, candles on the great *tenebrario* extinguished until but one remained, the washing of feet on Maundy Thursday, the supreme Passion on Good Friday when one heard the clacking of the *matraca* in place of cheerful bells, the consecration of the paschal candle, and the supreme ecstasy of Easter morn—all that moved Columbus as no worldly honors could, and strengthened his conviction that his own toils and triumphs fitted the framework of the Passion. And it was pleasant to receive the congratulations of old friends who "always knew he would make it," to be presented to noblemen and bishops, and to have choice young *caballeros* introduced by their fathers in order to plead with Señor Almirante to take them to the Indies, where they would do anything he asked. (They meant, anything but work!)

What the Indian captives thought of it all we know not.

On or shortly after Easter Sunday, 7 April, the Admiral's cup of happiness overflowed upon receipt of a letter from Ferdinand and Isabella, addressed to "Don Cristóbal Colón, their Admiral of the Ocean Sea, Viceroy and Governor of the Islands that he hath discovered in the Indies." These were the exact titles they had promised him if he did reach the Indies, and the use of them indicated that they believed he had. They expressed pleasure at his achievements, commanded him to attend court, and "Inasmuch as we will that that which you have commenced with the aid of God be continued and furthered," ordered preparations for a second voyage to be started immediately.

Sweet words! Columbus promptly drafted a report for the Sovereigns on how Hispaniola should be colonized. As chance entries in his Journal prove, he had been thinking this over for several months. The result was a modification of the trading-factory idea with which he had begun his First Voyage. He now proposed to recruit two thousand settlers who would be required to build houses in a designated town in return for a license to trade for gold with the natives. Each must return to the town at stated intervals and hand over his gold for smelting to an official who would deduct the Sovereigns' fifth, the Admiral's tenth, and another tax to support the church. There should be a closed season on gold-hunting in order to ensure that the settlers would take time to grow crops. Foreigners, Jews, infidels, and heretics must be kept out of the Indies, but priests should be sent there to convert the natives.

Columbus had already realized from his contact with the Tainos that their wants were few and easily met, so that they could not be expected to flock to the beach to sell gold, as did the natives of Africa. To do much business, Spaniards would have to work the interior of Hispaniola and perhaps other islands too. But, in the interest of fiscal control, everyone must check in at a trading factory on the coast, and all transatlantic traffic must go through Cadiz.

After sending this report ahead by courier, the Admiral purchased clothes suitable for his rank, and organized a cavalcade, including a few of his officers and servants, and six long-suffering Indians in native dress, carrying parrots in cages. At Cordova the municipality gave him a reception, and he met his mistress Beatriz and picked up his two sons to join him. They arrived at Barcelona around 20 April 1493. As he entered the hall of the Alcazar where the Sovereigns held court, his dignity, gray hair, and noble countenance tanned by eight months at sea made the learned men present compare him to a Roman senator. As he advanced to the throne to make obeisance, Ferdinand and Isabella arose; and when he knelt to kiss hands, they bade him rise, and seated him on the Queen's right. The Indians were presented, the gold artifacts and samples of alleged rare spices were examined, a multitude of questions asked and answered; then all adjourned to the chapel where *Te Deum* was chanted. It was observed that at the last line, "O Lord, in Thee have I trusted, let me never be confounded," tears were streaming down the Admiral's face.

Columbus at this point could have had anything he wanted—castle in Spain, title, pension, or endowment. It would have been well for him had he then taken his profits and retired with honor, leaving to others the responsibility of colonization. But he was not that kind of a man. Had he been, this great voyage would never have taken place. He must see that the islands he discovered were settled by Christians; he must put the gold trade on a proper footing, and start conversion of the natives; he must meet the Grand Khan or some Oriental potentate of higher rank than Guacanagarí. The rights already granted to him, incident to his offices of Admiral and Viceroy, promised to be far more lucrative than any estate in Spain; and so they would have been, had the crown respected them. Moreover, he was in good health, full of energy, in the prime of life (aged forty-one), and he regarded the work for which God had appointed him to be just begun.

His sense of a divine mission also appears in the curious Graeco-Latin signature he now adopted, and of which no contemporary explanation exists. In the entail of his property he describes it as "an X [by which he probably meant a Greek chi] with an S over it and an

M with a Roman A over it and over that an S, and then a Greek Y
[by which he probably meant a capital upsilon] with an S over it,
preserving the relation of the lines and points." The way he wrote
it is as follows:

. S .

S . A . S

X . M . Y

: Xpo FERENS

Many attempts have been made to solve the riddle. My suggestion is
that the initials stand for *Servus Sum Altissimi Salvatoris, Christoû
Mariae* Υἱοῦ (Servant am I of the Most High Saviour, Christ Son of
Mary). The last line, *Xpo Ferens,** is a Graeco-Latin form of *Christopher*, emphasizing his most cherished mission, to carry Christianity
to lands beyond the sea. Even on such brief chits as have survived, he
signed himself *Xpo* FERENS, the Christ Bearer.**

Columbus tarried at court over Whitsuntide, Trinity Sunday, and
Corpus Christi. The King and Queen and Infante Don Juan having
graciously consented to act as godparents, six Indians were baptized.
The first in rank, kinsman to Guacanagarí, they christened "Ferdinand
of Aragon"; another, "Don Juan of Castile"; while the clever interpreter was named "Don Diego." Don Juan attached himself to the
royal household and died within two years; the other five returned
with the Admiral to the New World.

These christenings expressed good intentions of the Sovereigns and
of Columbus toward the natives, but in the Indies themselves, human
greed had to be satisfied first, and forced labor exterminated almost the
entire native population of Hispaniola within half a century. But the
Indians unwittingly had their revenge on Europeans through *Tre-
ponema pallida*, the spirochete of syphilis, which the conquerors contracted in the Indies and brought back to Spain. The first recorded
outbreak of syphilis in Europe took place in 1494 among the soldiers
of a French army which marched to Naples and back. Bishop Las
Casas, who admired Columbus, loved the Indians, and spent a large

---

* This is not to be read "Expo" but "Christo," the letters Chi Rho being a com-
mon Greek abbreviation of *Christ*.
** Sometimes he signed himself "El Virrey"; and on one occasion, "Virrey de
Asia."

part of his life in a vain effort to protect them, states in his *Apologetica Historia* of around 1530 that the disease was transmitted to the French army by Spanish women who were infected by the Indians brought to Barcelona by Columbus. He adds that, from repeated questioning of the natives of Hispaniola, he believed the disease to be one of long standing in the New World; so long, indeed, that the natives did not suffer greatly from it. Among Europeans, however, syphilis promptly assumed the most hideous and malignant forms, with many fatalities, just as measles and smallpox affected the Indians when introduced by Europeans. It seems, therefore, probable that the Indians whom Columbus brought to Barcelona were so joyfully and briskly entertained by the women of the town as to infect these women, who either infected Spanish volunteers in the army of Charles VIII or accompanied that army as camp followers.

This subject is controversial; but it appears to me that Las Casas was correct. *Niña*'s crew for the return voyage cannot have contracted syphilis, for all were healthy and able to work the ship up to the moment of landing; Columbus more than once remarked on it with amazement, since on African voyages sailors were expected to sicken and die. Medical authorities assure me that it would have been almost impossible for a man infected with syphilis to make a tough voyage of two months without becoming very sick indeed. As for those in *Pinta*, a Spanish surgeon named Ruy Díaz de Isla, in his book on the disease printed at Seville in 1539, stated that the spirochete infected "a pilot of Palos called Pinzón," and implies that he attended him. It will be remembered that three Pinzóns shipped in *Pinta*, and that Martín Alonso, the captain, died shortly after her arrival; but Díaz de Isla admits that the disease also spread from Barcelona. It became a terrible plague in Europe and among the Spanish colonists of Hispaniola. They used a local Indian remedy, decoctions of guiacum or lignum vitae. This had no therapeutic effect whatsoever, but people, both natives and Europeans, thought it to be a sovereign cure.

Although Columbus tarried several weeks in Barcelona, he did not simply bask in the sunshine of royalty. He looked after their interests, and his own. The Sovereigns' letters patent granting him a coat of arms gave him the singular privilege of quartering the royal arms of Spain, the castle of Castile and lion of Leon, with an archipelago and five anchors, the symbol of admiralty. At the same time the rights and privileges granted him conditionally at Granada the previous April were confirmed. He and his heirs "now and forever" were to be styled Admiral of the Ocean Sea and Viceroy and Governor of "the said islands and mainland that you have found and discovered." As Viceroy he could appoint and remove all officials in the Indies and have complete civil and criminal jurisdiction; as Admiral he would have jurisdiction over all who sailed the ocean west and south of a line from the Azores to the Cape Verdes. Admiralty jurisdiction meant that he or his deputies could handle all disputes among fishermen or merchant mariners in American waters and try all cases of mutiny, piracy, barratry, and the like. It did not imply command of a fleet, or flag rank in the navy, but nonetheless was a very high and honorable distinction.

The Admiral also worked for the Sovereigns. His famous Letter on the voyage was printed at Barcelona, in Spanish, about the time that he arrived. A Latin translation, dated 29 April, appeared shortly after in Rome. The object of this prompt publication was not so much to spread the news but to obtain papal confirmation of the lands newly discovered, as the public law of Europe then required. The Sovereigns depended on Columbus to prove that his discoveries were outside jurisdiction previously granted to the king of Portugal. Pope Alexander VI, a Spanish Borgia who owed his election to Ferdinand and Isabella, let them practically "write their own ticket" in a series of papal bulls. The third and most important, dated 4 May 1493, drew a line of demarcation along the meridian one hundred leagues (318 nautical miles) west of the Azores. All undiscovered lands east of it would belong to Portugal; all west of it, to Spain.

Columbus undoubtedly suggested this line, because he believed that compass variation changed from east to west, and that the boisterous winds of Europe gave way to the gentle trades, on or about that meridian of longitude. According to Bishop Las Casas, it was an entomological boundary as well. He observed that seamen and passengers departing from Spain were tortured by lice and fleas until they reached a hundred leagues west of the Azores, when the insects began to disappear; but upon the return passage they emerged from hiding at the same longitude "in great and disturbing numbers!" A later form of this myth described insect life as disappearing at the Equator. Readers of *Don Quixote* will remember how, in that famous voyage in the enchanted bark, the Knight of the Rueful Countenance bids Sancho Panza search himself for vermin, in order to ascertain whether or not they have passed the Line.

Nevertheless, the line of demarcation set up by the Pope was not enforced. Portugal protested, and as the hostility of D. João II would have jeopardized their communications, Ferdinand and Isabella in the Treaty of Tordesillas (1494) consented to push the line to the meridian 370 leagues (roughly 1175 miles) west of the Cape Verde Islands. From that new division of the world, Portugal derived her title to Brazil and her claim to Newfoundland.

During the three months that Columbus resided at Barcelona, news of his discovery spread wide, by means of epistles from Italian residents in Spain, and from the printed Letter in many translations. But the news traveled very slowly beyond the Alps. The learned men of Nuremberg, center of geographical study in northern Europe, were ignorant of it as late as July 1493, and brother Bartholomew, living near Paris, did not hear of it in time to join the Admiral's Second Voyage.

Judging from the letters and chronicles, the items in the news that aroused the most attention were gold, the naked natives, and the opportunity to convert them. Columbus had stressed all three in his Letter, as well as opening a new trade route to China. Europe was then so short of specie that any gold strike made a universal appeal, as it would today. Fashions in 1493 required women to be heavily clothed from head to foot, so that a community where the natives wore less than a bikini for full dress was news indeed, besides suggesting the state of innocence before Adam's fall. And as Europe had an uneasy conscience at letting Christianity fall back before the Turks, this opportunity to gain souls and redress the balance aroused agreeable anticipation. Of the real significance of the discovery for Europe's future there was not one hint in contemporary comment, nor did anyone venture to suggest that Seneca's prophecy of a vast continent had been fulfilled.

Columbus's assertion that he really had reached the Indies was accepted by the Spanish Sovereigns and the Pope, but not by everyone. Peter Martyr d'Anghiera, an Italian humanist at the Spanish court, wrote to a correspondent that the size of the globe seemed to indicate that Columbus could not have reached Asia, and in November 1493 he described the Admiral in a letter to Cardinal Sforza as "Novi Orbis Reportor," "Discoverer of a New World." To him, as to other contemporaries, New World did not mean a separate, undiscovered continent, but land unknown to Ptolemy; a group of islands adjacent to the Malay Peninsula would be a New World. That is exactly the conclusion reached by Columbus himself in 1498, and by Amerigo Vespucci a little later. But Amerigo got the credit, as we shall see.

Columbus's Second Voyage

We must never forget that Columbus made three more voyages to America, any one of which would entitle him to top rank as a navigator. The Second Voyage, of 1493-94, Spain's follow-up to the First, employed a big fleet, and also set up the first European colony in America that survived. But it was also important for discovery— the Lesser Antilles, the Virgin Islands, Puerto Rico, the south coast of Cuba, and Jamaica.

Within a month of his arrival from the First Voyage, he agreed with the Sovereigns to lead a second expedition for further discovery, and to establish a colony in Hispaniola. They gave him full latitude as to means in their instructions issued 29 May 1493. Prime objective was to be the conversion of the natives, for which purpose six priests were assigned to the fleet, and the Admiral must see to it that the Indians are "treated very well and lovingly." Hundreds of laymen were to be recruited for the second declared objective: the establishment of a colony. Whilst in 1492 it required the utmost persuasiveness to induce any but the very young and adventurous to ship with Columbus, now the Admiral was embarrassed by the number of volunteers. Both his fame and public expectations were at their zenith; anticipation of finding gold and valuable spices was high; thousands of men and boys were eager to go with him, hoping to make their fortunes and, in any event, to have fun. Finally, the Admiral was charged to explore Cuba, in the hope that it might be a peninsula of Asia leading to the golden cities of Cathay.

In June 1493, accompanied by five of the six baptized Indians and his younger brother Diego, Christopher Columbus set forth from Barcelona. After passing through Madrid and Toledo, he took the pilgrims' road to Guadalupe in the Estremadura, passing through

Trujillo where a thirteen-year-old boy named Francisco Pizarro, future conqueror of Peru, was then engaged in caring for his father's herd of swine. Columbus prayed long and fervently before the famous Virgin of Guadalupe, and the monks asked him to name an island after her. En route to Seville, he passed through the little town of Medellin where a small boy named Hernándo Cortés must have seen him go by.

Columbus arrived at Cadiz, where the Second Voyage was mounted, in early July. Juan de Fonseca, archdeacon of Seville, had done an excellent job of organizing this fleet. He had bought or chartered seventeen vessels, victualed them for a round voyage of six months, recruited at least 1200 sailors, soldiers, and colonists, and collected the necessary seeds, plants, domestic animals, tools, and implements to plant a colony. Citizens of Jerez furnished wheat at 73 maravedis a bushel (about fifteen cents in gold value). Others were paid to grind it into flour and bake ship biscuit—the "hardtack" that formed the staple diet of sailors almost to our own day. Cattle and swine were slaughtered and pickled in brine. Wine, purchased by the pipe, should have been delivered in stout new oaken casks. Columbus complained bitterly that many of the casks were secondhand and let so much wine leak out that Spaniards in Hispaniola for months endured the incredible hardship of drinking only water! One curious element in the expedition was a cavalry troop of twenty lancers who sold their blooded barbs in Cadiz, purchased some sorry hacks, and lived high on the difference; but the substitutes proved good enough to terrorize the natives of Hispaniola.

Unfortunately the records do not allow us to compile a task organization of this fleet, unsurpassed even by Magellan's. The flagship, named *Santa Maria* (like that of the First Voyage) and nicknamed *Mariagalante*, was considerably bigger than her namesake; say 200 tuns' burthen. Two other *naos* were called *Colina* and *La Gallega*. There were about ten square-rigged caravels including gallant *Niña* of the First Voyage, at least two lateen-rigged caravels, and some small Cantabrian barques for shoal-water exploration. The Pinzón family was conspicuously absent, but four members of the Niño family of Moguer participated. Most of the sailors were from that region. Everyone was on the royal payroll except about two hundred gentlemen volunteers; no women were allowed.

On 25 September 1493, a bright autumn day with a light offshore breeze, "This fleet so united and handsome," as Columbus called it, departed white-walled Cadiz. Every vessel flew the royal standard of Castile. Every captain dressed his ship with brightly colored banners, and waistcloths emblazoned with the arms of gentlemen volunteers were stretched between forecastle and poop. A number of big seagoing Venetian galleys which happened to be in Cadiz harbor escorted the fleet to the open sea amid music of trumpets and harps and the firing of cannon.

On 2 October the fleet made the Grand Canary, and on the fifth called at Gomera, home of Doña Beatriz de Peraza y Bobadilla, lady captain of the island. Columbus, according to his shipmate Cuneo, had become *tincto d'amore* ("dyed with love") for her on his previous visit, and she now received his fleet with salvos of cannon and fireworks. But if Beatriz expected to play Circe to this Ulysses, she was disappointed. Columbus tarried but a few days and spent most of his time topping off the vessels with water, provisions, and livestock. She would indeed have been a very proper wife for the now "Very Magnificent Don Cristóbal Colón, Almirante del Mar Océano, Virrey de las Indias." Probably, however, as a practical young widow, she did not want a sailor for her second husband, but a man who would stay at home and look after her and her small boy.

The fleet ran into the usual Canary Islands calms and took its final departure from Ferro on 12 October 1493, first anniversary of the discovery of America. The course set by the Admiral was west by south. He planned to shorten the ocean passage and make discoveries in the Lesser Antilles. The captive Indians had told him that Matinino (Martinique) and Charis (Dominica) of the Lesser Antilles were the nearest islands to Spain, and he figured the course to them correctly, within half a compass point.

Sailing before the trades in a square-rigger is a sailor's dream of the good life at sea. You settle down to the pleasant ritual, undisturbed by shifts of wind and changes of weather; and this ocean crossing seems to have been pure joy for everyone who loved the sea. There is the constant play of light and color on the bellying square sails (gold at sunset, silver in moonlight, black in starlight, white as the clouds themselves at noon). The sea, flecked with whitecaps, is of a gorgeous deep blue, the schools of flying fish spring like a flash of silver from the bow wave. And on this Second Voyage there were seventeen ships in company, so that from the high-pooped flagship one could see white sails all around the horizon. Every day the faster vessels romped ahead, racing one another, but toward sundown each closed *Maria-galante* within hailing distance so that the Admiral could give night orders. As darkness fell, every ship lit her stern lantern or kindled light-wood in an iron cresset. Throughout the night, during which the trade wind blew full and steady, each tried to keep her assigned station, as in a modern convoy. Every half hour the voices of the ships' boys announced the turning of the glass. Just before 7:00 a.m., when the morning watch came on duty, a priest on board the flagship celebrated what was called a "dry Mass," in which he went through the motions but did not consecrate the sacred elements lest the ship's motion cause them to be dropped or spilled. On the other vessels the men watched for the elevation of the host, a signal to kneel and cross themselves. Then a hymn was sung, the glass turned, the watch relieved, and every ship cracked on sail to race the others during the daylight hours.

A thunder squall on St. Simon's Eve (26 October) split a number of sails and lighted ghostly "corposants" on the tips of masts and yards. All the rest of the outward passage, the ships enjoyed fair wind and made the 2500 nautical miles from Ferro to Dominica in 21 days, an average speed of about 5 knots. On All Saints' Day, 1 November 1493, the Admiral was so confident of making land within three days that he issued an extra allowance of water. As an experienced seaman he knew land was near at sundown, 2 November, by clouds gathering over the horizon ahead. That night he shortened sail lest his fleet over-run the land before moonrise, which came shortly before dawn. An anxious night it must have been, young men imagining that they saw lights or heard breakers, leadsmen heaving the deep-sea lead and sing-ing out, "No bottom!" At five in the morning of Sunday, 3 Novem-ber, just as the first faint gray of dawn appeared in the east, a lookout in *Mariagalante* sees a dark cone blotting out a small section of the star-studded horizon ahead. He sings out, *Albricias! Que tenemos tierra!* ("The reward! For we have land!") The cry of *Tierra! Tierra!* passes from ship to ship; all is bustle and excitement, and the Admiral sum-mons all hands to prayer on the quarterdeck, where they sing *Salve Regina* and other hymns "very devotedly, giving thanks to God for

The Grand Carbet waterfall, Guadeloupe. Just as Columbus saw it in 1493,
plunging from the clouds. David Crofoot photo.

so short and safe a voyage." Only 21 to 22 days land to land, one-
third less than the First Voyage, and a marked contrast to later
southern voyages of discovery.

From Dominica to Navidad

Columbus named the island of his landfall Dominica, and this Sabbath-
day island still is, in my opinion, the most beautiful of all the Carib-
bees. With no other aid then his captive Indians' advice, he had hit the
Antilles at the exact spot recommended by official sailing directions
for the next four centuries! For here the passage between the islands
is clear, with no dangerous reefs to avoid; and once inside the Caribbean you can count on fair winds whether bound for Venezuela and
the Spanish Main or Vera Cruz and Mexico, or the Leeward Islands,
Puerto Rico, Hispaniola, and Cuba.

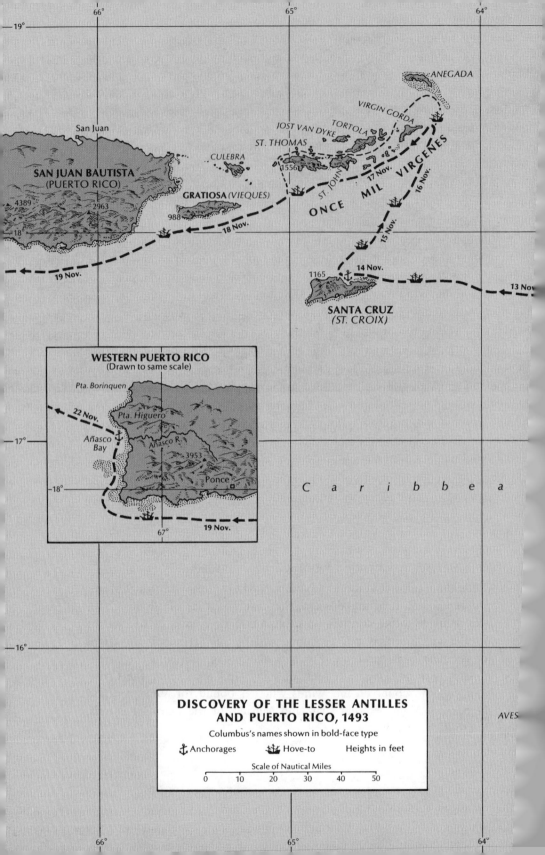

19°

66°   65°   64°

San Juan

ANEGADA

VIRGIN GORDA

JOST VAN DYKE   TORTOLA

ST. THOMAS

CULEBRA

SAN JUAN BAUTISTA
(PUERTO RICO)

1556   17 Nov.   VIRGENES

4389   ST. JOHN   ONCE   MIL   16 Nov.

2963   GRATIOSA (VIEQUES)

988   15 Nov.

18

18 Nov.   14 Nov.

1165   ⚓

19 Nov.   13 Nov

SANTA CRUZ
(ST. CROIX)

WESTERN PUERTO RICO
(Drawn to same scale)

Pta. Borinquen

22 Nov.   Pta. Higuero

17°   Añasco
Bay   Añasco R.

3953

18°   Ponce

5   C a r i b b e a

67°   19 Nov.

16°   AVES

66°   65°   64°

DISCOVERY OF THE LESSER ANTILLES
AND PUERTO RICO, 1493

Columbus's names shown in bold-face type

⚓ Anchorages   ⛵ Hove-to   Heights in feet

Scale of Nautical Miles

0   10   20   30   40   50

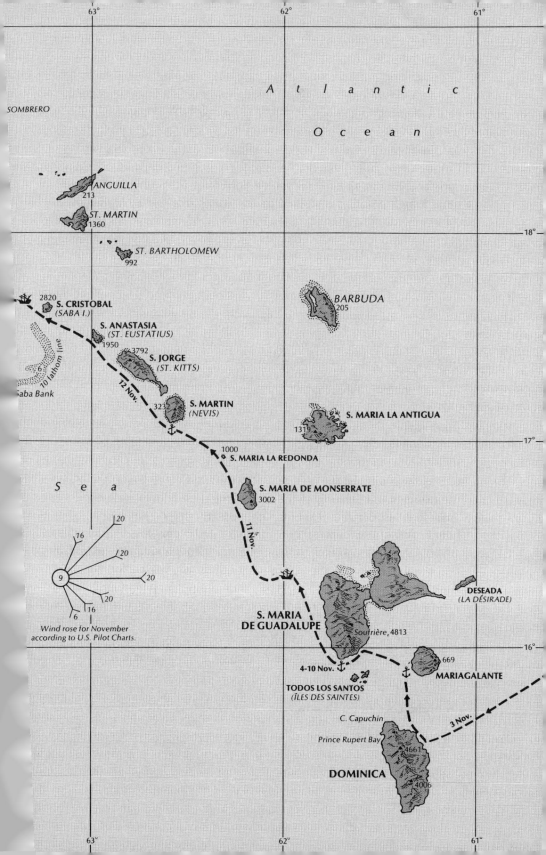

SOMBRERO

A t l a n t i c

O c e a n

ANGUILLA
213

ST. MARTIN
1360

ST. BARTHOLOMEW
992

BARBUDA
205

2820 **S. CRISTOBAL**
(SABA I.)

S. ANASTASIA
(ST. EUSTATIUS)
1950

3792
S. JORGE
(ST. KITTS)

12 Nov.

6
10 fathom line

6
Saba Bank

323 **S. MARTIN**
(NEVIS)

S. MARIA LA ANTIGUA
1319

1000
S. MARIA LA REDONDA

S e a

S. MARIA DE MONSERRATE
3002

11 Nov.

20

16

20

9

20

20

6 16

*Wind rose for November
according to U.S. Pilot Charts.*

**S. MARIA
DE GUADALUPE**

Soufrière, 4813

DESEADA
(LA DÉSIRADE)

4-10 Nov.

669

MARIAGALANTE

TODOS LOS SANTOS
(ÎLES DES SAINTES)

3 Nov.

C. Capuchin

Prince Rupert Bay

4661

DOMINICA

4006

63°   62°   61°   18°   17°   16°

As the light increased on 3 November and the fleet sped westward, they sighted a round, flat island which Columbus named *Mariagalante* as a tribute to his flagship, and a group of islands which he called *Todos los Santos* for the feast of All Saints just passed. (French since the seventeenth century, they are still Mariegalante and Les Saintes.) Columbus anchored on the lee side of the first-named, went ashore with his banners, and formally took possession for Spain. In the mean-time, a high island was sighted to the westward, and as Mariagalante offered little of interest, Columbus ordered anchors aweigh and shaped his course thither. This was the big kidney-shaped island which he named *Santa Maria de Guadalupe,* as he had promised the monks to do. (Guadeloupe, as the French called it, is now their oldest colony; it became a sugar island so valuable that the British in 1763 seriously thought of swapping all Canada for it.) As the fleet approached this island, they saw the strange and beautiful sight of a high waterfall, slender as a silver thread, which appeared to plunge out of the clouds hanging over the mountains. The vessels anchored under the southern slope of the island's 5000-foot volcano, in a sheltered bay now called Grande Anse, and there remained five or six days.

Columbus did not intend to stay more than one night, but his first shore party lost itself in the dense tropical rain forest. Since the natives here were the dreaded man-eating Caribs, these men were lucky to be located by one of four search parties of fifty men each. In the course of their wanderings, the searching Spaniards learned a good deal about the manners and customs of the Caribs, the tribe from which the word "cannibal" is derived. In huts deserted by the natives they found human limbs and cuts of human flesh partly consumed, as well as emasculated boys who were being fattened to provide the main dish for a feast, and girl captives used to produce babies for the hors d'œuvre. Two boys and "twelve very beautiful plump girls from fifteen to sixteen years old" were picked up by the Spaniards. These girls, who had been captured by the Caribs in a raid on Hispaniola, were useful as interpreters, and doubtless in other ways too.

From Guadeloupe on, the fleet enjoyed a spectacular sail along the leeward (western) coasts of the Lesser Antilles, with a quartering or beam wind. Each island is a mountain peak rising 3000 to 5000 feet from the Caribbean. Depths from a few hundred yards off each shore are deepest sapphire, whilst the shoals vary from brilliant emerald to a luminous golden yellow. At dawn the next island ahead is a vague

boriquen
las Virgines
Circulo cancro
s xpōbal s de lanieve
S cruz S martin
cnidi la gorda s: mjª de monsera
S: mjª de guadalupe
domjnjca s: mª galante
asencion
el falcon
las agulas
mayo los hermanos
pºyna
boca del drago

THE LESSER ANTILLES ON
JUAN DE LA COSA'S MAP

shadow, a dark shape against the celestial sphere. With the increase of light, and upon one's own swift approach, the land takes form, substance, and color. One can watch the sun kindle the mountain pinnacles to flame, the forested slopes turning from gray to green, and finally to a blue a few shades lighter than the sea. As the wind makes up during the forenoon watch, it forms a cloud over each island, and if you are off the leeward coast by noon, you are apt to be becalmed under the heights; that happened to Columbus at Guadeloupe. The sea then becomes a gently undulating mirror, reflecting the colors of the land and broken only by flights of flying fish and leaping dolphins. But the calm never lasts long. The wind springs up again, the island is left astern, and you gaze back at it, fascinated, as showers lash the forested slopes and the clouds turn orange with the declining sun.

And if the western horizon is clear, the sun as it dips below sends up a brilliant emerald flash.

Even more than most sailors, Columbus was devoted to the Virgin Mary, and for several days he named almost every island after one or another of her shrines. Some of his names were later transferred to other islands, but from the famous chart by Juan de La Cosa, the Admiral's shipmate on this voyage, we may trace the fleet's course with some confidence. Next after Guadeloupe it passed an island that Columbus named *Santa Maria de Monserrate* after a famous monastery near Barcelona; it is still called Montserrat, and is famous for the Irish brogue of the natives, black or white, inherited from Oliver Cromwell's captives with whom the English peopled it in the seventeenth century. Next came a tiny round island, *Santa Maria la Redonda;* this has never been settled, although a crazy American once claimed to be king of it. To windward Columbus saw but did not visit a large island which he named *Santa Maria la Antigua,* after a famous painting of the Virgin in Seville Cathedral. During the night of 11–12 November the fleet lay at anchor in the lee of an island which the Admiral named *San Martín* because it was the vigil of the feast of St. Martin of Tours. This was probably Nevis and not the present Franco-Dutch island of Saint-Martin or Sint-Maarten, which was too far off his course for

Les Saintes.

St. Eustatius.

Columbus to have visited or even seen. Originally, Nevis was *Santa Maria de las Nieves*, St. Mary of the Snow, so called from the pretty story that Santa Maria Maggiore in Rome was built on the Esquiline because the Virgin indicated the proper site by causing snow to fall there in August.

Next to the modern Nevis is the present St. Christopher (abbreviated St. Kitts), which Columbus traditionally named after his own patron saint because the shape of the mountain resembled a giant carrying someone pick-a-back. That answers better to the next island, St. Eustatius, but it is anybody's guess how to apply some of the northern names on Juan de La Cosa's map.*

The night of 12–13 November was spent by the fleet hove-to off

* As Mauricio Obregón has said, names on discoverers' maps are nomads. A good instance in my *Northern Voyages*, pp. 299, 322–23, is the wandering of *Arcadia* from North Carolina to Nova Scotia.

Scene of the first fight. Salt River Bay, St. Croix. David Crofoot photo.

the northern end of the island chain. That must indeed have been a
brave sight. Seventeen vessels under short sail, slowly drifting to leeward, lights from the stern lanterns of the big ships and the iron
cressets of the smaller vessels reflected in the water. At break of day
each vessel makes sail and scurries to the flagship for orders. The Admiral sets a course almost due west, to an island whose direction his
Indian guides pointed out and called *Ayay*.

The island, which the Admiral called *Santa Cruz*, and for which we
now use the French form St. Croix, is the first future United States
territory discovered by Columbus. Unlike the heavily forested islands
that they had passed, St. Croix was intensively cultivated by its Carib
inhabitants and looked like a great garden as they skirted its northern
coast. Missing the future Christiansted Harbor, owing to the outer
reef barrier, they anchored off a small estuary now called Salt River
Bay. And here the Spanish mariners had their first fight with American natives.

At noon 14 November, Columbus sent an armed boat with twenty-five men toward a small village at the head of this harbor. The inhabitants fled, but as the boat returned, a Carib canoe suddenly came around the point. The paddlers at first were stupefied by the sight of the great ships, but presently recovered their senses; and although they numbered only four men and two women, picked up their bows and arrows and let fly, wounding two Spaniards, one mortally. Columbus's boat rammed and upset the dugout; but the Caribs swam to a rock where they fought like demons until overcome and taken. A horde of natives in warpaint now ran down to the shore, eager for revenge, but they had no weapons that could reach the ships.

This skirmish at Salt River Bay gave the Spaniards a healthy respect for the Carib nation, which in general they left alone, visiting their islands only with strong armed parties. Probably the first Carib in history to be subdued was a "very beautiful girl," one of the canoe party, captured in the fight by Michele de Cuneo, Columbus's boyhood friend, and presented to him by the Admiral as a slave. "Having taken her into my cabin," wrote Cuneo, "she being naked according to their custom, I conceived a desire to take pleasure." She gave him a

Sir Francis Drake Channel, Virgin Islands.

severe working-over with her fingernails, he "thrashed her well" with a rope's end, and she raised "unheard-of screams," but "finally we came to an agreement in such manner that I can tell you that she seemed to have been brought up in a school of harlots."

Columbus did not care to tarry at St. Croix, lest the Caribs bring up reinforcements. Having already noted the rounded tops of a number of islands over the northern horizon, he decided to investigate them. As the ships approached, more and more islands appeared. The Admiral appropriately named them *Las Once Mil Vírgenes*, after the 11,000 seagoing virgins from Cornwall who, according to legend, were martyred by the Huns at Cologne after a long and pleasant yachting cruise.

To explore these Virgin Islands the Admiral used the smaller caravels and Cantabrian barques. He sent them through the easterly passage to look at Anegada, after which they squared away down the channel later named after Sir Francis Drake, with high, handsome islands on either hand. The sailors marveled at the dazzling colors of some of the rocks and at the pink coral beaches. In the meantime, *Mariagalante* and the larger vessels sailed in deep water south of the two larger islands, St. John and St. Thomas. On the morning of 18 November the fleet again united west of St. Thomas. That day they raised an island which Columbus named *Gratiosa*, after the noble mother of his friend Alessandro Geraldini, who had entertained him in his days of poverty. Unfortunately that name, recording filial piety and a deep friendship, has been replaced by Vieques, or Crab Island.

After another night hove-to, the fleet made the south coast of a big island which the natives called *Boriquén* or *Borinquen;* the Admiral named it for St. John the Baptist. All day 19 November Columbus's fleet sailed along the mountainous southern coast of Puerto Rico, and on the morning of the 20th rounded its southwest point, Cabo Rojo, and steered northwest "on a bowline," looking for a good passage through the reefs which protect the first twenty miles of the island's west coast.* Finally the reefs ceased to mask the land, and the fleet sailed in deep water right up to the land, in what is now Añasco Bay.

---

* Before seeing the island, I mistakenly followed earlier historians in stating that Columbus landed in the nearest harbor, Boqueron Bay. A glance at the chart should satisfy anyone that no good sailor would risk his fleet working through so narrow an unexplored channel.

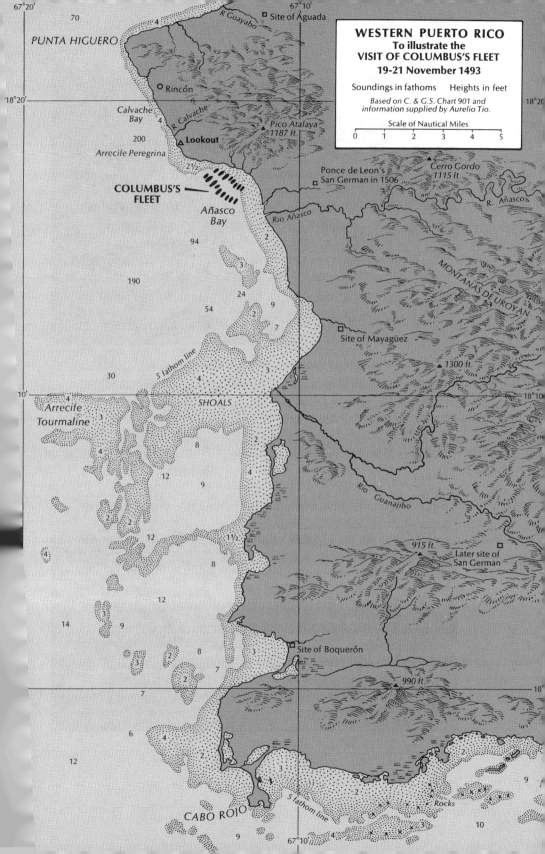

WESTERN PUERTO RICO
To illustrate the
VISIT OF COLUMBUS'S FLEET
19-21 November 1493

Soundings in fathoms   Heights in feet

Based on C. & G.S. Chart 901 and
information supplied by Aurelio Tio.

Scale of Nautical Miles

0   1   2   3   4   5

67°20'   70   R. Guayabo   67°10'   Site of Águada

PUNTA HIGUERO

18°20'   18°20'

○ Rincón

Calvache
Bay   R. Calvache   Pico Atalaya
          4   1187 ft.

200   ▲ Lookout   Cerro Gordo
Arrecife Peregrina   Ponce de Leon's   1115 ft.
                                    San German in 1506   R. Añasco

COLUMBUS'S —
FLEET
          Añasco
          Bay   Rio Añasco

                94   MONTAÑAS DE UROYAN

        190   Site of Mayagüez

                24   1300 ft.
        54   9
                2   7
                                    5 fathom line   18°10'
10'   30   18°10'
          4   SHOALS
Arrecife
Tourmaline   3
                              8
        4   2
        12   9   4
                                                    Rio Guanajibo
        2   2
        12   1½   915 ft.   Later site of
                                                    San German
        4   12   8

        12   Site of Boquerón
    14   9   3
        3   8
        2   7
        2   990 ft.
        7
                                                    Rocks
    6   4
        2   9
    12
              5 fathom line

CABO ROJO
        9   67°10'   4   10

Mouth of Añasco River and Añasco Bay.

Where Columbus's fleet landed in Puerto Rico.

Ensenada de Calvache, Añasco Bay.

Lookout Mound, Ensenada de Calvache.

It was a perfect place for watering a large fleet, as not only the big Rio Añasco rising in the mountains empties here, but a dozen other smaller streams of sweet water gave every vessel an opportunity to replenish her casks.

This area was heavily populated by Indians, but when the Spaniards visited a big village they found it completely empty. This branch of the Arawak lived in constant terror of raids from the eastern half of the island by Caribs and (as son Ferdinand noted) maintained a continual watch at a natural lookout on the shore whence they could be warned of an approaching fleet of war canoes. Sight of the Columbus fleet must have convinced them that the Caribs had grown wings, and they all fled to the mountains.

One of the Admiral's shipmates on this voyage, Ponce de León, decided that Borinquen would do nicely for him, and early in the next century conquered it, as we shall see in due course.

From Puerto Rico the fleet crossed the Mona Passage, and at eventide 22 November made landfall on Cape Engaño, Hispaniola. An Indian whom Columbus had picked up at Samaná Bay in January came out and directed the fleet to his home village. He was set ashore, well provided with trading truck, in the hope of mitigating the fears of the suspicious Indians there. Apparently that worked, as a number of Ciguayos visited the ships and traded. The sailor wounded in the fight at St. Croix, who had since died, was here given Christian burial.

Columbus now ranged a coast that he had already discovered coming home. On the evening of 27 November the fleet anchored outside the pass to Caracol Bay. In view of what had happened on the last Christmas Eve, the Admiral refused to enter in the dark. Flares were lighted and cannon fired, but no answer came from the shore. Late at night a canoe approached, manned by Indians calling *Almirante! Almirante!* and, when Columbus came on deck, they presented him with gifts from Guacanagarí. They assured him that the Spaniards at Navidad were all right—except that a few had died:—some understatement! "Diego Colón," the Indian interpreter, got the truth out of them, a tale so horrible that Columbus at first refused to believe it.

The Spaniards at Navidad had acted without restraint or reason. Two of the leaders, including Gutiérrez the crown official, formed a gang and roamed the island looking for more gold and women than Guacanagarí was able or willing to supply. They fell afoul of Caonabó, cacique of Maguana in the center of Hispaniola, a chief of stouter stuff than the feeble and complacent cacique of Marien. He killed the Gutiérrez gang and then marched on Navidad to wipe out the source of trouble. Only ten men were left under Diego de Harana to guard the fort. Caonabó disposed of them easily, hunting down and slaughtering every Spaniard who took to the bush. Thus ended the honeymoon between Christians and natives.

Columbus's immediate problem was to choose a site for his trading-post colony. Dr. Chanca, the fleet surgeon, ruled out the swampy shores of Caracol Bay where the natives were friendly, and Cape Haitien seemed far from the gold-bearing Cibao. So the Admiral decided to turn eastward in search of a good harbor. Sailing against the trades and westward-flowing current meant a long, tedious beat to windward, and it took the fleet 25 days to make good about 32 miles. Frequent shifting of sail and constant wetting with salt spray wore sailors down, exasperated the colonists, and killed a large part of the livestock. On 2 January 1494, when the fleet anchored in the lee of a peninsula that afforded shelter from the east wind, Columbus decided to pitch his city there and then. Although named Isabela after the Queen, this settlement was founded under an evil star.

Here for the time being discovery ended, as happiness had already ended for Columbus when he learned the fate of Navidad. Yet he must have derived great satisfaction from this voyage to Hispaniola. He had safely conducted across the Atlantic seventeen vessels, many of them very small, made a perfect landfall, and continued through a chain of uncharted islands with no accident serious enough to be recorded. He had discovered some twenty large islands and over two-score small ones upon which the eyes of no European had ever rested. Over the greatest fleet that had yet crossed the Atlantic, bearing 1200 seamen, colonists, and men-at-arms, he had kept discipline during a voyage that lasted fourteen weeks. In a region inhabited by man-eating Caribs he had avoided conflict save for one brief skirmish, and lost but a single man. Plenty of trouble was awaiting the Admiral when he left the deck of *Mariagalante* for dry land and exchanged the function of captain general for that of viceroy. The turn in his fortunes was sharp, and it came quickly. In years to come, when suffering in body from arthritis and in mind from the ingratitude of princes, Columbus must have sought consolation in the memory of those bright November days of 1493, the fleet gaily coasting along the lofty, verdure-clad Antilles with tradewind clouds piling up over the summits and rainbows bridging their deep-cleft valleys; of nights spent hove-to with his gallant ships all about, stars of incredible brightness overhead, and hearty voices joining in the evening hymn to the Blessed Virgin.

Evil Days at Isabela

Isabela was founded as a trading post, the only type of colony with which Columbus was familiar. Even as such the site was ill chosen, like so many of the first European colonies in America; for instance, Roanoke Island, Virginia, and St. Croix Island on the river of that name in Maine. Isabela had no proper harbor; only a roadstead open to the north and west, and no fresh water either. But Columbus was in a hurry to get his men ashore and send most of the ships home. He had wasted a month looking for a site which the Navidad garrison should have found, and the gold nuggets which they might have collected were not there. He must start trading quickly and produce something valuable to please his Sovereigns.

All the colonists and some of the seamen landed here. A town was laid out in classic form (for nothing less than a miniature Cadiz would suit the Admiral), with church and governor's palace fronting a square plaza—the pattern repeated wherever Spaniards settled in the New World. Men were put to work felling trees, cutting coral stone, and digging a canal to bring water from the nearest river, and some two hundred wattled huts were built as temporary housing. But insufficient wine and provisions had been brought over. Workers fell ill of malaria or from drinking well water and eating strange fish, although Dr. Chanca tried every new species on a dog before he would let any Christian touch it. Columbus, impatient to get things done, drafted some of the gentlemen volunteers for the hard labor, which caused great indignation; they had come out to fight or gather gold, not to do menial work. If they refused, they got no rations, and that was considered an abominable way to treat a Castilian hidalgo.

Many, however, were appeased by an early opportunity to gather gold. Isabela had been founded but four days when the Admiral organized an armed party to explore the Cibao and find the alleged mine. It was commanded by Alonso de Ojeda, an agile, handsome Andalusian who had attracted the Queen's attention and favor by the singular feat of pirouetting on a beam that projected from the Giralda, a tower 200 feet above the street in Seville.

With a score of Spaniards and native guides, Ojeda penetrated the great central valley of Hispaniola, the Vega Real, and reached the foothills of the Cordillera Setentrional in the Cibao. There he obtained three great gold nuggets, one with metal enough for a fifty-dollar gold piece. Within two weeks, on 20 January, he was back at Isabela bringing the first good news for many weeks. "All of us made merry," wrote Cuneo, "not caring any longer about spicery, but only for this blessed gold."

The Admiral feared that if he sent the ships home with nothing more than what Ojeda brought in, people might make nasty remarks about his line of samples—as they did. Yet he had to risk it, since the crews of seventeen ships were accumulating pay and eating up food, several hundred men were sick, Dr. Chanca had run out of drugs, and there were barely enough Spanish provisions left to see the fleet home.

So, retaining only *Mariagalante, Gallega, Niña,* and two smaller cara-vels, he dispatched the other twelve vessels under command of flag captain Antonio de Torres. Pierre Chaunu regards this eastward voyage of Torres as in a class with the Admiral's, for he not only made a record unbroken for centuries—35 days Isabela to Cadiz—but carried a real cargo. Thus Torres inaugurated the *carrera de Indias,* the regular trade between Spain and the West Indies. It is true that what Torres brought home was so-called cinnamon, only it tasted like bad ginger; strong pepper, but not with the flavor of Malayan pepper; wood said to be sandalwood, only it wasn't, not speaking of the 60 parrots and 26 Indian slaves; but gold to the value of 30,000 ducats sweetened the lot.

Antonio de Torres's fleet made Cadiz on 7 March 1494. As brother to the governess of Infante Don Juan, he had access to the Sovereigns and so was entrusted by Columbus with the outline of a report to present to them orally. This "Torres Memorandum" is a proof of Columbus's common-sense views on colonization. If he failed as a colonial administrator, it was not from odd ideas but from inability to control lazy and rough hidalgos who hated him as a foreigner. Las Casas wrote that the Archangel Gabriel would have been hard put to govern people as greedy, selfish, and egotistical as the early settlers of Hispaniola.

The gist of the Torres Memorandum was an appeal for more of everything—men, munitions, Spanish food and wine, tools, livestock, clothes, and shoes. Logistic supply in America was a major problem for all European pioneers; it will be remembered how the first English settlers in Virginia rotted and starved for want of their native bread, beef, and beer in a country abounding with maize, game, and good water; and how the French in Canada, a country teeming with fish, fowl, and venison, were always on the verge of starvation by spring.

Ferdinand and Isabella felt that most of their Viceroy's requests were reasonable. The only thing that the Queen rejected was his sug-gestion to build up a profitable export of Carib and other native slaves. Slavery was so taken for granted in those days, both by Europeans and Moslems (some of whom still practice it), that Columbus never gave a thought to the morality of this proposal. If he had, he would doubtless have reflected that the Indians enslaved each other, so why should we not enslave them, particularly if we convert them too, and save their souls? The Admiral concluded his memorandum by a generous tribute to Dr. Chanca and other subordinates, asked to have their salaries raised, and recommended that the two hundred gentlemen volunteers be placed on the royal payroll so that they could be controlled by him.

About a month after sending the fleet home under Torres, Columbus organized and in person led a reconnaissance in force of the interior, first of those overland marches of Spaniards in armor which set the pattern followed by Balboa, Cortés, Pizarro, and De Soto. In military formation with drums beating, trumpets sounding, and banners displayed, several hundred men set off from Isabela on 12 March 1494. Crossing the Cordillera Setentrional by a pass which Columbus named *El Puerto de los Hidalgos* after his gentlemen trailmakers, they soon came in view of a spacious valley "so fresh, so green, so open, of such color and altogether so full of beauty," wrote Las Casas, that "the Admiral, who was profoundly moved by all these things, gave great thanks to God and named it Vega Real," the Royal Plain. Guided by friendly Indians, they pushed up the northern slope of the cordillera to a mesa overlooking a bend of the Rio Janico, where Columbus left fifty men under Mosén Margarit to construct a rough earthen fort. "On that trip," wrote Cuneo, "we spent twenty-nine days with terrible weather, bad food, and worse drink; nevertheless, out of covetousness for that gold, we all kept strong and lusty."

Those left behind at Isabela were neither lusty nor strong. They had found no gold to compensate for living and working in that unhealthy spot. Almost the last of the Spanish provisions were spent. Discontent was rife, mutiny was seething, several troublemakers were in irons, and as a precaution Columbus placed all arms and munitions on board his flagship with brother Diego in command.

To raise morale and get rid of the troublemakers, he now planned a second reconnaissance in force under Ojeda, consisting of four hundred men with orders to march to Santo Tomás, relieve the garrison, and then explore the country and live off the natives. This was one of Columbus's worst decisions. He instructed Ojeda to do the Indians no harm, reminding him that the Sovereigns desired their salvation even more than their gold; but the first thing that Ojeda did was to cut off the ears of a native who stole some old clothes, and to send the cacique whom he considered responsible in chains to Isabela. Ojeda then relieved Margarit, who with some four hundred men roamed the Vega Real extorting gold from the natives, exhausting their food supplies, carrying off boys as slaves and young girls as concubines.

Before there was time for Columbus to learn of these doings, he had departed to explore Cuba, leaving his younger brother in charge at Isabela. That, too, was a mistake. Diego Colón, "a virtuous person, very discreet, peaceable and simple," was incapable of raising the morale of the colonists, much less of controlling people like Ojeda and Margarit. But Columbus felt that there was no one else in the colony whom he could trust.

Bibliography and Notes

The Papal bulls. These and the Treaty of Tordesillas (1494) are printed, translated, and discussed in Frances G. Davenport, ed., *European Treaties Bearing on the History of the United States and Its Dependencies* (Washington, D.C., 1914). Luis Weckmann has since gone extensively into the background of these bulls in *Las Bulas Alejandrinas de 1493 y la Teoría Política del Papado Medieval* (Mexico, 1949).

No official log or journal of this Second Voyage has survived, but we have detailed accounts from three participants: Dr. Diego Chanca the fleet surgeon; Michele de Cuneo of Savona near Genoa, a childhood friend of Columbus; and Melchior Maldonado, a former Spanish diplomat whose account is the basis of Peter Martyr's in his *Decades of the New World.* Columbus, moreover, told Andrés Bernáldez, a Spanish chronicler with whom he stayed at the conclusion of the voyage, many details of which Bernáldez set down in his *Historia de los Reyes Católicos;* the part about this voyage is to be found, both text and translation, in Cecil Jane, *Select Documents* (Hakluyt Society), I, 129–67.

Translations of Cuneo's and Syllacio's letters and of Ferdinand's account of the return passage in 1496 are in my *Journals and Other Documents,* pp. 197–256. Dr. Chanca's letter will be found in *Raccolta* I, part i, pp. 235–65 and, together with a biographical study, in my learned Puerto Rican friend Aurelio Tió's *Dr. Diego Alvarez Chanca* (San Juan, 1966). Cecil Jane, *Select Documents,* I, 20–73, has a good English translation. A royal cédula for the provisioning of the fleet, dated 1 June 1493, was published in facsimile by La Casa del Libro, San Juan, P. R., in 1961.

Identity of the Lesser Antilles. In the *pleitos* taken in 1512, II, 47 (see bibliography to Chapter I, above), one Pedro Anrriquez who was with Columbus on the Second Voyage, mentions, in this order, Dominica, Mariegalante, Guadeloupe, Montserrat, Antigua, Redonda, San Martín, San Jorge, San Cristóval, Ysla Gorda, Santa Cruz, Anegada, Las Vírgenes, and San Juan [Puerto Rico], "all discovered at one time." A comparison with Juan de La Cosa's map makes it evident that there is plenty of room for friendly discussion of Columbus's original names for islands discovered subsequent to Guadeloupe.

Puerto Rico. Aurelio Tió has for years pursued the problem of Columbus's landing place in *Borinquen* in local and Spanish archives; the articles which sum up his latest findings are "El Enigma del Descubrimiento de Puerto Rico," *Boletín* de la Academia Puertorriqueña de la Historia, I (San Juan, 1969), 13–49, and "Indicaciones Arqueológicas," pp. 59–65; and *Boletín* de la Academia de Artes y Ciencias de Puerto Rico, VI (1970), 495–578. My examination of the terrain with him on 17 February 1973 has left no possible doubt that the landing took place at Añasco Bay, the first bay Columbus could have anchored in after rounding Cabo Rojo without encountering dangerous reefs. It has ample anchorage for 17 sail; all the beaches are good for landing, and several rivers and streams flow into it from the hilly interior of Puerto Rico. Ferdinand Columbus adds, "Near the sea was a high, well made *palco* [platform, watch tower], that could hold ten or twelve persons" (chap. 48, Benjamin Keen trans. of the *Historie*, 1959, p. 117). This is easily identifiable by a natural stone outcrop at the mouth of García Creek and near the Pellegrina reef. From it one can see Cabo Rojo on the south, and Punta Higuero on the north. This coast later became a favorite watering place for outward-bound ships. A short, well-illustrated account by Señor Tió in English is in *Puerto Rican Living* (1970). pp. 5–13. Commander Roberto Barreiro-Meiro of the Museo Naval, Madrid, disagrees as usual (*Revista General de Marina*, April 1969).

✳ VI ✳

Jamaica, Cuba, and Rebellion

1494-1496

Jamaica and the South Coast of Cuba

Between voyages, Columbus decided that Cuba must be the Chinese province of Mangi, the name which Marco Polo gave to all South China; and as the Sovereigns had ordered him to look into it, Columbus lost no time resuming his congenial role of discoverer. *Niña* served as flagship; the other two vessels that accompanied her were lateen-rigged caravels *San Juan* and *Cardera*. They are described as "much smaller" than *Niña* and carried crews of only fourteen to sixteen as compared with her twenty-eight to thirty. For officers, Columbus had one of the Niños, Pedro de Terreros, and several other veterans of his First Voyage. Fortunately for history, his gossipy friend Michele de Cuneo shipped as passenger, and Juan de La Cosa the chartmaker as able seaman. "Diego Colón," the best of the Indian converts, came along as interpreter, as did one of the priests.

The three caravels sailed from Isabela 24 April 1494. It was the best season for navigating the Greater Antilles, when the trades can be depended on by day and there is an offshore breeze at night; the air is still cool, and there is no danger of a hurricane. On the 29th they crossed the Windward Passage to Cape Alpha and Omega, as Columbus had named Cape Maisi on his First Voyage. He landed there, set up a column and a cross, and again took formal possession of Cuba for Spain. On the advice of his officers, the Admiral decided to range the south rather than the north coast, "because should there be anything good it would rather be to the southward than the northward." This was Aristotle's ancient theory, supported by Portuguese experience in Africa, that the further south one sailed, the more gold and precious wares would be encountered.

From Cape Maisi on, the Spaniards made fresh discoveries. They sailed west by south for fifty miles along a cliff-rimmed coast, noting (as we did in our ketch *Mary Otis*) the sweet scent of the land, a combination of sea grape, cactus flowers, and other aromatic plants. As evening fell on the last day of April, they entered a great sickle-shaped harbor which Columbus named *Puerto Grande*. (This was Guantán-amo Bay, seat of an important United States naval base in the twentieth century). A shore party ascertained that the natives had fled in the midst of cooking a gigantic dinner of fish, iguana, and hutía (the small Cuban quadruped), to entertain a visiting cacique. Diego persuaded the cooks to return and share the feast with the Spaniards. They were well paid with hawks' bells and other trifles for their trouble of catching more fish to regale the cacique, and were relieved that their uninvited guests refused to touch iguana meat, roast iguana being the favorite native delicacy.

On May Day morning the fleet departed with the land breeze. As the ships sailed close to the bold shore, multitudes flocked to the water's edge or paddled out in canoes, offering cassava bread and sweet water, and begging the "men from the sky" to call. There had been no unfortunate incidents between Spaniards and natives in Cuba. Race relations there were still "of the Golden Age," and Columbus, to his credit, kept them so.

Forty miles west of Guantánamo the Admiral noted a break in the sierra and sailed through a narrow, cliff-bordered channel into the great bay where twenty years later Diego de Velásquez founded the city of Santiago de Cuba. Again, relations with the natives, who had "the loveliest gardens in the world," were idyllic. Departing at dawn 2 May, the fleet sailed through the waters in which, four centuries later, the Battle of Santiago concluded the long and glorious history of Spanish sea power in the New World.

After sailing all night, Columbus on 3 May, feast of the Discovery

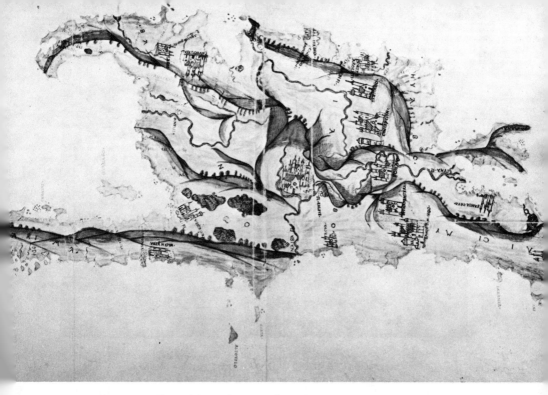

Peter Martyr's map of Hispaniola, 1516.

of the True Cross, landed at a cape that he named Cabo de Cruz, and it is still so called. Instead of turning into the Gulf of Guacanayabó, he decided to take off for Jamaica, of whose existence he had been told by the natives of Santiago. Here he hoped to find gold; for Cuba, so far as he could ascertain, had none.

The trades blew up strong and the fleet had a rough passage of two days, part of the time hove-to. When it moderated enough to make sail, and all hands had been on deck for many hours, the Admiral considerately sent everyone below to rest while he himself set about making sail all alone. I do not imagine he could have done much more than cast off a few gaskets and trim the braces before the sleepers were awakened by the slatting of sails and the change of motion, and came topside to help. But this incident illustrates a pleasant side of Columbus's character and helps to explain the loyalty of common sailors to him.

On 5 May the fleet anchored in St. Ann's Bay, Jamaica, which

Jamaica, Portland Bight. David Crofoot photo.

Columbus named *Santa Gloria*. He declared that this island, half the area of Sicily, was "the fairest that eyes have beheld," mountainous and heavily populated. Sixty or seventy Indian warriors came out in dugout canoes to meet the fleet and showed every sign of giving fight; but a blank cannon shot sent them paddling furiously shoreward. Columbus proceeded to the next port west, Rio Bueno. There the natives made another hostile demonstration, but Columbus attacked with his ships' boats, armed with crossbowmen who "pricked them well and killed a number." Then he set upon them a great dog which "bit them and did them great hurt, for a dog is worth ten men against Indians." These tactics of worrying Indians with big, savage dogs were practised in the New World, as earlier they had been on the Guanches in the Canaries. The natives of Rio Bueno, also Tainos, appeased the Spaniards with provisions but were unable to produce gold. So the Admiral made but one more call in Jamaica, at Montego Bay, then sailed back on the starboard tack to Cape Cruz.

The fleet now resumed its exploration of the south Cuban coast, alert for evidences of Chinese culture. They sailed around the Gulf of Guacanayabó, and at sunrise 15 May 1494 sighted an archipelago of small islands. These were the inshore group of the Laberinto de Doze Leguas. Columbus named this archipelago *El Jardín de la Reina*, the Queen's Garden. According to his description, these cays were then very beautiful; some under cultivation and others adorned with royal palms and calabash trees. The Spaniards admired the flamingoes— "great birds like cranes, but bright red"—and watched the natives hunting turtle with a fish hound. An Indian would catch and train a pilot fish (which has suckers on its head) and let it out on a leash when turtles were about. The fish would then attach itself to a shell, which his Indian master had only to haul in to capture the turtle; the pilot fish was politely thanked and rewarded with bits of meat. This was one of Columbus's tales that Europeans found most difficult to believe, but it was true; and when I sailed through those waters more than thirty years ago, I was told that native Cubans still practised the same method of catching turtle. But we found the "Queen's Garden" a sad disappointment. Mangrove had driven all other plants off the cays, and most of the mangrove had been killed in a hurricane. The channels are so intricate and shallow that we felt Columbus must have been as good a navigator in shoal water as on the ocean.

The three caravels put to sea through the Boca Grande, then shaped a course for the Sierra de Trinidad. As they sailed along this bold coast, natives again flocked to the shore bearing gifts and welcoming the Spaniards as "men from the sky." But not one Chinese junk or sampan or temple or bridge! Could it be that the culture of Cathay had not reached this outlying part of the Grand Khan's dominions? Or was this only one more big island?

Columbus missed the narrow entrance to the bay where Cienfuegos later rose, but investigated the Gulf of Cochinos, which in 1961 acquired notoriety as the "Bay of Pigs," scene of an abortive invasion by exiled Cubans. He observed the subterranean streams that break out from under the sea and enable sailors to fill their water casks without going ashore. "The water was so cold, and of such goodness and so sweet," said Columbus, "that no better could be found in the world." He and a shore party "rested there on the grass by those springs amid the scent of the flowers, which was marvelous, and the sweetness of the singing of little birds, so many and so delightful, and under the shade of those palms, so tall and fair that it was a wonder to see it all." Andrés Bernáldez set all this down from the Admiral's own lips.

We hardly need labor the point that Columbus's appreciation of the beauties of nature was equal to that of eighteenth-century romancers, and unique among pioneers in the age of discovery.

The little fleet now entered the Gulf of Batabanó, where the Admiral saw a phenomenon that has intrigued many later navigators: the sea water turning as white as milk, and then black as ink. The white is caused by fine marl becoming roiled by waves in the shallow waters, and the inky color by black sand similarly stirred up. The shores of this gulf, said the Admiral in vivid language, were of mangrove "so thick a cat couldn't get ashore." By 27 May he reached the tip end of the Zapata Peninsula, which he called *Punta del Serafín* because it was the feast of All Angels; he crossed the Ensenada Broa and anchored near the present town of Batabanó.

And as yet no sign of China!

Sailing westward along the southern shore of the Province of Pinar del Rio, the caravels became involved in the worst shoals yet experienced. They could get through some channels only by the laborious process of kedging—rowing an anchor ahead, dropping it, and hauling the vessel up to it by the windlass while her keel scraped the mud. They even passed the limit of Taino culture and entered the last stronghold of the Siboney. Diego the interpreter could not understand them.

Somewhere along this line, a contemporary manuscript called the Sneyd Codex states that Columbus took off to the southward and discovered South America. Nothing to it! He didn't have time.

Columbus now figured out by mathematics that he was at least half the way around the world; actually he was at longitude 84° West of Greenwich, less than one-quarter around. Assuming the Bahia Cortés, where Cuban land trends south, to be the Gulf of Siam, he believed that he was hot on the trail of the Strait of Malacca. So, why not return to Spain around the world, hooking up with the tracks of Bartholomew Dias and Vasco da Gama?

Fortunately the common sense of a good seaman came to his rescue. The caravels were leaky because of frequent groundings; their rigging had deteriorated to shreds and tatters; provisions were low, and the seamen were growling and grumbling. So the Admiral decided to reverse course. Following the precedent established by Dias in 1488 when forced to turn back from the very gates of India, Columbus took a deposition from almost every man in his little fleet to the effect that Cuba must be part of a continent, that it was useless to sail further to prove it, since no island of that length could exist! Actually, they were then about fifty miles from Cape San Antonio, the western promontory of Cuba. This procedure did not convince even Juan de La Cosa, who represents an insular Cuba on his famous mappemonde dated 1500.

The return to Isabela began on 13 June 1494. For the most part it was a tiresome beat to windward among the same cays as on the outward passage, because the fleet could make no progress in deep water against the trade winds and the westward-flowing current. "If the ships in the Indies only sail with the wind abaft the beam," wrote Columbus, "it is not from bad design or clumsiness; the great currents, which run there in the same direction as the wind, so make it that nobody attempts to struggle close-hauled, for in one day they would lose what they gained in seven; nor do I except caravels, even Portuguese lateeners." His good windward record with *Niña* and *Pinta* in 1493 had been made in deep water with little or no current. Sailing vessels never could cope with the conditions Columbus describes until the advent of the modern racing yachts, and even they usually do so by "turning on the juice." William Hickey, writing at St. Mary's, Jamaica, in the last years of the eighteenth century, tells of watching a ship trying to beat ten miles eastward from Kingston to Port Morant. Every day for eight days she stood out to sea close-hauled on the port tack, and every evening, sailing close-hauled on the starboard tack, she returned to the same position.

Columbus now learned that the only way to make progress to windward in the Caribbean was to stay in smooth water, avoid the current, and work the land breeze at night. It took him 25 days to make good about 200 miles. By the time he reached the Queen's Garden he could stand no more mud navigation, and made for blue water. And then it took him ten days to make 180 miles to windward. Provisions had to be rationed to a pound of weevily biscuit and a pint of sour wine a day, and the sailors worked constantly at the pumps. Finally, on 18 July, they reached Cabo de Cruz and were well entertained by friendly Indians. Rather than endure another long beat to windward along the ironbound coast of Oriente Province, the Admiral decided to ease off his sheets and learn more about Jamaica.

Montego Bay he again entered on 21 July. From that future scene of sport and fashion he passed close aboard the pretty harbor of

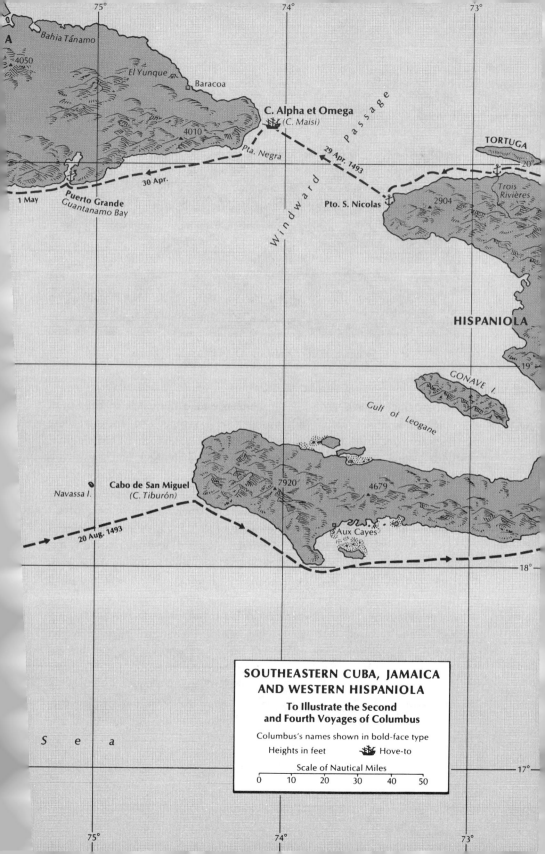

A

Bahía Tánamo

▲4050

El Yunque

Baracoa

4010

Pta. Negra

C. Alpha et Omega
(C. Maisi)

29 Apr. 1493

W i n d w a r d   P a s s a g e

30 Apr.

1 May

Puerto Grande
Guantanamo Bay

TORTUGA

20°

Trois Rivières

Pto. S. Nicolas

2904

HISPANIOLA

19°

GONAVE I.

Gulf   of   Leogane

Navassa I.

Cabo de San Miguel
(C. Tiburón)

7920

4679

20 Aug. 1493

Aux Cayes

18°

S e a

17°

SOUTHEASTERN CUBA, JAMAICA AND WESTERN HISPANIOLA

To Illustrate the Second and Fourth Voyages of Columbus

Columbus's names shown in bold-face type

Heights in feet   Hove-to

Scale of Nautical Miles

0   10   20   30   40   50

75°   74°   73°

Jamaica: Lucea Harbor. David Crofoot photo.

Lucea, then hauled around the western end of Jamaica to the south coast and edged along, anchoring every night. The Indians were friendly; one cacique embarrassingly so. He came out to the flagship with a fleet of canoes, his family and suite dressed in magnificent parrot-feather headdresses and little else. The cacique wore a coronet of small polished stones and some large disks of gold and copper alloy that he must have obtained from Central America. In the bow of his canoe stood a herald wearing a cloak of red feathers and carrying a white banner. His wife was similarly adorned with native jewelry, although she wore nothing that could be called clothing except "a little cotton thing no bigger than an orange peel." Their beautiful daughters, aged about 15 and 18, were completely naked. When they drew alongside, the Admiral was in his cabin, so absorbed in reading the office of terce that he did not notice them until they were on board. The cacique then proposed, through Diego Colón, that he and his family sail to Spain with the Admiral to visit the Catholic Sovereigns, "and to see the wonders of Castile." Here was a golden opportunity for Columbus to make a hit at court, but humanity prevailed. He thought of the cold weather on the voyage home, of the indignities that the pretty daughters might suffer from the sailors, and of the effect of a complete change of climate on these innocent souls. So he sent them ashore with gifts, after receiving the cacique's homage and fealty to Ferdinand and Isabella.

On 19 August the fleet cleared Morant Point, the eastern cape of Jamaica, crossed the Windward Passage, and sighted Cape Tiburón, Haiti. By the end of the month they reached Alta Vela, the sail-like rock which marks the southernmost point of Hispaniola.

Saona Island, behind which the three caravels anchored to ride out a hurricane, was so named for Savona, the home town of Michele de Cuneo, the Admiral's merry guest. A total eclipse of the moon took place on 14 September while the fleet lay there, and Columbus, who had an almanac which gave the time of the eclipse at Nuremberg, tried by timing it at Saona to calculate the longitude. It was a simple enough calculation—15 degrees to an hour's time—but something went wrong and the Admiral worked out a longitude too far west by 23 degrees. Building on that gross error, it was easy for Columbus to persuade

Alta Vela: David Crofoot photo.

himself that he had been well on his way around the world when he turned back from Cuba.

The Admiral intended to make a side trip to Puerto Rico, but in the Mona Passage he fell ill. His symptoms suggest a nervous breakdown as the result of lack of sleep, frequent drenching, and inadequate food. Probably he also had the beginning of arthritis, which troubled him gravely during the last ten years of his life. His officers held a council and decided to scud before the wind to Isabela, where the three caravels anchored on 29 September 1494. The Admiral had to be carried ashore in the arms of his seamen.

Although Columbus had not found the empire of the Grand Khan, he had accomplished a great deal on this round voyage of five months from Isabela. He had opened up what proved to be the most valuable of Spain's insular possessions. He had discovered Jamaica. He had demonstrated that he was no less apt at coastal piloting and island hopping than at charting a course across the ocean and conducting a fleet off soundings. Shipmates of that voyage never tired of extolling his feats of navigation, his humanity, and his consideration for them.

Hispaniola and Home

Good news met the Admiral upon landing at Isabela. His brother Bartholomew, whom he had not seen for six years, had arrived. News traveled so slowly from Spain to France that Bartholomew never heard about the success of the First Voyage until too late to embark on the Second. But Ferdinand and Isabella were highly impressed by "Don Bartolomé," as they called him, gave him command of three caravels to take provisions to Hispaniola, and conferred the title of *Adelantado*, advancer. He was not only an expert sailor and cartographer but a far better administrator than his brilliant brother. Intelligent without being an intellectual, he had an innate sense of leadership. Curt in speech and tough with subordinates, he lacked the "sweetness and benignity" that Las Casas saw in Christopher, but he never lost courage or fell ill. Unexpected situations on land or sea he met with promptness and resolution.

It is most regrettable that Bartholomew missed the Second Voyage because he, if anyone, could have averted the appalling situation in Hispaniola which his weak younger brother Diego had allowed to develop. It must be said, however, that the three Columbus brothers had two strikes against them from the start: they were Genoese and the colonists were Spaniards. Spain was the most fiercely nationalistic of European nations, and her sons who went to the New World to seek their fortunes were not only brave and rugged but often greedy and unreasonable. Oviedo, in his *History of the Indies* that came out in 1535, wrote that any early governor of Hispaniola, "to succeed, must be superhuman." And Christopher had already made two bad mistakes—appointing Diego his deputy, and turning Ojeda and Margarit loose in the interior.

During the Admiral's absence, Diego heard about the cruelty and rapacity of Margarit and sent him an order to mend his ways, which so enraged the Spaniard that he roared into Isabela demanding retraction—or else. When he didn't get it, he joined other malcontents in seizing the caravels which Bartholomew had brought out from Spain, and sailed home, where he circulated slanders against the Columbus brothers. A Sevillian goldsmith of the party even declared openly that none of the gold in Hispaniola was genuine.

Before the end of 1494, Antonio de Torres arrived at Isabela in command of four caravels bringing provisions and supplies. He delivered a friendly letter to the Admiral from the King and Queen, who urged him to leave Hispaniola in charge of his "brother or some other person" and come home to help them negotiate with Portugal. Columbus made a great mistake in not accepting this invitation; pride compelled him to try to master the local situation, and to provide a profitable export to Spain. To do that, he adopted the questionable policy of rounding up and enslaving Indians who had resisted Margarit's men. Time and again Columbus had asserted that the Tainos were the most kindly, peaceful, and generous people in the world, and the Sovereigns had particularly enjoined him to treat them as such. But, by the close of February 1495, when Torres was ready to sail to Spain, the Columbus brothers had collected 1500 Indian captives at Isabela. Torres loaded 500 of them, all his four ships could take. The Admiral then allowed every Spaniard at Isabela to help himself to as many of the remainder as he chose, and the rest were told to get out. Cuneo records how these wretched captives, when released, fled as far as they could from the Spaniards; women even abandoned infants in their fear and desperation to escape further cruelty. But at least they were free; the lot of the slaves shipped home was worse. Some two hundred died at sea. The survivors were landed at Seville where Andrés Bernáldez, the clerical chronicler, saw them put up for sale "naked as they were born." He added that they were "not very profitable since almost all died, for the country did not agree with them."

A cacique named Guatiguaná now tried to unite the Indians of Hispaniola, estimated to be at least 250,000 in number, against the Spaniards. He managed to collect a formidable army in the Vega Real to march on Isabela. The Spaniards took the offensive. The Admiral, Bartholomew, and Ojeda marched to the Puerto de los Hidalgos with 20 horse, 20 hounds, and 200 foot, half of them armed with arquebuses. The fire from these primitive muskets alarmed the Tainos more than it harmed them, but when Ojeda charged at the head of the cavalry, dashing into the closely huddled mass of Indians, and at the same time unleashed the savage dogs, their rout became complete. This, the first pitched battle between Europeans and Indians, took place at the end of March 1495. Ojeda followed up his victory by capturing Caonabó, toughest of the caciques, who had been responsible for exterminating the Navidad garrison.

The original Isabela beachhead now expanded to cover the entire island. The Admiral himself made a triumphal march across Hispaniola, which by 1496 was so thoroughly subdued that a Spaniard could safely go wherever he pleased and help himself to the Indians' food, women, and gold.

For almost a year the Columbus brothers were occupied with subjugating and organizing Hispaniola in order to obtain as much gold as possible. Several forts were built in the interior, and armed men were sent to force the natives to deliver a gold tribute. The *repartimientos* system, which later spread to all Spanish America, was begun by Columbus. This meant that grants were made to the individual colonist *with the natives there living,* who were his to have and hold, exploit, punish, or torture, as he chose; subject always (Spanish apologists are fond of pointing out) to the Laws of the Indies which enjoined conversion and kind treatment. But these were seldom enforced. This cruel policy initiated by Columbus and relentlessly pursued by his successors resulted in genocide. Of the estimated native population of 250,000 in 1492, not 500 remained alive in 1538.

Lest we become smug about modern progress and humanity, I wish to remind the reader that exactly the same policy of *repartimientos,* this time to obtain wild rubber and unpaid native labor, was applied to blacks in the Belgian Congo at the turn of this century, and a few years later to Indians in the Portumayo, the upper Amazon, by Peru and a British company. Brian Inglis's noble biography of Roger Casement, who did his best to abolish this atrocious state of things, has evidence that in the Portumayo, at least, virtual slavery of the Indians existed as late as 1970.

The calumnies of Fray Buil, Margarit, and others against Columbus made their mark on the Sovereigns, who sent Juan Aguado, a colonist who had returned to Spain with Torres, to investigate the charges and report to them. He arrived at Isabela in command of four provision ships in October 1495 and at once began throwing his weight around. Columbus now realized he had better return home to mend his political fences. The Spanish population of the island, mostly concentrated at Isabela, had now fallen to 630, partly owing to deaths from disease, partly because many had gone home. A large number of those left behind were sick, and all were discontented. In this rich, fertile land with beautiful climate, they were still dependent on imported provisions. Nobody, unless under compulsion, would trouble to sow grain, said Cuneo, because "nobody wants to live in these countries"; and the most potent oath heard at Isabela was, "As God may take me to Castile, I'm telling you the truth!"

Finally, naming brother Bartholomew governor in his absence, Columbus sailed home in *Niña* on 10 March 1496.

This return from the Second Voyage was a sad contrast to the pomp, pride, and superb equipment of the outward passage in 1493. *Niña*'s sole consort was a 50-tun caravel named *India* which had been built at Isabela from the timbers of two vessels wrecked in a hurricane. The two caravels were dangerously overcrowded with 225 Spaniards and 30 Indian slaves. Columbus was eager to make best speed home, but so few return passages had yet been made that nobody knew the quickest route; and he decided to jump off from the Leeward Islands. That was the shortest rhumb-line to Spain, but it turned out to be the longest in time, because of the necessity to buck headwinds most of the way. The caravels took twelve days to clear Hispaniola, and two weeks more to reach Guadeloupe, where the Admiral wished to lay in a supply of native provisions. Here his first shore party was met by an army of Carib women armed with bows and arrows, from which he concluded that this was the Isle of Amazons. Only by securing as hostages three boys and ten women, one of them a cacique's lady, were the Spaniards able to force the Caribs to provide a supply of cassava roots. These, if properly prepared so as to eliminate the poison, a process that the Indians taught the Spaniards, produced a flour which made a nourishing and palatable bread. The lady cacique and her daughter, so Columbus declared, volunteered to accompany him to Spain, and were accepted. They died en route, or shortly after.

On 20 April 1496, *Niña* and *India* departed Guadeloupe. We have no details of the next month's sailing except that it was very slow, and mostly beating to windward. After a month at sea, all hands were put on a short allowance of six ounces of cassava bread and a cup of water per diem. About that time, providentially, they caught a westerly breeze south of the Azores, but hunger increased daily. Some Spaniards proposed eating the Indians, starting with the Caribs who were man-eaters themselves; it wouldn't be a sin to pay them in their own coin! Others proposed that all natives be thrown overboard so that they would consume no more rations. Columbus, in one of his humanitarian moods, argued that after all Caribs were people and should be treated as such. The debate was still undecided on 8 June when they made landfall on the Portuguese coast almost exactly where the Admiral intended, about 35 miles north of Cape St. Vincent. The several pilots on board thought they were still hundreds of miles from shore and heading for Galicia. Columbus's success at hitting the land "on the nose" after six weeks at sea, much of it sailing a zigzag course, convinced all the seafaring tribe of his high competence at dead-reckoning navigation. The only doubts have been raised by library navigators of recent decades.

On 11 June 1496, Columbus's Second Voyage to America ended in the Bay of Cadiz. Every available banner was broken out and all pendants run up to make as brave an appearance as possible, but it was a sad show at best, what with the miserable Indians and Spanish passengers whom an onlooker described as wasted in their bodies and with "faces the color of saffron."

Two years and nine months had passed since the Admiral's great fleet of seventeen sail departed Cadiz with hearts high and grandiose expectations of founding a valuable colony and locating the emperor of China. From the point of view of the average intelligent Spaniard, all that had been a phantom, and Columbus now seemed an impractical dreamer. Cuba was no limb of China; anyone who talked with a member of the exploring expedition could see that. His town of Isabela, instead of being a rich trading factory like the Portuguese São Jorge da Mina on the Gold Coast, was a miasmic dump which even the Columbus brothers were abandoning. Instead of the promised gold mine of the Cibao, gold was diffused in small quantities over the island and could only be produced by slave labor. Instead of golden-age simplicity and peacefulness, the natives were beginning to show fight. Nor was there even the consoling thought that before being killed the Indians had been assured of eternal life; none save the few brought home to Spain had yet been baptized. And so loud and angry were the cries of returned Spaniards against the Columbus brothers that the Sovereigns must have been tempted to dismiss them and forget about the Indies. Possibly that is what they would have done had they not heard that the king of Portugal was about to fit out a new expedition to India (Vasco da Gama's), and that Henry VII of England had engaged John Cabot to find a short, high-latitude ocean route to China.

Notes

The Sneyd Codex. Alleged discovery of the Continent in 1494. Besides pearls along the coast behind Margarita, Columbus found women who were not only *amorosas* and *desnudas* but *blancas* and *discretas!* Although C. E. Nowell in *Hispanic American Historical Review*, XXII (1942), 193–210, demonstrated that the writer of this "Sneyd Codex" was describing a fictitious voyage, impossible to sandwich into Columbus's itinerary, it was revived in Spain in 1972 and played up by the press. Columbian myths and hoaxes never die.

Juan de La Cosa and his world map are also subjects of interminable controversy. In the first place, was the recreant master-owner of *Santa María* on the First Voyage the same as the mariner-cartographer on the Second? In my *Admiral of the Ocean Sea*, I, 186–89, 198, I argued that he was not, that there were two of them; and I understand that Miss Gould came to the same conclusion. But Capitán de Corbeta Roberto Barreiro-Meiro of the Museo Naval, Madrid, in a pamphlet, *Juan de La Cosa y su Doble Personalidad* (Instituto Histórico de Marina, 1970), has impugned some of my evidence and plumps for a single La Cosa. The same author, in a pamphlet that appeared in 1972 with the same imprint, *Algo Sobre la Carta de Juan de La Cosa*, suggests that Vicente Yáñez Pinzón circumnavigated Cuba in 1499, points out that several important people did not follow Columbus in calling it mainland, and that the date 1500 in the La Cosa mappemonde may

Autograph Letter of Columbus. To the Bank of St. George, Genoa, 2 April 1502, with his signature. Relating to his *mayorazgo*, or entail, which the Bank is to administer. Courtesy Archives of Genoa.

be correct. Peter Martyr in his First Decade, written in 1500–1501, states that several navigators had circumnavigated Cuba. The late Admiral Guillén told me that he regarded the 1500 date as a mere *incipit*, that it had not been finished before 1505, and I agree with him, finding no good evidence for those alleged circumnavigations of Cuba.

Saul Jarcho, "Jaundice During the Second Voyage of Columbus," *Revista* de la Asociación de Salud Pública de Puerto Rico, II (1958), 24–27, is an interesting medical study of the sickness on board *Niña* in 1496.

✳ VII ✳

Third Voyage, Mainland Discovered

1498-1500

Preparations

Columbus frequently "wrestled with God" to find out why things turned out so badly for him. He performed his religious duties regularly and did his best to convert the Indians to the True Faith; so why did Providence frown on his undertakings? He had served the Sovereigns faithfully, respected their every wish and guarded their interests, and had won for them a new empire overseas; why, then, did they listen to his enemies and send out a low fellow to insult him? He had made all practical preparations, kept his ships staunch, his people healthy, and his powder dry; but now, it would seem, every Spaniard's hand was against him. Why? Why? Why? The Book of Job afforded him consolation, but no clue. Perhaps it was because he had embraced the deadly sin of pride after his First Voyage, had worn excessive apparel (as befitted the rank of admiral), had consorted too much with high company, partaken of rich viands and rare vintages? Pride, to be sure, is a deadly sin. So, upon arrival at Cadiz and ever after, Columbus assumed the coarse brown habit of a Franciscan as evidence of humility, and instead of accepting invitations to castles and palaces, he put up in religious houses with rough quarters and coarse fare. While awaiting a royal command to appear at court, he stayed with a priest named Andrés Bernáldez, chaplain to the archbishop of Seville.

The Admiral might be ostentatiously simple in his habits, but he knew very well the value of publicity. So, when an invitation came from the Sovereigns to visit them, he organized another impressive cavalcade. Two members of the cacique Caonabó's family accompanied him on muleback. Servants rode ahead with cages of brightly colored parrots whose screams heralded the arrival of the hero and his suite. Whenever they entered an important town, Caonabó's brother wore around his neck a massy gold collar, and on his head the cacique's crown, "very big and tall, with wings on its sides like a shield and golden eyes as large as silver cups." Unfortunately, none of these priceless objects has survived, but many others of the kind have since been dug up and preserved in the museums of Europe and America.

Columbus found the King and Queen and his sons Diego and Ferdinand, pages to the Queen, at Valladolid. He was courteously received, especially after presenting the Sovereigns with a clutch of gold nuggets as big as pigeons' eggs. Promptly he put in a plea to be outfitted for a Third Voyage. Five ships he wished to be laden with provisions for Hispaniola and three for himself, to seek out a continent which, as he put it, the king of Portugal believed to be in the ocean south or southeast of the Antilles, and the existence of which had been confirmed by hints received from the Indians. D. João II of Portugal was dead, but the fact that he believed in the existence of this continent stimulated Ferdinand and Isabella to get there first. But Columbus could get nothing but vague promises from the Sovereigns until news from Portugal indicated that João's successor, D. Manuel I, was fitting out a big overseas expedition under Vasco da Gama that was almost ready to depart, destination unknown. Might he not be looking for this same part of the world?

The Sovereigns confirmed Columbus's rights, titles, and privileges and ordered him to recruit three hundred colonists for Hispaniola at the royal expense. Wages started at about fourteen cents a day for a common workman or soldier and rose to forty-two gold dollars a year for farmers and gardeners, plus eight cents a day for keep. Also, they authorized Columbus to recruit for the expedition thirty women who received neither pay nor keep but were expected to work their passage and marry upon arrival. These were the first Christian women to go to the New World since Leif Ericsson's scandalous kindred. All malefactors confined in jail, excepting traitors and heretics, were offered pardon if they would sail with the Admiral to the Indies and stay a year or two. Hispaniola had been so discredited that this was supposed to be the only way to obtain emigrants to the future "Land of Promise." Columbus sent these fellows in the squadron direct to Hispaniola, which he later had reason to regret.

The Admiral found it very difficult to equip his new fleet, because most of it had to be done on credit. He had numerous rows with Bishop Fonseca, who had immediate charge of preparations, and on one occasion became so exasperated with a rascally ship chandler as to knock him down. But, as may be seen by the following task organization, every ship and most of the officers came from Palos. This indicates a lasting confidence in the Admiral by the shipowners and seamen of the town where he obtained his first recruits in 1492.

In January 1498 *Niña* and *India* left for Hispaniola; and three more caravels followed shortly with supplies. These were commanded respectively by Alonso Sánchez de Carvajal, one of Columbus's most faithful captains, and a veteran of his Second Voyage; Pedro de Harana, brother to the Admiral's mistress; and "Gianetto" Colombo, the Admiral's first cousin. We shall encounter this fleet later. The list of those on the Third Voyage of Discovery, and of a second Hispaniola replenishment squadron, follows:—

THIRD VOYAGE TASK ORGANIZATION *
CAPTAIN GENERAL: CHRISTOPHER COLUMBUS

DISCOVERY SQUADRON

Flagship, SANTA MARIA DE GUÍA, *nao* of 101 tuns. Cristóbal Quintero of Palos, master and owner; Bartolomé Ruiz of Palos, assistant master.
Caravel LA CASTILLA (nicknamed VAQUEÑOS), 70 tuns, Pedro de Terreros, captain; Andrés García Galdin, master.

Caravel LA GORDA (nicknamed CORREO), 60 tuns, Hernán Pérez, captain.

The Hispaniola Squadron, which went direct from Ferro to Santo Domingo, consisted of three more caravels under Carvajal.

* Compiled from Capitán de Corbeta Roberto Barreiro-Meiro, "Las Naves del Tercer Viaje de Colón," *Revista General de Marina*, Feb. 1970, which corrects and augments my *Admiral of the Ocean Sea*, I, 228–32.

Third Voyage, to Trinidad

Both squadrons assembled at Seville and departed during the last week of May 1498—the same week that Vasco da Gama arrived at Calicut in India. All six dropped down the Guadalquivir to the roadstead of Sanlúcar da Barrameda, where the Admiral came on board, and on 30 May the Third Voyage to America began.

Columbus decided to sail a more southerly course than heretofore, both in hope of finding D. João's predicted continent, and to seek more gold, holding to the ancient belief that all precious things were to be found in abundance near the Equator. So he planned to sail south to the supposed latitude of Sierra Leone, where the Portuguese had found Guinea gold, and then sail due west. Again, old-fashioned latitude sailing. The Admiral knew very well that he must do something spectacular on this voyage or the whole Enterprise of the Indies might be abandoned. He sometimes compared himself to David, who was commanded to perform incredible tasks and did so, but each time fell into greater disfavor with Saul. He had discovered a western route to the Indies, but that was not enough. He had led a great fleet to Hispaniola, founded a colony there, discovered the Lesser Antilles, Puerto Rico, and Jamaica, explored Cuba, but that was not enough. He must now discover more gold and a continent (which he did)—even that was not enough. Of course he could now have retired with a title, a castle, and a pension, and left brother Bartholomew to rule Hispaniola; but he felt that there was a lot more discovering to be done in the Indies, that he was the one person capable of doing it; and he owed it to the Sovereigns to do just that. Columbus was not the kind of man to sell out. Had he been, we would never have heard of him.

At Funchal in Madeira, where he had formerly resided, he was now received as a hero. Thence he made a three-day run to the familiar roadstead of San Sebastián, Gomera. The romance with Doña Beatriz had evidently died, since all that Columbus or anyone else wrote about this call at her capital was, "We loaded cheeses." It was probably well for the Admiral that this flirtation never ripened into marriage, for Doña Beatriz was cruel as well as beautiful. A gentleman of Gomera who spread rumors of her unchastity after Columbus's previous call was invited to visit her at the castle. This "tea for two" abruptly ended when the lady rang for her retainers and ordered them to hang her guest on a rafter in the castle hall, until he died. To rub it in and discourage gossips, she then had his corpse strung up outside his own residence. Eventually she married D. Alonso de Lugo, captain and conqueror of the Grand Canary, a very suitable husband.

At Gomera, Carvajal's Hispaniola squadron of three caravels, one commanded by the Admiral's cousin "Gianetto" Colombo, parted from the exploring expedition. They made the Dominica landfall as directed, but afterward got into trouble, as we shall see.

From the Canaries, Columbus shaped a course for the Cape Verde Islands, covering 750 miles in six days. He made a brief stop at Boavista to salt down goat mutton, the only meat available; then, on 1 July, called at Santiago in the hope of obtaining cattle to breed in Hispaniola. After staying a week there in heat so intense that many of his people fell ill, he departed with no cattle. On 7 July the trades sprang up, and Columbus shaped a course southwest, seeking the parallel of Sierra Leone. But the wind grew more and more soft, and finally died completely on 13 July when the fleet had reached about latitude 9°30′ N, longitude 29° W. They were in the doldrums, and for the next eight days drifted with the equatorial current. Their crews, who would have thought it suicidal to strip down and cultivate sun-tans, sweltered in their thick woolen clothes. The Admiral profited (as he thought) from the calm to observe the North Star with his quadrant, but as usual in his efforts at celestial navigation, made so many mistakes that he found the latitude to be 5° N, over 250 miles too far south. He was pleased to believe that he had reached 5° N for a curious reason. Many years before, José Vizinho, a famous Portuguese navigator, had taken the latitude of the Los Islands off the coast of Sierra Leone and found it to be 5° N, as Columbus had been informed. But even Portuguese navigators were not always impeccable; the true latitude of the Los Islands is 9°30′ N, very close to where Columbus's fleet actually was! The only result of his four-and-a-half-degree error was to throw off all subsequent latitude calculations on this voyage.

On 22 July 1498, a fresh trade wind sprang up from the ESE, slack lines became taut, limp sails bellied out, the ships quickly gathered way, the temperature dropped, and the sailors, who had half expected to rot and die in mid-ocean (for none had before experienced whole days of calm), began talking about the gold they were going to find. The

Cabo de la Galera, Trinidad.

Admiral set the course due west, and for nine days, with a prosperous blast from the trade winds, his fleet made an average speed of six knots or better.

This leg of the voyage must have been almost pure delight to Columbus and his men; we know that, as we followed the same route in our *Capitana* in 1939. Day and night the fleet made exceptional speed. In the trades, vessels always roll a good deal, but the fair and steady wind singing in the rigging, the sapphire white-capped sea, the rush of great waters alongside, and the endless succession of puffy trade-wind clouds lift a seaman's spirits. The old-time Spanish mariners called these broad waters *El Golfo de las Damas*, the Ladies' Sea; so easy is the navigation, so mild and genial the climate. Occasionally a black squall makes up from windward but passes harmlessly with a brief lash of rain. For days the sheets and braces need no attention except to alter the nip on the block so that the lines will not chafe. Flying fish and dorados play about, and the pelagic birds, petrels and the like, pay brief visits.

Sailors can always find something to grumble about and now it was the continual fair wind. How will we ever get back to Spain if we go on this way? said they. But even though the Admiral's latitude was screwy, he was keeping a good dead reckoning and knew almost exactly where he was, relative to the discoveries of the Second Voyage. On 31 July he announced that he was on the meridian of the Lesser Antilles, which was correct, and since the supply of fresh water was dangerously low, he would make a northern detour to water up in Dominica or some other Caribee isle. That very morning he altered the course to N by E.

At noon the Admiral's servant Alonso Pérez, having gone aloft, sang out that he saw land to the westward in the form of three hills. "All glorified the divine bounty and with great joy and merriment they repeated, singing, the *Salve Regina* with other devout canticles and prayers which glorify God and Our Lady, according to the custom of mariners." Columbus, having placed this voyage under the special protection of the Holy Trinity, regarded the three hills of the landfall an answer to prayer, and named the island Trinidad.

Changing course to approach the land, they sighted the southeastern point of the island. Columbus named it *Cabo de la Galera*, Galley Cape, because its peaked cliffs resemble lateen sails, and diagonal marks on the rocks suggest a bank of oars. The fleet arrived off this cape about 9:00 p.m. and, as the moon was nearly full, jogged westward all night.

Next day, the first of August, the Admiral continued along the south coast of Trinidad, searching for a bay that would have a river emptying into it. With his usual good judgment, he chose the best watering place on that coast, now called Erin Bay, where a stream of cool, sweet water crosses the beach. The men went ashore, washed their clothes, wallowed in the fresh water to sluice the caked salt and sweat from their bodies. and had a fine time splashing and yelling, and hallooing into the jungle in the hope that some pretty native girls might respond.

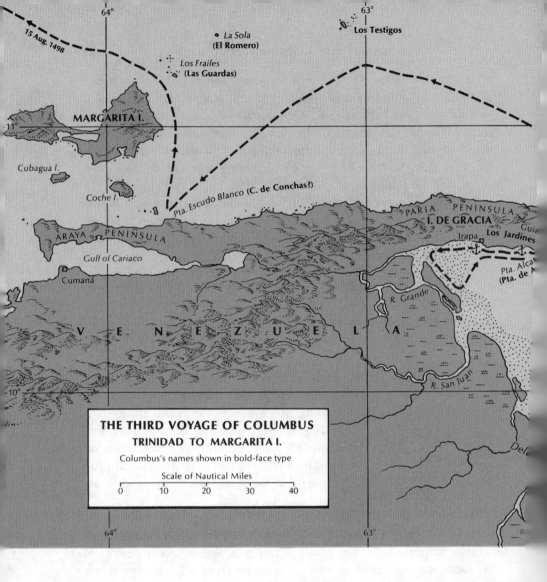

THE THIRD VOYAGE OF COLUMBUS
TRINIDAD TO MARGARITA I.

Columbus's names shown in bold-face type

Scale of Nautical Miles

0   10   20   30   40

First Continental Landing

Columbus weighed anchor at Erin Bay on 2 August and sailed through the Boca de la Sierpe into the great Gulf of Paria that lies between Trinidad and the mainland. He must have sailed through the Boca at turn of tide, for he made no remark about the current that swirls dangerously around the mid-channel rock, which he named *El Gallo* (the cock); it is now Soldado. Columbus anchored in the lee of Icacos Point, Trinidad, and ordered all hands ashore in relays for a few days'

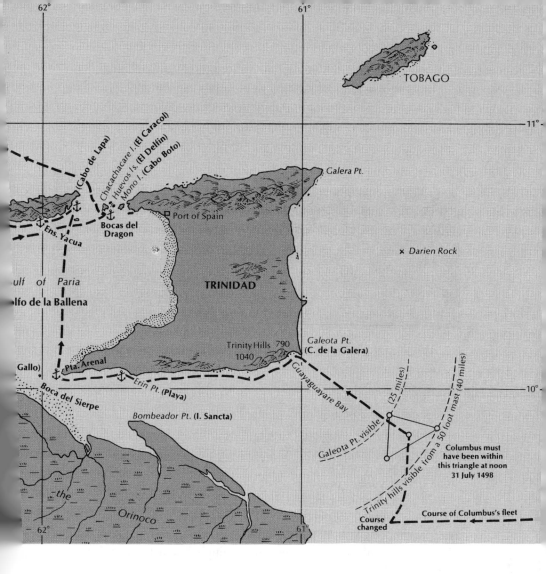

62°   61°

TOBAGO

11°

(Cabo de Lapa)

Chacachacare I. (El Caracol)
Huevos Is. (El Delfin)
Mono I. (Cabo Boto)

Galera Pt.

⚓

⚓
Bocas del
Dragon

⚓

Port of Spain

Ens. Yacua

× Darien Rock

ulf of Paria

lfo de la Ballena

TRINIDAD

Trinity Hills 790
1040

Galeota Pt.
(C. de la Galera)

Gallo)

⚓ Pta. Arenal

⚓

Erin Pt. (Playa)

Cuayaguayare Bay

Galeota Pt visible from a 50 foot mast (40 miles)

(25 miles)

10°

Boca del Sierpe

Bombeador Pt. (I. Sancta)

Galeota Pt visible

Columbus must
have been within
this triangle at noon
31 July 1498

the

Orinoco

Trinity hills visible

Course
changed

Course of Columbus's fleet

62°   61°

relaxation. They amused themselves fishing and gathering oysters, while the Admiral caused the Boca to be sounded, and marveled at the speed and fury of the current.

His only contact with the natives at this point was mildly comic. He had been hoping to encounter either Chinese mandarins or black potentates like those on the Gold Coast. But when a dugout canoe approached, he observed with disgust that it contained only naked Indians looking very like Caribs. Fortunately, they had better manners. He derived some consolation from the fact that they wore cotton

El Gallo (Soldado Rock).

bandannas like those obtained by the Portuguese in Sierra Leone. With this apparent confirmation of Aristotle's theory of the same latitude producing the same things the world over, he was sure to find Guinea gold around the corner! The Admiral, hoping to start trade, caused some brass chamber pots and other shining objects to be enticingly displayed over the bulwarks, but the Trinidad Indians were not impressed by these common objects of the European home. Next, the Admiral tried putting on a show for their benefit; he ordered a pipe-and-tabor player to sound off, tambourines to be jingled, and the ships' boys to dance. The Indians mistook this to be the strangers' method of warming up for a fight, and let fly a shower of arrows, none of which hit.

On 4 August, as the ships were weighing anchor and about to explore the Gulf, the Spaniards had probably the greatest fright of their lives. An enormous bore or tidal wave, evidently caused by a volcanic disturbance, roared through the Boca, snapped the anchor cable of *Vaqueños*, raised the flagship to what seemed an immense height, and dropped her so low that one could see bottom. The Admiral decided that this was no place to linger, and named that strait *La Boca de la Sierpe*, the Serpent's Mouth.

He now steered due north, attracted by the sight of mountains across the Gulf, on the Paria peninsula. Approaching the tip end of the peninsula, he enjoyed the same gorgeous view that greets a sailor today. Astern lay the placid Gulf, its far shores below the horizon; westward under the setting sun stretched a succession of mountains and rugged headlands; eastward were the high, broken islands that divide the famous Bocas del Dragón, and behind them rose the mountains of Trinidad. Far to the northeast, as it was a very clear evening, Columbus sighted an island which may have been Tobago but more probably was a northern promontory of Trinidad. He anchored for the night at Bahia Celeste near the tip of the Paria peninsula, and next day turned west to explore its southern shore along the Gulf.

Of many harbors, Ensenada Yacua, a little round cove with a sand beach between two rocky headlands, is probably the one that Columbus chose for a landing. He found a large thatched house and a fire burning; but the natives had fled, their places taken by swarms of monkeys who chattered indignantly at the Spaniards. This was the first place where the Admiral or his men set foot on the mainland of America; the first time, indeed, that any European had done so since the Vinland voyages.* As usual, the Admiral did not know what he had discovered; he still believed that Paria peninsula was an island. The date was Sunday, 5 August 1498.

Since it would have been undignified to take formal possession for Spain with only monkeys as audience, Columbus postponed the ceremony until two days later when a horde of friendly natives appeared at the mouth of the Rio Guiria. The Admiral, suffering severely from sore eyes, stayed on board and sent his senior captain, Pedro de Terreros, to take formal possession of this region, which the Indians told him was called Paria. It is still called the Paria peninsula, part of the Republic of Venezuela.

After a preliminary distribution of beads, sugar, and hawks' bells the Indians came out in a fleet of canoes, bringing fruits of the country and a beer called *chicha* fermented from maize. This they still brew in Venezuela. As ornaments they displayed great polished disks made of an alloy of copper and gold that they called *guanin*, and which

---

* John Cabot in 1497 may be credited only with an insular landfall (see my *Northern Voyages*, pp. 170–74) and Vespucci's alleged 1497 landing on the mainland should be dated 1499, as we hope to demonstrate later.

First landing on continent. Ensenada Yacua. David Crofoot photo.

modern archaeologists have named *tumbaga*. By smelting copper with gold, the melting point is greatly reduced, an advantage to these primitive metallurgists; and as they had to import the copper from Central America, it was more valuable to them than gold. So, greatly to the Spaniards' delight, these natives of Paria were willing to swap their gold for articles of the same weight in brass or copper. Columbus had entered a new area of native culture which extends from the Guianas to Honduras.

On 8 August the fleet resumed exploration of the Gulf, rounded the long, tapering Punta Alcatraz (which Columbus called *Aguja*, the Needle), and found a rich lowland with native gardens and groves of big, glossy-leaved mahogany and fustic. So he named it *Los Jardines*. The women of one village came on board wearing necklaces of fine pearls which Columbus ascertained came from the other side of the peninsula. That caused great excitement among the Spaniards. The Indians were willing to sell what pearls they had for the usual trading truck, but unfortunately they had few to spare; so the Admiral begged them by sign language to accumulate a few bushels against his return. At this pleasant place the natives were so friendly that a whole boat's crew accepted an invitation to a feast in a big thatched house, and returned to the ship fat and happy.

Again the Admiral turned west in search of an outlet to the sea. The water, already brackish, shoaled and became fresh and turbid. Caravel *Correo*, sent ahead to reconnoiter because of her light draft, reported four river channels to the westward. These were the mouths of the Rio Grande, and a mouth of the Orinoco emptied a few miles away. Columbus, stubborn as usual in his geographical ideas, would not yet admit that this river flowed from a continent, but he gave up the search for an outlet that was not there and turned east again at the rising of the moon, on 11 August.

All day the land breeze held, and with a favoring current from the river, he reached the Bocas the same night and anchored in a neat little port named *Puerto de Gatos* (Monkey Harbor) on Chacachacare Island. In the small hours of the 13th, the fleet weighed and stood into Boca Grande. There they found the usual turmoil between the fresh water flowing out and the salt tide roaring in, and "thought to perish" when the wind dropped and the caravels drifted toward the rocks; but the fresh water prevailed over the salt, carrying them slowly out, and to safety. Columbus named this strait *Boca del Dragón*, and the name is still used for all four channels that connect the Gulf of Paria with the Caribbean. Dangerous they still are for small craft.

On the way out, Columbus sighted to the northward, over sixty miles distant, the island of Grenada and named it *Asunción* because it was the vigil of the Feast of the Assumption. At dawn 15 August, he sighted an island that he named Margarita, after the charming and witty Infanta Margarita of Austria.

Columbus did not tarry to look for the pearls that were there in abundance, as he was in a great hurry to get to Santo Domingo. That decision, as it turned out, was a mistake. Conditions in Hispaniola would have been no worse had he stayed another month; bringing home a quantity of pearls would have enhanced his prestige, and, worst of all, Ojeda and Bastidas stole his secret of the Pearl Coast and cashed in on it.

Puerto de las Cabañas. Huevos Island, Boca del Dragón. David Crofoot photo.

An "Other World"

On this Feast of the Assumption it suddenly dawned on the Admiral that he had seen the mainland. In his Journal he recorded, "I believe that this is a very great continent, until today unknown. And reason aids me greatly because of that so great river and fresh-water sea, and next, the saying of Esdras . . . that the six parts of the world are of dry land, and one of water. . . . And if this be a continent, it is a marvelous thing, and will be so among all the wise, since so great a river flows that it makes a fresh-water sea of 48 leagues."

This passage, "his very words," Las Casas assures us, is typical of the workings of Columbus's mind. For two weeks he had been sailing along the coast of the continent that he sought, yet refused to believe that it was one because it did not match his idea of a continent. Finally, the evidence of the vast volume of fresh water changed his mind, and at once the old Esdras "six parts out of seven," odd scraps of Scholastic learning, and vague gestures of Caribs, flew together in his mind to prove it.

These lands, he said, are an Other World (*otro mundo*), as indeed they were. It was mere chance that he did not write *nuevo mundo*, New World, which would have entitled him to the credit afterward accorded to Amerigo Vespucci for having recognized it as such. Actually, the two phrases as Columbus and Vespucci used them (and as Peter Martyr had already used *mundus novus*), meant the same thing: a region hitherto unknown to Europeans, not mentioned in Ptolemy's Geography. It distinctly did not mean the "New World" that we use to denote the two Americas. Columbus believed that the mainland he had just coasted along had the same relation to China and the Malay Peninsula as the present Republic of Indonesia actually does.

But Columbus was never satisfied to make two and two equal four; they must make twenty-two. A couple of days later, he confided to his Journal that this continent was the Terrestrial Paradise, the Garden of Eden! Several medieval writers quoted in his favorite bedside book, *Imago Mundi*, on the basis of Genesis ii.8, "And Lord God planted a garden eastward in Eden," located that famous garden at the furthest point of the Far East, where the sun rose on the day of creation. Turning again to the second chapter of Genesis, Columbus read of trees "pleasant to the sight, and good for food," and of the river with "four heads" that watered the garden; and caravel *Correo* had reported four mouths. "And the gold of that land is good;" certainly it was, even though the silly natives liked copper better. He then jumped to the wild conclusion that the globe at this point had a bump on it like a woman's breast, in order to bring Terrestrial Paradise nearer Heaven!

Did not the violent currents in the Bocas prove that water was running down a steep slope?

Although Columbus did suffer from arthritis and inflamed eyes, he was not out of his mind, as these weird theories might suggest; equally strange hypotheses were common among stay-at-home geographers in that era. And he always kept account of his daily positions by dead reckoning. From Margarita on 15 August he set a course NW by N for Saona Island off Hispaniola, as a good point whence to coast down-wind to Santo Domingo, the new island capital. And that *was* the correct airline course! Imagine all the factors Columbus had to feed into his mental computer to get this result—Hispaniola to Cape St. Vincent and Cadiz in 1496; Sanlúcar to Madeira, Gomera, and the Cape de Verdes in 1498; Cape de Verdes to Trinidad, and then through the Gulf of Paria and out by the Bocas to Margarita. And without sighting any land known to Europeans after the Cape de Verdes.

Although he had the direct course to Saona, two factors prevented him from making his desired landfall. One was the westward-running equatorial current which he had no means of gauging; the other, due to his very proper fear of running a reef in the dark of the moon, was cautious navigation. He ordered the caravels to jog or heave-to every night, heaving the lead frequently, and to make sail only by day when dangerous reefs could be detected by changes in the color of the water. This lengthened the passage and so increased his set to leeward. The result was that the fleet made landfall on Alta Vela, 120 miles southwest of Santo Domingo. "It weighed on him to have fallen off so much," wrote Las Casas, but he decided correctly that his miscalculation was caused by a strong current. Could any modern navigator, amateur or professional, provided only with Columbus's knowledge and instruments, have done the like? If not superb dead reckoning, he must have had divine guidance; perhaps a combination of the two!

On 21 August when anchored near Alta Vela in the shelter of Beata Island (which the Admiral named *Madama Beata*, the Blessed Lady), they saw a little caravel approaching from the direction of Santo Domingo. This was the first ship his fleet had sighted since leaving Spain. The stranger fired a gun, luffed up alongside the flagship, and to the Admiral's delight he was hailed by brother Bartholomew. The Adelantado was engaged in pursuing the provision squadron under Carvajal, which he had sighted from shore but which had stupidly continued to sail westward. After this happy reunion, the four caravels beat up to the new capital in eight days, good going against wind and current.

The flagship, *Correo*, and *Vaqueños* anchored in the Ozama River, the inner harbor of Santo Domingo, on the last day of August 1498. Another voyage had been brilliantly carried through. The Admiral had found the gateway to a vast territory for the expansion of the Spanish race, language, and culture, extending from the Rocky Mountains to the Strait of Magellan. What matter if he did think it to be the Garden of Eden? Note his prophetic words in his Journal of this voyage on the day he reached furthest west in the Gulf of Paria:

> And your Highnesses will gain these vast lands, which are an Other World, and where Christianity will have so much enjoyment, and our faith in time so great an increase. I say this with very honest intent and because I desire that your Highnesses may be the greatest lords in the world, lords of it all, I say; and that all may be with much service to and satisfaction of the Holy Trinity.

Superb faith, marvelous prophecy! At a time when Spain's first overseas colony was languishing, and settlers had to be recruited from the jails; when few people of any importance believed in Columbus or thought his discoveries worth the smallest of the Canary Islands, he foretold the vast revenue that Spain would obtain from these conquests, making her the first power in Europe. He predicted that Christianity, whose territory had been shrinking since the rise of Islam, would advance triumphantly into his Other and New World.

Home in Chains

At court, in the meantime, the Admiral's stock was falling. Spaniards who returned from Hispaniola, claiming overtime, were making nuisances of themselves, assaulting King Ferdinand whenever he stirred abroad with cries of, "Pay! Pay!" Columbus's younger son remembered bitterly how he and his brother Diego, pages to Queen Isabella, were mortified by these wretches hooting at them and shouting, "There go the sons of the Admiral of the Mosquitoes, of him who discovered lands of vanity and delusion, the ruin and the grave of Castilian gentlemen!"

Yet we must admit that the three Columbus brothers had failed as administrators. They had been weak when they should have been firm, and ruthless at the wrong time; they had not saved the Indians from exploitation, and had alienated most of the Spaniards. The Sovereigns, before receiving news that the rebel Francisco Roldán had made his peace with the Admiral, appointed Francisco de Bobadilla to go to Hispaniola as royal commissioner, with unlimited powers over persons and property. Bobadilla arrived at Santo Domingo 24 August 1500, when the Admiral was at La Vega, brother Bartholomew at Xaragua, and brother Diego in charge of the city. The first thing that the Spaniard saw upon landing was a gallows from which seven Spanish corpses were hanging, and Diego cheerfully remarked that five more were due to be hanged next day. These men, having rebelled under Adrián de Moxica, had been defeated and captured with Roldán's assistance. Bobadilla, without waiting to hear the Columbus side, took over both fort and government, tossed Don Diego into the brig of his flagship, impounded all the Admiral's effects, won over the populace by proclaiming a general freedom to gather gold anywhere; and, when the Admiral appeared in obedience to his summons, had him fettered and confined in the capital's calaboose. Bartholomew, then in the interior with a loyal army, might have marched on the capital and released his brothers, but the Admiral neither dared nor cared to defy the royal authority Bobadilla represented. On his advice, Bartholomew, too, submitted and was thrown into jail.

The royal commissioner, after compiling a file of anti-Columbus depositions from discontented and mutinous Spaniards, decided to send all three brothers home for trial. In early October of 1500 the Admiral and Diego, both chained, were placed on board caravel *La Gorda*, bound for Spain; Bartholomew sailed in another vessel. The captain of *La Gorda* "would have knocked off the Admiral's irons," says son Ferdinand, but his father "would not permit it, saying that they had been put on him by regal authority and only the Sovereigns could order them struck off."

To a sensitive man like Columbus, these indignities were far more humiliating than they would have been to the average tough *hombre* of that era. On his way home he wrote to a true friend at court, Doña Juana de Torres, a long letter which is at once a cry of distress, a bill of complaints, and a proud vindication of his own conduct. Our Lord, he said, had made him the messenger of the "new heavens and a new earth" envisioned in the Apocalypse and prophesied in Isaiah lxv.17. The Queen, as a reward for understanding this, had been made heiress to this Other World, and in her name he went out and took possession. Yet none of her subjects is so vile that he cannot now insult the Admiral with impunity. He is accused of illegal actions, although he put down two rebellions against the Sovereigns' authority. He safeguarded their Highnesses' interests in the collection of gold. Then Bobadilla arrived, listened to the calumnies of rogues, threw him and his brothers into jail, and removed all restrictions on gold collection so that one rascal made a small fortune in four hours! Columbus ended with a poignant expression of outraged dignity and sense of justice:—"By divine will I have placed under the sovereignty of the King and Queen our lords an Other World, whereby Spain, which was reckoned poor, is become the richest of countries." That was the plain truth.

Fair winds attended the homeward voyage of *La Gorda,* as if the Ocean Sea had wished to shorten the miseries of her Admiral. Before the end of October 1500 he landed at Cadiz, still in chains. Accompanied by his jailer, he lodged at the monastery of Las Cuevas in Seville. The spectacle of Columbus in chains is said to have made a lamentable impression on the populace, but six weeks elapsed before the Sovereigns ordered him released from his fetters, and summoned him to court.*

The three brothers presented themselves to the King and Queen at the Alhambra in Granada shortly before Christmas, 1500. Diego Colón, now in his twenty-first year, was there too, with Ferdinand, a boy of twelve. Imagine their mortification to see their father dressed in Franciscan brown and with marks of iron fetters on his wrists!

The Sovereigns now spoke to Columbus in a kindly and consoling manner, and promised that justice would be done and privileges restored. Weeks stretched into months, but nothing happened. More urgent business than the affairs of distant Hispaniola occupied the atten-

---

* As Ogden Nash summed up the Admiral's career, with a poet's economy:

> So Columbus said, Somebody show me the sunset
>   and somebody did and he set sail for it.
> And he discovered America and they put him in jail for it,
> And the fetters gave him welts,
> And they named America after somebody else.

The Face Is Familiar (Boston, 1940), p. 209, by permission of Mrs. Ogden Nash.

tion of Ferdinand and Isabella. Nothing less than complete restoration of his rights, properties, titles, and offices would satisfy Columbus. He spent time and effort compiling a Book of Privileges, containing all his agreements with and orders and letters from the Sovereigns. But it was futile for him to expect to get everything back. He and his brothers had made too much of a mess of things in Hispaniola, to be entrusted again with the overseas government. And as the coast of South America gradually opened up, it was idle to suppose that the Sovereigns would confirm tithes and similar privileges over a vast continent which originally had been granted in the expectation of his setting up a trading factory or discovering a few islands. Again, Columbus would have been well advised to settle for a castle, a pension, and a new title; but he was not the man to give up anything. Had he been, he would never have discovered the New World.

After waiting eight months from New Year's Day 1501, Columbus learned the worst in September. Instead of being returned in triumph to Hispaniola, he was formally replaced as governor by Don Nicolás de Ovando. Columbus did obtain permission to keep his now empty titles of Viceroy and Admiral, and to send out an agent in Ovando's fleet to make Bobadilla disgorge the moneys which were his. Ovando departed in February 1502 with a magnificent fleet of 30 sail, carrying 2500 sailors, soldiers, and colonists.

Eager to embark once more on his proper element, Columbus now asked for the means to make a Fourth Voyage to the Indies. The Sovereigns so ordered, only a month after Ovando sailed for Hispaniola.

Bibliography and Notes

Sources. Las Casas abstracted the now lost Columbus *Diario* or Journal of the Third Voyage. Facsimile and printed text by Carlos Sanz, *Descubrimiento del Continente Americano* (Madrid, 1962), in his serias *Biblioteca Americana Vetutissima.* Translation in my *Journals and Other Documents*, pp. 259–312, together with Columbus's letters, to the Sovereigns of 18 October 1498, to Juana de Torres of October 1500, and the Royal Mandate of 27 September 1501 ordering restitution of the Admiral's property and rights. My *Admiral of the Ocean Sea*, II, 269–74, discusses various controversies about Columbus's route in the Gulf of Paria.

Landfall. We in our *Capitana* in 1939, twenty days out from the Canaries, reached a position within a mile or two of the one where Columbus made that landfall, and had the pleasure of watching, as they rose from the sea, the three hills which seemed to Columbus a happy omen on the last day of July 1498. The name *Cabo de la Galera*, through a misunderstanding, has been transferred to the northeast point of Trinidad; Columbus's landfall is now called Galeota Point.

The Infanta Margarita. Columbus had attended the wedding at Burgos of Margarita and the Infante D. Juan, heir to the throne of Castile, in 1497. She had been betrothed in infancy to Charles VIII of France, who jilted her, and at seventeen she was affianced to D. Juan. In the course of her voyage from Flanders to Spain, a violent storm arose, in the midst of which Margarita composed this epitaph for herself:

> *Ci gist Margot la gentil demoiselle*
> *Qu'a deux maris et encore est pucelle*

> Here lies Margot that proper young girl,
> Who with husbands twain has preserved her pearl.

Margarita Island is worthy of its namesake—fertile and beautiful, with mountains at each end rising two and three thousand feet from the sea, and lowlands between.

Hispaniola. See my article on Columbus's changing colonial policy, in reaction to his difficulties in Hispaniola, in *Bulletin* of the Pan American Union, October 1942, which also contains important articles by Afrânio Peixoto on "Columbus in the Literature of Portugal and Brazil," and by Enrique de Gandía on "The Glory of Columbus." The three volumes of *Studi Colombiani* issued by the Civico Istituto Colombiano of Genoa in 1951 to honor the 500th anniversary of the Admiral's birth, contain numerous important articles, as well as mine on "Columbus as a Navigator" (II, 39–48).

* VIII *

The Mariner's Day

Time and Watches

Before we take up the several voyages to the Caribbean and Brazil which were launched immediately after Columbus's Third, suppose we describe a day at sea in his time, which will also go for the entire sixteenth century. Information on this subject, since everyone then took knowledge of it for granted, is very scarce; one can only pick up bits and pieces from sea journals. Fortunately, a humorous Spanish official, Eugenio de Salazar, wrote a very detailed account of what he observed in a voyage from Spain to Santo Domingo in 1573. Without him this chapter would have been mostly blank.

A decent formality has always been observed in ships at sea. The watches are changed and the tiller or wheel is relieved according to formula, solar and stellar observations are made at fixed hours, and any departure from the settled custom is resented by mariners. In Spanish and Portuguese ships these formalities were observed with a quasi-religious ritual, which lent them a certain beauty and served to remind the seamen every half-hour of the day and night that their ship depended for safety not only on her staunchness and their own skill, but on the grace of God.

Until the late sixteenth century, the only ship's clock available was

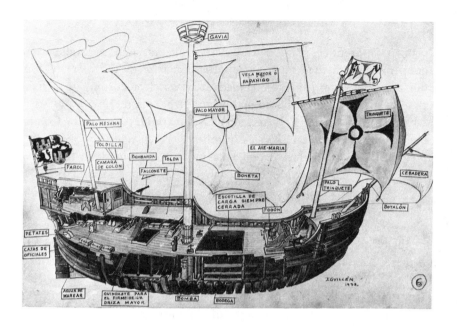

Admiral Guillén's "cut-out" of *Santa Maria*. Courtesy of Naval Museum, Madrid.

the *ampoletta* or *reloj de arena* (sand clock), a half-hour glass containing enough sand to run from the upper to the lower section in exactly thirty minutes. Made in Venice, these glasses were so fragile that many spares were usually carried—Magellan had eighteen on his flagship. It was the duty of a ship's boy in each watch to mind the *ampolleta* and reverse it promptly when the sand ran out. A very rough sea might retard the running of the sand, or the boy might go to sleep; Columbus on one occasion expressed indignation with a lazy lad who lost count. As a ship gains time sailing east and loses it sailing west, even the most modern ship's clock has to be corrected daily by radio. The only way one could mark correct sun time in the era of discovery was to erect a pin or gnomon on the center of the compass card, and watch for the exact moment of noon when the sun's shadow touched the fleur-de-lis that marked north (or, if in the Southern Hemisphere, south) and then turn the glass. Even that could not be counted on to give true noon nearer than 15 or 20 minutes.

The *marineros*, *grumetes*, and *oficiales* of the ship's company (able seamen, apprentice seamen, and petty officers such as caulker and cooper) were divided into two watches (*cuartos* or *guardias*) of four hours each. An officer commanded each watch according to a fixed rule of precedence: captain, pilot, *maestre* (master), *contramaestre* (master's mate or chief boatswain).* From sundry entries in Columbus's Journal, it is clear that his watches were changed at 3, 7, and 11 o'clock. These hours seem odd to a modern seaman, who by immemorial usage expects watches to change at 4, 8, and 12, and I believe they were so changed from 1500 on. Presumably the afternoon watch was "dogged" (i.e., split into two 2-hour watches) as the merchant marine still did in the nineteenth century, in order that the men might change their hours nightly. On a sailing vessel which might be many weeks or even months at sea, it was fairer to dog the watches daily so that each man would have the unpopular "graveyard watch" from midnight to 4:00 a.m. (or from 11 to 3) on alternate nights.

Mariners in those days thought of time less in terms of hours than of *ampolletas* and *guardias*, glasses and watches, eight glasses to a watch. The system of half-hourly ship's bells that we are familiar with began as a means of accenting the turning of the glass. No ship's bell is mentioned in any of the Spanish sea journals of the sixteenth century that I have seen, and García de Palacio's *Instrucción Náutica* (1587), the Mexican seaman's first Bowditch, says nothing of them. Drake's flagship *Golden Hind* carried no bell, but his men "liberated" one from the church at Guatulco, Mexico, in 1579. They hung it in an improvised belfry on board, where a Spanish prisoner reported that it was "used to summon the men to pump." Since pumping ship was the first duty of every watch, it is evident that the bell was used for summons, and that this use of the bell was new to Spaniards, if not to Englishmen.

At night in the Northern Hemisphere whenever the weather was clear and the latitude not too low, your sixteenth-century navigator could tell sun time from the Guards of the North Star. The Little Bear or Little Dipper swings around Polaris once every 24 hours, sidereal time. The two brightest stars of that constellation, *beta* (Kochab) and *gamma*, which mark the edge of the Dipper furthest from the North Star, were called the Guards; and if you knew where Kochab (the principal Guard) should be at midnight, you could tell time as from a clock hand. The early navigators constructed a diagram of a

* In Portuguese ships, curiously, pilot came below master.

little man with Polaris in his belly, his forearms pointing E and W, and
his shoulders NE and NW.* That gave eight positions for Kochab. As
this star moved from one major position to another in three hours, you
could tell time at night if you knew its position at midnight on that
date. For that purpose a very simple instrument, the nocturnal, sufficed.
It had a hole in the center through which you sighted Polaris, and a
movable arm representing the Guards, which you moved until it
pointed at Kochab; then you read the time off a scale on the outer
disk. Nocturnals were in use for centuries. With a little practice,
almost anyone on a long voyage can learn to tell time by this method
within a quarter-hour.

Ritual and Religion

In the great days of sail, before man's inventions and gadgets had
given him a false confidence in his power to conquer the ocean, seamen were the most religious of all workers on land or sea. The
mariner's philosophy he took from the Vulgate's 107th Psalm: "They
that go down to the sea in ships and occupy their business in great
waters; these men see the works of the Lord, and his wonders in the
deep. For at his word, the stormy wind ariseth, which lifteth up the
waves thereof." It behooved seamen to obey the injunction of the
Psalmist, "O that men would therefore praise the Lord for his goodness, and declare the wonders that he doeth for the children of men!"
That is exactly what they did, after their fashion. The Protestant Reformation did not change the old customs of shipboard piety, only the
ritual; Spanish prisoners on Drake's *Golden Hind* reported a daily
service which featured the singing of psalms.

Although the captain or master, if no priest were present, led morning and evening prayers, the little semi-religious observances which
marked almost every half-hour of the day were performed by the
youngest lads on board, the *pajes de escober* (pages of the broom).
This I suppose was on the same principle as having family grace said
by the youngest child; God would be better pleased by the voice of
innocence.

According to Eugenio de Salazar, the ritual which he describes
always prevailed when venturing on unknown seas where the divine

* See my *Northern Voyages*, p. 154.

protection was imperatively needed. No pious commander would have omitted aught of these traditional observances. I repeat them here just as Salazar reports them, with a translation.

A young boy of the dawn watch saluted daybreak with this ditty:

Bendita sea la luz,	Blessed be the light of day
y la Santa Veracruz	and the Holy Cross, we say;
y el Señor de la Verdad,	and the Lord of Veritie
y la Santa Trinidad;	and the Holy Trinity
bendita sea el alma,	Blessed be th'immortal soul
y el Señor que nos la manda;	and the Lord who keeps it whole,
bendito sea el día	blessed be the light of day
y el Señor que nos lo envía.	and He who sends the night away.

He then recited *Pater Noster* and *Ave Maria*, and added:

> *Dios nos dé buenos días; buen viaje; buen pasaje haga la nao, señor Capitán y maestre y buena compaña, amén; así faza buen viaje, faza: muy buenos días dé Dios a vuestras mercedes, señores de popa y proa.*
>
> God give us good days, good voyage, good passage to the ship, sir captain and master and good company, amen; so let there be, let there be a good voyage; many good days may God grant your graces, gentlemen of the afterguard and gentlemen forward.

Before being relieved the dawn watch was supposed to have the deck well scrubbed down with salt water hauled up in buckets, using stiff besoms made of twigs. At 6:30 or 7:30 the *ampolleta* was turned up for the seventh and last time on that watch, and the boy sang out:

Buena es la que va,	Good is that which passeth,
mejor es la que viene;	better that which cometh,
siete es pasada y en ocho muele,	seven is past and eight floweth,
mas molerá si Dios quisiere,	more shall flow if God willeth,
cuenta y pasa, que buen viaje faza.	count and pass makes voyage fast.

As soon as the sands of the eighth successive glass ran out, the boy in turning up said, instead of his usual ditty:

> *Al cuarto, al cuarto, señores marineros de buena parte, al cuarto, al cuarto en bueno hora de la guardia del señor piloto, que ya es hora; leva, leva, leva.*
>
> On deck, on deck, Mr. Mariners of the right side,* on deck in good time you of Mr. Pilot's watch, for it's already time; shake a leg!

---

* Meaning the watch, port or starboard, that is due on deck.

The new watch need no time to dress, for nobody has undressed; when they went below in early morn, each man sought out his favorite soft plank, or some corner wherein he could brace himself against the ship's rolling and pitching. The mariners coming on duty are soon awake, rubbing their eyes and grumbling, and each man grabs a ship biscuit, some garlic cloves, a bit of cheese, a pickled sardine, or whatever is on for breakfast, and shuffles aft to the break in the poop. The helmsman gives the course to the captain of his watch, who repeats it to the new helmsman, who repeats it again. Little chance for error! A lookout is posted forward, another aft, the off-going captain of the watch transfers his reckoning from slate to logbook, and the ship's boy wipes the slate clean for the new captain. Chips the carpenter (or *calafate* the caulker if he goes on watch) primes the pump, and if the ship has made water during the night, two or three hands pump her dry. The off-going watch eat breakfast and curl up somewhere out of the sun to sleep.

Now the decks are dry, the sun is yardarm high, and the ship is dancing along before the trades with a bone in her teeth. The captain, whose servant has brought him a bucket of sea water, a cup of fresh water, and a bit of breakfast in his cabin, comes on deck, looks all around the horizon, ejaculates a pious *gracias a Dios* for fair weather, and chats with the master or pilot.

Each watch is responsible for the ship during its hours of duty, except in case of tempest or accident, when all hands are summoned. The usual duties are keeping the decks both clear and clean, making and setting sail as required, trimming sheets and braces; and when there is nothing else to do, scrubbing the rails, making spun yarn and chafing-gear out of old rope, and overhauling other gear. In the morning watch, as soon as the running rigging has dried from the night dews, it has to be swayed up, and every few days the lanyards or tackles that connect the shrouds with the bulwarks must be taken up—but not too taut.

One question to which every old salt wants the answer is about "Crossing the Line." Since the principal southern voyages after 1498 crossed the Equator and entered the Southern Hemisphere, did they do it with ceremony? Did the Portuguese and Spanish navigators relieve the tension of a long voyage with the now time-honored ceremony of Crossing the Line? Did a burlesque Neptune and court come on board over the bows, subjecting the "pollywogs" or neophytes to various humorous indignities to turn them into "shellbacks"? Existing sources indicate that they did not; this ceremony belonged to the northern nations. It was derived from the medieval custom of Norman, Hanseatic, and Dutch sailors holding a quasi-religious service when they passed a well-known landmark such as the Pointe du Raz in Brittany or the Berlingas off Portugal.

The earliest known reference to a ceremony at the Equator is a contemporary account of the voyage of the Parmentier brothers of Dieppe to Sumatra in 1529. "Tuesday 11 May in the morning, about 50 of our people were made *chevaliers* and received the accolade in passing below the Equator; and the mass *Salve Sancta Parens* was sung from notes to mark the day's solemnity; and we took a great fish called albacore and some bonito, of which a stew was made for supper, solemnizing this feast of chivalry." The next, in order of time, occurred on the voyage of a French ship captained by Jean de Léry, to Brazil in 1557. Here is the first reference to the now traditional pranks: "This day the 4th of February, when we passed the World's Center, the sailors went through their accustomed ceremonies . . . namely, to bind [a man] with ropes and plunge him into the sea, or blacken his face well with an old rag rubbed on the bottom of the kettle and then shave it off, so as to give those who had never before passed the Equator something to remember. But one can buy oneself off and be exempt from all that by paying for wine for all hands, as I did."

Parmentier's and Léry's ships were French. When did the Portuguese and Spanish adopt this genial way to break the monotony of a long voyage? Gossipy Pigafetta, who sailed with Magellan and Elcano around the world in 1519–22, never mentions anything of the sort, which suggests that they had not yet done so.

Sixty years passed, and the account by Jan Huygen van Linschoten of a voyage to Goa in an official Portuguese fleet indicates that sailors of this nation had taken over the custom and developed it in their own fashion. Linschoten's ship sailed in February 1583; on 26 May she passed the Equator off Guinea, and on the 29th the business began. Each ship, following "an ancient custome," elected someone as "Emperor," who became lord of misrule. On this occasion the pranksters and the drinking went too far, and "by meanes of certain words that passed out of their mouths, there fell a great strife and contention among us at the banquet; at the least a hundred rapiers drawne, without respecting the Captaine or any other, for he lay under foote, and they trod upon him, and had killed each other," had not a distinguished passenger, the new archbishop of Goa, burst forth from his cabin, and commanded every man, under pain of excommunication, to hand over his weapons. This they did, and the strife ended.

No record exists, to my knowledge, of any Spanish ship holding a Crossing the Line ceremony before the eighteenth century. The Portuguese must have adopted it from their many North European friends.

Returning to daily life at sea, on big ships the master's or pilot's orders were transmitted to the men through the *contramaestre* or chief boatswain, who carried a pipe or whistle on a lanyard around his neck and on it played a variety of signals. There is no mention of a pipe on Columbus's ships, probably because they were so small that the captain of the watch gave orders orally. Salazar said he had never seen an order so well and promptly obeyed by soldiers as those of his pilot. Let him but cry, *Ah! de proa!* (Hey, up forward!) and they all come aft on the run "like conjured demons" awaiting his pleasure. Here are some samples of the orders.

dejad las chafaldetas	well the clewlines
alzá aquel briol	heave on that buntline
empalomadle la boneta	lace on the bonnet
tomad aquel puño	lay hold of that clew
entren esas badasas aprisa por esos ollaos	pass them toggles through the latches quick
levá el papahigo	hoist the main course
izá el trinquete	raise the foresail
dad vuelta	put your back into it
enmará un poco la cebadera	give the spritsail a little sheet
desencapillá la mesana	unbend the mizzen
ligá la tricia al guindaste	belay the halyard on the bitts
tirá de los escotines de gabia	haul in on the topsail sheets
suban dos á los penoles	two of you up on the yardarm
untá los vertellos	grease the parrel trucks
amarrá aquellas burdas	belay them backstays
zafá los embornales	clear the scuppers
juegue el guimbalete para que la bomba achique	work that pump brake till she sucks

Nautical Castilian, like nautical English of the last century, had a word for everything in a ship's gear and a verb for every action; strong, expressive words that could not be misunderstood when bawled out in a gale.

For any lengthy operation like winding in the anchor cable or hoisting a yard, the seamen had an appropriate *saloma* or chantey, and of these Salazar gives an example which it is useless to translate. The chanteyman sang or shouted the first half of each line, the men hauled away on the "o" and joined in on the second half, while they got a new hold on the halyard:

> *Bu izá*
> *o dio—ayuta no y*
> *o que somo—servi soy*
> *o voleamo—ben servir*
> *o la fede—mantenir*
> *o la fede—de cristiano*
> *o malmeta—lo pagano*
> *sconfondi—y sarrahin*
> *torchi y mori—gran mastín*
> *o fillioli—dabrahin*
> *o non credono—que ben sia*
> *o non credono—la fe santa*
> *en la santa—fe di Roma*
> *o di Roma—está el perdón*
> *o San Pedro—gran varón*
> *o San Pablo—son compañón*
> *o que ruegue—a Dio por nos*
> *o por nosotros—navegantes*
> *en este mundo—somo tantes*
> *o ponente—digo levante*
> *o levante—se leva el sol*
> *o ponente—resplandor*
> *fantineta—viva lli amor*
> *o joven home—gauditor*

And so on, improvising, until the halyard is "two-blocks," when the captain of the watch commands, *Dejad la driza, amarrá* (Well the halyard, belay!).

When not ordering the men about, the captain of the watch kept station on the high poop, conning the helmsman through a hatch in the deck just forward of the binnacle. On all but the smaller vessels the helmsman had a second compass to steer by, but he could not see ahead, and so had to be an expert at the feel of the ship to keep her on her course. Salazar gives us some specimens of the orders to the helmsman:—

botá a babor	port your helm
no boteis	steady
arriba	up helm
governá la ueste cuarta al sueste	steer W by S

Besides a nautical language, a nautical slang had developed. Just as modern seamen with mock contempt speak of "this wagon" or "the old crate," a Spaniard called his ship *rocín de madera* (wooden jade) or *pájaro puerco* (flying pig). The nickname for the firebox meant "pot island." People on board got in the habit of using nautical phrases for other things; Salazar, for instance, says, "When I want a pot of jam I say, *saca la cebadera*, break out the spritsail; if I want a table napkin I say, *daca el pañol*, lead me to the sail-locker. If I wish to eat or drink in form I say, *pon la mesana*, set the mizzen. When a mariner upsets a jug he says, *oh! cómo achicais*, Oh how she sucks! When one breaks wind, as often happens, someone is sure to cry, *Ah! de popa*, Hey there, aft!"

Naturally there was a good deal of joking about the seats hung over the rail forward and aft, for the seamen and afterguard to ease themselves. These were called *jardines*, perhaps in memory of the usual location of the family privy. Salazar writes in mock sentiment of the lovely views they afforded of moon and planets, and of the impromptu washings that he there obtained from the waves. A later voyager, Antonio de Guevara, complained of the indecency of thus exposing a Very Reverend Lord Bishop to the full view of the ship's company, and adverts bitterly to the tarred rope-end which performed the function assigned by North American folklore to the corncob.

Food and Drink

Apparently the seamen on Spanish and Portuguese ships enjoyed but one hot meal a day. This must have come around noon, so that the watch below could get theirs before coming on deck, and the watch relieved could eat after them.

Who did the cooking? I wish I knew! There was no rating of cook on any of Columbus's ships or even on Magellan's. The earliest man especially designated as cook that I have found on a ship's roll sailed on Sebastian Cabot's flagship in 1526. García de Palacio's *Instrucción Náutica* of 1587, which gives all ratings and tells everyone's duties, mentions neither cook nor cooker; although the steward, he says, has charge of the fire. My guess is that the hard-worked ship's boys took turns at the firebox, except that the captain's servant would naturally have cooked for him, and pages of gentlemen volunteers served them. On board the big Mexico-bound galleons described by Palacio, a table was set for the men forward, the boatswain presided, and the pages served and cleared away. On small ships it is probable that foremast hands took their share in a wooden bowl and ate it with their fingers wherever they could find a place. How the little *fogón* or open firebox could cook food for over a hundred people on a small caravel, as it must have on *Niña*'s voyage home in 1496, staggers the imagination.

The only drinks mentioned in Spanish or Portuguese inventories are water and wine, both of which were kept in various types of wooden casks. It was the cooper's job to see that these were kept tight and well stowed or lashed down so that they would not roll. South Europeans, unlike the English and French, did not carry beer or cider, which always went sour on a long voyage; coffee and tea did not reach Europe until the following century. The staff of life for Spanish seamen was wine, olive oil, salt meat, salt codfish, and bread in the form of sea biscuit or hardtack baked ashore from wheat flour and stowed in the driest part of the ship. The only sweetening came in the form of honey, sugar being too expensive. Columbus's ideas of the proper provisioning of vessels on an American voyage are given in a letter to the Sovereigns of about 1498–1500:

> Victualling them should be done in this manner: the third part of the breadstuff to be good biscuit, well seasoned and not old, or the major portion will be wasted; a third part of salted flour, salted at the time of milling; and a third part of wheat. Further there will be wanted wine, salt meat, oil, vinegar, cheese, chickpeas, lentils, beans, salt fish and fishing tackle, honey, rice, almonds, and raisins.

Olive oil, carried in huge earthenware jars, was used for cooking fish, meat, and legumes. Salted flour could be made into unleavened bread and cooked in the ashes, as Arab seamen do today. Barreled salt sardines and anchovies are frequently mentioned among ships' stores of the time, and garlic would certainly not have been forgotten. The sixteenth-century mariners fared as well as peasants or workers ashore, except during a storm, or weather so rough that no fire could be kept— or when provisions brought from Europe gave out.

Dinner for the afterguard was announced by a ship's boy in this wise:

> *Tabla, tabla, señor capitán y maestra y buena compaña, tabla puesta; vianda presta; agua usada para el señor capitán y maestre y buena compaña. Viva, Viva el Rey de Castilla por mar y por tierra! Quien le diere guerra que le corten la cabeza; quien no dijere amén, que no le den á beber. Tabla en buena hora, quien no viniere que no coma.*

> Table, table, sir captain and master and good company, table ready; meat ready; water as usual for sir captain and master and good company. Long live the King of Castile by land and sea! Who says to him war, off with his head; who won't say amen, gets nothing to drink. Table is set, who don't come won't eat.

Salazar describes how the pages would slam on the officers' table a great wooden dish of stringy, ill-cooked salt meat, when everyone would grab his share and attack it with a sheath knife as if he were a practitioner of anatomy; and how every bone was left "clean as ivory." The table conversation, he says, was mostly sighing for what you couldn't have—"Oh! how I'd fancy a bunch of Guadalajara white grapes!—I could manage a few turnips of Somo Sierra!—If we only had on board a plate of Ilescas strawberries!"

What they longed for, obviously, were anti-scorbutics. Nothing then was known about vitamins, and, for want of fresh vegetables, fruit, or fruit juice, scurvy in its most hideous forms raged among the seamen on almost every long voyage. The officers fared better, as they always carried personal luxuries such as figs, raisins, prunes, and pots of jam which kept the dread disease away. By the end of the next century (as Abbé Labat tells us) the French managed to sail with salad plants set out in flats, so that the afterguard enjoyed green salad almost daily; but they had to set a twenty-four-hour guard over their shipboard garden to keep off rats and sailors.

Although Chaunu's compilation of voyages to the Indies mentions several instances of food giving out on an unduly long return voyage, that was comparatively rare on the West Indies routes. But, as we shall see, no master mariner prior to Drake managed to feed his crew adequately on voyages that went south of the Line, especially those which reached the Pacific. There simply was not room enough, or storage tight enough, to preserve basic foodstuffs such as wine, hard bread, flour, and salt meat for so long a time. Hence the resort to penguin meat, seal, and other loathsome substitutes; and occasionally to the desperate eating of rats and chewing leather chafing-gear. Drake's men made out comparatively well, only because he stripped every prize ship of all desirable food stores, gear, and weapons. There is not one of these southern voyages on which the modern blue-water yachtsman, used to refrigeration and canned goods, would have been happy.

Navigation

On this subject I have little to add to what has already been related in my *Northern Voyages* (pages 136–42). During the sixteenth century, "rutters," manuals of navigation, such as Medina's *Arte de Navegar* (1545) proliferated; but sailors, the most conservative of men, were reluctant to try anything new. It was the pilot's business to keep track of the ship's position; but despite the education given pilots before they could be licensed as such, throughout the sixteenth century most pilots depended on dead reckoning.

Captain Teixeira da Mota, after meticulous search into both manuscript and printed rutters of the sixteenth century, has concluded convincingly that the best Portuguese pilots early in that century had plotted the trade winds (which they called *os ventos gerais*), as well as the equatorial current which runs from the bulge of Africa to the Caribbean. They pointed out very early the important fact—known to any square-rig master in the last century—that vessels sailing from the Cape Verde Islands to Brazil must not allow themselves to be carried to the north (leeward) to Cape San Roque, but steer for Cabo Santo Agostinho. Similarly the Spaniards, owing to their increasing trade with Hispaniola, Cuba, and Mexico, found out about the Gulf Stream and so planned their return routes to Spain that this mighty ocean current would help them to whip around Florida and up into the zone of the westerlies.

If one studies the rutters rather than actual voyages, one too easily concludes that Portuguese pilots of the sixteenth century knew every-thing. But when we read the *Tratado da Sphera* of 1537 by Pedro Nunes (Nonius), the famous Portuguese-Jewish mathematician who discovered the vernier, we wonder how useful these pilots really were. "Why do we put up with these pilots, with their bad language and barbarous manners?" wrote Nunes. "They know neither sun, moon nor stars, nor their courses, movements or declinations; neither latitude nor longitude of the places on the globe, nor astrolabes, quadrants, cross staffs or watches, nor years common or bissextile, equinoxes or solstices." Yet they were supposed to have learned all these things before being licensed by the Casa de Contratación, or by the cor-responding board at Lisbon.

Columbus was a dead-reckoning navigator. He made colossal mis-takes every time he tried to determine latitude from a star until, marooned at Jamaica, he had plenty of time to make repeated observa-tions. He knew no way (nor did anyone else in the sixteenth century) of determining longitude except by timing an eclipse. Regiomon-tanus's *Ephemerides* and Zacuto's *Almanach Perpetuum* gave the predicted hours of total eclipses at Nuremberg and Salamanca respec-tively, and by comparing those with the observed hour of the eclipse by local sun time, multiplying by 15 to convert time into arc, you could find the longitude west of the almanac-maker's meridian. This sounds simple enough, but Columbus with two opportunities (1494 and 1503) muffed both, as did almost everyone else for a century. At Mexico City in 1541 a mighty effort was made by the intelligentsia to determine the longitude of that place by timing two eclipses of the moon. The imposing result was 8h 2m 32s (120°38′) west of Toledo; but the correct difference of longitude between the two places is 95°12′. Thus the Mexican savants made an error of some 25½ degrees, putting their city into the Pacific! Even in the late seventeenth century Père Labat, the earliest writer (to my knowledge) to give the position of Hispaniola correctly, adds this caveat: "I only report the longitude to warn the reader that nothing is more uncertain, and that no method used up to the present to find longitude has produced anything fixed and certain."

In the previous chapter we related a telling example of Columbus's excellent dead-reckoning on his Third Voyage. Dead-reckoning is still the foundation of celestial navigation, but the modern navigator

Boxwood Nocturnal "for both Bears," dated 1724. Courtesy Peabody Museum, Salem.

checks his D.R. daily (if weather permits) by latitude or longitude sights or both, which Columbus never learned to do. And, as an error of half a point in your course will mean an error of about 250 miles in landfall on an ocean crossing, it is evident that Columbus's dead-reckoning was extraordinarily careful and accurate. Andrés Bernáldez, who had information directly from the Admiral after his Second Voyage, wrote, "No one considers himself a good pilot and master who, although he has to pass from one land to another very distant without sighting any other land, makes an error of 10 leagues, even in a crossing of 1000 leagues, unless the force of the tempest drives and deprives him of the use of his skill." No such dead-reckoning navigators exist today; no man alive, limited to the instruments and means at

Columbus's disposal, could obtain anything near the accuracy of his results.

By the time Magellan sailed, in 1519, great advances had been made in taking meridian altitudes of the sun with a quadrant or mariner's astrolabe, and working out latitude from a simple formula. Albo, Magellan's pilot whose logbook we have, recorded latitudes of newly discovered places fairly accurately. And there was considerable improvement during the century, as we can ascertain by the positions recorded in Drake's voyage.

The most surprising thing about Columbus's voyages, after his uncanny perception of profitable courses, was the speed that his vessels made; *Niña* and *Pinta*, for instance, making 600 miles in four days of February 1493 and approaching a speed of 11 knots. He and the

Shooting the Sun with an Early Quadrant. Engraving by Ph. Lansbergen, 628. The caption says, "Here we reckon how far off Heaven is. Psalm 6.5 (Thy mercy, O Lord, is in the heavens.) Courtesy Maritiem Museum "Prins Hendrik," Rotterdam.

Heere uwe goetheyt reyckt foo wijt als den hemel is, Pfalm. 36.verf. 5

Pinzón brothers must have been what men in the clipper ship era called "drivers," not comfortable joggers-along; they refused to shorten sail every night or at the appearance of every black cloud. On his first two voyages Columbus made the Grand Canary in six and seven days from Andalusia; compare that with the average time of that run for Spanish merchantmen in the half-century 1550–1600—just double. His first three ocean crossings of 2500 to 2700 nautical miles—33 days in 1492, 29 days in 1493, 40 days on the Third Voyage in 1498, were good; and that of 21 days on the Fourth Voyage, 1502, was phenomenal. According to Pierre Chaunu, it has seldom been equaled and never surpassed in the colonial era. Even the twelve-ship convoy under Antonio de Torres, by following his master's directions, arrived home in 35 days from Isabela, a record never equaled under sail. For 53 homeward-bound convoys from Havana, 1551–1650, the average time was over 67 days.*

Part of the explanation of these remarkable bursts and sensational stretches of speed lies in the lines and sail plan of the caravel. Would that one of these brave little vessels were dug up, like the Viking ships in Norway, so we could guess at her secret! Naturally a lightly laden caravel, in the early voyages, could sail circles around a heavily laden 200- or 300-tun *nao* on the later trade routes. But the design of those full-rigged and wide-hulled ships also improved through the century. The "round tuck" at the stern of the first *Santa Maria* gave way to a square stern, upon which the high superstructure was built, as an integral part of the vessel. Toward the end of the century, the Dutch began to save manpower by cutting sails smaller and shortening the yards. Perhaps the most important improvement was that of sheathing, to thwart the teredos. Drake's flagship was double-planked, and toward the end of the century Henri IV of France, when outfitting a fleet against Spain, insisted on not only double sheathing but a pad of superior German felt between the planks, and copper-plating below the waterline.

End of a Day at Sea

At 3:00 or 4:00 p.m. the first dog watch is set. The day's work of scrubbing, splicing, seizing, and making repairs is now done; and if the

* See above, Chapter III, for the speed of *Niña*.

wind is such that the sails need no handling before nightfall, the men sit about talking and spinning yarns, tending a fishline, washing in buckets of salt water. Peninsular seamen were a cleanly lot. Columbus, at least twice on his First Voyage, mentions their going swimming in a mid-ocean calm, and they never missed a chance to wash themselves and their clothes upon landing near a river. They certainly needed it, since hygiene (in the sixteenth century) required them to wear woolen clothes from neck to feet no matter how hot the climate.

In the second dog watch and before the first night watch is set, all hands are called to evening prayers. The ceremony begins with a ship's boy trimming the binnacle lamp and singing, as he brings it aft along the deck:

> *Amén. Dios nos dé buenas noches, buen viaje, buen pasaje haga la nao, Señor Capitán y Maestre y buena compaña.*
> Amen. God give us a good night and good sailing; may the ship make a good passage, Sir Captain and Master and good company.

The boys then lead the ship's company in what was technically called *la doctrina cristiana*. All hands say *Pater Noster, Ave Maria,* and *Credo,* and sing *Salve Regina.* This beautiful hymn, one of the oldest Benedictine chants, fittingly closed the day. The music has come down to us so that we can in some measure re-create that ancient hymn of praise to the Queen of Heaven that floated over uncharted waters every evening as a fleet of discovery slipped along.

We are not to suppose that the seamen kept very close to this music. Columbus once refers to the "*Salve Regina,* which the seamen sing or say after their own fashion," and Salazar wrote his friend: "Presently begins the *Salve,* and we are all singers, for we all have a throat. . . For as mariners are great friends of divisions, and divide the four winds into thirty-two, so the eight tones of music they distribute into thirty-two other and different tones, perverse, resonant, and very dissonant, as if we had today in the singing of the *Salve* and *Litany* a tempest of hurricanes of music, so that if God and His glorious Mother and the Saints to whom we pray should look down upon our tones and voices and not on our hearts and spirits, it would not do to beseech mercy with such a confusion of bawlings!"

The boatswain or boatswain's mate, whichever is on watch, extinguishes the cooking fire before the first night watch is set. As the *ampolleta* is turned up, the boy chorister sings:—

Bendita la hora en que Dios nació,	Blessed be the hour in which God was born
Santa María que le parió	Saint Mary who bore Him
San Juan que le bautizó.	Saint John who baptized Him.
La guarda es tomada,	The watch is called,
La ampolleta muele,	the glass floweth;
buen viaje haremos	We shall make a good voyage
si Dios quisiere.	if God willeth.

On sail the ships through the soft tropic night. Every half hour the boy turns his *ampolleta* and sings his little ditty:

Una va pasada	One glass is gone
y en dos muele;	and now the second floweth;
más molerá	more shall run down
si mi Dios querrá	if my God willeth.
á mi Dios pidamos,	To my God let's pray
que bien viaje hagamos;	to give us a good voyage;
y á la que es Madre de Dios y abogada nuestra,	and through His blessed Mother our advocate on high,
que nos libre de agua de bomba y tormenta.	protect us from the waterspout and send no tempest nigh.

Then he calls to the lookout forward:

Ah! de proa, alerta, buena guardia! Hey you! forward, look alive, keep good watch!

At which the lookout was supposed to make a shout or grunt to prove that he was awake (like our "Lights burning brightly, sir!"). Every hour the helm and the lookout are relieved, but the captain of the watch keeps the quarterdeck for the whole watch, pacing up and down and peering into the binnacle to see if the helmsman is holding his course. If the night is quiet, all members of the watch not on lookout or at the helm lean over the fore bulwarks, watching entranced the phosphorescent sea, dreaming of epic morrows in that marvelous New and Other World.

Notes

Diego García de Palacio, *Instrucción Náutica Para Navegar* has been reprinted in facsimile from the rare Mexico, 1587 edition (Madrid, 1944),

SALVE REGINA

Sal - ve Re - gi - na   Ma - ter Mi - se - ri - cor - di - ae,

Vi - ta,   Dul - ce - do,   et   spes   no - stra   sal - ve.

Ad Te cla - ma - mus   ex - su - les Fi - li - i E - vae.

Ad Te sus - pi - ra - mus Ge - men - tes et flen - tes

In hac la - cri - ma - rum val - le.   E - ia   er - go

Ad - vo - ca - ta   no - stra,   il - los   tu - os

Mi - se - ri - cor - des o - cu - los   ad nos con - ver - te.

Et Je - sum Be - ne - di - ctum fru - ctum ven - tris tu - i,

No - bis post hoc ex - si - li - um   o - sten - de.   O   cle - mens,

O   Pi - a,   O   Dul - cis Vir - goMa - ri - a.

edited by Admiral Guillén. Very, very informing. For the chanteys, Eugenio de Salazar, *Cartas Escritas á Muy Particulares Amigos Sujos* (Madrid, 1866). For later eds., see my *Admiral of the Ocean Sea*, I, 237.

Shipboard religion. Captain John Smith showed that the Protestant Reformation made no break on English ships, for in describing the mariners' day he writes: "They may first go to prayer, then to supper, and at six a-clocke sing a Psalme, say a Prayer, and the Master with his side begins the watch, then all the rest may doe what they will till midnight; and then his Mate with his Larboard men with a Psalm and prayer releeves them until foure in the morning."

Crossing the Line. References and quotations from Harry M. Lydenberg's excellent book of this title (New York Public Library, 1957). In addition, Alexis de Saint-Lo, *Relation du voyage du Cap-Verd* (Paris, 1637), tells of blacking neophytes' faces and ducking them upon crossing the Tropic of Cancer.

Food and Drink. Jean-Baptiste Labat, *Voyages aux Isles de l'Amérique 1693-1705* (Paris, 1931), I, 15. The date of his voyage to Martinique was 1693. The menus on the king's ship, the *Loire*, make one's mouth water: for breakfast, about 9:00 a.m., ham or paté, a ragout or fricassee, cheese, fresh baked bread and butter, "et surtout de très bon vin." For dinner (after shooting the sun at midday), a rich soup, two courses of fresh meat with salad; cheese, compote, fruit, chestnuts and confitures for dessert. Each member of the afterguard opened his private cellar to all comers and threw the key overboard; all except the ship's secretary. In consquence, he suffered the indignity of having his bottles of liquor emptied and refilled with salt water by the young fellows. Served him right, observed Père Labat!

Navigation. The numerous articles written in recent years on the navigation of the late fifteenth and sixteenth century are well summarized in English by Captain Teixeira da Mota in Royal Society of Edinburgh *Proceedings*, § B, LXXIII (1942) 59-67 (International Congress on Oceanography); and in Portuguese, "Evolução dos Roteiros Portugueses," in *Publicações do Agrupamento de Estudos de Cartografia Antiga*, XXXIII (Coimbra, 1969). For Nunes's complaint of pilots, see his *Tratado da Sphera* (1537), p. 126; quoted in D. João de Castro, *Primeiro Roteiro da Costa da India* (Oporto, 1843), p. 241 ff., along with other complaints of professional pilots by Portuguese navigators. The Newberry Library published in 1972 a magnificent facsimile edition of Pedro de Medina, *Libro de Cosmographía* (1538), with Introduction and translation by Professor Ursula Lamb of Yale.

For speed of ships, see my *Admiral of the Ocean Sea*, I, xli-xliii, 410-14, and Pierre Chaunu, *Séville et l'Atlantique*, VIII (1959), i, 95-98. The distances I quote are by great circle courses, worked out for me from Bowditch by Commander John Gordon; but of course the actual miles logged were much greater, owing to wind fluctuation.

Valuable monographs resulted from the Portuguese government's Agrupamento de Estudos de Cartografia Antiga, and are published as separates by the Junta de Investigações do Ultramar (Coimbra, 1965-70). These are: VII, Luis Mendonça de Albuquerque, *Observação de Estrelas na Náutica dos Descobrimentos* (1965); XV, David Waters, *The Sea or Mariner's Astrolabe* (1966); XVI, Albuquerque, *A Determinação da Declinação Solar* (1966); XXXI, Ernst Crone, *How Did Navigators Determine . . . Speed . . . and Distance Run?* (1969). XXXV, W. E. Washburn, *Representation of Unknown Lands in XIV–XVI Century Cartography* (1969); XXXVII, Waters, *Iberian Bases of English Art of Navigation in XVI Century* (1970); XLI, R. A. Skelton, *The Seaman and the Printer* (1970); XLIV, Albuquerque, *Contribução das Navegações do Séc. XVI . . . Magnetismo Terrestre* (1970); XLVIII, R. Laguarda Trías, *Interpretación de los Vestigios del Uso de un Metodo de Navegación Preastronomica en el Atlantico* (1970); LIV, Albuquerque, *Um Processo Gráfico . . . do Século XVII na Determinação da Amplitude de um Astro* (1970). The interesting discussion following each original presentation is also printed.

* IX *

"Minor Voyages":The Spanish Main

1499-1526

Alonso de Ojeda and Juan de La Cosa

While Columbus wrestled with rebels in Hispaniola and sailed home in chains, a number of Spanish expeditions immediately resulting from his enterprise swarmed into the Caribbean, and Cabral accidentally discovered Brazil for Portugal. These "minor voyages," as Navarrete called them, are the subject of this chapter. They covered the mainland from the bulge of Brazil to the Gulf of Darien, overlapping one another, and the Admiral's Fourth; but it will be convenient to follow each *adelantado* separately to his end, usually miserable or tragic.

Most of the Spanish expeditions were commanded by Columbus's former shipmates, but unauthorized by him. According to his agreement with the Sovereigns, no Spaniard should have sailed to the New World without the Admiral's license and permission; but the New World discovery already had become too vast for one man to manage, or even to supervise. So it is not surprising that the Sovereigns tolerated other ambitious men thrusting into what, strictly speaking, was Columbian territory. All were financed, at least in great part, by merchant shipowners of Seville, eager to share the fabulous wealth of "the Indies." The three most important merchant shipowners were the Guerra brothers of Triana (across the river from Seville) whose main business was the baking of *bizcocho*—ship biscuit or hardtack—for provisioning ships. Antón, the eldest, took a leading part in outfitting Columbus's Third Voyage, and the relief squadron for Hispaniola. He himself went out in the ship commanded by "Gianetto" Colombo, and returned in her to Spain with the first pearls from Margarita and the Admiral's chart of the Pearl Coast.

Before the Guerras were ready to do business, came the first and most amusing of all interlopers, a merry devil named Alonso de Ojeda. Born about 1470 to a respectable family of Cuenca, New Castile, he was slim, handsome, and attractive alike to men and women—and also courageous, ruthless, greedy, and exceptionally cruel. As a youth he became a squire to the Duke of Medina Celi and fought in the war with the Moors, and he also became a favorite of Bishop Fonseca. The bishop gave him a small painting of the Virgin Mary which he carried everywhere and to which he attributed his good fortune not to suffer wounds in his numerous brawls and scuffles.

Alonso, as we have seen, attracted the attention of the Queen by an athletic feat; and it was probably to please her or conciliate Fonseca that Columbus appointed this young man—(twenty-two or twenty-three years old)—captain of a caravel on his Second Voyage. The Admiral found him to be an excellent leader in his expeditions to the Cibao, and in battles with the natives.

Four years later, Ojeda was back in Seville. Through the influence of Fonseca he obtained a sneak preview of Columbus's October 1498 report to the Sovereigns on the Pearl Coast, and his chart of the waters between Margarita Island and the Spanish Main. He decided there to make his fortune, and received a license from the Bishop to try. Merchants of Seville financed him, and at least two distinguished men sailed with him: Juan de La Cosa the mapmaker and Amerigo Vespucci, a Florentine merchant banker and ship chandler resident in Seville. (This is the voyage that Vespucci antedated by two years in his Soderini Letter of 1504 and made into a round-the-Caribbean junket.) Of Juan de La Cosa, almost a generation older than Ojeda, Navarrete well wrote that he was "a great mariner in the common concept, and in his own not inferior to the Admiral, whose shipmate and disciple he had been on the Cuba-Jamaica expedition" of 1494. La Cosa became warmly attached to his young captain without being able

Malapascua on the Paria peninsula. Ojeda sailed by but did not stop. David Crofoot photo.

to cool the younger man's ardent and reckless temperament. What Amerigo Vespucci thought of him he never recorded.

Ojeda sailed from Puerto de Santa Maria near Cadiz, in May 1499. His backers furnished him with three caravels, one of which he so disliked for her unseaworthiness that he returned to Santa Maria where he hijacked a better vessel, leaving the old one in exchange. Another he picked up at Huelva. Continuing his way southward, Ojeda improved his own equipment by helping himself to the gear of various vessels that he encountered. This was done by a boat crew of selected cutthroats who, looking harmless enough but really armed to the teeth, would row their captain to a passing ship, whose master allowed him to board on the plea that his fleet was short of food or water. Then they threw off their disguise, showed fight, and picked up anything that took their fancy. At Safi in Morocco he sold powder and arms to the Moors. At Lanzarote in the Canaries, various sea-stores were obtained by plundering the town house of Doña Inés de Peraza, daughter of Columbus's Gomerian lady-love. Ojeda also tried to steal another caravel there, but failed. In a way, this was a better method of obtaining a proper sea outfit than trusting to Bishop Fonseca and the land sharks!

After a short crossing—24 to 26 days—this half-piratical fleet reached the New World somewhere in the Guianas, several hundred miles east of the Gulf of Paria. Ojeda's five-degree error in landfall is readily explicable. Columbus, having estimated the latitude of the entrance to the Gulf of Paria to be 5° N instead of the actual 10 degrees, doubtless entered the lower latitude on his chart of the Third Voyage. Ojeda's sail of 660 miles coastwise to reach Trinidad must have started in Cayenne, around latitude 5° N.

Sailing past the mouths of the Orinoco, and marveling at the volume of water being discharged, they entered the Boca del Dragón. There, the local Caribs who had resisted Columbus's song and dance act the previous year, fought back when Ojeda insisted on their producing free food. Then he passed through the Gulf of Paria and sailed downwind to Margarita. Ojeda considered himself to be the real discoverer of this island because he went ashore, whilst Columbus had merely seen and named it. He gathered few pearls, the primary object of his voyage, probably because of his rough way with the natives; "he went along killing and robbing and fighting," says the later perquisition against him, "although these natives were peaceful and quiet." At the site of a place called Naracapana, Ojeda either terrified or ingratiated the Indians, who supplied him with food. There his men built a small bergantina * on shore, and in her or one of the caravels he obliged his hosts by attacking a Caribee island (probably one of the Grenadines) from whence they had been raided. He burned the

---

* A shoal-draft lateener with banks of oars in which it was possible to sail to windward, up rivers, and against a contrary current.

Margarita from the south. Columbus discovered it, Ojeda claimed it. David
Crofoot photo.

houses of the guilty natives and retired with a lot of spoil. After this
exploit, one would suppose that the natives of Naracapana would have
showered pearls on Ojeda; but they may have been outside the pearl-
oyster belt and not on friendly terms with the pearl gatherers.

Ojeda resumed his voyage westward into virgin territory for

Europeans. He must have been the first to sight Aruba and Bonaire, although they are not mentioned in the sources. He does mention a group of islets that Columbus named *Las Guardias,* and which he named *Los Frailes,* and that name has stuck; and a big island he called *Gijantes,* as the natives were big fellows. We now call it Curaçao. Next, he entered the Gulf of Maracaibo. There the first thing that met the Spaniards' eyes was an Indian village built over the water on piles, a veritable "Little Venice"—*Venezuela.* This name, which we owe to Ojeda, not only survived but became that of an American republic. The amphibious natives at first were suspicious, then over-friendly, swarming on board the Spanish ships and surrounding them with dugout canoes. Suddenly they took alarm at something, we know not what; the old women left behind in "Little Venice" started an ungodly screeching and tore their hair, the girls and all other natives on board dove overboard, and those in canoes shoved off and shot arrows harmlessly at the ship. Ojeda, in contrast to Columbus's laughing off a similar misunderstanding at Trinidad, insisted on replying with firearms, killing fifteen or twenty natives, capturing prisoners, and afterward ransacking their poor huts in search of gold. Fortunately all prisoners escaped excepting one pretty girl whom Ojeda detained as mistress-interpreter, and brought back on the next voyage. One wonders how Vespucci, a Florentine gentleman, liked these goings-on. He used the Little Venice episode in his account of the fake 1497 voyage but has not left us any estimate of his captain.

Ojeda now sailed around the Guajira peninsula as far as Cabo de la Vela, and the famous map dated 1500 by his shipmate Juan de La Cosa is fairly accurate for this part of the Spanish Main. He loaded logwood, and turned north to replenish supplies and repair his caravels. On 5 September 1499 he anchored in Jacmel Bay (then called Yaquimo) in Xaragua, the southwestern kingdom of Hispaniola. Here the worst of the caravels was abandoned.

Columbus, unwilling to risk leaving this feckless character at large in Hispaniola, sent the reformed rebel Francisco Roldán with three caravels to deal with him. There followed an amusing comedy, each trying unsuccessfully to force the other into his power. Ojeda attempted to put himself at the head of Spanish rebels living in Xaragua, sail to the opposite end of the island to pick up Ciguayos, (reportedly eager to fight), and then, with this rag-tag army, sail into Santo Domingo and depose Columbus. He tried to capture Roldán's flagship on pretext of going on board to parley, but only succeeded in losing his longboat. Finally he promised Roldán to leave Hispaniola if the boat were returned, which Roldán promptly did, regarding this as a cheap price to get rid of Ojeda and his ruffians.

Our hero now raided the Bahamas for slaves and carried off from an unidentified island that Vespucci calls Iti some 232 of the gentle tribe who had welcomed Columbus. Thirty-two of these wretched creatures died at sea, the rest were sold in Cadiz. Although the Queen had strictly forbidden enslavement of American natives, Ojeda knew that he could get away with this, and he did.

In the spring or early summer of 1500, Ojeda's two caravels arrived in Spain. Despite the fact that he had committed enough piracies to deserve hanging, Ojeda was still Bishop Fonseca's fair-haired boy who could do no wrong; he even escaped the usual stretch in jail with which Spain rewarded her most eminent discoverers. On the contrary, the Sovereigns on 8 June 1501 ordered their businessman-bishop to issue Ojeda a new license to return to the Pearl Coast and recoup his fortunes by establishing a trading post. This time he had an official title—Governor of the Province of Coquivacoa (the native name for "Little Venice"), and the crown gave him a fleet of respectable strength with good commanders. The alleged reason for this unusual favor was the "slight profit" he had made on his former voyage. Here is a list of this fleet:

SANTA MARIA DE LA ANTIGUA, ship commanded by García de Ocampo

SANTA MARIA DE LA GRANADA, ship commanded by Juan de Vergara

MAGDALENA, caravel commanded by Pedro de Ojeda, the captain's nephew

SANTA ANA, a *caravelón* (little caravel), commanded by Hernando de Guevara, who had been on Ojeda's first voyage.

Juan de Vergara worked for a wealthy canon of the Seville Cathedral, and Ocampo (or Del Campo) was a merchant of that city. These two made a contract with Ojeda to be his partners for two years and split profits three ways. The fleet sailed from Cadiz early in January 1502.

A minor object of this voyage was to root out any Englishmen who might be found on the Spanish Main. Rumors of English activities there had reached Spain; and as nothing had been heard from John Cabot's 1498 voyage, it was feared that he might have tried to start a colony in the Caribbean. But no Spanish explorer of this area ever saw hide or hair of any Englishman. Men of that nation, and also of France and the Netherlands, eventually came to the Caribbean to plunder and claim the Lesser Antilles which Columbus had discovered but Spain overlooked.

Ojeda had not changed his methods. Anticipating that he would be unwelcome in the Canaries after his earlier piracies, he called for replenishment at Santiago in the Cape de Verdes. There, with his usual genius for trouble-making, he got into an armed brawl with the Portuguese authorities, as a result of which his principal caulker was arrested and detained by the governor. Ojeda retaliated by capturing one white man and one black, and stormed out of the harbor firing a salvo of round shot at the governor's palace. Fortunately he made a fast passage from the Cape de Verdes to the Gulf of Paria, as upon arrival (about 10 March 1502) the men were almost starving. On the 24th, within sight of Margarita, the little caravel *Santa Ana* was wrecked, and on 12 April Ojeda sent Juan de Vergara to Jamaica in *La Granada* to procure supplies. A month later, not having heard from Vergara, he sent another ship in search of him.

Why Ojeda did not pitch his trading post on the Pearl Coast we know not. He continued westward, bypassed the Gulf of Maracaibo, and founded his would-be colony at Bahia Honda on the outer coast of the Guajira peninsula, in what is now Colombian territory. Quiquevacos, or Coquivacoa as Ojeda named the place, was a miserable failure. Neither pearls nor gold could be had, the Indians were surly and offish, and Ojeda's captains mutinied, put him in irons, and sailed for Santo Domingo. There he was thrown into jail and his belongings and property in Hispaniola confiscated. It took Fonseca's intervention to have him released and returned to Spain in this same year 1502.

For the next year or two we know not what mischief Ojeda was up to. The crown, in 1504, signed an elaborate *capitulación* with him to set up a mainland colony somewhere on the Gulf of Urabá, provided he kept off the territory already discovered by Columbus and Bastidas, and that any commerce that he initiated should pass through Santo

Domingo. These restrictions were hardly to Ojeda's liking, and he probably could not raise the necessary money; anyway, he did not sail.

Juan de La Cosa's credit, however, was still very good. On St. Valentine's Day 1504 he received permission from the crown to make a voyage to the Gulf of Urabá "and other islands of the Ocean Sea which have or will be discovered," at his own expense. Financial backers who accompanied him were Martín de los Reyes who had been on Columbus's Fourth Voyage, and Juan de Ledesma who had in part financed the Bastidas expedition in which La Cosa served as pilot. This voyage was enormously profitable. La Cosa with four ships (names unknown) crossed the ocean by the already classic Canaries–Dominica route, sailed along the Pearl Coast, and at the Bay of Cartagena encountered the Guerra expedition, first instance of two minor voyages meeting. La Cosa found one Guerra brother dead and their crews suffering from scurvy. The two expeditions made a joint attack on Tierra Bomba, a big island in the bay, capturing the amazing total of 600 natives. After plundering various other Indian villages in the Gulf of Darien and once more rescuing the surviving Guerra brother, Juan and his partners returned to Spain in 1506. They realized some 2,500,000 maravedis (about $17,500) from the sale of gold, pearls, and slaves after paying one-fifth to the royal treasury. King Ferdinand, however, did not keep all the crown's share; on 14 March 1508 he ordered his treasurer "out of the 6000 ducats of gold that you recorded at my order from Juan de La Cosa and Amerigo Vespucci" each be paid back 6000 maravedis. How Vespucci got in on this deal I cannot explain; probably he had lent money to La Cosa.

One would expect the now aging pilot to settle down—but not he! When on 9 June 1508 the new queen of Castile, Doña Juana, appointed Alonso de Ojeda and Diego de Nicuesa joint governors of the coast from Maracaibo to Darien, Juan de La Cosa was ready for yet another voyage. This would be his last.

Nicuesa was a young nobleman not unlike Ojeda in character, and his natural rival; he was more skilled than Ojeda in tournament and other gentlemanly feats of horsemanship, and in addition a notable ballad singer and performer on the guitar. He had come to Hispaniola with Ovando to seek his fortune, and here was his chance. He and Ojeda, who now first met at Santo Domingo, hated each other at first sight, and so wisely agreed to divide their granted territory by the Gulf of Darien, Ojeda taking the eastern side which Bastidas had discovered. Ojeda and Nicuesa took in as third partner Martín de Enciso, a bachelor of laws who had made a small fortune pleading for litigants in the viceregal courts. Enciso was to stay in Hispaniola to obtain recruits and send out supplies, while the other two went out a-colonizing. Enciso seems to have been a "nice fellow" who lost all his money by joining his fortunes with those of Ojeda and Nicuesa. But we hope he got some of it back when he wrote a good descriptive book, *Suma de Georgrafía*.

With rare good judgment, Ojeda selected the magnificent harbor of Cartagena de las Indias for his projected colony. We know very little about this effort. The three hundred settlers recruited in Santo Domingo were no sooner ashore than they began raiding the interior to capture Indians—for a Spanish hidalgo must have slave labor to live. As a consequence, sixty-nine Spaniards were killed by poisoned arrows, and among their number was old Juan de La Cosa. His body was later recovered, bloated and disfigured by poison. One arrow wounded Ojeda, but he saved his life by ordering a soldier to cauterize the wound with a red-hot sword blade.

At the time of his death, 28 February 1510, Juan de La Cosa, about sixty years old, was the senior and most knowledgeable pilot in the service of Spain. He had already made five or six round voyages to America when he met this cruel death. Queen Isabella, commenting on Bastidas's request for a license in 1503, remarked, "I would prefer that Juan de La Cosa make this voyage, for I believe he would do it better than anyone else." And on another occasion, she said to Cristóbal Guerra, "In navigation, I command you to follow what appears best to Juan de La Cosa, for I know that he's a man who knows well what he is talking about when he gives advice." Posterity has confirmed these sagacious judgments by Doña Isabel.

Alonso de Ojeda now shifted his colony to a point on the eastern shore of the Gulf of Urabá which he called San Sebastián. True to form, he began raiding the neighboring country in search of gold, food, and slaves; but the Indians here were as tough as those around Cartagena. They not only drove the Spaniards back into their fort, but besieged them within it. Ojeda dispatched his one remaining vessel to Hispaniola to seek help. He himself, leaving his settlers under

the command of Francisco Pizarro, future conqueror of Peru, made his
way to Cuba on a passing ship owned by a pirate named Bernaldíno de
Talavera. The ship ran ashore on Cuba whence Ojeda made his way
to Hispaniola in hope of obtaining help. But his partner Enciso had
already sent a ship to take off the survivors from San Sebastián, and
Ojeda was detained by a fresh prosecution for "crimes committed in
his province . . . and elsewhere." He died in extreme poverty at
Santo Domingo in 1515.

What, then, did this feckless adventurer accomplish? He discovered
or at least explored about a thousand miles of coast from the Guianas
to Trinidad and from Margarita Island to Cabo de la Vela, as his
shipmate Juan de La Cosa recorded on his famous mappemonde.
That, in addition to his attractive personality when he chose to be-
have himself, excused all Ojeda's villainies in the eyes of the Spanish
government. He seems to have been first to sail along the Guianas, but
Bastidas preceded Ojeda along the Guajira peninsula and so is regarded as the discoverer of the Colombian shore, later called *Castilla
del Oro,* Golden Castile. Las Casas, who detested Ojeda for his
brutality to the natives and his disloyalty to Columbus, said, "Though
he had not been born, the world would have lost nothing." But at this
long interval we welcome a jolly rascal between the austere Columbus
and the somewhat faceless navigators who immediately followed.

Peralonso Niño and the Brothers Guerra

Peralonso Niño of Moguer, pilot of the first *Santa Maria,* had the
most distinguished career of the three Niño brothers who originally
accompanied Columbus. Later he commanded a replenishment caravel
to Hispaniola and brought back to Spain a cargo of Indian slaves. The
proceeds of their sale he turned over to Columbus toward the expenses
of the third Columbian voyage, for Peralonso always remained loyal
to his admiral. In the *Pleitos* a retired mariner named Miguel de Toro
declared that he had sailed several times with pilots Niño and Juan de
La Cosa, both of whom attributed their knowledge of the "Arts of
the Sea" to Columbus. But loyalty did not prevent Niño from being
the second person to obtain a preview of Columbus's map of the
Pearl Coast, and the first to cash in on this information. Like other
minor voyagers he was ordered not to land within fifty leagues of

the coast discovered by Columbus, but like all the rest he paid no attention to this prohibition.

The Guerra family of Triana was in on this too. Niño had no trouble recruiting a crew from his family and friends in the Niebla, but he had no money. So he persuaded Luis Guerra to stake him, in return for making Luis's younger brother Cristóbal the captain. The Queen not only appointed Cristóbal Guerra captain, but her *receptor* to see that she got the crown's 20 per cent of the profits. That odd relationship portended shipboard quarreling, since Niño had all the maritime experience and Guerra paid the bills; but they managed to get along until the very end. With but one caravel (name unknown) of 50 tuns, and a crew of 30 to 33 men, they sailed from Palos in early June of 1499, shortly after Ojeda and La Cosa. Both expeditions arrived at Paria and the Pearl Coast about the same time.

Before they reached the Pearl Coast, Niño and Guerra, outside the Boca del Dragón, encountered a flotilla of 18 canoes manned by Caribs. These they drove off by a salvo of cannon, and one big dugout was captured. In it were one Carib and a native of the nearby coast, the latter bound hand and foot and destined for his captor's homecoming dinner; six of his friends had earlier furnished the materials for a banquet. Niño, angered by this display of cannibalism, allowed the prisoner to take it out on his now disarmed enemy. He promptly complied, with fists, feet, and cudgel, while the Spanish crew looked on, doubtless enjoying the bloody exhibition. This unequal contest ended by the captive's chopping off his captor's head and parading it on a pole.

No other fight is recorded for this voyage; there would surely have been a terrific one if the two seekers after pearls, Ojeda and Niño, had encountered one another. In any case, it was Niño who got the pearls. He and Guerra must have been more polite to the natives than the rude and boisterous Ojeda, and they had more patience in exploring the Pearl Coast. The *Paesi Novamente Retrovati* tract, printed in 1507, states that "in obedience to the king they sailed into a province called *Curtana* by its inhabitants and there found a harbor similar to that of Cadiz where there was a village of 80 houses . . . in the midst of a thickly inhabited locality." This was probably the place that the natives called *Curiana* on the base of the Paraguana peninsula, just south of Aruba; but it might have been Cubagua Island south of

Margarita, later the center of the pearl fishery, where the harbor did resemble that of Cadiz. No European had been to Curiana before, the natives were friendly, and Niño obtained fifteen ounces of pearls. He and Guerra, having only thirty-three men in their ship's company, were very careful not to offend or frighten anyone. They noted tall and handsome trees, *pavoni* "not feathered like ours," * but no gold. Andrés de Morales, pilot of the Niño caravel, deposed many years later that he sailed up to Isla Margarita, "and there gathered many pearls," then down to Cumaná (still so called) on the bay of that name, contacted a friendly cacique, and "gathered a great quantity of pearls," even some "blacker than the blackest jet," says Las Casas.

After trading from place to place on the Pearl Coast for three months, the Niño caravel sailed west for six days to a province called *Cauchiete* or *Canchiete*, probably on the east coast of the Guajira peninsula. Ojeda had not been there, and it turned out to be wholly delightful. The natives were so friendly and fearless that the men even came on board to spend the night; but, doubtless to the Spaniards' disappointment, forced their women to stay ashore. Niño and Guerra here spent about three months, attracted by the kindness of the natives, "with whom they became as intimate as if they were fathers and sons." For the standard trading truck that Columbus used—scarlet cloth, hawks' bells and glass beads—they bought a great quantity of maize, cassava, fruit, fish and fowl of every kind, and some gold. And no doubt the prohibition of female intercourse came to a mutually agreeable end.

Departing Cauchiete with a flock of parrots screaming in the rigging and monkeys chattering, the Niño caravel sailed ten days westward to a place called Chichiriviche, where the natives were of magnificent physique but, in comparison with the others, "highly rustic"; i.e., rude in their manners. There are still two fishing ports of that name on the coast of Venezuela, but these Chichiriviche must have been on the coast of Colombia. The natives here could afford to be rude, since they were able to mobilize an army of 2000 warriors armed with clubs and bows and arrows, to prevent the Spaniards' land-

---

* *Crax globicera*, the currasow bird, a species of wild turkey, which Columbus described as "a great fowl with feathers like wool." See photo in Morison and Obregón, *Caribbean as Columbus Saw It*, p. 190. Still called *pavón*, the Spanish name for peacock, in Central America.

ing. So the invaders sailed back to Curiana and gathered more pearls.

On 8 February 1500 the Niño-Guerra caravel departed Curiana for home. It took so much time to work north into the zone of westerlies that over two months were required to reach Bayona in northern Spain. There the two partners fell out. Guerra accused Niño and others on board of trying to smuggle their share of the valuables through the royal customs; he denounced them to the local authorities, who flung them all into jail. Nothing could be proved, however, and the Queen not only released Niño but restored him to government service. He lived for many years and went on several official missions to Hispaniola as captain or pilot. Peralonso Niño was one of the most amiable and successful of the band Washington Irving immortalized as "the Companions of Columbus."

This voyage was the least costly and most profitable yet undertaken to the New World. With only one caravel, a crew of thirty-three, and a barrel of cheap trading truck, they brought home buckets of pearls, some "as big as hazel nuts," weighing (according to Las Casas), "150 pounds or marks." They also obtained a quantity of the native gold-and-copper alloy called *guanin*, and plenty of logwood for ballast.

The Sovereigns evidently decided that since pearl fishing proved to be lucrative, they would enter the game, which they did by appointing their honest representative Cristóbal Guerra captain general of an official expedition. He departed Andalusia early in 1501. Another enterprising native of Triana, Diego Rodríguez de Granada, equipped two caravels for him at the charter rate of 110 maravedis per tun per month each, and went along. The main interest of this expedition is the surviving table of wages and salaries: 1500 maravedis monthly for each pilot and master, 900 for able seamen, 850 for men-at-arms, and 300 for pages. The total roll numbered 72 men and boys. Finding lean pickings on the Pearl Coast after Niño and Ojeda, this precious pair raided the island of Bonaire and carried to Spain (arriving about 1 November 1501) a cargo of Indian slaves. That had been all right for the commendador Mendoza and Luis Guerra,* since their slaves were considered Portuguese; but the Queen was furious when she learned that her own Spanish subjects were being openly sold in Castile, and ordered them released and returned to Bonaire at Guerra's expense. Cristóbal, however, seems to have crawled out of this situation—as Ojeda had

* See Chapter X, below.

done the previous year—and the Queen issued an order in 1503 permitting the enslavement of natives of Cartagena and the Gulf of Darien, on the ground that they were incorrigible pagans and a menace to honest Christians. The Indians always lost.

Before we turn to Bastidas, the next native of Triana to venture on a voyage, let us conclude the adventurous career of the three Guerra brothers. Cristóbal, Luis, and a fellow biscuit baker named Monroy sailed from Seville in command of three vessels in the summer of 1504. After ranging the Pearl Coast, they headed toward the Gulf of Darien, where the Queen had declared open season on slaving. Near Cartagena they captured a cacique and set his ransom at a basket of gold worth some 30,000 pesos. Yet unsatisfied, they raided the interior, and on one of these forays Cristóbal was killed. At this point arrived Juan de La Cosa, and without the aid of that doughty Basque it is probable that all would have perished. Luis Guerra, who succeeded brother Cristóbal as captain general, managed to run his caravel ashore near Cartagena, and she became a total loss. The second vessel had already been scrapped, and the third, under Monroy's command, tried to rejoin La Cosa but (again owing to teredos) had to be abandoned somewhere near the present Colombia-Panama boundary. La Cosa's own vessels, stranded on the Gulf of Darien near the village of Urabá, met the same fate. Somehow La Cosa and the Guerras were rescued and returned to Spain early in 1506; but the six hundred captured Indians never tasted the presumed benefits of Christian civilization. No more voyages were made by the two surviving Guerras, but we still have to relate their part in the discovery of Brazil.

Rodrigo de Bastidas

In this breezy first age of Spanish-American discovery, it is remarkable how many civilians of good repute and fortune suddenly rushed into maritime adventure without any prior experience of the sea; and how many got away with it. We have already seen Alonso de Carvajal, mayor of Baeza, abandoning politics to sail under Columbus, and the Guerra brothers, and some of Ojeda's captains, too. The story of Rodrigos de Bastidas, another adventurous dweller in Ariana has, however, suffered from a mistake made by Navarrete a century and a half ago. Navarrete misread the description of Bastidas in a document as *vecino* (native) of Triana, as *escrivano* (public scribe) of Triana. In consequence, Bastidas has been ridiculed as a notary public with quill pen behind his ear, giving up a respectable profession to go to sea. Actually he was a retired mariner who had become a small-time merchant, and who now wanted to share directly in the profits of discovery and exploration.

So off from Seville sailed Bastidas with two caravels on 5 July 1500. With him was Juan de La Cosa, who never missed a voyage if he could help it. Bastidas also had had a good look at Columbus's chart of 1498, and received a contract for his voyage with the monarchy. He topped off at Gomera in the Canaries, made the same landfall as that of Columbus on his Second Voyage (Juan de La Cosa doubtless acting as pilot), and steered west to Cabo de la Vela. Thence he continued in the same general direction to the Gulf of Urabá (Darien), thus covering almost the entire coastline of the present Republic of Colombia, including the sites of Santa Marta, Barranquilla, and Cartagena. After making a fair haul of gold and pearls, he took off for Hispaniola to careen and grave his teredo-riddled ships. Both were wrecked on Cabo Tiburón, the southwestern promontory of Hispaniola. Bastidas and his men then walked to Santo Domingo, carrying their treasure; presumably they used Indian guides and porters. Having arrived at the colonial capital, tattered, hungry, and weary, Bastidas reported to Governor Bobadilla, the one who sent Columbus home in chains. Bobadilla threw Bastidas into jail and impounded all his valuables.

Now came a stroke of good luck for Bastidas. Governor Ovando, Bobadilla's successor, sent him and La Cosa home on *Aguja*, the one ship which survived the vicious West Indies hurricane of July 1502.* There, after repeated efforts, Bastidas succeeded in having his impounded treasure (rumored to be worth many thousands of pesos) returned by the crown. The Sovereigns also conferred pensions on him and La Cosa, to be paid from the still non-existing revenues of the Province of Urabá which they had discovered. "Such," observed Washington Irving cynically, "was the economical generosity of King Ferdinand, who rewarded the past toils of his adventurous discoverers out of the expected produce of their future labors."

In the meantime, Balboa had discovered the Pacific Ocean—of him presently.

* See Chapter XI, below.

One would suppose that Bastidas had enjoyed enough adventure for a lifetime, but nothing could keep this old sailor from the sea. In 1524, when he must have been at least forty-five years old, he received a license from Charles V to start a colony on the Spanish Main. As preparation, he spent a couple of years stock-raising in Hispaniola where he recruited his colonists. With four caravels and 500 colonists including women and children, he sailed from Santo Domingo in May 1526, and on 25 July founded Santa Marta, whose site he had discovered. A happy choice; here lay one of the best harbors on the Spanish Main, cut into the slope of a snow-crowned sierra. But the early story of the colony is anything but happy.

Warned by the native enmity aroused by Ojeda's rough treatment of Indians, Bastidas protected those living near Santa Marta from enslavement; but, not warned by the Columbus brothers' attempt to make Spanish hidalgos work, he insisted that his colonists do the necessary hewing and digging. Nothing put an *adelantado* in worse odor with his colonists than forcing them to perform manual labor. One Juan de Villafuerte raised the standard of rebellion. An epidemic of dysentery broke out; and with no medicaments left, Bastidas, himself sick, sailed in one of his caravels for Santo Domingo before the end of 1526. Twelve days out, he died at sea.

Balboa Discovers the Pacific

All captains of "minor voyages" were men of unusual energy and force of character, but the most outstanding, one who lost his life and became a popular hero, was Vasco Núñez de Balboa. He was born in humble circumstances about 1475 at Jerez de los Caballeros in the Estremadura. After accompanying Bastidas on his first voyage and noting the Gulf of Darien with an appraising eye, Vasco Núñez settled in Hispaniola as a planter. There he went broke, and became harassed by creditors. In desperation, taking only his sword and one suit of clothes, he stowed away on a ship that Enciso was loading at Santo Domingo with reinforcements for the Ojeda-Nicuesa colony on the Gulf of Darien. This he effected by heading himself up in a provision cask from his own farm, now abandoned to the creditors, and seeing to it that it was lowered into the hold with the rest of the cargo. (This perhaps has something to do with the tradition that Balboa was short and dumpy,

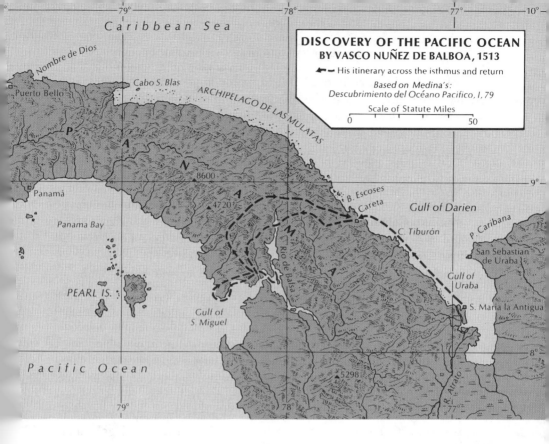

DISCOVERY OF THE PACIFIC OCEAN
BY VASCO NUÑEZ DE BALBOA, 1513

◄— His itinerary across the isthmus and return

Based on Medina's:
Descubrimiento del Océano Pacifico, I, 79

Scale of Statute Miles

0   50

Nombre de Dios

Cabo S. Blas

ARCHIPELAGO DE LAS MULATAS

Puerto Bello

Panamá

P

A

N

A

8600

4720

M

A

Panama Bay

Rio de Balsa

B. Escoses

Careta

Gulf of Darien

C. Tiburón

P. Caribana

San Sebastian de Uraba

Gulf of Uraba

S. Maria la Antigua

R. Atrato

PEARL IS.

Gulf of S. Miguel

5298

Pacific Ocean

but very tough.) Enciso, surprised and not at all pleased, soon learned to make use of Vasco's remarkable qualities.

Finding Ojeda's settlement San Sebastián deserted, Enciso took his stowaway's advice, and on the western side of the Gulf of Darien founded the settlement of Santa Maria de l'Antigua del Darien at the end of 1509 or early in 1510. It was located on the bank of the Rio Darien, some thirty miles from the entrance to the Gulf and several miles inland. Balboa chose this place because, when sailing with Bastidas, he heard that the Indians on that side of the Gulf did not use poisoned arrows. This was the earliest European settlement on the continent.

The community so promisingly founded became rent by factions. First Enciso was banished and returned to Spain, where he wrote his *Suma de Geografía*, printed in 1519. Nicuesa, the gentleman-explorer, Ojeda's rival, showed up and made himself so unpleasant that Balboa gave him a worn-out bergantina and told him to get out. That he did, and disappeared. Diego Colón the Second Admiral, from his capital at

Santo Domingo, authorized Balboa to act as governor of Santa Maria de la Antigua, and Balboa dispatched a ship to Spain to seek royal confirmation. Her commander reported back that the governor had better do something important, and quickly, if he did not wish to be recalled to Spain to account for himself.

Spanish conquistadors seem to fall into two classes: the haughty and arrogant like Ojeda who always had trouble with the natives and usually with their own men too; and the affable, humane, and diplomatic sort like Columbus, Bastidas, and Cabeza de Vaca who liked Indians and got along well with them, but who often were hated by fellow Christians. Balboa belonged to the second class. He became bloodbrother to Comaco, cacique of a local tribe, and married one of his pretty daughters. This tribe provided plenty of provisions for the Spaniards who, in return, helped them to fight a local war. At the end of the campaign, says Peter Martyr (as translated by Richard Eden), the cacique gave Balboa a quantity of gold ornaments weighing some 4000 ounces. While the Christians were weighing it, and "brabbling and contention arose" over the crown's share, a son of the cacique, disgusted with their greed, dashed the scales from their hands, scattering the gold, and rebuked them thus: "What is the matter, you Christian men, that you so greatly esteeme so little portion of gold more than your owne quietnesse . . . If your hunger of gold, bee so insatiable, that onely for the desire you have thereto, you disquiet so many nations, . . . I will shewe you a region flowing with golde, where you may satisfie your ravening appetites." To which he added, "When you are passing over these mountains (poynting with his finger towarde the south mountaines) . . . you shall see another sea, where they sayle with shippes as bigge as yours, using both sayles and ores as you doe, although the men be naked as wee are." The natives had no such boats, but his report of their gold was no exaggeration.

Balboa's famous crossing of the cordillera began 1 September 1513 from a point on the coast about fifty miles west of Santa Maria, near Puerto Escocés. Although the isthmus is there only forty-five miles wide and the peaks are not more than a thousand feet high, this crossing was a marvelous exploit. True, Balboa had with him 190 Spaniards and several hundred native guides and porters to hack out a path with machetes; but the tropical rain forest was so thick and heavy that an explorer named Prevost in 1853 could not see the sky for eleven days, and not one man of a German botanical expedition which tried to follow Balboa's route in the same decade came out alive. Worse than the forest were the swamps and lakes frequently encountered in the valleys. The only way the party could cope with them was to strip naked, make a bundle of their clothes to be carried on the head, and swim or wade to the other side. That sometimes took many hours, and it went on for day after day. And they had to fight a battle with the army of a cacique named Quaraqua, whose court was "soiled by the infamous vice" of homosexuality. Balboa captured about forty members of Quaraqua's male harem and had them torn apart, alive, by dogs. Vasco Núñez is lauded by Herrera for his "compassion toward the sick and wounded, whom he visited one by one to console them," but like other Christians of his era he had no compassion for sodomites.

One of the most dramatic moments in the history of discovery came on 25 September 1513 when Balboa, "alone upon a peak in Darien," sighted a vast ocean glittering in the sun. As Herrera described it, when near the summit of the sierra, Balboa "commanded his armie to halt, and himselfe went alone to the toppe, where, having sighted the *Mar del Sur*, he knelt down, and raising his hands to Heaven, pouring forth mighty praises to God for His great grace in having made him the first man to discover and sight it. Having made this pious demonstration, he signalled all his people to come up, and they in their turn fell on their knees, rendering thanks to God for this great favor, while the Indians stood amazed at the rejoicing and ecstasy of the Castilians." One ocean more or less was nothing to them.

Four days later, on 29 September (Michaelmas) 1513, Balboa reached the shore of a bay that he named San Miguel after the archangel; and when breakers came roaring in over the sand flats, he waded in, sword in hand, and took possession of this *Mar del Sur*, as he called it, for the Sovereigns of Castile.

For priority, however, we must not forget Alonso Martín, who reached the Pacific a day before Balboa, paddled out in a dugout and shouted to his comrades to bear witness that he was the first to sail on that ocean.

Alas, the news of this spectacular discovery, confirming Columbus's reports of a narrow isthmus on his Fourth Voyage, reached Spain too late to forestall the sailing of one Pedro Arias de Ávila (generally called Pedrárias Dávila) to replace Balboa as governor of Darien. His qualifications were merely courtly; he had married a daughter of Beatriz de Bobadilla, marquesa de Moya, an intimate friend and lady in waiting to Queen Isabella. He turned out to be exceedingly rough, tough, and cruel, though not lacking in energy.

Pedrárias arrived at Antigua on 29 June 1514 with a fleet of twenty sail, and in his company, numbering 1500 or more men, were several future *adelantados*, such as Hernando de Soto and Bernal Díaz del Castillo. Santa Maria de l'Antigua now became a respectable city, first European settlement on the mainland, complete with a royal charter and a bishop.

While Vasco Núñez crossed the Isthmus repeatedly, overseeing the building of several bergantinas, discovering the Pearl Islands, and preparing to sail south and take a look at Peru, Pedrárias and his captains, who belonged to the "get tough" school of native relations, were undoing his good work locally. Using their superior fire power to force the natives into providing food and slave labor, they ended, as Vasco Núñez said, in changing sheep-like Indians into "fierce lyons." Before Balboa could begin his great design of sailing south to reconnoiter Peru, Pedrárias, jealous of his success, decided to do him in, accusing him of intending to cast off Spanish authority and set himself up as emperor of Peru. So, one day in 1517, Vasco Núñez de Balboa, as kindly, loyal, and competent a conquistador as ever brought the cross and the banner of Castile overseas, was seized by order of Pedrárias, tried, and condemned to death on the charge of treason and murder. Next day he and four companions were beheaded in the public square and their bodies thrown to the vultures. Balboa was only forty-two years old.

About the year 1525 Pedrárias removed the capitol of Castilla de Oro to Old Panama and Santa Maria de l'Antigua del Darien reverted to jungle. None but Indians live in that region today.

These are by no means all the minor voyages to the Caribbean and northern Brazil in the years 1499–1526. Every year several vessels sailed from Spain to Hispaniola with emigrants and supplies, returning with gold, cotton, and Indian slaves. Had we flown over the Caribbean and the Spanish Main in any one of those years, we would have flushed Spanish ships every two or three hundred miles. We have not yet narrated the most important of these voyages, Columbus's *Alto Viaje* of 1502–4; but first we must relate the discovery of northern Brazil in 1500

by one of the most fortunate explorers of his generation, Vicente Yáñez
Pinzón.

Bibliography and Notes

GENERAL

Los Viajes Menores (Navarrete's phrase) have been so neglected during
the last century that when starting research on them I found the best
sources and secondary works in the library inherited from my grandfather,
who died in 1898! These are: (1) Bartolomé de Las Casas, *Historia de las
Indias*, especially chaps. 164–174 (1927 ed., II, 38–88), and lib. iii, chaps.
39–56 (II, 515–77), chap. 246 (III, 594). (2) Washington Irving, *Companions
of Columbus* (1831); in the revised edition of 1851 it is Volume III of his
Life and Voyages of Columbus. (3) in Justin Winsor's *Narrative and
Critical History of America*, II (Boston, 1886), 187–216, Edward Channing's
chapter on "The Companions of Columbus," Winsor's critical essay on the
sources, and his chapter on the early cartography of the Gulf of Mexico.
(4) Martín Fernández de Navarrete's *Colección*, III (1829). These are the
bases of every relatively modern account such as E. G. Bourne, *Spain in
America* (New York, 1904), R. B. Merriman, *Rise of the Spanish Empire*,
II (New York, 1918), and the opening chapters of José Toribio Medina,
El Descubrimiento del Océano Pacífico, I (Santiago de Chile, 1914). In
Seville in 1972 I found Professor Louis-André Vigneras working in notarial
records in the Archives of the Indies for material on the captains; and the
proof of his having done so to very good purpose appeared in his article,
"The Three Brothers Guerra of Triana and their Five Voyages to the New
World, 1498–1504," *Hispanic Am. Hist. Review*, LII (1972), 621–41.
Herein he really opened up the entire subject of the Andalusian voyages, as
he calls them; for all were mounted at Seville or (in the case of Pinzón) the
Niebla.

OJEDA

(Also spelled Hojeda and Doxeda.) Washington Irving did not know of
the existence of the records of Ojeda's iniquities; they are printed in Duquesa de Berwick y de Alba, *Autógrafos de Colón* (Madrid, 1895), pp. 25–
38. My Harvard Columbus Expedition shipmate Albert Harkness, Jr.,
when in the U.S. Foreign Service in Chile, wrote two good articles on Ojeda
for *The Andean Quarterly* of Santiago, numbers for Christmas 1942, pp.
40–49, and Fall 1943, pp. 10–19. The main sources are very scattered. Ojeda's
task organization for his first voyage and instructions for his second voyage
and other data are in Navarrete, *Colección*, III (1829), 28, 85, 116–17, 120–
21. The *Colección de Documentos Inéditos Relativos al Descubrimiento
. . . de las Antiguas Posesiones Españolas de América y Oceania*, XXX

(1878), 535–44, and XXXI (1879), 258–71 contain Ojeda's *asientos* with the crown of 5 December 1501 and 30 September 1504. *Pleitos de Colón* (Duro, ed.), in the *Colección de Documentos Inéditos . . . de las Antiguas Posesiones Españoles de Ultramar*, 2nd series, VII (1892) contains (pp. 203–8) Ojeda's testimony taken at Santo Domingo in 1512, in which he admits that he was shown Columbus's map by Fonseca, and (p. 206) that "Emerigo Vespuche" accompanied him. Although Ojeda found no trace of English activity on this coast, this has not prevented certain "English first" enthusiasts from claiming that John Cabot came this way on his 1498 voyage and had been observed by Spaniards. The Venezuela episode is largely based on Vespucci's narrative in his Soderini Letter of 1504 (Princeton Reprints, 1916, pp. 12–14). He says that all prisoners escaped, and another early authority says that Ojeda picked up his interpreter-mistress elsewhere.

On Ojeda's fight with the Caribs, Washington Irving complains of the "discrepance" of the sources (*Companions*, III, 27). Irving claimed to have "collated the narratives of Vespucci, Las Casas, Herrera and Peter Martyr," as well as the *pleitos*, and to have "endeavored to reconcile them." Your present author sympathizes, so often has he had to do just that. One must remember that the early historians of America, although endeavoring or at least pretending to relate exactly what happened, were primarily concerned with telling a good story, and that most of their data were obtained orally and at second or third hand.

JUAN DE LA COSA

For this senior pilot there are several brief biographies in Spanish, of which Antonio Vascano, *Ensayo Biográfico* (Madrid, 1892), with French translation; Antonio Ballesteros y Beretta, *La Marina Cantabra y Juan de La Cosa* (Santander, 1954), pp. 318–44, and Victor Andresco, *Juan de La Cosa* (Madrid, 1949), seem to be the best. Andresco concluded that he was born at Santa Maria del Puerto (now Santoña) in 1449; but Vascano insists that his birth date was "about 1460."

THE NIÑO-GUERRA VOYAGE OF 1499–1500

With the exception of L. A. Vigneras's above-mentioned article, nothing important about this voyage has come out, to my knowledge, since Navarrete's *Colección*, III (1828), 11–19. In an appendix to Volume II that he calls "Colección Diplomatica," Navarrete includes the essential *pleitos*. The tract of 1507, *Paesi Novamente Retrovati*, devotes three chapters (cix, cx, cxi; Princeton Reprints, pp. 126–28) to the voyage of "Pietro alonso chiamoto el negro," as the anonymous Italian writer calls Peralonso. The Las Casas reference to their take is in his *Historia* (1927 ed.), II, 74. The *Paesi* tract reduces this to 96 pounds of pearls.

Chronology. E. G. Bourne, *Spain in America*, p. 69, following Navarrete, III, 3, declares that Niño arrived at the Pearl Coast "a few days before" Ojeda; but think he is wrongly translating the statement of Nicolás Pérez in the *pleitos* (Navarrete, III (1829), 541, line 3 from foot) that they returned to Spain "a pocas dias" before Ojeda. Medina, *El Descubrimiento del Océano Pacífico* (Madrid, 1913–20), I, 5, says that Niño arrived 15 days after Ojeda. In case of doubt, I always follow Medina.

BASTIDAS

See Morison, *Admiral of the Ocean Sea*, II, 364, for evidence that Bastidas sailed no further west than the Gulf of Darien. Certain Colombian historians claim that he went as far as the little harbor on the Panama coast that Columbus named *Retrete*. At Eastertide 1973 an air-surface expedition mounted by the Colombian government and headed by Mauricio Obregón located the site of Santa Maria de l' Antigua del Darien. From a harbor called La Gloria, about 30 miles SE of Cape Tiburón, a mule track leads inland to the Rio Tanela which was formerly called Darien. At the junction of this track with the river, preliminary digging revealed several 16th-century artifacts. This must have been the site of the city. Señor Obregón's *Breve Informe* dated Bogatá, June 1973.

BALBOA

General sources for this chapter are the early Spanish historians such as Oviedo, Las Casas, and Herrera, who have nothing but praise for him. For Peter Martyr I have used Richard Eden's translation of 1612. Las Casas used a report by one of Balboa's followers, and Herrera improved on it. The one good modern monograph is the 400th-anniversary contribution of José Toribio Medina, *El Descubrimiento del Océano Pacífico*, I (Santiago, 1914), which fully supports the favorable verdict of earlier historians.

ENCISO

Martín Fernández de Enciso, *Descripción de las Indias Occidentales*, was reprinted in 1897 by Medina with a biographical introduction. The text is a digest of Enciso's 1530 edition; the title of his first edition (Seville, 1519) was *Suma de Geografía*. *El bachiller Enciso* was almost as eager as Peter Martyr to exhibit his classical learning. But he does give the mileage to all known points south to Rio de Janeiro, with their latitudes. He mentions "Sant Jerman" in Puerto Rico and says that much fine gold was found there. An early English translation is John Frampton, *A Briefe Description of the . . . Bayes and Havens of the West India* (London, 1578); and there is a good estimate of Enciso in John Parker, *Books To Build an Empire* (Amsterdam, 1965).

SPANISH TRANSATLANTIC VOYAGES

Generalities, covering not only this chapter but the entire volume. Here the classic work is that of my late colleague Clarence H. Haring, *Trade and Navigation Between Spain and the Indies in the Time of the Hapsburgs* (Cambridge, Mass., 1918). Almost forty years later, Huguette and Pierre

Chaunu began publishing their stupendous multivolume *Séville et l'Atlantique* (8 vols. (vol. 8 in 4 parts); Paris, 1955–59) devoted to what the Spaniards called *la carrera de Indias*, the trade between Spain and the West Indies. This is based primarily on the ms. *Libro de Registros* in the Archives of the Indies, Seville, dating from 1503. In Volume I, especially pp. 36–61, this fundamental source is described. Freights and frauds are described on pp. 97–111. There is a chapter on tunnage, telling exactly what Spain meant by a *tonel* and a *tonelada* (pp. 130–46), and many pages on costs. Volume II (1955) gives the statistics of the movement of merchantmen and merchandise between Spain and America, 1504–60, printing the entries in the Register, with vessels' names, tunnage, names of masters and owners, and destinations. Here we find many ships formerly owned by discoverers, such as Columbus's *Santa Maria de Guia*, doing duty as humdrum cargo carriers. Unfortunately the registered names, mainly those of saints, are commonly given, not the nicknames. As an index of the importance of these sea routes, one may cite the statistics for sample years:—

Year	Number clearing for Indies	Number returning from Indies
1506	23	12
1512	33	21
1522	18	33
1533	60	37
1537	42	28
1542	86	59
1549	101	75

All destinations are in Hispaniola until 1513, when San Germán (Puerto Rico) and Concepción (Cuba) begin to figure. Ten years later we find Yucatan a destination; then for several years no destination is recorded, and then "T.F." (*Tierra Firme*) is common. Until the 1540s the recorded tunnage of each ship is so uniformly 110 or 100 as to suggest that these figures are not accurate. The smaller number of returns over clearances does not necessarily mean that the others were wrecked or captured; many vessels remained in the Indies for traffic between the Islands, Mexico, and Panama; many were worn out and broken up. The New World was, in fact, a "graveyard of shipping."

Volumes IV and V are on the traffic from 1596 to 1650. Volumes VI and VII (1957) are statistical tables with charts of trade winds and currents, of the frequency of convoys for each month, of the lengths of passages out and home, the percentage of different kinds of ships, comparative tables of tunnage bound for each West Indies port, by decades (note, VII, pp. 94–96, the sudden surge of Nombre de Dios in 1541 over Vera Cruz, which catches up again in 1561), and that Florida attracts almost no shipping except in 1561–70; and of ship losses 1550–1650 (pp. 120–23)—a particularly interesting chart showing that Vera Cruz, Havana, Bermuda, and the Azores took the heaviest toll, and that the hurricane months were the worst.

Volume VIII, Part i (1959), of 1212 pages, is Chaunu's inferences from the sources, with an original chapter on Columbus and the Conquest, an appendix (pp. 234–37) with a fine tribute to Clarence Haring, tables of traffic in and out of all Spanish-American ports; and chapters on the colonization of Cuba, Puerto Rico, Mexico, Peru, and Chile.

Volume VIII, Part ii (1959), of 840 pp, subtitle *La Conjuncture*. Brilliant chapters: on "Grandeur et fin du monopole des îles (1510–22)"; on "Le cycle de la Nouvelle Espagne (1522–30)," and "Le Pérou entre en scène (1533–44)." In short, nobody should presume to write on the Spanish Empire of the sixteenth and seventeenth centuries without consulting this magistral work.

X

The Discovery of Brazil

1500-1508

V. Y. Pinzón and A. Vélez de Mendoza

Most fortunate of all "Companions of Columbus," and one of the first Europeans to see any part of Brazil, was Vicente Yáñez Pinzón, captain of *Niña* on the Discoverer's First Voyage out and home. Unlike other members of the Pinzón family, he always remained loyal to his onetime commander, and in the probings of the *pleitos* he resisted every official effort to draw out of him anti-Columbus statements.

In December 1495 he received a royal license to make a voyage to a secret destination (to be revealed at Barcelona) with two caravels named *Vicent Yáñez* and *Fraile*, each of about 50 tuns.* Although this voyage apparently never even started, the detailed *asiento* or agreement is of interest as showing prices and salaries. Charter rate, 110 maravedis per tun; Pinzón's salary, 20,000 maravedis (about $1400) annually; pilot's salary, 15,000 maravedis; sailors and soldiers to be paid each 15 maravedis (about 10 cents) per diem, and Pinzón to have 10 maravedis each more for their maintenance; 500 maravedis a month to be allowed for *sebo* (tallow for keeping blocks oiled and topsides tight), and repairs.

---

* *Toneles*, i.e., tuns of 4 hogsheads or two pipes each. The other Spanish measure of a vessel's capacity, *tonelada*, was about 20 per cent less; 10 *toneles* equaled 12 *toneladas*.

Vicente Yáñez apparently received an advance payment of 169,187 maravedis from Bishop Fonseca to cover purchase of the caravels and other expenses; yet he never sailed, we know not why. It could not have been for lack of men, because this best liked of all early navigators could always recruit a crew from among friends and neighbors at Palos and Moguer.

Two or three years later, when about thirty-seven years old, Pinzón had a preview of Columbus's Letter of 1498 about the Pearl Coast, and Bishop Fonseca issued him a license to make a voyage thither. On 18 November 1499, with four caravels (names unknown), he sailed from his native town of Palos in Andalusia, dropped down to the Cape de Verde Islands, and took his departure from Fogo or Santiago on 6 January 1500. Determined, apparently, to strike the American mainland further south than had anyone else, he steered two or three points west of south and had very good luck. *Una terribilissima fortuna de mare*, a violent gale, made up, and one hell of a wind it must have been to blow Pinzón's fleet at top speed across the usual zone of calms, allowing him to make a record crossing of the Atlantic Narrows which stood for centuries—only twenty days.

This must have been a fascinating sail. As the Cuban poet José-Maria de Heredia described such a voyage, in imperishable alexandrines:—

> Chaque soir, espérant des lendemains épiques,
> L'azur phosphorescent de la mer des Tropiques
> Enchantait leur sommeil d'un mirage doré;
>
> Ou, penchés à l'avant des blanches caravelles,
> Ils regardaient monter en un ciel ignoré
> Du fond de l'Océan, des étoiles nouvelles.

Unforgettable when sailing south in the southern hemisphere is the first sight of Canopus, Capricorn, the constellation Argo with its false cross, and Crux the true Southern Cross, trailed by Hadar and Rigil Kentauri. Pinzón had already seen some of these from Hispaniola, but most of his men and boys, like himself, were new to the waters below the Line, and one can well imagine their leaning entranced over the forward bulwarks, watching for new stars and seeing in the phosphorescent sea an augury of gold to come.

Vicente Yáñez was probably the first European to cross the Equator on the American side of the Atlantic. On 20 or 26 January 1500 (the

Cape San Roque. M. Obregón photo.

sources differ) he raised a cape that he named *Santa Maria de la Con-*
solación. Later he identified it as the one which the Portuguese named
Santo Agostinho, adjoining Recife, at 8°20′ S; others, however, insist
that Ponta do Mucuripe next Fortaleza, at 3°42′ S, was it. Both are
definitely in Brazil, the one south of, the other north of the "bulge."
Pinzón anchored in 16 fathom, landed, and took formal possession for
Spain. In his later testimony in the *pleitos* he admitted that his Cape
Consolation was on the Portuguese side of the Line of Demarcation.
The natives, said to be of gigantic stature, were offish and unfriendly,
not even submitting to the blandishment of jingling hawks' bells.

If his landfall really was Santo Agostinho, Pinzón had hit the bull's eye—just as Columbus had done in his Dominica landfall in 1493. For, after studying repeated voyages from the Cape Verdes to Brazil, the Portuguese writers on navigation advised ships to aim for this very cape, rather than Cape San Roque.

Sailing west and northwest from his landfall, Pinzón took five months to reach the Gulf of Paria. This can be explained by frequent stops, by his excursion up the Amazon, and by entering the Intertropical Converging Zone between the northeast and southeast trades, where it is always stormy in February and March. At one place, still unidentified but not improbably Cabo Primero at Angla de San Lucas, he fought a pitched battle with the toughest Indians that Europeans had yet encountered; his men were driven back to their boats after losing eight of their number. As these natives had no visible huts, Pinzón concluded that they were nomads, "like gypsies or rather Tartars."

It must have been a rather tedious sail, whether it began at 8°20′ or 3°42′ S. After rounding the inconspicuous but ever dreaded Cape San Roque with sand dunes (and nowadays a red candy-striped lighthouse), one encounters numerous reefs near shore, and the coast is low and barren. Extensive sand banks and dunes confront the navigator to the site of Fortaleza, where the outstanding Ponta do Mucuripe, which Captain Guedes of the Brazilian navy believes to have been Pinzón's original landfall, is now part of the city, bristling with quays. Sailing west from Fortaleza one loses the view of interior mountains, and the shore, reef-rimmed, is low, backed by heavy jungle and laced with as numerous rivers and creeks as Veragua. Even today it is the least developed part of coastal Brazil; flying over it, you cross one big bay after another, the eye vainly searching for a boat or some other evidence of human life. This terrain continues with little change along the Guianas and the coast of Venezuela to Trinidad.

At one point, Pinzón found the sea water fresh enough for drinking, for the fleet was off one of the mouths of the mighty Amazon, which he called *Marañón*. After escaping unhurt from a gigantic bore where the fresh water met the salt, he sailed up the Amazon some fifty miles. The natives here were simple, friendly, and gaily painted. Pinzón "requited their hospitality," says Washington Irving, "in a mode too common among the early discoverers by carrying off thirty-six of them captive," together with one monkey. Pinzón, loyal to Columbus's ideas as well as to his person, reported that they were now sailing along the coast of India *extra Gangem*. Was the Amazon the Ganges? He probably thought so.

After crossing the Gulf of Paria and sighting Tobago, which he named *Isla de Mayo*, Pinzón sailed to Santo Domingo, arriving about 23 June 1500. Thence he proceeded to the Bahamian islands east of Crooked Island Passage which he had visited in *Niña* in 1492. Pinzón's memory of this region probably saved him from destruction in a hurricane which blew up in July. Two caravels dragged anchors and were wrecked on shoals then known as *Los Ojos de la Babura*, with the loss of all hands; the cables of a third caravel parted, and she drove out to sea, and the fourth seemed so close to sharing her fate that the crew took to their boats and made for shore. Here they found a few native Tainos who appeared to be friendly; but, fearing lest they summon natives of the neighboring islands to kill them (a natural thing for them to do after Ojeda's and many other slaving raids), the officers discussed whether it would not be wise to put this lot to death. Fortunately, that proved to be unnecessary. The flag caravel which had been driven out to sea returned, and the one deserted by her crew rode out the storm unattended but uninjured; so that the crew returned on board and, with the other, sailed to Hispaniola to refit. Having repaired the damages sustained in the hurricane, Pinzón made sail for Spain and arrived at Palos on 30 September 1500. There he discharged a cargo of logwood and twenty Indian slaves.

"Thus ended," wrote Washington Irving, "one of the most checkered and disastrous voyages yet made to the New World," one in which half the men were lost, most of them being Pinzón's neighbors. Nor did the safe arrival of the survivors put an end to the troubles of Vicente Yáñez. During his absence, merchants who had financed the expedition cracked down on the Pinzón family for payment, so that at the end of this adventurous voyage he was faced with debtors' prison. A petition to the government to be allowed to sell the 350 quintals of logwood that he brought home was granted, but that did not pay all the debts, and next year he received royal permission to export some 4800 bushels of wheat to get free of his creditors. He was also named captain and governor of the coast he had discovered, a purely honorary appointment.

A second Andalusian voyage to Brazil in 1500 was undertaken by

Ponta do Mucuripe, near Fortaleza.

Cabo Santo Agostinho.

Alonso Vélez de Mendoza, Comendador of the Order of Santiago. Like Niño he had no money, but the two Guerra brothers Antón and Luis agreed to provide one caravel and to go along as captain and *escribano*. One ship, *Sancti Spiritu*, belonged to Luis Rodríguez de la Mezquita of the Parish of Santa Ana, Triana. Mendoza himself commanded the other caravel, *San Cristóbal*, which apparently he borrowed from the Ramírez family. Pilot for *Sancti Spiritu* was Antón García of Triana, a brother of the pilot for Columbus and Niño. The *asiento* from the crown for this voyage, 5 June 1500, required the partners to not intrude on Columbus's or Ojeda's territory, and that prohibition they respected. Few others did.

The Mendoza-Guerra expedition sailed from the Torre del Oro, Seville, on or shortly after 18 August 1500 and returned within ten months. The two caravels dropped down to the Grand Canary, then to Santiago in the Cape de Verdes; and, steering SSW at least for part of the way, hit the Brazilian coast a short distance north of Cabo Santo Agostinho. We cannot, however, credit this expedition with the discovery of Brazil because both Cabral and Vicente Yáñez Pinzón had been there earlier in the same year. They anchored for Christmas 1500 at the mouth of what they called the *Rio de Cervatos;* probably the Rio San Francisco at latitude 10°30′ S. Either there or elsewhere, some of Guerra's men, exploring inland, encountered a band of tough Tupi Indians who killed several Spaniards. This led to a sordid quarrel between Vélez de Mendoza and Luis Guerra about the dead men's share of the booty in logwood and Indian slaves. From the subsequent litigation one gathers interesting facts about this Spanish-Brazilian slave trade. Luis Guerra, for instance, sold a girl for 6000 maravedis to a swordsmith, who demanded his money back when the wench fell ill, but didn't get it; neither did a local tanner who bought a twenty-five-year-old man from Vélez. The Comendador made so little profit from this voyage that he had to borrow money to go home after reaching Spain, but Guerra did very well.

Almost in the wake of Pinzón sailed Diego de Lepe, of whom almost nothing is known except that he belonged, somewhat remotely, to the Pinzón family of Palos. Bearing a license to explore the mainland, and commanding one or two caravels, he sailed from Seville in December 1499, took departure from Fogo in the Cape Verdes, and on 28 February 1500 made a bay or river on the Brazilian coast south of Cape San Roque. Lepe called it San Julián, but it was certainly not the Patagonian

San Julián, memorable for executions. Captain Guedes believes that he crossed the mouth of the Amazon when Vicente Yáñez was sailing up-stream.

Luis Guerra's later voyage to the site of Cartagena we have already covered; Pinzón's later voyage we shall return to after relating that of Cabral, the most important one of 1500 or in the discovery of Brazil.

Pedro Álvares Cabral

From the Treaty of Tordesillas of 7 June 1494, in which the Spanish and Portuguese Sovereigns adopted the meridian 370 leagues west of the Cape de Verde Islands as their world-girdling Line of Demarcation, relations between the two courts remained close and friendly for many years. D. João II died on 25 October 1495, and his successor D. Manuel "the Fortunate" married Doña Isabela, Infanta of Castile; and after her death he married in 1500 her younger sister Doña Maria. Portu-guese raids on the Canary Islands ceased, and the Hispano-Portuguese spheres of influence in North Africa were amiably settled in 1509. But how about America, as the New World would shortly be called?

As may be read in my *Northern Voyages*, Portuguese discovery and exploration in America were confined to the Labrador and Newfound-land until 1500. That year, a stroke of good fortune established Portugal on the shoulder or "bulge" of Brazil, clearly on her side of the de-marcation line. According to the treaty, each party should have ap-pointed a commission of pilots and navigators to meet at the Cape de Verde Islands, where they would sail in company due west until they found land, or agreed that the proper meridian had been reached; in the latter event, they would change course 90 degrees to due south and, where they first made land, would set up a stone pillar. Considering that nobody then had the foggiest idea of how to ascertain longitude, it is probably fortunate for international relations that this voyage never came off.

Vasco da Gama returned from India, around the Cape of Good Hope, in the summer of 1499. It was a splendid voyage, although costly in men, opening the ages-old Asiatic world to Portugal as Columbus's voyage opened a fresh, unknown world to Spain. But it had to be followed up quickly, and the Indian trade promptly exploited, to be of any value. As da Gama felt too depleted to undertake a second voyage himself, the command as *Capitão-Mor* (Captain General) was offered

Pedro Álvares Cabral's fleet. From *História da Colonização Portuguesa do Brasil*, II, 51.

to, and (15 February 1500) accepted by, Pedro Álvares (or Pedrál-vares) Cabral. He had been born in 1467 or 1468, second of eleven children to a family of country nobility in their ancestral castle of Belmonte, a little town which nestles under the Serra da Estrela about fifty miles east of Coimbra. Pedro Álvares attended the pages' school at the court of D. João II and, when he reached his majority, became (along with two of his brothers) a *fidalgo* of the council of D. Manuel and a knight of the Order of Christ. There is no record of his ever having been to sea. But he was a handsome, well-built young man, thirty to thirty-two years old, of fine presence and sense of command, whom both Vasco da Gama and the King trusted; and their trust was not misplaced. Nevertheless, there are few important figures in the era of discovery of whom we know so little as we do of Cabral.

Nor do we know much about his fleet of thirteen or fourteen vessels, the finest yet sent out from Lisbon. Only three can be named: *Anunciada*, *São Pedro*, and *El Rei* which Captain Tovar cast ashore in East Africa. We do not even know their tunnage, or whether they were ships or caravels; possibly Coelho's ship was the same *Berrio* which he had commanded in Vasco da Gama's voyage. The picture that we have reproduced is from the Livro das Armadas manuscript in the Lisbon Academy of Sciences, which depicts all Portuguese East Indian fleets 1497 through 1566.* The ships are generalized and only their captains named. For want of something better it may serve as a rough sort of

* Max Justo Guedes, *O Descobrimento do Brasil* (São Paulo, 1966), pp. 61–63, where the complete text will be found as well as that from a later manuscript by Simão Ferreira Paes at the Biblioteca da Marinha, Rio de Janerio. Discussion of the ships and equipment on pp. 72–78. Referring to the picture, from left to right and then down, the captions, abbreviated or expanded from other sources are: (1) Luis Pires's ship which peeled off near the Cape de Verdes and returned to Portugal; (2) Gaspar de Lemos's storeship which Cabral sent back from Brazil; (3) Pero (really Diogo) Dias, brother of Bartholomew, who discovered Madagascar en route; (4) Caravel *São Pedro*, lost on the shoals of San Lázaro; (5) Vasco de Ataide, lost in the tempest; (6) Cabral's flagship; (7 and 8) Nicolau Coelho and Nuno Leitão in collision, the latter's ship was named *Anunciada*, and Coelho captained her home; (9) Simão de Miranda, collided in the tempest with the flagship but miraculously survived; (10) Aires Gomes da Silva, a high-ranking nobleman, lost in the tempest; (11) Simão de Pina, lost in the tempest; (12) Sancho de Tovar (a Spaniard and second in command to Cabral); his ship, named *El Rei* (200 tuns), ran aground on the return passage and was abandoned and burned off Melinde. (13) The caravel of Bartholomew Dias the discoverer, lost in the tempest off Cape of Good Hope.

task organization, although the only accurate thing about the ships is the red cross of the Order of Christ on their sails. Most of these captains were chosen from the nobility, both to impress the East Indians and to give jobs to young gentlemen. Unfortunately, good family connections failed to compensate for total lack of maritime experience, and this lack, added to the hazards of the sea, caused Cabral's fleet to lose many ships. The total complement of 1200 included interpreters, friars, and priests, whose efforts at conversion seem to have secured but one Indian yogi for the Christian faith.

The Tagus, with its backdrop of green hills sloping away on each side, lends itself to pageantry. Anyone who has witnessed the annual blessing of the Greenland fishing fleet can imagine the scene when Cabral's fleet set sail off Restelo, where the Jerónimos convent later rose, and the naval museum is now housed. D. Manuel and members of his court, archbishops, bishops, and ministers of state, bands of musicians and marching soldiers came to Restelo to see this armada off for India; and at the water's edge a royal standard of Portugal, representing the five wounds of Christ, was personally presented by the King to his Captain General.

Barros the historian, a child at the time, said that the liveries and blazonry of Cabral's ships and of the boats filled with spectators made the river "as gay as a spring garden in full flower." But "what was most spirit-stirring was to hear drums, trumpets, tambours and tambourines, the flute and the shepherd's pipe, which hitherto had been heard only afield with the flocks, now for the first time going upon the salt waters of the ocean; and from that time forward they were taken in every fleet, that the men in so long a voyage might want no solace which could lighten the wearisomeness of the sea."

This happened 8 March 1500, and as the wind blew foul for crossing the Tagus bar, the fleet sailed next day. Vasco da Gama had already dictated Cabral's instructions and sailing directions. The usual system of signals was set up for changing course, and taking in or making sail, by fires kindled in the iron cressets at the flagship's stern. Cabral was instructed to bypass the Canaries and Cape de Verdes if the shipboard water supply held out. Vasco da Gama had learned from the Arabs how to make wooden tanks to hold fresh water, a great improvement over carrying it in rolly and leaky casks; Cabral's fleet was evidently equipped with them, for it passed the Canaries and Cape de Verdes

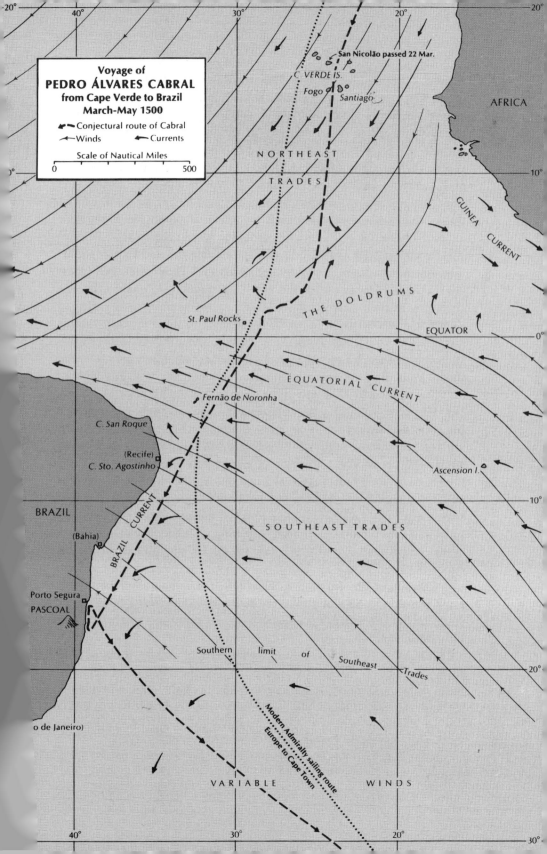

Voyage of
PEDRO ÁLVARES CABRAL
from Cape Verde to Brazil
March-May 1500

- ➤ Conjectural route of Cabral
- ◄— Winds   ◄— Currents

Scale of Nautical Miles
0 _____ 500

San Nicolão passed 22 Mar.

C. VERDE IS.
Fogo
Santiago

AFRICA

N O R T H E A S T

T R A D E S

GUINEA CURRENT

THE DOLDRUMS

St. Paul Rocks

EQUATOR

E Q U A T O R I A L   C U R R E N T

Fernão de Noronha

C. San Roque

Ascension I.

(Recife)
C. Sto. Agostinho

BRAZIL

(Bahia)

S O U T H E A S T   T R A D E S

Porto Segura
PASCOAL

BRAZIL CURRENT

o de Janeiro)

Southern   limit   of   Southeast   Trades

Modern Admiralty sailing route
Europe to Cape Town

V A R I A B L E   W I N D S

without watering up. And it was not the least of Da Gama's glories that on his first round voyage to India he had figured out how to take advantage of the northeast and southeast trades by making a wide sweep to the westward to reach the zone of variables and westerlies beyond latitude 20° S. (He instructed Cabral to take approximately the same course for the Cape of Good Hope as the one recommended by the Hydrographic Office and the Admiralty for sailing ships today.) He should steer as near due south as possible until he caught the southeast trades, then sail close-hauled until the Cape of Good Hope (latitude 34°21' S) bore due east. And, he adds, "In the said region they will not want weather, with Our Lord's help, to double the said Cape." Right! The appended map will show what good sense these directions made. By making optimum use of the northeast trades, you could cross the doldrums at their narrowest neck, and at the same time get a good slant for crossing the zone of the southeast trade winds into that of westerlies and variables. Remarkable indeed, and a tribute to his superb seamanship, that Vasco da Gama after one round voyage to India, should know the best course to follow.

Cabral sighted São Nicolau in the Cape de Verdes on 21 or 22 March, but did not call. During the dawn watch next day nobody could see the vessel commanded by Luis Pires, and the fleet spent two days looking for her unsuccessfully. Proceeding south with a fresh trade wind astern, they crossed the Equator (according to Captain Guedes's calculations) at longitude 24°30' W. In crossing the doldrums, the fleet could not have averaged over one knot speed, and would have drifted some eighty miles west with the equatorial current. Now the southeast wind made up, almost dead ahead, requiring all braces, tacks, and sheets to be close-hauled. Luckily the fleet passed far enough east of the St. Paul Rocks and Fernão de Noronha so that these places were not seen, and Cabral was not tempted to head into the difficult waters around Cape San Roque. So along sped the fleet, each ship with a bone in her teeth, racing the others during the day, and reporting to the Captain General at nightfall.

On Tuesday, 21 April, the appearance of birds and seaweed told seasoned mariners that land was near. And as the office of vespers was being sung on Wednesday of Easter week, 22 April 1500, a keen-eyed lookout shouted, *Terra!* The landfall, on the starboard beam, was a conical mountain which Cabral appropriately named *Monte Pascoal*,

Monte Pascoal. M. Obregón photo.

and it is still called by that name. This Easter Mountain's elevation is such (1758 feet) that, even though it rises eighteen miles inland at latitude 16°53′ S, it can be seen from many miles out to sea. Cabral changed the fleet's course westerly to head for it. When a cast of the lead showed a depth of eighteen fathom and good holding ground, the fleet dropped anchor, twenty miles off shore. Next morning, the 23rd, it weighed and stood shoreward, the smaller vessels in the van to warn the big ones of impending shoals. At about a mile and a half from the beach, the fleet anchored off the mouth of a small stream, the Rio Cahy, at about latitude 17° S.

Cabral named the country, which he supposed to be an island, *Ilha da Vera Cruz,* Isle of the True Cross, because on Low Sunday following his landfall occurred the feast of the Discovery of the True Cross at Jerusalem in A.D. 326.

The Captain General sent ashore Captain Nicolau Coelho, who had sailed with Vasco da Gama, to parley with a crowd of natives assembled on the beach. They seemed friendly enough, but he soon returned on board as the wind was freshening and the sea making up. That night it blew hard from the southeast, and the flagship and others dragged anchors. So next morning (24 April), the Captain General ordered all twelve ships to weigh and proceed northward along the coast, close to shore, in search of a good harbor. After a sail of about forty miles they found what they wanted, and anchored. Cabral named the place Porto Seguro—Safe Harbor.* He reported it to be big enough to hold 200 ships; no exaggeration if you include the adjoining bay to the north, now called Santa Cruz. Here is a long sand beach, wooded hills rising to 120 feet elevation, a sizable river (Santa Cruz, or João de Tiba), and a small stream. Protection from the sea is afforded by breaking reefs, and the modern coast pilot, which describes both Cabrália and Porto Seguro Bays with as much enthusiasm as official publications permit, states that "the sea is never heavy in either part of the bays, even during southeasterly winds."

It all seems simple enough to a sailor—the fleet being deflected from the optimum course for India by a shift of wind or a stronger current than the navigator anticipated. Although nobody has seriously disputed the locality of Cabral's Brazilian landfall, the question whether he was the first European to sight Brazil, and whether or not he intended to do it, has been fiercely debated by historians of Portugal and Brazil. I am content to follow the great Alexander von Humboldt, William B. Greenlee, and my correspondent Professor T. O. Marcondes de Sousa of the University of São Paulo, in asserting, emphatically, that the discovery was purely accidental; and that, except for the visit of Vicente Yáñez Pinzón a few months earlier in the same year, no European prior to Cabral had visited any part of Brazil. In any case, the progressive opening up of the country stemmed from Cabral's rather than Pinzón's discovery.

Cabral promptly sent his storeship home under command of Gaspar de Lemos, to inform D. Manuel of this discovery. The news got around Europe very quickly, and in time to be recorded both on the Juan de La Cosa mappemonde dated 1500, and the Cantino mappemonde of

---

* Not the modern port of that name, but a port six miles further north, at latitude 16°20' S, now called Baia Cabrália after the discoverer. Charts and detailed discussion in Guedes, pp. 100–111.

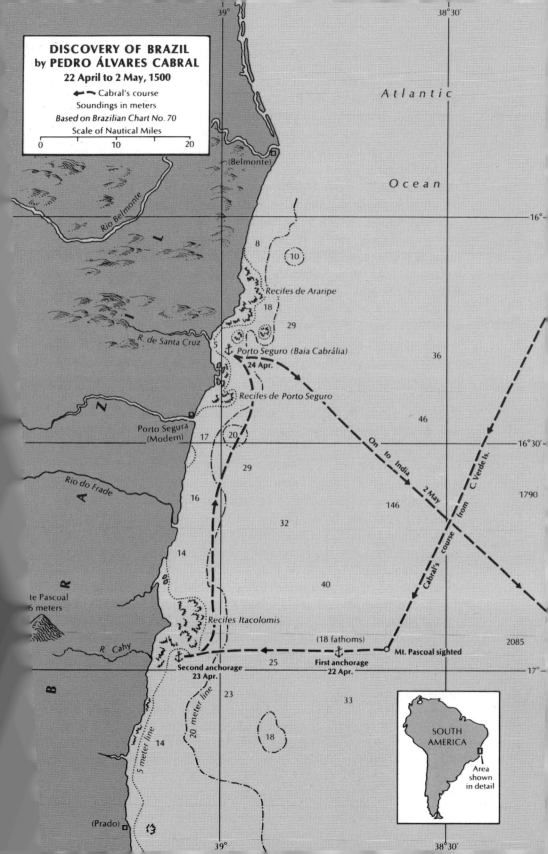

DISCOVERY OF BRAZIL
by PEDRO ÁLVARES CABRAL
22 April to 2 May, 1500

◀━━ Cabral's course
Soundings in meters
Based on Brazilian Chart No. 70
Scale of Nautical Miles

0   10   20

39°   38°30′

Atlantic

(Belmonte)

Ocean

Rio Belmonte

16°

8

⑩

Recifes de Araripe

18

29

R. de Santa Cruz

5   Porto Seguro (Baía Cabrália)
24 Apr.

36

Recifes de Porto Seguro

46

Porto Segura
(Modern)   17   ⑳   On to India   2 May   C. Verde Is.   16°30′

29   1790

Rio do Frade   16

32

146   Cabral's course from

14

40

te Pascoal   Recifes Itacolomis   2085
6 meters

R. Cahy   (18 fathoms)   ○ Mt. Pascoal sighted
⚓ Second anchorage   ⚓ First anchorage   17°
23 Apr.   25   22 Apr.

23   33

⑱

B   14   SOUTH
AMERICA

Area
shown
in detail

(Prado)   ⑬

39°   38°30′

1502. La Cosa merely dubbed in an island he calls *isla descubierta por portugal,* off an indefinite Brazilian coast; but Cantino's anonymous Portuguese cartographer put the discovery on the mainland, and against Porto Seguro placed an inscription stating that Cabral "fell in" with this land "which they believe to be mainland" on a voyage to India, and that the natives went naked.

Cabral tarried at Porto Seguro only eight days, for he had to be getting on to India. In the meantime, Pedro Vaz de Caminha had time to make observations, which he related in a long letter to D. Manuel on his way home in the storeship. An intelligent and well-educated man, Caminha goes at great length into the manners and customs of the Tupi or Tupi-Guarani nation which then occupied almost the entire Brazilian coast. For personal adornment they made good use of the feathers of the macaw and other birds and lavish use of paint, and their lack of shame in revealing their bodies proved that they were living in a pre-lapsarian state of innocence. A delegation trustingly came aboard and were formally received by Cabral seated in a chair on the flagship's quarterdeck, in full dress and wearing a gold collar. They tested the food and wine offered and found both not much to their liking; but (doubtless owing to the wine) stretched out on deck stark naked to nap, shocking the Portuguese sailors, who hurriedly provided covering.

The Captain General permitted no mass liberty, except twice when about twenty or thirty men went ashore, "made merry" with the Tupi, loaded wood, and swapped trading truck for macaws. Some of these talkative and brilliantly hued birds must have survived the voyage to India, as they are accurately depicted on the Cantino map of 1502; and their popularity led to their land being named on some of the old maps, "Tierra de Papagalli" (Land of Parrots). Cabral did allow small groups of officers to "visit" with the Indians. Among them, Diogo Dias (brother to Bartholomew the discoverer), an "agreeable and pleasure-loving" customs official of Sacavém, went ashore with a bagpipe player, to accompany an Indian dance. Diogo participated, "taking them by the hands, and they were delighted and laughed," especially when he performed solo, "making many light turns and a remarkable leap which astonished them." Diogo later spent a night in a hammock at an Indian village some five miles inland, and reported their dwellings to be long houses (like those of the Iroquois), and that they lived mainly on bread from the manioc or cassava, wild seeds and berries, and fish. Nobody in Cabral's fleet suspected their not infrequent feasts of human flesh.

Coelho, Caminha, and Dias also went ashore and apparently had a good time enjoying four young and pretty girls whose plump thighs concealed the *mons Veneris.* "One of the girls, all painted from head to foot . . . was so charming that many women of our land, seeing such attractions, would be ashamed that theirs were not like hers." (One may conjecture that the reactions of the Portuguese ladies would have been somewhat different!) The outstanding thing about these Tupi Indians was not their nudity, common to all natives in warm regions, but their timidity. None showed any desire to fight, and at the slightest excuse they would take fright and scatter "like sparrows at a feeding place." Thus, in native relations, Cabral's discovery of Brazil reads like a repeat performance of Columbus's discovery of San Salvador.

Wanting a stone *padrão* to set up as emblem of Portuguese sovereignty (since they had not expected to discover new regions), Cabral's men fashioned a substantial wooden cross, carved on it the arms of Portugal, and set it up near the mouth of the Santa Cruz River. On the first Sunday after Easter, Mass was said ashore in a tent, the gospel side adorned with the banner of the Order of Christ that Cabral had brought from Lisbon. On Monday, 27 April, the fleet took on water, and Mestre João, a converted Jewish physician whom D. Manuel had sent along to make celestial observations, went ashore to shoot the sun with his astrolabe and work out the latitude. He found it to be 17° S, a mistake of forty miles. He also made a diagram of the Southern Cross and adjacent constellations that was not too bad. The Tupi here were as friendly and helpful as the Indians whom Columbus had found in the Bahamas; they even helped the Portuguese to load wood, and were rewarded by being allowed to spend a night on board in "a bed with mattresses and sheets to tame them better." We wonder how people who were accustomed to sleep in hammocks liked that. This is the earliest reference I have seen to sheets and mattresses on board ship; they must have been reserved for the top officers.

On 2 May, leaving ashore two convicts to "civilize" the natives, Cabral's twelve ships set sail from their Safe Harbor in Brazil. It had been a delightful interlude in a long voyage, unmarred by any untoward incident or brutality. Later discoverers, as we shall see, reported the Tupi to be not quite so innocent as they appeared to Cabral; but that was part of the pattern. American natives were almost invariably friendly to Europeans who gave evidence of moving on, and the more quickly they moved, the warmer the friendship.

The few days of shore liberty at Porto Seguro were the last days of pleasure for two hundred or more members of Cabral's fleet. Departing 2 May 1500, they followed Gama's instructions, making best way toward the Cape of Good Hope. A comet appeared on 12 May and was visible for ten days; the sailors regarded this as highly sinister. It was. When sailing before a strong west wind in the high-pressure area east of Tristan da Cunha, one of the most dangerous of all Atlantic zones, the entire fleet was thrown aback by a tornado, with no warning. Four ships capsized and sank with all hands before the others could lend a hand; the remaining seven drove under bare poles for twenty days, losing sight of each other and rounding the Cape of Good Hope without even sighting it. Eventually they rendezvoused at Mozambique and stayed until 20 July, making extensive repairs. Piloted by natives, they reached Calicut on 13 September 1500.

Cabral's stay at Calicut was stormy too, in a different sense. Owing to opposition from Arab competitors, he was able to load only two of his seven ships. Although he obliged the ruler of Calicut by sending a caravel to capture an Indian vessel with a cargo of elephants, the same magnate, allied with local Arab traders, opened war on the Portuguese. After severely bombarding Calicut, Cabral began his return passage on Christmas Eve 1500.

His greatly reduced fleet straggled into Lisbon between 23 June and 27 July 1501. Of the thirteen that left Lisbon the previous year, six had been lost at sea, two returned empty, and only five brought valuable cargoes of spices and other Indian products. These, to contemporaries, were the important results of the voyage, for they proved that Far Eastern spices could be imported by the Cape route independent of the costly caravans. The discovery of Brazil, a country destined far to surpass Portugal itself in area, wealth, and population, was considered valuable only as a place to replenish food, water, and wood on a passage to India. João da Nova did that in 1501, but most Portuguese captains found it more convenient to top off in the Cape de Verdes than risk shipwreck on the reef-ringed shores of Brazil. Greenlee well said,

"Few voyages have been of greater importance to posterity, and few have been less appreciated in their time."

Despite all losses, Cabral completed this voyage to the satisfaction of D. Manuel, who chose him to command the third Portuguese voyage to India. He worked assiduously on the preparations for eight months, but then was superseded by Vasco da Gama, who set sail with a fleet of fifteen vessels on 25 March 1502. Da Gama as senior sea lord to Cabral, could not be denied if he wanted the command. Disappointed, the discoverer of Brazil retired to a small estate at Jardim near Santarém. There he found comfort and financial support by wedding a lady of royal lineage. Dona Isabel de Castro, one of the queen's ladies-in-waiting. She bore him six children, through one of whom, Fernão Álvares, the Cabral line has descended to this day.

Pedro Álvares Cabral died in 1530 and was buried in the chapel of the Asilo de Santo António, a small church in Santarém. He was a great seaman and an important discoverer, even though his discovery was accidental, like that of Columbus. He must have been a good leader of men because, alone among important fleet commanders in the southern hemisphere, he was never troubled by insubordination or mutiny. He had the good fortune to discover an unusually beautiful part of the spectacular coast of Brazil, under idyllic circumstances.

Last Voyages of Vicente Yáñez Pinzón

Undismayed by the results of his first voyage to Brazil, Vicente Yáñez between 1502 and 1504 made a second, over much the same territory but in reverse order. He called first at the Gulf of Paria where he trafficked profitably with the Indians, loading 3000 ounces of gold, a quantity of odoriferous gum, hangings of cotton-silk, and parrots, already in great demand as pets. He then coasted eastward and southward to latitude 7° S, a little beyond Cape San Roque, and returned via Santo Domingo, where he met Columbus in July 1504 after the Admiral's enforced stay in Jamaica.

Vicente Yáñez next turned his eyes to Puerto Rico as a profitable island to exploit. King Ferdinand, now regent of Castile, first appointed him captain of a fortress (to be constructed at his own expense) and then, on 24 April 1505, governor and captain general of that important

"Isola de Sant Xoan in the Ocean Sea." He seems never to have gone there and taken over. Later the same year, the King gave him a gratuity of 10,000 maravedis and authorized him to go on a joint voyage with Juan de Solis. Peter Martyr, our only source of any consequence, states that they did so in 1506, following the same route in Central America that Columbus had on his Fourth Voyage, with no results important enough for him to relate.

In 1508 extensive preparations were made in Spain for a voyage along South America in caravel *Isabeleta* and ship *Magdalena* of 50–60 tuns each, with Juan de Solis and Pinzón as joint commanders. Details of the contract indicate that the crown considered this voyage to be very important, its principal object being discovery of an inter-oceanic strait. Pinzón and Solis each are to receive a salary of 50,000 maravedis, but Pinzón would command ashore and Solis at sea. Anticipating the trouble that Magellan later had over precedence, this *asiento* instructs the two captains to speak to each other morning and evening "without observing any formality or deferring the one to the other," excepting that the ship which has the windward gauge must look out for the one to leeward. Very sensible!

From the little recorded of this expedition, it seems that they coasted the Caribbean Sea, searching for the strait, and then returned because of dissension between the two captains. After the voyage ended, in 1509 or 1510, Solis received the usual stretch in a Spanish jail; but, as we shall see, he got out in time to make two more southern voyages and to leave his well-picked bones on the shores of the River Plate.

This was the last voyage by Vicente Yáñez Pinzón. He died at his home in Palos in 1514, unfortunately not living long enough to enjoy the gracious act of Emperor Charles V ennobling the entire Pinzón family and granting them a coat of arms. Vincente well earned the following tribute from the historian Oviedo: "He had the reputation of being the most skillful of the pilots of the King and of that time. I knew him and liked him; he was as fair-spoken as any seafaring man I have ever seen, and one of those who best understand their art." To which historian Gómara added that Pinzón and Solis knew far more about navigation than did Amerigo Vespucci.

Yet Pinzón is still a controversial figure. Most Portuguese and Brazilian historians, encouraged by the eminent Duarte Leite, are unwilling to admit any discovery of Brazil by a Spaniard. Asserting that Pinzón could not possibly have crossed the Atlantic Narrows in the brief time that he gives, they insist that Santa Maria de la Consolación must have been Cape Orange on the border of Brazil and the Guianas, or even Cayenne, at about latitude 5° N; that he neither crossed the Equator nor even sighted the Amazon. Unfortunately, the sources are so few and the descriptions of scenery therein are so scanty that positive identifications are impossible. My own belief is that Pinzón did discover Cabo Santo Agostinho and first sailed up the Amazon. But Cabral's later landfall south of the bulge was well the most important, since settlement of Brazil followed him, after an interval. Brazil is a big enough country to admit two discoverers, like North America.

Bibliography and Notes

VICENTE YÁÑEZ PINZÓN

A fair biography is James R. McClymont's *Vicente Añes Pinçon* (London, 1916, edition of 150 copies). He translates most of the scattered sources in Navarrete and the *Documentos Inéditos*, but makes few and feeble attempts to identify landfalls; there is great need of a Vicente Yáñez Pinzón expedition by yacht or airplane to accomplish this. Pinzón himself testified in the *pleitos* of 1513 that he explored "from the Cabo de Consolación, which is in the territory of Portugal and now is called Cabo de S. Agostin" (Navarrete, III, 547). But Captain Max Justo Guedes (*O Descobrimento do Brasil*, Rio de Janeiro, 1966) believes it to have been Ponta do Mucuripe, the headland next Fortaleza, at latitude 3°42' S.

A contemporary narrative by Angelo Trevisan, printed in his *Libretto de Tutta la Navegatione de Re de Spagna* (Venice, 1504), chaps. 112–13, and reprinted in *Paesi Novamente Retrovati* (1507), and in T. O. Marcondes de Sousa, *O Descobrimento do Brasil* (São Paulo, 2nd edition, 1956), pp. 244–46. Portuguese historians, led by the redoubtable Duarte Leite, in "Os Falsos Precursores de Álvares Cabral," (*Hist. Col. Port. do Brasil*, I, 109–229), deny that Pinzón crossed the Equator or saw the Amazon or sighted any part whatsoever of the Brazilian coast. Others, notably Marcondes de Sousa, pp. 89–102, insist that he did make Cabo Santo Agostinho. His Atlantic crossing, however, was phenomenally short. Hans Stade, on a Portuguese merchant ship, took 84 days in 1547 to sail from Arzila to Santo Agostinho, and 108 days to reach the Azores from somewhere south of Pernambuco. *Captivity of Hans Stade* (Hakluyt Society, London, 1874, LI, pp. 19, 25).

For the Amazonian part, McClymont, pp. 14–15, quoting pilot Juan de Umbria in the lawsuit. Pinzón was apparently the first European to note the phenomenon of fresh water out to sea, all the more remarkable when the shore is shrouded by mist. My father told me, early in this century, a story that he was told by Captain Josselyn of barque *Nuuanu*. A ship whose crew were dying of thirst, sailing off the mouth of the Amazon yet out of sight of land, spoke a passing vessel and begged for water. "Lower a bucket, you bloody fools!" was the seemingly heartless reply. "Well, let's try it anyway," said the captain; and behold, the water *was* fresh!

Diego L. Molinari, *El Nacimiento del Nuevo Mundo* (Buenos Aires, 1941), Map No. 14, shows Pinzón's routes as disputed by historians.

The ·agreement, dated 5 September 1501, is translated by McClymont, pp. 43–48, from *Colección de Documentos Inéditos Relativos al Descubrimiento . . . de las Antiguas Posesiones Españoles de América y Oceania,* XXX (Madrid, 1878), 535–42. Navarrete, III, 112, has a similar but later one dated 25 March 1505, useful as describing the extent of the coast starting at Santa Maria de la Consolación, passing a place called *Rostro-Hermoso* which Captain Justo Guedes identifies as the Curu River mouth at Ceará, a beautiful shore; a great river called *Santa Maria de la Mar Dulce* (the Orinoco?), and Cabo de San Vicente. Duarte Leite will allow the Spaniard but a smidgeon of Brazil, Cape Orange, just across the border of French Guiana.

I favor the Cabo Santo Agostinho landfall because (1) Pinzón, as an expert caravel captain who at times got 11 knots out of Columbus's *Niña*, was capable of making a quick Atlantic crossing to this point; (2) he identified it as his Cabo de Consolación, and (3) he took five months to sail thence to Trinidad. But I must admit that Captain Guedes has made a cogent argument for Ponta do Mucuripe, based on Pinzón's southwesterly course from the Cape de Verde Islands, and an intense study of the Juan de La Cosa mappemonde. This was compiled after Pinzón returned to Spain, and its nomenclature begins well north of the bulge.

Pinzón in the Bahamas. McClymont, pp. 22–23, 49–50; *Colección de Documentos Inéditos Relativos al Descubrimiento . . . de las Antiguas Posesiones Españoles de América y Oceania,* 2nd Series, VII (Madrid, 1892), 203, 270. On page 50 McClymont translates from another set of *Documentos Inéditos* a document dated 13 March 1508 in which King Ferdinand orders the Casa de Contratación to buy four caravels for Amerigo Vespucci and Pinzón to go on a joint voyage recommended by Amerigo. This probably refers to the 1508 voyage with Juan de Solis; but if it does, Vespucci dropped out.

Mendoza's voyage is told briefly in D. L. Molinari, *Nacimiento,* p. 14 and Maps 15 and 16. See also Henry Harrisse, *Discovery of North America,* pp. 680, 682, and pp. 690–91 for Lepe's second voyage (probably 1502), of which almost nothing is known.

The Pinzón-Solis voyage of 1508. The *asientos* or contracts are translated in McClymont, pp. 64–73, from *Documentos Inéditos,* XXII (1874), 5–13 and XXXVI (1881). They include an interesting inventory and list of complement allowed—24 mariners, 16 gromets, 6 boys, and a pilot, master, carpenter, caulker, master gunner, and cooper for each caravel. The provisions were 11 *arrobas* of wine and quantities (not stated) of dried fish, beans, pulse, cheese, and honey. The 1508 agreement specifies (p. 72) the exact dimensions of the chests in which seamen were allowed to bring home the goods they bought from the natives. Reported in his return cargo were "canes" (hardly sugar canes this early), an "odoriferous gum," probably copal, and "sandalwood," a case of wrong identification. The nearest wild sandalwood grew on the West Coast of Africa and in Hawaii.

Watches at Sea. The Portuguese, according to Guedes, *op. cit.*, p. 68, divided the night from 8 p.m. to 8 a.m. into the first, the *Modorra* ("sleepy") —what American sailors used to call the "graveyard"—and the *Alva* (dawn) watches.

CABRAL

The *magnum opus* in English for Cabral is a Hakluyt Society volume (2nd series, LXXXI, London, 1938), translated and edited by William B. Greenlee, entitled *The Voyage of Pedro Álvares Cabral to Brazil and India.* Following a scholarly and comprehensive introduction, Greenlee translates and liberally annotates the leading documentary sources. These are:—Pedro Vaz de Caminha's Letter of 1 May 1500 to D. Manuel, Mestre João's Letter of the same date to the king, the so-called Anonymous Narrative of a gentleman who went the whole way with Cabral, and important letters written after the return of the fleet to Lisbon. He also has an excellent appendix on ships and men.*

Captain Max Justo Guedes, *O Descobrimento do Brasil,* is an excellent short book, with maps, and includes the principal documents, such as Cabral's Letter of Appointment, 15 February 1500 (p. 11). As he says (p. 40), these documents are *pouquíssimos,* very, very few; so everyone reprints them and too many read into them things that are not there. Captain Guedes is a Brazilian naval officer who knows his coast with its winds and currents. He has made the most detailed study, on the spot, of Cabral's Brazilian landfall and of his movements ashore. T. O. Marcondes de Souza, *O Descobrimento do Brasil* (São Paulo, 2nd ed., 1956), is an excellent compendium of the subject, with an appendix of documents in the original languages. The author was professor of history at the University of São Paulo.

S. E. Morison, *Portuguese Voyages to America in the Fifteenth Century* (Cambridge, Mass., 1940; 2nd ed., New York, 1965). In this book, written independently of the two preceding, I reached the same conclusions as their authors, on the unlikelihood of any European's having come to Brazil before 1500. What has the other side to offer? The deathbed declaration in

---

* Mr. Greenlee (1872–1953), whom Professor H. Morse Stephens interested in Portuguese history while at Cornell University, retained his interest during a long business career in Chicago, and left his manuscripts to the Newberry Library there. He was working on a Life of Vespucci at the time of his death. See Francis M. Rogers, "William Brooks Greenlee," *Hispanic American Historical Review,* XXXIII (1953), 587–89.

1580 by an aged gaffer who when making his will said that he had been in Brazil more than fourscore years; declarations of seamen who were witnesses in a damage suit or trying to get out of jail; Robert Thorne's report in 1527 of Sevillian gossip; forced construction of sentences out of context; and, to fill gaping holes in the evidence, an imaginary "policy of secrecy" for which no rational motive has been adduced. This hypothesis that one or more Portuguese reached America before Columbus and returned with the news, which the King promptly suppressed so that it escaped notice until the Cortesão brothers discovered it after 450 years, belongs in the realm of fantasy. My translation of the sailing instructions of Vasco da Gama to Cabral is in *Mariner's Mirror*, XXIV (October 1938), 402–7.

If the documents of the Tordesillas negotiation ever turn up, it may be found that D. João II possessed actual knowledge when he predicted to Columbus the existence of a southern continent such as Brazil. I believe that this sagacious monarch was merely reflecting the medieval antipodean school of cosmography. Writers such as Vincent de Beauvais argued that there simply *had* to be a continent over there to balance Africa.

Barros's description of the fleet's departure is quoted in Robert Southey, *History of Brazil*, I (London, 1810), 10. Caminha's Letter (Greenlee, p. 22) adds bagpipes, which were as native to Portugal as to Scotland.

Cabral's landfall. There is no doubt about this, but on the map that Vaughn Gray has prepared for me I am placing Cabral's course just prior to the sighting further out than do most authorities, so that (except for the Banco Royal Charlotte) he will approach in deep water.

Inscription on Cantino map:

> The Vera Cruz † called by name, the which Pedralvares Cabral nobleman of the household of the King of Portugal found, and he discovered it going as Captain General of fourteen ships that the said king ordered to Calicut, and on the route thither he fell in with this land which they believe to be mainland, and in which there are many people who all go naked men and women as their mothers bore them, and they are more white than dark and they wear their hair very smooth. This land was discovered in 1500.

Facsimile in T. O. Marcondes de Souza, p. 160. A world map by Hieronimus Marinus dated Venice, 1511 (British Museum facsimile from original in Brazil Foreign Ministry) is the earliest to show name BRASIL, right on the bulge. "Munich-Portuguese" map of 1519 calls it Brazil, "from the wood which is brought thence in quantities."

In 1968, fifth centenary of Cabral's birth, the Agência-Geral do Ultramar in Lisbon brought out *Os Sete Únicos Documentos de 1500 Conservados em Lisbon Referentes à Viagem de Pedro Álvares Cabral*. These, for the most part, are those already translated by Greenlee; but the comments of the editors, Captain Fontoura da Costa and Dr. António Baião, and those of Professor Pereira da Silva on Mestre João's Letter on navigation and the stars, are new and important.

The three-volume folio *Historia da Colonização Portuguesa do Brasil* (Porto, 1921–24) contains many chapters on Cabral and those who followed, and is illustrated liberally. Helio Vianna, *Historia do Brasil* (8th ed., Vol. I, São Paulo, 1970), has an informing chapter on the logwood industry and era.

In December or early January 1928–29, after being sighted from Tristan da Cunha headed for the Cape, Danish training barque *København* disappeared without a trace, and with loss of all 59 men and boys on board. Alan Villiers, *Posted Missing* (New York, 1956), pp. 205–7.

No portrait of Cabral earlier than the nineteenth century exists, and no contemporary has told us anything about his physique or disposition.

✳ XI ✳

Columbus's Fourth Voyage

1502-1504

The "High Voyage"

We left Columbus in Spain in early 1502, forlornly watching the fleet of Governor Ovando, his successor, depart for Santo Domingo. He felt that the only thing left for him to do, now that he had been deprived of all governmental privileges, was to embark on a new voyage. Hence his Fourth, and last, Voyage to America, a highly interesting one to sailors. The Admiral evidently thought so too, as he always referred to it as *El Alto Viaje*.

Almost fifty-one years old at the start and fifty-three when he returned, the Admiral was already an old man by the standards of the day, but on this voyage he showed the highest qualities of seamanship, courage, and fitness to command. Unfortunately, by sailing out into the blue he did not dispense with court influence and administrative problems. The treasurer of Castile, on whom he depended for the seamen's pay, insisted on his taking two Porras brothers, one as captain of a caravel and the other as crown comptroller, since their sister was his mistress. An odd way of pleasing a mistress; but that is what she and the "boys" wanted, and they would have returned as heads of the expedition had the Columbus brothers not been a little too much for them.

The celerity with which the Admiral got away this time, and the ample provision made for his fleet, strongly suggest a desire on the part of Ferdinand and Isabella to get rid of him. He asked for the fleet on 26 February 1502; the Sovereigns authorized it on 14 March, and ordered him to make all convenient speed westward, "since the present season is very good for navigation" (which it was not!). He actually organized an expedition of four caravels in a little more than two weeks.

The main object of this voyage was to find a strait between Cuba (still assumed to be a promontory of China) and the continent discovered in 1498. As we have seen, Ojeda, Bastidas, and others had pushed along the Spanish Main as far as the Gulf of Urabá or Darien; but the shores and waters of the Caribbean west of a line drawn from Darien to Bahia Cortés, Cuba, including the entire Gulf of Mexico, were still unexplored by Europeans. Here, Columbus believed, was the key to the great geographical riddle: the relation of his discoveries to Asia. Here he expected to find the strait through which Marco Polo had sailed from China into the Indian Ocean. And the Sovereigns gave him a letter of introduction to Vasco da Gama, outward bound on his second voyage to India around the Cape of Good Hope, in the hope that the two would meet somewhere in the Indian Ocean! Everyone still regarded *the* Ocean Sea as one and indivisible, and the "great sea of India" as a mere bay of it, like the Mediterranean, which would be readily accessible from Europe if only you could find an opening in the western Caribbean.

The Admiral had hoped to have built for him some bergantinas, shoal-draft lateeners with banks of oars, which would make it possible to sail to windward, up rivers, and against a contrary current—but there was no time for that. He had to take what ships he could get, and they were not too bad. Each of his four caravels was square-rigged with small main topsails, and of about the same burthen as *Niña*. Columbus and his son Ferdinand sailed in the largest (70 tuns), the name of which we do not know. He always referred to her as *La Capitana*, the flagship. Diego Tristán, who had been with the Admiral on his Second Voyage, served as her captain. She carried a crew of two officers, 14 able seamen, 20 boys, and 7 petty officers, including trumpeters, presumably to provide a dignified entrance for the Admiral to Oriental ports. The second vessel of this fleet, called *La Gallega* (the Galician), mounted a bonaventure mizzen, a tiny fourth mast stepped on the taffrail like the jigger of a modern yawl. Pedro de Terreros, the only man who is known to have sailed in all four of Columbus's voyages, commanded her; and Juan Quintero, her owner, shipped as master. She carried a boatswain, 9 able seamen, 14 gromets, and one gentleman volunteer. Next in burthen came *Santiago de Palos,* nicknamed *Bermuda* after her owner and master Francisco Bermúdez. Her captain was the lord treasurer's crony Francisco Porras, whose brother Diego sailed with him as comptroller. Since this precious pair had never been to sea, Columbus fortunately insisted on brother Bartholomew's sailing in *Bermuda* as a passenger, with orders to take command in time of stress, when the Porras brothers cowered below. She carried 11 able seamen and a boatswain, 6 gentlemen volunteers, 12 boys, and 4 petty officers. Smallest of the fleet, measuring about 50 tuns, was *Vizcaina* (the Biscayan), commanded by Bartolomeo Fieschi, scion of a leading Genoese family which had befriended the Colombos in times past. She carried a boatswain, 3 gentlemen, 8 able seamen, 10 boys, and the fleet chaplain Fray Alejandro.

All except the Columbus family were on the royal payroll; the captains touched 4000 maravedis (about $27 in gold) a month; able seamen were paid one-quarter of that, and apprentice seamen about $5. Everyone received an unusual advance of six months' pay, and those who survived the voyage had a pot of money coming to them. Collecting it, of course, was another matter.

Comparing the crew list with that of the First Voyage, the only other that we have, one notes the large number of boys between 12 and 18 years old carried in this Fourth Voyage. The Admiral had evidently learned that on a voyage of discovery and high adventure, young fellows make better seamen and obey orders more briskly than old shellbacks who grumble and growl. "What's the idea? Old Captain So-and-So didn't do it that way!" and declare that the new islands are not worth a ducat apiece, and hanker after the fleshpots of Marseilles, Naples, and Lisbon.

The fleet sailed from Seville, 3 April 1502, and on the way down river careened at Casa de Viejo to cleanse the ships' bottoms and pay them with pitch to discourage teredos. On this voyage, unfortunately, the teredos seemed to like pitch; they ate right through it and, within a few months, had riddled the planking. From the river mouth the caravels proceeded to Cadiz, where Columbus and his twelve-year-old son Ferdinand came on board.

At Cadiz the fleet was delayed by foul winds until 11 May, when it sailed with a favoring northerly. After a courtesy call at Arzila on the coast of Morocco, where the Portuguese were reportedly hard-pressed by the Moors, the fleet reached Las Palmas on 20 May and sailed from the Grand Canary on the 25th. "West and by South," the same course as the Second Voyage, was set by the Admiral. We have no details of the ocean passage, completed in only 21 days, a middle-Atlantic record for many years. On 15 June they made landfall on Martinique, next island south of Dominica, tarried there three days for rest and refreshment (apparently undisturbed by Caribs or Amazons), and then ranged the chain of Antilles discovered on the Second Voyage.

On 29 June the Admiral hove-to in the roadstead off the Ozama River mouth, Santo Domingo. He had been forbidden by the Sovereigns to visit his viceroyalty lest he and Ovando run afoul of each other; but the Admiral had several good excuses, if not reasons, to look in at his former capital. He knew that Ovando was about to dispatch a fleet home and that a hurricane was making up, and he wished to take refuge. Columbus had already experienced two hurricanes and recognized the portents only too well. An oily swell rolled in from the southeast, veiled cirrus clouds tore along through the upper air, light gusty winds played over the surface of the water, low-pressure twinges were felt in his arthritic joints, and (a sign unknown to modern hydrographers) various denizens of the deep such as seal and manatee gamboled on the surface in large numbers. So, heaving-to in the outer roadstead, the Admiral sent Captain Terreros ashore with a note to Governor Ovando, predicting a hurricane within two days and requesting permission to take refuge there, and begging the governor to keep all ships in port and double their mooring lines. Ovando had the folly not only to disregard both warning and request but to read the Admiral's note aloud with sarcastic comments to his heelers, who roared with laughter over this "soothsayer" who pretended to be able to predict the winds. And the great fleet proceeded to sea as the governor had planned.

Retribution came swiftly. Ovando's fleet had just rounded into

Mona Passage with the harborless southeastern coast of Hispaniola on the port hand, when the hurricane burst upon it from the northeast. Ships foundered at sea or were driven onto the lee shore and destroyed; and among those that went down with all hands was the flagship commanded by Antonio de Torres, carrying Bobadilla as passenger and a cargo estimated at over half a million dollars in gold. Nineteen ships sank with all hands, six others were lost but left a few survivors, and four scudded safely around Saona into Santo Domingo, arriving in a sinking condition. The only ship that got through to Spain was the smallest, named *Aguja*, bearing Columbus's agent Carvajal with gold belonging to the Admiral which he had forced Bobadilla to disgorge.

Denied shelter at Santo Domingo, the Admiral sought it off the mouth of the Rio Jaina, a short distance to the westward. For he rightly estimated that the hurricane would pass through the Mona Passage and along the north coast of Hispaniola, so that the wind would blow off the southern shore, affording a lee to his ships. As night closed in, the north wind reached the height of its fury, probably a hundred miles per hour. The three smaller caravels parted their cables and drove out to sea, but were well handled (*Bermuda* by Bartholomew Columbus, as Captain Porras took to his bunk) and escaped with only superficial damage. The Admiral had every bit of ironmongery on board frapped to *Capitana*'s cables, and she rode it out. As he remarked in a letter home, "What man ever born, not excepting Job, would not have died of despair when in such weather, seeking safety for son, brother, shipmates and myself, we were forbidden the land and the harbor that I, by God's will and sweating blood, won for Spain!"

By God's will and good seamanship his little fleet came through and made rendezvous in the landlocked harbor of Puerto Viejo de Azua, some fifty miles to the west of Santo Domingo. Columbus and his captains could not have done better if they had received storm warnings by radio. One ship's boat and three anchors were the only serious losses.

After resting a week or ten days at Azua, they put to sea again, steering southwest to the Alta Vela Channel and then west across the Windward Passage, and along the south shore of Jamaica; thence northwest to a cay, probably Cayo Largo off the south coast of Cuba.

Bonacca Island. Señora Obregón photo.

On 27 July the wind turned northeast and the fleet crossed the Caribbean, 360 miles wide at this point, in three days. When the wind moderated, a lookout sighted a group of islands off the coast of Honduras.

At Bonacca or Guanaja, first of the lofty, highly colored, and spectacular Bay Islands, where the Spaniards anchored, they encountered the biggest native canoe any of them had seen: "Long as a galley," beamy, with a cabin amidships for passengers. She carried cotton cloth, copper implements and crucibles for smelting ore, gourds full of beer made from the hubo fruit, and cacao beans which the Jicaque Indians of Honduras used, even recently, as currency. The canoe had come from the mainland, and after trading with the Bay Islands, was bound for Coronel Island off the Yucatan coast, a native emporium for Caribbean traffic. Columbus forcibly detained the skipper, whom he renamed Juan Pérez, as guide and interpreter.

After crossing the thirty-mile strait to Cape Honduras (now called Punta Castilla) on the mainland, the fleet anchored off the site of Trujillo, later founded by Cortés. Here began in earnest the Admiral's search for *the* strait. Should he turn west or east? West would be easier going but hard to get back from against the prevailing wind. So eastward he turned, and that let him in for a long and distressing beat to windward lasting twenty-eight days, from Rio Romano to Cape Gracias a Dios.

> It was one continual rain, thunder and lightning [wrote Columbus]. The ships lay exposed to the weather, with sails torn, and anchors, rigging, cables, boats and many of the stores lost; the people, exhausted and so down in the mouth that they were all the time making vows to be good, to go on pilgrimages and all that; yea; even hearing one another's confessions! Other tempests I have seen, but none that lasted so long or so grim as this. Many old hands whom we looked on as stout fellows lost their courage. What griped me most were the sufferings of my son; to think that so young a lad, only thirteen, should go through so much. But Our Lord lent him such courage that he even heartened the rest, and he worked as though he had been to sea all of a long life. That comforted me. I was sick and many times lay at death's door, but gave orders from a doghouse that the people clapped together for me on the poop deck. My brother was in the worst of the ships, the crank one, and I felt terribly having persuaded him to come against his will.

The wind blew steadily from the east, and the current too ran counter to their course. Every morning the caravels had to weigh anchor, make sail, and claw off shore on the starboard tack, often in heavy rain. At noon the fleet wore to the port tack, stood inshore again, and at sundown anchored off a sodden coast in an open road-stead, the caravels pitching and tossing all night, and the crew fighting mosquitoes from the swamps. Some days they gained a few miles; on others they fetched up opposite the same grove of mangroves off which they had spent the previous night. The average distance made good was only six miles a day. But the Admiral had to be getting on; he dared not tarry for a fair wind, nor to stand out to sea lest he miss the strait. It was the most exhausting sail of his entire career.

At last, on 14 September 1502, the fleet doubled a cape that the Admiral named *Gracias a Dios* (Thanks be to God). Since the land here trended southward, this marked the end of his long dead-beat; now they were able to jog along on the port tack a safe distance from shore.

A Nicaraguan beach, Cape Gracias a Dios in distance. Señora Obregón photo.

They anchored off the Rio Grande de Nicaragua, 120 miles south of Gracias a Dios, to obtain wood and water; Columbus sent a boat over the bar safely, but on the return it was capsized and two sailors were drowned, so the Admiral named this place *Rio de los Desastres*. Off its mouth today there is bar which the chart says is dangerous, and it certainly looks so from the air. They passed at night at Rio San Juan del Norte, missing a chance to sail up to Lake Nicaragua within fifteen miles of the Pacific, and entered a region that the Indians called Cariai, the present Costa Rica.

Ten days were passed at anchor behind Uvita Islet, off the present Puerto Limón. Here they had friendly though somewhat aloof relations with the local Talamanca Indians. The usual roles were reversed, the natives eager to do business and the Spaniards somewhat coy. First, the Indians swam out to the caravels with a line of cotton shirts and ornaments of *guanin*, the gold and copper alloy that Columbus had found in Paria on the Third Voyage. Evidently *guanin* did not sell in Spain, for Columbus would have none of it, but gave the would-

243

be traders some presents to take ashore. Next, to break down "sales resistance," the Indians sent on board two virgins, one about eight and the other about fourteen years old. "They showed great fortitude," recorded Ferdinand (who was then about the same age as the elder), "gave no signs of grief or fear but always looked cheerful and modest. The Admiral . . . had them clothed and fed and had them sent ashore." (Columbus, on the contrary, wrote that they were immodest hussies.) Spanish continence astonished the natives; and when, next day, Bartholomew went ashore to take formal possession, the Indians took his writing materials (ink in a cow's horn, quill pen and paper) to be magical apparatus, and tossed brown powder into the air as "good joss" to counteract these apparently sexless sorcerers from Spain.

To reconnoiter this part of Costa Rica, Columbus sent an armed party upcountry. They reported an abundance of game—deer, puma, and the turkey-like currosow bird. And they brought back as a pet a spider monkey which one of the crossbowmen had wounded. In the meantime, the Indians at Puerto Limón had presented the Admiral with a pair of peccaries, one of which he kept. It was so fierce and aggressive that his Irish wolfhound remained below deck as long as the porker was on board. Piggy met his match, however, in the spider monkey which, wounded though it was, coiled its tail around the peccary's snout, seized him by the nape of the neck, and bit him until he screamed with pain. This "novel and pretty sport," as Columbus called it, he wrote about in full detail to the Sovereigns. Ferdinand, at least, would have enjoyed it.

On 5 October the search for the strait was renewed, and toward evening Columbus believed that he had found it in a channel, the Boca del Dragón, that leads into a great bay now named *Almirante* after him. Once inside, he found Indians wearing on their breasts "mirrors," disks of fine gold. For the standard price of three hawks' bells, value about a penny, the Spaniards were able to buy a gold disk worth ten ducats, about twenty-five dollars.

Having allowed "Juan Pérez" to go home, the Spaniards from now on had no interpreter. So, when Columbus asked in sign language for a strait to a wide ocean, the Indians waved him on to a narrow passage (now Split Hill Channel) that led out of the lagoon. The caravels sailed through this channel, so narrow that their yards brushed

Split Hill Channel in foreground. Columbus sailed through, but not to Indian Ocean. Señora Obregón photo.

the trees, and were rewarded by the sight of a great expanse of water. But, alas, there were mountains on every side; this was not the Indian Ocean but Chiriqui lagoon.

For ten days the fleet idled about the shores of this lagoon, the Guaymi Indians plying a brisk trade in gold disks and bird-shaped amulets which the Spaniards called eagles. Columbus learned from them that he was on an isthmus between two seas, but a high cordillera barred his way. He also picked up from the Indians, or misunderstood them to say, that the Ganges River was only ten days' sail away. Referring to his Bible, the Admiral inferred that this region was the Ophir of 2 Chronicles viii. 18, whence the servants of Hiram brought 450 talents of gold to Solomon. Apparently he also satisfied himself that no strait existed, since from now on he concentrated on gathering gold and establishing a trading post.

On 17 October 1502, a day of westerly wind, the fleet left Chiriqui lagoon by the eastward channel, passed a little shield-shaped island that the Admiral named *El Escudo,* and sailed along Miskito Gulf, working its way east against the trades. From here to Limón Bay (now the Caribbean entrance to the Panama Canal), a distance of over 125 miles, there are no harbors except where a river mouth has built up a bar over which only a canoe can enter, and only when the bar is not breaking. Because of this, and also because the Indians made menacing gestures (howling, spitting, beating drums, blowing conch-shell trumpets, and brandishing spears) at the roadsteads where he anchored, Columbus pressed forward as fast as westerly winds would take him, hoping to find a more hospitable spot for a trading post. On 2 November the four caravels entered a fine harbor which he named *Puerto Bello* and is still so called; during the Spanish colonial regime it became a thriving city at the northern end of the trans-isthmian mule track.

Had Columbus decided to locate there, his garrison would certainly have heard of the Isthmus of Panama and obtained a glimpse of the Pacific Ocean ten years before Balboa did. But the local Indians, though friendly, could not be understood. The Admiral stayed less than a week, obtained provisions and cotton, and continued his voyage on 9 November, when the wind forced them back several miles to a harbor which Columbus named *Puerto de Bastimentos*, Harbor of Provisions. Ten years later, Diego de Nicuesa renamed it *Nombre de Dios* and founded a town which long shared the transit trade with Puerto Bello, and so was sacked by Francis Drake. There the Columbus fleet remained twelve days, making minor repairs while the wind stayed in the east. Again, the Admiral missed a chance to start a settlement at a suitable site.

Their next stop was at a tiny harbor which they called *El Puerto del Retrete*, now called Escribanos. It was so small that the four caravels had to tie up alongside the banks, as to a wharf. This gave the men a chance to sneak off to Indian villages and do private trading with a gun, and that made trouble. Indians gathered on the beach and made threatening gestures, and the Admiral had to mow down a few with gunfire before the rest would disperse.

Tired of waiting for the wind to change, Columbus now decided to sail back to Veragua and take measures to obtain more of the gold which the natives displayed so abundantly in their personal jewelry. On 5 December the fleet returned to Puerto Bello. Next day the wind whipped around into the west again. For a month, the caravels were batted back and forth. The current always changed with the wind;

it was no use trying to buck it. The weather was unusually foul. "I don't say it rained," recorded Columbus, "because it was like another deluge," with thunder and lightning whenever the wind changed. Once the fleet was threatened by a tremendous waterspout, but it passed harmlessly after the Admiral had exorcised it by reading aloud from the Gospel according to St. John the account of that famous tempest on the Sea of Galilee concluding, "It is I: be not afraid." Then, clasping the Bible in his left hand, with drawn sword he traced a cross in the sky and a circle around the fleet. That night *Vizcaína* lost sight of her consorts but found them again after three very dark, tempestuous days. The people were so worn out, said the Admiral, that they longed for death to end their sufferings. Then came two days of calm, during which great schools of shark lashed around the caravels; many were taken and some eaten, as provisions were running low. Ferdinand remembered that the hardtack had become so full of weevils that some men waited for darkness to eat a porridge made of it, but others did not even trouble to wait, "because they might lose their supper had they been so nice."

Two days before Christmas, the fleet put in at the present harbor of Cristóbal, Panama Canal Zone, and there kept Christmas and New Year's Day 1503, very miserably, riding at anchor off the site of the present-day Coco Solo naval base. Here, had he only known it, Columbus was within a few miles of solving the riddle of the strait. He might have gone up the Chagres in borrowed Indian canoes. From the head of navigation he would have been only twelve miles by land from the Pacific Ocean. But he and his men were so beaten down by their long buffeting, so drained of energy and enterprise, and so incapable of communicating with the natives, that they did nothing. Thus Columbus missed by a few miles the most important geographical discovery he could have made on the High Voyage.

Santa Maria de Belén

Sailing back, westward along the inhospitable coast of Veragua, Columbus searched for a likely place to found a trading post which would draw on the abundant gold of that region. On 6 January he anchored off the mouth of a river that he named *Belén* (Bethlehem) because it was Epiphany, the Feast of the Three Kings who brought gifts of gold, frankincense and myrrh, to the infant Jesus. A good omen! Sounding from the boats, he found seven feet of water over the bar and towed his caravels inside, where the river forms a deep basin. They were just in time, as next day another storm worked up a heavy sea which broke on the river bar.

The coastal plain here narrows to a few hundred yards' width, and behind it rises rugged, broken country covered by an impenetrable rain forest; and behind that, mountains whose summits are usually concealed by clouds. The coast consists of long sand beaches separated by rocky bluffs. It is a dangerous place to anchor, and in most places impossible to land from small boats. Rainfall is so excessive that agriculture on any large scale is unprofitable. The few people who live along that shore today have no means of communication with the outside world except by dugout canoes, which can be launched only when the sea is exceptionally calm. We on the Harvard Columbus Expedition found this the most difficult region of all discovered by the Admiral, to examine. Only through the co-operation of the Panama government, providing us with a diesel-powered trading sloop and a good native pilot, did we manage to effect a landing (after sundry tumblings in the surf) at the Rio Belén.

A few days after the Feast of the Epiphany, Bartholomew Columbus took the ships' boats westward along the coast and rowed up the next river (the Veragua) toward the seat of a cacique known as the Quibián. Dignified but friendly, the Quibián came downstream with a fleet of canoes to greet the visitors, and next day called on the Admiral in *Capitana*.

Veragua has one of the heaviest rainfalls in the world, and the ground is so thoroughly soaked that every storm starts a freshet. Columbus experienced this on 24 January 1503. Following a rainstorm in the mountains, a torrent roared down on the caravels in the Belén mooring basin. *Capitana* dragged, fouled *Gallega*, and carried away her bonaventure mizzen; and only by smart work with the ground tackle were both vessels kept from broaching on the bar. Two weeks of rain and flood followed; it was not until 6 February that the sea was calm enough for the boats to come out. Bartholomew then made a return visit to the Quibián and marched upcountry along an Indian trail with native guides. In one day, with no other implements but their knives, the Spaniards collected about ten dollars' worth of gold apiece.

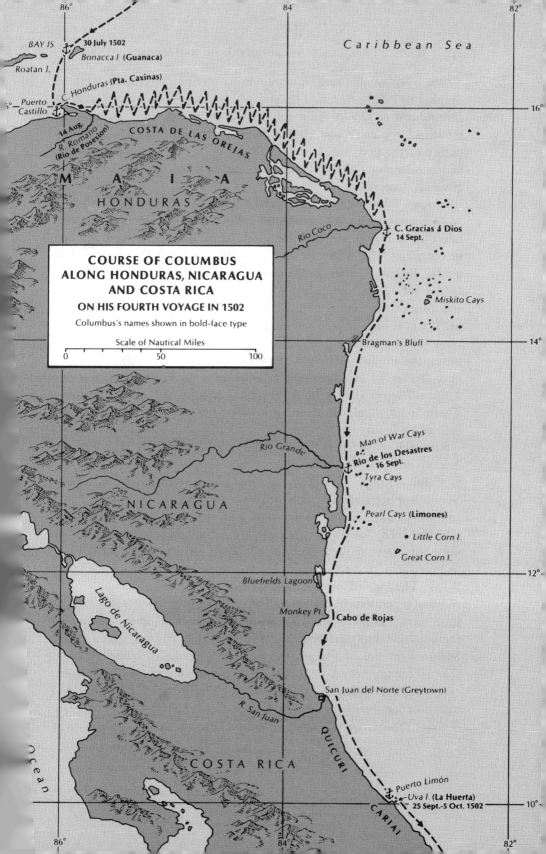

86°

84°

82°

BAY IS.
30 July 1502
Bonacca I. (Guanaca)

Caribbean Sea

Roatan I.

C. Honduras (Pta. Caxinas)

Puerto
Castillo

16°

14 Aug.
R. Romano
(Rio de Posesion)

COSTA DE LAS OREJAS

M   A   I   A

HONDURAS

Rio Coco

C. Gracias á Dios
14 Sept.

Miskito Cays

**COURSE OF COLUMBUS
ALONG HONDURAS, NICARAGUA
AND COSTA RICA**

ON HIS FOURTH VOYAGE IN 1502

Columbus's names shown in bold-face type

Scale of Nautical Miles

0   50   100

Bragman's Bluff

14°

Rio Grande

Man of War Cays

Rio de los Desastres
16 Sept.

Tyra Cays

NICARAGUA

Pearl Cays (**Limones**)

• Little Corn I.

Great Corn I.

12°

Lago de Nicaragua

Bluefields Lagoon

Monkey Pt.

Cabo de Rojas

San Juan del Norte (Greytown)

R. San Juan

Ocean

COSTA RICA

QUICURI

Puerto Limón
Uva I. (**La Huerta**)
25 Sept.-5 Oct. 1502

CARIAI

10°

86°

84°

82°

Discovery of this auriferous region so pleased the Admiral that he decided to build a fortified trading post at Belén, leave his brother in charge, and return to Spain for reinforcements. A little hill near the mouth of the river was chosen for the site, and the men began to construct the post, which Columbus named *Santa Maria de Belén*. He had chosen about the worst spot on the coast of Central America to establish a beachhead.

In 1940, when we were ranging this coast to check up on Columbus, we encountered an old prospector who explained why Veragua had never been really exploited for gold. Years before, he went up one of the rivers with a partner and an Indian guide. "Where do we find gold?" he asked, after paddling many miles. "Right here!" said the Indian, who pulled out a clasp knife, dug some clay from the river bank and panned out plenty of gold grains! The prospector and his partner began at once to plan how to spend their first million dollars. They returned to the nearest town for supplies and lumber and built sluice boxes, the product of which should have made them rich. But in the next freshet all this gear was washed into the Caribbean. That has happened again and again during the last four and a half centuries. There is still "gold in them thar hills," but only the Indians know how to get it out.

Rio Belén now fell so low that the caravels could not cross the bar. And at this juncture, when they were trapped inside, there came the inevitable change of attitude on the part of the Guaymi Indians. Sailors had been sneaking off by twos and threes to trade with a gun and get women. The Quibián could put up with a good deal of that if he believed that his importunate visitors would shortly depart; but since they now showed every intention of settling down, he decided to give them "the treatment." He sent men in canoes to reconnoiter Belén. They acted so suspiciously that Diego Méndez, one of the Admiral's gentlemen volunteers, offered to row along the coast to learn what was going on. After a few miles he came upon a camp of a thousand howling warriors. Méndez, with that amazing nerve of the Spaniard in face of danger, stepped ashore alone to confront them; then, returning to his boat, kept just out of arrow range all night, observing the Indians' movements. They, realizing that surprise had been lost, retreated to the Quibían's village. Méndez followed them thither, and in the midst of a horrible uproar, coolly pulled out a barber's kit and had his hair cut by his companion, Rodrigo de Escobar. This not only stopped the yelling but so intrigued the Quibián that he ordered his hair to be trimmed. Méndez did so and presented him with the shears, mirror, and comb, after which the Spaniards were allowed to return in peace.

Columbus should now have taken the hint that his trading post would be untenable in the face of the hostility of thousands of Indians who could sneak up under cover of the jungle and overwhelm it. Instead, he made another bad decision—to seize the Quibián and hold him as hostage for his people's good behavior. The cacique and about thirty others were ambushed by an armed party of Spaniards and carried down river. But the Quibián broke his bonds, escaped, and raised his people against the intruders.

In the meantime, seamen were towing three of the four caravels over the bar, intending to leave behind *Gallega* as a floating fortress for the use of Bartholomew and the Belén garrison. On 6 April, while farewells were being said and only twenty men and the Irish wolf-hound were guarding the fort, it was attacked by hundreds of Indians armed with bows and arrows and spears. They were beaten off, largely through the rough work of the hound. But the Indians promptly got their revenge by killing Captain Diego Tristán of *Capitana* who, with a boat party, insisted on carrying out orders issued by the Admiral before the fight started, to fill the flagship's water casks upstream. Only one Spaniard of the boat party escaped, and ten were killed. Ferdinand contrasts this Spaniard's stolid courage with that of Bastiano, an Italian member of the garrison. Méndez caught him running away from the fight and ordered him "About face!" to which Bastiano replied, "Let me go, you devil! I am going to save myself!" and did.

The Admiral, ill with malaria, remained alone on board *Capitana* anchored outside the bar; all his crew had gone ashore to help the garrison. He climbed to the main top and shouted to the men to return, but they could not hear his voice above the hideous screams of the Indians. He became delirious, saw visions, and heard a voice which he believed to be that of God Almighty reminding him that He had done as much for Columbus as for Moses and David, that his tribulations were "written on tablets of marble," and that he was to fear not but trust Him.

Rio Belén. Santa Maria de Belén was on the left-hand hill.

Here was a tough situation. Three caravels were lying in the open roadstead outside the bar, at the mercy of any storm that might blow up; one (*Gallega*), which the Admiral intended to leave for the garrison's use, lay trapped inside. Indians continued to prowl about the settlement, raising horrid whoops and yells; and there were no hostages for their good behavior, since those imprisoned on board the flagship either escaped or hanged themselves in the hold. Columbus now realized that he had made the Indians implacable enemies and that the trading post must be evacuated or the garrison would meet the fate of Navidad. Having only one small boat left, and that too deep to get over the bar, Columbus had to send orders to his brother by a stout swimmer, Pedro de Ledesma. He returned with Bartholomew's urgent request that the garrison be evacuated promptly, and Columbus consented. Diego Méndez built a raft upon which all the Spaniards ashore, with most of their stores and gear, were lightered across the bar.

Gallega was abandoned, and Santa Maria de Belén reverted to wilderness.

No subsequent attempt to found a European settlement on that coast ever succeeded. The descendants of the Guaymi have retreated to the interior, and except for a few clearings where a handful of half-breeds live in poverty, the coast of Veragua is as wild, wet, and forbiddingly beautiful as when Columbus landed there on the Feast of the Three Kings in 1503.

Marooned in Jamaica

On Easter Sunday, 16 April 1503, *Capitana*, *Bermuda*, and *Vizcaina* departed Belén roads, hoping to make Santo Domingo by Whitsuntide. Columbus, estimating his longitude to be many degrees west of the meridian of Hispaniola, and knowing by experience that it was almost

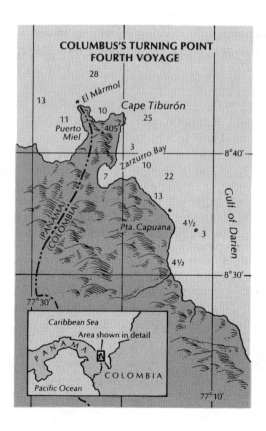

impossible to beat against the easterly trades and the equatorial currents, planned to edge along the coast by working the land breeze and anchoring in bad weather. Then, when he had reached an estimated point due south of Hispaniola, to fetch Santo Domingo on the starboard tack. This sensible decision caused murmurings among the men because the pilots, wrong as usual, estimated that they were already due south of Santo Domingo, or even Puerto Rico. And the three caravels were riddled with teredos. Columbus, being blamed for this, answered thus in his report to the Sovereigns:—

"Let those who are fond of blaming and finding fault, while they sit safely at home, ask, 'Why did you not do thus and so?' I wish they were on this voyage; I well believe that another voyage of a different kind awaits them, or our faith is naught."

In other words, to hell with them!

As the coastwise voyage progressed, all hands were kept busy at the pumps or bailing with buckets and kettles. Nevertheless, *Vizcaina* had to be abandoned in a hopelessly leaky condition at Puerto Bello, where her carcass was found by Nicuesa in 1509. Her crew was divided between *Capitana* and *Bermuda*. These two crawled along into the Gulf of San Blas. All hands were too busy trying to keep afloat to admire the scenery, where a jagged cordillera rises behind gleaming white beaches and a tropical rain forest of mahogany, ebony, and other hard woods. Their foliage makes a glossy-leaved canopy above which an occasional giant of the forest thrusts a top bursting with pink or orange blossoms, as though a torch were being held up from the dark jungle. And the Cuna Cuna or San Blas Indians have retained their integrity and independence to this day.

On 1 May the two caravels reached a headland that Columbus named *El Mármol*, the Marble Cape, because of conspicuous white strata on the cliffs. In that aspect it is unique on this coast, and so has enabled Señor Obregón and myself to identify it positively as Cape Tiburón, on which a small monument marks the boundary between the republics of Colombia and Panama. As the coast here trends southeast into the Gulf of Darien, the pilots and captains, hopefully figuring that they were already east of Guadeloupe, ganged up on Columbus and practically forced him to leave the coast and strike northward. Actually they were on the meridian of Kingston, Jamaica, and about

El Mármol (Cape Tiburón) with its white strata. Señora Obregón photo.

900 miles west of Guadeloupe! The Admiral was so beaten down by arthritis, malaria, and apparent failure that he gave in.

So, on May Day 1503, worm-eaten *Capitana* and riddled *Bermuda* stood northward, sailing as close to the wind as possible, but continually set to leeward by the current. Ten days later they passed the Little Cayman island northwest of Jamaica, and on the 12th made a most unwelcome landfall on the Cuban archipelago which Columbus had formerly named the Queen's Garden. "Full of hunger and trouble," as Ferdinand records, the caravels dropped anchor in a little harbor with poor holding ground at Cayo Breton. The people had "nothing to eat but hardtack and a little oil and vinegar, exhausted by

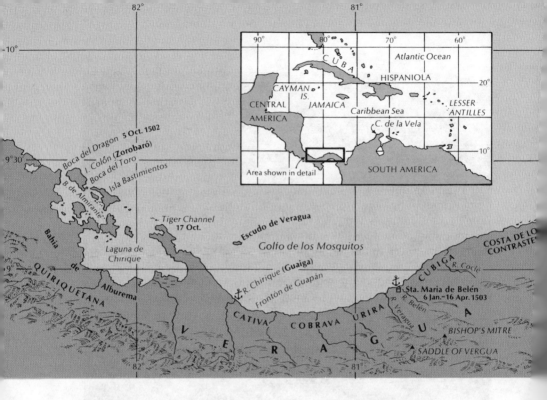

working three pumps day and night because the vessels were ready to sink from the multitude of worms that had bored into them." On top of that, one of the night thunderstorms for which this coast is notorious burst upon them, causing *Bermuda* to part her cable and foul *Capitana*. The flagship passed her a line, and *Capitana*'s one remaining anchor fortunately held them both.

After six days the wind moderated and the caravels, with planking "like a honeycomb" and the sailors "spiritless and desperate," continued to struggle eastward along the Cuban coast. By about 10 June 1503 when they were still west of Santiago, Columbus decided that the only way to save their lives was to stand out to sea on the port tack, hoping for a favorable slant that would take them across Windward Passage to Hispaniola. But when the caravels had reached a point estimated to be about a hundred miles from Cape Tiburón, the water gained on *Bermuda* at so alarming a rate that the Admiral ordered both caravels to square away for Jamaica. Since wooden ships labor less and sail faster with the wind aft, his decision to seek refuge in Jamaica saved their lives.

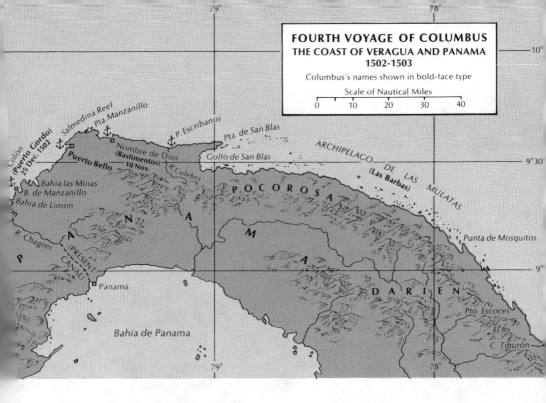

FOURTH VOYAGE OF COLUMBUS
THE COAST OF VERAGUA AND PANAMA
1502-1503

Columbus's names shown in bold-face type

Scale of Nautical Miles

0   10   20   30   40

On 25 June the wretched vessels, their decks almost awash, entered St. Ann's Bay, Jamaica, which Columbus had named *Santa Gloria* on the Second Voyage. (Here Spain founded her first Jamaican settlement, in 1509.) He ran them aground side by side on a sand beach, and shored them up to keep them on an even keel. High tides rose almost to their decks, upon which palm-thatched cabins were built for the 116 people.

And there they stayed for a year.

These Spaniards marooned on Jamaica were fairly well situated for defense; the ships' hulks made a dry home and no mean fortress. A large and friendly Indian village lay nearby. Columbus, who knew by bitter experience that the natives would not long remain friendly if his people were allowed to mingle with them, allowed nobody to go ashore without his permission.

The first thing that needed attention was food. Diego Méndez and three men set forth on a foraging expedition. They traveled almost to the east end of the island, purchased a dugout canoe, loaded it with native provisions, and returned to Santa Gloria in triumph; and, to en-

257

Santa Gloria (St. Ann's Bay), Jamaica, where Columbus spent a year. The clearing at right center indicates the excavation for Nueva Sevilla, the first Spanish settlement, founded in 1509.

sure a continuing supply, Méndez drew up a tariff agreement with the neighboring Indians to sell a cake of cassava bread for two glass beads, two of the big rodents called hutia for a lace point, and a great quantity of anything, such as fish or maize, for a hawk's bell. Why these Spaniards and Genoese could not fish for themselves or plant their own cornfields has never been explained; it is clear that if the Indians had not fed them they would have starved to death.

But how to get home? This final resting place of the two caravels commanded a wide sea view, but the chance of any Spanish or other vessel coming there was infinitesimal, since Columbus had broadcasted "no gold in Jamaica." *Capitana* and *Bermuda* were beyond repair. In later voyages we find Spaniards and Englishmen cheerfully constructing bergantinas and pinnaces on any wooded coast; but these crews appear to have been as incapable of building a small vessel as of feeding themselves. So the only possible way to avoid spending the rest of their lives in Jamaica was to send a messenger to Hispaniola.

As usual, everyone said, "Let Diego Méndez do it!" That faithful and indefatigable Spaniard hauled out the big dugout canoe he had purchased, fixed a false keel and washboards, and fitted a mast and sail. On his first attempt he was captured by Indians somewhere near Northeast Point, escaped, and returned to Santa Gloria. On the next he had plenty of assistance. Bartolomeo Fieschi, the Genoese captain of *Bermuda*, undertook to pilot a second canoe with him to Hispaniola, and the Adelantado organized an armed escort in the shape of a fleet of dugouts to protect them in Jamaican waters. At or near Northeast Point, farewells were exchanged and the two canoes pushed out into Windward Passage.

More to-do was made about this canoe trip than about anything else on the High Voyage. In comparison with numerous lifeboat and raft voyages in World War II, it does not seem a particularly long or difficult passage—only 108 miles from island to island, with a break at Navassa 78 miles out; and the month was July, when the trades die down and hurricanes are few. But neither the Spaniards nor these Indians were used to small-boat journeys, and they certainly took this one hard. Each captain had a crew of six Christians and ten Indian paddlers. The first day out was calm and the following night cool, but the natives drank up all their water rations. By the second sunset, one Indian had died of thirst and others were too weak to paddle.

And a third night fell with no sight of land. But when the moon rose, Diego Méndez observed the outline of Navassa Island against its lower limb. They reached the island in about 72 hours from Jamaica, a little better than a mile an hour. On Navassa everyone drank his fill of fresh water (some of the Indians dying of it), a fire was kindled and shell-fish cooked. Now they could see the lofty mountains of Hispaniola, and the following evening they made Cape Tiburón, Haiti. Obtaining fresh Indian paddlers, Méndez and Fieschi continued along the coast to Azua, and thence marched inland to meet Ovando and request succor for the Admiral. It was now August 1503. The governor, by no means grieved at the prospect of Columbus dying in Jamaica, re-fused to send one of his station ships to rescue him and for seven months continued putting off Méndez. Finally, in March 1504, he was allowed to go to Santo Domingo and there charter a vessel.

Columbus and his men had no means of knowing whether their messengers had arrived or had perished. After six months had elapsed and the winter northers began to make their position on the grounded ships uncomfortable, a mutiny formed around the Porras brothers, the political appointees. They spread the word that Columbus was serving out a term of banishment and had no desire or intention to go to Santo Domingo. So, me lads, if you want to get out of this hell hole and back to Spain, join us; we'll grab a few guns, impress some Indian paddlers, and get ourselves to Hispaniola. Let that cursed Genoese and his infatuated followers stay here and rot!

Forty-eight men, about half the total, began the mutiny on the day after New Year's, 1504. Crying the watchword "To Castile! To Castile!" the mutineers piled into ten dugout canoes and started east-ward along the coast, robbing the Indians wherever they called. They had made only about fifteen miles toward Northeast Point when a freshening breeze from the east forced them to put back. All their plunder had to be thrown overboard, and most of the Indian paddlers too. Two more attempts were made to cross, but both failed. So the Porras party abandoned their canoes and trudged back to Santa Gloria, living off the country.

In the meantime those loyal to Columbus were becoming very hungry. The Indians had no surplus stocks of food, and "consumer demand" for beads, lace points, and hawks' bells was exhausted. Moreover, said Ferdinand, every Spaniard consumed enough food for twenty Indians. At this critical juncture, the Admiral pulled his famous eclipse trick. He had an almanac which predicted a total eclipse of the moon on the last night of February 1504. So that day he summoned the nearby caciques and chief men on board stranded *Capitana*, told them that God desired the Indians to supply his people with food, and would presently give them a clear token from Heaven of divine displeasure at their failure to do so. Let them watch the moon that night! The eclipse began at moonrise, and as the blacked-out area increased, the Indians flocked to the ships, howling and lamenting, praying the Admiral to stop it. Columbus retired to his cabin while the eclipse lasted, emerged when he was sure that the total phase was almost over, and announced that he had interceded with the Almighty and promised in their name that they would provide the food the Christians wanted, in return for which God consented to take away the shadow. It worked perfectly, and there was no more food shortage.

At the end of March 1504, more than eight months had elapsed since the canoe messengers had left for Hispaniola, and nothing had been heard of or from them. Suddenly a small caravel sailed in to St. Ann's Bay and anchored near the Spanish camp. It had been sent by Ovando to report on Columbus, especially whether he were still alive. The governor was mean enough to order the captain, Diego de Escobar, not to take anyone to Hispaniola—but she did bring a message from Méndez that he was doing his best to charter a rescue ship. And also a welcome gift—two casks of wine and a side of salt pork.

The morale of the Spaniards hit an all-time low when this caravel disappeared over the horizon. Columbus made advances to the Porras party, knowing that he would be blamed if that pair of brothers did not get home. The Porrases rejected his offers (which included a share of the salt pork), in the hope of suborning the Admiral's men and seizing the stranded boats. They marched on Santa Gloria and the Columbus brothers mustered loyal men to meet them. A pitched battle, fought with knives and swords for want of gunpowder, took place on 29 May, and the loyalists won. The local Indians, who had ringside seats for this fight, doubtless enjoyed seeing the Christians carve each other up. One man had the sole of one foot sliced so neatly that it hung down like a slipper!

Rescue was not much longer in coming. Diego Méndez finally managed to charter a little caravel in Santo Domingo and sent her to

The Morisons and Obregóns home from their flight covering Columbus's Last Voyage.

Jamaica under command of Diego de Salcedo, a loyal servant of the Admiral. He made Santa Gloria in the latter part of June 1504, took everyone on board, and on the 29th departed for Hispaniola. The survivors of the Fourth Voyage, about a hundred strong, had been in Jamaica a year and five days. The little caravel was in poor condition with a sprung mainmast, rotten sails, and a foul bottom; she leaked so badly that they feared she would founder, and it took her six and a half weeks to reach Santo Domingo. There Columbus chartered another vessel and embarked for Spain on 12 September with his brother, his son, and twenty-two others of his company. A majority of the Fourth Voyage survivors elected to remain in Santo Domingo rather than risk another ocean passage. They had had enough work on the pumps to last ten lives.

We know not the route taken by this chartered ship, but the passage of fifty-six days was long and tempestuous, and although the mainmast broke, the Columbus brothers contrived a jury mast out of a spare yard. They finally reached Sanlúcar de Barrameda on 7 November 1504.

The High Voyage was over, after two and a half years at sea, including the year marooned in Jamaica. The most adventurous of the Admiral's four voyages, it was also the most disappointing. He had not discovered the Strait, since none there was; the isthmus that he reported was of no interest to the Sovereigns, and the gold-bearing Veragua that he discovered was unexploitable. But he had done his best. As he wrote to son Diego shortly after his arrival:

"I have served their Highnesses with as great diligence and love as I might have employed to win paradise and more; and if in somewhat I have been wanting, that was impossible, or much beyond my knowledge and strength. Our Lord God in such cases asketh nothing more of men than good will."

Death of the Admiral

After this long and distressing voyage, Columbus expected at least to be summoned to court to tell his story, a favor accorded to almost every captain of an overseas voyage, however insignificant. But the report he had sent home by Diego Méndez did not make a good impression. This *Lettera Rarissima* is rambling and incoherent. It contains some interesting information, together with a superfluity of self-justification and numerous unconvincing "proofs" that he had been sailing along the Malay Peninsula or somewhere in the Far East.

By the time the Admiral reached Seville, 8 or 9 November, the Sovereigns were holding court at Segovia and the Queen was suffering an illness that turned out to be her last. She died on 26 November 1504, greatly to Columbus's grief and loss. Isabella had never sneered at him. She understood what he was trying to do, respected his rights, and protected him from envy and detraction. Ferdinand, too, had supported him, but the Indies were the Queen's overseas kingdom, not his.

The Admiral, now living in a hired house in Seville, was sick in heart and body, but not badly off in this world's goods. He retained a share of the gold acquired on the Fourth Voyage, and Carvajal had brought home a substantial sum for him in *Aguja,* which survived the hurricane of 1502. Two years later, Ovando delivered to him a chest of gold, and he claimed about $180,000 more, still at Hispaniola with his mark on it. But Columbus felt that he had been defrauded and repeatedly besought his son to obtain confirmation of what he called his tithes, eighths, and thirds. The tithe meant 10 per cent of the net exports from all lands that he discovered, as guaranteed by the original contract of 1492. Columbus complained that the government allowed him only a tenth of their fifth of the gold; that is, 2 instead of 10 per cent. The eighth meant the Admiral's guaranteed investment in one-eighth part of the lading of any vessel trading with the Indies. He complained that Bobadilla or Ovando impounded his eighth in sundry cargoes without payment. The third was preposterous. Columbus's grant as Admiral of the Ocean Sea stated that it carried "pre-ëminences and prerogatives . . . in the same manner as . . . the Grand Admiral of Castile." Having ascertained that this Grand Admiral collected 33⅓ per cent tax on trade between Spain and the Canary Islands, Columbus claimed a similar cut on the entire inward and outward trade between Spain and the Indies! Obviously, if the crown had admitted that, little profit would have been left for anyone. As it was, even by collecting a mere 2 per cent of the gold, the Admiral was a rich man according to the standards of his day, and able to leave substantial legacies to his sons.

There is no evidence known to me to indicate that Columbus ever changed his cosmographical ideas, or realized the vast extent of the continent which he had discovered. Peter Martyr very early and Rodrigo Fernández de Santaella (the editor of the first Spanish edition of Marco Polo) in 1503, among others, questioned whether Columbus's Indies were the real Indies, but the Discoverer ignored them. He died believing that his *Otro Mundo* was but an extension of the Malay Peninsula for several hundred miles.

Even on his deathbed Columbus planned to finance a new crusade, and tried to provide for it in his last will and testament. He spent practically nothing on himself or on keeping up appearances, and he always intended to use the profits of his discoveries to recover the Holy Sepulchre from the infidel. But he also concerned himself over collecting pay for his seamen on the Fourth Voyage who had returned with him. Poor men with no other means of support, they now had two years' wages due. Thrice the Admiral begged the treasurer of Castile to pay them off, without result. They even sent a delegation to court to demand their back pay, with letters from the Admiral to his son and to other persons of influence backing them up; but for years nobody received anything.

Columbus now wisely concluded it was hopeless to expect to be sent back to Hispaniola as viceroy and governor; his poor health and "advanced age" of fifty-three made that impracticable. So he concentrated on having the viceroyalty and admiralty conferred on his son Diego. That boy, a clever courtier, had made himself solid by marrying a lady of royal blood, Doña Maria de Toledo. And, three years after his father's death, Diego was appointed governor of Hispaniola and confirmed in some of his father's hereditary titles.

By the spring of 1505 Columbus felt well enough to travel, provided he could ride a mule; a horse's gait was too rough for him. The crown, under pressure by the horse breeders of Andalusia, had forbidden the use of mules for riding, so the Admiral had to beg for a special permit. That the King granted, and in May 1505 the Admiral started on his long journey to the court at Segovia, north of Madrid.

Ferdinand received him graciously and proposed that an arbitrator be appointed to settle his claims against the crown. Columbus refused because the King insisted that his viceroyalty and admiralty be adjudicated as well the pecuniary claims, and he was too proud to arbitrate anything to which he had a clear legal title. The King then hinted that if he would renounce all titles, offices, and revenues, he would be granted a handsome estate with a fat rent roll. Columbus rejected that absolutely. He considered it dishonorable. He would have all or nothing, and nothing he got.

As the court moved to Salamanca and on to Valladolid, the Admiral painfully followed. A year passed, nothing happened, and in the meantime his arthritis grew worse, and he became bedridden. But he felt so certain of justice being done that he made a will providing legacies out of his expected revenues, such as a sinking fund for the crusade, a house in Genoa to be kept open perpetually for his descendants, a chapel in Hispaniola so endowed that daily Masses might be said for his soul forever. In his simplicity he seemed to feel that these pious bequests would attract the attention of the Almighty, who would compel the King to make them practicable.

Almost at the last moment of his life, Columbus had his hopes raised by the arrival in Spain of the Infanta Doña Juana to claim her mother's throne of Castile. She had been at court when Columbus first returned from the Indies, and looked wide-eyed at his artifacts and his Indians, so he hoped that she might confirm the favors granted by her sainted mother. He was too ill to move, so he sent brother Bartholomew to kiss the young sovereign's hands and bespeak her favor.

During Bartholomew's absence, the Admiral failed rapidly. On 19 May 1506 he ratified his final will, creating son Diego his principal heir and commending to his benevolence all other relatives, including Ferdinand's mother Beatriz de Harana. Next day he suddenly grew worse. Both sons, brother Diego, and a few faithful followers such as Diego Méndez and Bartolomeo Fieschi gathered at his bedside. A priest, quickly summoned, said Mass, and everyone in the devoted circle of relatives, friends, and domestics received the sacrament. After the concluding prayer, the Admiral, remembering the last words of his Lord and Saviour, murmured as his own, *In manus tuas, Domine, commendo spiritum meum*—"Into Thy hands, O Lord, I commend my spirit."

A poor enough funeral followed for the "Admiral of the Ocean Sea, Viceroy and Governor of the Islands and Mainlands in the Indies." The court sent no representative; no bishop, no great dignitary attended, and the official chronicle failed to mention either death or funeral. Columbus had the ill fortune to die at the moment when his discoveries were slightly valued and his personal fortunes and expectations were at their lowest ebb.

Little by little, as his life receded into history and the claims of others to be the "real" discoverers of America faded into the background, his great achievements began to be appreciated. Yet it is one of the ironies of history that the Admiral himself died ignorant of what he had really accomplished, still insisting that he had discovered a large number of islands, a province of China, and an "Other World"; but of the vast extent of that Other World, and of the ocean that lay between it and Asia, he had neither knowledge nor suspicion.

Now, more than five hundred years after his birth, when the day of

Columbus's first landfall in the New World is celebrated throughout the length and breadth of the Americas, his fame and reputation may be considered secure, despite the efforts of armchair navigators and nationalist maniacs to denigrate him. A glance at a map of the Caribbean may remind you of what he accomplished: discovery of the Bahamas, Cuba, and Hispaniola on the First Voyage; discovery of the Lesser Antilles, Puerto Rico, Jamaica, and the south coast of Cuba on his Second, as well as founding a permanent European colony; discovery of Trinidad and the Spanish Main, on his Third; and on the Fourth Voyage, Honduras, Nicaragua, Costa Rica, Panama, and Colombia. No navigator in history, not even Magellan, discovered so much territory hitherto unknown to Europeans. None other so effectively translated his north-south experience under the Portuguese flag to the first east-west voyage, across the Atlantic. None other started so many things from which stem the history of the United States, of Canada, and of a score of American republics.

And do not forget that sailing west to the Orient was his idea, pursued relentlessly for six years before he had the means to try it. As a popular jingle of the 400th anniversary put it:

> What if wise men as far back as Ptolemy
> Judged that the earth like an orange was round,
> None of them ever said, "Come along, follow me,
> Sail to the West and the East will be found."

Columbus had his faults, but they were largely the defects of qualities that made him great. These were an unbreakable faith in God and his own destiny as the bearer of the Word to lands beyond the seas; an indomitable will and stubborn persistence despite neglect, poverty, and ridicule. But there was no flaw, no dark side to the most outstanding and essential of all his qualities—seamanship. As a master mariner and navigator, no one in the generation prior to Magellan could touch Columbus. Never was a title more justly bestowed than the one which he most jealously guarded—*Almirante del Mar Océano* —Admiral of the Ocean Sea.

Bibliography and Notes

The Royal Instructions for this Voyage, crew list, task organization and payroll, Ferdinand's account (chapters 88–92 of his *Historie*), Columbus's

Lettera Rarissima, and the will of Diego Méndez, are translated in my *Journals and Other Documents,* pp. 307–98; other sources are indicated on p. 308, note 2. My joint work with Mauricio Obregón, *The Caribbean as Columbus Saw It* (Boston, 1964), chapters ix and x, follows Columbus's course, with photographs.

There is a good account of the Fieschi family in Alejandro Cioranescu, *Primera Biografía de C. Colón, F. Fernando Colón y Bartolomé de Las Casas* (Tenerife, 1961), and of Diego Méndez, by L. A. Vigneras in Institut Français au Portugal, *Bulletin des Études Portugaises,* n.s., XXX (1969), 39–47.

The old seaman's rhyme about West Indies hurricanes:

> July—stand by,
> August—you must,
> September—you'll remember,
> October—all over

is not very accurate. *Brown's Almanac,* quoting the U.S. Weather Bureau's *Manual of Marine Meteorological Observations* (1963), p. 45, gives a 50-year count of tropical cyclones in the North Atlantic and Caribbean: May—4; June—24; July—25; Aug.—71; Sept.—112; Oct.—91; Nov.—23; Dec.—2; none for January–April.

For identification of the Marble Cape, Morison and Obregón, *Caribbean as Columbus Saw It,* pp. 217–18.

Sevilla Nueva, Jamaica. Mr. Charles S. Cotter of Lime Hall describes recent excavations in *Jamaica Journal,* June 1970. The name of Peter Martyr, titular abbot of Sevilla Nueva, may still be seen on a stone of the ruined church. It remained the capital of Jamaica until 1534. Excavations have been made in St. Ann's Bay for remains of the stranded caravels, without success.

Cosmographical Ideas. Francis M. Rogers, "Valentim Fernandes, Rodrigo de Santaella, and . . . the Antilles," *Boletim* of the Sociedade de Geografia de Lisboa, July 1957, and *The Quest for Eastern Christians: Travels and Rumors in the Age of Discovery* (Minneapolis, 1962), pp. 92–93.

COLUMBUS'S HEIRS AND DESCENDANTS

Ferdinand (Hernando), the young boy who sailed on this Fourth Voyage, became a noted humanist, book collector, and correspondent of Erasmus. The legitimate son, D. Diego, married Doña Maria de Toledo, a cousin of King Ferdinand, who appointed him governor of Hispaniola in 1508. He died in 1526. His only legitimate son D. Luis was a disgrace to the family. His mother did well to persuade the crown to settle on him and his descendants the titles Duke of Veragua and Marquess of Jamaica, plus a pension of 10,000 ducats, in return for renouncing all other claims of his grandfather. D. Luis returned to Santo Domingo as governor of Hispaniola in 1540 and exercised that function, usually in absentia and always with conspicuous inefficiency, until 1551. He first married in 1542; five years later, while his wife was still alive, he married again. In 1546 he sent an expedition under Cristóbal de Peña to take over his duchy of Veragua, but found the Indians there to be as warlike as in 1503, and his force was driven off with great loss, including that of Francisco Colón, bastard son of D. Diego. In 1556 Philip II created D. Luis Duke of the Vega in Hispaniola and allowed him to continue to call himself Admiral of the Indies, in return for renouncing the exercise of admiralty jurisdiction and his now useless fief in Veragua. He also gave him an extra pension of 7000 ducats. Luis celebrated these favors by marrying a third time while two earlier wives were still alive; and for this he was tried and convicted of polygamy, and confined for five years in various fortresses. Stone walls, however, could not keep D. Luis from the women. By bribing his jailers he managed to get out at night and acquire a mistress whom he married, Nos. 1, 2, and 3 all still alive! This final indiscretion earned him an additional sentence to exile in Oran, Algeria, where such manners were understood; and there he died in 1572. Henry Harrisse, *Christophe Colomb*, II, 251-62.

The duchy of Veragua was inherited by one of D. Luis's legitimate daughters, and, after her death, by Nuño Colón de Portugal, a great-grandson of D. Diego. Nuño Colón's great-great-granddaughter, Catalina Ventura, married Fitz-James Stuart, son of the famous Duke of Berwick and grandson of James II of England and Arabella Churchill. In the meantime, the descendants of Cristóbal Colón de Toledo, a younger brother of D. Luis, had married into the Larreátegui family. By an arrangement made around 1790, the house of Stuart renounced the Veragua title (since, as the late Duke of Alba told me, "We already had three dukedoms in the family") in favor of the Larreátegui. The present incumbent, whose full name is Cristóbal Colón de Carvajal y Maroto Hurtado de Mendoza y Pérez del Pulgar, was born in 1925. He styles himself the 17th Duke of Veragua (counting D. Diego as No. 1), 15th Duke of the Vega, Marquess of Jamaica, and Grand Admiral of the Indies; by virtue of which, while still a lieutenant in the Spanish Navy, he wore a full admiral's uniform on ceremonial occasions. He married another descendant of Columbus and has an heir, born in 1949. Rafael Nieto y Cortadellas, *Los Descendientes de Cristóbal Colón* (Havana, 1952), with photo of the 17th Duke at p. 311.

COLUMBUS'S REMAINS

Where are they? Rudolf Cronau, *The Discovery of America and the Landfall of Columbus. The Last Resting Place of Columbus* (New York, privately printed, 1921), J. B. Thacher, *Life of Columbus*, III, 506-13, and Armando A. Pedroso, *Cristóbal Colón* (Havana, 1944), pp. 451-71, contain everything essential. The facts may be thus summed up: Columbus died in Valladolid, possibly in the house now a museum. His body, first buried in the Church of San Francisco there, was removed in 1509 by order of his son D. Diego to a chapel in the monastery of Las Cuevas, Triana, where Columbus had stayed between his Third and Fourth Voyages, and which he had made the depository of his muniments. There too were buried the Adelantado Bartholomew, in 1514, and the second Admiral, D. Diego, in

1526. Las Cuevas was secularized in the nineteenth century and the buildings are now part of the Triana tile factory.

In 1541 or shortly after, in accordance with the wishes of D. Diego, his and his father's remains were placed in small lead caskets, removed to Santo Domingo and interred before the high altar of the Cathedral, Christopher's on the gospel side. A monument or inscription was provided near or over the vault, but in 1655 when it was feared that an English expeditionary force would capture and sack the city, it was removed and subsequently lost. When Santo Domingo was ceded to France by the Treaty of Basel in 1795, the then Duke of Veragua, believing it unseemly for his distinguished ancestor's remains to rest on French republican soil, obtained permission from the Cathedral chapter to have them transferred to Havana. Excavations were made next the high altar on the gospel side, a small stone vault was found, and in it human remains. On the assumption that these bones and ashes were those of Christopher Columbus, they were placed in a new coffin, transferred to Havana, and there reinterred in the cathedral. After Cuba became independent, this coffin was transported to Seville where it was placed in a modern monument in the Cathedral, as containing the remains of Christopher Columbus.

In 1877, when the presbytery of the Cathedral of Santo Domingo was being enlarged, a vault was found next the wall on the gospel side of the altar, and in it a lead casket measuring 42 by 21 centimeters. Upon examination it was found to contain bones, dust, and a small lead bullet. The casket had the letters CCA, probably standing for *Cristóbal Colón Almirante*, on its front and ends. Inside the lid is this inscription, cut into the lead in gothic letters:—

Ill^{tre} Es^{do} Varon
D^{n} Criztoval Colon

(Illustrious and famous gentleman Don Cristóbal Colón.) On top of the lid is the inscription

D. de la A. P^{er} A^{te}

This is variously interpreted as (1) *Descubridor de la América Primer Almirante* and (2) *Dignidad de la Almirantazgo, Primer Almirante* (Discoverer of America, or, Dignity of the Admiralty, First Admiral). The second reading does not make much sense, and the first has been challenged because Spaniards seldom if ever used the word *America* as early as 1541, when the Admiral's remains made their first transatlantic voyage. Supposing, however, the inscription had been cut by a German or Flemish workman in Spain, and many such were there in the era of Charles V and Philip II, this man might well have thought of the New World as "America" and not as "The Indies." In 1878, when the casket was returned to the Cathedral after the repairs were completed, a small silver plate was found on the bottom, evidently the original coffin plate. On one side is the inscription

U^{a}p^{te} de los r tos
del p mer Al te D
Cris toval Colon Des^{r}

which probably stood for *Ultima parte de los restos del primer Almirante D. Cristóbal Colón Descubridor.*

At the same time, under the pavement on the epistle side of the altar was found a lead casket with the inscription

se el almirante donluis
colon ducue de iamaica
marques de la vagua

"His Excellency the Admiral Don Luis Colón Duke of Jamaica and Marquess of Veragua." These were the old scamp's two titles, reversed.

This discovery gave rise to a nasty controversy with charges of trickery and forgery against the ecclesiastics of Santo Domingo, especially the archbishop, who happened to be an Italian. Rudolf Cronau, who examined the remains and the casket in 1891, reports the inscriptions to be undoubtedly ancient, and as here given. The casket was opened again on 14 April 1945 in the presence, among others, of Professor Pedroso, who describes the contents in great detail in *Studi Colombiani*, III, 39–42.

There need be no doubt that the authentic remains of Christopher Columbus are under his monument in the Cathedral of Santo Domingo. It is the intention of the Dominican government eventually to transfer the lead casket to the other side of the Rio Ozama and bury it under a colossal Columbus monument.

Veragua: Rio Chiriqui. Señora Obregón photo.

* XII *

Vespucci and Solis

1499-1516

The Cantino Mappemonde

This magnificent colored mappemonde, measuring 10½ by 22 centimeters, and of which our reproduction here of certain parts gives but a
faint idea of its beauty, is the oldest but one of European maps showing America; or, if the La Cosa is really post-1500, the very oldest. It
is also the most accurately known as to date and provenance.

Ercole d'Este, Duke of Ferrara, a typical Renaissance prince, took a
keen interest in the new discoveries. To Lisbon he had sent a secret
agent, one Alberto Cantino, not only to find out all he could about
them but also to buy horses and mules for the ducal stables. Already
the Portuguese had become very close-mouthed about their discoveries;
but Cantino in his quality of horse jockey managed to get about to the
right places, and to persuade a cartographer, name unknown, to design and draft this map from data he had picked up at the waterfront.
It is generally called the Cantino map.

We can, fortunately, pinpoint the date of composition. It not only
records the discovery of Brazil, as reported by Cabral from Porto
Seguro, but indicates discoveries in Asia brought to Lisbon by João da
Nova on 13 September 1502. Furthermore, according to a letter from
Cantino to Duke Ercole that is still extant, he sent the completed

Cantino map of 1502. The Spanish Main. Collotype reproduction of 1883.

map to him from Lisbon on 19 November 1502. It reached Ercole at Ferrara shortly after, was transferred to the ducal palace at Modena in 1592, and has been there ever since—except in mid-nineteenth century when it was thrown out of the palace window during a popular riot and for several years did duty as a screen in a local butcher shop. Rescued from this ignominious use, it may now be seen in all its pristine glory in the Biblioteca Estense at Modena. Thus this map was compiled when Columbus was at sea on his Fourth Voyage, and when Vespucci was making his first voyage with Coelho along the Brazilian coast.

The accurate east coast of Newfoundland on the Cantino map has already been depicted in my *Northern Voyages*. Here I am confining myself to the West Indies part: *Las Antillas del Rey de Castella*, as Cantino calls them, reflecting the Portuguese notion that these islands had nothing to do with the real Indies (true enough), but were merely

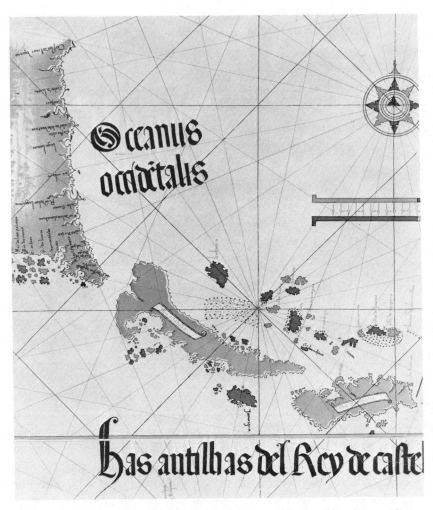

Cantino map of 1502. The Greater Antilles and the Mysterious Coast. Collotype reproduction of 1883.

extensions of the fabulous Portuguese island of Antilia (which they were not).* *Colombo almirante* is credited with their discovery, in a short inscription; but the Cantino map is much less accurate on the West Indies than that of Juan de La Cosa, who had been with Columbus.

* See my *Northern Voyages*, pp. 97–102, 224.

The chain of islands ends with the Guadeloupe group, leaving a vast gap between them and the *Rio de Agua Dolce* (the Orinoco), where Pinzón's 1500 voyage is recorded. Nor is the outline of the Spanish Main as accurate as Juan de La Cosa's.

But the controversial feature of this chart, one which has driven historians and geographers almost frantic, is the continental area jutting out from the western border of the map, next the inscription *Oceanus Occidentalis*. What does it represent?

Anyone's first guess would be Florida. But Florida is supposed to have been discovered by Ponce de León in 1513, and this map was made in 1502! Very well, a "secret voyage" to Florida before Ponce? Cantino's Newfoundland records unknown Portuguese voyages in its jagged outline, so why not here too, in the Antilles? Because this outlined coast bears no resemblance whatever to the east coast of Florida in detail or in character. Henry Harrisse and John Fiske insisted that this area records a real voyage by Vespucci in 1497. The next person to come up with a theory was George E. Nunn. In a small book printed in 1924, he argued that the mysterious peninsula was the Cuban mainland of Columbus's imagination, whilst the real Cuba is represented by an island shaped like a savage dog about to bite the continent. He pointed out that the eastern cape of the unknown peninsula is named *Cabo fim de abrill;* and Columbus passed Cape Maisi on 30 April 1494. (True indeed, but he named it Cape Alpha and Omega.) *Rio de don Diego* might be named after Columbus's older son, the one who stayed at home; *Rio de los Largatos* might be any river full of nasty alligators. But there is no name or configuration that you can identify with Columbus's voyage along Cuba's south shore.

Next, in 1956, the careful Dutch historian Edzer Roukema asserted in an article in *Imago Mundi* that this was "A Discovery of Yucatan prior to 1503." The outline is somewhat like that of Yucatan (without the important Cozumel Island) and the alligators belong there too; but in order to believe that it represents Yucatan you have to twist that peninsula sideways, place it on the wrong side of Cuba—and find a pre-1503 discoverer.

Over thirty years ago, I suggested that the unknown discoverer might have been the Portuguese hero Duarte Pacheco Pereira, who in his *Esmeraldo de Situ Orbis* written between 1505 and 1508, states that in 1498 D. Manuel ordered him to "discover [or explore] the western region," where he found "a very large land mass with many large islands adjacent, extending 70° North of the Equator" and "28° toward the South Pole." Possibly he got carried to leeward of Cape San Roque, worked up to the northwest, and made a discovery of Florida that his royal patron put "on ice" until such time as he could use it.

For this suggestion my old friend Admiral Gago Coutinho took me to task so roundly that I hardly dare bring it up again; but I now find more "evidence" on the Cantino map. Not only are its names on this peninsula Portuguese, but some of the names on the Spanish Main are Portuguese, although a few given by Columbus like Punta de la Galera and Boca del Dragón are included. The island of Margarita, for instance, is *Ilha de la Raposso*, or *Raposa*, and there is an *Ilha do Brasill* and a *Rio de Fonfoca*, names unknown to previous voyagers or maps. So, why may not Duarte or some other Portuguese mariner who reported to him, have sailed along the Pearl Coast and Castilla del Oro, and then to Florida?

There I leave the question. Some day, no doubt, an historian more clever than myself will unlock the secret of Cantino's mysterious land.

Enter Vespucci—and Coelho

On the way home from India, Cabral's ship *Anunciada*, together with the one commanded by Diogo Dias, entered the little West African harbor of Bezeguiche or Beseguiche under Cape Verde, identical with (or very near to) the modern Dakar. It had become a convenient port of call for vessels sailing between Portugal, South Africa, and India. There, about 1 June 1501, Cabral met a fleet of three Portuguese caravels commanded by one Gonçalo Coelho. His mission was to follow up Cabral's discovery of Brazil, of which D. Manuel had heard from Caminha and others who came home in the storeship direct from Porto Seguro. On board, as passenger and self-appointed navigation officer, was a Florentine resident in Seville, Amerigo Vespucci, who would become famous within a decade for having his name attached to the New World.

Amerigo * Vespucci, born in the parish of Ognissanti, Florence, on

---

* Named after an uncle, and he after an obscure saint. Amerigo in northern languages is Emerich; in Spanish, Amalaric. The family bore as coat of arms, gold wasps (*vespe*) on a bend azure, and field gules.

Simonetta Vespucci, by Piero di Cosimo, at Chantilly. Lauros-Giraudon
photo.

9 March 1454, and baptized on the 18th, is the most controversial character in the history of discovery. Estimates of him run the gamut from a charlatan who never even saw the New World, to a great navigator and discoverer after whom America is appropriately named. Born third of four sons into a leading upper-class family, which included an ambassador, a bishop, and a banker; all being friends of the powerful Medici. Amerigo's fame, prior to the next century, was based on his being related to Simonetta Vespucci, the model for Botticelli's Birth of Venus and Primavera. Simonetta, crowned queen of beauty in a Florentine fete of 1471, was one of those rare young women whose grace, beauty, and kindness impressed everyone she met; "so amiable and charming that all men praised her and no woman maligned her." Married to Amerigo's cousin Marco at the age of fifteen, and of the same age as Amerigo, he must have passed her almost daily; but she died in 1476 at the age of twenty-three.* Of about the same date is Domenico Ghirlandaio's painting of the Vespucci family group in a lunette at the Ognissanti, "Madonna della Misericordia," in which young Amerigo appears as a handsome boy next to the Virgin. It is the only known portrait of him from life.

Amerigo had to cross Florence twice daily to attend a private school at the Convent of San Marco conducted by his uncle, Father Giorgio Antonio Vespucci. There one of his schoolmates was Pier Soderini— who rose to be gonfaloniere (prime minister) of the Florentine Republic—to whom he addressed his famous *Lettera*. Amerigo entered the commercial house of Lorenzo di Pier Francesco de' Medici, who sent him in 1491, after twenty years' service, to Seville as head employee of a Medici affiliate, Juanoto Berardi. He was then almost forty years old. At Seville his main business was merchant banking and ship chandlery. Upon the death of Berardi in 1495, Vespucci became head of the house, and as such helped to outfit Columbus's fleet for the Third Voyage in 1498. In so doing he earned the Discoverer's rare praise, in 1505, as an honest ship chandler.

Everyone seems to have liked Amerigo until he began publishing an account of a voyage in 1497 that never took place. He first went to sea on Ojeda's voyage which began in May 1499, as a gentleman

---

* Piero di Cosimo, who painted this portrait from memory years later, is said to have put the live snake about her neck as a symbol of the tuberculosis that killed her.

Amerigo Vespucci as a boy. Detail of Madonna della Misericordia, by Domenico Ghirlandaio. Alinari/Scala photo.

volunteer, and had probably helped to finance it. Apparently he found
Ojeda's methods too rowdy, for he jumped ship in Hispaniola and
returned to Seville in June 1500 ahead of his captain, whose voyage
he describes as if it had been his own with no Ojeda present.

Apparently Amerigo's talk about this voyage, as well as the reputation for navigation that he had acquired in the course of it, reached
D. Manuel of Portugal. He had just appointed Gonçalo Coelho to
reconnoiter the land allotted to Portugal under the Treaty of Tordesillas, and Amerigo received a royal invitation to go along, and write
about it. That he did, in a printed *Lettera* dated 4 September 1504 to
his old school friend Soderini, and also in a shorter tract called *Mundus
Novus* addressed to his former Medici employer, which had a great
circulation. Both were printed at Florence in 1504–6, and led to a continent's being named after Amerigo. But they led to no fame for
Coelho, whom Vespucci never even mentions by name. *Mundus Novus*,
and the Bartolozzi Letter quoted later in this chapter, are the chief
sources for this, Vespucci's second voyage (which he claimed to be
his third).

From now on I am telling the story of the two voyages to Brazil
very much as Vespucci does, warning the reader that many items have
been challenged as false or exaggerated. Especially blown up is Amerigo's claim that all would have been lost but for *his* knowledge of
navigation. "Though a man without practical experience," says he,
"yet through the teaching of the marine chart for navigation, I was
more skilled than all the shipmasters of the whole world." And he
stretches his furthest south to "within 17.5 degrees of the Antarctic
Circle," a gross exaggeration.

The Captain General of this fleet of three caravels which homecoming Cabral met at Cape Verde in June 1501, was Gonçalo Coelho.
This skillful mariner, whose fame has been completely eclipsed by
that of his voluble subordinate, belonged to one of the prominent
families of northern Portugal. He had satisfactorily executed a royal
mission to Sierra Leone some years earlier, and although he gained
no fame from his voyages with Vespucci, D. João III rewarded him by
creating his son, Duarte Coelho, donatory captain of Pernambuco. And
his place in the history of discovery may now be considered secure,
since there has turned up in an obscure Italian library, the Biblioteca
Comunale Federiciana at Fano, a world map by the celebrated Genoese

cartographer Vesconte de Maiollo of about 1504–5, in which Brazil is called *Tera de Gonsalvo Coigo vocatur Santa Croxe.**

The object of this Portuguese voyage was to reconnoiter the land which Cabral had discovered, to report what products were to be expected from it, and to "nail down" what Portugal was entitled to under the Treaty of Tordesillas.

According to Vespucci's *Lettera* to Soderini, the Coelho-Vespucci fleet sailed from Lisbon 10 May 1501, tarried eleven days at Bezeguiche taking on wood and water, and then sailed SW by S for 700 leagues in 67 days, in very tempestuous weather. They raised a rocky island which must have been Fernão de Noronha. This was so named a year later after a wealthy merchant-shipbuilder of Lisbon who made a contract with D. Manuel to start a colony in Brazil in return for a two-year monopoly of logwood. Next, on 17 August 1501, they made landfall on Brazil itself. Vespucci gives the latitude as 5° S, that of the mouth of the Rio Massoró, about 75 miles south of Fortaleza; but it might have been under Cape San Roque at latitude 5°29′ S.

Natives appeared in great numbers, but Vespucci's shipmates' experience of them was very, very different from that of Cabral. As these Indians would neither talk nor trade, Coelho sent ashore two men bearing trading truck, to parley. After five days, during which these men failed to return, a crowd of girls and women gathered at the harbor's edge close to where the caravels were anchored. Coelho then sent ashore a handsome young sailor, hoping he would charm them with his beauty and virility. Charm them he did, fatally. While the girls were admiring and fingering him, raising his expectations of a delicious orgy, a stout wench armed with a great club crept up behind and killed him with one blow on the head. While native archers covered this operation by shooting flights of arrows at the Portuguese in the boats, the girls dragged the poor lad by the feet up the nearest hill, where they defiantly roasted him and ate collops of his flesh before the horrified gaze of his shipmates.

Coelho refused (to Vespucci's indignation) to lay on a counterattack, and his fleet sailed on, rounding Cabo Santo Agostinho on latitude 8° S; Vespucci takes credit for the latter name, which now

---

* Teixeira da Mota, *Novos Documentos* (1969), p. 6. He points out that in the Genoese dialect the Portuguese *lh* is represented by a simple *g;* hence *Coigo* for *Coelho.*

became fixed. A few days later they encountered a friendly tribe of Indians, three of whom volunteered to accompany the Christians back to Portugal. And at Porto Seguro they picked up and brought home the two Portuguese convicts left there by Cabral in 1500; they had not done much to civilize the natives, but at least had stayed alive.

Making frequent and long stops, including the mouth of the São Francisco River and the site of Salvador da Bahia, they reached (according to Captain Guedes's estimate) Guanabara Bay at latitude 23° S, which they named Rio de Janeiro because it was New Year's Day 1502.* With no more trouble from cannibals or warriors, Coelho's caravels sailed down to a latitude which Vespucci calculated to be 32° S, about that of the later city of Rio Grande; but most authorities believe that they got no further than Cananéia on latitude 25° S. Ursa Minor had disappeared, and Ursa Major the Great Bear "stood over us very low . . . almost to the horizon's edge," says Vespucci. Captain Coelho, having run out of the logwood country and discovered no mineral wealth, now decided to strike off in another direction. Vespucci (according to himself) took complete charge of the navigation. But the flagship, commanded by a representative of Fernão de Noronha, here parted from the other two caravels and returned directly to Lisbon, calling at the island named after Noronha, on Midsummer Day, 24 June 1502.

Coelho's caravel, with Vespucci on board, together with the third caravel, departed Brazil on 13 February 1502. On 3 April, having logged (by Vespucci's calculation) about 1500 miles from their last Brazilian harbor, "the South Pole had an elevation of full 52° above our horizon," and neither Great nor Little Bear was visible.** There a tempest forced the caravels to run for four days under bare poles before a stern wind and horrendous seas. They then "sighted new land,"

---

* The name Rio de Janeiro first appears on the Turkish Piri Re'is map of 1513 as *Sano Saneyro*.

** Soderini *Lettera*, translated in Princeton Reprints, p. 39. Even assuming (as Guedes does) that 52° was a printer's error for 32°, this observation was very inaccurate. Von Humboldt stated in his *Histoire de géographie*, V (1837), 18n, that the Great Bear (Big Dipper) disappears at lat. 25°35' S (Guedes, p. 259), and such is the reputation of that great German scholar that no sailor-historian checked him for over a century. Finally, Francis M. Rogers did, in his *Skies of Vasco da Gama* (Lisbon, 1972), p. 18. He states that a modern navigator in a northbound vessel may observe the first three stars of Ursa Major between lat. 10° S and the Equator, thus it may be said to disappear below lat. 10° S.

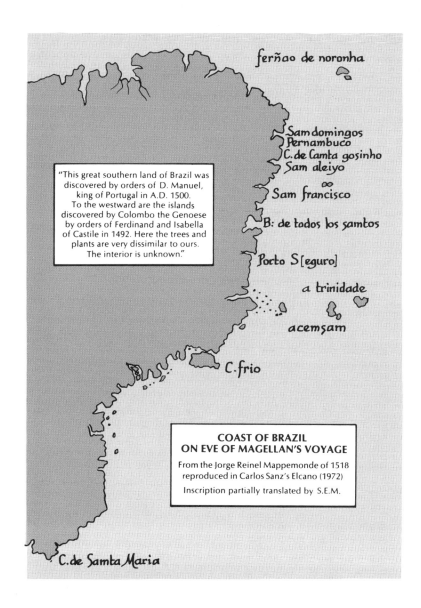

ferñao de noronha

Sam domingos
Pernambuco
C. de Camta gosinho
Sam aleiyo

Sam francisco

B: de todos los samtos

Porto S[eguro]

a trinidade

acemsam

C. frio

"This great southern land of Brazil was
discovered by orders of D. Manuel,
king of Portugal in A.D. 1500.
To the westward are the islands
discovered by Colombo the Genoese
by orders of Ferdinand and Isabella
of Castile in 1492. Here the trees and
plants are very dissimilar to ours.
The interior is unknown."

**COAST OF BRAZIL
ON EVE OF MAGELLAN'S VOYAGE**

From the Jorge Reinel Mappemonde of 1518
reproduced in Carlos Sanz's Elcano (1972)

Inscription partially translated by S.E.M.

C. de Samta Maria

an ironbound coast with roaring surf, but no sign of life. If Vespucci
and his printer reported the 52° latitude accurately, this would have
been South Georgia at latitude 54° S, some 900 miles S by E of the
Falklands; but it is more likely to have been Ilha da Trinidade at
20° S—a considerable difference! Finding no anchorage there, the men

prevailed upon Coelho to shape a course for Portugal. The weather then grew warmer, and on 10 May 1502 they reached a port in Sierra Leone, where they burned one badly beat-up caravel. The other, after touching at the Azores, entered Lisbon 7 September 1502.

This voyage disappointed the crown by bringing back no gold or silver, only logwood, parrots, and monkeys; discoveries on the southern slope of Brazil were not yet appreciated.

Vespucci was the first explorer of Central or South America after Columbus to show any interest in or appreciation of native scenery, fauna and flora; and one of the few to observe carefully the human beings he encountered. Here is what he writes in a manuscript indisputably his, the so-called Bartolozzi Letter to Lorenzo di Pier Francesco de' Medici, his former employer, written from Lisbon in the autumn of 1502 after returning from his first Brazilian voyage. It includes the earliest and best description we have of the Guarani.

> Let us now proceed to a description of the land, of the people, of the animals and plants and other common matters, which in these places we found pertaining to human life. This land is very delightful, and covered with an infinite number of green trees and very big ones which never lose their foliage, and throughout the year yield the sweetest aromatic perfumes and produce an infinite variety of fruit, grateful to the taste and healthful for the body. And the fields produce herbs and flowers and many sweet and good roots, all of which are so marvelous in their suave fragrance of herbs and flowers, and the savor of these fruits and roots, that I fancied myself to be near the terrestrial paradise. And what shall I say of the quantity of birds and their plumage and colors, and their songs, and of such variety and beauty? I wish not to enlarge upon this, for I doubt whether it would be credible. How shall I enumerate the infinite variety of wild animals, lions, panthers, cats (not like those of Spain but of the antipodes), such as wolves, stags and monkeys of every sort, and many very big? And so many more animals we saw that I believe it would have been hard for them to have entered Noah's ark, such as wild pig, kid, deer, hare and rabbit; but no domestic animals whatsoever, they do not have any.
>
> Now we come to the reasoning animals. We found all the earth inhabited by people completely nude, men as well as women, without covering their shame. They have bodies well proportioned, white in color with black hair, and little or no beard. I tried very hard to understand their life and customs

because for 27 days I ate and slept with them, and that which I learned of them follows:

They have no laws or faith, and live according to nature. They do not recognize the immortality of the soul, they have among them no private property, because everything is common; they have no boundaries of kingdoms and provinces, and no king! They obey nobody, each is lord unto himself; no justice, no gratitude, which to them is unnecessary because it is not part of their code. They live in common in houses made like very large cabins; and for people who have no iron or other metal, it is possible to say that their cabins are truly wonderful, for I have seen houses which are 200 *passi* long and 30 wide and artfully made by craftsmen, and in one of these houses were 500 or perhaps 600 souls. They slept in nets [hammocks] woven of cotton, exposed to the air without any other covering; they eat seated on the ground; their food is roots of herbs and many good fruits, an infinity of fish and great quantities of shellfish; crabs, oysters, lobsters, crayfish, and many other things which the sea produces. The meat which they eat commonly is human flesh, as shall be told. When they can have other flesh of animals and birds they eat that too but they do not hunt for it much because they have no dogs and their land is very full of woods which are filled with fierce wild beasts, so they do not ordinarily enter the woods unless with a crowd of people.

The men are accustomed to bore holes in their lips and cheeks and in these holes they place bones and stones; and don't believe that they are little. Most of them have at least three holes and some seven and some nine, in which they place stones of green and white alabaster, and which are as large as a Catalan plum, which seems unnatural; they say that they do this to appear more ferocious; an infinitely brutal thing. Their marriages are not with one woman but with as many as they like, and without much ceremony, and we have known someone who had ten women; they are jealous of them, and if it happens that one of these women is unfaithful, he punishes her and beats her and puts her away.

They are a very prolific people, but have no heirs because they hold no property; when their children, that is the girls, reach the age of puberty, the first man to corrupt them must be their nearest relative except the father, after which they can be married. The women in parturition do not use any ceremony as ours do; they eat everything, go on the same day to the fields and wash themselves; and it seems that they hardly feel their parturition. They are people who live many years, and according to their succession we have known many men who have four generations [living]. They know not how to count the days, years or months save that they reckon the time by lunar months, and when they wish to demonstrate anything they count their time with stones, placing a stone for each moon, and I found a very old man who signaled to me with stones that he had lived 1700 lunar months, which counted up to 130 years, figuring 13 lunars to the year.

They are a warlike people, and among them is much cruelty and all their arms and weapons are (as Petrarch says) *commessi al vento*, which are bows, arrows and darts and stones, and they wear no body armor because they go [to war] almost as naked as they were born. Nor do they follow any tactics in their war, except that they take counsel of the old men; and when they fight they do so very cruelly, and that side which is lord of the battlefield bury their own dead, but the enemy dead they cut up and eat. Those whom they capture they take home as slaves, and if women they sleep with them; if a man, they marry him to one of their girls, and at certain times when a diabolic fury comes over them they sacrifice the mother with all the children whom she has had, and with certain ceremonies kill and eat them, and they did the same to the said slaves and the children who were born of them; and this is true because we found much human flesh in their houses, placed in the smoke; and we purchased of them 10 creatures male and female, who had been marked for the sacrifice which one might better call the crime. We rebuked them much, but I know not whether they will mend their ways, and the more astonishing thing about their wars and cruelty is that we could find no reason for them, since they have no property or lords or kings or desire for plunder, or lust to rule, which seems to me to be the causes of wars and of disorder. When we asked them to tell us the cause, they could not give other reason except what they said before, that this crime began among them and they wish to avenge the death of their ancestors. In conclusion it is a beastly thing and one of their men confessed to me that he had eaten of the flesh of more than 200 bodies and this I believe for certain; and that's enough." *

This is easily the most vivid description of a New World country since the writings of Columbus, and the natives' views on war, in the last paragraph, are worth pondering.

* This translation from the Bartolozzi Letter was made from the original manuscript by S.E.M. with the aid of Dr. Gino Corti. All texts of it hitherto printed are corrupt.

For Vespucci's third and last voyage we have little but what is related in the Soderini *Lettera* (the one which includes the mythical 1497 voyage), but we do know that it took place and that Amerigo commanded one vessel in a fleet of six under Gonçalo Coelho. Vespucci never mentions him by name but insults him on several occasions. The 300-tun flagship (name unrecorded), unusually large for an Atlantic voyage, was not intended to perform a mere Atlantic voyage. They planned, says Vespucci, "to go in quest of an island toward the east, called *Melaccha*, of which we have information that it is very rich." Thus his destination, which he never reached, was the Far East, to follow up Cabral's report of the spice trade.

Sailing from Lisbon 10 May 1503, the fleet topped off at the Cape Verde Islands. Coelho, "a very presumptuous and headstrong man" (says Vespucci) thence steered for Sierra Leone but dared not anchor or seek harbor because of foul weather. From off this part of Africa they steered SSW, and after an estimated 950 miles, found themselves to be three degrees south of the Line. There they found "an island in the midst of the sea," uninhabited, and "only two leagues long and one wide." No island there exists; but (by Francis M. Rogers's electronic calculator), Coelho's course and distance would have taken them to latitude 6°07′ S, longitude 19°16′ W; and since Ascension Island is at latitude 7°55′ S, longitude 14°25′ W, we may assume that this was it.

Here on 10 August the flagship struck a reef and went down, but all her crew were saved. Coelho sent Vespucci's caravel to spy out a harbor, which he did; but only one of the surviving vessels showed up there. She and Vespucci's caravel took on wood and water, and after sailing seventeen days, entered in November 1503 at latitude 13° S, an already discovered great bay of Brazil, naming it *Todos os Santos*, a name it still bears. At its entrance, situated like San Francisco with broad views both bayward and seaward, is now the great city of Bahia or Salvador. The time Vespucci gives for this passage from either island to Bahia was not too short, as the fleet had a brisk trade wind behind it; but his statement that it was "a full 300 leagues"—over 900 nautical miles—is too short for Ascension, the great circle course being 1453 nautical miles. As that works out as an average day's sail of only 85 miles, it is acceptable.

Vespucci's ship and her consort waited in vain for the rest of the fleet for over two months, off the site of the city of Salvador. They then sailed very leisurely along the coast of Brazil. At a harbor whose latitude Vespucci gives as 18° S (but actually must have been behind lofty Cape Frio at 23° S), they tarried five months, building a fort and loading their vessels with logwood. Leaving this fort garrisoned with twenty-four survivors of the wrecked flagship to prepare more logwood for export, Coelho and Vespucci in the other vessel steered NNE for home, "and in 77 days, after much hardship and danger," entered Lisbon 28 June 1504. They were well received, despite having suffered many losses, "all through the pride and folly of our admiral," says Amerigo. Poor Coelho, no writer, had no chance to reply.

America So Named

Most of the above account of Vespucci's last voyage is from his own printed *Lettera* dated 4 September 1504 to his Florentine friend Soderini, and as usual, he shamelessly exalts his own role.

Although the other printed letter *Mundus Novus* is very brief, there are several reasons why it enhanced Vespucci's reputation as a discoverer beyond his deserts. First, its timeliness. Columbus's own account of his Third Voyage was not printed, except for a dull and brief digest in the *Libretto de Tutta la Navigatione* of 1504, and the *Paesi Novamente Retrovati* of 1507. Second, whilst Columbus's letters and reports were written for the eyes of a chaste queen whom he did not wish to offend, Vespucci went in detail into native sexual customs that appealed to the public in the early sixteenth century—as they do in the late twentieth. In *Mundus Novus* he describes how the women of Brazil, "being very lustful," apply a local poison to their men's genitals to make them swell. Completely promiscuous, "Son cohabits with mother, brother with sister," and "urged by excessive lust," they were delighted to take on Christian visitors. Finally, Vespucci insists that he has found "what we may rightly call a New World . . . a continent more densely peopled and abounding in animals than our Europe or Asia or Africa; and, in addition, a climate milder and more delightful than in any other region known to us." Columbus, to be sure, had called the Spanish Main an "other" and "new" world, but he did not see enough of it to be convincing; whilst Vespucci went "rolling down to Rio," and claimed to have gone even as far as the latitudes below 50° S. Within a few years some forty editions of *Mundus Novus* in Latin, Italian, French, German, Flemish, and even Czech came out. Even so, it is astonishing that a young professor of geography in an obscure college at Saint-Dié in Lorraine should have persuaded first Northern Europe and finally the whole world to name this New World *America*.

Martin Waldseemüller, the name of this man (who should be the patron saint of all library navigators) was getting out a new edition of Ptolemy, entitled *Cosmographiae Introductio*, a sure step to academic fame and fortune. He decided to print a Latin translation of Vespucci's Soderini Letter as an appendix or *pièce justicative* to his pregnant suggestion in the text:—

> . . . *et quarta orbis pars (quam quia Americus inveunit* [sic] *Amerigen / quasi Americi terram / sive Americam nuncupare licet)* (. . . and the fourth part of the Globe, which, since Americus discovered it, may be called *Amerige* or *Land of Americus*, or *America*. . . .)

And later he repeats his plea:—

> . . . *quarta pars per Americum Vesputium (ut in sequentibus audietur) inventa est / quam non video cur quis iure vetet ab Americo inventore sagacis ingenii viro Amerigen quasi Americi terram / sive Americam dicendam: cum & Europea & Asia a mulieribus sua sortita sint nomina.*
>
> (. . . Since another fourth part [of the world] has been discovered by Americus Vesputius (as will be seen in what follows), I do not see why anyone should object to its being called after Americus the discoverer, a man of natural wisdom, Land of Americus or America, since both Europe and Asia have derived their names from women.)

Also, on his big wood-engraved map of 1507, which appeared at the same time as the *Introductio*, Waldseemüller placed a bold AMERICA on South America, at some distance north of Monte Pascoal, the mountain discovered by Cabral at Eastertide 1500.

Waldseemüller had probably tried this pun on Vespucci's name— America- Ameriγη—at the St. Dié high table, where it was so well received that he ventured to put it into his book, hardly expecting the great men of his profession to take it seriously. We may imagine his surprise and pleasure when they did, and the still keener satisfaction of the Florentine so complimented. The name *America* was so neat, so analogous to Europe, Asia, and Africa, and Vespucci's *Mundus Novus*

APARCTIAS

Mare glaciale.

CIRCVL⁹   ARCTIC⁹

Caput de la nó trouatis

India superior

ASIE PARS

Terra incognita

MARE GLACIALE

CIRCVL⁹

100 200 210 220 230 240 250 260 270 280 290 300 310 330

90

80

140   160

Vespucci and *Mundus Novus*, on Waldseemüller's 1507 map. Courtesy Señor Carlos Sanz.

became so widely circulated, that every subsequent writer or cartographer in England and Northern Europe fell for it. So did certain Portuguese; Diogo Homem's atlas of 1558 has not only *America* but *quarta orbis pars*. Spanish writers and map-makers, however, held out against it for centuries, continuing to call the New World *Las Indias*. Owing (one assumes) to indignant outcries from the Peninsula, Waldseemüller actually dropped the name America from his 1513 edition of Ptolemy, therein calling the New World simply *Mundus Novus*. But the deed was done. *America* gradually worked onto the maps, and by mid-century included North America.

Please observe that Waldseemüller suggests the name America because that "fourth part of the world has been *discovered* by Americus." By that he meant that Vespucci discovered the mainland in 1497, a year before Columbus.

Why Vespucci performed that colossal if well-planned deception, nobody has ever succeeded in explaining. Many of his adherents, for no good reason, have tried to shrug it off as a trick of the Florentine publisher, but that won't do; there are authentic bits of Ojeda's voyage in 1499 embedded in Vespucci's fake one of 1497. Vespucci's false claim was first challenged by another noted story-teller, Sebastian Cabot, and shown up by Columbus's friend Bishop Las Casas. The next exposé came from the pen of Michael Servetus in that very edition of Ptolemy (1535), whose disagreement with Holy Writ as to the fertility of Palestine figured among the heretical charges against him by John Calvin. From the many expressions of vanity and self-esteem in Vespucci's accounts of his Brazilian voyages, I conclude that he deliberately invented the 1497 voyage in order to claim that he, not Columbus, discovered the mainland at the Gulf of Paria. The deception certainly worked; for by the time almost everyone had agreed that Columbus reached the mainland first, the name America was too well fixed to be changed to Atlantis, Columbiana, or any of the other names suggested.

This is not to say that everything Vespucci wrote is false. His accounts of his two Brazilian voyages under Coelho contributed greatly to European knowledge of the vast country. They were the earliest to explore the coast from Salvador to Rio de Janeiro, and the *feitoria* they founded behind Cape Frio may be called the first European attempt at a permanent settlement in Brazil. The data they brought back were sufficiently novel and impressive for Queen Juana of Castile to appoint Vespucci *piloto mayor* (22 March 1508), with power to license

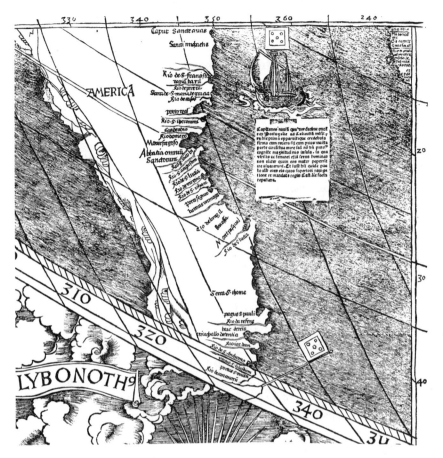

The first AMERICA, on Waldseemüller's 1507 map. Courtesy Señor Carlos Sanz.

all blue-water pilots sailing under the Spanish flag, and to keep up-to-date a *padrón real* or standard map of the world. She had already naturalized him as a Spanish subject.

Amerigo's last years were tranquil. He died at Seville on 22 February 1512, leaving his Spanish widow and nephew Giovanni, but no children. His embalmed body was transported to Florence and buried in the family vault of the Ognissanti church, almost under the Ghirlandaio Madonna della Misericordia which shows his innocent features as a young boy. Juan de Solis succeeded Amerigo as *piloto mayor* and was required to pay his widow one-fifth of his salary of 50,000 maravedis in lieu of pension. The descendants of Amerigo's brothers remained prominent in the life of Florence for three centuries.

Conclusion on Vespucci

There remains the question, What did Vespucci amount to as a celestial navigator? For that was what he mainly counted on for fame. Not only his printed letters, but the manuscript ones to his Medician friend, are full of alleged navigational discoveries, with sundry conceited remarks about his self-taught skill at shooting the heavenly bodies.

It so happens that of the many secondary writers on Vespucci, the only one qualified by mathematical and navigational training to make a correct estimate of Amerigo's astronomical pretensions was Duarte Leite. In his posthumously printed *História dos Descobrimentos* (1959), he concluded (p. 650): "The portrait of Vespucci, a renowned astronomer, acute cosmographer, skilled navigator and audacious discoverer, is purely imaginary, and was made up by his compatriots, whom other admirers followed, thanks to the printing press. In truth Vespucci was a cunning Florentine, vain, ambitious and with a superficial knowledge of exact sciences, who as a merchant made two voyages with Spaniards and Portuguese, whom he assisted in their discoveries."

That is just about the conclusion reached by my colleague Professor Francis M. Rogers * and myself, in the year 1973. We regard all the pretentious apparatus of celestial navigation in Vespucci's writings as so much dust thrown in the eyes of important Spaniards and leading Florentines. Herein, as in his claim to have discovered the continent in 1497, he succeeded beyond his wildest dreams. It would weary the reader to pick out every inaccurate statement so confidently made by our genial faker. His distances are palpably wrong; for example, the statement in his Vaglienti Letter of 18 July 1500 that he and Ojeda sailed for 1300 leagues southwest from Cadiz, would have brought them across the continent to Antofagasta, Chile. His claim

---

* Professor Rogers kindly discussed this with me, and allowed me to see an early draft of his forthcoming book, *Astronomical Navigation: Its Practice and History*. In this work, Vespucci's famous triangle (*Mundus Novus*, Northup translation, p. 12) is explained.

Americus Discovers America by Theodor De Bry. Courtesy Burndy Library, Norwalk.

to have used lunar distances to find longitude is fantastic. This method is generally supposed to have been discovered by John Werner of Nuremberg and published in his 1514 edition of Ptolemy. Vespucci is to be praised for having heard about it earlier, but he is merely pulling his reader's leg in implying that he was able to use it. His method, he says, was to turn a primitive plumb-line quadrant or a mariner's astrolabe on its side to measure the angular distance between the moon and a planet, which is impossible, especially at moonrise, with the instruments at his disposal. And the particular longitude that he claimed to have worked out by this method would have taken him to the Galapagos Islands in the Pacific. Actually, the lunar distance method requires such complicated figuring and the use of logarithms that it never became generally used until Nathaniel Bowditch's famous *American Practical Navigator* came out in the early nineteenth century. Lunar distance tables were still included in Bowditch when I was young (and in the British *Nautical Almanac* until 1906), but thereafter were dropped as too complicated for the average mariner, who then had radio signals to check an inaccurate chronometer, or lack of one.

So, too, with Vespucci's calculations of latitude. Most of them were a long way off; some were fairly accurate, but no more so than those of Columbus in Jamaica, and far less accurate than those of pilot Albo on Magellan's voyage. That he studied navigation is evident from his remarks on lunars, but that he practiced it with any accuracy is not true. Nevertheless, he was able to convince the Casa de Contratación and the Queen that he was sufficiently expert to be appointed *piloto mayor* of Spain, and to persuade sundry popular writers of our day that he was one of the world's great navigators.

So, what shall we say about the gentleman for whom the New World is named? Remember that Amerigo grew up at Florence in the wonderful *quattrocento* with a galaxy of great artists and writers—Botticelli, Ghirlandaio, Leonardo da Vinci, Ariosto, Michelangelo, Machiavelli, Verrocchio, and a host of others. His own uncle, Giorgio Antonio, was a noted teacher. Amerigo I suppose to have been a tricky kid but a poor scholar, the stupid boy of his class who flunked Greek and so had to go into business. That took him to Seville where, when working for Berardi, he decided to make a reputation as a navigator and discoverer. No Florentine had done that for two centuries; so if he accomplished something notable his name would go down in history as one of the greats. He had no trouble getting a berth under Ojeda, the clever young man of Seville, and squeezed two voyages out of that one. He went on two more, to Brazil, under Coelho, and let it be inferred that he commanded them all. The first, fictitious one of 1497 he antedated so it would appear that he, not Columbus, discovered the Spanish Main.

A French translation of the Soderini *Lettera* dedicated to René d'Anjou, that *bon roi René* of happy memory, was brought to the attention of René's subject, Professor Waldseemüller, with the suggestion that here was something to be played up. And that the St. Dié professor did, to very good purpose. The bad Italian of the *Lettera*, natural for a poor scholar who had spoken only Spanish for years, did not come through in the French translation. And a little earlier appeared *Mundus Novus*, translated into good Latin. This little tract established Amerigo's European reputation so that by the time he died, Florence regarded him as a distinguished son.

And do not forget that he was an honest ship chandler!

Defenders of Vespucci, when cornered, declare their hero to be a proper person to have a continent named after him, on the ground that he first demonstrated that the South American continent was indeed *Mundus Novus*, having nothing to do with Asia; thus, he was the first to recognize what it really was. Alas, that also is not true. Over a century ago the sapient Alexander von Humboldt wrote, "It is certain that Columbus and Vespucci died in the belief of having only touched at a part of Eastern Asia."

In his Vaglienti Letter of 18 July 1500 Amerigo wrote, "After having sailed about 400 leagues continually along the coast, we concluded that this was a mainland, as I say, and within the eastern bounds of Asia, and the beginning of the west." This is exactly what Columbus was thinking when he named the eastern promontory of Cuba, Cape Alpha and Omega. Again, Vespucci wrote, "We were about 13 months on this voyage, incurring immense perils, and discovering much land of Asia.* These quotations are from his letter on his voyage with Ojeda; but there is nothing in his later writings to indicate any change of mind. His real scientific accomplishment was to demonstrate the vast extent of South America, far beyond anything conceived of by Columbus; and his ship (under Coelho) was probably the first from Europe to enter the great bay of Rio de Janeiro. The extensive coast that he and Coelho reconnoitered is reflected in the maps of that era, especially in Waldseemüller's, and led others in the right direction.

So, here's to you, Amerigo! Liar though you were, you made three long transatlantic voyages, wrote entertainingly about them, and played your cards so cleverly as to be elected to the exclusive club of the immortals. Without you, the history of American discovery would be infinitely poorer.

Discovery of the River Plate

The decade prior to the start of Magellan's voyage in 1519 was one of growing rivalry between Portugal and Spain for the east coast of

---

* The text of the Vaglienti Letter of 1500, as collated by Dr. Corti and myself, reads, "Dipoi d'aver navicato al pie di 400. leghe di continuo per una costa, concludemo che questa era terra ferme, che la dico, e' confini dell' Asia per la parte d'occidente . . ."

South America. Spain admitted that the Line of Demarcation cut across the bulge of Brazil, but insisted that the Terra de Vera Cruz discovered by Cabral in 1500 was an island (as he first supposed it to be), and that the mainland belonged to Spain. Portugal, on the contrary, demanded all the mainland from Cape San Roque south, not only by virtue of the Treaty of Tordesillas but because the Coelho-Vespucci voyages had explored that coast as far as latitude 50° S, which was far from true.

Waldseemüller's completely-new-world concept for America did not gain many converts prior to Magellan's voyage. A common notion was to separate Brazil Inferior from Brazil Superior by a strait somewhere near the River Plate, and to join Brazil Inferior to the Spice Islands by an Antarctic continent running around the globe. Lopo Homem's planisphere of 1519 did much to spread this concept, and library geographers seem to have preferred it to the small Tierra del Fuego of Magellan, Loaysa, Drake, and other mariners; they went right on depicting the blown-up Antarctic continent for over a century.

In 1506 Ferdinand of Aragon and Philip I of Castile planned an expedition (1) to figure out where the Line of Demarcation crossed the South American coast, and (2) to search for the Strait. Two years later, it took off. The captain, Juan Diaz de Solis, recommended by the Casa de Contratación as the best deep-sea mariner available, had been a Portuguese subject, but where or when he was born is still unknown. He had served Portugal well at sea, but in order to escape punishment for murdering his wife, had taken refuge in Spain, where his maritime talents were put to work. Vicente Yáñez Pinzón went along with him as joint commander and Vespucci too would have joined had he not just been appointed *piloto mayor*. This Solis-Pinzón expedition consisted of two vessels, caravel *Isabeleta* and ship *Magdalena*, respectively of 50 and 60 tuns. They accomplished nothing, since all their strait-searching took place in the Caribbean, retracing the course of Columbus's Fourth Voyage in the hope of finding a strait that he had missed. When they returned to Spain empty-handed (28 August 1509), King Ferdinand, furious, gave Solis the usual treatment—a stretch in jail; but like most of the imprisoned discoverers, he managed to get free and go on to greater things. Released in the latter part of 1511, Solis rose suddenly in his sovereign's favor, being appointed *piloto mayor* after the death of Vespucci on 22 February 1512.

If gold were the first valuable product to be found in America, wood of the *Caesalpina* species, known in English as brazilwood, or simply logwood, had become the second by 1510. Formerly imported from India at great expense, it made up for the worthlessness of American "spices" reported by Columbus. When properly processed for dyeing wool, this logwood yielded washable red, blue, and black colors and brought enormous sums in European textile centers such as Rouen and Antwerp. Although logwood grew close to the shore all around the Caribbean, it seems to have been particularly abundant in Brazil; so much so that its name became applied to the vast country first named after theTrue Cross by Cabral.* A Venetian agent in Lisbon reported to his Senate in 1506–7 the magnitude of this dyewood business:—20,000 quintals (hundred-weights) were there imported annually, and it sold at Lisbon for two ducats per quintal. A wealthy merchant, Fernão de Noronha, had a ten-year monopoly for which he paid the crown 4000 ducats a year; but for illicit imports in Spanish and French ships we have no figures. You could cut your own logwood almost anywhere on the Brazilian coast—we have already seen the work of French interlopers—but the most economical way to conduct the business was to set up a *feitoria* (factory) in some deserted harbor, to leave a crew (or impress local Indians) to work the year round, felling trees and sawing them into lengths suitable for shipping. A vessel or two came out every summer to load the valuable wood for home.

One factory was set up by a Portuguese group on the island at the entrance to Bahia de Todos os Santos, opposite the site of the future city of Salvador. There a Portuguese ship named *Bertoa* or *Bretoa*, owned by a group of Lisbon merchants including Noronha, loaded logwood between 17 April and 12 May 1511, then proceeded to Cabo Frio where more wood was cut in June and July, and returned to Lisbon 22 October of the same year. Her pilot was João Lopes de

---

* The name BRASIL first appears on the Jerónimo Marini map of 1511, reproduced in *Hist. Col. Port. Brasil*, II, 332. The name refers to the bright red color of the wood, suggesting coals in a brazier, and has no connection with the mythical island of Brazil or Hy-Brasil off Ireland.

Carvalho who nine years later piloted Magellan's fleet to Rio de Janeiro (close to Cabo Frio) and there encountered the native mistress he had acquired on *Bertoa*'s voyage. *Bertoa*'s total take was over 5000 logs, 35 Indian slaves, and a quantity of parrots and *saguim*, small monkeys of the hapalidean family, also in great demand as pets.

When Solis succeeded Vespucci as *piloto mayor* in 1512, King Ferdinand conceived the idea of sending him to occupy the Spice Islands, on the ground that the Line of Demarcation, if run around the world, would pass through Ceylon. The Portuguese were naturally suspicious of this project, and protested. Ferdinand assured them that Solis had no orders to discover anything, only to ascertain where the Line ran: D. Manuel replied that indeed he hoped so! Before the end of the year, however, Ferdinand cancelled this expedition. At the same time he ordered the Spanish authorities at Santo Domingo to "look for a Strait" and to arrest any nosey Portuguese ships found in the Caribbean.

The first to suffer from this order was a Portuguese vessel, name unknown, commanded by one Estéban Froes, whom Spaniards called Flores. He was accompanied by a second caravel commanded by a famous Portuguese pilot, João de Lisboa, and they were financed by Cristóbal de Haro, originally of Burgos, who had branches in Antwerp and Lisbon and settled permanently in Spain in time to become Magellan's principal financial supporter.* Unfortunately, Froes's ship on her return passage turned out to be in such poor shape that he felt obliged to visit the Caribbean and repair her before attempting an Atlantic crossing. In the meantime he was detected doing a bit of slaving along the Spanish Main and sent into Santo Domingo. There the viceregal admiralty court condemned his ship, not for slaving, but because of her Portuguese flag, and her entire crew was thrown into prison.

A brief account of this voyage is found in one of the little German newssheets, precursors of the newspaper, which the banking house of Fugger in Augsburg circulated to keep its customers informed as to what was going on in the world. One of these, undated but printed not earlier than 1514, came out under the title *Newen Zeytung auss*

---

* See my *Northern Voyages*, pp. 260–61, for the importance of these merchant princes in financing voyages. Haro was in a class with the Ango of Rouen and the Gherardi of Lyons.

Presillg Landt (Fresh News from Brazil Land). It tells about a voyage to the River Plate, naming neither ship nor captain. Colonel Laguarda Trías, in his latest book, has meticulously analyzed this newssheet and concluded that the story it tells is that of a caravel under João de Lisboa and Froes, in 1511–12. Froes, as we have seen, got in trouble by poaching in the Caribbean; but the other caravel, commanded by the famous pilot, loaded logwood at Cabo Frio and sailed back to Cadiz, calling at Funchal. There or at Cadiz an agent of the Fuggers interviewed João de Lisboa and obtained his story of the voyage. João gave out that somewhere in South America there was a long strait (probably the not yet explored River Plate) through which one could sail to the East Indies. In any case, this voyage was the first, so far as our records go, to enter the River Plate.

In 1514 King Ferdinand, having received the news of Balboa's discovery of the Pacific, decided to make a fresh try for the strait and organized a fleet under Juan Diaz de Solis, *piloto mayor*, now considered the No. 1 active mariner in Spain since La Cosa's death and Pinzón's retirement. On 24 November the king granted an *asiento* to Solis "to discover in the back parts (*espaldas*) of Golden Castile"— by which he meant the south side of the Isthmus of Panama. Solis was to take three ships, one of 50 tuns and two of 30 tuns each, and 70 men, and the crown was to pay one-third of the expenses, the other two-thirds to be contributed by private merchants. When and if he reached the back side of Panama, he was to report to Governor Pedrárias, the slayer of Balboa. It was expected that the voyage would be long and that he must provision his ships for two years and a half.

Sources for this last voyage of Juan de Solis are fragmentary up to its tragic conclusion. He did not sail until 8 October 1515. Exactly where he made his Brazilian landfall we know not; but he "doubled Cape St. Augustin," according to Peter Martyr, rounded Punta del Este, Uruguay, and entered the great estuary of the River Plate. Solis named it *La Mar Dulce*, the Fresh-Water Sea. In mid-February 1516, somewhere on or near the coast of the present Republic of Uruguay, probably the island later named Martín García, Solis observed natives of apparently friendly aspect. Incautiously he landed with seven men. No sooner were they ashore (quoting Peter Martyr's account as translated by Richard Eden), when "sodenly a great multitude of the inhabitants bruist forth upon them, and slue them every man with clubbes, even in the sight of their fellowes, not one escaping. Their furie not thus satisfied, they cut the slayne men in peeces, even uppon the shore, where their fellowes might behold this horrible spectacle from the sea. But they being stricken with feare through this example, durst not come foorth of their shippes, or devise how to revenge the death of their Captayne and companions. They departed therefore from these unfortunate coastes, and by the way lading their shyppe with Brasell [wood], returned home agayne with losse, and heavie cheare. Of these thynges I was advertised of late by their owne letters." Francisco del Puerto alone survived the massacre, to be later picked up by Sebastian Cabot.

After the natives had unwittingly avenged Solis's murdered wife by killing and eating him, his now famished survivors slaughtered seal on the Lobos Islands and salted down their meat. When sailing along the Brazilian coast, one of his ships was wrecked at a place that the survivors called *Puerto de Patos*. This, Colonel Laguarda Trías has identified as Massiambu, at latitude 27°50′ S, where Sebastian Cabot's flagship later came to grief. The other two vessels sailed on to Cabo Frio to load logwood. This they did successfully, returning to Seville in September 1516.

The same year, 1516, a Portuguese ship commanded by a famous Frenchman named Cristóvão Jacques, who was running a sort of coast guard operation along the Brazilian coast, rescued seven shipwrecked survivors of the Solis fleet at Puerto de Patos and carried them to Lisbon, where they were flung into jail. More survivors were found many years later by Loaysa's *San Gabriel*.

Thus, Solis lost his life, about one-third of his company, and one of his three vessels. Hardly a successful voyage, but the River Plate estuary was called Rio de Solis by Spain until about 1525, when it was changed to Rio de la Plata. Esteban Froes, it seems, was the real discoverer.

After a long series of heavily polite letters between the Spanish and Portuguese governments, the P.O.W. question was settled by the exchange of Froes and his men in Santo Domingo, after spending four years in jail, for the seven Solis survivors brought home by Jacques. João de Lisboa, Esteban Froes, and Juan de Solis were firm believers in the existence of a big strait somewhere between latitudes 35° and

50° S. No doubt their views came to Magellan's attention and encouraged him to concentrate on the Patagonian coast in his search.

The year 1519 is a good date to leave the Discovery of Brazil, by no means complete. In that year Brazil was still almost a virgin land. Spotted along its 3000 miles of coast were only two Portuguese *feitorias* (Bahia do São Salvador and Cabo Frio), where for a year or two sailors cut logwood until the groves easily accessible from the sea were exhausted. Besides magnificent harbors such as Bahia and Rio there were dozens of places south of Cabo Santo Agostinho, like Cabral's Porto Seguro, where natural harbors were formed by reefs, behind which a small ship or even fleet could moor and load in comparative safety. The number and scattered nature of these temporary establishments gave rise to the English always referring to this country in the plural—"The Brazils"—until the end of the eighteenth century.

We shall now take up the greatest voyage in recorded history, that of Ferdinand Magellan.

Bibliography and Notes

THE CANTINO MAP

The best annotated reproduction to date is in Armando Cortesão and Avelino Teixeira da Mota (eds.), *Portugaliae Monumenta Cartographica*, I (Lisbon, 1960), 7 ff. Yet even here most of the names cannot be read, so I have had parts of it photographed from the collotype reproduction published in 1883. There are other good though reduced colored reproductions of the American part in Duarte Leite, *História dos Descobrimentos* (1959), II, 88; *História da Colonização Portuguesa do Brasil*, II 174, and, with good discussion, in the Cumming, Skelton, and Quinn *Discovery of North America* (1972), chap. ii. I personally examined the original at Modena, and it is magnificent. Why will not historians of Renaissance art include superb maps like this?

George E. Nunn's book of 1924 is called *Geographical Conceptions of Columbus*. Edzer Roukema's important articles are "A Discovery of Yucatan Prior to 1503," in *Imago Mundi*, XIII (1956), 30–38, and "Brazil in the Cantino Map," *ibid.*, XVII (1963), 7–26. On XIII, 38, he lists the toponymy of the mysterious land compared with those of the Caverio (1502–5), Waldseemüller and Ruysch (1507), Ptolemy (1513), Waldseemüller (1516), and Gemma Frisius (1525) maps, all of which followed Cantino. Thereafter it dropped out of the maps. See also Luis de Albuquerque and J. Lopes Tavares, "Algumas Observações sobre o Planisférico Cantino," offprint from *Revista do Centro de Estudos Geográficos*, III (Coimbra, 1967). D. O. True,

"Some Early Maps Relating to Florida," *Imago Mundi*, XI (1954), 73–84, is devastated by Giuseppe Caraci, *ibid.*, XV (1960), 32–39; and in 1974 we are no nearer to a solution.

Latest contribution of the D. O. True school is by Horace Sutton in *Boston Sunday Globe*, 11 March 1973. Key Biscayne, Florida, now the eastern seat for sheltered presidential relaxation, was discovered by John Cabot in 1497! It was Cabot who named Cape Florida on the southern tip of Miami, " 'The Cape of the End of April,' for that was the month he returned here after meandering about in the Gulf of Mexico." One of Sebastian Cabot's tall tales come to life!

For the controversy with Admiral Gago Coutinho, my *Portuguese Voyages to America in the Fifteenth Century* (Cambridge, Mass., 1940; reprint, New York, 1965), pp. 132–41; Kimble translation of the *Esmeraldo* (Hakluyt Society, London, 1937), p. 12; C. V. Gago Coutinho, *A Naútica Descobrimentos*, II, 90–91. I was momentarily assured by finding the great Duarte Leite supporting me in 1931 (*História dos Descobrimentos*, I, 498–502), but cast down again on ascertaining that in a later article, written in 1945, he had changed his mind (*ibid.*, II, 276n).

AMERIGO VESPUCCI

BIBLIOGRAPHY AND SOURCES

During a visit to Florence late in 1973, profiting by the gracious hospitality of the Mason Hammonds at Villa I Tatti, I studied the Vespuccian sources at the Biblioteca Nazionale with the help of Dr. Gino Corti, a learned palaeographer. We found the 18th-century printings of the letters to be very inaccurate, yet reprinted in all modern editions such as Levillier's. There is need of a new and accurate edition of all Vespuccian sources before any further progress can be made in this thorny subject.

The best bibliography is *Mostra Vespucciana, Catologo*, a catalogue of the Vespucci Exhibit in Florence (Firenze, Palazzo Vecchio, 1954–55). There is also a folio *Raccolta di Carte e Documenti* issued by the same *Mostra*, same date.

The two printed tracts are:

1. The *Mundus Novus*, of which the full title is *Mundus Novus Albericus Vespucius Laurentio Petri de Medicis* * *salutem plurimam dicit*. A Latin translation of Amerigo's Florentine original (long since lost) to his former Medicean employer. Covers his first Brazilian voyage only. The above *Catalogo* lists 15 editions, undated but probably 1503–7, printed at Florence, Venice, Paris, Augsburg, Antwerp, and Nuremberg, including two retranslations from the Latin to German and Dutch. And it appears also in Fracanziano da Montalboddo's *Paesi Novamente Retrovati* from 1507 on.

---

* Lorenzo di Pier Francesco d' Medici (d. 1525), married to a Soderini; best known as the father of Lorenzaccio ("Bad Lorenzo") de' Medici, who murdered his cousin Alessandro.

João Vidago, *O Nome de América* (Lisbon, 1968), p. 7, counts 36 imprints in 5 languages. An astonishing circulation!

2. The *Lettera* to Soderini: *Lettera di Amerigo Vespucci delle Isole Novamente Trovate in Quattro Suoi Viaggi.* Only one edition, generally assumed to have been printed by Paccini of Florence in 1505–6, but finished (as the colophon states) on 4 September 1504, at Lisbon. This one edition is in Italian. Facsimile of the Princeton copy in *Vespucci Reprints* (see below), Vol. II (1916) with English translation in Vol. IV.

In addition, there are four early 16th-century copies of Vespucci's ms. letters in Florentine libraries or collections:

1. *The Vaglienti Letter,* of 18 July 1500, to the same Medici; ms. copy by Pero Vaglienti (d. 1514) in the Biblioteca Riccardiana. The inaccurate 18th-century text is repeated in all collections of Vespucci's letters— Levillier's, Markham's, and Uribe White's. Dr. Corti and I collated the quotations I have used, from the original Vaglienti copy. Very important for the voyage with Ojeda.

2. *The Cape Verde Letter,* of 4 June 1501, to the same Medici. Early 16th-century ms. copy in the Riccardiana. Mostly about Cabral's voyage, since Vespucci, outward bound, met at Cape Verde two of Cabral's ships homeward bound.

3. *The Bartolozzi Letter* of September or October 1502, from Lisbon to the same Medici, late 16th- or early 17th-century ms. copy in the Strozzi collection, Biblioteca Nazionale. Bartolozzi was the scholar who unearthed it in 1789 and printed a very inaccurate text which appears in all collections of Vespucci's Letters. Dr. Corti and I collated the translation that I used in this chapter. See comment in the *Mostra Vespucciana,* No. 49. Tells story of first Brazilian voyage with Coelho.

4. *The Fragmentary Letter,* of September–December 1502. This was discovered by Roberto Ridolfi in the muniments of the Ginori Conti family at Florence and printed in *Archivio Storico Italiano,* Vol. I (1937), as *Una Lettera Inedita di Amerigo Vespucci Sopra Il Suo Terzo Viaggio.* In 1973 I ascertained that the original has since disappeared; some say it was bought by a collector, others that it went with the great flood of 1966. Evidently written to the same Medici, Vespucci defends himself from criticisms of his earlier remarks on astronomy, and repeats details that were in No. 3, and others on the voyage with Ojeda (here undated). Best available text, with translation, in Levillier's *Cartas, pp.* 154–58, translation on pp. 293–99.

COLLECTIONS OF VESPUCCIANA

1. *The Vespucci Reprints,* issued by Princeton University Library in 1916. Unfortunately never finished. Volumes published are: II, *The Soderini Letter* 1504, in facsimile; IV, translation of same; V, *Mundus Novus;* VI, *Paesi Novamente Retrovati & Novo Mondo 1508,* in facsimile; VII, *Sensuyt le nouveau monde & navigations faictes par Emeric de Vespuce* (Paris,

1505), a French popularization of *Mundus Novus* and the *Lettera* which gives Amerigo no fewer than seven voyages!

There are two other collections of Vespucci's letters. Sir Clements Markham, *The Letters of Amerigo Vespucci* (London, Hakluyt Society, 1894), which includes a translation of what Las Casas wrote about him; Uribe White, *Edición Facsimilar de las Cartas de Vespucio* (Bogotá, 1942), Latin and Italian texts, with Navarrete's Spanish and White's English translations, and valuable notes by this eminent Colombian soldier and scholar.

The tradition that the boy Amerigo is depicted next the Virgin in Ghirlandaio's Misericordia at the Ognissanti goes back to the 1591 *Guide to Florence* by Francesco Bocchi (facsimile edition of 1971, p. 101). For Simonetta, R. Langton Douglas, *Piero di Cosima* (Chicago, 1946), pp. 74–75, Germán Arciniegas, *Amerigo and the New World* (New York, 1955), pp. 33–36.

Fernão de Noronha. Duarte Leite, *História dos Descobrimentos* (1959), I, 644–46; *História da Colonização Portuguesa do Brasil*, II, 320, and the Columbian *Raccolta di Documenti e Studi*, Pt. III, vol. ii, pp. 120–22.

The first Coelho-Vespucci voyage to Brazil. The cannibal episode is illustrated on the so-called Kunstmann II Map of 1502; a young white man being spitted and grilled by a native. Levillier, *América la bien llamada*, II (Buenos Aires, 1948), 10–14. This map is the first to note many of the Brazilian names given to the coast on this Coelho-Vespucci voyage, and enables us to date the progress of the voyage by the saints' days. For instance, C. San Roche, 17 August; C. Sancta Cruz (Agostinho), 28 August; Bay of All Saints, 1 November; Serra de S. Thomá, 21 December; Monte de S. Vicente, 22 January. The toponymy of this map in Harrisse, *North America*, p. 427. is incorrect. Best reproduction is in Friedrich Kunstmann, *Atlas zur Entdeckungsgeschichte Amerikas* (1859).

A BRIEF HISTORY OF THE VESPUCCI QUESTION

America's eponym is still the most enigmatic and controversial figure in early American history. As one of my Portuguese friends remarked, you have only to mention the name to another historian to see his face grow red, his eyeballs protrude, his blood pressure rise, and his voice become emotional!

As early as 1515 Sebastian Cabot, himself no mean fabricator of false voyages, questioned whether any faith be placed in the voyage of 1497, "which Americus says he made." Later in the century, Las Casas (*Historia de las Indias*) demonstrated in detail that Vespucci was a liar, and so did Michael Servetus; whilst others like Peter Martyr simply left him out of their histories of the New World. By 1600 almost everyone regarded Amerigo as a charlatan who had thrust himself forward at the expense of Columbus, had written an account of a voyage which never took place, and so was unworthy of any credence.

In Justin Winsor, *Narrative and Critical History of America*, II (Boston,

1886), the chapters on Vespucci (pp. 128–79) by Sydney II. Gay and the editor are excellent summaries of all that had been written up to that time. The summary of early opinions (pp. 174–78) is masterly. The Sebastian Cabot quotation is on p. 156.

Alexander von Humboldt, in his classic *Examen critique de l'histoire de la géographie du nouveau continent* (Paris, 5 vols., 1836–39), went as thoroughly into the question as available sources permitted, and concluded that the "First" Voyage of 1497 was impossible (IV, 268); but did not impugn his two Brazilian voyages except to point out that Vespucci did not command them (V, 87, 107). The Portuguese historian M. F. de Barros e Sousa, better known by his title Visconde de Santarém, summarized a series of anti-Amerigo papers in his *Recherches historiques . . . sur Améric Vespuce et ses voyages* (Paris, 1842). The translation of this work by E. V. Childe (Boston, 1850) came to the attention of Ralph Waldo Emerson, who in his *English Traits* (1856) remarked: * "Strange that . . . broad America must wear the name of a thief. Amerigo Vespucci, the pickle dealer at Seville, who went out, in 1499, a subaltern with Hojeda, and whose highest naval rank was boatswain's mate in an expedition that never sailed, managed in this lying world to suppress Columbus and baptize half the world with his own dishonest name."

Had the Sage of Concord been able to read Portuguese, he would probably not have gone out on that particular limb. For in 1854 a scholarly Brazilian historian, Francisco Adolfo de Varnhagen ** (1816–78), in his *História Geral do Brasil* (2 vols., Rio de Janeiro, 1854–57), pronounced all that Vespucci wrote in the *Lettera* to be true, and even compiled a chart of the 1497 voyage. According to Varnhagen, Amerigo sailed directly from Spain non-stop to Columbus's Cape Gracias a Dios in Honduras, and then around the Gulf of Mexico and Florida to the Chesapeake, Bermuda, and home! Bermuda (though no Indians ever got that far) was the "Iti" where Ojeda loaded slaves for sale.

One of Emerson's younger neighbors, John Fiske (1842–1901), popular philosopher and historian, did read Varnhagen to very good purpose. In his *Discovery of America*, Vol. II (Boston, 1892), 25–91, he presented Varnhagen's views with infectious enthusiasm, scoring everyone who had doubted the existence of the 1497 voyage as "critics of mingled dullness and flippancy." He even converted the skeptical Henry Harrisse. Fiske asserted that the unexplained peninsula on the Cantino map of 1502 must be Florida, discovered by Vespucci in 1497–98; and *Lariab*, in Vespucci's letter to Soderini, which others shrugged off as a mere misprint for *Parias*,

---

* Centenary edition of Emerson's *Complete Works*, V, 152.
** Appropriately created Baron and Viscount of Porto Seguro by the Emperor of Brazil, but generally known as Varnhagen. He also wrote *Vespuce et son premier voyage* (Paris, 1838) and *Amerigo Vespucci, son caractère, ses écrits . . . sa vie et ses navigationes* (Lima 1865). Portrait in Vianna, *História do Brasil*, I (1970), 96.

must be an actual place in Central America where numerous native names ending in *-ab* can be found. It follows that the lacustrian Venezuela must have been near Tabasco in Mexico. Fiske did make one good point, that Vespucci had nothing personally to do with Waldseemüller's naming the New World America. He was embarrassed by the corrupt Italian of the Soderini Letter—"a jargon salted with Atlantic brine," as he called it. The same salty Italian has been made an argument by Magnaghi and others for Vespucci's Letters having been forged in Florence; but surely fakers would have done their job in classical Tuscan.

Fiske wrote with such verve that the Florentine began creeping back into schoolbooks as a great discoverer. But few historians of repute followed Fiske and Varnhagen in putting the 1497 voyage back on the map. And one of the chief talking points for it—the name *Lariab*—was finally ruled out when a lost manuscript of the *Lettera* to Soderini turned up in the Magliabechiana Collection at the Biblioteca Nazionale, Florence. There it is indeed *Parias*. *Lariab* is in the printed copy of the *Lettera* to Soderini, on folio b.i.v°, line 15. In the ms. copy in the Magliabechiana Collection at the Biblioteca Nazionale, *Parias* appears at folio 124 r°, third line from foot.

Several popular writers such as Germán Arciniegas,* Stefan Zweig, and others, follow Varnhagen and Fiske in stamping the 1497 voyage with their approval. But, alas, Visconde de Santarém, over a century ago, proved from Spanish documents that Amerigo, during 1497 when he claimed to be discovering America's mainland, was living at Seville, engaged in business. And other unkind historians have pointed out that if Vespucci's courses were followed literally, he would have had to cross Mexico and would have ended up at Puget Sound. But you cannot convince anyone who has the Vespuccian faith. Henry Vignaud, after spending most of his life trying to drag down Columbus, decided to build up Vespucci; and at the age of ninety-two published his *Americe Vespuce, 1451–1512* (Paris, 1916), which again supports the 1497 voyage.

Apart from the above, the important works that so far have appeared in the twentieth century are:

Alberto Magnaghi, *Amerigo Vespucci* (2 vols., Rome, 1924; revised ed., one vol., 1926), well illustrated with clear photos of early maps. Magnaghi (1874–1945) was professor of geography in the universities of Palermo and Turin. He concludes that both the *Lettera* and *Mundus Novus* were pirated (see especially pp. 43–51, 55–56). Dr. Corti and I are not impressed by this argument. To us, the *Lettera* is in good though inelegant Tuscan, with a few Spanish words and turns of phrase, natural to a ship chandler turned sailor who had not been home for twelve years.

A fresh spate of books and articles on Vespucci began with the publica-

* Devastatingly reviewed by Wilcomb E. Washburn in *William and Mary Quarterly*, XIII (1956), 102–5. Arciniegas's reply and Washburn's rejoinder are on pp. 449–53. But Arciniegas did contribute fresh data on Amerigo's Florentine background and relatives.

tion in 1948 of *América, la bien llamada* by Roberto Levillier (1881–   ),
a leading Argentinian historian. He followed this up by a revised edition,
Américo Vespucio (Madrid, 1966). Levillier attempts rather feebly to
rehabilitate the 1497 voyage, but his main interest is to establish how far
south Vespucci actually sailed on his two voyages under Gonçalo Coelho.
According to him, Amerigo discovered the River Plate, Patagonia to latitude 50° S, and even the Falkland Islands! Both Levillier's works are rich
in reproductions of early maps; his scholarship is impressive even though
his interpretations often seem unjustified by the facts. But he has not succeeded in convincing many people. Vice Admiral Ernesto Basílico of the
Argentine navy, for the Instituto de Publicaciones Navales at Buenos Aires,
brought out in 1970 *El Tercer Viaje de Américo Vespucio*, with the subtitle, *Vespucio no descubrió el Rio de la Plata, ni la Patagonia, ni Las Malvinas*. Even earlier, in an article, "Vespucio y Levillier," in *Revista General
de Marina* for October 1968, Capitán de Corbeta Roberto Barreiro-Meiro of
the Museo Naval Madrid cracked down on Levillier. By an economical use
of tracings of early maps that cover Brazil (such as the Kunstmann II of
about 1505, the Waldseemüller of 1507, the Kunstmann III of *c.* 1515, and the
Turin of *c.* 1522) he convinces me that the Rio Cananéia at latitude 25° S
was the place whence Vespucci took off into the deep blue.

Ernesto Greve, *América la Bien Llamada* (Santiago de Chile, 1951), is a
highly favorable review of Levillier. Giuseppe Caraci the eminent Roman
geographer savagely reviewed Levillier in "The Vespuccian Problems—
What Point Have They Reached?" *Imago Mundi*, XVIII (1964), 12–23,
with foonotes listing polemical articles by himself and others. Caraci's critique is super-severe.

Comparing *Mundus Novus* with the Bartolozzi Letter that Vespucci wrote
to his Medici friend from Lisbon in September 1502, I cannot agree with
Caraci (p. 16) that *Mundus Novus* is merely the Bartolozzi Letter "altered
by many additions and amplifications for the sake of lucre, by an anonymous
author." Why may not Vespucci have written several letters to Pier
Lorenzo? *Mundus Novus* seems to me much more than a blown-up Bartolozzi. Amerigo states therein that he planned to use data from this voyage
for "a small work, which when I am at leisure, I shall find occupation in
completing, and which will acquire for me some fame after my death."
May not *Mundus Novus* have been a trial balloon for this work? Why
should it be assumed that everything in *Mundus Novus* not in the Bartolozzi was invented by some unknown person "for the sake of lucre"? And
let it be remembered that Vespucci lived until 1512 and thus had plenty of
time to disassociate himself from both the Soderini and the Medici printed
letters, had he chosen to do so.

At the end of his review (p. 22n), Caraci takes on Arthur Davies the
English geographer, for his article on Vespucci's alleged 1497 voyage in
Geographical Journal, CXVIII (1952), 331 ff.

Edzer Roukema's scholarly article, "The Mythical 'First Voyage' of the

Soderini Letter," *Imago Mundi*, XVI (1962), 70–75, tears apart the navigational data in the alleged 1497 voyage, in a manner that should convince all but those whom the author (p. 73) describes as "Vespucci's hopelessly bedazzled advocates."

Coeval with Levillier was Duarte Leite. His revised "Américo Vespúcio" is a large part of his posthumously printed *História dos Descobrimentos* (Lisbon, 1959), 549–650; earlier he wrote the chapter on him in the *História de Colón*. The most eminent Brazilian historian of his day, Leite (1864–1950) held the chair of Astronomy and Geodesy at the University of Coimbra. Thus he was able to prick the bubble of Vespucci's pretentious remarks on the stars of the Southern Hemisphere and, without fear of contradiction, pronounce him a "pure charlatan" on such matters. But he covers the entire course of the Vespucci question and exhibits great zeal in pulling apart other authorities such as his compatriot T. O. Marcondes de Sousa,* especially his notion that the Florentine discovered Puerto San Julián in Patagonia and gave this name to Magellan. He points out that the Caverio map, usually dated 1504–5, supports the theory that the voyage's furthest south on Brazil was Rio Cananéia at latitude 25° S.

On the Oliveriana world map at Pesaro the Brazilian coast names end with Porto Seguro, although a bay with many islands south of it suggests Rio de Janeiro, and the coast continues to the latitude of Rio Cananéia. See notes and reproduction in my *Northern Voyages*, pp. 242–44 (better reproduction in Levillier, II, 17). This map has been dated as early as 1502, but I would now place it no earlier than 1507 or 1508, after the appearance of Waldseemüller's *Cosmographiae Introductio*, owing to its naming South America *Mundus Novus*. I managed to read the Brazilian names in the Oliveriana Library in 1970 by practically standing on my head, and dictating them to my wife. All but *cauo s. roqe* are identical with those on Waldseemüller's map of 1507, and all are on the Caverio map, which is generally dated 1504–5, but may be later. All three maps reflect Vespucci's first voyage with Coelho, but which one comes earlier is anyone's guess.

A new era of Vespucciana began very recently with the works of historians who also are sailors; especially Avelino Teixeira da Mota of the Portuguese Navy, and Max Justo Guedes of the Brazilian Navy. Everything they write on it is important. Note especially Teixeira da Mota's appendix to Duarte Leite, *História*, I, 680–83 on the Maiollo maps. His *Novos Documentos Sobre uma Expedição de Coelho ao Brasil* (Lisbon, 1969) produces the petitions for pardon from two sailors who deserted this last voyage at the Cape de Verdes, which proves that it did take place, which some have

---

* Not the *Descobrimento* mentioned in Chap. X, notes on Cabral, but *Amerigo Vespucci e Suas Viagens* (São Paulo, 1946, 1947) in that university's *História da Civilização Brasileira*, No. 10; revised edition, São Paulo, 1954, and "Amerigo Vespucci e a Prioridade do Descobrimento do Brasil," *Revista da História*, VIII, No. 18 (1954). I believe Marcondes de Sousa to have been a much more thorough and objective scholar than Duarte Leite cared to admit.

doubted. His learned paper on "Duarte Coelho, Capitão-Mor de Armadas" does much to clear up the life of this hitherto forgotten captain. And Max Justo Guedes, *As primeiras expedições portugueses e o reconhecimento da costa brasileira* (separata da *Revista Portuguesa de História*, XIV, Coimbra, 1970), is a keen summary of all Vespucci's voyages, with useful tables of names from the earliest maps. I have, however, ventured to differ from my Brazilian friend in the order of events of Vespucci's last voyage.

The Naming of America. Here the best work to date is Carlos Sanz, *El Nombre América, Libros y Mapas que lo Impusieron* (Madrid, 1959), with numerous facsimiles and a bibliography of Waldseemüller's editions of the *Introductio* and of his maps. The well-documented story of Waldseemüller's responsibility was challenged by Jules Marcou, professor of French at Harvard, in *Nouvelles Recherches sur l'origine du nom d'Amérique* (Paris, 1888), and *Derivation of the Name America*, from the Smithsonian Institution Report of the same year. He attributed it to Amerrique, name of a mountain range and a tribe of Indians in Nicaragua, both of which were discovered by Columbus on his Fourth Voyage. This theory has met little acceptance outside Nicaragua, whose historians have taken it up with great enthusiasm. Dr. João Vidago of Lisbon has studied the origin and diffusion of the name in articles on *América, origem e evolução deste nome*, in *Revista Ocidente*, LXVII (1964), 93–110, and LXXV (1968). These may be considered definitive until and unless fresh sources are discovered.

Portraits of Vespucci. Winsor, II, 109–41, lists those known to him, all posthumous, and each differing radically from the others. The only surviving portraits of Amerigo are those here reproduced: —the child in the Ghirlandhaio Misericordia, and Waldseemüller's on his world map of 1507; here the enormous dividers are authentic—there is a similar pair in the Museum of Science, Florence—but this cartographer never saw Vespucci. The Johannes Stradanus allegorical engraving of *c.* 1580, "Americus Discovers America," in which Vespucci, holding a mariner's astrolabe and a banner with a cross, surprises Miss America in a hammock, with a human-flesh barbecue in the background, cannot be called a portrait of Vespucci, but it at least reflects a contemporary opinion of him.

The Vespucci family, collateral descendants of Amerigo, were still respected citizens of Florence in mid-nineteenth century when they spawned an adventuress who called herself America Vespucci. For participating in a "Young Italy" rising of 1832, she had to quit Florence and seek asylum in Paris where she became mistress of the Duc d'Orléans, son of King Louis-Philippe. He got rid of her in 1838 by sending her to the United States on a French warship. A beautiful and talented woman, Miss America was feted on this and a subsequent visit in every city of the Atlantic seaboard as well as in Louisville, New Orleans, and St. Louis, but failed in her principal object to obtain a land grant from Congress. By way of compensation she became the mistress of a wealthy Scots entrepreneur named George Parish, Jr., and lived with him from 1841 to 1859 at his mansion in

Ogdensburg, New York, now (1974) called the Remington Memorial, which contains a room devoted to memorials of "Miss America." John F. McDermott, "America Vespucci or Abroad in America," Missouri Historical Society *Bulletin*, XI (1965), 371–78; Prince de Joinville, *Vieux Souvenirs* (1895). There is also a novel about her called *Parish's Fancy* by Walter G. Kellogg. I am indebted to Mrs. Howard T. Fisher of Cambridge, for this information.

FROES AND SOLIS

I am highly grateful to Colonel Rolando Laguarda Trías of Montevideo, who kindly allowed our common friend Comandante Teixeira da Mota to lend me an advance copy of his work *El Predescubrimiento del Rio de la Plata por la Expedición Portuguesa de 1511–12* (Lisbon, 1973). Earlier important writings on this period are in *História da Colonização Portuguesa do Brasil*, II (Porto, 1923).

José Toribio Medina, *Juan Diaz de Solis* (2 vols., Santiago, 1897), is still the capital work on that unfortunate explorer. It is paged according to Medina's peculiar system: historical introduction of 252 pp., numbered Roman (Vol. I), and 252 pp. of documents numbered Arabic (Vol. II)— both *impreso en casa del Autor*. Solis's *Asiento* and *Instrucción* are in Navarrete, III, 134–37. For his death, Richard Eden's translation of Peter Martyr, 3rd decade (London, 1512), pp. 149–50.

Also Medina's *Solis*, notes 87–89, pp. ccxc–ccxci; D. L. Molinari, *Nacimiento del Nuevo Mundo*, pp. 80–82 and Map. No. 26.

✳ XIII ✳

Ferdinand Magellan

It is an old saying that God gave the Portuguese a very small country to live in, but all the world to die in. A son of Lusitania who nobly exemplified this is the navigator known to a large part of the world as Ferdinand Magellan. About the year 1480 he was born in one of the northernmost provinces of Portugal, either Trás-os-Montes or Entre-Douro-e-Minho. Forty years later he died in the Philippines after conducting the crucial part of the most remarkable voyage in recorded history, the first circumnavigation of the globe.

Trás-os-Montes is in a sense the Portuguese Switzerland. The Serra do Gerez on the Galician (Spanish) border rises to a height of over 5000 feet. Another serra, the Marão, divides it from the province of Entre-Douro-e-Minho on the west. Along its southern border the River Douro flows through deep gorges. Snow lies late on the ground. Hunting deer, wolves, and the wild boar were more important than agriculture in Magellan's day, and in our day they still afford good sport. Guillemard, the English biographer of our hero, found nothing in Trás-os-Montes to interest the tourist "save a certain gloomy grandeur in its scenery," and quotes a Portuguese observation about the climate: *Nove meses de inverno, e três de inferno*—Nine months of winter and three of hell! He declares that our hero inherited the

FERDIN·MAGELLANVS·SVPERATIS
ANTARTIC¹   FRETI·ANGVS
TIIS·   CLARISS·

Portrait of Magellan. Courtesy Kunsthistorisches Museum, Vienna.

"gloomy and superstitious" character of the people. On my brief incursion into Trás-os-Montes I found the scenery, with steep valleys and intensively cultivated small farms, strikingly beautiful; and the people, pleasant and polite to the stranger from overseas—whither a large proportion has emigrated in search of work. To me, this region was no more gloomy than Switzerland or Norway. My guess is that the province contributed to her most famous son a tough but not a gloomy character; rugged strength and the power of prompt decision, qualities which may be learned hunting the wild boar as well as in warfare.

Fernão de Magalhães * was probably born in the Quinta de Souta, parish of Sabrosa, Trás-os-Montes. At least such was his accepted origin until this present century, during which several Portuguese scholars have argued that Terra da Nóbrega, in the adjoining province of the Minho, was the family seat; and still others that he was born and brought up in Oporto, the metropolis for both provinces. The Magalhães were a noble family who had come to Portugal from Normandy with the Count of Boulogne, who became Afonso III in 1248. By more than one marriage they were allied with the great Sousa family who were cousins to the royal house of Aviz. We shall see later how these arms got Ferdinand into trouble in Seville. His first cousin, trying to recover debts to the navigator's heirs in 1563, stated that two brothers, Rui (Ferdinand's father) and Lourenço, had "similar tastes and adventurous inclinations, friends of navigation, and ingenious and extraordinary pilgrims." The mother of the great navigator was Alda de Mesquita, and he had one or two sisters and a brother. His parents having died when he was ten or twelve years old, it was arranged by his Sousa cousins that he be received as a page in the household of Dona Leonor, queen of D. João II, who died in 1495. D. João's successor, D. Manuel I, took the young nobleman into his service; and finding him to be a likely youth, tough and ambitious, allowed him to volunteer under D. Francisco de Almeida, who was about to embark for India as the first Portuguese viceroy.

Few European governors have left India with a better reputation than Almeida, a man of honor, blameless in his actions, devoid of arrogance and greed. His fleet of at least twenty sail departed Lisbon 25 March 1505, and 22 July made Kilwa on the east coast of Africa. After capturing that town and laying the foundations of a fortress, Almeida continued to Mombasa, took this important Arab trading center by storm, left a garrison, and sailed to Anjidiv Island,

* As he signed himself, and this has become the usual Portuguese spelling of his name. It became Anglicized and Gallicized shortly after his death as Ferdinand Magellan, the form now followed in almost all Western languages except Spanish, where it is Hernando de Magallanes.

the key to Goa; that place became a Portuguese colony and so remained until the end of 1961. Almeida's policy was to establish as many
fortified trading posts as possible on the shores of the Indian Ocean and
to co-operate with local potentates tired of the Arab monopoly of sea
trade. The "Moors" did not take this lying down; there were sea fights
and land battles, almost all won by the Christians. Magellan was
wounded in one of them and always walked with a slight limp.

We know little else about Magellan's part in the successful campaigns
of the Portuguese in the Far East. In 1508, with his bosom friend
Francisco Serrão, he sailed in a small fleet of four ships from Cochin
on the Malabar coast to Malacca, which commanded the important
strait of that name and had become an emporium similar to Singapore.
Here Magellan distinguished himself by giving warning of a Malay
plot to capture the ships when most of their crews were ashore, and
thereby thwarting it.

An episode which early Portuguese historians took pains to relate
shows the measure of the man. In January 1510, when he was about
thirty years old, two ships of a homeward convoy from Cochin, with
Magellan on board, struck on the Padre shoals near the Maldive Islands.
Magellan took command, sent the ships' boats with the captains and
gentlemen passengers to Cannanore—a journey of eight days—and
himself remained in charge of the two wrecks with the greater part of
their crews. They, but for confidence in him, would have rushed
the boats to get away, or starved. During the several weeks before a
rescue vessel arrived, Magellan had the wrecked hulks shored up for
safety, kept constant watch against a pirate attack, took care that rations were served out fairly and that there was no pilfering of the
valuable cargo. It was considered so remarkable for an officer to do that
instead of saving himself, that even the early historians who considered
him a traitor to Portugal, praised his courage and his men's loyalty.
Magellan was always a sailor's sailor, and *os rudos marinheiros*, as
Camoëns called the common "matlow" of that era, always stood by
him in his contests with officers.

Governor Afonso de Albuquerque now sent a fleet under António
d'Abreu to conquer Malacca in the summer of 1511, and Magellan
sailed with him. Malacca fell after a siege of six weeks. Here the Portuguese received breath-taking accounts of the Spice Islands (the Moluccas) that more than substantiated the earlier reports of the Italian

traveler Varthema, and Albuquerque decided without delay to reconnoiter this spicy paradise. Three ships were equipped under Abreu, who commanded *Santa Catarina;* Magellan's friend Francisco Serrão commanded the *Sabaia,* and Magellan himself the third, a caravel. This little fleet, destined to open a new era of opulence for Portugal, departed Malacca at the end of 1511, and with a local pilot reached Ambon and Banda. There nutmegs were so plentiful that Abreu loaded up and turned back to Malacca. Serrão's vessel struck a reef and became a total loss. By a ruse he captured the vessel of some pirates who were looking for him, and in her sailed back to Ambon and on to Ternate. Thence he wrote enthusiastic letters to his friend Magellan about the amenities of the Spice Islands and the abundance of clove, cinnamon, and nutmeg.

The fact that Magellan sailed with Abreu as far east as Ambon and Banda justifies us in naming him as the first person of any race to circumnavigate the globe. For Ambon is on longitude 128° E of Greenwich, and Banda is two degrees further east; whilst Mactan in the Philippines, where Magellan met his death, is on longitude 124° E. Thus his furthest west in 1521 overlapped his furthest east in 1511 by four to six degrees of longitude. Later, we shall consider the counterclaim of Magellan's slave Enrique to be first around the world.

Serrão stayed on in Ternate as an unofficial Portuguese resident, and hoped to meet his friend on his way westward around the globe; but both were killed before they could meet.

Magellan returned to Portugal a veteran sailor and soldier, expert at navigation, and with an important plan. He was certain that the Moluccas could be got at more easily by following Columbus's original idea, sailing west, than by the long, difficult voyage around the Cape of Good Hope and through Malacca Strait. From his own, or Serrão's, observations, the Spice Islands were relatively civilized, with local governments under Moslem or pagan sultans who were eager to trade with Europeans. But an essential part of this grand design was to find a strait through Spanish America. Magellan believed he knew where he could find one.

While waiting for a proper opportunity to present this project to D. Manuel, Magellan embarked as a volunteer in a Portuguese army sent to Morocco. There he got in trouble with his commander on the charge of selling surrendered cattle back to the enemy. He therefore

left Africa for Lisbon to clear himself with his sovereign. At the interview he tactlessly asked for an increase of his *moradia* or retaining fee
by the modest sum of about one gold dollar a year.* D. Manuel refused
to listen and sent him back to Morocco to answer the charges. There
they were dropped by his military superiors. They probably had been
involved in the graft, if graft there were; but, after all, what could you
do with a captured herd of cattle but sell it, if you couldn't eat it all?
So Magellan returned to Lisbon, where the king again turned a deaf ear
to his grand design, "The king always loathed him," wrote Barros, a
chronicler of D. Manuel's reign; nobody knows why. The refusal to
increase his *moradia* rankled in Magellan, as he saw hundreds of subordinate officers and mere hangers-on at court receiving more than he
did; Portuguese courtiers were rated socially according to the amount
they received. Far more important, however, than the *moradia* was the
king's rejection of Magellan's enterprise to find the American strait
through which he could sail west to the Spice Islands.

While living under the shadow of royal displeasure, Magellan made
a personal alliance with a fellow countryman named Rui Faleiro, a
scholar in celestial navigation, of which Magellan by this time was no
mean practitioner himself. Together they worked out the theory that
the famous Line of Demarcation between Spanish and Portuguese
spheres of influence laid down in the Treaty of Tordesillas (1494), if
continued around the globe, would pass west of the Spice Islands, and
thus place them in the Spanish half of the world. A Spanish voyage to
prove it would be their anchor to windward, in case D. Manuel were
so stupid as to sneer at the westward route. The king, however, already
controlled one good route to the Spice Islands and he had sent Gonçalo Coelho on two American voyages, looking for another without
success. So he declined. Thus D. Manuel lost his chance to promote
one of the world's two greatest voyages, as his predecessor D. João II
had dismissed the other, that of Columbus.

What kind of a man was Magellan when, at the age of about thirty-
seven he shook the dust of Lisbon from his feet and entered the
Spanish service? Dark-complexioned, somewhat short in stature but
broad in body, strong and agile in all his members; but above all, tough,
tough, TOUGH. Fortunately for us, Bishop Las Casas, then at Valladolid,

---

* The *moradia* in varying amounts was paid to all courtiers as commutation of
the king's obligation to feed and lodge them. The increase demanded by Magellan
was a beggarly 850 reis per annum.

recorded his impression of Magellan at an interview with the king of
Spain:—

> Magellan brought with him a well-painted globe showing the
> entire world, and thereon traced the course he proposed to
> take, save that the Strait was purposely left blank so that no-
> body could anticipate him. . . . I asked him what route he
> proposed to take, he replied that he intended to take that of
> Cape Santa Maria (which we call Rio de la Plata) and thence
> follow the coast up [south] until he found the Strait. I said,
> "What will you do if you find no strait to pass into the other
> sea?" He replied that if he found none he would follow the
> course that the Portuguese took. But, according to what an
> Italian gentleman named Pigafetta of Vicenza who went on
> that voyage of discovery with Magellan, wrote in a letter,
> Magellan was perfectly certain to find the Strait because he had
> seen on a nautical chart made by one Martín of Bohemia, a
> great pilot and cosmographer, in the treasury of the King of
> Portugal the Strait depicted just as he found it. And, because
> said Strait was on the coast of land and sea, within the boun-
> daries of the sovereigns of Castile, he [Magellan] therefore had
> to move and offer his services to the king of Castile to discover
> a new route to the said islands of Molucca and the rest.

Las Casas now gives us the most vivid picture we have of Magellan's
appearance and personality:—

> This *Hernando de Magallanes* must have been a brave man,
> valiant in thought and for undertaking great things, although
> his person did not carry much authority, since he was of small
> stature and did not look like much, so that people thought they
> could put it over him for want of prudence and courage.

They certainly learned better! Three Spanish courtiers and a priest
left their bones in Patagonia for having underrated Magellan's valor
and toughness.

His finest qualities of courage, decision, and leadership he now
offered to Spain. This change of allegiance brought upon him furious
attacks by Portuguese writers for more than two centuries after his
death. It is difficult to figure out why, since Columbus of Genoa and
the Cabots of Venice had offered their enterprises to four different
courts, and were thought of none the worse for that. Señor Mauricio
Obregón suggests that the reason was this: Magellan, no *roturier* like
Columbus or Cabot, belonged to a royal court, which made his desertion of his monarch reprehensible. Yet the law recognized that a

vassal could change his allegiance at will. And Magellan's reputation fared no better with his new associates. His short way with mutineers was bitterly resented, and both Esteban Gómez and Juan Sebastián de Elcano brought home a cargo of lies about him to Spain to cover their own misdeeds. His sea journal and other personal records were impounded by the Portuguese when they seized his flagship in the Spice Islands, and are lost. No letter of his written during the voyage has survived. Yet, Magellan's greatness stands out, despite all attempts to disparage him. He not only had the gift of making the right decision at the right time; he was able to outwit enemies who were plotting to kill him, and to keep the loyalty of his men. And, as the Portuguese sailor who wrote the Leiden Narrative recorded, he was "an industrious man, and never rested," the kind of sea captain who slept little and woke at a moment's notice for anything like a change of wind. As a mariner and navigator he was unsurpassed; and although he did not live to complete the greatest voyage of discovery in the world's history, he planned it, and discovered the "Strait that shall forever bear his name," as well as the Marianas and the Philippines where no European had touched before. I cannot do better than quote Edward G. Bourne's masterly summary:

> There was none of the prophetic mysticism of Columbus in the makeup of the great Portuguese. Magellan was distinctly a man of action, instant, resolute, enduring. . . . The first navigation of the Straits of Magellan was a far more difficult problem of seamanship than crossing the Atlantic. . . . Columbus's voyage was over in thirty-five days; but Magellan's had been gone a year and weathered a subarctic winter before the real task began—the voyage over a trackless waste of waters exactly three times as long as the first crossing of the Atlantic. . . . Magellan is to be ranked as the first navigator of ancient or modern times, *and his voyage the greatest single human achievement on the sea.*

Aye, aye, say I!

Bibliography and Notes

GENERAL BIBLIOGRAPHY ON THE MAGELLAN-ELCANO VOYAGE
Martin Torodash, "Magellan Historiography," in *Hispanic American Historical Review*, LI (1971), 313–35, comprehensive yet critical, is recommended to readers who wish to pursue the subject further.

SOURCES

There are three accounts by members of the expedition. Of these, the most important are the several editions of Antonio PIGAFETTA's narrative:—

(1) *Primo viaggio intorno al mundo.* Title of a manuscript in the Ambrosian Library, Milan, which James A. Robertson printed very accurately, with an excellent parallel English translation and copious notes (3 vols., Cleveland, 1906); his title is *Magellan's Voyage Around the World.* The same text and translation are in Blair and Robertson's 55-volume *History of the Philippine Islands,* Volumes I and II (Cleveland, 1903). I have generally used this admirably produced and annotated edition of Pigafetta, and refer to it as "Robertson ed." * Robertson's translation has been reprinted by the Filipiniana Book Guild, Carlos Quirino (ed.), as *First Voyage Around the World* (Manila, 1969).

(2) *Navigation et descouvrement de la Inde supérieure et isles de Malucques ou naissent les cloux de Girofle.* This is the title of the Beinecke (formerly Philipps) manuscript, now in the Beinecke Library, Yale University. Printed as *Magellan's Voyage: A Narrative Account of the First Circumnavigation* (New Haven, 1969). Volume I, English translation with notes by R. A. Skelton; Volume II, facsimile of the manuscript in color. See reviews by C. R. Boxer in *American Anthropologist,* LXXIII (April 1971), 452–54; S. E. Morison in *New England Quarterly,* XLIII (June 1970), 325–28; and Armando Cortesão in *Studia,* No. 29 (April 1970), 319–25. Referred to here as "Yale ed." Here Skelton joins the "heresy" of denying that Magellan ever intended to sail home around the world (despite Pigafetta's explicit statement that he did); but Cortesão in his above-mentioned review tears that concept apart. Just as Columbus's First Voyage makes no sense unless his object was the Indies, so Magellan's makes no sense unless he intended to (1) sail through a strait, (2) cross the Pacific to the Spice Islands, and (3) return home around the world, by a route most of which he already knew.

(3) *The Voyage of Magellan. The Journal of Antonio Pigafetta* (William L. Clements Library, Ann Arbor, 1969). Facsimile of the earliest printed edition of Pigafetta—*Le Voyage et navigation faict par les Espaignolz es Isles de Mollucques* (Paris, probably 1525), with an English translation by Paula S. Paige. A good text and translation, not annotated.

(4) *The Denucé edition:* a manuscript in the Bibliothèque Nationale, Paris, edited by the eminent Belgian scholar Jean Denucé, printed at Antwerp and Paris in 1923 and 1956 as Antonio Pigafetta: *Relation du premier voyage autour du monde par Magellan.* Collated with other manuscripts, and excellent footnotes.

* James Alexander Robertson (1875–1939), historian and editor, was the most distinguished North American scholar on Latin-American and Spanish-American history in the generation that followed E. G. Bourne (see below). The Ambrosian Ms. had earlier been printed in the *Raccolta Colombiana,* Pt. V, vol. III (Rome, 1893), with notes by Marco Alegri.

Pigafetta's maps are so grossly inaccurate that one suspects that he got them up after his return.

For other Pigafetta manuscripts and early printed editions and translations, see Robertson ed., II, 240–304; Yale ed., I, 1–32, and Henry Harrisse in the series *Biblioteca Americana Vetustissima* (Carlos Sanz facsimile ed., Madrid, 1958), I, 228–29. Of the translations, Richard Eden's, first printed in his *Decades of the Newe Worlde or West India* (London, 1555), is important for its influence on English voyages.

For discussions of Pigafetta, see Torodash's bibliography, p. 327.

There are three other important narratives by participants:

1. Francisco Albo, *Diario ó Derrotero del Viage de Magellanes*. A careful, indispensable pilot's log of the voyage, from Brazil to Spain. First printed in Navarrete, IV (1837), 209–47, translated in part in Stanley, pp. 210–36 (see below). Facts about Albo are in J. T. Medina, *Descubrimiento* (see below), III, chap. xvi, No. 7.

2. The anonymous Leiden Narrative, in Portuguese; unsigned ms. in the library of the University of Leiden, probably by an apprentice seaman named Vasquito Gomes Gallego. This covers the entire voyage, and is important for the Cebu massacre and the last voyage of *Trinidad*. It was printed at Coimbra as *Um Roteiro Inédito* in 1937, M. de Jong, editor.

3. The *Roteiro* of the "Genoese Pilot," variously identified as Juan Bautista de Punzorol, León Pancaldo, and others—but he was neither a Genoese nor a pilot. First published by the Lisbon Academy of Sciences in *Notícias Para a História e Geografia das Navegações Ultramarinas*, IV and VI (Lisbon, 1825). Translated in Stanley (see below), pp. 1–29. A factual account, important for navigation and for details after Magellan's death.

Note that Pigafetta and the other sources often differ by one day in the dates they assign to events of the voyage. That happened because Albo, like all ships' log-keepers down to 1925, counted days from noon to noon, whilst other writers used the standard calendar. For instance, an event on the morning of 11 June would be put down by Albo as happening on 10 June. A further "one day out" came as a result of the fleet's crossing the international date line without knowing it.

For minor accounts by other participants, see Torodash's bibliography, pp. 319–21.

Manuscript sources are mostly in the Archivo de Indias, Seville, where the Director, Doña Rosario Parra Cala, has been most helpful. So far as I can ascertain, all documents on Magellan and Elcano have been published by Navarrete, Medina, and Pastells (see below), with the exception of a very full accounting of the costs and profits of the voyage done by Cristóbal Haro in more than 50 folios. Any young scholar who wishes to contribute new knowledge to this voyage cannot do better than to transcribe and print this document. There is a typed copy of it in the Goldfarb Library of Brandeis University.

COLLECTIONS OF SOURCES

NAVARRETE. Martín Fernández de Navarrete, *Colección de los Viages y Descubrimientos* . . . , IV (1837). (For this great Spanish editor see bibliography to Columbus, Chapter I, above). Volume IV opens with his own 90-page history of the voyage. It is followed by the Task Organization (pp. 3–26), a partial list of the dead (p. 65) and survivors, including *Victoria*'s men abandoned at the Cape Verdes (p. 94). There are documents on the organization of and preparations for the voyage (pp. 110–89), the elaborate royal instructions (pp. 130–50); Magellan's memorial on positions of the Spice Islands (p. 113), investigations of mutinies (pp. 189–208); Francisco Albo's *Diario ó derrotero* (pp. 209–47); investigation of Elcano, 18 October 1522 (pp. 285–301), letter of Admiral Brito about the fate of *Trinidad* (pp. 305–11), and documents on the Congress of Badajoz and the Line of Demarcation (pp. 312–69). This entire volume of Navarrete is reprinted in *Biblioteca de Autores Españoles*, LXXVI (Madrid: Ediciones Atlas, 1955, 1964), but the documents are somewhat cut down in this edition.

STANLEY. Lord Stanley of Alderley (ed.), *The First Voyage Round the World, by Magellan. Translated from the Accounts of Pigafetta and Other Contemporary Writers* (London, Hakluyt Society, No. LII of their *Publications*, 1874). This member of the distinguished if erratic Stanley family, born in 1827, was the eldest son of the second Baron of Alderley and Henrietta Maria Stewart (both in the *Dictionary of National Biography*, XVIII, 952–53). He entered the British diplomatic service after a year at Cambridge, traveled extensively in the Near and Far East, became an excellent linguist and a convert to Islam; his brother Algernon, a Catholic convert, rose to be titular Bishop of Emmaus. Stanley's *First Voyage* contains an inferior translation of Pigafetta's narrative but good ones of his *Treatise of Navigation* (pp. 164–74) and *Roteiro* of the "Genoese Pilot" (pp. 1–29). Also, Magellan's orders of 21 November 1520 in the Strait (pp. 182–78); the account of Maximilianus Transylvanus (see below), pp. 179–210; Francisco Albo's *Diario*, translated incompletely from a manuscript in the British Museum (pp. 210–36); contemporary accounts of the mutiny at Port San Julián, from Navarrete, and (pp. 244–56) what the Portuguese historian Gaspar Correia (d. 1563) has to say about the voyage in his *Lendas da India*.

MEDINA. The Chilean historian José Toribio Medina (1852–1930) may well be called the South American Justin Winsor, and he was even more productive than Winsor. His first important publication was *Historia de la Literatura Colonial de Chile*, opening with researches on the Chilean epic *La Araucana*. His main enthusiasm soon turned to history, and in the course of a long life he published over 300 volumes of original historical narratives, collections of documents, and bibliographies. He visited Spain frequently and worked extensively in the Archives of the Indies. Finding relations with the university press and private publishers unsatisfactory, he set up his own press, which he called the Elzeviriana, in his house. Of his documentary works, one of the most important is *Colección de Documentos Inéditos para la Historia de Chile desde el viaje de Magallanes hasta la Batalla de Maipo* (30 vols., Santiago, 1888–1902). Volumes II and III deal with Magellan and his companions. An extensive appendix to these are his *El Descubrimiento del Océano Pacífico, Balboa, Magallanes y sus Compañeros.* Three volumes (usually bound in one and numbered III; Santiago, 1920), with an indispensable detailed list of Magellan's shipmates. The same title with the subtitle *Documentos* added (Santiago, 1920), contains more documents, a fresh crew list, and Index to the *Documentos Inéditos.* On pp. 320–21—not, unfortunately, found in every copy—is a useful plotting of *Victoria's* crossing of the Indian Ocean.

Medina did not merely edit documents; he was a fine narrative historian. His vast collections of previously unedited documents long have been and will ever continue to be of great use to scholars. Equally important are his voluminous and painstaking bibliographies of the Hispano-American press. The best available account of his long and distinguished career is in Maury A. Bromsen (ed.), *José Toribio Medina, Humanist of the Americas,* published by the Pan American Union in 1960, with chapters by Guillermo Feliú Cruz and Irene Wright; digest in *Américas,* XXIV (Oct. 1972), pp. 41–43. Señor Feliú Cruz, one of Medina's disciples and assistants, describes him as short, and erect in bearing, walking with sure, quick steps. Although nervous and sometimes curt, close friends found him vivacious and communicative. I felt it a privilege to have studied in the sumptuous Medina Library which is part of the Biblioteca Nacional in Santiago.

NOWELL. Charles E. Nowell (ed.), *Magellan's Voyage Around the World. Three Contemporary Accounts* (Evanston, 1962). This handy little book of 350 pages includes an excellent 70-page introduction by the editor, the Robertson translation of Pigafetta's narrative minus most of the notes, and Stanley's translations of Maximilianus and Correia. He concludes with a few pages on later expeditions through the Strait.

PASTELLS. P. Pablo Pastells, *El Descubrimiento del Estrecho de Magallanes* (Madrid, 1920, illus.). This work, by the then Director of the Archivo de Indias, is mainly useful for its 579-page appendix of documents and for reprinting Ladrillero's and Sarmiento's narratives (pp. 239–308). Unfortunately it is not indexed.

SECONDARY AUTHORITIES

The earliest printed account of Magellan's voyage is one of those little German newsletters that the Augsburg banking house of Fugger sent to their important customers. Its abbreviated title is *Eine schöne Newe zeytung so Kayserlich Mayestet ausz getz nemlich zukommen seind* (Augsburg, 1522, 8 leaves). See Harrisse, in the series *Biblioteca Americana Vetustíssima* (Carlos Sanz facsimile ed., Madrid, 1958), No. 115; and Sanz's own *Ultimas Adiciones* to Harrisse (1960), II, 909–12. A highly inaccurate summary of American discovery from Columbus through Magellan! The final paragraph records the setting forth of a fleet *mit iiij Hundert personen* under one *Wagelanus*, the return of one ship, unnamed, on 6 September 1522, *mit xviij personen . . . und der selb Wagelanus*, which had *die gantzen Welt umbgefaren* and brought some spices. There are copies of this very rare tract in the John Carter Brown Library of Providence, and James Ford Bell Library of Minneapolis whose librarian, Dr. John Parker, kindly furnished me with a transcript.

Fortunately we are not dependent on this tract, or on the next one in order of time:—*Maximiliani Transylvani Caesaris a secretis Epistola, de admirabili & novissima Hispanorum in Orienttius navigatione . . . cum ipsis etiam Moluccis insulis beatissimis, optimo Aromatum genere refertis . . .* (Cologne, January 1523-24).

This young man, one of Charles V's secretaries and a protégé of Peter Martyr, ambitious to acquire fame as a writer, adopted a suggestion of his father, the Cardinal Archbishop of Salzburg, that he interview survivors of *Victoria* and write up the voyage. This little tract of 15 unnumbered leaves is the result. I had the pleasure of reading one of the few surviving copies of the first edition in the Beinecke Library of Yale University, and of the second (also 1523) at the Scheepvaart Museum, Amsterdam. Spanish translation in Navarrete, IV, 249–84, and English ones in Stanley, Nowell, and the Filipiniana Book Guild edition of Pigafetta (see above); this last, the best, is well annotated by the Philippine historian Carlos Quirino. The tract is about what one would expect of a high school boy interviewing Shackleton or Byrd, and it failed to promote Max as an author; his Latin is poor, and he had no sense of narrative. But he did conclude that Elcano's *Victoria* better deserved a place among the constellations than Jason's *Argo*.

Of the 16th- and 17th-century Spanish and Portuguese historians, Correia may conveniently be consulted in Stanley or Nowell (above). Antonio de Herrera's *Historia General de los Castellanos en las Islas y Terra Firme del Mar Océano* (4 vols., Madrid, 1601–15), by the official historian of the Indies, is the most comprehensive. I used the translation by John Stevens entitled, *The General History of the Vast Continent and Islands of America* (London, 1740), which covers Magellan in Volumes II, 174–77, and III, 8–24, 145–54. There are shorter accounts of the voyage in Oviedo, López de Gómara, *Historia de las Indias* (1554), cap. xci, Peter Martyr, and others. These historians must be used with caution; their manifest inaccuracies are numerous, but they do give some seemingly veracious details not found elsewhere.

Skipping over several unworthy biographies of Magellan, we come to one which I consider the best to date: F. H. H. Guillemard, *The Life of Ferdinand Magellan and the First Circumnavigation of the Globe* (London, 1890; 353 pp.). This is in the series The World's Great Explorers and Explorations. Guillemard (1852–1933), a geographer and explorer (see obituary in *Geographical Journal*, LXXXIII, 350), had traveled over parts of Magellan's route. Thorough and honest in his research, he gave his readers plenty of good maps and wrote in excellent narrative style. His own travels are related in *The Cruise of the Marchesa* (1886).

Andrea da Mosto, "Il primo viaggio intorno al globo," a long chapter in the *Raccolta Colombiana* of 1894, Part V, Vol. III, tells everything known about Pigafetta. G. Berchet in the same *Raccolta*, Part III, Vol. I, 172–84, adds a bibliography of Italian sources. R. A. Skelton's introduction to Yale ed., I, has biographical and bibliographical data on Pigafetta.

Edward Gaylord Bourne, *Spain in America* (Albert Bushnell Hart's series *American Nation: A History*, Vol. III, New York, 1904). Chapter ix is on Magellan's voyage. This book, which I purchased when in college, first interested me in Magellan. Rereading it after sixty-five years, I still think that the chapter on Magellan by this Yale professor, whose untimely death deprived America of a second Parkman, is the best compendium of the great voyage in existence, and I am proud to quote two of his superb paragraphs.

Visconde de Lagoa, *Fernão de Magalhãis* (2 vols., Lisbon, 1938). The most important biography in Portuguese. Volume I is devoted to Magellan's ancestry, his service in the Far East under D. Manuel, and preparations for the voyage. Volume II includes a Portuguese translation of Pigafetta, well annotated, a nautical study of the voyage by Admiral Freitas Ribeiro (pp. 217–36), an appendix of documents, and a bibliography. Admiral Gago Coutinho, *A Náutica dos Descobrimentos*, II (1952), chaps. vii, viii, is an excellent summary by the great Portuguese sailor-historian.

Charles McKew Parr, *So Noble a Captain: The Life and Times of Ferdinand Magellan* (New York, 1953; London, 1955). The second edition (1964) is called *Ferdinand Magellan, Circumnavigator*. This work, by an enthusiastic amateur, is to be recommended for its fine narrative style; but it is a fictionalized biography, containing imaginary episodes.

Recommended for background is Boise Penrose, *Travel and Discovery in the Renaissance 1420–1620* (Cambridge, Mass., 1952). Armando Braun Menéndez, *Pequeña Historia Austral* (Buenos Aires, 1971), is an excellent manual covering three centuries. Chilean and Argentinian historians have not been idle, but I postpone a list of those I particularly recommend, to the Notes to Chapters XXII and XXIV.

J. G. Kohl, *Geschichte der Entdeckungsreisen u. Schifffahrten zur Magellan's-Strasse* . . . *mit acht karten* (Berlin, 1877), is a brief but valuable account by a learned German geographer-historian (1808–78), a contemporary of Justin Winsor, covering all important voyages through the Strait from Magellan's through Dampier's. Kohl, while in the United States (1854–57), worked out a method of reproducing the essential features and toponymy of old maps for modern printing that, in my opinion, has never been surpassed; and his originals are accessible in the Library of Congress. See Memoir by Charles Deane in Massachusetts Historical Society *Proceedings*, XVI (Dec. 1878), 381–85. He quotes from Kohl's last letter to him, sending affectionate greetings and memories of Maine to Professor Leonard Woods of Bowdoin College, and the poet Longfellow. Happy days, a century ago, when despite slow communication the *Américanistes* of both continents knew each other and gave friendly mutual assistance!

Captain A. Teixeira da Mota has favored me with copies of several yet unpublished papers of his on Magellan's navigation and his preparations, in which he brought out the resemblance of Rui Faleiro's and Pigafetta's works on longitude. Miss Helen M. Wallis of the British Museum Map Room has been equally generous in allowing me to read her unpublished Oxford doctoral dissertation, *The Exploration of the South Sea, 1519-1644.*

MAGELLAN'S BIRTHPLACE

Antonio Baião, "Fernão de Magalhães, o problema de sua naturalidade rectificado e esclarecido," *História e Memorias da Academia das Sciencias de Lisboa,* n.s., XIV (1922), 25-81 (summarized in Lagoa's opening chapter), is the basic study which most later writers have followed, shifting Magellan's birthplace from Sabrosa to Nóbrega. A collateral descendant, Manuel de Magalhãis e Menenzes Villas-Boas, of Lisbon, has made extensive genealogical researches which he kindly communicated to me. He believes that our Magellan belonged to the Sabrosa branch of the family but was not necessarily born there. Baião prints a lengthy legal document on an effort by Magellan's cousin Lourenço in 1563 to collect some of the moneys owed to the navigator by the Spanish crown. Lourenço claimed that he and Magellan were respectively sons of two brothers, born and brought up in Nóbrega. This effort for financial restitution failed; but in 1796 a more remote collateral descendant, a gentleman of Sabrosa, married to a niece of the famous Spanish minister of state Godoy, tried again. The 1509 will was then discovered "in an old book"—which Baião considers evidence that the Sabrosa gentleman forged it. But even today wills are found in old books, under rugs, and all manner of unlikely places. It reads like a genuine will, and I still believe that Sabrosa was our hero's birthplace. All agree, however, that he settled in Oporto, the metropolis of northern Portugal, when he returned from the Far East. There is a good review of this birthplace question by Damião Péres in *Revista Chileña de Historia y Geografía,* No. 120 (Santiago, 1952), pp. 7-12.

Magellan's portraits and personality. J. T. Medina, *Descubrimiento del Océano Pacífico* III (1920), cvii-cxi, starts with a reproduction of the portrait commonly known, that of a rather sinister-looking man all in black—black hat, black beard, heavy black moustache, and thick lower lip. It first appeared in the *Relación del Último Viage al Estrecho de Magallanes de la Fragata de S. M. "Santa Maria de la Cabeza"* (Madrid, 1788); Medina thinks it came from the celebrated picture gallery of famous men belonging to Paulo Jovio at Como, and dates it 1568. Herrera, in the first edition of his *Hechos de los Castellanos* (1601), has a small portrait of Magellan apparently founded on this, as were 37 later versions listed by Medina. The frontispiece in the Visconde de Lagoa's biography reproduces a much more convincing portrait, now in the Kunsthistorisches Museum, Vienna, whose

The probable birthplace of Magellan, Sabrosa, Quinta de Souta. Courtesy Senhor Manuel de Magalhãis e Menenzes Villas e Boas.

Entrance which dates from Magellan's time. Courtesy Senhor Manuel de Magalhãis e Menenzes Villas e Boas.

Director, Dr. E. M. Auer, has kindly sent me the photograph reproduced here, as well as this information. Artist and date are unknown, but Archduke Ferdinand II (1529–95) had it painted for his collection of portraits of celebrities in his Schloss Ambras near Innsbruck; thence it was transferred to the imperial collection in Vienna, and finally to the Ambraser Portrait-Sammlung in the Kunsthistorisches Museum, Vienna. The inscription reads: "The Illustrious Ferdinand Magellan, Conqueror of the Narrow Antarctic Strait."

Another portrait, frequently reproduced, an engraving done at least a century after Magellan's death by Crispin Van de Passe senior (d. 1637), is in the Albertina Library of Vienna, whose Director kindly sent me a photograph. It is in the 17th-century style of *Heroölogia Anglica* (1620) to which Crispin and his sons contributed.

The modern painting by António Menendes, in the Museu da Marinha at Lisbon, is based on careful study of the old ones, and appeals to me as *the* Magellan of the great voyage.

A second, long-posthumous, engraved portrait, by one L'Aumessin in the Bibliothèque Nationale, is reproduced in Lucien Mazenod (ed.), *Les Explorateurs célèbres* (Geneva, 1947), p. 52. This Magellan is curly-haired and looking at a constellation, with a pair of dividers in one hand and a rolled-up chart in the other.

Las Casas's description of Magellan is in his *Historia de las Indias*, lib. iii, chap. ci (1927 ed., III, 145–46).

Magellan's arms. The blazon of the simple Magellan family arms, delineated in Guillemard (p. 20), is, on a field argent three bars checky, gules and argent; crest an eagle with spread wings. But Magellan in his last will, of 1519, directed that these be quartered with the Sousa arms, which include the royal arms of Portugal—the five *quinas* or wounds of Christ.

Magellan's Far Eastern experience. The best account is by Jean Denucé in *Mémoires de l'Académie Royale de Belgique*, 2nd ser., IV (1908), 100–138. Varthema's travels were published at Milan in 1511 as *Ludovici Patritii Romani Novum Itinerarium Aethiopiae, Aegipti, utriusque Arabiae, Persidis, Siriae ac Indiae, intra et extra Gangem.* A new edition was published by the Hakluyt Society (No. 35, London, 1866). A Portuguese manuscript now at Barcelona, is translated by Stanley, *A Description of the Coasts of East Africa and Malabar by Duarte Barbosa.* This Barbosa was either Magellan's brother-in-law who became an officer in his expedition, or, possibly, that Barbosa's uncle. Written about 1514, it is a chatty sort of *roteiro* of the Far East, and includes an account of the trade of Malacca with Timor and the Spice Islands (pp. 192–93), and the clove trade (199–204, 219–20). Magellan probably read one of the copies of this manuscript, which circulated in Spain and Portugal; it mentions his friend and correspondent Serrão.

A more comprehensive account of the Far East, and detailed narrative of Abreu's voyage, written by a Portuguese before Magellan came to Spain, is *The Suma Oriental of Tomé Pires* (2 vols., London, Hakluyt Society, 1944), rendered the more valuable by the scholarly footnotes and introduction (p. lxxx ff.) of the translator and editor, Armando Cortesão. Barros (*Decadas*, No. 3, lib. V, chap. viii) is the authority for D. Manuel's detestation of Magellan. For the Padre Shoals episode, Gaspar Correia, *Lendas de India*, II, 28, 625; and Fernão Lopes de Castanheda, *História do Descobrimento & Conquista da India pelos Portugueses* (Coimbra, 1551–52, lib. iii, chap. v). Las Casas has the story, too, in *Historia de las Indias*, chap. ci (1927 ed., III, 145). See also Stanley, pp. xvii–xx.

Portuguese viceroys of India were entitled to use the regal "Dom;" mere governors were not. Albuquerque, a governor, succeeded Almeida in 1509.

✳ XIV ✳

Armada de Molucca

1517-1519

Preparations

In the fall of 1517 Magellan broke with Portugal. He had the civility
to seek a final audience with D. Manuel and there formally to ask permission "to go and live with someone who would reward his services."
The King coldly replied that he could do as he pleased. Magellan requested the honor of kissing the hand of the monarch he had served
so long and faithfully, but D. Manuel refused even that slight boon.
Magellan promptly went to Seville, arriving 20 October 1517. Shortly
after, he signed the formal papers making him a Spanish subject.

In contrast to eastward-oriented Lisbon, Seville was humming with
Western Ocean and New World activity, and Magellan found himself
in the midst of it. The year before he arrived, Charles I, son of Felipe
el Hermoso of Austria and grandson of Ferdinand and Isabella, had
become king of Castile, Leon, and Aragon at the age of sixteen; and
in June 1518 he was elected king of the Romans, meaning that he
would be Emperor as soon as he could get the Pope to crown him in
Rome. That did not take place for two years, but the Pope consented
that he adopt the style and title of emperor at once. Thus he is known
to history as Carlos Quinto, Charles-Quint, or Charles V, Emperor
of the Holy Roman Empire.

Let us pause for a few words on that remarkable young man, successor to the Caesars at the age of nineteen. Charles was an intelligent man of great energy, in both respects above contemporary monarchs. He cared a good deal about exploration and discovery, certainly much more than did his contemporaries Henry VIII and François-premier. But, although he adopted as a motto *Plus Ultra* (More Beyond), wrapped around the Pillars of Hercules, the king's primary interest was Spain's position in Europe. He regarded America and the Far East principally as sources of specie and other convertible wealth, to pursue his European objectives. And these objectives were so costly as to be unobtainable:—to recover for his empire the old kingdom of Burgundy with its capital at Dijon and western boundary on the Rhône, to dominate Italy by balance-of-power politics, and to fight that "upstart" power France. It cost Charles almost a million ducats ($2,320,000 in the gold of 1934) to bribe the electors of the Holy Roman Empire to elect him King of the Romans; he had to borrow most of it from the bankers, who never got it all back. The specie flowing in from Mexico and Peru helped, but he never had enough to get out of the red; and many master mariners who devoted their lives to discovery were rewarded either with a pittance or a jail sentence.

Please look at this portrait of the Emperor at the age of about twenty-five by the Dutch painter Jan Cornelisz Vermeyen. This is the Charles V whom Magellan met, before he began dressing his hair in the new Italian fashion and letting his beard grow. Note the pendulous lower lip and the "whopper-jaw," Hapsburg characteristics which he inherited from his father, Philip of Austria, and transmitted to his descendants, even to Alfonso XIII. When he first came to Spain, Charles could hardly speak Spanish; but he soon learned, and did other things to please his new subjects such as showing a good leg on horseback, taking command of infantry in the field, and even jumping into the ring and killing a bull in a *corrida*.

More often than not, Charles V was absent from Spain—visiting his Burgundian inheritance at Brussels, traveling through Italy, on campaigns against France. Like Columbus, his great dream was to head a new crusade to liberate the Holy Land from the infidel; but it was all he could do to prevent the Ottoman Empire's able sultan, Suleiman the Magnificent, from conquering Vienna. On the whole, Charles V paid more attention to problems of discovery, exploration, and overseas conquest than did any contemporary monarch. Although individuals like Magellan generally took the initiative for a voyage of discovery, and merchants like Cristóbal Haro paid most of the bills, Charles V did leave to his son Philip II a greater empire than the modern world had ever known. And that, forty years before England, France, or any other country had established a single colony in the New World.

Everything seemed to be on the move during the first four years of Charles's reign. In the same month that Magellan came to Seville, Martin Luther nailed his famous Ninety-Five Theses against current Catholic practice to the church door at Wittenburg. While Magellan was at sea. Cortés conquered Mexico for Spain. In 1516–17 were written or published some of the greatest books of the High Renaissance:—Machiavelli's *Prince*, Erasmus's *Institution of a Christian Prince*, Thomas More's *Utopia*. Nationalism was rising, and there were other ambitious princes besides those on the Iberian Peninsula, eager to contest a threatened Spanish world hegemony based on the wealth of "the Indies."

Despite the rivalry between Spain and Portugal for this wealth, many Portuguese entered the Spanish service. Among those at Seville who supported Magellan were Diogo Barbosa, alcalde of the arsenal and knight commander of the Order of Santiago. He invited Magellan to stay in his house. His son Duarte (probably the man of that name who had sailed the Eastern seas for Portugal and written a book about them) joined the great voyage. Magellan fitted into the Barbosa family so agreeably as to woo and win Beatriz, Diogo's daughter and Duarte's sister. They were married in 1518, and she brought him a sizable dowry, 600,00 maravedis (about $42,000 in gold). A boy, Rodrigo, was born of this marriage about six months before Magellan sailed; but he died while his father was at sea. Doña Beatriz, wounded by the lies about her husband that successful mutineers brought to Spain, and hearing from Portuguese sources of his death in battle, died of a broken heart in 1521. With her, Ferdinand Magellan's line became extinct. Unlike Columbus, he left no sons to maintain his honor and confound malicious enemies.

Although Magellan had promised his partner Faleiro not to breathe a word of their joint project before Faleiro joined him at Seville, Magellan felt he could not miss an opportunity to lay it before the

The Emperor Charles V. Portrait by Jan Vermeyen; R. Todd-White photo.
Courtesy of owner, Lady Merton of Maidenhead Thicket.

The Empress Isabel. Portrait by Jan Vermeyen; R. Todd-White photo.
Courtesy of owner, Lady Merton of Maidenhead Thicket.

Casa de Contratación. This was the official board at Seville which handled most of Spain's colonial business. The Casa heard and shelved Magellan's scheme; but one member, Juan de Aranda, took the Captain aside, wormed every detail out of him, and promised to promote his cause at court in return for a 20 per cent cut of the expected profits. Faleiro, having arrived in Seville, became so furious over his partner's apparent breach of faith as to quarrel and subsequently break with him; but he did accompany his partner and Aranda to court at Valladolid. Magellan brought along a slave he had bought at Malacca, christened Henrique, who was destined to accompany him on his circumnavigation, and also a pretty girl slave from Sumatra.

At this conference (a description of which by Las Casas we have already quoted), Magellan put up a strong argument for the Spice Islands' being on the Spanish side of the Line of Demarcation if the line were carried around the world. His guess received influential support from Cristóbal Haro, an international figure in merchant banking who had outstanding claims against Portugal which the government of D. Manuel ignored.

It must be emphasized that Magellan had not the remotest idea of the width of the Pacific Ocean, uncrossed as yet by any European. Schoener's globe of 1515, a copy of which Magellan probably showed to Charles V,* places Japan a few hundred miles off Mexico; and the historian López de Gómara asserts that, in his negotiation with Charles V, Magellan declared that the Spice Islands were "no great distance from Panama, and the Gulf of San Miguel which Vasco Núñez de Balboa discovered."

A great personage with whom Magellan had to deal was Juan Fonseca, bishop of Burgos and the most influential member of the Casa de Contratación. He had done his best to hamper and discourage not only Columbus but Balboa and Cortés. Fonseca pretended to like Magellan, and as he was also a member of the royal council immediately under the king, that was important. But it is highly probable, though not proved, that, after placing several relatives and favorites as captains of Magellan's ships, Fonseca encouraged them to take over the command and run away with the expedition. They very nearly did, as we shall see.

The king, a hard-headed young man, snapped at a chance to enlarge

* See Below, Chapter XVI.

his already extensive dominions by annexing the Spice Islands, or at least sharing their trade with Portugal. On 28 March 1518 Charles issued a *capitulación* or agreement pertaining to it. He promised to provide Magellan and Faleiro, joint "captains general of the armada," with an annual salary of 50,000 maravedis each (about $1200), and almost tripled Magellan's before sailing. A fleet of five ships carrying some 250 officers and men would be provided; the partners would receive one-fifth of the profits, and the king promised to send out no rival expedition within ten years. Hypocritically, Charles ordered them not to explore within the territories of his "dear and well-beloved uncle and brother the King of Portugal" *—which was the main object of the expedition. If they discovered any new lands not claimed by any Christian prince, they could become hereditary adelantados thereof, but that chance never occurred. Members of the expedition found it more expedient to trade with the sultans and rajahs of the Far East than to conquer their kingdoms; Magellan lost his life trying to prove the contrary.

The preparations for this important voyage took much longer than expected—as with almost every great voyage under sail for the last four hundred years. In Magellan's case the usual difficulties of equipping ships for sea were multiplied by waterfront rascality and by the inveterate opposition of Portugal. Letters of Portugal's ambassador to Spain prove that he did everything possible to wreck the enterprise before it started, even offering Magellan a bribe to drop the whole thing and return to Portugal. One of D. Manuel's counsellors and confessors, Bishop Vasconcellos, even advocated the assassination of Magellan. Another difficulty was the irascible interference of Rui Faleiro, obviously going mad; he finally had to be left behind. The Casa de Contratación, lukewarm about the enterprise, needed several strong letters from the king to help Magellan get to sea. Portugal's consular agent at Seville noted with pleasure that the five ships procured for Magellan were "very old and patched up"; he "would not care to sail to the Canaries in such old crates; their ribs are soft as butter." Sour grapes, no doubt. Magellan could never have been fobbed off with a rotten ship for a long ocean voyage. The fleet went to sea sound and

---

* Charles V's elder sister Leonor had already married D. Manuel, and his younger sister Catarina married D. Manuel's heir who became D. João III in 1521. In 1525 Charles V married D. Manuel's daughter the Infanta Isabel.

Exterior, Church of Santa Ana, Triana, Seville.

staunch, and none of the many casualties on this voyage were due to defects in the vessels but to wear and tear, inadequate provisioning, and human depravity. Bishop Fonseca's hostility did not extend to the fitting out, as he expected his friends to take over the armada at sea; but he winked at cheating by the fleet's furnishers.

Faleiro had been acting so strangely that on 26 July 1519, only a fortnight before the fleet sailed, Charles V ordered him replaced by Juan de Cartagena as captain of *San Antonio* and inspector general of the fleet. "Señor" Cartagena, as he was called in the letter of appointment, had neither rank, title, nor sea experience. A bumptious young courtier, he owed this extraordinary promotion to the fact that he was Bishop Fonseca's "nephew"; i.e., the fruit of some episcopal indiscretion. Antonio de Coca, a bastard of the bishop's brother, was appointed *contador*, fleet accountant. Two other ship's captains, both royal appointees, were Luis de Mendoza, described as a "friend" of the archbishop of Seville, captain of *Victoria* and fleet treasurer with an annual salary of 60,000 maravedis; and Gaspar de Quesada, captain of *Concepción*, also a "servant of the Archbishop" (Fonseca), but beyond that we know naught of his country or family. Thus Fonseca had his men, mostly bastards, spotted in very significant positions in the fleet. But we must credit the episcopal nepotist with one excellent royal appointment, that of Gonzalo Gómez de Espinosa as *alguacil mayor* (chief marshal) of the fleet, commanding all shipboard soldiers. He remained steadfastly loyal to Magellan, and after Magellan's death commanded flagship *Trinidad*. The only captain Magellan could really count on was Juan Serrano of little *Santiago*, like himself a voluntary exile from Portugal. Brother or cousin to Francisco Serrão, Magellan's intimate friend whom he hoped to meet in the Spice Islands, Serrano was an experienced mariner. Portuguese, too, was Esteban Gómez, flag pilot; but he hated Magellan and pulled off the only successful mutiny of the voyage.

Further to emphasize Cartagena's exalted position, Fonseca allowed him to bring along ten servants, all on the payroll, and the Emperor permitted him to draw his court stipends during the expedition in addition to his pay of 60,000 maravedis a year. Was he also joint captain general with Magellan, as Faleiro would have been? The royal cédula of 26 or 28 July 1519, appointing Cartagena captain of *San Antonio* in place of Faleiro, does indeed describe him as *conjunta persona* with Magellan. Cartagena naturally regarded this as giving him joint authority with Magellan; but that is certainly not what Charles V intended. For in his commission and other documents the Emperor always referred to Magellan as *Capitán Mayor* or senior captain, which is usually translated Captain General. And he ordered all officers of the fleet at the before-sailing ceremony in Seville to swear to obey Magellan *en todo*, in all respects.

Everyone who has written about this voyage has had to decide whether Cartagena was legally joint commander with Magellan. In my opinion, the *conjunta persona* phrase in the July cédula was simply a clerical oversight, the scribe assuming that the king wished to grant Cartagena all Faleiro's rights and duties. Had there been any doubt of his position, surely Cartagena would have raised it before the fleet left Sanlúcar, instead of waiting until they had been at sea for over a month and then challenging Magellan in a manner which led to his death.

Charles V made Magellan knight commander of the Order of Santiago before sailing, an honor he did not confer on Cartagena or, after the voyage, on Elcano.

One would like to know what age these captains were, and what maritime experience, if any, they had had. I infer from the fact that José Toribio Medina was unable to find anything about them prior to 1519, that they were all fairly young and completely inexperienced. By exception, he found that Espinosa was then thirty-two. Magellan himself had reached his thirty-ninth birthday when he embarked. Curiously enough, we have data on the ages of many of the common sailors in 1519. The youngest was a page fourteen years old; the eldest, an ancient mariner of forty-four.

Besides the usual wrangles and jangles on getting ready for sea, Magellan, in common with Columbus, had the extra handicap of being a foreigner. For this reason, probably, the King warned him not to engage more than five Portuguese for the fleet. An incident on 22 October 1518 indicated that he was on slippery ground at Seville. His intended flagship, *Trinidad*, was being careened to cleanse her bottom. On such occasions, naval etiquette required a king's ship to show the royal ensign at a masthead, and the captain's flag on each capstan head. Since all her royal ensigns and other Spanish flags had been sent to be newly painted, Magellan had nothing to show aloft, and he used flags with his own arms to cover the capstan. On them the Magalhães family arms were quartered with the Portuguese royal arms, owing to their relationship with the Sousa family. A crowd of idlers gathered on the Seville graving beach to view this interesting operation. Pretty soon they began to growl and grumble that the banners and ensigns of their own king had been replaced by Portuguese arms on the capstans. One of Magellan's friends, Canon Marienzo of the cathedral, suggested that he remove his arms from the capstans to appease the mob. That he did, but to slight effect; for the captain of the port and other officials appeared, roaring with patriotic zeal, to arrest Magellan for *lèse majesté*. When the Canon tried to dissuade them by pointing out that the Captain General was a royal officer, they rushed upon him with drawn swords, screaming threats of murder. Magellan kept his cool, and with furious Sevillians thrusting naked swords under his nose, remarked that the vessel was in a dangerous position with an inrushing tide, and if they did not leave him and his crew to do what had to be done, she would be swamped through the open hatches, and they would be responsible for the loss of a king's ship. That sent the officials slinking away, and the shore mob contented itself with more muttering and bawling. Magellan recounted the whole sorry affair in a letter to the King, who ordered all officials who had had a part in the riot to be severely punished. There is no evidence that they ever were.

As this incident shows, the Portuguese were very unpopular in Andalusia. Magellan had to send all over Spain to obtain sailors for his armada; the final lists show, besides a majority of Spaniards, numerous Portuguese, Genoese, Sicilians, French, Germans, Flemings, blacks, and one Englishman. Charles V himself discharged Rui Faleiro and had to order another troublemaker, Luis de Mendoza, flag treasurer and captain of *Victoria*, to render unhesitating obedience to Magellan. This he notoriously failed to do, and it would have been well for him had he been left in Spain instead of providing food for the vultures in Patagonia. The Portuguese historian A. Teixeira da Mota argues that Faleiro must have been responsible for Magellan's general ideas on cosmography, or he would not have taken him to Spain. Pigafetta's *Regole sull' Arte del Navigare* (Rules on the Art of Navigation), it now appears, is merely a free translation of Faleiro's *Regimento da Altura de Leste-Oeste* (Rules for Finding Longitude); but neither tract helped Magellan to determine longitude. Faleiro apparently did not stay long in the *casa de locos* in which he was placed when Magellan sailed. He quarreled with his family, returned to Portugal (where he was put in jail), and after serving the sentence came back to Spain to sue for the salary he would have been paid had he gone to sea. He died in 1544 in poverty.

From Barcelona on 8 May 1519 Charles V issued minute instructions for the voyage—no fewer than 74 paragraphs! Magellan's initial reaction must have been, "Does His Highness suppose I have never been to sea?" Most of the instructions were routine, such as never to overload, always to be kind and just to the natives, to treat the crews "lovingly," and to forbid gambling, brawling, bawdry, and blasphemy. Every member, from captains down to the smallest ship's boy was to have a designated amount of free freight—the system later known as "primage"—for his personal investment in the Far East; captains could bring 8000 pounds' weight; ship's boys 75 pounds each, an unusually generous allowance. Someone close to the king tried to imagine everything that might happen, to include in these instructions; but never anticipated the terrible things that did happen—starvation, mutiny, and the leader's death.

Ships and Crews

From documents in the Spanish archives we know many details of Magellan's fleet and complement. To spare my non-nautical readers, I have relegated these to an appendix to this chapter, here stating the bare outline.

Flagship *Trinidad*, 100 tuns, Magellan captain, succeeded by Duarte Barbosa, João Carvalho, and Gonzalo Gómez de Espinosa.

San Antonio, ship of 120 tuns, Juan de Cartegena captain, succeeded by Antonio de Coca, Álvaro de Mezquita, and Hierónimo Guerra.

Concepción, ship of 90 tuns, Gaspar de Quesada captain; succeeded by Rodríguez Serrano and Luis de Gois.

Victoria, ship of 85 tuns, Luis de Mendoza captain, succeeded by Duarte Barbosa, Cristóbal Rebelo, and Juan Sebastián de Elcano.

Santiago, caravel of 75 tuns, Juan Serrano captain.

Nothing is known about the antecedents of these vessels, except that *Victoria* was built in Guipuzcoa. No contemporary painting or model can be identified as one of them. *Victoria* does indeed appear crossing the Pacific, winged Victory perched on her bowsprit, in Ortelius's atlas of 1589, a picture often copied (even for Drake's flagship!), but she has only two masts and is of a later design than any Magellanic ship. *La Dauphine*, Verrazzano's flagship in his attempt to find a northern strait in 1524, measured 100 tuns; and we have at least a conjectural portrait of her.* The nearest ship pictures, in time, to those of our *Armada de Molucca* (the official name of Magellan's fleet) are those in the Diego Ribero mappemonde of 1529, where two pair of ships, each captioned *voyamaluco* ("I'm going to the Moluccas"), are shown; one pair sailing before the wind off the Chilean coast, the other approaching Surigao Strait. These may (somewhat cautiously) be assumed to be Ribero's idea of *Trinidad* and *Victoria*. The ships in João de Castro's *Roteiro de Goa a Suez* (1541) and those in the Miller Atlas (1525) may also be considered similar to Magellan's. All these are depicted by Portuguese; but so far as I can learn there was then no

* See my *Northern Voyages*, p. 286.

difference between the architecture and rigging of Spanish and Portuguese ships, except that the Portuguese went in heavily for caravels, and only one of Magellan's was of that rig. According to the historian Herrera, Magellan's vessels had exceedingly high sterncastles, to accommodate the unusually large number of officers. The sterncastle had by this time evolved from a square *toldilla* looking like a loose box, to a functional, two- to three-deck superstructure, carrying out the lines of the afterbody and the square stern. That had replaced the neat round "tuck" of Columbus's ships.

This "cage work" (as the English called it) or *obras muertas* "dead wood" (the Spanish phrase) was not so great a detriment to navigation as one might think; the very light woodwork and the high sides helped a ship to sail. Each of Magellan's vessels carried three masts, two square-rigged and the mizzen lateen. The high turn of speed shown by the fleet between Guam and Samar (see Chapter XVII, below) suggests that Magellan's vessels crossed very long main yards and spread big billowing courses, as shown in the Miller I and Ribero maps.

The fleet was amply armed, with 62 culverins, 10 falconets, and 50 arquebuses, in addition to the ordnance that came with the ships. But, as explorers still depended on *l'arme blanche* rather than gunpowder, hundreds of steel pikes, halberds, and swords were carried as well as one hundred complete suits of armor, and the personal suits of mail and plumed helmets owned by the leading officers. Several hundred crossbows, and many long bows, were also taken. The provision of navigation instruments reflects Magellan's interest in the science, as well as that of Andrés de San Martín, the *astrólogo* or top navigator of the fleet. There were 23 charts by Nuño García, an Italian cartographer employed by the Council of the Indies; 6 pair of dividers, 7 astrolabes (one of brass), 21 wooden quandrants such as Columbus used, 35 magnetized needles for the compasses, and 18 half-hour glasses for keeping time. The Portuguese who seized *Trinidad* in the Spice Islands impounded San Martín's books, two planisphere maps by Pedro Reinel, and all other charts and instruments. None have survived.

The fleet carried chests full of trading truck to barter with natives, such as 20,000 hawks' bells in three sizes, 500 pounds of glass beads, brass bracelets, fishhooks, silk, cotton, and woolen cloth of many colors, 400 dozen German knives "of the worst quality," a thousand "little hand mirrors, 100 of them better quality," and a ton of mercury—this, presumably, for medical purposes as its metal-extracting properties had not yet been discovered. When Vasco da Gama presented this sort of truck to the sultans and rajahs of the Indian Ocean, they indignantly rejected it as cheap junk; so Magellan, having had experience with Far Eastern potentates, saw to it that his fleet also carried presents suitable for royalty. Unfortunately we have no list of them, but in the Phillipines and the Moluccas he presented the chieftains with silk robes "made in the Turkish fashion," and sundry bolts of woolen and silk cloth.

As in Columbus's ships, there was no rating of cook. Apparently, apprentice seamen still took turns at the skillet, using a wood fire in an open cook box under the overhang of the forecastle. Important people like Cartagena had personal servants and possibly their own particular cook boxes; in the bigger ships, these were probably below decks. The list of equipment shows utensils of iron and copper, and the provisions included seemingly ample quantities of wine, olive oil, vinegar, beans, lentils, garlic, flour, rice, cheese, honey, sugar, anchovies, sardines, salt cod, salt beef, and salt pork. Each ship carried a few live cattle and swine to slaughter en route. One curious item is 35 boxes of *carne de membrillo*—quince jelly or preserve—for *Trinidad*, whilst other vessels rated but four boxes each. The flagship, too, carried twice as many raisins as her consorts.

Officers and gentlemen volunteers such as Pigafetta had individual cabins or at least bunks in the sterncastle. Some petty officers such as the chief gunner may have lodged there too; but the common sailor slept anywhere on the main deck, in his clothes. Each ship had a *batel*, a longboat, which was usually towed, and several small boats which could be nested in the waist or taken apart and stowed below. The fleet had so many small boats that the simple natives of Rio de Janeiro, seeing them all in the water alongside the ships, assumed them to be the ships' children being suckled like a farrow of pigs! The ships were amply provided with anchors, cables, spare sails, and colors. Charles V and Magellan intended their *Armada de Molucca* to make a brave show.

Information about officers is scarce, especially on the three Spanish captains Cartagena, Mendoza, and Quesada. Magellan himself managed to sign on four relatives—his brother-in-law Duarte Barbosa, his natural son Cristóbal Rebelo, and two cousins, Álvaro de Mezquita and

Martín de Magallanes; the first three rose to command, but Mezquita proved to be a weakling. Barbosa—murdered at Cebu—had had sea experience under the Portuguese almost equal to Magellan's. Born in Lisbon, he spent the years 1501–16 in Portuguese service in the Far East. Happening to be at his father's house in Seville when Magellan married his sister, he signed up with no definite rating but proved a tower of strength to the Captain General, whom he survived for only a week.

Magellan had so much trouble recruiting sailors that he persuaded the king to raise the permitted number of Portuguese from five to more than thirty; even so, we find that a number of Portuguese sailors were put on the beach at the last minute and Spanish substitutes found, because the allotted number had been exceeded. Enemies later accused Magellan of having purposely beefed up his Portuguese contingent to ensure loyal support against mutinous Spaniards—and, God knows, he needed them! But it is not necessary to believe this. Spanish sailors were by now a privileged class, like American-born sailors in the American merchant marine during the last century. There were hardly enough of them to man the well-established and profitable routine voyages to the West Indies, to which they naturally preferred sailing, with prospects of gold, silver, and girls, rather than embarking on a dubious enterprise; and although Magellan attempted to conceal his destination lest recruits be repelled by anything so extraordinary, some rumor of it must have leaked out on the waterfront. Little *Santiago* was more than half manned by foreigners; *Concepción*'s crew, on the other hand, was mostly Andalusian, and *San Antonio* had a large number of Galicians; flagship *Trinidad* and *Victoria*, the one that finally rounded the world, were very mixed in their complements. All the gunners were French, Flemish, German, or English. Charles V must have considered the artillerymen of northern Europe to be better than Spaniards. All five ships had Portuguese pilots. This was natural, as only Portuguese had navigated the coasts of Brazil, East Africa, and Indonesia; everyone bound away wanted a Portuguese pilot, just as all British tramp steamers in the nineteenth century insisted on Scots engineers. All Magellan's pilots were professionals, certified by the board that preceded the Casa de Contratación. They drew 10,000 maravedis annual pay from the crown, and a few thousand extra for piloting Magellan. There were many Genoese, the most prestigious seamen in

Europe, and a scattering of Greeks, Cypriots, and Sicilians. Also one Englishman, "Master Andrew of Bristol," and the inevitable Irishmen from Galway, Guillermo Ires and Juanillo Ires—"Irish Bill" and "Irish Johnny." The five or six blacks on board were slaves to the top officers—"Antón de color negro" followed his master Gonzalo Gómez de Espinosa as a prisoner to India. No such internationally-manned fleet had ever put forth for discovery; at least not since Jason's Argonauts, to whom classically educated writers like Maximilianus were wont to compare Magellan's crew—to the Argonauts' disadvantage.

The sources used by Medina for seamen's pay indicate that a *marinero* (able seaman) drew 1200 maravedis a month, gromets or apprentice seamen 800 maravedis, and the men-at-arms the same. Everyone on board, even Juan de Cartagena's ten personal servants and Magellan's Malay slave Enrique, was on the payroll, and almost everyone received four months' advance pay.

One important foreigner who joined the flagship as a gentleman volunteer and who appears on her crew list as "Antonio Lombardo," was Antonio Pigafetta of Vicenza in Lombardy, where his family house is still (1974) standing and marked by a tablet. Despite the fact that he wrote the most famous sea narrative of his century, we have slight knowledge of Pigafetta's life before he came to Spain in the suite of the papal ambassador to Charles V. Since this envoy and Peter Martyr d'Anghiera were opposite numbers—protonotaries—at the papal and Spanish courts, it was natural for them to get together, and for Pigafetta to pick up information about the forthcoming expedition. He tells us himself that, "prompted by a craving for experience and glory," he applied for and received permission from the king and ambassador to sign up with Magellan. In May 1519 he arrived at Seville in time to participate in last preparations, to collect more navigational instruments, and to attend a solemn ceremony in the chapel of Santa Maria de la Victoria in Triana, Seville. There Magellan was presented with a royal standard, all officers swore to obey him in every respect, and every member of the expedition received communion. Several of those who swore obedience to Magellan were already plotting to kill him and take over.

On the face of it. Magellan's fleet, ships, matériel, and people were well suited to the enterprise. The one thing wrong with it came from the apparent political necessity of filling top ranks with bishops' bas-

Nuestra Señora de Victoria, in Church of Santa Ana. Sanchez Obregón photo.

tards, and letting them bring along a pack of pages and other "idlers" "only fit to keep the bread from moulding," as North American sailors used to say. With fewer idle hands and hungry bellies there might have been less starvation and suffering than the crews of *Trinidad, Concepción,* and *Victoria* endured in their long, lonely crossing of the Pacific.

Under Way

The Emperor showed himself very eager for Magellan to get going, and that he did on 10 August 1519. Even with expert river pilots it took the fleet several days to drop down the Guadalquivir to Sanlúcar de Barrameda, the outport for Seville. There it anchored in a wide bend of the river, almost under the castle of the Duke of Medina Sidonia. Shipmasters favored this anchorage because, no matter from what direction the wind blew, they could weigh and fill away without making short tacks. And there they stayed for more than a month, until 20 September. A good part of this time was spent in adding to the provisions. Owing to the discovery that "land sharks" had cheated on supplies, furnishing short-weight or putrid meat and old, weevily biscuit, Magellan refused to put to sea until these deficiencies were made good. This meant boat trips to Seville and finding barges to float fresh supplies down to Sanlúcar. Even so, he did not discover half the cheating until the fleet reached Patagonia.

Nuestra Señora de Barrameda, the waterfront church of Sanlúcar where the mariners worshipped, has disappeared. But the Capuchin monastery on the high part of the town still shelters a celebrated image of the Virgin and Child, called Our Lady of the Good Voyage, she holding a silver ship in one hand. In 1519 this image was in a little hermitage on the same spot, and many of Magellan's men must have gone there to pray for a safe voyage. At Sanlúcar the sailors were given daily shore leave on condition that they attend Mass. That duty accomplished, they were free to drink and otherwise disport themselves, for Magellan absolutely refused to allow women on board.

At Seville on 24 August 1519 Magellan signed his last will and testament. Therein he describes himself as Hernando de Magallanes, Comendador (of the Order of Santiago) and His Imperial Majesty's Captain General of the Armada bound for the Moluccas. He declares his firm belief in the Christian faith and in Our Lady as intercessor. He makes several tiny legacies to churches, shrines, and *cofradías* in Seville, and to the sacristy chapel in Seville Cathedral where he usually received holy communion. He hopes to be buried in a grave that he has reserved at Santa Maria de la Victoria in Triana; or, if he dies at sea, to be buried in the nearest church dedicated to Our Lady. The

Sanlúcar de Barrameda: Sketch by Samuel de Champlain, 1598. Courtesy
John Carter Brown Library.

View from the city in 1971. Courtesy D. Alfonso d' Orleáns y de Borbón.

600,000 maravedis that he had received as dowry should be repaid to his widow before any other legacies. One-tenth of all he may gain from the voyage to the Moluccas is to be set apart for legacies; one-third to build a new chapel around Santa Maria de la Victoria, where the monks may forever pray for the repose of his soul; two-thirds to be divided three ways—between Santa Maria de Monserrate near Barcelona, San Francisco at Aranda in the Douro valley, and Santo Domingo de las Dueñas in Oporto. His servant (and natural son) Cristóbal Rebelo is to receive 30,000 maravedis; and his slave "Enrique, mulatto, native of Malacca," his freedom and 10,000 maravedis "because he is a Christian, and that he may pray God for my soul." There are elaborate provisions for a *mayorazgo* or trust fund for the benefit of his widow, their children, his sister Isabel, and his Sousa cousins. His executors are his father-in-law Diogo Barbosa and Canon Marienzo of Seville, the one who intervened during the graving of *San Antonio*.

Alas, none of these generous and pious provisions were ever carried out. Doña Beatriz, their son, and the baby not yet born died before *Victoria* returned to Spain. Enrique deserted in Cebu. All attempts of the Barbosa and Magellan families to recover the Captain General's property from the crown, or even to have his long-overdue salary paid, failed. Had he been a convicted murderer, his family could not have been worse treated by the king-emperor whose dominions he had so notably increased, and in whose reign Magellan's voyage stands out as one of the most glorious events.

In September, when ready to sail, Magellan addressed to the king-emperor a memorial stating what he believed to be the longitude of certain islands in relation to the Line of Demarcation. Again he expressed the opinion that the already famous Spice Islands or Moluccas—Ternate, Tidore, and the rest—discovered for Portugal by Serrão in 1512, lay on the Spanish side of that north-south line. This confirms the belief that he expected to enlarge the Spanish empire at the expense of the Portuguese. The positions correspond closely to those on a world map by Maiollo, a copy of which he may have seen or acquired.

On Monday, 19 September 1519, all hands went ashore in relays to confess and receive absolution, and on Tuesday the 20th every ship weighed anchor and shaped her course southwest. Three years would elapse before any of these men except successful mutineers would return.

Bibliography and Notes

Salaries and Exchange. Guillemard, *Life* . . . , pp. 106–8; later raised to 146,000 maravedis for each, plus 30,000 for initial expenses. Juan de Cartagena's salary was 110,000, and Mendoza's 70,000. One thousand Spanish maravedis in Columbus's day was worth about $7.00 in gold, according to my calculations, but Guillemard (p. 107) calls it 11*s* 6*d*, about $3.00.

Faleiro. Stanley, *The First Voyage* . . . , pp. 164–74, Nowell, p. 65. A. Teixeira da Mota, *O Regimento da Altura de Leste-Oeste de Rui Faleiro* (Lisbon, 1953). This scholar and naval officer has really restored Faleiro to fame.

Esteban Gómez. Medina, *El Descubrimiento*, III, ch. xvi, No. 106; for later career, see my *Northern Voyages*, pp. 326–36.

Conjunta persona. Navarrete, *Colección*, IV (1837), p. 156, and p. 28. The phrase is, "Se quede é vaya en su [Faleiro's] lugar el señor Juan de Cartagena como su conjunta persona, asi como su Alteza lo manda por su carta."

Task Organization and Other Details. Original in Archives of the Indies, printed in Navarrete, IV (1837), 12–22. English translation in Robertson ed. Pigafetta, I, 205–15. José Toribio Medina reprinted a partial list, with the pay that each man received, in his *El Descubrimiento del Océano Pacífico —Magallanes y sus Compañeros* (Santiago, 1920), pp. 60–98, and his three-volume work of that same title devotes a long chapter (xvi) in volume iii (also 1920) to an alphabetical list of all who sailed with Magellan, with every bit of information he could find about them. Little more has been found in the last 50 years.

See my *Northern Voyages* (1971), p. 156, and my *Samuel de Champlain* (Boston, 1972), pp. 282–83, for descriptions of contemporary naval ordnance. Magellan's are listed in Navarrete, IV, 4–6.

Duarte's *Livro* . . . *do que Viu e Ouviu no Oriente* (Book of What I Saw and Heard in the Orient), first printed in 1813, translation by Lord Stanley in Hakluyt Society Vol. of 1866. But was he identical with our Duarte?

Magellan's 1519 will is translated in Guillemard, pp. 317–26.

Mulatto (mule) then meant anyone of mixed blood. Henrique was probably Malay or Visayan, possibly mixed with Portuguese.

Magellan's objectives. The late R. A. Skelton in his introduction to the Yale ed. of Pigafetta, p. 1, declared that when Magellan sailed in 1519 "he had not conceived a voyage round the world." Armando Cortesão, to my great joy, demolishes this heresy (*Studia*, April 1970, pp. 323–25). This theory is comparable to Cecil Jane's declaration that Columbus, when he set sail in 1492, had no definite objective. Of course Magellan intended to sail to the Moluccas, through an American strait if he found one, if not, via the Cape of Good Hope; and whilst he might have attempted to return via America if the strait had not proved to be so remote and difficult, Pigafetta states directly that at the time of his death he intended to return around the world, apparently the shortest way home.

Chapel of Santa Maria de la Victoria. This was in the Minorite convent of San Francisco de Paulo, erected in 1516, but the much older Virgin commemorated the victory over the Moors at Malaga. José Sebastián y Bandarón, "Breve noticia de las Imagenes de la SS Virgen Maria Venerada con especial Devoción en Sevilla," *Boletín* de la Real Academia Sevillana de Bonas Letras, No. 69, 144. Convent and chapel were destroyed in 1868, but the site is commemorated by a memorial tablet let into the wall facing the river. The statue of Santa Maria de la Victoria was saved, removed to the Church of Santa Ana less than a mile away, and carefully restored in 1928.

Appendix to Chapter XIV

MAGELLAN'S TASK ORGANIZATION

The names of all Magellan's ships and of those who sailed with him from Spain or the Canaries, have already been printed, several times.[*] This task organization is simplified. I have inserted the monthly pay for those in the flagship only, as it was the same for men in the other ships.

Capitán Mayor de la Armada: HERNANDO DE MAGALLANES
(Captain General of the Fleet: FERDINAND MAGELLAN)

TRINIDAD, *nao* (ship) of 100 tuns

Captain: Magellan. "Pilot of His Highness":[**] Esteban Gómez, formerly Portuguese. Master: Juan Bautista de Punzorol, salary 3000 maravedis per month. *Contramaestre* (assistant master or chief boatswain): Francisco Albo of Axio (Actium), a citizen of Rhodes, 2000 maravedis. Albo acted as flag pilot. Surgeon, Juan de Morales of Seville (the only one paid by the year), 25,000 maravedis. *Escribano* (secretary): Leon de Espleta. *Alguacil* (marshal, the military commander): Gonzalo Gómez de Espinosa (1800 marevedis). Petty officers: a barber-surgeon (1200 maravedis), a carpenter (Genoese), a steward (salary 1200 maravedis), a caulker (Genoese), a cooper. *Condestable* (chief gunner), Master Andrew of Bristol (salary 5 ducats monthly). Chaplain: Pedro de Valderrama (1500 maravedis). There were 11 *marineros* (able seamen), 4 or 5 of them Genoese (salary 1200 maravedis) and two gunners (salary 4 ducats), 10 or 11 *grumetes* (gromets,

---

[*] Navarrete, IV, 12–25, translation in Robertson ed. Pigafetta, I. My facsimile page is from the original document in Archivo de Indias; it covers only a part of the flagship's complement.

[**] Meaning that he had already been licensed by the Casa de Contratación, and was drawing a yearly salary.

apprentice seamen), including 2 Portuguese and 1 Genoese (salary 800 maravedis). Many *criados* (servants), including four of the Captain General's; one, a Portuguese named Cristóbal Rebelo (salary 1200 maravedis). He rose to command *Victoria*, fought beside his father at Mactan, and was killed at the fatal Cebu banquet. Magellan's slave Enrique de Molucca went on the roll as *lengua*, interpreter, and drew 1500 maravedis monthly. The *sobresalientes* (supernumeraries) included Duarte Barbosa, Magellan's brother-in-law, and Álvaro de Mezquita, his cousin or nephew; both rose to command. Pigafetta, incidentally, drew pay of 1000 maravedis per month, and the men-at-arms got 800. Total on board flagship: 61

SAN ANTONIO, ship of 120 tuns

Captain, *veedor* (inspector general of the fleet) and second in command to Magellan, Juan de Cartegena. *Contador* (accountant): Antonio de Coca. Secretary: Hierónimo Guerra. "His Majesty's Pilot": Andrés de San Martín* "Pilot of His Highness": Juan Rodriguez de Mafra. Master: Juan de Elorriaga (salary 3000 maravedis). Assistant master: Diego Hernandez (salary 2000 maravedis); chief gunner: Maître Jacques of Lorraine, and 2 gunners, both Flemish. A barber, a steward, a cooper, 2 caulkers, 2 gunners, 9 mariners (1 French, one of Actium), 10 gromets (3 Italian), 2 boys, 15 servants (including Cartagena's 10), drew 800 to 1500 maravedis per months; and several men-at-arms. Chaplain: Bernardo Calmeta, a Frenchman. Total: 57.

CONCEPCIÓN, ship of 90 tuns

Captain: Gaspar de Quesada. "Pilot of His Highness": João Lopes Carvalho, a Portuguese. Master: Juan Sebastián Elcano (later commander of *Victoria*). Assistant master: Juan de Acurio. Secretary: Sancho de Heredia. A barber, a caulker, a carpenter, and a steward. Chief gunner: Hans Vargue (German) and 2 gunners, (both Flemish) 10 mariners, 10 gromets, 11 pages and supernumeraries including 2 Portuguese, an Azorean, and 2 Genoese. These were mostly men-at-arms, drawing 800 to 1000 maravedis per month. Total: 44.

VICTORIA, ship of 85 tuns

Captain and flag treasurer: Luis de Mendoza. "Pilot of His Highness": Vasco Gallego, Portuguese. Master: Antón Salomón, Sicilian. Assistant master: Miguel of Rhodes. Secretary: Martín Méndez. *Alguacil:* Diego de Peralta of Navarre. Steward: Alonso Gonzales, Portuguese. A caulker from La Rochelle, a carpenter, 2 coopers, and a blacksmith; 11 mariners (including 2 from Rhodes, 3 Neapolitans, and a Genoese). Chief gunner: Jorge Alemán (i.e. a German) and 2 gunners (a German, and one of Lorraine), 10 gromets (one Genoese, one Portuguese, one from Narbonne); 10 servants, men-at-arms, and other supernumeraries. Total: 45.

* Elsewhere called *astrólogo*, the chief celestial navigator of the fleet.

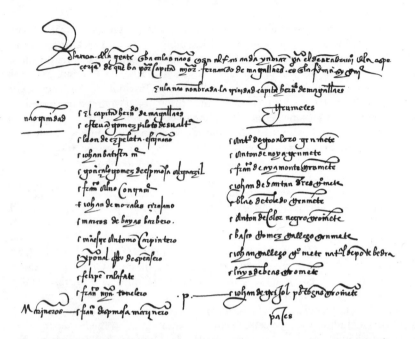

Part of the ship's roll of *Trinidad*. "Roll of the people going in the ships bound to the Indies and the discovery of the Spicery, of which Fernando de Magallanes was Captain General." Courtesy Archivo General de Indias.

SANTIAGO, caravel * of 75 tuns

Captain and "Pilot of His Highness": Juan Rodríguez Serrano of Seville, formerly Portuguese. Master: Baltazar, Genoese; assistant master: Bartolomé Prior of Saint-Malo, Brittany. Secretary: Antonio de Costa. Steward: Gaspar Diaz of Graciosa, Azores. Caulker: Joan Garcier of Genoa. Carpenter, Ripart of Normandy. Eight mariners (one Fleming, one from Boulogne, and one from Bordeaux); 2 gunners (both French); 8 gromets (one the captain's black slave, one a Breton); 5 men-at-arms and pages (one a Fleming). Total: 31.

Thus the grand total (according to Navarrete, IV, 32) of those leaving Spain is 239. But from other sources we know that 25 men signed up in the Canaries, mostly as apprentice seamen; four of these were Portuguese, two Genoese, and one a black slave bought by pilot Carvalho. Later, in Brazil, Carvalho enrolled his seven-year-old son by an Indian woman. This gives

* Sometimes referred to as a *nao*, but I agree with Admiral Gago Coutinho that a vessel of that tonnage, with so small a crew, must have been a caravel.

us a grand total of 265. Of these, about 50 returned to Spain in the *San Antonio* which defected, 18 returned to Seville in the *Victoria* in 1522, 15 more were returned from the Cape Verdes, and four or five more straggled back from the Portuguese Indies.

All in all, this was a formidable fleet, although Portugal had already sent bigger ones to the Far East. One ship and a caravel would have been enough. The prime reason for this show of strength was prestige; the second was the possibility of tangling with Portuguese warships or with a fleet of armed junks in the Far East where native potentates knew the use of gunpowder. And, too, there was the consideration of losing ships on so long and potentially dangerous a voyage.

The cost of the fleet amounted to 8,751,125 maravedis, which Guillemard translated as £5032, or $24,405 in gold prior to the Anglo-American devaluation of 1934. The ships alone cost the crown £2249. Of the grand total, Cristóbal Haro contributed three-quarters, and the king-emperor the rest. Yet the cargo of cloves brought back by *Victoria*, the one ship that returned, more than repaid all this expense.

✳ XV ✳

Magellan's Voyage to the Strait

1519-1520

From Sanlúcar to the River Plate

Before finally setting sail from Sanlúcar on 20 September 1519 in the dark of the moon, Magellan issued stringent rules and regulations designed to keep his fleet together and under his control. Flagship *Trinidad* at all times will sail ahead of the others. Each vessel must approach her toward nightfall and ask for orders, and then follow lights kindled in iron cressets on her stern; the *farol*, the principal light, to be made from a torch of pitchy wood or an old hemp rope soaked in oil. The flagship will show two lights if the fleets is to come about or wear, three as a signal to reduce sail, four to strike sail. Any ship from which land is sighted should fire a gun. Three watches were set on each ship nightly: the first at nightfall, the second (called the *modeno*) at midnight, and the third (the *diane*) at daybreak. All men accordingly were divided into three watches, the first under the captain or the *contramaestre*, the second under the pilot or the boatswain's mate, and the third under the master. Instead of "dogging" the watches, as in recent times,* their order was changed nightly to ensure that every three days only did the men have to stand the *modeno*, which American sailors used to call the "graveyard watch."

---

* Splitting 4:00 to 8:00 p.m. watch in two, thus bringing the next day's watch on duty at a different hour.

Once outside the harbor of Sanlúcar, Magellan set the course *sudo-este*—southwest, and with a fair wind his fleet romped south and reached Tenerife in the Canaries on 26 September. There they topped off with water, wood, and fresh meat, bought a load of salt codfish from a caravel, and pitch for caulking seams. Before they cleared from Tenerife, another caravel arrived with an ominous message to Magellan from his father-in-law, Diogo Barbosa. It warned him that his three Spanish captains Cartagena, Mendoza, and Quesada were planning to kill him. Pigafetta confirms this: "Although I don't know why they hated him, except that he was Portuguese and they Spaniards." Magellan sailed handicapped by the bitter hostility of his top Spanish officers; and it is not the least of his glories that he had the wit and fortitude to dispose of them.

Magellan sent a stout reply to Barbosa by the caravel, that what e'er betide he would do his duty as a servant of the king-emperor, if it took his life.

The fleet departed Tenerife at midnight 3 October 1519 with a soft land breeze and a first-quarter moon. At sea it followed a southwest course down to latitude 27° N, and then changed to south by west. Juan de Cartagena, running *San Antonio* under the flagship's stern, demanded of the Captain General why he had changed course? Magellan replied, *Que le siguiessen y no pidiessen mas cuenta*—"Follow me and ask no questions!"

Magellan had good reason to follow a course skirting the African coast. The shipmaster who sold him the salt fish told him that the king of Portugal had sent out a fleet to apprehend him on his Atlantic crossing. D. Manuel had, in fact sent two intercepting fleets, just as D. João II did to catch Columbus. Magellan figured that the way to elude them was to avoid the direct course to Brazil and parallel the African coast to a low latitude, then nip across the Atlantic Narrows. He was right, but the maneuver cost the fleet both time and discomfort.

On 18 October, off Sierra Leone with a last-quarter moon shining balefully through overcast, the fleet underwent a series of storms that sorely tried the seamen. There were furious squalls succeeded by flat calms, in which shoals of sharks cruised around. St. Elmo's fire—Camoëns's "living light, which sailors hold as sacred"—blazed for two hours from the flagship's masthead. Pigafetta, whose natural history

observations are somewhat lacking in accuracy, blew up the St. Elmo's
fire to a light so powerful that the entire crew went blind for "near a
quarter hour" after it went out! He also states that they saw a bird
which had no anus, and another bird whose hen, having no feet, laid
her eggs on the back of the cock and never touched earth. Here is the
ancient myth of the bird-of-paradise, about which the Spaniards heard
more in the Moluccas. There was a good deal of Sinbad in Pigafetta;
but his tall tales, though sometimes incredible, are always amusing.
He repeats the story, already told by Columbus and still current among
sailors, of the boatswain bird's eating other birds' excrement. This was
based on the big bird's mean practice of watching a booby stuff himself with fish, then swooping at him, screaming, and frightening the
poor booby into vomiting; the boatswain bird then caught and swallowed the regurgitated fish.

The fleet now paid for the Captain General's cautious sailing close to
the African coast, by running into equatorial calms after shaping a
southerly course for Brazil. For many days the five ships were becalmed. The heat became oppressive, as it had been for Columbus in
the more northerly doldrums, and inactivity proved a good medium
for sedition.

Cartagena probably brooded over the snub he had received from
Magellan on changing course; after all, the king had named him *conjunta persona*. In any event, he decided to take issue over a matter
of ceremony at sea. The Captain General had ordered each vessel to
close the flagship every evening to hail him and receive his oral orders;
they could do that even in a flat calm by manning their sweeps. The
proper hail, as used on Columbus's voyages, was, *Dios vos salve, señor
capitán-general, y maestro y buena compaña*—"God keep you, sir
Captain General and master, and good company." One evening, Juan
de Cartagena caused the *general* to be omitted and sent a petty officer
to sing out—a double insult to Magellan, who answered that in future
he expected to be addressed properly, and by the captain himself.
Cartagena impudently retorted that he had sent his best man to give
the hail, and if Magellan didn't like it he would send a page to do it
next time. Magellan has been criticized for treating Juan de Cartagena
too roughly. But remember that the Captain General was a Portuguese nobleman of ancient stock who would not suffer insolence

from a bishop's bastard, especially one who was plotting to usurp his command and take his life.

Three days later, still in a flat calm and after two repetitions of the insult, Magellan summoned all four captains on board the flagship to participate in a court-martial of *Victoria*'s quartermaster for sodomy with a ship's boy. After the trial (in which both parties were found guilty and condemned to death), Magellan remained in the flag cabin with Captain Cartagena of *San Antonio,* Captain Quesada of *Concepción*, Captain Mendoza of *Victoria,* and Captain Serrano of *Santiago*. The first three were in the plot. Cartagena, hoping to provoke a fight in which the Captain General would be killed, taunted Magellan for having got them into the calm belt through bad navigation. The Captain General kept his cool; Cartagena, mistaking this for timidity, roared out that he for one would no longer obey Magellan's orders. The Captain General expected this. At his signal, the alguacil of *Trinidad*, Gonzalo Gómez de Espinosa, well armed and armored, broke into the cabin, closely followed by Duarte Barbosa and Cristóbal Rebelo with drawn swords. Magellan sprang on Cartagena, grabbed him by the front of his elegant shirt, forced him to stay seated, and cried out, "Rebel, this is mutiny! You are my prisoner, in the king's name!" Cartagena screamed at his confederates Mendoza and Quesada to plunge their daggers into Magellan "according to plan"—thus giving away his prior intention—but they dared not move; Gómez de Espinosa hustled Cartagena down to the main deck and clapped him into a pair of stocks normally occupied by common seamen guilty of petty offenses. Mendoza and Quesada begged the Captain General to afford him more dignified treatment; and as neither of them had committed himself as a mutineer, Magellan consented to release Cartagena and entrust him for safekeeping to Mendoza in *Victoria*. Then, after sounding trumpets to attract everyone's attention in the fleet, the Captain General announced the appointment of Antonio de Coca captain of *San Antonio* in Cartagena's stead.

Ocean currents finally floated the armada out of the doldrums, the blessed trade wind made up, and the ships filled away and gathered speed. Magellan called *Concepción*'s pilot, João Lopes Carvalho, to the *Trinidad* to be flag pilot, because he knew the coast better than

Entering Rio de Janeiro, 1971. Courtesy of the Brazilian Consul at Barcelona.

Gómez did. Magellan also had a copy of the *Livro da Marinharia*, by the chief pilot of Portugal, which gives fairly accurate latitudes of places on the Brazilian coast down to 35° S; and he must have learned from earlier Portuguese experience that if you hit the coast near Cape San Roque at 5° S, the hump of the Brazilian bulge, you are likely to be stuck there for a long, long time. Consequently he aimed for Cabo Santo Agostinho (which marks the harbor of Pernambuco, now Recife) at latitude 8°20′ S, and made it on 29 November 1519.

Since Magellan knew that the Portuguese had already established a *feitoria* at Recife, and wished to avoid being sighted, he did not stop but headed south, keeping the shore in sight. Finally, on Carvalho's assurance that no Portuguese would be encountered at Rio de Janeiro (latitude 22°54′ S), he decided to call there for rest and refreshment. In the small hours of 13 December 1519 the fleet passed Cape Frio, and that afternoon rounded into the spectacular bay. *Trinidad* proudly led the way through the channel, past the now famous *Pão de Açúcar* or Sugar Loaf, and anchored further up the harbor, off the site of the city, in seven fathom. Since this was the feast day of St. Lucy, Magellan named the bay *Santa Luzia* after her. But Coelho and Vespucci had already entered it in the first week of January 1502 and then named it *Rio de Janeiro*, River of January.

The happiest part of the voyage for all hands, and the last fun for most of them, was spent in the two weeks that they tarried at Rio, although the quality of the fun would have shocked St. Lucy, virgin and martyr. Immediately after anchoring, swarms of naked Indians boarded each ship. Carvalho warned the sailors that Guarani husbands were jealous and would resent advances to their wives; but that young girls were free for all, provided their brothers were paid for their services. And the pilot arranged a good deal: every sailor could have his girl for the price of one of those German knives "of worst quality" carried in the slopchests, paid to her brother. Mariners and Indian girls certainly enjoyed each other; nightly revels were held ashore, under a waning moon, and the more attractive lassies earned bonuses, in the shape of Venetian beads, hawks' bells, and red cloth, over the agreed-upon ten-cent knife. One day a beautiful young woman, says Pigafetta, selected her own gift. Coming on board alone when most of the crew were ashore, she peered into the unoccupied master's cabin and spied a long iron nail, more valuable to her than gold. "Picking it up, with great skill and gallantry, she thrust it between the lips of her vagina and, bending low, departed, the Captain General and I having witnessed this."

Carvalho himself collected a bonus: his former Brazilian mistress turned up with their seven-year-old son. The pilot signed up the boy as a *criado* or servant, but he could not persuade Magellan to take the mother along. The Captain General never allowed women on board ship at sea. Before he left any port where there had been goings-on, he caused the alguacil to search every nook and corner of each ship to root out girl stowaways.

The Christians found good trading at Rio, and not only in girls. The Indians loved playing cards and would give eight chickens for one king out of a pack. You could buy a slave with a hatchet; but Magellan forbade slave trade, not only to avoid offending the Portuguese, but because he wanted no extra mouths to feed.

At Rio, mutiny raised its ugly head for a second time. On board *San Antonio* Captain Coca, Bishop Fonseca's nephew, released Juan de

Cartagena and other prisoners. Magellan sent Gómez de Espinosa with men-at-arms to put the mutiny down, but once more entrusted the safe-keeping of Coca and Cartagena to Captain Mendoza of *Victoria*. He then appointed his cousin Álvaro de Mezquita, who had shipped as supernumerary in the flagship, captain of *San Antonio*. That was a mistake; Mezquita, promoted over many others, was not tough enough to deal with such hardbitten *hombres* as he now found under him.

Magellan and his pilots put their heads together and tried to determine the longitude of Rio by timing a conjunction of the moon and Jupiter and comparing it with the time that their almanac gave for it in Cadiz. As usual in such attempts, starting with Columbus's in Jamaica, they messed up the figures so that the result was worthless; later, however, they made a good educated guess at the longitude of Rio Santa Cruz. Magellan's pilots and navigators were the best of their era at celestial navigation. They managed to take an almost correct latitude of Cape Frio, 23° S—only a mile out; even João de Lisboa had made it 25° S.

The fleet kept Christmas off the site of the city of Rio de Janeiro and departed next morning, 26 December 1519. It weighed anchor to the sound of dolorous music, the wailing of abandoned native "brides." Goodby forever to the magnificent bay and harbor, and to the hospitable native Cariocas.

And, as they sailed south, it was goodby to many familiar stars. The Great Bear or Dipper which Homer described as "ever circling . . . with no part in the baths of Ocean," dipped below the northern horizon astern, and already had risen the Southern Cross, almost outshining even brilliant Orion.* The great southern stars only fitfully seen in the north, golden Canopus and Fomalhaut, ruddy Antares and Achenar, dominated the sky.

Now began the serious search for the Strait. Unlike his emulator Verrazzano who sailed so far off shore that he missed all the big bays, Magellan sailed as close to shore as he dared, frequently heaving the lead and investigating every big opening. Once only, between Rio de Janeiro and the River Plate, on 8 January 1520, did the fleet anchor at

* *Odyssey*, v, 274–75. Camoëns in *Lusiads*, V, 15 and VIII, 72, alludes to the "now-bathing Bear." The Southern Cross is apt to disappoint travelers from the north at first sight; but in comparison with other stars of the Southern Hemisphere, one ends in feeling, with Dante, "Heaven in their flames seemed to rejoice."

Punta del Este, Uruguay. Magellan's Cabo de Santa Maria, where he anchored for several days in January 1520. Courtesy of the American Embassy, Montevideo.

night, the moon but four days full. Two or three days later Pilot Carvalho recognized, by three conspicuous hills, Cabo Santa Maria, which he had seen on an earlier voyage. (It is now Punta del Este, Uruguay.) Rounding the Isla de Lobos where now a tall lighthouse marks the eastern entrance to the great Rio de la Plata estuary, Albo's shot of the sun worked out as latitude 35° S. Correct; latitude 35° passes halfway between the Point and the Island. Keeping the coast close aboard, they sighted a conspicuous mountain, doubtless the 1640-foot Cerro Las Animas which loomed up as we steamed by Punta del Este in 1972. Magellan cried out, "Monte Video!" and Montevideo is the name of the modern city and capital of Uruguay, sixty miles to the westward.

Magellan, eager to explore the Rio de la Plata (later Englished as the River Plate) then opening up, sailed on. He called it Rio de Solis after the man murdered there by natives in 1516. Hoping that this estuary would turn out to be the Strait (which the Schöner globe of 1515 placed at about latitude 35° S, and both Juan de Solis and João de Lisboa reported it to be there), the Captain General sent *Santiago*, his lightest-draft vessel, up-river to look for an outlet. Captain Serrano found the bay narrowing and shoaling, and reported plenty of evidence that one or more big rivers emptied into it. But, in order to make sure that he had not missed anything, Magellan sent the longboat of each ship to make a detailed search, while the fleet lay at anchor under Punta del Este, off the present beach resort. This boat exploration found the water becoming brackish and then fresh, proving it to be no arm of the sea, but a river.

Convinced that the Strait could not be much further south, the Captain General insisted on going on, hoping to find it before the Antarctic winter closed in.

The Coast of Patagonia

A very difficult part of the voyage now began. The ships departed their anchorage near Montevideo on Candlemas Day, 2 February 1520. This was the right season for a coastal voyage; the official Pilot Chart shows mostly force-four winds from the northwest quadrant and few calms or variables, and Magellan started with a full moon. He crossed the great estuary on course due south, and first anchored off the mod ern Cabo San Antonio. He usually anchored at night so as not to miss anything—for João de Lisboa's sailing directions ended at Cabo Santa Maria; and sailing within sight of shore was not difficult. Sailors have a rule of thumb for this coast—"as many miles as fathoms"; i.e., on an eight miles' offing you will find a depth of eight fathom. This works very well from Cabo San Antonio to Mar del Plata; the ten-fathom line runs just about ten miles from shore.

At anchor 13 February (off the modern lighthouse of Bahia Blanca), their cables held during a terrific thunderstorm, during which *Victoria* took a number of *culadas* (literally, "arse-hits") on her keel. A particularly beautiful corposant or St. Elmo's fire played about the spars, a "spiritual comfort" to the sailors. Magellan thought Bahia Blanca worth investigating, and they threaded their way among the islands of that now important port and beach resort. Here, or earlier, Magellan adopted a twenty-four-hour schedule, sailing one league from the land by day, and five or six leagues off shore by night.

On 24 February, at latitude 40°40′ S, Magellan opened the mouth of a sixty-mile-wide bay receding more than eighty miles. He brushed this off as a dead-end (which it was) and because his dipsey lead would not

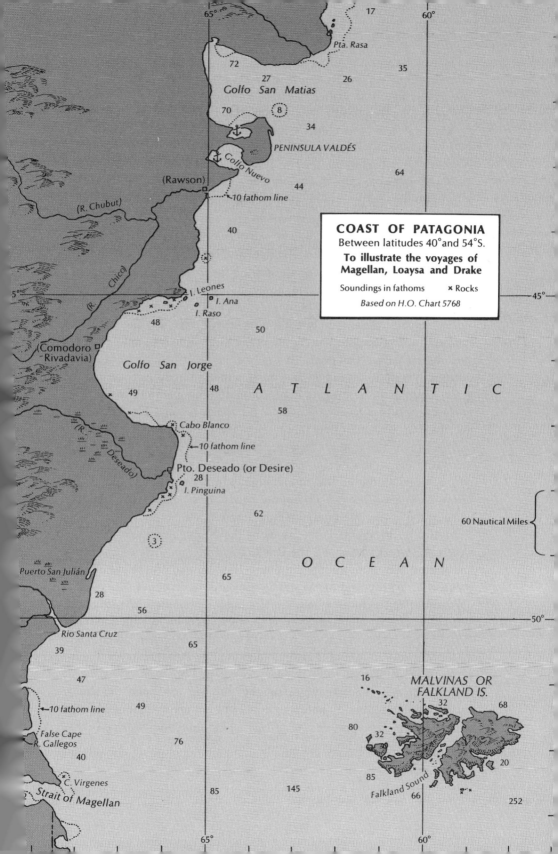

17

60°

72

Pta. Rasa

27

26

35

Golfo San Matias

70

8

34

64

PENINSULA VALDÉS

Golfo Nuevo

(Rawson)

44

←10 fathom line

(R. Chubut)

40

COAST OF PATAGONIA
Between latitudes 40° and 54° S.
**To illustrate the voyages of
Magellan, Loaysa and Drake**

Soundings in fathoms   × Rocks

Based on H.O. Chart 5768

(R. Chico)

5°

I. Leones

45°

I. Ana

48

I. Raso

50

(Comodoro
Rivadavia)

Golfo San Jorge

A T L A N T I C

49

48

58

Cabo Blanco

(R. Deseado)

←10 fathom line

Pto. Deseado (or Desire)

28

I. Pinguina

62

60 Nautical Miles

3

O C E A N

Puerto San Julián

65

28

56

50°

Rio Santa Cruz

65

39

MALVINAS OR
FALKLAND IS.

47

16

32

68

49

80

32

False Cape
R. Gallegos

76

40

20

C. Virgenes

85

145

Strait of Magellan

85

Falkland Sound

66

252

65°

60°

reach bottom—on the Ribero map of 1529 it is called *Bahia sin fondo*, Bottomless Bay. For shelter he chose a snug little harbor just south of Valdés, which he named *Puerto de San Matias* since this was the vigil of St. Matthias. It is now called Golfo Nuevo, a pleasant, well-protected spot to spend a few days. On 27 February they lay off a broad bay that they called *Bahia de los Patos*, owing to the immense number of penguins, for which Europeans as yet had no name except *patos sin alas*—wingless ducks. The boat sent ashore to replenish found plenty of elephant seal and penguin, which the men were still slaughtering when an offshore gale sprang up and blew the fleet out to sea. The wretched shore party had to cover themselves with dead seal and rotting penguin to avoid freezing to death. When the fleet, returning, rescued them, they were smelling horribly. This locality I take to have been the shallow bay at Cabo dos Bahias, and the three islands off it.

The name of these islands, Sanson, evidently refers to the stature of the natives; for Magellan had discovered (and shortly would name) a vast region called Patagonia. It was often described by nineteenth-century travelers, usually in uncomplimentary terms. But the natural grass, nutritious for sheep as it had been for the guanaco, made Patagonia eventually a rival to Australia for sheep raising. The country is not flat but undulating, covered with grass, green in the Antarctic spring, brown the rest of the year. It is well watered, crossed by numerous rivers which rise on the eastern slopes of the Andes, some of which Magellan felt he had to investigate. In his time, these undulating plains were pastures for enormous herds of guanaco, the southern llama, and of puma and rhea, the American ostrich.

Physically, Patagonia corresponds to the North American West between the Great Plains and the Rockies and it, too, inspires both love and hatred. Martinic quotes the farewell of an early explorer: "Patagonia, thou art the land of the strong man and the free soul!"

Storm after storm now pursued the fleet. These were the infamous *pamperos*, line squalls that blow with great ferocity off the land. Six stormy days were ridden out in a small bay that Magellan called *Bahia de los Trabajos*, "Bay of Travail," identified as Port Desire or *Puerto Deseado* at latitude 47°46′ S. Darwin, who kept Christmas 1833 there in *Beagle*, called it "a wretched place," but in 1972 we found the shores neither so rugged nor so picturesque as Darwin's artist Conrad Martens depicted them. The present-day official sailing directions warn one that

Port Desire in 1833. Drawing by Conrad Martens of the *Beagle* expedition.

"heavy gales . . . rising without warning" are prevalent. Magellan's fleet, once outside, suffered more battering, and for three weeks they made only about 120 miles southwesterly, and no sun appeared. Finally they entered *Puerto San Julián,* as Magellan named it, on the last day of March, the eve of Palm Sunday. Summer (January, February, March) was almost over in these high latitudes, and winter so near that the Captain General announced the fleet would stay there until better weather offered some prospect of finding the Strait. And there they stayed for five months, until 24 August.

Puerto San Julián still offers a spacious inner harbor, but a depressing aspect. The entrance between the hundred-foot-high gray cliffs (Cabos Curioso and Desengaño) narrows to a half-mile-wide bottleneck. The tidal range is twenty to twenty-five feet, and the current at the narrow entrance runs up to six knots. So, when things got sticky, Magellan found it wise to moor his flagship in the bottleneck so that any vessel trying to escape would have to cross his cannon range.

Two months elapsed before the Spaniards met one soul ashore. According to Pigafetta, "One day suddenly we saw a naked man of giant stature on the shore of the harbor, dancing, singing, and throwing dust on his head. When the giant was in the Captain General's and our presence, he marveled greatly, and made signs with one finger raised upward, believing that we had come from the sky. He was so tall that we reached only to his waist, and he was well proportioned."

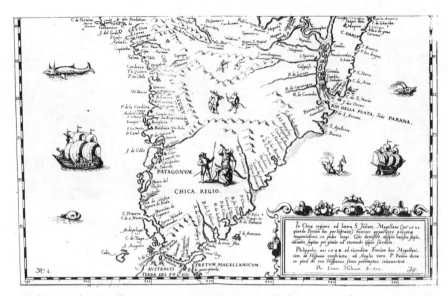

A Patagonian swallowing an arrow. From the Hulsius map of 1602, courtesy
British Museum.

He was painted all over and partially dressed in guanaco skins. His
feet, shod with guanaco-hide buskins stuffed with straw, looked enormous, which caused Magellan to name him *patagón* (big-foot), and
his country, Patagonia. Although Pigafetta greatly exaggerated the
Patagonian's stature, many later explorers described these natives as
taller than the average European. They led a nomadic and pastoral life,
"like Cingani" (gypsies), said Pigafetta, following the wild herds of
guanaco which they caught by using captured calves as decoys.
They lived largely off that animal, much as the North American Indians of the Great Plains used to do off the buffalo.

This first encounter between Europeans and natives of the region
passed off well. The Captain General gave the "man of giant stature"
a clutch of rosary beads, some tinkly hawks' bells, a comb in the hope
that he might use it on his filthy, tangled locks, and a mirror. This
last gift set off a comic scene. The poor savage was so terrified at
seeing his hairy mug in the glass that he recoiled, knocking down, as
he did so, four little Spaniards. Other natives turned up with their tame
guanaco and their beasts of burden—the women. These were short

and squat, with breasts hanging down half a fathom, repulsively ugly to Magellan's crews. The men, to amuse the Spaniards, performed a primitive version of the old sword-swallowing trick, shoving arrows down their gullets and drawing them out without hurt.

Some eighteen Patagonians were entertained on board the ships, and later one stayed with them for at least a week, allowed himself to be christened Juan, and learned to say *Jesu, Ave Maria,* and a few other words; he was delighted to eat all the rats and mice that were caught on board, and left clothed and apparently happy. But he never turned up again.

A fortnight later, however, four natives appeared and Magellan kidnapped two by a very mean trick. He heaped their cupped hands with trading truck, and then brought out two pair of leg irons. The giants admired them (as they did everything of iron) but indicated they could hold no more. Carvalho suggested that they could be carried on the legs, and the innocent giants acquiesced "When they saw later that they were tricked," wrote Pigafetta, "they raged like bulls, calling for their god Setebos to aid them." These were the only contacts with the natives that Magellan made in the five dreary months at Puerto San Julián.

Now for the mutiny, which began earlier. Maximilianus Transylvanus, first to interview the few Spaniards who returned home to Spain, recorded shipboard gossip and what he calls a "shameful and foul conspiracy" among the Spanish officers and men. They accused Magellan of planning to cast away the entire fleet, or else of luring Charles V for years with vain hopes of doing the impossible—reaching the Spice Islands via the Antarctic. Anyway, he was a Portuguese, so to hell with him!

Elcano's excuse for participating in the disloyalty, when examined in 1522 was this: Magellan and Cartagena were joint commanders; hence the latter should have been consulted before every decision. In an earlier chapter I concluded emphatically that Cartagena was never joint commander—but he may well have imagined that he was. Magellan alone was the Emperor's Captain General. He alone had the title. In his commission he is given absolute power over all persons sailing with him; or, as Correia put it, *poder de baraco e cutello*— "power of rope and knife." And in the religious ceremony before departure, all officers swore to obey him, and no other commander.

The Narrows, Puerto San Julián. James F. Nields photo.

The very eve of their arrival at San Julián, 31 March, Magellan, after reducing rations, held a colloquy with deputations from all five ships. The men urged him to restore full rations and return to Spain; they doubted whether any strait existed, feared that to continue the voyage southward would lead only to starvation and a frozen death. Magellan replied that he would rather die than give up his quest for the Strait, which the king had ordered; that plenty of food could be found in Puerto San Julián, and they still had enough bread and wine from Spain; and he pointed out that the Strait, which would certainly be found, would lead them to languorous islands and girls even kinder and more beautiful than those of Rio. Finally, he exhorted them not to be wanting in the valor for which Castilians had ever been distinguished. The men, apparently placated, returned to their duty. But the conspiracy continued among the officers.

Next day, Palm Sunday, Magellan summoned all officers to hear Mass ashore, and invited the captains to dine with him afterward in the flag cabin. Only his kinsman Álvaro de Mezquita accepted. That was ominous, and a most unholy Holy Week followed. On Palm Sunday night the mutineers took possession of three ships—*San*

370

Antonio (Captain Mezquita), *Concepción* (Captain Quesada), and *Victoria* (Captain Mendoza). Cartagena, the deposed captain of *San Antonio*, stabbed but failed to kill Elorriaga, the loyal master of *San Antonio*, and clapped Captain Mezquita in irons; this took care of the biggest ship, while Quesada and Elcano overawed the crew of *Concepción*, and Mendoza got control of *Victoria*.

On Monday of Holy Week Quesada sent a message in *Concepción*'s longboat (manned by stout oarsmen to breast the strong current) to Magellan in flagship *Trinidad*. Coca commanded the boat. The message, signed by the three leading mutineers, took the high ground that the Captain General was disobeying royal instructions by leading them so far south. No longer would they recognize him as Captain General, but would follow his lead as senior captain if he promised to take them back to Spain. Magellan made no reply, but performed a very clever bit of strategy. Detaining this boat and crew, he dressed thirty of his own men in their clothes so that they would not be recognized, manned the boat with them, and let her out on a long hawser so that the tide would carry her near enough to *Victoria* in case she was wanted. (There was a strong ebb current from the flagship to her, and they had plenty of light under the paschal moon, two nights short of full.) Magellan then dispatched alguacil Gómez de Espinosa in his own gig with five or six armed men to *Victoria* with a letter ordering Mendoza to return to his duty and report on board the flagship; if the rebel captain refused to obey, Magellan instructed Espinosa to kill him. Mendoza allowed the alguacil and his men to board *Victoria*, and admitted Espinosa and one man-at-arms to his cabin on the alguacil's assertion that he had a private message for the captain. Mendoza, after reading Magellan's letter, crumpled it as if to throw it away, laughing scornfully. That was his last laugh. Espinosa, stretching forth his left hand as if to take the rejected letter, grasped Mendoza's beard, jerked back his head, and with a dagger thrust in the throat killed him, while his man-at-arms, to make it certain, stabbed the victim's head.

The longboat, full of armed men and commanded by Duarte Barbosa, was standing by a few yards upstream, awaiting a signal. Espinosa waved a cloth, Barbosa ordered his hawser to be cast off, the current quickly took the boat alongside *Victoria*, and the men-at-arms swarmed aboard that ship before her people even knew of their captain's death. Barbosa, promptly appointed by Magellan captain of *Victoria*, ordered anchors aweigh, and with sweeps working, a foresail to catch the evening breeze, and the longboat towing, approached the flagship and anchored alongside. Loyal Serrano followed, anchoring his caravel off *Trinidad*'s other board.

Quesada, captain of *Concepción*, seeing that Magellan now controlled three of the five ships, lost his nerve and tried to sneak out of Puerto San Julián under cover of night in company with *San Antonio*, of which Cartagena had usurped command. This scheme did not work because, before Quesada was ready to sail, a loyal sailor cut *Concepción*'s cable and she drifted with the evening ebb tide within range of Magellan's flagship *Trinidad*. And the almost-full moon helped. When she came near enough, the Captain General gave her a point-blank broadside, and men in the fighting tops raked her decks with crossbow fire and lances. Quesada in full armor on the sterncastle of his ship, with arrows and crossbow bolts bouncing off his steel corselet, vainly tried to rally his crew to fight back. Magellan now had himself rowed to *Concepción*, boarded her, and with drawn sword forced Quesada to surrender his ship.

The Captain General, after clapping both Quesada and Coca in irons on board *Trinidad*, continued the good work. Rowed by Espinosa to *San Antonio*, he hailed her. Cartagena, in armor, abjectly answered the hail in loyal terms. Espinosa boarded the ship and placed him under arrest.

Thus by sheer audacity, wit, and ability to seize opportunities, Magellan who in the morning was master only of his flagship and *Santiago*, by evening ruled the entire fleet. A very serious mutiny had been quenched with injury to but one loyal man, Juan de Elorriaga. As the author of the Leiden Narrative wrote, "After the punishment of these persons all the people were in peace, and there were no more mutinies." Nobody dared again to challenge Magellan's authority—at least not when he was around.

Next day—Tuesday of Holy Week—Magellan had Mendoza's body taken ashore and quartered, and cried him through the fleet as a traitor. He then called a formal court-martial which found Mendoza (represented by his quartered corpse), Cartagena, Coca, Elcano, Quesada, and Quesada's servant Molino, guilty of treason and condemned them to death. There followed a grim celebration of

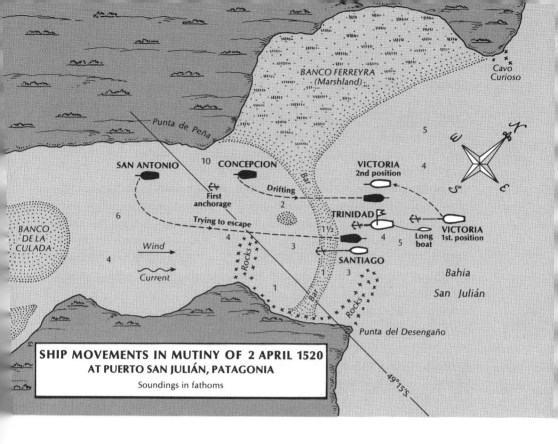

SHIP MOVEMENTS IN MUTINY OF 2 APRIL 1520
AT PUERTO SAN JULIÁN, PATAGONIA
Soundings in fathoms

Easter Sunday. Molino won his life as reward for executing his master, which apparently he did with relish; and Quesada's body was hanged on a gibbet next to Mendoza's remains, probably on the Isla Justicia upriver. Magellan commuted all other sentences to hard labor, and all except Cartagena were organized into a sort of chain gang, cutting wood and pumping out ships through the rest of that long winter. Elcano laid this up against Magellan and did his best, after returning to Spain, to destroy his reputation.

Magellan's leniency to Cartagena was misplaced. He was caught using one of the chaplains, Pero Sánchez de Reina, to stir up the men to fresh mutiny. Another court-martial found both, layman and priest, guilty and sentenced them to be marooned.

One force that helped Magellan to quell this serious mutiny was the loyalty of the enlisted men. They had sailed under him long enough to size him up as an experienced mariner, firm yet just; but the three Spanish captains, as they had ample opportunity to observe, were not even sailors.

During the five and a half chilly months at San Julián, Magellan had his men build barracks ashore and (as he well knew sailors must be kept busy) set them a-fishing, hunting game, and curing their catch with salt extracted from natural salt pans at the head of the bay. Sailors also made themselves guanaco and sealskin coats to keep out the bitter cold. More provisions were urgently wanted because, when the ships were unladen in preparation for "rummaging" * them ashore, the scribes and clerks made the appalling discovery of more dirty work by the Sevillian land sharks. Owing to an ingenious method of fraudulent checking, the ships had stores for only six months instead of for a year and a half.

Alan Villiers' curse on rascally ship chandlers, purveyors of rotten spars, substandard cordage, and spoiled or insufficient food, I cheerfully second. Magellan's men, Captain Cook's, and countless others suffered from the diabolical cheating of these human teredos. Their callously selfish peculations have sent countless thousands of poor sailors prematurely to Fiddler's Green. Damn their eyes, one and all!

In search of provisions, and because Captain Serrano was "an industrious man and never rested" (as the author of the Leiden Narrative said), the Captain General sent *Santiago* south under him to try to locate the Strait. Through no fault of her captain, *Santiago* met her fate about three leagues south of the entrance to Rio Santa Cruz, on 3 May 1520. She anchored off a beach, an onshore wind suddenly arose, and before she could make sail her anchor cables parted and she drifted ashore. The men jumped aground dry-shod, all except black Juan, the captain's slave. *Santiago* floated off on the next spring flood, only to ground again a short distance away; this time they could not get her off. Later, much of her cargo was salvaged. After the first grounding, two members of the crew volunteered to walk to San Julián for help. First they had to build a boat from *Santiago*'s timbers to cross the river. From there the distance overland, as the crow flies, is a good sixty miles, and their route must

---

* Careening, and throwing out the stone ballast to be cleansed by the tide; scraping out accumulated filth in the hold, sprinkling it with vinegar and replacing the ballast. Magellan also had topsides below the waterline smeared with pitch to keep out teredos.

have been at least half again as long. It took them eleven days' stumbling over the partially snow-covered pampas, and with very little to eat as they were unable to shoot guanacos or big birds. Magellan promptly sent a rescuing force by boat to Santa Cruz, and all *Santiago's* survivors were brought back safely after a month's privation.

Weary of inaction and eager to get on, Magellan now resolved to spend the rest of the Antarctic winter at Rio Santa Cruz. The last sight his men saw as they departed unhappy Puerto San Julián in September, was Juan de Cartagena and the priest kneeling at the water's edge and bawling for mercy. Firearms, gunpowder, wine, and hardtack were left with them, but whether they starved to death or were killed by the Indians we know not. Theirs are not the only bones of marooned men left at San Julián. Drake executed Thomas Doughty, convicted of attempted mutiny, at the same spot fifty-one years later. A sinister place indeed.

Magellan has been criticized by sundry armchair admirals for tarrying so long in Patagonian ports. They point out that Drake got through the Strait in seventeen days in August-September 1578, the Antarctic winter. But Drake, on leaving the Strait, ran into a series of northerly and westerly gales which delayed him over a month, and lost two of his three ships; whilst Magellan debouched into a calm, pacific sea. That alone was worth waiting for.

It took the fleet but two days to reach Rio Santa Cruz, so named because they entered on 14 September, feast of the Exaltation of the Holy Cross. The people, however, called it the River of Shad, because they caught so many of that tasty fish. The Genoese pilot estimated this harbor to be on latitude 50° S, and he was correct. There they stayed until 18 October. Santa Cruz, unlike San Julián, lay at the mouth of a navigable river, as Magellan realized after ascertaining the water to be fresh. Captain FitzRoy of H.M.S. *Beagle,* and Charles Darwin, explored 140 miles of Rio Santa Cruz in 1834, and forty-three years later an Argentinian, F. P. Moreno, reached the source in Lago Argentino.

Magellan's officers now thought up a new scheme to avoid worse cold and discomfort; to sail east to the Spice Islands around the Cape of Good Hope. The Captain General rejected this out of hand, but promised to consider it if he found no strait above latitude 75° S.*

* Navarrete, IV, p. lvii. I think this is a misprint for 57° S.

This did not satisfy the officers, and Esteban Gómez, now pilot of *San Antonio*, proposed another mutiny, but Captain Mezquita decided to follow Magellan. Gómez bided his time.

By 17 October, Magellan judged the Antarctic spring to be sufficiently advanced to proceed. All hands went ashore, confessed to Pedro de Valderrama the flag chaplain, and attended Mass. Next day the four ships, *Trinidad*, *San Antonio*, *Concepción*, and *Victoria*, sailed out of Rio Santa Cruz; and this time they were not disappointed in finding *el paso*, the Strait.

Bibliography and Notes

Peter Martyr, *De Orbe Novo* (Gaffarel translation, 1907, p. 489, in 5th Decade). Guillemard, *Life* . . . p.149, quoting Gaspar Correia, *Lendas da India*, II, 627. *Magellan's rebuke to Cartagena* is in Herrera, but not in English translation.

The Africa-Brazil route. This subject is badly in need of investigation. I have been unable to ascertain what Portuguese experience considered to be the optimum route, in Magellan's time or later, Captain Teixeira da Mota, in his important pamphlet *As Rotas Marítimas Portuguesas no Atlântico* (Lisbon, 1970), studies the journal of ship *Bertoa* to Brazil in 1511, printed in *Hist. da Col. Port. do Brasil*, II, 343–47. This shows the kind of trade going on between Portugal and Brazil eight years before Magellan sailed, suggesting that he might have obtained plenty of information in Lisbon. Manoel de Figueyredo, in the first edition of *Hydrographia* . . . *Roteiros de Portugal pero o Brasil* (Lisbon, 1608; copy at Yale), advises ships after passing Madeira to leave Isla Palma in the Canaries 10 to 12 leagues to port, and from latitude 26° N steer S by E to the Cape Verde Islands, then S to 14° N, thence SSE and SE by S to a point off the Bay of Santa Ana, Guinea, (on Sherbro Island, Sierra Leone), at about 7°30′ N. Then lay a course for Fernão de Noronha. That is indeed the shortest crossing (about 1300 nautical miles), but according to the modern Pilot Chart a sailing ship taking it would encounter equatorial calms and run the risk of being carried to the wrong side of Cape San Roque. Admiral Gago Coutinho (*A Náutica dos Descobrimentos*, II, 97) wrote that Magellan continued further along the Guinea coast to use the SE trades, but at that season he would not have caught them until about latitude 3° N, off Cape Palmas.

Sources on the mutiny. Robertson's notes to Pigafetta, I, 230–34, quote Navarrete (who wrote the earliest connected account of it), and others. The interrogations when *San Antonio* and *Victoria* returned to Spain, and documents abstracted by the Portuguese from *Trinidad*, are printed in Navarrete, IV, and some are translated in Stanley's *First Voyage*. Other less direct sources are statements in early Portuguese and Spanish historians such as Correia, *Lendas da India* (translated in Nowell), and Herrera, *Historia General*. The former heard a great deal of talk about the voyage after *Victoria* returned. Pigafetta says almost nothing about the mutinies. It is significant that almost all existing accounts of them, bringing out Magellan's fortitude, patience, and power of decision, come from sources unfriendly to him.

Cabo Santa Maria and Montevideo. Uruguayan historians agree that Punta del Este was Magellan's Cabo Santa Maria, a name which has been moved 45 miles east and given to a less conspicuous cape with neither anchorage nor mountains. Others think the mountain in question was the much lower hill one sees on the port hand entering Montevideo Harbor, but which is not visible from afar.

The Falklands—Islas Sanson—Islas Malvinas question. This is a subject of great pith and moment to the Argentinians, who claim that wicked England stole them from their young republic, with the connivance of the United States. Enrique Ruiz Guiñazú, *Proas de España en el Mar Magallánico* (Buenos Aires, 1945), beautifully illustrated, with big maps, is excellent on this subject. At page 78 he discusses the map from Alonso de Santa Cruz's *Islario* (1541), which shows a group of islands off Patagonia labeled *ys de sanson*. Admiral Basílico (see p. 309) argues convincingly (p. 104) that these islands were *not* the Falklands but the Penguin Island group (Pingüino, Chata, Gernelos, and Blanca) off Rio Deseado, in latitude 47°55′ S, and that they were named after the hero of the Book of Judges because of the gigantic stature of the nearby natives.

The English title to the Falklands goes no further back than John Davis, who sighted them on his return from Cavendish's second voyage in 1592 (see Chapter XXX). The French name *Isles Malouines* dates from visits by sailors of Saint-Malo, Brittany, in 1706-14, and the name *Les Malouines* for the group appears on the Frézier chart of 1717. The famous Sieur de Bougainville established a short-lived French colony there in 1764, Commodore John Byron ("Foul-weather Jack") took formal possession for England in 1766. After a diplomatic hassle, during which war was threatened, France ceded her claims to Spain, and Spain hers to England in 1771. The Argentine Republic, regarding the English title as invalid for want of a settlement, raised her flag in 1820 on *Las Islas Malvinas*, and established a cattle ranch. Trouble ensued between the Argentine *gauchos* and American sealers from Stonington, Connecticut, in consequence of which President Jackson ordered U.S.S. *Lexington* (Commander Silas Duncan) to clear out the offenders; he did so in 1832, deporting to Buenos Aires all the gauchos, who were nothing loath, having had no pay for over a year. Just at that time, when the Falklands were temporarily unoccupied, the British moved in, and there they have stayed. The Argentine Republic is still trying to get the islands back. Ricardo R. Caillet-Bois, *Las Islas Malvinas* (Buenos Aires, 1949), comprehensive and well documented; Julius Goebel, Jr., *The*

Struggle for the Falkland Islands (New Haven, 1927), the best work in English. Alexander G. Findlay, *A Sailing Directory for the Ethiopic or South Atlantic Ocean* (London, 1883), pp. 272–75, has a good account of the islands' later history.

Patagonia and the Patagonians. I used Argentine Chart No. 52 (Santa Cruz–Golfo Nuevo), and H. O. 5284 (San Julián to Magellan Strait). H. Dosserres (pseudonym for Captain Hector R. Ratto of the Argentine navy), "La Derotta de la Armada de Magallanes en la Costa Patagónica," *Boletim del Centro Naval,* año XLIV (Buenos Aires, 1927), with maps, is the authoritative work on the Patagonian part of Magellan's voyage, Captain Ratto having cruised along it many times, Albo's log in hand. Capitán de Navío Laurio H. Destéfani of the Argentine navy, to whom I am deeply indebted for many favors, called my attention to this valuable article. A succinct description of the land is that of the present distinguished Director of the Institute of Patagonia, Mateo Martinic Beros, *Patagonia, Materia y Espiritu* (Punta Arenas, 1970); and among the earlier descriptions are W. Parker Snow (commander of missionary yacht), *Two Years' Cruise off Tierra del Fuego, the Falkland Islands, Patagonia, and the River Plate* (2 vols., London, 1857, illustrated with colored plates); Florence Dixie, *Across Patagonia* (New York, 1880, illustrated); Charles Darwin, *Voyage of the Beagle* (published as *Narrative of Voyages of H.M.S. Adventure and Beagle,* 1839; revised 1845 ed. now in paperback, Doubleday, 1962, bibliography on p. xvi); Alan Moorehead, *Darwin and the Beagle* (New York, 1970); F. P. Moreno, *Viaje a la Patagonia Austral* (2 vols., Buenos Aires, 1879); Robert FitzRoy, *Narrative of the Surveying Voyages of H.M.S. Adventure and Beagle, 1826–1836* (3 vols., London, 1839; Volume III is *Darwin's Journal and Remarks*). Also, the works of Aguiles D. Ygobone, especially *Renacimiento de la Patagonia* (Buenos Aires, 1964).

Penguin (see my *Northern Voyages,* p. 347) originally meant the Great Auk of Newfoundland waters. *New English Dictionary,* VII, 641, tells in detail how the name came to be applied, in Drake's time, to the southern bird which is a very different species; in the meantime the Spanish had no name for it but *pato sin alas.* The southern penguin, salted down, probably saved many sailors from starvation. Sir John Narborough stocked up on Isla Pingoïns off Port Desire. Here or elsewhere John Davis, parting from Cavendish in 1593, revictualed his ship with 14,000 penguin, which failed to save his crew from starvation. For at best it is a "hungry sort of food," as Michael Miskell said of periwinkles in Lady Gregory's play *The Workhouse Ward.* Captain James Cook, however, insisted that penguin and shag boiled in the ship's coppers were "exceeding good eating." Beaglehole edition of his *Journals,* II, 606–7.

Patagonians' stature. Darwin excuses Magellan's exaggeration, observing that their guanaco mantles, flowing hair, and straw-packed moccasins made them seem taller than they really were. The real name of this tribe was Tehuelche. A Dutch 17-century map used by Rockwell Kent in his *Voy-*

aging Southward from the Strait of Magellan (New York, 1926) makes them 10 feet tall! As late as 1891 it was authoritatively stated that their height was 6′ to 6′4″ (Daniel G. Brinton, *The American Race*).

Setebos. Here the poor savage unwittingly contributed a name to Western literature. Shakespeare, who must have read Richard Eden's early translation of Pigafetta, has Caliban invoke Setebos in *Tempest*, I, ii.

Bahia Blanca. My late esteemed correspondent the eminent Argentinian historian José Luis Molinari argued convincingly in *Las Expediciones Marítimas a la Patagonia y al Estrecho de Magallanes . . . Descubrimiento de la Bahia Blanca* (Bahia Blanca, 1927), that this now well-populated center was visited by Magellan's fleet, and Ratto agrees.

Puerto San Julián and the mutinies. Albo gave the latitude of Puerto San Julián as 49°40′ S; fleet navigator San Martín figured it out as 49°08′ S; Pigafetta says 49°30′ S, and Maximilianus, 49°12′ S. The British Admiralty's *South Atlantic Pilot* (10th edition, London, 1959), p. 609, puts the northern entrance. Cabo Curioso, on latitude 49° 11′ S, longitude 67°36′ W. Magellan must have meant the southern entrance, at 49°12′ S. So Max really hit it! Even Sir John Narborough, in 1670, was a couple of miles out.

Magellan's speech to his men. Herrera, dec. II, lib. vii, chap. ii (Stevens trans., III, 14), and López de Gómara, cap. xcii, give paraphrases of the speech out of Pigafetta.

The mutinous priest enlisted in the Canaries. Herrera says he was French, also known as Calmette.

Elcano's version. In his interrogation after returning in *Victoria*, Juan Sebastián (Navarrete, IV, 287-91) made two inadmissable statements: (1) that the boat from *Concepción* to *Trinidad* was trying to prevent rather than incite mutiny; and (2) he, being present, saw Magellan pay Gómez de Espinosa 5 ducats to kill Mendoza. Elcano was not on board but helping Quesada hold down *Concepción*, and a Castilian hidalgo such as Espinosa did not have to be paid to carry out orders. But it must be admitted that both Albo and Bustamente, when examined, supported Elcano.

Santa Cruz. Captain Destéfani in *Santa Cruz y Su Historia Naval* (Buenos Aires, 1968) gives the later history of Santa Cruz, which was not formally taken possession of by Argentina until 1878. The same author, in *La Armada Argentina y Su Acción en la Patagonia* (1969), treats interestingly of the later history of Patagonia, which has been the "neglected child" of the Republic. With about 25 per cent of the area, it had barely 3 per cent of the population by the census of 1960.

* XVI *

"The Strait
That Shall Forever Bear His Name"

October-November 1520

Strait Discovered

On 21 October 1520, the feast of St. Ursula and the Eleven Thousand Virgins, the fleet raised a prominent peninsula which Magellan named after the seagoing Cornish princess and her martyred shipmates. Cabo Vírgenes or Cape Virgins it still is, on latitude 52°20′ S, longitude 68°21′ W. Albo was only twenty miles off in latitude, and made a good guess at the longitude. The Cape is a long flat stretch of grass-topped clay cliffs rising about 135 feet above the water. The landmarks for it (said Uriate on Loaysa's voyage) are a white sand hill four leagues north and "three great mountains of sand which look like islands but are not." On top of this cape the Chile-Argentine boundary turns a right angle and reaches the Atlantic a few yards east of the Chilean lighthouse on Punta Dungeness, the flat and gravelly extension of Cape Virgins. It then drops due south, leaving to Argentina one-third of Tierra del Fuego down to the Beagle Channel, and giving Chile both sides of the Strait.

Although the cape is conspicuous enough, the fact that a strait opens here is by no means obvious, and the tidal currents are so strong and confusing that an uncertain mariner would be tempted to sheer off. (Note in a later chapter what happened to Loaysa and Camargo.)

America and Asia on the Schöner globe of 1515, simplified and reduced.
From História da Colonização do Brasil.

Joshua Slocum in 1898 was blown outside Cape Virgins for thirty hours by a southwest gale; the next "loner," Louis Bernicot in *Anahita*, also without power, was twice blown out to sea; even steamers have been forced to scud all the way to the Falklands and there await a change of wind. Pigafetta writes that but for Magellan they would never have found the Strait, "for we all thought and said that it was closed on all sides." (The men evidently imagined a strait as something one could look through, like that of Gibraltar.) Pigafetta continues: "But the Captain General found it. He knew where to sail to find a well-hidden strait, which he saw depicted on a map in the treasury of the king of Portugal, made by that excellent man Martin de Boemia." That "excellent man" must have been Martin Behaim, to whose globe of 1492–

Sketch of Cape Virgins, in Guillemard's *Magellan*.

93 we have already referred; but what was the map? Behaim died in 1507; he never, so far as we know, went on a voyage of discovery, and no chart by him subsequent to the famous globe is known to exist.

Every biographer of Magellan, and many historians, have discussed the question, "What chart did Magellan see in Lisbon?" To me, the most reasonable answer in that he had seen one or more charts which ended South America with a strait, on the south side of which was the supposed Antarctic continent running around the world. The globe made in 1515 by the German geographer Johannes Schöner (1477–1547) is a good example of the chart that Magellan might have seen and thought to be Behaim's, since both Behaim and Schöner were Nurembergers, and their style was very similar. As we have seen, Magellan brought a painted globe to the Spanish court to prove his point; may not this have been a copy of Schöner's? Pigafetta's word *carta* need not put us off, since in those days the word could mean a flat map or one spread on a globe.

A globe like this could have assured Magellan that a strait existed either at the River Plate or further south. And Schöner makes the Pacific Ocean encouragingly narrow. *Zipangri* (Japan) is smack up to *Parias* (Central America), and the Spice Islands are no farther from the west coast of South America than the Lesser Antilles are from Florida. Had they indeed been so near to America, Magellan's idea that a round-the-world extension of the Line of Demarcation would give them to Spain would have proved correct. Spain, in fact, would have got all Asia up to the Ganges.

Two geographical factors unknown to Magellan thwarted him, although, curiously enough, he discovered both. One was the Strait's extreme southern position, and the other was the enormous breadth of the Pacific Ocean. These, combined, made the western route to the Far East so long and arduous as to be almost impracticable until ways were found to cross Mexico. Even so, the Portuguese Cape of Good Hope route remained the shorter and less difficult of the two. Magellan shared Columbus's basic idea of sailing from Europe to Asia "in a few days." America and the unexpected width of the Pacific thwarted both discoverers. And Magellan's exploits were never properly appreciated until Schouten and Le Maire capped them with the discovery of Cape Horn.

From Cape Virgins to Cape Pillar

It was now 21 October 1520; moon two days past first quarter. Having passed Cabo Vírgenes and avoided the many off-shore rocks and shoals which there await unwary mariners, the Captain General determined to investigate this break in the coast, and make sure whether it really was *the* Strait. He nipped around Punta Dungeness, the flat southern prolongation of Cabo Vírgenes. Mooring his flagship and *Victoria* in Bahia Posesión, hoping that this would turn out to be fair holding ground (which it was not), the Captain General sent ahead *Concepción*, now commanded by his faithful friend Serrano, and *San Antonio*, commanded by his kinsman Mezquita, to reconnoiter.

One of the sharp northeast gales characteristic of this region blew up the night of 21–22 October. *Trinidad* and *Victoria* weighed and jilled around inside the bay; the two others, too deeply embayed to beat against the gale, sailed west, giving themselves up for lost. Miraculously, as it seemed, the two-mile-wide Primera Angostura (First Narrows) opens up, and they roared through into Bahia Felipe where they found shelter and holding ground. Further on, they found another and broader narrows (Segunda Angostura) which led to a big bay, Paso Ancho (Broad Reach). Serrano and Pilot Carvalho put their heads together and decided that they really were in *the* Strait. After the gale had blown itself out and the wind turned west, *Concepción* and *San Antonio* returned to Bahia Posesión and announced themselves to *Trinidad* and the Captain General by breaking out gay banners, sounding trumpets, firing gun salutes, shouting, and cheering. Each pair had feared the loss of the other.

When all four ships were safely anchored, they "thanked God and the Virgin Mary," and Magellan decided to follow whither *San Antonio* and *Concepción* had led. Since it was now 1 November, All Saints' Day, the Captain General named the strait *Todos los Santos.* On early maps that name appears only for sections of the Strait; the whole Strait is almost invariably called *Estrecho de Magallanes,* Magellan's Strait.

The Captain General and his shipmates would have roared with laughter, could they have read the modern official sailing directions for the Strait: "The passage is safe for steamers"; but in thick weather, "both difficult and dangerous, because of incomplete surveys, the lack of aids to navigation, the great distance between anchorages, the strong current, and the narrow limits for the maneuvering of vessels." Magellan might say, "What about us? With no power, other than sail and oar, no survey, no aid to navigation?" The same manual assumes that no ship without power would be so foolhardy as to try the Strait.

Captain James Cook stated in his Journal of the *Endeavour's* voyage (1769), "The doubling of Cape Horn is thought by some to be a mighty thing, and others to this Day prefer the Straits of Magellan." After Cook's fast passage of Cape Horn became known, the big sailing ships in general shunned the Strait and suffered all the buffetings of "Cape Stiff" rather than face the dangers of the shorter route. But the Strait has since come back as a major sea highway. Not only small freighters destined for Chile and Peru, but the mammoth oilers of the 1970's, use the Strait regularly, and an average of about three a year run aground or are lost there. Few realize how long the Strait is—334 nautical miles. This is equivalent to the entire length of the English Channel from Bishop Rock to Dover Strait, or from the Gulf of St. Lawrence to Montreal, or from the Panama Canal entrance to Barranquilla.

Magellan and his captains wisely did not attempt to sail here at night; but as they entered the Strait in the Antarctic spring, darkness lasted but three to five hours.

A boat sent ashore from *Trinidad* in Bahia Felipe between the two Angosturas, reported a dead whale and a native cemetery with a couple of hundred corpses raised on stilts, but nothing alive. No Magellan source mentions his fleet having had any contact with live natives in the Strait. He saw their signal fires almost every night—hence the name that he gave to the country on the south side, *Tierra del Fuego.* The name is particularly applicable today, since this region has struck oil;

the gas from sundry oil wells burns in smoky flares on each side of the Strait's eastern entrance.

In seeing no Fuegians, Magellan's men missed viewing these examples of human fortitude in the face of hostile nature. Probably among the first arrivals from the Asiatic invasion tens of thousands of years earlier, continually pushed south by more powerful and enterprising tribes, these Indians had reached a dead end. Accommodating themselves to available food, though not to dress as the Eskimos did in the far north, they lived on the big, succulent mussels of the Strait and on such fish and birds as they could shoot or snare, burning the wood of the Tepu tree (*Tepularia stipularis*), and stripping bark for canoe hulls from various species of the evergreen Antarctic beech (*Nothofagus antarctica pomilio*, etc.) which clothe the lower slopes of the mountains. Charles Darwin thus described a canoeful of Fuegians whom he encountered in the *Beagle:* "These poor wretches were stunted in their growth, their hideous faces bedaubed with white paint, their skins filthy and greasy, their hair entangled, their voices discordant, and their gestures violent." They seemed not to mind sleet falling on their almost naked bodies.

Undeterred by sinister hints of the native graveyard, Magellan's fleet worked through the wider Second Narrows and came to an anchor in Paso Real between Isabel Island and the main. Here, and well into Paso Ancho or Broad Reach, the landscape on each side is pampas: green-to-brown rolling country with no hint of a strait. Even Paso Ancho looks like a dead-end because in clear weather, sixty miles to the southward, the mountains on Dawson Island and on the Cordillera Darwin rise like an impenetrable barrier. On the land side the aspect today is pastoral. In February, hayfields white with daisies roll down to the sea, sheep and cattle pastures are everywhere, and a few neat villas planted with evergreen to shield them from the furious winds, indicate that this region is livable winter or summer. Paso Ancho (15 miles broad), when low-hanging clouds hide the distant snowy mountains, looks very much like any broad bay in Maine, Nova Scotia, or Scotland. The great scenery begins within sight of Cape Froward.

Magellan's fleet, continuing south through Paso Ancho and passing the site of Punta Arenas, again separated. The Captain General sent *San Antonio* and *Concepción* to investigate two openings eastward which turned out to be dead-ends—Bahía Inútil (Useless Bay) and

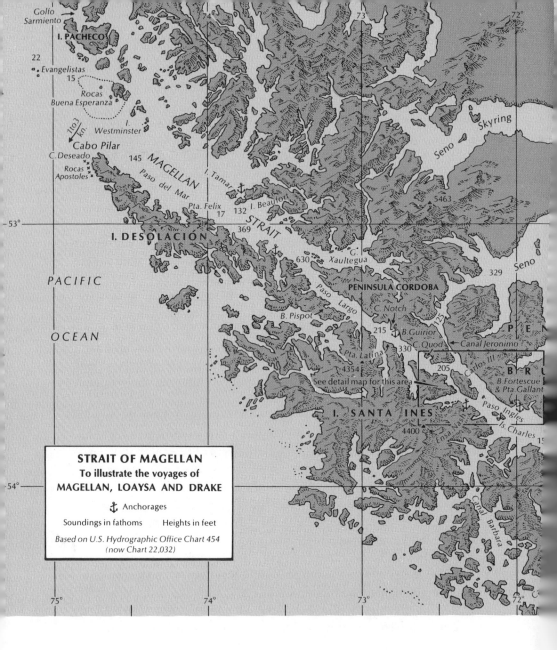

Golfo
Sarmiento

I. PACHECO

22
• Evangelistas
15
Rocas
Buena Esperanza

1 to 3
km
I.
Westminster

Cabo Pilar

Seno Skyring

C.Deseado
Rocas
Apostoles

145 MAGELLAN

Paso del Mar

I. Tamar

5463

Pta. Felix
17   132 I. Beaufort

— 53° ——————————————— 369 ——— STRAIT

I. DESOLACIÓN

630   Xaultegua   329   Seno
G.

PACIFIC

Paso Largo

PENINSULA CORDOBA

C. Notch

B. Pispot

125

OCEAN

215 B.Guinor   P E

Pta. Latina   330 C. Quod ← Canal Jeronimo

4354   205   B R

Carlos III

See detail map for this area   B.Fortescue
& Pta. Gallant

Paso Inglés

I. SANTA INES   Is. Charles 15

4400   Ensa.Va

Canal Barbara

STRAIT OF MAGELLAN
To illustrate the voyages of
MAGELLAN, LOAYSA AND DRAKE

⚓ Anchorages

Soundings in fathoms   Heights in feet

Based on U.S. Hydrographic Office Chart 454
(now Chart 22,032)

— 54° —

75°   74°   73°   72°

71°

70°

ARGENTINA
(CHILE)

Cabo Virgenes

ATLANTIC OCEAN

B. Posesión

Loaysa ships dragged ashore

Cerros San Gregorio
1184

C. Gregorio

Pta. Gracia

18

First
Narrows

12

22

3

2 to 4 kn.

MAGELLAN STRAIT

Punta
Dungeness

29

37

5 to 8 kn.

20

Bahia
Victoria

4

2

C. Espíritu Santo

Second Narrows

Paso Royal

Sn. Vicente

23

I. Sta. Marta

5

32

I. Isabel

53°

Otway

104

50

TIERRA   DEL   FUEGO

Punta Arenas

Paso
Ancho
(Broad Reach)

127

Los Tres Morros
3000

70

68

Bahia   Inútil

53°30'

N S U L A

270

100

S · W · I · C · K

Pta. Santa Ana

30 Nautical Miles

Andrews

Mt. Tarn
2184

P. del Hambre

Holland

B. Woods

Mt. Victoria
3018

C. San Isidro

(CHILE)

(ARGENTINA)

Pta.
Ovidia

210

C. Froward

301

ISLA
DAWSON

284

54°

Paso
Froward

B. George

Seno
Magdalena

Admiralty

3100

Sound

Canal Magdalena

ockburn

71°

7218

70°

69°

387

Seno del Almirantazgo (Admiralty Bay)—while he in the flagship with *Victoria* sailed along what fortunately turned out to be the real Strait.

Just before this separation, Magellan held a captains' conference to decide whether or not to push on. All were in favor of doing so except Esteban Gómez, now pilot of *San Antonio*. Although a Portuguese, Gómez "hated the Captain General exceedingly" (says Pigafetta), because he had hoped to command the entire fleet, and his simmering hate blew hot when Magellan, after eliminating Cartagena, conferred the captaincy of *San Antonio* on his cousin Mezquita instead of on Gómez. Magellan, *muy compuesto* (with his usual cool), replied that he was resolved to go on, "even if they had to eat the leather chafing-gear on the ships' yards." And that is exactly what they did.

While *San Antonio* was exploring Useless and Admiralty bays, Esteban Gómez pulled off the one successful mutiny of this long voyage. He managed to suborn the stoutest fellows in the crew, clapped weak Captain Mezquita in irons, gave his fellow conspirator Hierónimo Guerra command of the ship, and piloted her back to Spain, arriving at the end of March 1521. He made no attempt to put in at San Julián to pick up marooned Cartagena and the priest. At Seville, both Gómez and his victim Mezquita were flung into jail. Gómez managed to parley his way out and into the royal favor to such good purpose that he got a new ship to go in search of a better strait than Magellan's. But poor Álvaro de Mezquita, the most frustrated officer of the fleet, remained in jail until after *Victoria* arrived home, when he found witnesses to put his conduct in a more favorable light. Charles V eventually ordered Mezquita to be released, and he returned to Portugal on D. Manuel's invitation.

In the meantime Magellan in *Trinidad* with *Victoria* sailed west again down Broad Reach. About thirty miles south of the site of Punta Arenas they passed, behind Punta Santa Ana, the site of Rey Don Felipe, one of two outposts established by Sarmiento de Gamboa in 1583 to guard the Strait. Port Famine, the name given to it by Cavendish in 1587, is still the southernmost settlement on the Strait; not a soul lives to the south and west. Near here, wrote Captain Slocum in 1900, "I had my first experience with the terrific squalls called williwaws, which extended from the point on through the Strait to the Pacific. These were compressed gales of wind that Boreas handed down over the hills in chunks. A full-blown williwaw will throw a ship, even

without sail set, over on her beam ends." Sailing directions warn mariners always to be prepared for a williwaw. They give no notice of their coming, and are apt to hit a vessel with such force as to strip off her sails, or even to capsize her.

Magellan's fleet sailed into spectacular scenery as soon as it passed Mount Tarn, which Darwin was the first to climb. Magellan's people had never seen anything like this combination of ocean strait with snow mountains; nor had Darwin. They rounded Cape Froward, a noble headland rising almost 1200 feet at latitude 53°54′ S, the southernmost point on the American continent. Here the Strait, about five miles wide, turns abruptly northwest, and after another twenty-five to thirty miles becomes a deep, narrow cut through the Andes, as if some giant hand had cleft the mountains millions of years ago.

Entering this part of the Strait, as we did in February 1972, one seems to be entering a completely new and strange world, a veritable Never-Never Land. The Strait never freezes except along the edges, and the evergreen Antarctic beech, with its tiny, matted leaves, grows thickly along the lower mountain slopes. The middle slopes support a coarse

Down the Strait: Cape Froward (above). Antarctic beech groves (below).

grass which turns bronze in the setting sun; and above, the high peaks are snow-covered the year round; when it rains in the Strait, it snows at 6000 feet. One misses, in the Antarctic autumn, the brilliant colors of New England and Canada (since Patagonia and Tierra del Fuego lack birch and other deciduous trees); but by way of compensation, they harbor no mosquitoes, which cannot stand the wind! There is no sign of human life south and west of Port Famine, except for a few small unattended lighthouses at dangerous points. The Indians are extinct, and with no coastal road or path or any means of land transportation, neither Chilean nor foreigner has attempted to settle or even to camp here.* Even the birds are different—the sinister gray *Carnero* which picks out the eyes of shipwrecked sailors, the Steamboat Duck whose whirling wings, resembling the churning paddle wheels of early steamers, enable him to pace an eight-knot vessel on the surface. In spring, when Magellan sailed through, both banks are gay with many-colored flowers, and saturated peat moss makes a sort of tundra in the hollows. Although glaciers are everywhere visible and some descend nearly to the sea, icebergs are missing; the glaciers "calve" only small bits of ice, not bergs. Waterfalls tumble directly into the bays. It is "fascinating sailing," wrote H. W. Tilman, who sailed through in his little sloop *Mischief* in an Antarctic summer not long ago. One rounds miniature capes and peeps into hidden coves: "It had the powerful appeal of an untrodden land." In several places, such as Paso Inglés by Rupert and Carlos Islands, and Crosstides, the channel is less than a mile wide, but in the center the depths run to 800 fathom; and from the narrow ribbon of practicable holding ground near shore, a ship is liable to be wrenched by a sudden williwaw.

The little bight which Magellan named River of Sardines, because its waters were swarming with small edible fish, one can identify as Fortescue Bay, just east of Cabo Gallant at latitude 53°42′ S. The Captain General may even have entered the inner landlocked harbor, Caleta Gallant. Both have excellent holding ground; the Chilean *Derrotero* (Sailing Directions) calls Fortescue the best anchorage in the Strait for all classes of vessels. And it is an exceptionally charming spot. The soft summer night of 24 February 1972, when we lay there in *Orompello* of the Chilean Navy, will be ever memorable for the Milky Way

---

* An exception: Bahia Cutter, up the Canal San Jerónimo, where there is a small copper mine with about a dozen employees.

rising in a great "whoosh" of sparkling light, and on top of it the Southern Cross flashing brilliantly. Next morning we went ashore on the pebble beach of Bahia Fortescue, wreathed with white flowers resembling gigantic marguerites; a few rods inland we found other flowers, brightly colored, and calafate bushes bearing big red berries. Magellan evidently chose this fair place to celebrate the first Mass in the future Chile. The inner Caleta Gallant, "difficult of access," says the modern *Derrotero*, but not too difficult for Magellan's ships, offers perfect protection and holding ground, with two rivers to replenish water and plenty of beechwood for fuel.

While he waited here, the Captain General fitted out, provisioned, and manned his flag longboat to explore the Strait further in the hope of finding an outlet. "The men returned within three days," says Pigafetta, "and reported that they had seen the cape and the open sea." Roldán de Argote, a Flemish gunner of the fleet, climbed a mountain (later named after him), sighted the ocean, and reported it to the Captain General who "wept for joy," says Pigafetta, "and called that *Cabo Deseado*, for we had long been desiring it." The name is still applied to one of the two prongs of Desolation Island which mark the Pacific entrance to the Strait; Cabo Pilar, the better known later name, is the northern prong.

Solicitous about his other two ships, Magellan turned back to search for them. Having already roughly charted the eastern half of the Strait, he avoided the great masses of kelp that mark rocky ledges, and had leisure to examine the striking scenery. Here, as Herrera tells us, "is the most beautiful country in the world—the Strait a gunshot across, separating high sierras covered with perpetual snow, whose lower slopes were clothed with magnificent trees."

Soon they met *Concepción* sailing alone. Captain Serrano had no news of *San Antonio*, but Magellan refused to write her off, and spent five or six days searching for her, even up Admiralty Sound; *Victoria* sailed all the way to Cape Virgins to look for the errant ship. The Captain General now turned to his chief pilot Andrés de San Martín, who combined astrology with navigation. After plotting the stars and consulting a book, Andrés, reported that she had returned to Spain with Captain Mezquita in chains. He was right, as we have seen.

After *Victoria* rejoined the flagship, Magellan decided to press forward, and information from the boat exploration saved him from wast-

Our landing at Fortescue Bay (Magellan's *Rio de Sardinas*), 24 February 1972. Sanchez Obregón photo.

Going ashore. Flowers at Caleta Gallant, the inner harbor. Sanchez Obregón photo.

ing time on dead ends. He sailed up the main channel, Paso Inglés, the most dangerous reach of the Strait (although not the most narrow), and passed Carlos III Island (where Captain Joshua Slocum in his sloop *Spray* foiled an attack by Fuegians by sprinkling carpet tacks on her deck at night). On this island of many hills Magellan erected a cross.

As one approaches the meeting of waters that some English navigator appropriately named Crosstides, where Canal San Jerónimo empties into the Strait, anyone might wonder which was the Strait and which the Canal. But the longboat crew must have observed as they got nearer, what Ensign Thornton of *Orompello* pointed out to me, that the waters of the Canal are lighter in color than those of the Strait, and that the nearer one approaches, the wider the real Strait appears to be. So Magellan wasted no time, and avoided the dead end. He passed safely through Paso Tortuoso witih its 330-fathom deep, and entered Paso Largo with depths up to 810 fathom.

Here again the character of the scenery changes. The mountains of Desolation Island on the port hand are of ribbed granite with stunted vegetation only in the clefts, reminding one of the Labrador; no more trees. Great Pacific surges roll in and break on both sides. You feel that you are coming out into something enormous and unpredictable. Magellan passed Bahia Corkscrew, Cape Providence, and the bold is-land of Tamar, off which a 2½-fathom rock has wrecked many an in-cautious ship. Here in mid-Strait, with 800-foot deeps on each side, is the dangerous Bajo Magallanes which breaks when heavy swells roll in from the ocean. At the end of Paso del Mar is the worst of many bad places in the Strait to be caught in a strong westerly.

After thirty miles of this, on 28 November 1520 (moon four days past full) *Trinidad, Concepción,* and *Victoria* passed Cabo Pilar (which Magellan named *Deseado*) on Desolation Island. Only one of these ships, and about 35 out of the 150 members of their crews, ever re-turned to Spain.

Antonio de Herrera, the late-sixteenth-century Spanish historian who seems to have cared most for Magellan, wrote of his entry into the great Pacific: "On the 27th of November he came out into the South Sea, blessing God, who had been pleas'd to permit him to find what he so much desir'd, being the first that ever went that way, which will perpetuate his Memory for ever. They guessed this Streight to be about one hundred Leagues in Length. . . . The sea was very Black and

Out of the Strait: Desolation Island begins (above). Cabo Pilar, from the west (below).

Boisterous, which denoted a vast Ocean. Magellan order'd publick Thanksgiving, and sail'd away to the Northward, to get out of the Cold."

All in all, Magellan had a "very good chance," as sailors say, especially as he had sailed thrice over at least 250 miles of the 334-mile length of the Strait, looking for *San Antonio*. He did not experience, or at least none of his three literary shipmates noted, any sharp squalls or particular hazards. He managed to moor safely every night by running a hawser from the stern to a tree ashore in one of the many anchorages suitable for small ships. Frequently the sailors landed to gather an excellent anti-scorbutic, the wild celery (*Apium australe*) which grew in abundance near springs or rivers. Later voyagers described the natural bowers that wind-blown beech and pine made in the woods. Their matted branches kept out excessive snow and cold; in this shelter herbs flourished the year round, and in the spring there is a gorgeous show of wild flowers. Magellan's men caught plenty of fish—albacore, bonito, and flying fish. After they had passed safely through, Pigafetta wrote, "I believe that there is not a more beautiful or better strait in the world than that one." Beautiful, yes, but terrible as well; and one must study the history of later voyages through the Strait, and if possible traverse it oneself, to appreciate the grandeur and the magnitude of Magellan's achievement. For say what you will of him, detractors, *he did it*. As Alonso de Ercilla wrote in *La Araucana*,

> Magallanes, Señor, fué el primer hombre
> Que abriendo este camino, le dió nombre.*
> Magellan, Sir, was the first man
> Both to open this route and to give it name.

"Wednesday, November 28, 1520," writes Pigafetta, "we debouched from that Strait, engulfing ourselves in the Pacific Sea." One of the great moments of a great voyage. The Pacific, shimmering under a westering sun, spread for half a circumference before Magellan's eyes. Vasco Núñez de Balboa, to be sure, had seen the ocean from a peak in Darien seven years before, and even earlier Abreu had sailed into its western edge which laved the Moluccas. But Magellan now faced a waste of water thousands of miles wide, and entered it without fear or hesitation. Here too he navigated well, for this forefront of the great ocean is studded with breaking reefs; the entire coast is smoky with

* Canto 1, strophe 8; first published in 1569.

their white spray. If you let a west wind and flood tide throw you off from Cabo Pilar, you are likely to strike the extensive rocky shoals hopefully if unsuitably named by early sailors *Buena Esperanza* and *Las Evangelistas*—Good Hope and The Evangelists.

Albo tells us that from Cabo Deseado they steered northwest, north, and north-northeast for two days and three nights, and on the morning of 1 December sighted land and found their latitude to be 48° S. They were well on their way to penetrate the greatest of oceans, hitherto unknown to Europeans except by rare glimpses of its distant verges.

Bibliography and Notes

STRAIT OF MAGELLAN

The main sources have already been given in the bibliography to Chapter XIII.

The U.S. Hydrographic Office *Sailing Directions for South America*, II, the British Admiralty's *South American Pilot*, II (10th ed., 1959), and the Chilean *Derrotero de la Costa de Chile*, IV, *Estrecho de Magallanes* (5th ed., 1968), are useful; and the last-named (a copy of which Admiral Pablo Weber of the Chilean Navy kindly gave me) is indispensable. For the Strait I use the modern official Chilean names, as noted on Navy Oceanographic Office Chart H.O. 454 (1969), and Chilean Navy Charts 1126 (entrance), 56 (entire length), 1111 (details, center), and 1000 (western entrance), which my friends in the Chilean navy obtained for me. The English names on British Admiralty charts are used in the older books. At an era when no South American nation did much charting, Captain FitzRoy of H.M.S. *Beagle*, and others, surveyed the Strait and naturally attached English names, most of which Chile has respected. Thus we have, in or around the Strait, a Punta Let Go, Puerto Hook, Bahia Good Luck, and Fundeadero Spiteful. Among books descriptive of the Strait and Tierra del Fuego are:—Joshua Slocum, *Sailing Alone Around the World* (1900), a classic; Rockwell Kent, *Voyaging Southward from the Strait of Magellan* (New York, 1924), illustrated by himself; Alberto M. de Agostini, *Magallanes y Canales Fueginos* (Punta Arenas, 1960), beautifully illustrated and with good chapters on fauna and flora; James Bryce, *South America, Observations and Impressions* (New York, 1912), chap. viii; E. Lucas Bridges, *Uttermost Part of the Earth* (London, 1948), life on Beagle Channel at the turn of the century; and H. W. Tilman, *"Mischief" in Patagonia* (1957), a well written and illustrated account of a small-yacht voyage.

Albo's longitude 52°31′ W presumably was counted from the meridian of Hierro (Ferro), which is 18°10′ W of Greenwich. Adding the two makes the longitude of Cape Virgins 70°41′ W; actually it is on 68°21′ W. A mistake of only 2°20′ in longitude was amazingly accurate for that era, but

Albo never repeated this good calculation. The landmarks are in Clements Markham (ed.), *Early Voyages to Magellan's Strait* (London, 1911), p. 90.

Question of Magellan's map. On the Schöner globe of 1515, America follows the Waldseemüller pattern, except for breaking a strait through the Isthmus of Panama. It ends in a cape, separated at about latitude 45° S by a strait from a land which Schöner calls *Brasilie regio*, which extends indefinitely around the world. (In his next globe, of 1520, Schöner corrects *Brasilie regio* to *Brasilia inferior.*) The west coast of South America Schöner calls *terra ulterior incog.*, "land hitherto unknown"; but he makes a good guess at its trend. See George E. Nunn, *The Columbus and Magellan Concepts of South American Geography* (privately printed, Glenside, Pa., 1932). According to Nordenskiöld, *Periplus*, p. 152, sec. 28, there are two copies of the Schöner globe of 1515, at Weimar and Frankfurt am Main. Since both are made from printed gores, D. Manuel may well have obtained a third copy, and as both Schöner and Behaim were Nurembergers, Magellan may have confused one with t'other and, as Schöner did not sign his globe, assumed that Behaim made it. The Schöner globe is reproduced in E. F. Jomard, *Les Monuments de la géographie* (Paris, 1862), and described in Franz Wieser, *Magalhães-Strasse . . . auf den Globen des Johannes Schöner* (Berlin, 1881). For Schöner's later globe, of 1520, repeating the same concept of South America and the Strait, see Nordenskiöld, *op cit.*, § 31. Justin Winsor's discussion of this mysterious map in *Narrative and Critical History*, II, 112–36, has never been bettered. J. G. Kohl, in *Geschichte . . . zur Magellan's-Strasse* (1877), pp. 8–9, taf. I, has a plausible reconstruction of the map that was in Magellan's mind when he sailed. Marcel Destombes, "The Chart of Magellan," *Imago Mundi*, XII (1955), 66–71, features a chart oriented from south to north, but it has no strait, so I doubt whether Magellan ever knew it. The best recent discussion is Carlos Sanz, *Juan Sebastián Elcano . . . Problema Histórico Resuelto?* (Madrid, 1973), amply illustrated. He decides on the Reinel mappmonde of 1518, an outline of which I have reproduced in Chapter XV, above.

Captain James Cook on the Strait. Cook never sailed through the Strait, but any remarks on it by so eminent a navigator are important. See Hakluyt Society ed., *Journals of Captain Cook, Voyage of Endeavour*, I (1955), 58. The Introduction by the New Zealand editor of this set, John C. Beaglehole, is a spirited and scholarly summary of all Pacific voyages between Magellan's and Cook's.

Early names for the Strait. Magellan never named the Strait after himself, but almost everyone else did. Kohl, discussing this question on page 47 of his *Geschichte . . . zur Magellan's Strasse*, reports that Pigafetta stated that the Captain General called it after the Eleven Thousand Virgins; but I find no authority for that, and believe that he called it *Todos los Santos* in honor of the day he entered it. The earliest English map, by Robert Thorne (in Hakluyt, *Divers Voyages*, 1582), calls it *Strictum Omnium Sanctorum*. Sailors, however, persisted in calling it after Magellan, and that name became fixed on the maps. Sarmiento de Gamboa proposed that it be officially renamed *Buena Madre* but Philip II refused, and declared that the Strait should always be called after its discoverer. Cheers for the old bigot!

Length of Strait. The distance from Punta Dungeness to the Evangelistas, as given in *Brown's Almanac* for 1971, p. 151, is 334 nautical miles. From Dungeness to Cabo Pilar is 311.5. These figures, representing steamship masters' count by patent log, are more reliable than simply stepping it off on a chart with dividers. To realize what this distance means, here are a few comparative distances from Brown and H.O. 117, *Table of Distances Between Ports* (Washington, 1968):—

	Miles
Bishop Rock to Calais	333
St. Lawrence River, Matane to Montreal	340
Colón, Panama, to Barranquilla, Colombia	336

Thus, the only narrow-seas exploit of the 16th century comparable to Magellan's was Cartier's sail up the St. Lawrence River.

Natives of the Strait. Samuel K. Lothrop, *The Indians of Tierra del Fuego* (New York, 1928, lavishly illustrated), is best, with a colored ethnographical map on page 24. In 1520, the north side of the Strait to Isla Isabel was occupied by the Tehuelche, named *Patagónes* by Magellan, but the east side of the Strait, and the rest of Tierra del Fuego was the land of the Ona and the Haush, whom Lothrop calls "foot Indians," as they lived off the land. The west side of the Strait from Isla Isabel down and the south side, starting at Dawson Island and Admiralty Sound, was occupied by the Alacalaf, one of two tribes called by Lothrop "canoe Indians." The Yaghan, the other canoe tribe, occupied Beagle Channel and the shores west to Breakneck Peninsula, and everything to the southward. See especially pp. 143–45 for description of the Yaghan beech-bark canoes. All these Indians were nomadic within definite limits. The Ona and Haush were linguistically allied to the Tehuelche, whom they equaled in stature; figures on p. 41; tallest Ona, slightly over six feet. They must have come from Patagonia, but how? In recent times they had no boats and could not swim. None of these Indians wove or made pottery, and they lacked such simple implements as fishhooks and cooking utensils. Except for a few wretched remnants they are now (1974) extinct. As Darwin wrote, "Wherever the European has trod, death seems to pursue the aboriginal."

Antarctic flora. My remarks are the result of personal observation, contact with the Instituto de la Patagonia at Punta Arenas, talking with its learned botanist Dr. Edmundo Pisano V., reading his mimeographed sheet *Descripción Esquemática de Algunas Características Vegetacionales de la Bahía Fortescue* (1972), and examining specimens in the Instituto's excellent Antarctic herbarium. Careless writers call the beech an oak and describe wild celery as "umbelliferous parsley." Captain James Cook pronounced the wild celery to be as palatable as English garden celery.

Esteban Gómez. See my *Northern Voyages*, pp. 326–31, 336–7; but add L. A. Vigneras's article in *Terrae Incognitae*, II (1970), 25–28.

The Steamboat Duck is *Tackyeres plenéres*. Captain Cook called it the

The Great White Fleet rounding Cape Froward, February 1908, led by Chilean cruiser *Chacabuco:* Sketch by Henry Reuterdahl for his oil painting, in the Naval Academy Museum, Annapolis. Courtesy of the late Commander Robert Huntingdon, USN.

"race-horse duck," no doubt because it beat his ship. Beaglehole (ed.), *Journals*, II, 614.

Since Cape Gallant, western headland of Fortescue Bay, is 116 miles from Cabo Pilar, sailors are suspicious of the statement that Magellan's boat returned in three days with news of the Pacific Ocean. But they did not have to sail more than half that distance, since Roldán of the boat's crew climbed a mountain near the shore and from its summit saw the Strait's end. For Roldán, who survived this voyage and sailed again with Loaysa, see J. G. Kohl, *Geschichte . . . zur Magellan's-Strasse* (1877), p. 50. After talking with Chilean sailors who use the Strait constantly, I believe this could have been done, had the boat enjoyed a fair wind both ways and taken advantage of the long summer days to sail almost constantly. Pigafetta says that there were only three hours of complete darkness.

Date of leaving the Strait. Pigafetta says 28 November 1520, Herrera (1740 trans., III, 23) the 27th, and Albo, the 26th. Note what I say in Notes to Chapter X about dates at sea. Some date from passing the Evangelistas, the official end of the Strait today, rather than Cabo Pilar. Pigafetta's mention of *Pacific* is in Robertson ed., I, 83. Later voyagers, including Drake, who found this ocean anything but pacific, preferred the older name *Mar del Sur* or South Sea.

Passage of the great white fleet. Most spectacular passage of the Strait of Magellan since days of sail was that of a United States fleet comprising 16 battleships (*Connecticut,* flag), commanded by Rear Admiral Robley D. Evans USN, in February 1908. The late Admiral H. Kent Hewitt USN told me some of the incidents. Chilean cruiser *Chacabuco* led the column. The American battleships, painted white with buff superstructures and stacks, were coal burners capable of making 15 to 17 knots, and with 12- and 13-inch main batteries. They had no aids to navigation that we now take for granted, such as voice radio, radar, and gyro compass. They did have long-range wireless for shore communication by Morse code, but their primitive radio worked so ill that inter-ship communication had to be by flag signal and semaphore. The chip log was still in use to determine speed, patent logs being considered unreliable. Passed Midshipman Hewitt went ashore at Punta Arenas to make longitude observations with artificial horizon, in order to correct the chronometers, and also to time the vibrations of a magnetic needle to determine the strength of the magnetic field at that remote part of the globe. After coaling at Punta Arenas, the battleships departed before dawn 7 February 1908 in order to round Cape Froward at first light. Steaming at 10 knots with 400 yards' interval between ships, they sortied from the Strait in a thick fog after nightfall same day. Henry Reuterdahl's painting, now in the Naval Academy Museum, Annapolis, shows the fleet rounding Cape Froward but omits *Chacabuco*. I reproduce here the artist's preliminary drawing, which President Theodore Roosevelt once owned; his son gave it to my late friend Robert Huntingdon, Jr., who kindly had it photographed for me.

✳ XVII ✳

Across the Pacific

North from Cabo Pilar

The fleet that Magellan led out of the Strait on 27 or 28 November 1520 comprised flagship *Trinidad, Concepción* now commanded by Juan Serrano, and *Victoria* commanded by Duarte Barbosa. According to Pilot Albo, they steered northwest, north, and north-northeast for two days and three nights; proper courses for avoiding the dangerous southern coast of Chile, especially the Buena Esperanza and Evangelista rocks which lie in wait for the unwary mariner. This portion of the Chilean coast resembles that of Norway, deeply indented with fjord-like bays, rocky and lofty shores; the modern sailing directions four and a half centuries after Magellan warn: "not yet closely examined; strangers should be on their guard!" "On the morning of 1 December," says Albo, "we saw bits of land like hillocks" sticking over the horizon. These ran together to make a mountainous promontory, a "bold and remarkable headland" rising to 1300 feet. This sounds like Cabo Tres Montes in latitude 47° S. Albo says 48°, the latitude of Campana Island; but Campana is not nearly so conspicuous as Tres Montes, so we must allow the pilot an occasional error. He usually calculated his latitude too far south.

From this place Magellan really shoved off into the Pacific Ocean, as he then named it, the winds being steady and the weather fair in comparison with what he had experienced in the Atlantic. "Well was it named Pacific," wrote Pigafetta, "for during this period"—three months and twenty days—"we met with no storm."

Here let us pause a moment and contemplate what lay ahead of Magellan. The Pacific Ocean was a watery wilderness as completely unknown to Europeans as Australia or Amazonia. Balboa had sighted it and the Portuguese had touched its western verge; but in the absence of any method to find longitude, nobody knew how wide this ocean could be; and all estimates in Magellan's hands, whether literary or cartographical, were at least 80 per cent short of the truth. Although Polynesians for centuries had been circulating through the thousands of Pacific islands and atolls in their outrigger canoes, Europeans knew nothing of them whatsoever. Magellan's lengthy voyage from the mouth of the Strait to Guam traced almost as many new routes for commerce as Columbus; and, in fact, realized (after the deaths of both men) Columbus's dream of tapping the wealth of the Indies by sailing west. Actually, mapmakers for a century after Magellan underestimated the width of the Pacific by as much as 40 per cent.

Pigafetta at this point gives us one of the earliest descriptions of the constellations in the Southern Hemisphere. "The Antarctic Pole is not so steady as the Arctic. Many small stars clustered together are seen, which have the appearance of two clouds of mist." These are *nubecula major* and *minor*, now the Magellanic Clouds. "In the midst of them," continues Pigafetta, "are two large and not very bright stars, which move but slightly. Those two stars are the Antarctic Pole." He probably meant two stars of the constellation Hydra which moves around the southern celestial pole, just as Ursa Minor circles its northern counterpart. "When we were in the midst of that Gulf," continues Pigafetta, "we saw a cross with five extremely bright stars straight toward the west, and they are equally spaced one with the other." Richard Eden's early translation of Pigafetta adds, "This crosse is so fayre and bewtiful, that none other hevenly body may be compared to it." Since the Southern Cross would have been low in the southeastern sky, Pigafetta must have made a mistake in identification. It could not have been Orion's Belt, which would have been due west at that time, since Orion was familiar; it might have been a cross-like constellation, *Grus* the Crane, which shone low in the southwest, about to set.

At Cabo Pilar, Pilot Albo picks up his narrative, which enables us roughly to plot the fleet's course across the Pacific. Here is a sample of it; the dates begin at noon of the day mentioned:

2–3 Dec. 1520, course NW, taking the fleet to latitude 46° 30′ S.

12–13 Dec. 1520, course NE by N, taking them to latitude 40° S.

1–2 Jan. 1521, course WNW, taking them to latitude 24° S.

19–20 Jan. 1521, course NW by W, taking them to latitude 15° S.

All fair winds and good sailing so far. Albo records southwest courses for two days, 21–22 January 1521, indicating head winds for the only time on this fourteen-week voyage to Guam. Correia the Portuguese historian declared that they sailed for five months (really three, Cabo Pilar to Guam) without shortening sail; and evidently very little shifting of the lines except to freshen a halyard's nip in the block.

It is a disappointment to the historian that none of Magellan's chroniclers, not even Pigafetta, has a word to say about the beauty of the Pacific or the day-by-day ritual. Nevertheless, anyone who has "spoomed" before Pacific trade winds can imagine the scene. *Trinidad*, *Concepción*, and *Victoria* roll along with wind astern or on the quarter, all square sails set and mizzen furled to help the steering. Bluest of blue seas, white fleecy clouds flying to leeward, frequent bursts of flying fish pursued by dorados, and (until February or March) plenty to eat; ships' boys singing their little ditties every half-hour when the glass is turned, and longer ones at change of watch; at dusk, *Concepción* and *Victoria* closing *Trinidad* so that Captains Serrano and Barbosa can make the proper hail: *Dios vos salve, capitán general y señor maestro y buona compaña!* At noon Pilot Albo shoots the sun and figures out the latitude. Velvet nights with the old familiar stars returning—the Bear (no longer indulging in his daily bath), Orion, and friendly Polaris, the navigator's best friend, appear. The incredible beauty of dawn at sea, heralded by the zodiacal light in the east. Does not the memory of it wring the heart of every old salt?

Magellan had no ship's bells to mark the passing time, only half-hour glasses; but he and his captains held morning and evening prayers regularly, just as all the great navigators did.

On the respective sailing qualities of his three ships I can find no data in any source. *Trinidad,* 110 tuns' burthen, was presumably faster than *Concepción* of 80 tuns, or *Victoria* of 85 tuns; but by this time they had learned to adjust their speed by lacing on or removing bonnets from their sails, to keep the fleet speed uniform. And from Guam to Samar, even if Albo slipped a couple of days in his log, they made the amazingly fast speed of eight knots, considering that they had not been careened and their bottoms cleansed since Patagonia.

Alan Villiers's poignant words on Captain Cook's fleet apply equally to Magellan's: "On sailed the little vessels, feeble, man-made, windblown chips upon a hostile immensity, held to their course only by the ability and iron will of the great seaman commanding them." * In Magellan's case, the Pacific was unusually kind to the man who first named her and crossed her. Fair winds wafted him on, and by following where they took him, he avoided possible shipwreck in the dark of the moon on any one of a thousand islets and atolls. He could have done no better had he enjoyed full information about the great ocean's winds and currents. Drake later in the same century, Bougainville and Wallis in the eighteenth, learned to their cost that no sailing vessel could safely stretch out to the westward right after clearing the Strait; she must sail north, preferably to latitude 25° S between November and March, before benefiting from the southeast trade winds.

Why, when all this was unknown, did Magellan sail north before turning west? The obvious, common-sense seaman's answer is, "to stay with fair winds." His "Genoese pilot" gives us an additional reason: "As he had information that there were no provisions at Maluco [the Spice Islands], he said that he would go in a northerly direction as far as 10° or 12° North. And they reached to as far as 13° N, and in this latitude they navigated to the W, and W by S."

It is true that not much food except rice and fresh fish could be had in the Spice Islands, as we shall see from *Victoria's* later experience; Magellan's friend Serrão had probably so informed him. Several modern historians argue that Magellan was heading for Okinawa and the Ryukyus. Duarte Barbosa called the Ryukyus *los Lequíos* in his book, which Magellan may have read, and identified them with biblical Tarshish and Ophir. Señor Obregón and I, however, believe

* Villiers, *Captain James Cook,* p. 245.

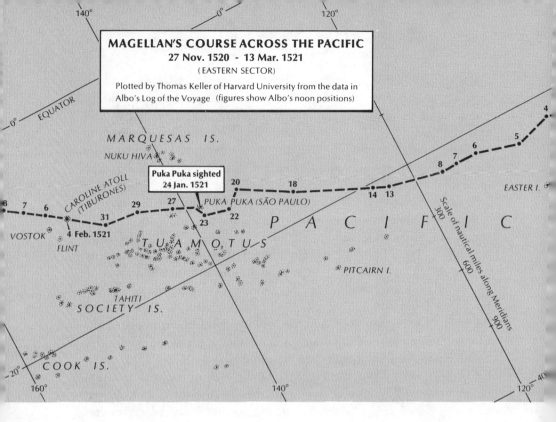

MAGELLAN'S COURSE ACROSS THE PACIFIC
27 Nov. 1520 - 13 Mar. 1521
(EASTERN SECTOR)

Plotted by Thomas Keller of Harvard University from the data in
Albo's Log of the Voyage (figures show Albo's noon positions)

that, apart from the provision problem, Magellan had learned about prevailing winds in the Moluccas during his early Portuguese voyage, and wanted to be in a good position to coast down to the Spice Islands when the northeast trades struck in. Be that as it may, we need no better motive than simple acquisitiveness to lead Magellan so far north. He must have heard of the Philippine Islands in Malacca, where there was a colony of some five hundred Filipinos, and he probably hoped to secure them for Spain before proceeding to his main objective, the Spice Islands.

Referring to our chart where Albo's courses are plotted, the fleet could not have sailed a more lonely course across the Pacific if Magellan had been the captain of a modern solo, non-stop cruise looking for publicity and prizes. First, he missed the two Juan Fernandez Islands well off Valpariso. Then, crossing a wide space where there are no islands, he left to port the Tuamotou and Manihiki archipelagos except (as we state below) for two uninhabited atolls. Had Magellan

406

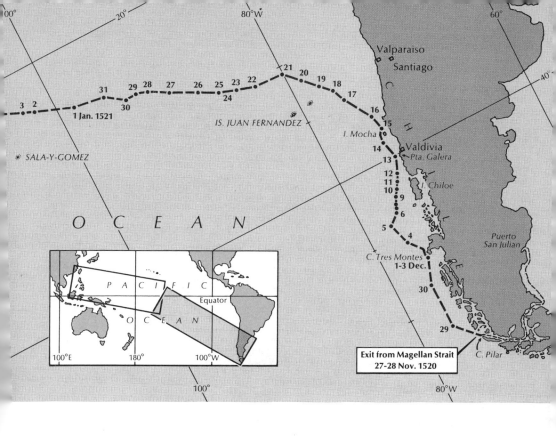

steered only three degrees further north, he would have seen the lofty Marquesas, which would have led to Nuka Hiva and the rest of that superb archipelago. Had he steered the same distance south, he might have made glamorous Tahiti. His fleet must have passed within a hundred miles or so of the northernmost Marshall Islands—Bikar, Bikini, and Eniwetok.

In considering this course, I agree with Alan Villiers that a kind providence was looking after Magellan. Further south he would have run into hundreds of islands and atolls, each a coral-baited trap for European ships. Semi-starvation and scurvy were bad, but better than running aground and being stripped bare by nimble Polynesians. He could hardly have shaped a better course if he had had modern sailing directions, not only avoiding dangerous, island-studded waters but making best use of prevailing winds and currents. Cast your eye over the United States government Pilot Chart of the South Pacific for January and February, and you will see that Magellan followed

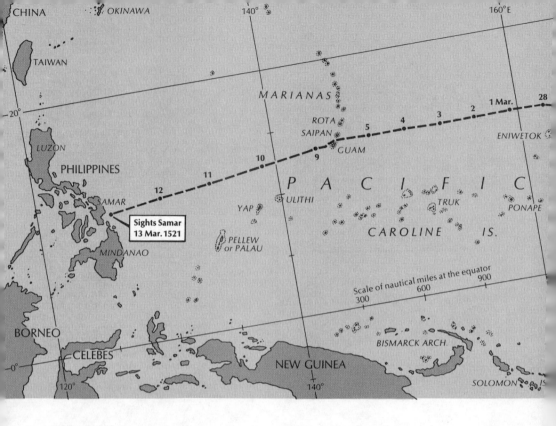

the recommended sailing route from Cape Horn to Honolulu until he got into the zone of the southeast tradewinds, and then steered before them, northwesterly, into the great open spaces.

Magellan's logistics have also been criticized. Why should his men have starved and been forced to eat chafing-gear and rats? First, because (at the government's behest) he had too many pages and other idlers on board. Second, because of cheating by the ship chandlers of Seville. Third, because of the unprecedented and unexpected length of the voyage. Have you never heard of hunger and scurvy on a long sailing voyage? Even three centuries after Magellan, with courses laid down on accurate charts, sailors expected to suffer both and often did. Instead of criticizing Magellan for his losses and sufferings, one should praise him for getting as far as Cebu. Note also that the Loaysa Expedition of 1525, although piloted by the experienced Elcano, fared even worse than Magellan's fleet; and so did most of the other trans-Pacific voyages whose fortunes we shall describe.

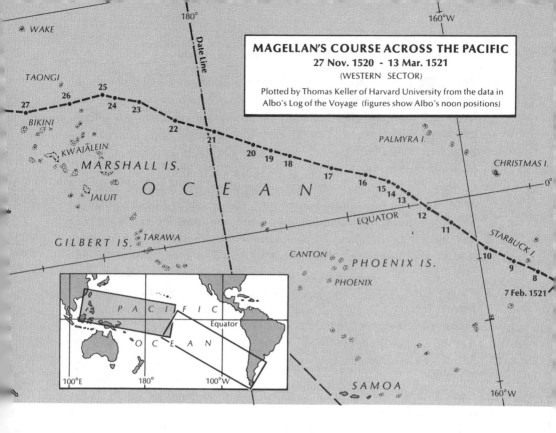

MAGELLAN'S COURSE ACROSS THE PACIFIC
27 Nov. 1520 - 13 Mar. 1521
(WESTERN SECTOR)

Plotted by Thomas Keller of Harvard University from the data in
Albo's Log of the Voyage (figures show Albo's noon positions)

In plotting the fleet's course we have to consider whether or not to apply the compass variation, which in that part of the Pacific is now 15° to 20° East, and we can only assume that it was probably about the same in 1520. The "Genoese pilot" (as quoted by Skelton) says, "We northeasted the compass box two points," which indicates that Albo's courses were taken from a compass adjusted for 22.5° E. variation. This can be proved by checking Albo between two known points, Guam and the entrance to Leyte Gulf. There we find his west by south course to be exact to the "true" bearing within a quarter-point, or 2.8°. This seems to indicate that Albo's compass bearings were accurate but that his day ran too short; that the fleet was making better speed than he allowed. The northward Humboldt Current along the west coast of South America is not strong enough to explain the discrepancy.

A remark on navigation by Pigafetta has aroused no end of controversy. "Daily," he says of the earlier part of the Pacific voyage, "we made runs of 50, 60, or 70 leagues *a la catena ho apopa*" (at the *catena*, which was at the stern). What does *catena* mean? Some have identified it as the chip log—but that was not yet invented. Others, including my respected Dutch acquaintance Mr. Crone, believe it to have been a trailed line for measuring the angle between a vessel's keel and her wake, in order to determine leeway. But no sixteenth-century log or book on navigation mentions anything like that, and every old salt to whom I have put the question answers that no accurate estimate of leeway could possibly be made by trailing a rope and measuring its angle to the wake. Furthermore, Pigafetta's mention of the word is in the context of speed, not angle of drift. My explanation is simple: *catena* in those days meant not only a chain but two important cross-beams in a vessel's hull, the first under the forecastle and the second well aft. Mariners stationed on the deck above each beam could time the seconds required for a piece of flotsam to pass between them as the ship sailed; when it passed the fellow at the stern, he sang out and the bow man stopped counting. Knowing the linear distance between these two beams, and the elapsed time, anyone who knew a little mathematics could figure out the ship's speed in knots—nautical miles per hour. This well known method of estimating a ship's speed was called by the English, "the Dutchman's Log." But, you may object, how could they count time without a watch? Why, just as navigators do today in counting seconds between a celestial observation with the sextant and consulting the chronometer, thus:

One chimpanzee, *two* chimpanzees, *three* chimpanzees, etc.; or,
One two three four, *two* two three four, *three* two three four, etc.

Las Islas Infortunatas

On 24 January 1521, after the fleet had dropped slightly south owing to a two-day head wind, and two days after full moon, they "found an islet wooded but uninhabited. We sounded and found no bottom, and so continued on our course, and this islet we named *San Pablo*, because it was the day of his conversion." So says Pilot Albo.

What was this deserted and unpromising island? Puka Puka, northernmost atoll but one of the Tuamotu archipelago. Albo says that they found it "in the neighborhood" of latitude 16°20′ S;

Las Islas Infortunatas: Puka Puka—Magellan's *San Pablo*. From the southeast, two miles distant. Courtesy of Captain Vallaux, French Navy (above). Caroline atoll—Magellan's *Isla de Tiburones*.

Pigafetta says flatly that it lay on 15° S. The center of Puka Puka, according to the latest French surveys, is on latitude 14°50′ S, only ten miles north of Piagafetta's estimate. Albo is definitely faulted on this point, for if Magellan really had sighted an island at 16°20′ S, he would have run into a flock of big atolls of the Palliser group.

There are other reasons, too, for a firm identification of Magellan's San Pablo as the modern Puka Puka. It rides out so far ahead of the Tuamotu archipelago as to catch the eye of anyone crossing the Pacific at around 15° S. To this day there is "no practicable anchorage," according to the French authorities. It was the first island after Juan Fernandez, seen in 1616 by Le Maire and Schouten, and it was the first island seen by Thor Heyerdahl in his voyage across the Pacific on the raft *Kon Tiki*.

After inspecting this island and deciding not to land, Magellan sailed NW, WNW, and W by N until on the eleventh day, 4 February 1521, he found (according to Albo) another "uninhabited island, where we caught many sharks, and so gave it the name *Isla de los Tiburones*." This, he says, lay on latitude 10°40′ S.

This shark-infested atoll must have been one of the three little islands which form an isosceles triangle with legs about 125 miles long: Flint (latitude 11°28′ S), Vostok (10°06′ S), and Caroline (10° 00′ S). It must have been Caroline, the biggest, and the only one with a lagoon; for it is common knowledge in the Pacific that lagoons attract sharks. And why did not Magellan at least call at one of these islands? Lack of holding ground, no doubt. The soundings nearest to them on the latest French chart are 2010 meters (Puka Puka), and 1370 meters (Caroline). We in 1971 could see plenty of coconut palms and pandanus on Caroline, but no sign of human life. Overcast prevented us from seeing Flint or Vostok Island, but both are rocky pinnacles rising from a great depth, and Flint has been such a favorite breeding and roosting place for sea birds that it became the scene of guano diggings in the last century.

Starvation at Sea, Relief at Guam

According to the "Genoese pilot," having reached latitude 13° N, "They navigated to the West by South, a matter of a hundred leagues, where on 6 March 1521 they fetched two islands inhabited by many people."

Albo, more convincingly, describes the course as northwest from 5 to 15 February, when the fleet reached latitude 01°45′ N, having crossed the Line on the 13th. They steered west-northwest from 15 to 25 February, and due west along latitude 13° N between 1 and 6 March.

Pigafetta is no help to us in tracking this last leg across the Pacific, but his description of the crews' sufferings is vivid and moving. The most trying part of the crossing took place after passing the two atolls, when they had already been two and a half months from the last place where they could have taken on food and water. "We were three months and twenty days without refreshment from any kind of fresh food. We ate biscuit which was no longer biscuit but its powder, swarming with worms, the rats having eaten all the good. It stank strongly of their urine. We drank yellow water already many days putrid. We also ate certain ox hides that had covered the top of the yards to prevent the yards from chafing the shrouds, and which had become exceedingly hard because of the sun, rain and wind. We soaked them in the sea for four or five days, then placed them for a short time over the hot embers and ate them thus, and often we ate sawdust. Rats were sold for half a ducat [$1.16 in gold] apiece, and even so we could not always get them."

Alan Villiers and I guess that the leather chafing-gear may not have been too bad as a hunger-stopper. Squareriggers needed an enormous amount of chafing-gear to prevent sails' slatting themselves threadbare against spars and rigging. Magellan, with his sea experience, would certainly have loaded plenty of guanaco hide in Patagonia for spares, and a relatively fresh guanaco hide would have made a more nutritious meal for a starving man than sawdust or old boots. Provided, of course, that the diner's teeth were sound and not rotted by scurvy!

The worst affliction, even above hunger and thirst, was scurvy. In Pigafetta's words, "The gums of both the lower and upper teeth of some of our men swelled, so that they could not eat under any circumstances." Thirty men got it in the arms, legs, and elsewhere, and, according to our chronicler, nineteen men died in the three ships. He, "by the grace of God, suffered no sickness," and neither did the Captain General. Magellan's supply of quince preserve doubtless came in useful as an anti-scorbutic for the afterguard; and let us hope that he issued some of it to the common sailors. "Had not God and His blessed mother given us such good weather," concluded Pigafetta, "we would

S. E. Morison, M. Obregón, and Pan Am crew. Sanchez Obregón photo.

Umatac harbor and village from site of old fort. Sanchez Obregón photo.

all have died of hunger in that exceeding vast ocean. I verily believe no such voyage will ever again be made."

Alas, Antonio, there have been very many such voyages, in which sailors have died of thirst, scurvy, and starvation after eating leather boots, scrapings from the inside of casks, and even, on occasion, each other. The nineteen deaths which he reports on Magellan's three ships were nothing extraordinary, and the official score is eleven. But why did not Magellan call at one of those *Islas Infortunatas* to fish, gather coconuts, and perhaps dig a well for fresh water? Probably because he felt that in another day or two he would raise some big island and find plenty of food.

On the next leg of their trans-Pacific run to Guam, which took exactly one month (5 February to 6 March 1521), they steered, according to Albo, northwest and west-northwest in February and west in March. Pigafetta here makes a curious statement: "We passed . . . a short distance from two exceedingly rich islands," one in latitude 20° N "by name Cipangu . . . and the other in 15° [N] by name *Sumbdit Pradit*." Cipangu means Japan, whose southernmost point of Kyushu lies on latitude 31° N and bears northwest from Guam many hundreds of miles. But a reference to Schöner's globe will show why Magellan thought he had passed it. What he meant by *Sumbdit Pradit* is still anybody's guess.

At last, on 6 March 1521, 98 or 99 days out from the Strait, the weary voyagers found their first relief, combined with plenty of excitement. They sighted two lofty islands, first lucky break of the Pacific voyage; for these were Guam and Rota. The fleet sailed between them, turned south, and followed the coast of Guam looking for a harbor. Soft green hills rose to jagged peaks, coconut palms lined the shore, and everything looked green and lush; but the hungry sailors could find no break in the reef until they were almost at the southern end of the island, when providentially a harbor now called Umatak, with no reef barrier, opened up. A group of thatched huts could be seen at the head of it, and a fleet of native sail engaged in fishing. These were *praos*, lateen-rigged dugout canoes, each with an outrigger. Marvelously fast and maneuverable, they sailed circles around the three ships. Magellan therefore called Guam and Rota *Las Islas de Velas Latinas*, Isles of Lateen Sails, but he soon found reason to change the name to the opprobrious *Islas de Ladrones*, Isles of Thieves.

Chamorro praos, sketched at Palau in late sixteenth century. Courtesy
Archivo General de Indias, Seville.

The natives promptly swarmed on board the flagship, which alone
had entered the harbor, and proceeded to pick up everything on deck
or below not nailed down; every bit of iron, crockery, belaying pin, or
length of line cut off the rigging. Doubtless they would have "stolen
the paint off the deck" (the traditional mariners' description of harbor
thieves), if paint there had been. The debilitated flagship crew could
neither dissuade them from stealing nor persuade them to go away;
so Magellan finally gave orders to his men-at-arms to shoot a few with
crossbows. That temporarily got rid of the boarders; one native pulled
a crossbow bolt right out of his side and looked with amazement at
the spurting blood. After this brawl terminated, the sailors observed
that the longboat had been stolen from right under *Trinidad*'s stern!

These people were Chamorros, an agile, handsome, brown-skinned
Polynesian race who had raided Guam several centuries earlier, con-

quered the native Macronesians, and become an arrogant ruling caste. Probably they had already dealt with errant Chinese junks; certainly they were neither awed by the ships nor afraid of Spaniards. In the next century, after having been converted by Spanish priests and their island group renamed *Las Marianas,* the Chamorros became friendly, peaceful, and charming. During their forty-two years under American rule (1899–1941), they conformed to Western ways, and under a harsh Japanese domination remained steadfastly loyal to the United States.

But that was in our time. Magellan's immediate problems were to procure fresh food and get back his boat. He acted with his usual coolness and decision. When night fell he ordered his fleet to jill about in the offing. At daybreak he approached the shore and attacked the village, having manned the other two ships' longboats with forty armed men. The landing force burned forty to fifty huts and many praos, recovered the stolen boat, and obtained a supply of rice, fruit, and fresh water which gave the fleet a comparatively balanced diet en route to the Philippines. Pigafetta notes that some of the sick on board begged the landing party to bring them a few buckets' full of the enemy's guts as a sure cure for scurvy—presumably a medical superstition of the time, or perhaps a means of satisfying their craving for fresh meat. Although seven Chamorros were killed in this brawl, hundreds of them cheerfully sailed out to the ships next day.

It was now 9 March 1521, the day after new moon, and Magellan immediately got under way. One wishes there had been an artist on board to depict his departure from Umatac. About a hundred praos made sail and romped around the slow-moving ships, their crews laughing and shouting; one fellow even had the impudence to sail right across the painter of a towed longboat. Others approached the ships holding up fish and offering by signs to toss them on board; if the Spaniards "bit" and bade them come nearer, they would drop the fish and throw a shower of stones at the sailors on deck, then sail away laughing their heads off. "Light-hearted masters of the waves," indeed.

From Samar to Cebu

The Captain General set course west by south. Whether he knew this would take him to Leyte Gulf, the best entrance to the Philippines, or simply made a good guess, we do not know. For five days they made unusual speed—an average of seven to eight knots. It was a happy run, with plenty of fresh food to cure the sick; all except Chief Gunner Andrew of Bristol, the only Englishman on board. Too far gone, he died the first day out from Guam.

On 15 March 1521 they saw the mountains of Samar rising from the sea. Magellan changed course to close; but, after observing the coast to be cliffy, with no harbor, altered his course again to due south, making the tiny but conspicuous island of Suluan on latitude 10°45′ N. There he anchored for the night. It was the fifth Sunday of Lent in the church calendar, dedicated to Lazarus; so Magellan named this archipelago after him. Only after the visit by Villalobos in 1542 was it renamed *Las Islas Filipinas*, after the Infante of Spain who became Philip II.

From Suluan they sailed to the much bigger island of Homonhon. *Trinidad, Concepción,* and *Victoria* were now in waters ever memorable for the greatest naval battle in recorded history, that of Leyte Gulf, 24–26 October 1944. Forty to forty-five miles across Leyte Gulf from Homonhon lies the coast of Leyte, where the American amphibious forces landed. Magellan, either by chance or acting upon information gained in his former Portuguese voyages to Malacca, had hit upon one of the two principal entrances to the Philippine archipelago, Surigao Strait.

The Captain General, solicitous for the health of scurvy victims, caused two tents to be pitched on Homonhon Island for their shelter, and a live sow (picked up at Guam) to be slaughtered to give them fresh meat. There, on Monday, 18 March, Europeans made their first contact with Filipinos, and sized them up as a far more civilized and sophisticated race than the Chamorros. A boat from Suluan approached with nine men on board. Magellan enjoined silence on his men while they landed and walked up to the tents. Their leader made "signs of joy" to Magellan, and left with him five of the best dressed members of his suite, says Pigafetta. Magellan, seeing that these were "men of reason," gave them something to eat and presented them with red caps, mirrors, combs, hawks' bells, ivory, fine linen cloth, and other articles. Impressed by the Captain General's courtesy, they presented him with fresh fish, a jar of palm wine "which they called *uraca*" (arrack), figs "more than a palm long" (bananas), and two *cochi* (coconuts).

Homonhon Island. Sanchez Obregón photo.

Limasawa Island. Sanchez Obregón photo.

That was all they had on hand. But the people made signs that they would return in four days' time bringing *umay* (rice), coconuts, and many other victuals, and they kept their word. Pigafetta describes in detail the native process of making palm wine and other products; he had never before seen a coconut or a banana. Two coconut palms, he said, can provide food and drink for ten people; and, he might have added, clothing, housing, and other things as well. "These people became very familiar with us," he says. "We took great pleasure with them, for they were very pleasant and talkative"—by the sign language, presumably. They are *caphri* (heathen) *, all except the chiefs go naked; they are "dark, fat and painted"—i.e., tattooed. Magellan showed them over *Trinidad*, exhibiting samples of spices and gold which he hoped to find in great quantities.

The ships stayed at Homonhon for a week, Magellan daily visiting the sick ashore, himself serving them drinks of refreshing coconut milk. On 25 March, as they were about to weigh anchor, Pigafetta fell overboard and just saved himself by seizing a main clewline trailing in the water, and hallooing for help. Apparently he had never learned to swim. He ascribed his rescue to "the mercy of that font of charity," the Virgin Mary, since it was the feast of her Annunciation.

Having made sail, the fleet shaped a west-southwest course into Surigao Strait, passing Hibuson, Dinagat, and other islands. (Here, 423 years and seven months later, occurred the last great naval action between battleships and their attendant destroyers. That night in 1944, Surigao Strait was brilliantly lighted by shell bursts and burning Japanese warships, and roaring with explosions.) But all was quiet on Thursday, 28 March 1521, when there occurred a dramatic and significant event.

The fleet had anchored off the little island of Limasawa at the southern entrance to Surigao Strait. A small boat put out and approached flagship *Trinidad;* eight men were on board. At the Captain General's order, his slave Enrique de Malacca hailed them. "They immediately understood him and came alongside." West had met East at last by circling the globe. Enrique may have been the first man to do it.

* From the Arabic *kafir*, non-believer; generally used in the Far East by Moors for people who did not worship God. Hence the Cafres or Kaffirs of South Africa.

Two hours later, two *balanghai* (native barges) full of men approached and on the quarterdeck of the larger sat a high personality under an awning of mats. He, the ruler Rajah Colambu, refused to come on board but allowed his people to do so, and Magellan showered them with gifts. His highness in return offered the Captain General a bar of gold and a basket of ginger, which were refused. Magellan's policy, which he impressed on all his men, was to pretend to undervalue gold, since he had observed that wherever European sailors showed greed for it, the price soared; he even refused to swap six strings of glass beads for a pointed coronet of massy gold. Both at Limasawa and Cebu he was rewarded for this continence by the natives' giving gold for iron almost pound for pound—"changey-changey," as sailors used to say.

Next day, Good Friday of 1521, Magellan sent Enrique ashore to assure the Rajah of his friendship and to buy food; Colambu himself came out with baskets of fresh provisions, embraced the Captain General and presented him with three dorados and three porcelain jars filled with rice. Magellan countered with a red cap and a red-and-yellow robe made "Turkish fashion," with which the Rajah was delighted. He was shown over the flagship and given a collation, after which Magellan demonstrated the value of European steel plate. A soldier put on a suit of armor, three others struck him repeatedly with swords and daggers, to no effect. The Rajah *resto casi fora dise* (was struck speechless) and then remarked that one such man in armor was worth a hundred local troops. Magellan capped that admission by boasting that he had two hundred such men on board each of his three ships—a gross exaggeration.

Next item in this West-meets-East business was a royal luncheon party attended by Pigafetta and two other officers. They took seats on a grounded *balanghai*, ate pork, and at every mouthful drank a toast in palm wine. The natives drank from a cup held in the right hand; at the same time they extended the left fist as if to strike their favored guest, but the Christians soon learned that this gesture was friendly. All became somewhat fuddled by the number of toasts. By suppertime Pigafetta had so far sobered up as to write down the names of things, phonetically of course, in the local language; and before leaving he had compiled a long vocabulary. Supper was served in the Rajah's palace, which reminded Pigafetta of a hay barn raised on stilts; and there they were joined by a brother rajah from Mindanao named Siaui. Dinner consisted of roast fish, fresh-gathered ginger, and more palm wine. The Italian and the guest rajah, who became intoxicated, spent the night there on a bamboo mat. When a boat came for Pigafetta and his two companions next morning, Rajah Colambu kissed their hands, and they reciprocated.

Now came the vigil of Easter Sunday, the first Easter that the fleet had passed at sea since leaving the Strait. Early next morning, Magellan caused High Mass to be celebrated on Limasawa by the flag chaplain. Fifty men landed "in theyr best apparel withowte weapons or harnesse" (i.e., armor), according to Eden's translation of Pigafetta, and marched with the two rajahs to the place where an altar had been set up. Both rajahs kissed the cross after Magellan, but were not allowed to partake of the sacred elements. At the elevation of the host, Magellan's body-guard fired a salvo from their arquebuses, and the ships discharged a blank broadside. Magellan next laid on a fencing contest between his men-at-arms, which greatly pleased the rajahs, and Colambu gave him permission to set up a cross on the nearest mountain. That they did on Easter afternoon. Each Christian present venerated the cross, repeating *Pater Noster* and *Ave Maria*, and the rajahs followed suit. Somewhere in the course of these entertainments, Colambu and Magellan performed the rite of *casi-casi* or blood brotherhood. This consisted, mainly, of each tasting a drop of the other's blood.

Although a good time was had by all who went ashore at Limasawa, not many provisions were available; and Colambu, upon being asked where more could be obtained, not only suggested Cebu but offered himself to pilot them there as soon as his own crop of rice was gathered. Magellan, to expedite this, sent details of mariners to help get in the harvest; they became so drunk on palm wine the first day ashore that they were not much good to anyone.

The gentle Limasawans, says Pigafetta, went about nearly naked, but the men were tattooed all over and the women wore tapa-cloth skirts. Both sexes wore heavy earings of gold and ivory, and constantly chewed betel nut. Here, and at Cebu, he describes a sexual practice known as *palang*. "The males, large and small, have their penis pierced from one side to the other near the head, with a gold or tin bolt as large as a goose quill. In each end of the bolt some have what resembles a star, with points; others are like the head of a cart nail. . . . In the middle of the bolt is a hole, through which they urinate." Their excuse for this "lewd way of intercourse," as it was called by a Spanish official in Manila many years later, was that their women liked it that way, spur rowels and all; from the age of six he adds, young girls had their vaginas artificially stretched so as to admit this load of phallic hardware. Pigafetta, however, asserts that "the women loved us very much more than their own men."

After a stay of one week, the fleet left Mazaua (as Pigafetta calls Limasawa) and, piloted by the rajah in his private dugout canoe, sailed through Canigao Channel with Leyte on the starboard hand, into the Camotes Sea. They anchored one night at an island which Pigafetta calls Gatighan, (which Robertson identifies as one of the Cuatro Islas off Leyte—but I rather think it was one of the Camotes). Here the men killed and ate a big fruit-eating bat and said it tasted like chicken. They then coasted into the principal harbor on the east coast of Cebu, behind the small but fatal island of Mactan.

It was now Low Sunday, 7 April 1521. On approaching the town of Cebu, on the same site as the present city, Magellan ordered his ships to be dressed with all their colors, struck all sails, and fired salutes as they dropped anchor. This created consternation ashore, but when the Captain General sent "a foster-son of his"—probably his bastard Rebelo—as ambassador to the sultan, accompanied by Enrique, the natives were reassured. Enrique told them that the Christians came in peace, their master the Captain General, subject to the greatest prince in the world, was "going to discover Malucho" (the Spice Islands). He now called on the sultan of Cebu at the suggestion of his blood-brother Colambu, to exchange merchandise for provisions. The sultan (named Humabon) consented, provided the Europeans paid tribute, which a Moorish junk from Siam had done only four days before. Enrique officiously replied that his master was subject of too great a king to pay tribute to anyone, and if Humabon "wanted peace, peace he would have; if war, war." At that the Moslem master of the junk (who was standing by) interposed, saying, "Watch out, sir; these are the same lot who have conquered Calicut, Malacca and Greater India. If well treated they will respond in kind, but if treated ill they will raise hell." Humabon replied that he would think it over. Next day, Colambu landed and backed up the Moro; and after the flag notary had explained through Enrique that the Captain General demanded no tribute

from him, Humabon not only consented to trade but performed the
casi-casi ceremony. A plentiful supply of food was purchased with
hawks' bells and glass beads.

All this inaugurated a precarious peace. The Sultan, his heir apparent, the Moro junk captain, eight chief men, and Rajah Colambu came
on board *Trinidad*. Magellan received them seated in a red velvet chair,
leather chairs were set out for the Spanish officers, and rugs or mats for
the visitors, as it embarrassed them to sit on chairs. The Captain General
made a long speech describing the elements of the Christian religion
and inviting them to be converted. Sultan Humabon appeared willing
to have all his people baptized. Magellan promised to present him with
a suit of armor that he admired; and added that if the girls too were
baptized, his men "could have intercourse with their women without
committing a very great sin"—a strange if amusing argument for Christian conversion! The Sultan and the Rajah promised to do everything
he wanted. Magellan embraced them, weeping with joy; and, clasping
hands with Sultan Humabon and the crown prince, promised that "by
his faith in God and in the Emperor his lord, and by the habit of Santiago which he wore," * he would give them perpetual peace with the
king of Spain.

Following an exchange of gifts, Pigafetta, Enrique, and a few others
walked up to the town and were received by the Sultan. "He was
short and fat and tattooed in various designs," noted Pigafetta, clad
only in a G-string, an embroidered head scarf, and jewelry. He was
regaling himself with a beaker of palm wine drunk through no fewer
than four straws, and occasionally reached out to pluck a turtle egg
from a porcelain bowl. The Italian, after investing his highness with an
Oriental-style robe, red cap, and string of Venetian beads, proceeded
with Enrique to the young prince's house, where they were entertained
by a four-piece orchestra of "very beautiful, almost white" girls playing on gongs and drums; after the music they threw off their already
scanty clothes and danced with the delighted Christians. The two visitors returned on board that night.

A crew member having died, Magellan obtained permission to bury
him in the public plaza after consecrating the spot, and set up a cross
over the grave. He also obtained the Sultan's consent to hold a sort of

* This habit featured the Santiago cross, whose arms and head are tipped with
fleurs-de-lys. It is shown in our frontispiece portrait of Magellan.

bazaar in a bamboo shed ashore. The Christians there displayed a variety of trade goods, which they swapped for gold, livestock, and rice. For fourteen pounds of iron the natives gave ten pieces of gold weighing a ducat and a half each.

The Sultan, having shown a wish to be baptized, now caused a platform to be set up in the plaza. On Sunday, 14 April, the ceremony was performed by the flagship's chaplain with all the pomp and circumstance the Christians could lay on, Magellan appropriately wearing a white robe. Humabon was renamed Don Carlos after the Emperor; Rajah Colambu became Don Juan after the Infante, and the Moslem junk captain, who also desired to be converted, became Don Cristóbal. Threatened with death if they did not conform, most of the chiefs did. Following their baptisms, at least 500 male subjects were christened. Mass was said ashore and the ships discharged their artillery as a salute to this new batch of converts. Next, the Sultana and forty women were baptized, and Magellan gave the lady a small image of a smiling Christ Child. This *Santo Niño* is the only object still preserved that once belonged to Magellan.

These picturesque and moving ceremonies, especially the conversion of the Moslem junk captain, mark another historic meeting of East and West. Islam had moved around the world from Arabia eastward; Christianity had moved westward from Jerusalem and Rome. Here they met. Which way would they go now? For the moment, the cross prevailed over the crescent, but not for long, and the conflict has never entirely ceased. When we were flying over these waters at Christmastide 1971, Christians and Moros were fighting in Mindanao.

The next four days were spotted with ceremony. Magellan came ashore daily to hear Mass celebrated by the flag chaplain, Father Valderrama. The Sultana (now christened Lisabeta), "young and beautiful and entirely covered with a white and black cloth," wearing a palm-leaf hat crowned with a sort of tiara, attended Mass and brought her ladies-in-waiting and many of her subjects. "Altogether we baptized 800 souls," recorded Pigafetta; and "before that octave had elapsed, all the persons of that island and some from the other islands were baptized." The Spaniards followed their now standard procedure of cross in one hand, sword in t'other. "We burned one hamlet in a neighboring island because it refused to obey the king or us," recorded Pigafetta. That was on Mactan, and Mactan did not forget.

Views on Cebu and Mactan: prao anchored off a village, and the Magellan
monument, Mactan.

Religious ecstasy reached its height when Magellan accepted a challenge to cure a sick brother to the crown prince, if he would burn a set of heathen idols to which he was making daily sacrifices. Magellan and Father Valderrama put on "a procession from the plaza to the house of the sick man with as much pomp as possible." They found him speechless and unable to move. The priest baptized him, together with both his wives and ten girls. Magellan asked him how he felt; he spoke at once and declared that he already "felt very well." Magellan administered a draught of specially prepared *mandolata* (milk of almonds), set up a complete bed to replace his crummy mat, and plied him daily with various soothing concoctions. On the fifth day the man began to walk, and people ran about the island shouting, "Castilla! Castilla!" and destroying every idol they could lay hands on.

Up to a point, the stay at Cebu was the most delightful of the entire voyage, even better than Rio de Janeiro. The men had plenty to eat and drink; the women were kind both before and after conversion. Magellan felt very proud over being the means of saving a thousand souls and acquiring a new province for Spain. Alas, if he could only have let well enough alone!

Battle of Mactan and Death of Magellan

Magellan was obsessed by the urge to attack Sultan Humabon's enemies. At Limasawa he had asked Rajah Colambu whether he would not like to take him on a raid to chastise his nearest enemy, but the cagey rajah declined on the ground that it was not the right season. Now Magellan intervened between Cebu and Mactan, although the newly baptized sultan showed no enthusiasm for battle. Tiny Mactan had two rajahs: Zula, friendly to Cebu, and hostile Lapu Lapu; but Humabon could live with that situation. Nevertheless, he accepted Magellan's offer to attack the recalcitrant Lapu Lapu, and contributed a thousand men to the expeditionary force.

There was nothing new in Magellan's strategy. Almost every group of European intruders into Africa and America felt that to cement an alliance with the nearest tribe of natives they must deploy fire power against next-door enemies. The Portuguese had done it repeatedly in Africa and India. Cortés marched on Mexico City against Montezuma with more native rebels than Spanish soldiers; Champlain pleased his

Canadian allies by fighting the Iroquois, inaugurating a century of warfare between them and the French. Even the English, who in general
managed to stay out of native rivalries, pitted one tribe against another
in the Carolinas. But for Magellan to do it here, when he had the local
situation well in hand, was utter folly. And what made it worse is the
fact that Humabon did not even demand this military action against
Lapu Lapu. Zula, who did ask for it, requested but one boatload of
men-at-arms, but the Captain General decided to send three, in the
ships' longboats. "We begged him repeatedly not to go," said Pigafetta,
"but he, like a good shepherd, refused to abandon his flock." He insisted on attacking on Saturday, 27 April, believing it to be his lucky
day.

In this fatal operation, Magellan broke every rule of amphibious
warfare, as we learned them in World War II; and the comparison is
not irrelevant because amphibious assault is the oldest form of naval
warfare, and many of its principles have never changed. Briefly, he
did not attempt surprise, he made no provision for gunfire support,
he chose an unsuitable beach full of natural obstacles which prevented
the boats from getting within shooting distance of the shore, he timed
the assault at low water when the rocks were most prominent, and he
failed to co-ördinate his attack with native allies, who remained idle
spectators of the ensuing slaughter.

Here is what happened; the sources are in surprising agreement. At
midnight 26–27 April 1521, the Christian assault force of sixty men
embarked in the three ships' longboats, and Sultan Humabon, some of
his chief men, and numerous warriors embarked in twenty to thirty
big native canoes and mostly played a spectator role. The moon was
five days past full. All boats were rowed or paddled through the narrow channel between Cebu city and Mactan, rounded Bantolinas Point
and paused before the big cove (now called Magellan Bay) on the
northeast side of Mactan. *Trinidad*, *Victoria*, and *Concepción* anchored within cannon shot of the shore, but, coming late, took no
significant part in the fight. Magellan's and Humabon's landing craft
reached their objective three hours before the break of day. Here was
an excellent chance for surprise, which Magellan lost by sending a
message via the Siamese trader to Lapu Lapu, "that if his subjects
would obey the king of Spain and recognize him as their lord, and pay
tribute, he would be their friend; if they wished otherwise, they would

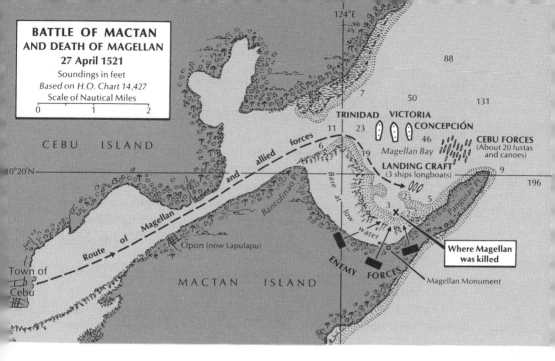

BATTLE OF MACTAN
AND DEATH OF MAGELLAN
27 April 1521
Soundings in feet
Based on H.O. Chart 14,427
Scale of Nautical Miles

CEBU ISLAND

Town of Cebu

Route of Magellan

MACTAN ISLAND

Opon (now Lapulapu)

and allied forces

Bantolinao P.

Bare at low water

ENEMY FORCES

TRINIDAD VICTORIA CONCEPCIÓN
CEBU FORCES
(About 20 fustas and canoes)
Magellan Bay
LANDING CRAFT
(3 ships longboats)
Panguian Pt.

Where Magellan was killed

Magellan Monument

124°E

feel the iron of our lances." Lapu Lapu replied that he feared not the
Christians' steel, having plenty of "fire-hardened spears and stakes of
bamboo," and Magellan could attack when he chose.

At first light, the landing craft having approached as near the beach
as they could at low water, Magellan and forty-eight of his men leaped
into water knee to thigh deep, and slowly waded toward shore. The
other eleven Spaniards guarded the boats, which stood by, distant from
the beach "two crossbow flights"—a little over a mile. By the time
the Christians landed, Lapu Lapu had organized his forces, "more than
1500 men," in three divisions—one at the head of the wide bay in
front of their village, and one on each flank. "When they saw us,
they charged down upon us with exceeding loud cries," wrote Pigafetta. The assault force swivel guns were out of range and the ships
had not yet come up, so Magellan received no gunfire support. He
formed his pitifully small landing force into two groups and fought
back, both to the right and to the left, with arquebuses and crossbows. It was no use; the shots, at too great a range, were deflected
by the enemy's wooden shields. Magellan ordered *no tirar*, "cease
firing," but his men paid no attention and shot off all their ammunition.
Now the enemy yelled even louder and "leaped about, covered by

429

their shields" and "shooting so many arrows and hurling so many bamboo spears (some tipped with iron) that we were put on the defensive." At this point, Magellan should have retreated, but he counter-attacked, landed, and set fire to native huts ashore, "to terrify them." That aroused the enemy to greater fury. The Captain General, shot through the right leg with a poisoned arrow, ordered his landing party to retire to the boats, and most of them did so precipitately; but Magellan with six or eight faithful men, including Pigafetta, covered their retreat. The enemy pursued them into the water, hurled spears abundantly, and knocked Magellan's helmet off twice; "but he always stood firmly like a good knight." Finally he made a fatal tactical error, taking a stand with his devoted band beyond the range of ships or armed boats.

"Thus did we fight for more than one hour," wrote Pigafetta, up to their knees or more in water, and with no help from anyone—a valiant little group about their Captain General. He could have saved himself by retreating helter-skelter with the rest, but like a *preux chevalier* of old, he felt obliged to cover the retirement of his men. With more and more native warriors swarming about, the end was inevitable. A man of Mactan hurled a spear at Magellan's face, missed, and was immediately killed by the Captain General's lance. Since the lance stuck fast in the native's body, Magellan tried to draw his sword but could not because his sword arm had been wounded; and when the Mactanese observed this weakness, all hurled themselves upon him. One wounded him in the leg with a scimitar, he fell face down in the water, the enemy rushed upon him with spear and sword and slashed the life out of him.

"Thus," wrote Pigafetta, "they killed our mirror, our light, our comfort and our true guide. When they wounded him, he turned back many times to see whether we were all in the boats. Then, seeing him dead, we wounded made the best of our way to the boats, which were already pulling away. But for him, not one of us in the boats would have been saved, for while he was fighting the rest retired." At the last moment, too late, the three ships started to cannonade the crowded ranks of the enemy.

Pigafetta's eulogy of his captain is a classic: "Among the other virtues which he possessed, he was always the most constant in greatest adversity. He endured hunger better than all the rest, and, more ac-

Magellan Bay, Mactan. Site of Magellan's death.

Quipit, Zamboanga Peninsula, Mindanao.

curately than any man in the world, he understood dead reckoning and celestial navigation. And that this was the truth appeared evident, since no other had so much talent, nor the ardor to learn how to go around the world, as he almost did." "I hope," said Pigafetta to the man to whom he dedicated his narrative, "that through the efforts of your illustrious self the fame of so noble a captain will never die."

Bibliography and Notes

Magellan's departure from Chile. Albo (Navarrete, IV, 216) describes their Chilean landfall on 1 December 1521 as *unos pedazos como mogotes.* This suggests mountainous, 1300-foot-high Cabo Tres Montes, Chile; and we regret that overcast prevented us from seeing either it or the less conspicuous Campana Island next south.

Eastern Pacific winds. J. C. Beaglehole's introduction to Hakluyt Society *Journals of Captain Cook,* pp. xxxiv–xxxvi. The U.S. Pilot Chart of South Pacific for Dec.–Feb. shows the SE trade-wind zone extending from 1° S to 30° S, suggesting that Magellan, had he so chosen, could have turned westward much earlier than he did. But, *creda experte,* the trade winds are not so constant and well behaved as the books and charts would have us believe.

The Pacific Crossing. On our conjectural track of Magellan's fleet, which Mr. Thomas Keller plotted, we use Albo's *roteiro,* but we first have to subtract to some 10° E from his courses, representing our guess at compass variation, to prevent Magellan from running afoul of the Chilean coast. Many find it incredible that Magellan crossed the Pacific and sighted only two islands. Keep in mind, however, that a Pacific atoll is flat and low and that one's approach to it is signaled neither by piled-up clouds nor shoaling water changing color, nor indeed by anything except the tops of coconut palms. One can therefore sail within 20 miles (often within 10 miles) of an atoll without having any hint of its existence; and they are much farther apart than one would expect after consulting a small-scale chart. You cannot appreciate the size of the Pacific until, after sailing for days or flying for hours over waters which many maps lead you to believe are sprinkled with islands, you have seen no land.

Why did Magellan sail so far north? Discussed in Nowell, pp. 19–29, and in Yale ed. Pigafetta, p. 153n. The "useful . . . hard-working" Luzon colony at Malacca is mentioned by the Portuguese traveler Tomé Pires, writing about 1513. He adds that the Luzon people "have in their country plenty of foodstuffs," and that Luzon lies ten days' sail beyond Borneo. Filipiniana Book Guild, *Travel Accounts of the Islands* (Manila, 1971); A. Cortesão (ed.), *The Suma Oriental of Tomé Pires* (Hakluyt Society, London, 1944), I, 134. Magellan presumably heard about this when he visited Malacca, and he may well have met Pires who was there from 1511 to 1513. My quote from the "Genoese Pilot" is from Stanley's Hakluyt Society volume, p. 9. For the Ryukyus hypothesis, Yale ed. Pigafetta, I, 158n, and Nowell, pp. 19–29.

Length of the league, and the catena *identified* L. A. Bauer in *U.S. Magnetic Declination Tables and Isogonic Charts for 1902* (Washington, 1902). Navarrete, IV, 55, states that the league used by Spaniards and Portuguese in Magellan's day equaled 3¾ (3.43) nautical miles, "or 17.5 to the degree," which works out as almost 3.5 nautical miles. An interesting table of varying guesses as to length of a degree of longitude by Colin Jack-Hinton is in *Journal* of the Malaysian Branch, Royal Asiatic Society, XXXVII (1964), Part 2, 125–61. Having laboriously worked out Columbus's league as 3.18 n.m., and so far unchallenged, I stick to that. Robertson discusses *catena* at length in notes to his edition of Pigafetta, I, 245; see also Yale ed., p. 158. The hypothesis that *catena* is a misprint for *antena* (yard) makes no sense.

Las Islas Infortunatas (Miserable Islands). Albo in Navarrete, IV, 218. Pigafetta and the "Genoese pilot" agree that Magellan bypassed both atolls; Correia (Stanley, p. 251) states that he stopped at one, and Maximilianus declares that he stopped two days at each and found "fair fishing" (Nowell, p. 292). Donald B. Brand's chapters in Herman R. Friis (ed.), *The Pacific Basin—A History* (New York, 1967), gives a good straightforward account of Magellan's Pacific crossing; but (p. 118) he considers it "ridiculous to insist on any identifications" of the *Islas Infortunatas*. Obregón and I, apparently, are fools to have attempted it! One who did so earlier, and made a botch of it, was George E. Nunn in "Magellan's Route to the Pacific," *Geographical Review*, XXIV (1934), 615–33.

Actually, Magellan's two islands are shown on Ribero's 1525 and 1529 world maps, about one-third of the way across the Pacific, and on latitudes corresponding to 10° S on the coast of Brazil. On 16 December 1971 Mauricio Obregón and I flew from Tahiti 1000 miles north to Caroline Island, to examine and photograph it. Magellan's *Tiburones* (sharks) Island was certainly Caroline, an atoll with a lagoon where sharks congregate to eat the little fish; whilst Flint and Vostok are solid, cliffy islets where sea birds used to roost and breed in such quantities that in the nineteenth century it was profitable to export their guano. Magellan's shipmates mention sharks, but no birds. These three islands have been under British sovereignty since 1868, and were included in the Gilbert and Ellice Island Colony in 1972. Caroline Island was rediscovered and so named in 1795 (probably after the just-married queen of George IV) by Captain Broughton of H.M.S. *Providence*. It was then thinly settled by Polynesians, but none are there now. Vostok Island was discovered and named (after his ship) by Captain Bellingshausen of the Russian navy in 1820 (his *Voyage . . . to the Antarctic*, Hakluyt Society, London, 1945, II, 295). It was worked sporadically for guano and copra to 1943. Flint Island was so named by one Captain Keen in 1835, and visited by the Charles Wilkes Exploring Expedition (*Narrative*, IV, 1845 ed., p. 277) on 6 February 1841. It was then thickly wooded, but no landing place could be found. There are detailed maps of all three islands in the National Geographic *Map of the Pacific Ocean*. At latest accounts they were leased to Omer Darr of Tahiti. Information from *Pacific Islands Year Book* (11th ed., Sydney, 1972), and Mr. G. Owlett of the British Embassy, Washington.

Puka Puka we were unable to visit on account of foul weather, but the French authorities at Papeete gave us plenty of information and a good photograph. It was annexed to French Oceania in the 19th century. When Le Maire and Schouten rediscovered Puka Puka on 10 April 1616 (Andrew Sharp, *Discovery of the Pacific Islands*, Oxford, 1960), they landed and found no people but three dogs, so named it *Honden*, Isle of Dogs. Service Hydrographique de la Marine, Chart No. 6036 (1969), and "Renseignements relatifs à Puka Puka," furnished to me by Commandant Vallaux at Papeete, give its position as lat. 14°38′ S, long. 138°19′ W. Admiral J. Freitas Ribeiro in Lagoa's biography of Magellan (Lisbon, 1938), II, 225, agrees with my identification of the islands. Puka Puka, according to the last census, had 98 native inhabitants under a native *chefesse*, engaged in the production of copra. It still has no anchorage and no good landing place; but a *goélette* from Papeete serves it monthly, and manages to land a small boat at a pier on the northwesterly end, usually the best lee.

Casualties. Navarette, IV, 54, counting the official list of deaths in the Simancas archives, states that 11 men, 7 of them before touching Guam, died between the Strait and the Philippines. Gómara and Herrera state that Magellan lost 20 men by feeding them rice boiled in salt water. This is another instance of these early historians' untrustworthiness. My old friend Jack Adams used to boil both potatoes and rice in salt water on his yacht, and nobody was the worse for it. Many instances of greater casualties on long voyages, right down to that of Cavendish, will be found in this volume; and in the next century, on ten Dutch East Indiamen, 2653 men died before even reaching the Cape of Good Hope, where 915 survivors were hospitalized. C. R. Boxer, "The Dutch East-Indiamen," *Mariner's Mirror*, XLIX (May 1963), p. 86.

Sumbdit Pradit. The usual guess is that this is a corruption of *Septe Cidades*, i.e. Antilia or the Seven Cities, but that seems too far-fetched; Antilia, a mythical island constantly moved about by cartographers, is always in the Atlantic. In any case, Pigafetta later contradicts himself and makes Sumbdit and Pradit two islands off the coast of China. Robertson ed., II, 181.

Umatak. Magellan's choice is vindicated by the fact that Umatak was the principal port of Guam throughout the Spanish colonial period; the governor had a second "palace" there and used to occupy it whenever a ship came in. The University of Guam's Research Center for Micronesia has a fine collection of early maps and descriptions of Guam, and I am indebted to Professor Paul Carano the Director, and his assistant Miss Emily Johnston, for valuable information.

Albo gives the latitude of Suluan as 9°40′ N, one of his bad shots, and a worse one on the difference of longitude between it and Cabo Pilar—106°30′. The correct measurement is 159°21′.

Philippine products. Pigafetta (Robertson ed., I, 101) gives a detailed description of the coconut palm and its products. The Spaniards had already introduced the banana from the Canaries to the West Indies; and about this time the coconut palm, sprouting from nuts that had floated across the Pacific, made its American debut on the west coast of Central America.

Enrique de Malacca. Where did he come from? He was baptized Enrique at Malacca, where Magellan bought him, and Pigafetta says that he came from Sumatra. My historian friends in the Philippines, however, point out that Sumatra could not have been his original home, since the language there was completely different from that of the Visayas; a native Sumatran could not possibly have made himself understood in Limasawa or Cebu. They make the plausible suggestion that Enrique came originally from the Visayas, had been captured young by slave raiders from Sumatra, and thence taken to the Malacca slave mart. Or, he might have belonged to the Philippine colony at Malacca. See *Travel Accounts of the Islands, 1573–1787* (Filipiniana Book Guild, XIX, Manila, 1971), pp. 1–3. If originally from the Philippines, he was the first person to circle the world and return to his starting point.

The notion that Enrique was an Egyptian (Thor Heyerdahl would have loved that!) comes from a misunderstanding by Navarrete of a statement by López de Gómara (*Historia de las Indias,* cap. xciii, p. 86 of 1740 ed.), who says that the Chamorro at Guam were thieves like gypsies and "said they came from Egypt, acording to Magellan's slave, who so understood." Anyway, Enrique's language attainments hardly included Chamorro, and the fleet's brief call at Guam offered no opportunity for palaver.

The Palang. Although certain writers, more prudish than judicious, have either omitted this story or called it one of Pigafetta's tall tales, *palang* did exist. It persists to this day in Borneo and parts of the Philippines, despite the efforts of Christian missionaries over a period of four centuries to put a stop to it. Robertson ed., I, 128–29, 167–69; Yale ed., I, 85–86. Antonio de Morga, *Sucesos de las Islas Filipinas,* written between 1593 and 1636 when he was a Spanish official in Manila (Hakluyt Society translation by J. S. Cummins, London, 1971, p. 278), confirms this extraordinary practice. Tom Harrisson, "The 'Palang,' Its History and Proto-History in West Borneo and the Philippines," *Journal* of Malaysian Branch, Royal Asiatic Society, XXXVII (1964) Pt. 2, 162–74, is a scientific study, with illustrations and personal observations down to 1960. Theodor DeBry, *Tertia Pars, Indiae Orientalis* (1628), pp. 23, 109, illustrates natives wearing this peculiar jewelry.

Cebu. The fleet evidently took three days to sail about 100 miles from

Statue of Lapu Lapu at Mactan. Courtesy of Mr. Esteban de Ocampo.

Limasawa to Cebu. The distance of Cebu harbor from "Gatighan," according to Pigafetta, 15 leagues—45 to 50 nautical miles—fits either Himuquitan or the Cuatro Islas or Poro, easternmost of the Camotes Islands.

The odd argument for conversion is in Robertson ed., I, 141.

The cross in Plaza Santa Cruz at Cebu City is said to contain fragments of Magellan's original. The Santo Niño, the statue of the Christ Child, which Magellan gave to the Sultana was piously preserved by a Christian convert after the island relapsed into paganism, and saved from a burning house by Legazpi in 1565. Subsequently placed in the Augustinian church, it is still there, an object of popular veneration; we could hardly get near enough to it to take a photo, owing to the swarms of worshipers. The church was made a basilica by a recent Pope in honor of the Santo Niño.

Lapu Lapu and Battle of Mactan. Robertson ed., I, 171–77; other contemporary accounts in notes on pp. 264–66. This rajah of Mactan, called *Cilapulapu* by Pigafetta ("Ci meaning "the"), commander of the natives of

Mactan who defeated and killed Magellan, has become a local hero. Opon, the principal town on Mactan, has been renamed after him, and bronze tablets in his honor have been put up on the stone monument to Magellan which Isabella II of Spain erected in 1869 on the beach near where Magellan fell. It is commonly believed locally that Lapu Lapu himself struck the lethal blow to Magellan, and with a bolo. According to a story picked up by Lieutenant Louis C. Moore USNR at Cebu (and supported by photos), the bow and arrow with which Lapu Lapu's statue was originally provided, pointed directly at the mayor's office; but after two mayors in succession had died there, the local authorities changed the bow and arrow for a big bolo, known as *kampilan*, pointing skyward! Pigafetta, who was beside Magellan when he fell, makes it clear that the lethal instruments were spears and swords, and there is no evidence that Lapu Lapu fought personally with his warriors. Our visit to Mactan unfortunately triggered a fresh batch of nonsense in the local press.

Firearms. Pigafetta's word for the arm carried by the landing force is *squiopeti* (modern spelling *schioppetti*); in the Yale ms. it is *haquébutiers;* in the Clements. Library ms., *choppetiers.* At Mactan it must have meant an arquebus, and Magellan's men were each armed with one. For illustration, see Morison, *Samuel de Champlain* (Boston, 1972), p. 282. The arms and armor museum in the Castel Saint' Angelo, Rome, has several specimens contemporaneous with Magellan. Robertson translates Pigafetta's *le bombarde de li batelli* (Robertson ed., I, 174–75), "the mortars in the boats." Skelton translates the phrase in the French manuscript (Yale ed., I, ii and II, xxvii), "the big guns in the ships." But *lombardo* or *bombardo* was a carriage gun (not a mortar) of about 6 to 7 cm. calibre, heaviest ordnance carried by Columbus on his First Voyage, and *batelli* in this case must mean the three ships.

Pigafetta on Magellan's navigation and fame. The phrase in the Ambrosian ms. *carteava et navigava* (Robertson ed., I, 176). The first word does not mean "make charts" but "navigated by the chart," i.e. by dead reckoning, whilst *navigava* means using celestial navigation. The Italian expression on his fame is *la fama duno si generoso capitano non essere extinta neli tempi nostri.* Yale's French manuscript, II, end of cap. xxvii, reads, *que la renommée d'un tel vaillant et noble capitaine ne sera point extincte ne mise en oubly en notre temps.* Very well said, as many efforts have been made in Portugal to denigrate Magellan, and in Spain to promote the fame of Elcano over his.

✴ XVIII ✴

Philippines and Spice Islands

Massacre at Cebu

Sultan Humabon wept when he heard of Magellan's death. He demanded the Captain General's body, asking the victorious rajah to name his own price; but Lapu Lapu refused to give it up "for all the riches in the world," and nobody knows what happened to Magellan's remains. A skull dug up on Mactan in 1971, with the remains of a Spanish sword, may possibly be his, but there is nothing to identify it.

The casualties in this fight, few but important, were eight Christians, including Magellan and Cristóbal Rebelo who had been promoted to captain of *Victoria*, together with four recently baptized natives of Cebu, and an estimated fifteen of the enemy. That afternoon the surviving officers chose Duarte Barbosa, Magellan's brother-in-law, to be captain of *Trinidad* and Captain General, dignities he enjoyed for barely three days.

Enrique de Malacca, the slave who had fought beside Magellan at Mactan, now turned lazy and surly when he could have been most useful, for he knew Spanish as well as Malay, and handled all communications with the rulers and people of Cebu. Enrique now declared that his master's death released him from servitude, which was correct; Magellan's last will and testament not only freed him but left him a legacy of 10,000 maravedis. So the former slave took to his bunk, nursing a slight wound he had received in the fight. This exasperated Captain General Barbosa, who spoke to Enrique somewhat in this wise: "Rise and shine, you lazy son-of-a-bitch, or I'll have you triced up and well flogged!" At any rate, he called him a dog and threatened to have him whipped, thus arousing all the man's native pride and vindictiveness, and costing Barbosa and some twenty-five shipmates their lives.

Enrique's revenge, doubtless sweet to him, widely outmeasured the offense. He convinced Sultan Humabon that the Christians planned to kidnap him, and then plotted to forestall treachery by treachery. This the Sultan did by means of a state banquet on 1 May, in the dark of the moon. Christians of every rank and rating were invited, and about thirty accepted, including Serrano and Barbosa. Of these, only Gómez de Espinosa and Carvalho survived because, smelling treachery, they sneaked out in time to save their lives and returned to their ships. Carvalho, now in temporary command, heard the tumult and saw natives throwing down the cross set up by Magellan and kicking it about. It took no great wit to guess what was up; Carvalho ordered each vessel to weigh and make sail, first approaching near enough to throw a few broadsides into the town. When *Trinidad* came within hailing distance, Captain Serrano was led to the shore, bound and bleeding, begging his countrymen to ransom him.

Carvalho is accused by Pigafetta and others of cold-bloodedly sailing away, leaving shipmate Serrano to his fate; but the Portuguese author of the Leiden Narrative tells a different story. Serrano called out that the ransom demanded for his life was two lombards, ships' cannon. Carvalho agreed, and sent a pair of these guns ashore in his skiff. The natives then declared these were not enough, and bargained for more. The boat party said they would give anything to recover Serrano, but he must be put in a safe place where they could pick him up. That they refused to do, and Serrano nobly urged his shipmates to break off the parley and get out, as he believed the natives were stalling until reinforcements arrived, to try to capture the ships, and they had better escape quickly "since it were better for him to die than that all should perish." Even as they were shifting sail to stand off shore, the Spanish sailors saw the men guarding Serrano turn on him, and heard shrieks which told only too well that another murder was being committed. The other victims of Enrique's revenge and the Sultan's treason in-

Route of
MAGELLAN'S FLEET
through the
PHILIPPINES AND MOLUCCAS
1521 - 1522

Based on a map prepared for
"Growth of the American Republic"
Scale of Nautical Miles

0   100   200   300

SOUTH

CHINA

SEA

LUZON

PHILIPPINES

From Guam

PHILIPPINE

SEA

SAMAR

13 Mar. 1521

PANAY

CEBU

LEYTE

Homonhon I.

Surigao Str.

NEGROS

Limasawa I.

PALAWAN

Magellan killed
27 Apr. 1521

SULU SEA

Quipit

MINDANAO

PELLEW o
PALAU IS

PACIFIC

Sulu Archipelago

Sarangani I.

Bruneí

OCEAN

Victoria and Trinidad
at Brunei 29 July 1521

CELEBES SEA

Talaud Is.

BORNEO

Morotai I.

JILOLO or HALMAHERA

Ternate

Arrival 8 Nov. 1521

Tidore

Victoria leaves 21 Dec.

Equator

SPICE IS.

NEW GUINE

CELEBES

CERAM

Ambon

Strait of Macassar

Molucca Passage

BANDA SEA

FLORES SEA

SUMBAWA

ARAFURA

FLORES

Alor Strait

TIMOR

SEA

SUMBA

Victoria leaves Timor
11 Feb. 1522

cluded three captains (Barbosa, Serrano, and Luis Alfonso de Gois), Andrés de San Martín, Father Valderrama, two secretaries, several petty officers and servants, and a dozen mariners and apprentice seamen. All were killed in the brawl or shortly after, sold as slaves to China. What became of Enrique we do not know; presumably he enjoyed an ill-earned eminence at the Sultan's court.

Cebu immediately relapsed into paganism, and every evidence of its brief experiment with Christianity was destroyed except El Santo Niño, the statue of the Christ Child.

Through the Philippines to the Spiceries

The three Spanish ships sailed to a beach somewhere on Bohol Island, and there reorganized. A conclave of officers elected Carvalho captain general, a responsibility he did not deserve and proved incompetent to perform. The alguacil, Gonzalo Gómez de Espinosa, then replaced him as captain of *Trinidad*. Since the fleet's complement had been reduced by starvation, fighting, and massacre to about 110 men, only enough properly to man two ships, it was decided to scrap *Concepión*, already riddled with ship worms. They saved anything that might be of value on the long voyage home, dividing her gear and stores between the two other ships, and burned her hull to the water's edge so that the natives could not pick her bones. Elcano, her master, soon emerged as captain of *Victoria*.

Sailing south-southwest, *Trinidad* and *Victoria* passed close to the tiny island of Panglao off southern Bohol, and were surprised to find it inhabited by "black men like those living in Ethiopia," says Pigafetta. These were the Negritos, as primitive a people as the Australian aborigines. Thence they made a leisurely tour of the southern Philippines and parts of the future Indonesia, apparently in no hurry to reach the Spice Islands. Probably they felt that, having come so far, they might as well discover all they could for Spain and pick up valuables for themselves. They were not, to be sure, discovering "new" countries like those of America, or even Guam. For the rest of the voyage they were visiting civilized communities with organized governments which had well established trading relations with China, Thailand, and India, as well as islands already familiar to the Portuguese. Nonetheless, to the crews of *Trinidad* and *Victoria* all these places were new and exciting, and I beg the reader to indulge me in carrying the story of this wonderful voyage to its conclusion.

Debouching into the Sulu Sea, the two ships called at a place called Quipit (now Kipit) on the Zamboanga peninsula of Mindanao. Here is a lofty, beautiful green-clad coast where rivers with ochre-colored water empty into the Sulu Sea, creating a golden pool amid the ocean sapphire; and the tiniest of white beaches nestle between rocky headlands. Calanao the local rajah performed the *casi-casi* ceremony with Carvalho, but had no food to spare. Pigafetta and other officers were rowed for two hours up river by the completely naked Rajah and his chiefs, introduced to the Ranee, and served a supper of rice and excessively salt fish, washed down by palm wine. There they passed the night, returning on board ship next day.

Sailing almost due west across the Sulu Sea, the ships called at the little island of Cagayan Sulu, whose inhabitants were Moros banished from Borneo. They shot game with poisoned arrows from blow-pipes. Again, no food; but the next island, about 120 miles to the northwestward, was lengthy, fabulous Palawan, where provisions of all kinds were abundant. "We called that land the Land of Promise," says Pigafetta, "because we suffered great hunger before we found it." At one of the numerous bays on the south coast of this opulent island, not improbably the future Puerto Principesa, they traded with friendly people, some pagan and some Moslem. Here the Christians saw their first cock fight, a form of sport that apparently had not reached Spain, and enjoyed the local arrack (rice wine) which had more kick than the palm wine of Cebu.

At beautiful Palawan, still an island paradise, they lingered a full month. There is a dreamy quality about summer sailing in the Philippines. The winds are mild, the sun warm, the sea teeming with fish. The land is so fertile that for more than half the year, after the main crops are gathered, the people have nothing to do but enjoy themselves. There was nothing very dreamy, however, in the way these Spaniards treated the natives. Wanting a pilot from Palawan to Borneo, they captured a ship about to enter the harbor and impressed her three Moro pilots to conduct them. The two ships departed enchanted Palawan on 21 June 1521, day of the full moon, and arrived at Brunei in northeastern Borneo on 9 July.

No "wild men of Borneo" greeted them here, but a most sophisticated society; the Spaniards might have thought they had found the land of a Thousand and One Nights. The Shahbender (title of the ruler of Brunei) sent out to meet *Trinidad* and *Victoria* a beautiful prao with gilt work on bow and stern. She flew a blue-and-white banner surmounted by peacock feathers; a band on board played on native instruments, and eight elderly chiefs closed the Spanish ships and came on board bearing gifts. Next, the Shahbender sent three music-making praos which encircled the ships "with great pomp," presented the Spaniards with various foodstuffs made of rice, and granted them permission to land.

This man was the most prestigious prince the Spanish had yet en-countered; and his independent sultanate has lasted to our own day. Three hundred men-at-arms holding naked scimitars at the ready, guarded him in a vast, richly adorned palace. He remained in his pri-vate apartments adjoining the harem, refusing to communicate except by speaking tube, and that with a palace official. Pigafetta and the six men who went ashore to make a formal call and present gifts were transported from the harbor to an official's house on elephants bearing silk trappings and castles on their backs. A dozen porters fol-lowed to carry the gifts. Cotton mattresses were provided by their host. Next morning the elephants carried them to the palace to present their credentials and receive permission to trade. They observed the protocol of raising hands over head, stepping up each knee, and bow-ing deeply toward the Shahbender. At him they were graciously permitted to peek as he lolled on a sofa in his private apartments, chewing betel nut and playing with one of his many young sons. After a thirty-two-course dinner at the official's, and a second night in real beds, the deputation enjoyed another elephant ride to the port.

This visit to Brunei did not end on the same gay note. On the morn-ing of 29 July 1521 the Spanish sailors saw a fleet of over a hundred praos approaching their anchorage from one side, and a fleet of junks advancing from the other. Anticipating treachery, as at Cebu, they hastily made sail and attacked the junks, capturing four and killing a number of men. On board one junk was the son of the Rajah of Luzon who, as the Shahbender's captain general, had sacked and destroyed the town of a disobedient chief and carried off three beautiful girls. Carvalho released him (secretly receiving a fat ransom in gold) and kept the three girl captives to start a harem of his own. Having completed this steal, Carvalho found it expedient to leave Brunei, abandoning his own eight-year-old Brazilian son who had been invited ashore to play with a son of the Shahbender. This boy never saw his father again. What became of the three girls we are not told; probably they were released at Ternate after Carvalho's death. Magellan would never have allowed them to sail in his fleet, but discipline had become lax since his death and the Spaniards behaved as if they had all the time in the world.

Retracing their course toward Palawan, on 7 September 1521 *Victoria* and *Trinidad* called at an island they called Combonbon, which was probably Banguey on the south side of Balabac Strait. Here they stayed forty-two days, during which "we labored hard," said Pigafetta, to grave, caulk and repair the ships and lay in a supply of firewood, going "barefoot in the forest" to cut it. The service of graving and pitching to deter the teredo, essential to keep a wooden ship afloat in tropical seas, must have been properly attended to, as *Victoria* made the long voyage home despite leaks. At Banguey they found many kinds of fish and shellfish including *Tridacena gigas*, the giant clam which can kill a man by clamping down on his arm or leg.

Proceeding eastward again, they spoke an important junk in which were embarked Tuan Mahmud, the Shahbender's governor of Palawan, and his son and brother. As she refused to strike sail, they captured and sacked her. The Tuan was so liberal with gifts over and above what had been stolen from him, that the Spaniards gave him expensive presents such as a yellow damask robe, a green cloth robe, and a blue cloth cloak. At the September full moon the fleet officers, feeling that Carvalho was becoming much too big for his boots as well as a menace to their future safety by acts of piracy, degraded him to his former rank of flag pilot, elected Gómez de Espinosa captain general as well as captain of *Trinidad*, and appointed Juan Sebastián de Elcano captain of *Victoria*, fleet treasurer and accountant.

The two ships, directed by one of the impressed pilots, crossed the Sulu Sea, passed through Basilan Strait into Moro Gulf, and passed the site of the modern city of Zamboanga. En route they encountered the ancestors of the latter-day Sámal Laut or sea-gypsies, who live on board their boats and follow the monsoon. Although Carvalho had been deposed, the crews of *Victoria* and *Trinidad* continued to practise piracy. For no apparent need or reason, they captured a big prao

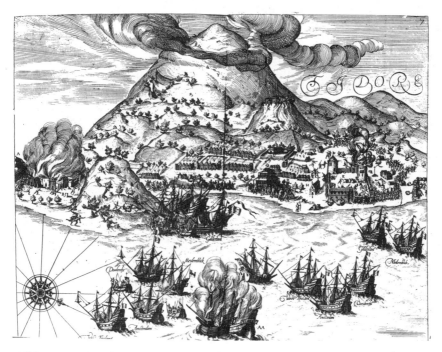

Tidore (really Ternate). A Dutch fleet attacking the Portuguese in early seventeenth century. After De Bry. From his *Peregrinates in Indiam Orientalem*, 1607.

with a crew of eighteen, all chiefs of Mindanao, killed seven and saved one to act as co-pilot, since he claimed to know the course to the Spice Islands. He did; this man knew his business.

On 26 October 1521 in the Celebes Sea and the dark of the moon, the two ships encountered their first storm since leaving the Strait of Magellan, and they had to strip down to bare poles. Three corposants—St. Elmo's on the maintop, St. Nicholas's on the mizzentop, and Santa Clara's on the foretop—appeared and "dissipated the darkness." The mariners promised, if saved, to donate a slave to each saint, but Pigafetta does not explain the proposed method of delivery.

At a harbor between the two islands of Bahut and Sarangani—latitude 6°07′ N, says Pigafetta, which is close—the Spaniards shanghaied two more native pilots who guided them southeasterly through the uninhabited Karakelong group and past the Sangi Islands, where all but

Ternate and Tidore, 1972. The two islands and the tiny one between.
Sanchez Obregón photo.

one of the impressed pilots managed to escape by swimming ashore. Finally, on 6 November 1521, they raised four conspicuous islands, and "The pilot who still remained with us told us that those four islands were *Maluco*"—the long-sought Spiceries. "So we thanked God, and for joy discharged all our artillery. And no wonder we were so joyful, for we had spent twenty-seven months less two days in our search for Molucca," counting from the day they left Spain.

They really had arrived. Here was what Columbus had been looking for, what Magellan had been sent to find. As Camoëns put it,

> Olha cá pelos mares do Oriente
> As infinitas ilhas espalhadas.
> Ve Tidore e Ternate co fervente
> Cume que lança as flamas ondeadas.
> As árvores verás do cravo ardente,
> Co sangue Português inda compradas.

Through all these Oriental waters / sprinkled with islands innumerable,/ behold Tidore and Ternate from whose burning / summit plumes

446

of fire flare; / trees of ardent cloves you may see, / which Lusitanian blood has purchased.

These were names to conjure with; John Milton tells of a fleet

> by equinoctial winds
> Close sailing from Bengala, or the isles
> Of Ternate and Tidore, whence merchants bring
> Their spicy drugs . . .

Henry Thoreau, wintering in his cabin on Walden Pond, mused that the ice there harvested "with favoring winds" would go "floating by Ternate and Tidore" to be "landed in ports of which Alexander only heard the names." *

On the afternoon of 8 November 1521, *Trinidad* and *Victoria*, firing another salute, entered the harbor of Tidore, most important of the five principal Moluccas. The others are Ternate, Motir, Makyan, and Batchian. They stretch in a north-south line, from latitude 4° N to the Equator, parallel to the big island of Halmahera (Jilolo), also counted as a Spice Island. All six islands are lofty and verdure-covered. Ternate and Tidore are so tiny—the first, almost round and only six and a half miles in diameter, and Tidore barely ten miles long—that it is difficult to believe that in the sixteenth century they inspired momentous voyages, supported independent rulers in high state, and caused thousands of deaths among Europeans fighting to control their fragrant riches.

And why were spices—especially clove, cinnamon, nutmeg, mace, and pepper—so avidly sought after in this era? They were part of life in both the European and Asiatic worlds. They flavored all kinds of cooked food. They were used in perfumes and (like myrrh) for embalming. Spices were among the most important ingredients of *materia medica*. Before tea, coffee, and chocolate had been introduced to Europe, spices pepped up beer and wine, and in lieu of refrigeration they masked the unpleasant savor of decomposing food. Even today, how would you like to live without pepper, nutmeg, or cinnamon?

Urdaneta reported to the king of Spain in 1537, after living several years in Molucca, that from all six Spice Islands the annual export varied from 5000 to 11,600 quintal (hundredweight) of cloves; that when he arrived there, the value of a *bahar* (over four quintal) of cloves was two ducats, and in five years it went up to ten. Maxi-

---

* Lusiads, x.132, *Paradise Lost*, ii.638, *Walden*, end of chap. xvi.

Morisons and Obregóns under clove tree, Ternate. Sanchez Obregón photo.

Informal reception committee, Ternate. Sanchez Obregón photo.

milianus Transylvanus, who obtained from *Victoria*'s survivors a fairly accurate account of how spices were grown, wrote, "The natives share groves of this tree among themselves, just as we do vineyards." Since about 1515 the Portuguese had been distributing the clove harvest from Lisbon throughout Europe, and also (by virtue of their superior navigation and business sense) throughout the Far East. No wonder that they, the first Europeans to reach the Moluccas, were determined to hold them in strict monopoly.

Returning to our voyage, on 9 November 1521, after the two Spanish ships had anchored in the harbor of Tidore, Sultan Abuleis, a Moslem about forty-five years old, came out to greet them in a prao. He was seated under a silk awning, accompanied by one of his sons bearing a scepter, two hand-washers with water in gold jars, and two men bearing gold caskets filled with betel-nut. The Sultan bade the Christians welcome; he had even dreamed of their coming. Boarding the flagship, he condescended to sit on a velvet-covered chair whence he "received us as children," says Pigafetta, and declared that he and all his people wanted nothing better than to be vassals of imperial Charles.

449

The Portuguese, who had been called in by his predecessor ten years earlier to break the Arab monopoly, had evidently outstayed their welcome.

Abuleis informed the Christians that Magellan's old friend Francisco Serrão had died on Ternate some eight months earlier, but tactfully concealed the circumstances. The rulers of Tidore and Ternate were enemies; Serrão supported Ternate, where he had been living since 1512, and so effectively that Abuleis put poison into his drink when, after concluding peace, he visited Tidore to buy cloves. Next, a few days after he had greeted the Spaniards, Abuleis himself was poisoned by his daughter, wife of the sultan of Batchian, "under pretext of trying to bring about peace between the kings of these two islands; but he recovered." Princely politics in the Moluccas are somewhat difficult to follow.

Pigafetta gives us some interesting figures on the sexual habits of these Moro princes. The sultan of Tidore had one principal wife and some two hundred girls in his harem; every family in the island had to furnish him with one or two daughters to keep it full. In the neighboring island of Halmahera (Jilolo) were two sultans who respectively fathered 526 and 660 children, surpassing Augustus the Strong of Saxony, who boasted only 364 bastards. Jessu, the elder with the top score, visited Ternate while the Christians were there and exchanged gifts, but not wives.

The weeks spent here were pure joy to Pigafetta. He describes how clove trees were grown and the harvest gathered, and the preparation of sago, the bread of these islands. The sultan of Ternate himself came to the Spanish ships and traded quantities of cloves. The sultan of Tidore swore "by Allah and the Koran" that he would always be a friend to the king of Spain. The sultan of Batchian made a state visit in a gaily beflagged prao, a veritable trireme with three banks of oars on each side and 120 rowers moving to the cadence of banging gongs. The Spaniards attended a banquet given in their honor by the local sultan; every man sat between two young girls "clad in silk garments from the waist to the knees."

New sails were now bent on the ships and painted with the cross of Santiago. The Christians left some of their arquebuses and culverins as a parting present with the sultan of Tidore, who gave them in return one slave, ten *bahar* of cloves, and two stuffed birds of paradise. These birds were supposed to live wholly in the air, never reaching earth until they died; and as the specimens which Elcano brought home had no feet, this was assumed to be true.

To have a double chance of getting home with these valuable cargoes, the officers of the fleet decided that, now the easterly monsoon had started, *Victoria* should return via the Cape of Good Hope, and *Trinidad* await the westerly monsoon and head for Nueva España. There her cargo would be carried across the Isthmus of Panama and shipped to Spain. Departure was delayed because *Trinidad* sprang a leak at anchor and the men had to careen and unload her to get at it. Leaving her in the harbor of Tidore, *Victoria* under Captain Elcano set sail 21 December 1521 with 47 of her original crew and 13 natives on board; Gómez de Espinosa stayed behind with 53 men to sail *Trinidad*. The last moon of the year had entered last quarter, a bad time to start. *Victoria* endured a nine months' voyage and many vicissitudes before Captain Elcano got her back to Spain with eighteen Christian and three native survivors.

Bibliography and Notes

Casualties are from Navarrete, IV, 65–67.

The Massacre. Maximilianus Transylvanus, who gives the most detail, declares that it was Serrano who threatened Enrique; but Pigafetta (who fortunately sent his excuses to the banquet invitation) wrote that it was Barbosa. Navarrete (IV, p. lxii), quoting Herrera, claims that Enrique was guiltless, that the instigators were the rulers of Mactan and two other rajahs who threatened to make war on Cebu unless Sultan Humabon got rid of the Christians and their ships; and that is what the Portuguese author of the Leiden Narrative says. The "Genoese Pilot" (Stanley, p. 14) says that Enrique was killed with Magellan. Several years later, Saavedra picked up at Mindanao a Spanish sailor from one of Loaysa's wrecked ships. He had been made a slave and taken by his Moslem master to Cebu, where he learned that five or six of the banquet victims were not killed, but sold as slaves to the Chinese.

Quipit. Variant spellings in Robertson ed., II, 196. On the modern map, Kipit Point is on Zamboanga peninsula, latitude 8°05′ N. Pigafetta (p. 17) gives the Quipit method of cooking rice: "They first put in an earthenware jar like ours a large leaf which lines it all. Then they add the water and the rice, and after covering it, allow it to boil until the rice becomes as hard as bread." The "Genoese Pilot" (Stanley, pp. 14–23) has many details on the fleet's visit to Mindanao and its course thence to Tidore.

Borneo. Robertson ed., II, 29–39, with Albo, the "Genoese," and Brito accounts on pp. 199–201. Pigafetta's description of Brunei, the houses built on piles in the harbor, which serve as fish pond, bath and sewer, would do for the same place even today. Brunei is still an independent sultanate attached to Malaysia, but much reduced in extent as the reigning sultan in 1841 gave the western half of his kingdom to Sir James Brooke in return for his putting down a rebellion of head-hunting Dyaks; and a good part of the eastern half became the British colony of Labuan, or North Borneo. For Brunei's (and all North Borneo's) successful resistance (with British assistance) to Sukarno's forcible attempt to annex them in 1962–66, see Harold James and Denis Sheil-Small, *The Undeclared War* (London and Totowa, N.J., 1971).

Changes in command. Cristóbal Haro's manuscript accounts in Archivo de Indias, leg. 37, doc. 38, around folio 9, state that Elcano's pay as captain of *Victoria* started 21 September 1521. See also Robertson ed., II, 47, 202–3, and depositions at the end of the voyage by Elcano, Albo, and Bustamente in Navarrete, IV, 286–95.

Spices and the Spice Islands. Frederic Rosengarten, Jr., *The Book of Spices* (1969), is my authority for the history and uses of spices and the spice trade. That is of great antiquity. In Genesis xxxvii. 25–27 we read how Joseph, after being cast into a pit by his brothers, was sold to a company of Ishmaelites from Gilead "with their camels bearing spicery and balm and myrrh, going to carry it down to Egypt," then the end of a caravan-borne spice line. Note also Song of Solomon, iii. 6, iv. 10–16, vi. 2. The Queen of Sheba came to Solomon with "camels that bare spices" (2 Chronicles ix. 1), and the main purpose of her visit was probably to prevent his navy from interrupting her spice line.

See Robertson ed., II, 206–8 for this leg of the voyage. There are many ways to spell the names of the Spice Islands. The Filipiniana Book Guild's Vol. XIV, p. 126, for instance, calls the three southernmost, Moter, Maru, and Mutjan; Tomé Pires (Hakluyt Society ed., II, 213) calls them Ternate, Tidore, Moter, Maqujem, and Pacham. Urdaneta's account is translated in Sir Clements Markham (ed.), *Early Spanish Voyages to the Strait of Magellan* (Hakluyt Society, London, 1911), pp. 84–85.

Ternate became the capital of the eastern part of the Portuguese empire. In 1619 the Dutch, having conquered the Moluccas, transferred the capital to Batavia (now Jakarta). The British captured the Moluccas in 1810 but returned them to the Netherlands after the Napoleonic wars. The Dutch, in order to control clove export, transferred the trade to Ambon, cut down all clove trees on the Spice Islands, and forbade the inhabitants, under pain of death, to grow any more. Perhaps that is why we found it difficult to locate a clove tree on Ternate in 1971! Clove trees later were smuggled into

China, Zanzibar, and Madagascar (now the principal sources), and Indonesia now has to import cloves to supply flavoring for her popular *kretch* cigarettes, one-third ground cloves and two-thirds tobacco (Rosengarten, p. 78).

Birds of paradise, and the history of their introduction into Europe and America, is the subject of the Chicago Zoölogical Society's publication *Bandar-Log*, No. 11 (Jan. 1954), edited by Ellen T. Smith.

✲ XIX ✲

Homeward Bound

1522

Trinidad's Fatal Attempt

Trinidad and *Victoria* have now sailed far beyond the limits set by this book. When they dropped Mindanao below the northern horizon, they had passed the last land which, by any stretch of imagination, could be called America, or new discoveries. Most of the native inhabitants, whether Moslem or heathen, were organized, sophisticated, and prosperous, and the Portuguese had been coming to Indonesia for fifteen years or more. Judging, however, that my readers would like to see this greatest of all voyages through, we shall finish the story of Magellan's two surviving ships.

First, let us relate the unsuccessful attempt of *Trinidad* to return home eastward. Owing to necessary repairs, she did not depart Tidore until more than three months after *Victoria*. Gonzalo Gómez de Espinosa commanded her, and Carvalho would have been her pilot had he not died at Tidore in February 1522. Juan Bautista de Punzorol, probably the one known to fame as the "Genoese pilot," replaced him.

Leaving one officer and four men ashore as nucleus of a trading factory to pursue the spice trade, *Trinidad*, carrying a cargo of almost 1000 quintal—nearly fifty ton—of cloves, set sail for Tidore 6 April 1522, in the full of the paschal moon. She passed Jilolo (Halmahera) and Morotai, into the Philippine Sea, revictualed at Komo, and for a time steered east by north; but head winds forced her to fall off to the northward. She called at one of the Marianas, where three men deserted; and, continually baffled by easterly winds, stormy weather, and what seemed to the crew to be intense cold, struggled as far north as latitude 43° N, that of Hakodate in Japan. Then Gómez de Espinosa decided to return to Tidore. It took him six weeks to reach an island that he calls Bonaconora, probably Morotai or another small island north of Jilolo. By that time, thirty of the crew of fifty-three had died, and so many more were disabled by scurvy that they had become incapable of handling the ship.

During her absence a fleet of seven Portuguese naval vessels under Captain António de Brito, who had been scouring the eastern seas looking for Magellan, put in at Tidore, mopped up the little Spanish garrison, and reduced the sultan to a tearful renunciation of his new friends and abject obedience to Portugal. Espinosa, at Bonaconora, received news of these doings, and in his helpless condition sent Brito a letter by boat, begging for succor. The pitiless Portuguese replied by sending a caravel to take possession of *Trinidad* and sail her to Ternate, where he impounded her papers and log-books, discharged her valuable cargo for his benefit, and stripped her of sails, lines, and all valuable gear. In that condition a squall struck her at anchor and she dragged ashore, broke up, and became a total loss.

Sad indeed was the once proud flagship's fate, and tragic that of most of her remaining crew. Brito beheaded a beachcomber whom Espinosa had picked up, on the ground that he was a Portuguese subject who had deserted. He seriously considered having the "Genoese pilot" and a few others slaughtered forthwith, but (he cynically explains in his letter to the king), "I detained them in Maluco because it is an unhealthy country, with the intention of having them die there," which most of them did. The boatswain and the carpenter were set to work for Brito himself, and the rest were sent to Governor Albuquerque of India, to dispose of as he chose. Their fate is unknown, except that Espinosa's slave, Antón "de color Negro," was presented by Albuquerque to his sister.

Of the four members of *Trinidad*'s crew who eventually returned to the Iberian Peninsula, Juan Rodriguez, at forty-four the oldest man in Magellan's fleet, escaped in a Portuguese ship. Espinosa and Ginés de Mafra were taken to the Banda Islands—Java, Malacca, and Cochin —where they endured hard labor for two years and were then shipped with Hans Vargue the German gunner to Lisbon. All three were there thrown into prison. Faithful Hans died in jail, pathetically bequeathing all his property—back pay and a packet of cloves and nutmegs— to his commanding officer. The Portuguese passed on Espinosa and Ginés de Mafra to Seville, where the Spanish authorities clapped them into jail. After seven months' incarceration, both were released and given their day in court in 1527—almost eight years after leaving home. Ginés found that his wife, believing him dead, had married again and spent all his property. After a legal hassle over that, he returned to the Indies. Pedro de Alvaredo employed him as chief pilot on a coastal voyage in the Pacific in 1536, and six years later he became pilot to Ruy López de Villalobos on his voyage to the Philippines. Espinosa, whose courageous support of Magellan in the San Julián mutiny saved the voyage, spent four and a half years in captivity in the East before returning to Spain.

Diogo Barbosa, Magellan's father-in-law, in a memorial to the king-emperor, remarked bluntly that mutineers in *San Antonio* "were very well received and treated at the expense of Your Highness, while the captain and others who were desirous of serving Your Highness were imprisoned and deprived of all justice. From this," he added, "so many bad examples arise—heartbreaking to those who try to do their duty." True enough. Magellan, too, had he returned to Spain, would certainly have been jailed on some excuse.

Charles V later made it up to Espinosa, so far as lay in his power. He granted him noble status and a coat of arms with a motto on a global crest differing slightly from Elcano's: "Thou wert one of the first to go around me." His back pay, even though the officials of the Casa de Contratación would allow him no salary for years spent in prison, amounted to a large sum of money. The king gave him 15,000 maravedis as heir of Hans Vargue, a pension of 30,000 maravedis, and a job paying 43,000 maravedis per annum as inspector of ships bound to the Indies. He still held that position in 1543, when we finally lose sight of this valiant captain and loyal supporter of Magellan. We do not know where or when he died. Peace to his soul!

Victoria's Voyage Home

Juan Sebastián de Elcano received full honors for sailing *Victoria* home, which caused his part in the San Julián mutiny to be overlooked and forgiven. A younger man than Magellan (born 1486 or 1487 at Guetaria in the northern province of Guipúzcoa, third of eight children to a middle-class family), he had commanded a ship bigger than any of Magellan's before the great voyage. Nobody ever denied the high quality of his seamanship. But what of his personality? Neither Pigafetta nor the Portuguese author of the Leiden Narrative, both of whom sailed with Elcano from Tidore to Seville, ever mentions him. Possibly they had not forgotten the mutiny at San Julián; more probably they had suffered personal slights. Since Magellan forgave Elcano for his part in the mutiny, so should we; but it is hard to overlook his lying at Magellan's expense about the mutiny at San Julián in 1527. Anyway, as captain of *Victoria* he never wavered on the difficult voyage home.

Her crew took leave of their fellow countrymen and new friends at Tidore on 21 December 1521 and sailed with a complement of sixty, thirteen of them natives. Steering almost due south along the line of Spice Islands, she called at the islet off Tidore to pick up a load of firewood that had been cut for her, left the other Spice Islands astern, saw the last new moon of 1521 arise, and passed to starboard the Xulla (Suela) Islands which tail off from the Celebes. In Manipa Strait between Ceram (Sarang) and Buru (Boeroe) she anchored in Jakiol Bay on 27 December and there obtained fresh provisions. Now turning southeast (having evidently shipped a native pilot who knew his business), *Victoria* passed through the great Indonesian island barrier by Alor Strait.* In the Savu Sea a severe storm arose, and all hands made vows to perform a pilgrimage to a shrine of the Virgin if she would deign to save them; but they had no opportunity to do that before Seville. *Victoria* scudded east before the storm along the ironbound south shores of Pantar and Alor Islands, reaching an island then called Malua, where she found a harbor and stayed a fortnight caulking and

---

* Most authorities say by the narrow Flores Strait, further west; but Albo makes it clear that they chose the wider Alor Strait, as any prudent pilot would do.

Beach on Timor

making other repairs. On 25 January 1522 she crossed the fifteen-mile channel to the great and lofty (9580 feet) island of Timor. The eastern half of this island remains Portuguese, last remnant except Macao of her Far-Eastern empire; but in 1522 no conquering Lusitanians had yet arrived.

Timor, described by Camoëns as that "isle which yields sandalwood salubrious and sweet to smell," received a good name from Pigafetta. "White sandalwood is found in that island and nowhere else. Also, ginger, water buffaloes, swine, goats, fowls, rice, figs [bananas], sugar-cane, oranges, lemons, wax, almonds, kidney beans, and other things. . . . We found a junk from Luzon there, which had come to buy sandalwood," and Elcano brought a packet of the fragrant wood home to Spain. The people were all heathen and (after some initial mis-understanding) willing to trade; but as they were riddled with the "disease of St. Job" (syphilis), the crew avoided the girls. For three weeks *Victoria* coasted the superb scenery of northwestern Timor, from Balibo (west of Dilli) to Kuping, buying provisions wherever they could be found.

Pigafetta, who seems to have understood the Moros with whom he conversed, picked up at Timor a series of yarns about China and the Far East. The tallest of them, which later European travelers have confirmed, is about a variation of the *palang* in the courtship habits of young gentlemen of Java. In his own words, "When the young men of Java are in love with any gentlewoman, they sew certain little bells between their member and the foreskin, stand under the window of their innamorata and, making a show of urinating and shaking their member, they make the little bells tinkle and so continue until the listening lady hears the sound. She then comes out and they take their pleasure; always with those little bells in place, for the women like hearing them ring inside."

On the night of the full moon, 10–11 February 1522, *Victoria* sailed from Timor with the land breeze into "the great open sea called Laut Chidol"—the Indian Ocean. Elcano dared not call at Bali, Java,

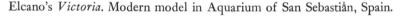

Elcano's *Victoria*. Modern model in Aquarium of San Sebastián, Spain.

or Sumatra for fear of being attacked by the Portuguese, and the fate of *Trinidad* proved the wisdom of his decision. But he paid for it with suffering. To double the Cape he steered straight across the Indian Ocean. Two more moons waxed and waned and a third became almost full, before he sighted Africa. This leg of the voyage reduced his crew to a state of misery equal to that which they had endured in the Pacific. Magellan's ships never could carry enough sea stores for a prolonged voyage. In this case, owing to the scarcity of salt in the Spice Islands and Timor, the barreled meat and fish, insufficiently pickled, turned putrid in the hold. And in early March the monsoon petered out and westerlies set in, head winds which raised enormous seas against which *Victoria* found it difficult to contend. Twice or thrice she had to lay-to, tossing and rolling, while the captain kept his men busy repairing leaks and splicing the now ragged rigging so that it would help get them home. Fortunately he had had a new suit of sails made in Tidore.

On 18 March 1522, just as Pilot Albo was shooting the sun, they sighted a "very high island." Twice they tried to fetch it but, thwarted by head winds, gave it up. This must have been the one that the Dutch later named Amsterdam, in latitude 37° 50′ S. Some of the sailors were so cold, hungry, and sick as to beg Elcano to put in at Portuguese Mozambique, which they wrongly estimated to be close at hand; but the majority, "more desirous of honor than of their own life, determined to go to Spain living or dead." Brave boys, hurrah for them!

For several more weeks *Victoria* shaped courses between west by south and west by north, twice venturing below latitude 40° S and being forced to lay-to for a couple of days. Elcano finally decided that sailing in the "roaring forties" did not pay, closed South Africa, sighted it on 8 May, and landed at a port, probably Mossel Bay or Port Elizabeth. No natives were encountered or food obtained here; and —O bitter disappointment!—they ascertained from the lay of the land, and the high mountains, that they had not yet doubled the Cape. So on *Victoria* struggled, bucking the Agulhas Current and contrary winds, carrying away her foretopmast and springing her main yard. Finally, on a fair May day she doubled Cape Agulhas, Africa's furthest south (latitude 34° 50′ S) and the nearby Cape of Good Hope, sighting both in the misty distance.

"Then we sailed north for two months continually without taking on any refreshment," wrote Pigafetta. On 8 June 1522, with a full moon, *Victoria* crossed the Equator for the fourth time since leaving Spain. Between Timor and the Cape de Verdes, she lost fifteen of her own men and ten Indonesians, more than had died on board Magellan's three ships in crossing the Pacific. Pigafetta thought it significant that when the corpses were committed to the sea, the Christians floated on their backs, facing heaven, and the pagans floated face down, toward hell!

On 9 July *Victoria* anchored in the port of Ribeira Grande on the Cape de Verdes island of Santiago. There the officers were disturbed to find that their count of the calendar was wrong; they thought it was Wednesday, but the people ashore assured them it was Thursday. This was a serious matter, since it meant that they had eaten meat (when they had it) on Friday, and kept Easter on Monday. A grievous if not mortal sin! Not until they reached Seville could anyone find the explanation that they had lost a day by sailing westward with the sun. In the meantime, all hands swore to do penance for this mistake, if they ever got home.

In order to deceive the Cape Verde Portuguese as to where they had been, Elcano instructed his shore party to declare that they had lost their way returning from the Caribbean. This worked at first, and the shore party brought out a boatload of rice. After resting at anchor four or five days with constant pumping, Elcano sent his biggest boat ashore manned by thirteen sailors, to get more food and buy slaves to spell out his exhausted men at the pumps. Having no cash, he sent several parcels of cloves for the purchase, and that put the Portuguese authorities wise to the fact that *Victoria* had been poaching on "their" Spice Islands. They detained the crew and sent out one of their own boats, ordering Elcano to surrender his ship. The Captain, unlike Columbus whose *Niña* had been similarly treated in the Azores in 1493, did not feel strong enough to shoot it out with the Portuguese; and, seeing several armed vessels in the harbor making sail apparently to overhaul him, he hastily departed on 15 July. This time, by the corrected calendar.

It was another long haul against the northerly "Portuguese trades" to get home, and in some respects this leg of the voyage was the toughest. For not only did the eighteen men have to do the work normally done by fifty; they had to work the pumps day and night to prevent *Victoria* from foundering. She sighted Tenerife 28 July. As usual with African traders returning home against the north wind, she had to make a wide sweep to the northwest on the starboard tack to the Azores. Tall Pico thrust its volcanic cone above the horizon on 7 August. With light variables, she jilled around the Azores for over a week, gravely in need of provisions but not daring to land in Portuguese territory. On 21 August she got a good slant for Cape St. Vincent and picked up that prominent landmark on 4 September, the eve of *Victoria*'s last full moon at sea.

The winds now favored the weary mariners. On Saturday, 6 September, *Victoria* entered the harbor of Sanlúcar de Barrameda. After one night (and, we hope, fresh food), Elcano procured a long boat with a crew of stout oarsmen, who helped pull her up the Guadalquivir on two flood tides. On the 8th she anchored off a quay at Seville hard by the Church of Santa Maria de la Victoria; and by a happy coincidence found that it was the feast day of this particular virgin, the friend of mariners. It was three years and one month from the time *Victoria* had sailed thence.

Only eighteen Christians were left to perform penitential vows. On Tuesday the 9th, barefoot and clad only in their shirts, each man carrying a long lighted candle, they marched into the Minorite convent at the Triana waterfront to pray before Santa Maria de la Victoria, then crossed the old pontoon bridge to Seville proper, and after a walk of well over a mile, entered the great Cathedral and worshipped at the venerated shrine of Santa Maria de l'Antigua.

Juan Sebastián de Elcano was not committed to jail, the fate of so many master mariners returning from a great discovery. He lost no time in making a brief report (translated in Appendix to this Chapter) to the Emperor, in which he shows a commendable concern for his fellow survivors. Charles V had returned to Spain after more than two years' absence, well pleased with himself; a rebellion in Castile had been suppressed, and although France had declared war, Henry VIII (whose daughter Mary the Emperor intended to marry) declared war on France. Elcano was summoned to his presence at Valladolid, together with picked members of *Victoria*'s crew, who first were issued

Arms of Elcano

new clothes and an installment of their wages. The Emperor received his captain graciously and granted him an annual pension of 500 ducats ($1160 in gold). The herald's office provided him with a very appropriate coat of arms. Here is the blazon: Chief, a castle *or* on field *gules*, and on the other half a field *or*, with two crossed cinnamon sticks, three nutmegs and twelve cloves. Crest: a globe bearing the motto *Primus circumdedisti me* (Thou first circumnavigated me). Supporters: two Malay kings, crowned, each holding a branch of a spice tree, proper.

Charles V demanded of his brother-in-law D. João III (now king of Portugal) the return of the thirteen sailors marooned in the Cape Verdes, and this was done fairly promptly. They with the rest of the eighteen Christians who finished this voyage were received at court; what happened to the three Indonesian survivors is unrecorded. Adding the five men from *Trinidad* who eventually reached the Peninsula, we have 35 survivors from the four ships which originally left Spain and the Canaries in 1519; *San Antonio*, which defected,

463

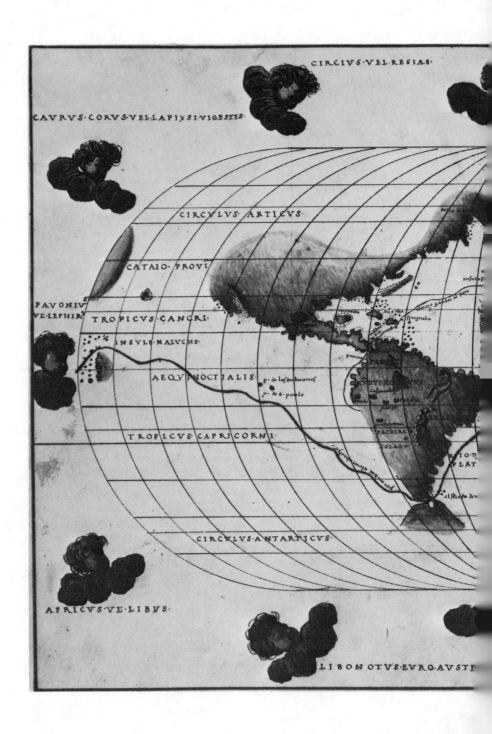

CIRCIVS·VEL·RESIAS·

CAVRVS·CORVS·VELLAPIXSI·VIGESTES·

CIRCVLVS·ARTICVS·

CATAIO·PROVI

FAVONIV
VE·ZEPHIR

TROPICVS·CANCRI·

INSVLE·MALVCHE·

AEQVTNOCTIALIS· p· d· los tubuenos·
                 p· d· s· paulo

TROPICVS·CAPRICORNI·

CIRCVLVS·ANTARTICVS·

AFRICVS·VE·LIBVS·

LIBONOTVS·EVROAVSTR

Battista Agnese map of 1568, showing course of Magellan and Elcano, and Panama route to west coast. Courtesy, Library of Congress.

would account for 50 to 55 more. Many had trouble collecting back pay. Miguel de Rodas, assistant master of *Victoria*, when presented to the Emperor, was given arms similar to Elcano's, and granted an annual pension of 50,000 maravedis; but three years later he testified that he had received none of it. Nevertheless, he liked seafaring so much that he shipped in the Sebastian Cabot expedition, to his subsequent sorrow. Juan de Acurio, one of the lucky eighteen, complained two years later that he had gained naught from *Victoria*'s voyage but "glory, experience, and a bale of cloves" weighing 75 pounds!

It is probable—although not provable—that the successful outcome of this great voyage convinced Charles V that God intended him to enlarge his empire to embrace the world. From his Hapsburg-Austrian forebears he had inherited not only a prominent jaw and a firm character, but the motto A.E.I.O.U., initials for *Austriae Est Imperare Orbi Universo* (Austria Is Destined To Rule the Entire Globe). Hitherto this prophecy had been supposed to apply only to the European world known to the ancients; but here was Elcano bringing home treaties with Oriental potentates. Perhaps Columbus's idea of Spain's drawing the Grand Khan into her diplomatic orbit was not extravagant? But, how could Charles V rule the Far East while he had the Grand Turk and France on his back? First things first; implementation of Magellan's voyage must wait.

The scientific value of this voyage is beyond doubt. There must have been old fogies who said, "What's the use? Everyone knew you could sail around the world, but who would want to?" Any European interested in geography knew that this was a great feat of navigation. Magellan and Elcano had contributed more to geographical knowledge than any navigator since Columbus. In the words of Edward Gaylord Bourne:

> The scientific results of Magellan's voyage were far more important than the political advantages derived from it. Once for all it gave a practical demonstration of the sphericity of the earth that convinced the ordinary mind unreached by the scientific proofs. It revolutionized all ideas as to the relative proportions of the land and water of the globe, and dissipated the traditional error on which Columbus's voyage and his whole geographical system were based, that the area of the land far exceeded that of the water. The vast width of the Pacific revealed that America was a new world in a more comprehensive sense than had been suspected.

Victoria, which should have been preserved as a monument, met her death in the merchant service. After extensive repairs to make her tight, she made one round voyage to the West Indies; but upon attempting a second, she disappeared with all hands.

Pigafetta traveled from court to court, presenting kings and queens with extracts from his narrative. From the Seignory of Venice he obtained permission to publish it there, but he never did; the first edition of his narrative, in French, came out in Paris in 1525. Through this, and several Italian editions prior to 1540, and the English translation by Richard Eden in 1555, knowledge of Magellan's voyage became well disseminated. Pigafetta, now created a knight of Malta, "dined out" on the Magellan voyage for several years but died fairly young in his home town Vicenza.

Cristóbal de Haro and others who financed the voyage struck it rich despite all losses. *Victoria* brought home 520 quintal (25 to 26 long tons) of cloves, which sold for 7,888,634 maravedis (about $22,680 in gold), and the packs of cinnamon, mace, and nutmeg brought about $1800 more. This exceeded by at least a thousand dollars the original cost of the entire expedition.

Almost everyone who knows the sea and has considered this subject, feels that Magellan's was the greatest and most wonderful voyage in recorded history. But for two centuries that "noble captain," the leader, organizer, and (until his death) Captain General, received little or no credit other than Pigafetta's encomium. The Portuguese denounced him as a traitor, the Spanish execrated him, owing to stories of his harshness and mistakes in navigation brought home by Esteban Gómez and Elcano. In Spain the Basque master mariner received all the credit; his home town and San Sebastián are full of monuments and memorials, and a heroic statue to him is about to be erected in Seville.

Doña Beatriz Magellan and her two little children died before *Victoria* reached Seville, and Magellan's legal heirs were unable to collect his salary from the government of Charles V. From the expedition to which he gave his life, Magellan reaped only fame. Killed when performing the last of many gallant acts, his remains lie in an unmarked grave, or were scattered to the winds near where he fell.

Of the three greatest navigators in the age of discovery—Columbus, Magellan, and Vasco da Gama—Magellan stands supreme. Gama first reached India, pushing the voyage of Dias to its logical conclusion. Columbus, with the boldest concept, broke the Atlantic barrier once and for all, and crossed the Western Ocean and back four times, but in its kindest zone. Magellan, however, conquered the tempestuous southern waters and overcame mutiny, starvation and treachery to cross the Pacific Ocean, which he named. Elcano, to be sure, finished the circumnavigation, but he was only carrying out Magellan's plan.

Magellan's real monument is the Strait that he opened to the world:

> Forever sacred to the hero's fame,
> Those foaming straits shall bear his deathless name.

Bibliography and Notes

Elcano is the only shipmate of Magellan to be the subject of a biography in English: Mairin Mitchell, *Elcano: The First Circumnavigator* (London, 1958). The best of those in Spanish is Eustaquio Fernandez de Navarrete, *Historia de Juan Sebastián del Cano* (Vitoria, 1872). See also J. T. Medina, *Descubrimiento del Océano Pacífico*, III, chap. xvi, No. 47. His last name is spelled many different ways; I have chosen *Elcano* on the advice of Don G. M. de Zúñiga, curator of the Museo Municipal de San Telmo, San Sebastián. See his article "Elcano y no Cano" in *Revue Internationale des Études Basques*, XVIII (1927), 302–4.

Trinidad's final voyage. The principal source is the examination of Gómez de Espinosa, Cristóbal de Haro, and Ginés de Mafra at Vallodolid in May 1527 printed in Medina, *Colección de Documentos Inéditos para la Historia de Chile*, I, 124–53. Captain Brito's account to his king, based on *Trinidad's* impounded documents, was first printed in Navarrete, IV, 305–11; translation in notes to Robertson ed., II, 217–18. Ginés de Mafra's account, translated in Stanley, pp. 24–29, tallies closely with Brito's. Medina, *Descub. del Océano Pacífico*, III, chap. xvi, Nos. 36 and 225, and note 16 to same, contains all that is known of Gómez de Espinosa's later life.

Products of Timor. Robertson ed., II, 163–67, 225–27. My old friend Rui Cinatti, poet, agronomic engineer, and colonial administrator, has published *Useful Plants in Portuguese Timor* (Coimbra, 1964) in which (p. 7) he identifies and gives the Latin name of everything mentioned by Pigafetta. Maize and potatoes were introduced later. He also has written *Esboço Histórico de Sândalo no Timor Português* (Lisbon, 1950), and *Brevíssimo Tratado da Província de Timor* (Lisbon, n.d.); both well illustrated.

The palang. Robertson ed., II, 168–69 and 230; cf. note to Chap. XIV, above. Duarte Barbosa had already told of this variation of the practice in Pegu and Burma, in his *Description of the Coasts of East Africa and Malabar* (Hakluyt Society No. XXXV, London, 1866). Urdaneta told about its existence in the Celebes to Oviedo, who records it in his *Historia General y Natural*, lib. XX, chap. xxxv (1852 ed., II, 105). Camoëns mentions it in *Lusiads* X, 122.

Amsterdam Island. Albo (Stanley, p. 233) says they sighted it 18 March at latitude 37°35′ S, only 15 miles south of the island's true position. His log of this stretch of the voyage, plotted by a German navigator for Medina's *Descubrimiento*, III (but not in every copy), shows that *Victoria* did not lie-to for weeks, as several historians, and Elcano's biographers, have stated.

Victoria in Africa. Robertson's conjecture that her place of call was Great Fish River (named by the Portuguese *Rio do Infante*), is challenged by my friend Professor Eric Axelson of Cape Town University, who knows that coast intimately. Every river there has a bar at the mouth and cannot be entered. He conjectures that *Victoria* made her call at Mossel Bay or Port Elizabeth. But may she not have anchored outside the bar at Great Fish River?

Victoria at Santiago. A different version is that a sailor, buying liquor with cloves, gave away her secret; but as Elcano at Seville had to account for 300 arrobas of cloves "lost" at Santiago, it would seem that his desire to help his crew with slave labor caused the leak. That is what Maximilianus says; and he talked with Elcano. For the Azores part of the voyage, see Albo in Navarrete, IV, 242–43, as this part of Albo is left out by Stanley.

Survivors from the Magellan voyage. Sir Clements Markham prints a complete list of survivors in *Early Spanish Voyages to the Strait of Magellan* (Hakluyt Society, London, 1911), pp. 25–27, but does not fully agree with the list in Navarrete's Vol. IV. No two people will make the same count, but here is my effort.

Total in expedition, including the 25 shipped at the Canaries, and the boy who joined at Rio	266
Of these, 55, more or less, were executed at San Julián or returned to Spain in *San Antonio*. This left to go through the Strait into the Pacific	211
Christians who finished the voyage in *Victoria*	18
Survivors of 15 Indonesians who joined *Victoria* at Tidore	3
Victoria's boat crew, abandoned at Santiago but later returned to Spain	13
Of *Trinidad's* crew of 53, there eventually returned to Spain	5
Total survivors of the Pacific part of the voyage	39
Total lost in the Pacific, including 12 Indonesians	184

The shrine in Seville. Santa Maria de la Victoria no longer exists as a church, but the Virgin of Victory is now in the nearby Church of Santa Ana. The victory she commemorated on 8 September was the Christian reconquest of Malaga from the Moors a few years earlier. She was removed to the Minorite Convent of San Francisco de Paula erected in Triana in 1576 and demolished in 1868, when she was transferred to Santa Ana. At that time the image was stripped of all dresses and ornaments down to bare wood; a photo of it in that state is in Pablo Pastells, *Descubrimiento del Estrecho de Magallanes* (Madrid, 1920), p. 83. But the Franco regime has since clothed the Christ Child in a pair of pants. *Boletín* de la Real Academia Sevillana de Buenos Libros, No. 69 (1944). Santa Maria de l'Antigua, in the Cathedral, is the painting (there ascribed to St. Luke) for which Columbus named Antigua in the West Indies.

Elcano's and Espinosa's arms. Elcano's blazon and achievements are in Guillemard, pp. 307n and 308, and in *Nobiliario de Conquistadores de Indias* (Madrid, 1892), p. 57 and plate XLI (this with unauthorized complications). Espinosa's blazon is in *Nobiliario*, p. 187 (wrongly dated 1522, should be 1527), and achievement on plate XLIII. J. G. Kohl well said (*Geschichte . . . zur Magellan's-Strasse*, p. 35) that Elcano's was "the most magnificent coat of arms ever conferred."

Pigafetta a Turk? My friend C. R. Boxer sends me the following reference to Pigafetta's becoming a Turk: Fr. G. Schwamner, *Gesammelte Studien*, II, *Orientalia* (Rome and Lisbon, 1963), pp. 455–61. A survivor of Magellan's fleet certainly joined the forces of the Turkish admiral Piri Re'is, author of the famous map, and Schwamner argued that this must have been Pigafetta, the only survivor who could have been of use to the Turks. But why not Pilot Albo, who disappears from Spain in 1524? Existing evidence indicates that Pigafetta settled down in Italy, enjoying his reputation as a raconteur and becoming a knight of Malta. He had no possible reason to defect; but Albo, a Greek, very possibly was ill treated in Spain. See bibliographies in appendixes to Robertson and Yale eds. of Pigafetta; for Albo, see Medina, *Descubrimiento*, III, No. 7.

Victoria's cargo is listed in Navarrete, IV, 247–48; calculations in Guillemard, p. 310. Pierre Chaunu, in his *Séville*, II, 134–36, lists a *Vitoria* clearing for the West Indies in 1523, and another as one of 53 vessels outbound in 1525, which never returned.

"Forever sacred" is from Sir Richard Burton's translation of Camoëns's *Lusiads*, x, 141.

The early Spanish historian López de Gómara, in his chapter 98, remarked that the travails of Ulysses were nothing in comparison with Elcano's in *Victoria*, which should have been preserved forever in the arsenal of Seville.

For other survivors of the voyage, see J. T. Medina, *El Descubrimiento del Océano Pacífico*, III (Santiago, 1920), especially Nos. 3, 47, 106, 107, and 212, and his one-volume *Descubrimiento . . . Documentos* (1920).

Magellan's finances. Medina prints some of Haro's accounts in *Descub. del Océano Pacífico* (1920), doc. LXVI, pp. 195–97. Magellan's salary was 8000 maravedis per month. He was paid six months' advance at Seville in 1519, but there is no record of Magellan's heirs having been paid the 116,533 maravedis due for the rest of his salary. The crown, however, repaid Haro 27,690 maravedis which he had advanced to Magellan at Sanlúcar before starting.

Appendix

ELCANO'S REPORT

At Sanlúcar on September 1522 Elcano made his report to the Emperor,* which for brevity and simplicity is comparable to Columbus's Letter to the Sovereigns:

> Most high and illustrious Majesty:
>
> Your high Majesty will learn how we eighteen men only have returned with one of the five ships which Your Majesty sent to discover the Spicery with Captain Ferdinand Magellan (to whom glory); and so that Your Majesty may have news of the principal things which we have passed through, I write and say briefly this:—
>
> First, we reached 54° S of the Equator where we found a Strait which passed through Your Majesty's mainland to the Sea of India, which Strait is of 100 leagues and from which we debouched; and, in the time of three months and twenty days, encountering highly favoring winds, and finding no land save two small and uninhabited islands; afterwards we reached an archipelago of many islands quite abundant in gold. We lost by his death the said Captain Ferdinand Magellan, with many others, and unable to sail for want of people, very few having survived, we dismantled one of the ships and with the two remaining sailed from island to island, seeking how to arrive, with God's grace, at the Isles of Maluco, which we did eight months after the death of the said Captain; and there we loaded the two ships with spicery. Your Majesty should know how, navigating towards the said Isles of Maluco, we found cloves, cinnamon and pearls.
>
> Wishing to leave the said Isles of Maluco for returning to Spain, there was found a very big leak in one of the ships, in such wise that it could not be repaired without unloading; and the season having passed in which ships navigate to Zabba and

* José T, Medina, *Magallanes y sus Compañeros* (1920), pp. 289–94. Señor Obregón corrected my translation.

Melua, we resolved either to die, or honorably to serve Your Majesty by informing him of the said discovery, to depart with one ship only, and she in such a [bad] state, because of the teredos, which only God knows; on this course we discovered many very rich islands, among them Banda, where ginger and the nutmeg grow, and Zabba, where pepper grows, and Timor, where sandalwood grows, and in all the aforesaid islands there is an infinite amount of ginger. The proof of all these productions gathered in the same islands in which they grow, we bring to display to Your Majesty.

The [treaties of] peace and amity of all the kings and lords of the said islands, signed by their own hands, we bring to Your Majesty, for they desire to serve and obey you as their king and natural sovereign.[*]

Having departed the last of these islands, in five months, without eating anything but wheat[*] and rice and drinking only water, we touched at no land for fear of the King of Portugal, who had given orders in all his dominions to capture this armada, to the end that Your Majesty obtain no information about it; and thus there died of famine among us twenty-two men; for which, and the lack of victuals, we arrived at the islands of Cape Verde, whose governor seized my boat with thirteen men, and sought to throw me and all my men into a ship which was sailing from Calicut to Portugal charged with spicery, saying that only the King of Portugal could discover spicery; and to this intent equipped four ships to seize me; but we resolved, with common accord, to die before falling into the hands of the Portuguese. And so with very great labor at the pumps, which we had to work day and night to free her of water, and as exhausted as any man ever was, with the aid of God and of Our Lady, and after the passage of three years, we have arrived.

So I beg Your Majesty that he procure from the King of Portugal the liberty of those thirteen men, who for so long a time have served you; and Your Majesty will know best that what we should esteem and admire most is that we have discovered and made a course around the entire rotundity of the world—that going by the occident we have returned by the orient.

I beg Your Majesty, in view of the many travails, sweats,

[*] An abstract of these treaties, by Elcano himself, has been found by Señora Kathleen Romoli Aveng, Colombian historian, in the Archives of the Indies, legajo 1525, Indiferente general, toward the end of the legajo.

[*] Wheat was extensively grown in the Far East in 1521. See Rui Cinatti's *Useful Plants in Portuguese Timor.*

famine and thirst, cold and heat, that these people have endured in the service of Your Majesty, to give us grace for the fourth and the twentieth * of their property and of what they brought with them. And with this I close, kissing the feet and hands of Your high Majesty.

Written on board the ship *Victoria*, in Sanlúcar, on the 6th day of September of 1522.

The Captain
JUAN SEBASTIAN DEL CANO

---

* The usual customs duties and royal share of profits, which but for the king's grace the men would have had to pay on their personal packets of spices.

✲ XX ✲

Spain's Follow-up to Magellan

1525-1565

The Organs of Spanish Maritime Control

Despite his long absences abroad, Charles V managed to keep in touch with American affairs through establishing a special Council for the Indies resident at Seville. Set up by the young king in 1517, it consisted of seven members with Bishop Fonseca as chairman; he was succeeded in 1521 by García de Loaysa, general of the Dominican order and the king's adviser. One of Loaysa's first acts was to give his brother command of an expedition to follow up Magellan. This council of eight members (exclusive of secretaries, attorneys, etc.) met twice daily to discuss colonial business. The Council for the Indies drafted all laws for the colonies, nominated all civil officers and bishops overseas, and served as a final court of appeal on judicial matters. The king signed its more important edicts.

The Casa de Contratación (Board of Trade), also appointed by the king, served as clearing house for all overseas matters and controlled piloting and cartography. This board, organized in 1524 but informally existing as early as 1503, consisted of a president, three other judges, and a growing body of subordinates, of which the most important was the *piloto mayor*. That office was always filled by a veteran navigator (or one who claimed to be such), as Amerigo Vespucci, Sebastian

474

Cabot, and Juan de Solis. The piloto mayor examined and licensed pilots for overseas voyages and tried to keep up to date a *padrón real*, or official map of the world, of which every captain bound for the Indies was supposed to have a copy. Historians have combed the archives in vain for a padrón real; the old ones seem to have been destroyed as soon as a new one was made. Certain world maps, such as Diego Ribero's of 1529, may have been copied from the padrón real, but one cannot prove it. In 1552 the Casa set up a chair of geography and navigation, whose professor gave courses which candidates for a pilot's license were supposed to pass. Later, in the reign of Philip II, the Casa required every captain and pilot to keep a log of his voyage, with a description of weather encountered and coasts seen, and to deposit a copy with them. Portugal, but no other country, had a similar system for regulating voyages and ruling overseas possessions; Englishmen such as Richard Hakluyt openly admired the Spanish regulations for training pilots.

Loaysa's Expedition, 1525–1536

Victoria arrived home in September 1522, but it took the Emperor about three years to follow up her outstanding voyage. Captain Elcano, in the meantime, gave himself a good time, spending in advance most of his pension, which was never paid until after his death. Judging from the shipboard inventory attached to his will, the Captain bought himself a complete outfit of new clothes, including six pair of shoes, 19 shirts and numerous jerkins, jackets, hats, caps, and other gentlemen's apparel; also a complete set of pots and pans for the galley, a book by Andrés de San Martín called *Astrológía*, a sphere, and a "Latin Almanac." All in preparation for another voyage. For present pleasure he acquired a mistress at Valladolid who bore him a daughter, and another at San Sebastián, who bore him a son named Domingo. This two-timing so enraged the men of one family that they threatened to beat him up, and Juan Sebastián found it expedient to hire an armed bodyguard.

Charles V seems to have been satisfied with Elcano's explanation of his part in the mutiny at San Julián, and pardoned him for having sold a government ship on a voyage prior to Magellan's. Encouraged by royal favor, Elcano petitioned to be made captain general of the next expedition to the Spice Islands, to command a fortress to be built there, for financial assistance to several poor relations, and for permission to wear the habit of the Order of Santiago. The king-emperor, who seems by this time to have become impatient with the circumnavigator's importunity, granted him none of these. It did seem rather hard that both Magellan and Faleiro had been created *comendadores* (knights commander) of the Order of Santiago, and not Elcano; but neither had Columbus made this grade. The Emperor replied evasively that only the knights could elect him and they, having no hint from the crown, never did.

Command of the next expedition went to a soldier, Francisco García Jofre de Loaysa, brother or near relation to two bishops, one the Emperor's confidential adviser García de Loaysa, bishop of Osma. He had served as officer in the imperial army and been named a comendador of the Order of Santiago. No wonder that Elcano refers to this captain general in his will as the "Muy Magnífico Señor Comendador Loaysa." Here is another instance of the Emperor's laissez-faire attitude toward his overseas empire. If anyone wished to enlarge the Spanish dominion overseas, he might do so at his own expense, but on condition that important commands be conferred on relatives of influential people, even though they lacked experience at sea. In this instance Charles V did appoint the highly experienced Juan Sebastián de Elcano second in command, chief pilot, and successor to Loaysa in case of the latter's death. This meant that Elcano practically ran the expedition while he lived.

In the meantime, a sincere attempt was made by the kings of Spain and Portugal to settle the question of sovereignty over the Moluccas. A congress of supposed experts met and organized on neutral territory, the bridge over the Guadiana River. The bridge proved to be so uncomfortable for a conference that it adjourned alternately to the two opposite frontier towns of Badajoz and Elvas. The mission of this Badajoz Conference, as it was generally called, was to decide where the Line of Demarcation, described in the Treaty of Tordesillas as 370 leagues west of the Cape Verde Islands, would lie if run through the poles around the world, a task altogether beyond the abilities of contemporary cosmographers. Many notables attended: Elcano, who contributed a brief of the Spanish case, Sebastian Cabot, Diego Ribero the mapmaker, Amerigo Vespucci's brother Giovanni, and Ferdinand Columbus. They accomplished nothing; in the general ignorance about longitude, no agreement could be reached.

Francisco López de Gómara, who found it amusing to enliven a rather poky subject with an off-color anecdote, told how the vulgar act of a little boy amused this pompous assembly. The Portuguese delegates en route to the conference were passing over the River Guadiana at a spot where a peasant woman had laid out her laundry to dry. Her little boy, who had been ordered to watch the clothes, asked the very magnificent Diogo Lopes de Sequeira, former Governor of India, whether they were coming to divide the world with the Emperor? He answered with a curt nod that they were. The kid then pulled up his shirt, displayed his bare behind, and drew his finger between the buttocks saying, "Draw your line right through this place!" The Portuguese, outraged, wanted the boy to be arrested and whipped, but the story got around and everyone else "turned it to a jest and laughed it off."

Where, then, should the Line have run? Stating the problem with Greenwich as the prime meridian, you start from Santo Antão in the Cape Verde Islands at latitude 17° N, longitude 25° W. A line measuring 370 leagues of 3.18 nautical miles each, west of Santo Antão, takes you to longitude 45°30′ W. This cuts across the bulge of Brazil, leaving the rest of the Americas to Castile. So far, very good for Spain. But if you run that Line of Demarcation across the poles and around the world, it becomes 134½° East longitude, which crosses the head of the New Guinea bird, leaving the Philippines, the Spice Islands, and almost all Indonesia on the Portuguese side; whilst Spain for her Pacific empire gets only the Marianas, the Palaus, and Micronesia. Since even after Magellan's voyage nobody knew exactly the width of the Pacific and no one could match a given longitude with a particular place on the earth's surface, each side left the Badajoz Congress claiming everything and conceding nothing. Diplomacy having failed, Charles V decided to plunge ahead and occupy the Spice Islands; but he little knew how strong were the Portuguese already there.

This Second Armada de Molucca, the official name of Loaysa's expedition, was financed by the firm of J. Fucar & Sobrinos to the amount of 10,000 gold ducats (2,570,000 maravedis), and four other persons contributed 4450 ducats. Planning for the expedition began in 1523, and it finally got off in the summer of 1525. Here is an abbreviated task organization:

Captain General of the Fleet FRANCISCO GARCÍA JOFRE DE LOAYSA

SANTA MARIA DE LA VICTORIA, *nao* (ship) of 300 tuns
Captain: Loaysa, succeeded by Elcano and the pilot Martín Iñigues Carquisano and Fernando Torre, the alguacil. Master: Juan Huelva. Pilot: Martín de Uriarte.

SANCTI SPIRITUS, ship of 200 tuns
Captain, second in command to the Captain General, and Chief Pilot: Juan Sebastián de Elcano; salary, 400 ducats (same as Loaysa's), of which two-thirds was to be charged against the 500-ducat pension which he himself never received! All other captains were paid 133⅓ ducats a year. Treasurer: Hernando de Bustamente, another Magellan survivor. Andrés de Urdaneta, seventeen years old, shipped as Elcano's page; he later transferred to the flagship, and eventually became a famous navigator in his own right.

ANUNCIADA, ship of 170 tuns
Captain: Pedro de Vera, *continuo* (official) of the royal court.

SAN GABRIEL, ship of 130 tuns
Captain: Don Rodrigo de Acuña.*

SANTA MARIA DEL PARRAL,** caravel of 80 tuns
Captain: Jorge Manrique de Najero. Pilot: Juan de Benevides.

SANTO LESMES, caravel of 80 tuns
Captain: Francisco de Hojas (Hoces or Hozes).

SANTIAGO, *pataje* (pinnace) of 70 tuns
Captain: Santiago de Guevara (Elcano's brother-in-law).

Seven vessels in all, the first three bigger than any of Magellan's, and a good 450 men. Yet not one of these ships returned, excepting the

---

* Acuña, after a hassle with Guevara, was demoted by Loaysa off the coast of Africa and relieved as captain of *San Gabriel* by Martín de Valencia, who started as "capitán de las caravelas," apparently a sort of division commander, with 133⅓ ducats salary. Markham, *Early Spanish Voyages* (London, 1911), p. 42, and Medina, *Documentos Inéditos Para la Historia de Chile*, III, 346–47.
** Named after a new but already famous convent in Segovia.

little pinnace which got as far as Mexico. Two reached the East Indies, but their bones were left there and only eight men survived for the alguacil Fernando Torre to bring back to Spain in 1536. Fortunately for history, among them were Andrés de Urdaneta, who wrote an excellent detailed account of the expedition, and Martín de Uriarte, who compiled a *derrotero* (sailing directions) for the Strait.

The Casa de Contratación, in the king's name, issued detailed instructions in 53 articles, beginning with a hypocritical "on no pretext was the Captain General to discover or touch at land within the limits of Portugal." Nevertheless, Loaysa should establish a trading factory in the Moluccas, build a fort, moor the three smallest vessels there with a garrison, and load the big ships with cloves and other spices. One odd article forbids the sailors "wrong doing with the women slaves lest a rebellion be raised"; and another promises all hands "full liberty to write home."

Elcano, as chief pilot, showed a singular disregard for the lessons of Magellan's voyage. The fleet sailed from Corunna on the vigil of the feast of St. James the Apostle, a day chosen for good luck; and on 14 August 1525 took its departure from Gomera in the Canaries. Rounding Cape Palmas and traversing the entire Gulf of Guinea, they raised an island off Gabon which they named San Mateo. This has been identified as Anobón in latitude 1°30' S, longitude 5°40' E. There they tarried ten days and topped off with fresh provisions. Elcano had criticized Magellan for standing too far east along the African coast before crossing the Atlantic Narrows to Brazil, but he piloted Loaysa's fleet several hundred miles farther (Anobón is only 180 miles west of Cape López). According to the wind-roses on the modern Pilot Chart of the South Atlantic, a sailing vessel would ordinarily require a 50-mile beat to windward from Anobón to cross the northern limits of the southeast trade wind, as against a 20-mile beat from Cape Palmas. They departed that island 31 October 1525 and sighted the coast of Brazil 4 December, fairly good time for the short but calm-cursed passage from Africa to America.

Their Brazilian landfall, recorded Urdaneta, was *los bajos de los Parbos*, identified as the modern Banco S. Tomé off the cape of that name, at latitude 22° S. From here on we have no record of their coastal course until, after passing the River Plate estuary, they ran into a storm in which *Santa Maria de la Victoria* and *San Gabriel* became separated from the rest off Rio Santa Cruz at 50° S. Elcano, taking the lead in *Sancti Spiritus*, persuaded *Anunciada*, the two caravels, and the pinnace to press on to the Strait lest they miss the summer season. For the two missing ships he left a message under a cross at Santa Cruz.

Then began a series of mishaps and disasters. Elcano mistook Cabo Buen Tiempo, the northern entrance to Rio Gallegos, for Cabo Vírgenes. Many later navigators have done likewise; even a recent authority, Findlay, warns mariners against making the same mistake. Upon ascertaining his error, Elcano led all five vessels on to the real Strait, and all but *Santiago* arrived at the Cape of the Eleven Thousand Virgins on 24 January 1526, six months out from Spain. Once inside, in Bahia Felipe between the two Narrows, a furious southerly gale caused *Sancti Spiritus* to drag her anchors and drive broadside onto the beach, where she broke up. Elcano and his page, Urdaneta the chronicler, now went on board *Anunciada*, Pedro de Vera's ship. A westerly gale then sprang up and blew *Anunciada* out to sea. Eventually she returned; and while her people were engaged in salvaging gear from *Sancti Spiritus*, the missing flagship, *San Gabriel*, and the little pinnace sailed in, to everyone's delight. The captain of *San Gabriel* ratted, like Gómez of Magellan's fleet, and sailed for Spain, but foundered somewhere off the coast of Brazil. A few men survived to be picked up years later by Sebastian Cabot.

A second westerly gale now made up. The two caravels *Parral* and *Lesmes* were blown out of the Strait and away down to latitude 55° S, where they claimed to have seen "the end of the land"; this may well have been the eastern end of Staten Island at 54°50′ S. *Anunciada* had no time to secure her boat or weigh anchors before the gale sent her roaring out to sea; nobody ever heard of her again, and there were no survivors. Elcano and Urdaneta had the good fortune to be ashore, salvaging gear from *Sancti Spiritus*, when this big wind hit the fleet. *Santa Maria de la Victoria* dragged all five anchors, struck several times, and grounded; but they managed to float her off, and on 17 February 1526 sailed her back into Rio Santa Cruz for repairs. There the people enjoyed killing *lobos marinos* (elephant seals) and *patos sin alas* (wingless ducks, i.e. penguins). By the time the flagship's repairs were completed, it was the last week of March and the Antarctic summer of 1526 had flown.

The armada, now consisting of *Santa Maria de la Victoria* (with both Loaysa and Elcano on board), the two caravels, and the pinnace, rounded Cape Virgins and Cape Dungeness on 5 April for their final and successful attempt to sail through the Strait of Magellan. It took them about seven weeks. Martín de Uriarte had time to write a *derrotero* (sailing directions) for the Strait, which he took back to Spain. It was grossly inaccurate, recommending several harbors that had neither holding ground nor protection, and describing others that nobody can identify; but no better mariners' guide was available until the next century.

From Bahia Felipe let us follow Uriarte's sailing directions. Starting 8 April, they "entered the first strait and passed through it in nine hours." A west-southwest course took them through the Second Narrows. Thence, he says, you make for the little island (now Santa Maria); leave it to port unless you choose to anchor behind the big island (Isabel) in a bay he calls *La Concepción* (the modern Paso Real).

Turning into Paso Ancho (Broad Reach), says Uriarte, "You will see a lofty mountain high in the center . . . forming four peaks, like the teeth of a French saw." A very apt description of the mountains of Dawson Island, and those rising to the southward, all prominent on a clear day as you enter Broad Reach. The site of Punta Arenas he did not notice, but he observed Mount Tarn and Cape San Isidro, "like the snout of a tunny. . . . Here is the entrance to the snowy [part of] the Strait." You must now whip around the southernmost point of the mainland (Cape Froward) instead of sailing into the dead-end Seno Magdalena. "You will then be in sight of Puerto Sardina." That name recalls Magellan's River of Sardines which we have identified as Bahia Fortescue, but Uriarte mistook its location, describing it as a mere beach, "a wretched place to be at," and returned to Bahia George (Urdaneta's San Jorge), where they took on wood and water and effected some repairs to the flagship. There a fire broke out on board the flagship; Loaysa took charge, stopped a panic, and vigorously quenched the fire. We are grateful for this evidence of the Captain General's strong, decisive personality.

On 25 April, with the boon of a light easterly wind, the fleet sailed from Bahia George and spent the next night off the southern shore of what Uriarte calls Buen Puerto. That must have been Ensenada Nash, identified by small islands at the entrance and a snug harbor in-

The Strait of Magellan. Approaching Mount Tarn and Cape Froward.
James F. Nields photo.

Passing Carlos III Island. James F. Nields photo.

Paso Cordova, a typical Strait harbor. James F. Nields photo.

side. The local Indians resented their presence, uttered blood-curdling cries, and flourished torches from their canoes, but dared not attack. Between this misnamed "Fair Harbor" and the opposite shore are four islands, one large (Carlos III) and three small (Charles, Rupert, and Monmouth), their names reflecting Sir John Narborough's devotion to the House of Stuart. From here on, says Uriarte, you favor the northern shore of the Strait and pass eleven islands.

Departing Ensenada Nash, the fleet, baffled by the strong tidal currents where Canal Jerónimo flows into the main Strait, anchored between "two large islands, named San Pedro and San Pablo. . . . A league beyond are two small islands, and a league further on is a wonderful port called San Juan Portalatina." This must have been Swallow Bay, for which the landmark is a great cascade which falls directly from a nearby mountain into the harbor. But, says the modern Chilean *Derrotero*, "The bottom is all rocky, so we can't recommend it." It snowed all the time Loaysa's fleet was there, and "no clothes could keep us warm," and in addition the lice were hungry and innumerable and the stench below almost insupportable.

After a short sail across the Strait, they entered "a very good harbor called *Puerto de la Ascensión*," for which Uriarte gives detailed sailing directions. It is now Bahia Guiror, a landlocked harbor where kelp has usurped almost all the good holding ground. Head winds now forced the fleet back to San Juan Portalatina. They arrived 10 May, departed the 14th, and next day anchored in Puerto de Mayo, not identified. It cannot have been much of a harbor, as Uriarte warns ships to anchor outside. But this neck of the Strait is full of tiny "gunk holes" which any exploring yacht might enjoy, provided she has plenty of ground tackle, and power. Oh to be forty again!

Uriarte noted on the starboard hand Golfo Xaultegua, which leads by the half-mile-wide Canal Gajardo to Canal Euston and Seno Skyring, whence you may proceed by the even narrower Channel Fitz-Roy to the great gulf of Seno Otway and back to the Strait by Canal Jerónimo. If you ever care to try it, you will find this a spectacular 150-mile sail.

They sailed from Puerto Mayo 25 May with a nice beam wind, and next morning arrived off Cabo Deseado (now Cabo Pilar), the Pacific entrance to the Strait. On Saturday, 26 May 1526, the eve of Trinity Sunday, they happily sortied from the Strait with a fair southeast

Western end of the Strait. A summer day, February 1972.

Canal that Loaysa avoided.

Pacific coast of Desolation Island with four capes and Twelve Apostles Rocks.

wind. Their passage lasted forty-eight days, if you count only the final attempt; but it was four months and a half since they had first raised Cabo Vírgenes. Although Elcano had already been through in *Victoria*, it would not be fair to blame him for all these contretemps; the weather treated the Loaysa armada far worse than it did Magellan's, and Loaysa made his passage in the Antarctic winter.

The fleet now consisted of *Santa Maria de la Victoria*, caravels *Parral* and *Lesmes*, and pinnace *Santiago*. Presently they were scattered by a severe storm "and never saw each other again," says Urdaneta. The flagship leaked badly, and with the need to feed the shipwrecked crew of *Sancti Spiritus*, their rations fell short. Caravel *Lesmes* simply disappeared; *Parral* crossed the Pacific alone (as we shall see later) and came to grief near the Spice Islands. Little *Santiago*, after sailing for fifty days, made Tehuantepec on the west coast of Mexico on 20 July 1526, provisions expended and her only boat lost. Captain Guevara, sighting an Indian village, tried to float ashore on a crate his chaplain, Fr. Juan de Arreizaga (dressed only in a shirt and drawers), carrying small wares such as scissors and mirrors for the natives. The crate capsized and the chaplain swam ashore clutching his trading truck, but he fell into friendly hands. A neighboring cacique entertained him and sent Indians on board with loads of food. This amphibious chaplain went on to Mexico City where he met Cortés and persuaded him to send succor to Loaysa in the Spice Islands. He intended to include *Santiago* in his relief squadron, but she was too shaky to leave Mexico for a trans-Pacific voyage.

On 30 July 1526 when the flagship, overcrowded with 120 men, lay wallowing in mid-Pacific around latitude 15° N, Captain General Loaysa died. The crew were suffering terribly from scurvy, but we are not told what he died of, except that part of it was constipation, for which in vain they tried an heroic remedy in the shape of broiled rat. As the king had ordered, the chaplain promptly swore in Juan Sebastián de Elcano as Captain General. But that stout Basque, too, was already on his way to Tom Tiddler's ground. He barely had time to dictate a long and elaborate last will and testament, when he too died, on 6 August 1526. Elcano left 100 ducats to the mother of his son, and "for discharge of my conscience," 50 ducats to the mother of his daughter, together with 400 ducats for her marriage portion. There are small legacies to the Church of San Salvador, Guetaria, where his ancestors were buried and where he wished his anniversary to be observed, and to ten or twelve other churches and hospitals in the Basque country, as well as to Santa Maria de Guadalupe. His clothes and other effects he left to surviving shipmates and to a brother. In the will he observes that all money legacies would be paid out of the thousand ducats' pension that the king still owed him when he sailed. Were they ever paid? We wonder.

As the third Captain General of this unfortunate fleet, the surviving officers elected pilot Martín Iñiguez Carquisano. *Santa Maria* still had 116 live men on board, but Urdaneta tells us that she and they were in sad straits. "The people were so worn out from much work at the pumps, the violence of the sea, the insufficiency of food, and illness, that some died every day." But they made Guam and there, as the Chamorros made no trouble, picked up plenty of fresh food as well as one of three sailors who had deserted Gómez de Espinosa's *Trinidad*.

Santa Maria de la Victoria, encountering variable winds, took 22 days (10 September–2 October 1526) to sail from Guam to a port on the east coast of Mindanao. There the people refused to sell them food; but at the Talaud Islands they obtained all they wanted, and after a stay of two weeks, sailed for the Spice Islands. "We were 105 people, 40 more having died during the voyage from the Strait," recorded Urdaneta, an even worse health record than Elcano's or Magellan's. Calms and variables prevented their making the next port of call, Morotai off the northern coast of Jilolo (Halmahera), until 6 November. There, through a Portuguese beachcomber, they heard the latest news of fighting in that part of the world. Tidore had been severely punished by the Portuguese for being friendly to Elcano and Gómez de Espinosa. The sultan of Jilolo, delighted to welcome a big armed ship full of Spaniards, sent a messenger with Urdaneta to the ruler of Tidore, then a refugee in the mountains, to say that happy days were here again. Presently word arrived from the Portuguese commander of the Ternate fort ordering *Santa Maria de la Victoria* to get out quick or be sent to the bottom with all hands. Captain Carquisano, in reply, declared that the Spice Islands belonged to His Catholic Majesty of Spain, and to hell with the Portuguese!

Unfortunately the fort captain was not bluffing. When the Spanish ship sailed to Tidore on 29 December 1526, a small Portuguese fleet threatened her but dared not fire when the commander saw what great guns the Spaniards mounted. Not long after, on 12 January 1527, when her sailors were being entertained at Tidore, *Santa Maria de la Victoria* was jumped by a bigger Portuguese fleet. They blazed away at each other intermittently for several days, and although *Santa Maria* drove the enemy off, she was so damaged that the Portuguese came back, captured her, and stripped her of guns, gear, and cargo of copper, iron, hollands, and woolens. With nothing of value left, the once proud flagship's crew burned her to the water's edge and shifted for themselves ashore.

So began a war between the Spaniards, with Tidore and Jilolo as allies, and the Portuguese allied with Ternate and other Spice Islands. Martín Iñiguez Carquisano was killed in July by poison treacherously administered by a Portuguese captain in a supposed cup of peace. Urdaneta wrote of this captain general, "He was a very clever and courageous man, feared as much by Christians as by Indians."

Fernando Torre, formerly commander of the flagship's men-at-arms, now became the fourth Captain General. He with a hundred stout fellows under his command still constituted a threat to the Portuguese; especially as he was building on Jilolo a new ship, a sailing vessel with seventeen sweeps. A Portuguese spy tried unsuccessfully to blow up this vessel, but the Spaniards, with native help, completed her by the end of 1527.

Charles V, if we read his mind aright, began to doubt whether more glory should be sought in the Far East, at the expense of a perpetual quarrel with Portugal. And he was about to cement his friendly relations with João III by marrying the Portuguese king's sister the Infanta Isabel, a charming young princess with whom he fell deeply in love. Also, as the years passed, it became more and more evident that Mexico and Peru, conquered by Cortés and Pizarro, would be mines of wealth to Spain; so why waste money on the faraway Spice Islands?

Prior to this détente respecting the Moluccas came the Saavedra expedition, mounted in Mexico. In obedience to an imperial cédula of 20 June 1526, Hernán Cortés built three ships at Zacatula and gave the command to his kinsman Álvaro de Saavedra Cerón, lieutenant governor of Vera Cruz. His primary objective:—cross the Pacific and lend a hand to Loaysa, the news of whose death had not yet

Triremes or galiots, and fustas of the Javanese. Torre's fusta presumably looked like the big one. From DeBry, *Collectiones . . . in Indiam Orientalem*, Part 2. Courtesy Harvard College Library.

reached Spain or Mexico. Little *Santiago*, whose arrival at Tehuantepec we have already noted, should have been one of the fleet, but a survey revealed her to be unfit for a cross-Pacific voyage, and a new *Santiago* with a crew of 45 and a new captain took her place. A 15- to 28-tun bergantina named *Espíritu Santo*, and a new, locally built caravel *Florida* with a crew of twelve and a landing force of thirty-eight, completed this fleet. It was well equipped and loaded with trading goods; the Viceroy claimed to have laid out 60,000 gold pesos on getting it to sea, and he provided Saavedra with as many letters of introduction to Oriental potentates as Columbus ever carried, besides one to Sebastian Cabot, news of whose change of destination (see Chapter XXII) had not reached Mexico. After a shakedown cruise to the Bay of Santiago north of Manzanilla, the little fleet sailed from Zihuantanejo, a few miles south of Zacatula on the west coast of Mexico, 31 October 1527.

Saavedra's voyage was unfortunate from the start. Two weeks out, *Florida* began leaking so badly that 30 hundredweight of provisions, enough to feed her crew for 50 days, were jettisoned to lighten her. Her crew grew so weak from constant pumping (landsmen can never appreciate how that takes it out of a sailor, especially when he never gets ahead of the leak), that they had to be relieved by men from *Santiago* and *Espíritu Santo*, standing by. The captains of the smaller vessels urged the Captain General to abandon *Florida* but he replied, "In that ship he had to be lost or saved." His stout spirit, like Sir Humfry Gilbert's in the *Squirrel*, saved him then, for in a heavy squall on 4 December *Santiago* and *Espíritu Santo* disappeared and were never heard of again; whilst *Florida*, after taking a bad knock-down to her beams' ends, righted, and by quick, expert work, the men stopped her leak.

Florida sighted Guam 29 December but did not call. Saavedra apparently dared not follow Magellan's example and sail through an opening in the reef, and found no bottom outside. She spent the first week of January 1528 at one of the Palaus, and on 2 February she called at a small island off Mindanao. There she picked up a survivor from Loaysa's wrecked caravel *Santa Maria del Parral* and ransomed two more from the natives of Sarrangani. By mid-March, five months out from Mexico, *Florida* reached Halmahera (Jilolo), where Torre's men sighted her and cautiously approached by boat. They could hardly believe their eyes when they saw the Spanish flag, and made the crew swear by the Holy Rood that they really were Spanish, not disguised Portuguese! Joyfully they escorted her to Tidore, arriving 30 March. There *Florida* was warmly welcomed by Fernando Torre, especially for her reinforcements, her medicine chest, and munitions.

"From that time the war proceeded with much greater heat," wrote Urdaneta. By May 1528 Torre's fusta, newly built at Jilolo, had been launched, rigged, and armed with *Santa Maria de la Victoria*'s cannon. In a fight with a big Portuguese galley and fourteen Moorish rowing boats, the fusta captured the galley and triumphantly brought her into Tidore.

Saavedra hopefully began his return passage to Mexico on 12 June 1528, with 70 hundredweight of cloves in the hold and a few Portuguese passengers and prisoners. At an island north of New Guinea, two of the Portuguese seized one of *Florida*'s boats and sailed in her back to Tidore. Torre had them tried for mutiny and sentenced to death; one was executed the same day. No permissiveness in the Moluccas!

This local war continued for over a year, first one side and then the other prevailing. In a fluid situation treachery and defection changed the balance of power overnight. Saavedra's *Florida* sailed up to latitude 14° N, gave up hope of finding westerlies, and returned to Tidore 18 November 1528. Like Magellan's *Trinidad*, she had been unable to make any significant progress toward Mexico, but, after a complete replanking and other repairs, she left Tidore for a second attempt on 5 May 1528.

It does not appear that Saavedra invited the Spanish survivors of the Loaysa expedition to return with him; but had he done so, they certainly would have refused. Their situation did not seem desperate like that of early colonists in Canada or Raleigh's Virginia. The French and English, surrounded by menacing savages and unable to procure food without the Indians' help, were only too glad of a chance to scuttle and run, but Loaysa's men were in a civilized country with plenty of friends and supporters. Their king had ordered them to hold down the Spice Islands for Spain, and that they would do at the cost of everyone's life if necessary. Unfortunately, their king let them down badly. A few days before *Florida* sailed a second time from Tidore, hoping to make Mexico, Charles V ceded all his Spice Islands claims to Portugal.

The European situation probably explains this complete change of policy on the part of the Emperor. François-premier, after being beaten to his knees at Pavia in 1525, again was making trouble. Suleiman the Magnificent was about to lay siege to Vienna. Italy was slipping through the imperial fingers, and the Emperor had become virtually bankrupt trying to keep his empire together. But D. João III of Portugal, wisely abstaining from European power politics, had plenty of money from the spice trade. So, by the Treaty of Saragossa of 23 April 1529, Charles V renounced all his claims to the Spice Islands in favor of Portugal, for the neat sum of 350,000 gold ducats —about a million dollars in gold. It was a smart deal on the part of the Emperor; he really got something for nothing, since to enforce his claims to the Moluccas by the long Pacific Ocean route would have cost far more than they were worth. Moreover, nothing was said in the treaty about the Philippines. They remained free-for-all, from the European point of view, and Spain later moved in.

The survivors of the Loaysa expedition, fighting for their king-emperor at the very ends of the earth, continued to resist the Portuguese on Jilolo, until *Florida* returned (8 December 1529) after her second unsuccessful attempt to reach Mexico. Saavedra had died on board, and his successor turned back from latitude 31° N. *Florida's* crew of twenty-two beefed up to fifty-eight the number of fighting Spaniards present, but the ship herself was too played out to be of any further use, and her bones were added to those of *Trinidad* and *Santa Maria de la Victoria*.

Charles V might have insisted in his treaty that the Portuguese repatriate any Spaniards taken in the Moluccas; but, assuming that Saavedra would pick them up, he did nothing about them. Torre wisely negotiated a local peace treaty, and begged the Portuguese governor of India to help him to get home. By that time the survivors numbered only a little more than a score. They had neither shoes nor money, and were living in Jilolo largely on wild fruit which they gathered, and wild pig which they hunted. Urdaneta, who had a sporting streak in him, really enjoyed this interlude in the fighting.

A few more facts illustrate the vicissitudes of P.O.W.'s in the Far East. In October 1533 (more than four years after the treaty), the Portuguese governor of India, Nuno da Cunha, sent a ship to carry Spanish survivors home. She sailed from Tidore 15 February 1534 with most of the pitiful handful, including Torre; but Urdaneta and Uriarte stayed behind, hoping to collect a quantity of cloves they had already paid for. A year later, after securing a part of the cloves, they embarked in a Chinese junk. She called at the Banda Islands and Java, and arrived at Malacca at the end of July 1535. There, on 15 November, they boarded a junk for Cochin, where they found Torre and four other survivors. These seven men on 10 and 20 January 1536 sailed in two different vessels which rounded the Cape of Good Hope at the end of March and arrived at Lisbon 26 June 1536, more than two years after they had left the Spice Islands. The

Portuguese authorities relieved Urdaneta of all his books and papers, so that he had to rewrite from memory a valuable account of his adventures. He dated it upon his release at Valladolid 26 February 1537, eleven and a half years after Loaysa's proud fleet of seven sail had left Corunna. Every one of these ships, as well as the three that Cortés sent to their rescue, had been lost, together with Loaysa, Elcano, Saavedra, and several hundred men.

But it took more than that to discourage the Spaniards of those days.

Urdaneta's Achievements

Urdaneta, seventeen years old when he left Spain as Elcano's page and twenty-eight when he returned, still had a great career ahead of him; and his activities were the one benefit to Spain from the pompous and futile Loaysa expedition. Fortunately, Urdaneta's merit had always been recognized. In the Strait and in the Moluccas his superiors gave him the command of several boat expeditions; and whether the mission was logistic, diplomatic, or military, this teenager always performed it acceptably. In addition, he accumulated useful navigational data under Loaysa and Saavedra, and learned more than one native language. The Royal Council examined him on 4 September 1536 and were favorably impressed; the Emperor received him at Valladolid and presented him with a purse of 50 gold ducats as a reward for his faithful service.

In April 1539 Urdaneta went out to Mexico as an officer under Pedro de Alvaredo, governor of Guatemala, who had a license from the Emperor to explore and discover "Islands in the West." It speaks well for Spanish energy and know-how that they took apart Alvaredo's ten ships at Vera Cruz, had the parts carried by slaves across Mexico, and put them together again at the Pacific port of La Navidad; a process which made them "cost more than 50 ships in Seville," as Alvaredo admitted. Unfortunately, the planned western exploring expedition was diverted to helping the governor to put down an Indian rebellion. Alvaredo fell in that campaign, and the cross-Pacific plan was shelved, but in 1542 the new viceroy of Mexico, Antonio de Mendoza, entrusted the enterprise to his nephew Ruy López de Villalobos.

The Villalobos expedition of six ships and some 370 men crossed the Pacific in three months, discovering dozens of islands that Magellan and Loaysa had missed, and reached Mindanao at the end of January 1543. It was Villalobos who changed the name of the archipelago to *Las Islas Filipinas* after the Infante who became Philip II. The Portuguese having disputed his presence, Villalobos, largely for want of food, surrendered to them at Tidore. He died at Ambon, not before one of his ships, *San Juan de Letrán*, had twice tried to sail back to Mexico. The first time she got as far as Iwo Jima; and the second, to Papua. On both occasions, like *Trinidad* and *Florida*, foul winds forced her to turn back, and eventually she too surrendered to the Portuguese. They returned to Lisbon the survivors, including an intelligent Augustinian friar who later communicated to Urdaneta valuable data on the trade winds.

Urdaneta fortunately did not accompany Villalobos. In 1552, now forty-four years old, he became an Augustinian friar and joined a group engaged in converting the natives of Mexico. This, however, did not satisfy his love of adventure. Soon he had another chance to go to sea, since Philip II, determined to nail down the Philippine Islands for Spain, had been told that this friar was the most competent Pacific Ocean pilot living, and his best chance for finding westerly winds to sail from the archipelago to Mexico. On 24 September 1559, when the King ordered the viceroy of Mexico to organize a new Philippine expedition, he sent a personal letter to Urdaneta, commanding him, in view of his knowledge of the winds and currents gained in the Loaysa expedition, to ship as chief pilot. He accepted, although (as he wrote to Philip II), "I am now over fifty-two and in poor health, and owing to the hard labors of my earlier years the rest of my life was to have been spent in retirement." Being in holy orders he was disqualified for a naval officer's billet, so the post of Prior of the Armada was created for Urdaneta, and the king allowed him to nominate the Captain General. He chose Miguel López de Legazpi, fifty years old, who had spent more than half his life as a Spanish official in Mexico.

Legazpi's fleet (*San Pedro*, over 500 tuns, *San Pablo* over 300, three pinnaces, and a small *fragata* as tender to the flagship) sailed from La Navidad on the west coast of Mexico 21 November 1564 with about 350 men embarked. This Legazpi-Urdaneta voyage vitally affected the future of Mexico and California, as well as Spain.

The fleet reached Guam 23 January 1565, departed 3 February, and raised Samar ten days later. This was not so fast a passage as Magellan's, although Legazpi's ships were much bigger than his. Threading her way through Surigao Strait, the flagship made Cebu 27 April and found so hostile a reception before landing that she treated Homonhon's old capital to a few salvos of cannonballs. The natives, short of ordnance, promptly caved in. Legazpi issued a blanket pardon for the massacre of 1521; the people provided his men with food; and, under Urdaneta's supervision, built a chapel for the Santo Niño. Cebu became the first Spanish and Catholic colony in the Philippines, and the center of trade with Mexico until 1571, when Legazpi transferred his colonial capital to Manila.

No time was lost in preparing *San Pablo* to seek a way home. The nominal captain was Legazpi's seventeen-year-old grandson Felipe de Salcado, but it was understood that he take orders from the Prior. Urdaneta managed this eastward voyage very well. First, he saw to it that the ship was amply provisioned. Departing Cebu 1 June 1565, the southwest monsoon carried *San Pablo* to the Marianas in time to catch the summer westerlies in the North Pacific. She had passed out into the Philippine Sea by the narrow San Bernardino Strait north of Samar, itself a very ticklish bit of navigation. She sighted a small, rocky islet covered with birds on 21 June, sailed up to latitude 39°50′ N, and there hit the westerlies, which carried her homeward for almost three months without sighting land. On 18 September she made her first landfall, San Miguel Island on latitude 34° N, marking the entrance to the Santa Barbara Channel of California. Urdaneta persuaded the boy captain to sail on, and *San Pablo*, after calling at La Navidad on 1 October 1565, terminated her epoch-making voyage at the much better port of Acapulco. According to a recent calculation, she had logged 11,160 miles.

Urdaneta had done it—found the sailing route home from the Philippines, which was a necessary preliminary to making them profitable for Spain. In 1567 began the annual service of the Manila galleons from Acapulco, so well described in the book of that name by my old friend William L. Schurz. These ships sailed west approximately by Magellan's route, and, laden with tightly packed China goods, returned eastward by Urdaneta's route, so far north of the Hawaiian chain as never to sight that very conspicuous archipelago. They made landfall on Cape Mendocino or elsewhere in Upper California and followed the coast to Acapulco. This system lasted until 1815.

Urdaneta's ambition to return to the Philippines as a missionary was defeated by ill health, and by what in those days passed as old age. He died at Mexico City on 3 June 1568, aged sixty.

With Urdaneta's return to Acapulco, and Legazpi's shifting his capital to Manila in 1571, we conclude a cycle of voyages which began with Columbus's First in 1492. The discovery of a practicable all-ocean route between Spain and the Orient, and the exchange of wares between China and Spain via Manila, fulfilled the Admiral of the Ocean Sea's dream. For we should never forget that his primary, overriding objective was to set up a trading post somewhere off the coast of Cathay, which would serve not only as a mart between Orient and Occident, but as a center for the propagation of Christianity. That is what Legazpi and Urdaneta finally accomplished, sixty-five years after the death of the man who said, "Sail to the West and the East will be found."

Bibliography and Notes

THE EMPEROR CHARLES V AND SPANISH MARITIME CONTROL

On this highly interesting monarch, who held the keys to peace in Europe and to empire in America, there is an enormous literature, most of which ignores his American and Far Eastern policy. Exceptions are: (1) Roger B. Merriman, *The Rise of the Spanish Empire in the Old World and in the New*, Vol. III, *The Emperor* (New York, 1925), and Vol. IV, *Philip the Prudent* (1934). Not many of the thousands of Harvard students who reveled in the sprightly and stimulating lectures of "Frisky" Merriman (1876–1945) realized that he was also an excellent Spanish scholar. These last two volumes of his great work are the only history of Charles V's and Philip II's reigns which weave in events outside the European orbit; and they are superlatively well done; (2) my late colleague Clarence H. Haring's *Spanish Empire in America* (New York, 1947, 1952, 1963) is arranged topically and is no less scholarly and interesting; (3) my present esteemed colleague John H. Parry has written an excellent synthesis, *The Spanish Seaborne Empire* (London and New York, 1966). Two other "background" books with more on Spain than on the Indies are: J. H. Mariéjol, *The Spain of Ferdinand and Isabella*, trans. and ed. by Benjamin Keen (New Brunswick, N.J., 1961), and J. H. Elliott, *Imperial Spain, 1469–1716* (London, 1963). Elliott is a Cambridge don. Of the Emperor's many biographies, Royal Tyler, *The Emperor Charles the Fifth* (London, 1956), is the best study of his personality and policy.

Organs of Spanish Maritime Control. Merriman, IV, chap. xxxii; Haring's chaps. vi, vii; Elliott, chap. v. Richard Hakluyt's praise of the system at "Civille" is in his "Discourse of Western Planting," *Original Writings . . . of the Two Richard Hakluyts* (Hakluyt Society, London, 1935), II, 272.

THE LOAYSA EXPEDITION

Principal sources are in Navarrete, *Colección de los Viages . . .* , V (1837). These include the narratives of Andrés de Urdaneta (pp. 401–39), Juan de Areizaga (pp. 223–25), the *derrotero* of Fernando Torre (pp. 241–312), the *Relación* of the Strait of Magellan by Francisco Dávila (pp. 225–33), but not Martín Uriarte's *derrotero* of the same, which is in J. T. Medina, *Documentos Inéditos Para la Historia de Chile*, III (Santiago, 1889), 387–88. Sir Clements Markham (ed.), *Early Spanish Voyages to the Strait of Magellan* (Hakluyt Society, London, 1911), translates Urdaneta, Uriarte, pinnace *Santiago*'s narrative, and narratives of later voyages by Saavedra, Alcazaba, and others. Medina, *loc cit.*, adds important documents, notably an anonymous narrative (pp. 387–88) and Francisco de Paris's "Declaration" (pp. 368–75). See also, "Documentos Relativos a Juan Sebastián del Cano," in the old Spanish *Colección de Documentos Inéditos, I* (Madrid, 1842), 244 and ff.

To the biographies of Elcano listed at the end of Chapter XIX above, add Pedro de Novo y Colson, *Magallanes y Elcano*, read at the Ateneo Científico in 1892. Juan Sebastián never drew his pension because it was assessed against the new Casa de Contratación de la Especería, a board set up at Corunna to handle the spice trade; and as the Emperor's deal with D. João III renounced the spice trade, the Casa had no money. Mairin Mitchell, Elcano's biographer, is also the author of *Friar Andrés de Urdaneta, O.S.A.* (London, 1964); a great little book. See especially his chapter xi on the adventures of Alonso de Arellano, who has been promoted over Urdaneta as discoverer of the Philippines-California route, unjustly I believe.

Congress of Badajoz. The story of the naughty boy, from López de Gómara's *Historia General de las Indias* (1552), is told by Richard Hakluyt in his "Discourse of Western Planting," Hakluyt Society ed. of his *Original Writings* (London, 1935), pp. 298, 306. Professor Rogers has kindly corrected my calculation of where the Line should have gone. I have not gone into the thorny question of the length of a degree of longitude.

Expenses and exchange. Navarrete, V, 3–4, and Medina, *Colección de Documentos Inéditos Para la Historia de Chile*, III, 344–46. Translated in

Markham, pp. 30, 39–40, with some changes. The financing and salary lists are useful in showing the value of a gold ducat; it was worth 375 maravedis, which is confirmed by E. J. Hamilton, *American Treasure and the Price Revolution in Spain 1501–1650* (Cambridge, Mass., 1934), p. 55n. The approximate value in gold pre-1934 dollars was $2.32, so better call it roughly $2.50 to $3.00.

San Mateo. Uriarte's and other early co-ordinates for San Mateo (lat. 1°50′ S, long. 21°10′ W) were so inaccurate as to give rise to a mythical "Island of St. Matthew." This stayed on the charts until the British Navy had proved, in 1817, that there was no such island. Markham, p. 42n.

The Atlantic crossing. My authority for the dates 31 October–19 November 1525 is Juan de Arreizaga (Navarrete, *Colección*, V, 223); and Urdaneta (*ibid.*, p. 402) gives the landfall. Markham, who has an irritating habit of making unheralded omissions from his translation, omits this clause. Captain Max Justo Guedes, author of the magnificent *Brasil Costa Norte, Cartografia Portuguesa Vetustíssima* (Rio de Janeiro, 1963), identified Urdaneta's *Bajos de los Parbos.* It should have been *Pargos*, the Portuguese name for the menhaden or porgy. This shoal lies off Cabo de S. Tomé. Although a 34-day crossing was not bad, there were shorter ones, such as Pinzón's controversial one of 1500, and the Portuguese expedition of Martim Afonso de Sousa in January 1531 which sailed from Porto da Praia, Cape Verde, to Fernão de Noronha in 21 days, and made Cabo Santo Agostinho 6 days later. *História Col. Port. do Brasil*, III, 134.

There is great need of a careful study of crossing the Atlantic at the Africa-Brazil narrows, which now became one of the main shipping routes for European, especially Portuguese, ships. By 1600 it had become sufficiently important to the English for Hakluyt to translate and reprint several rutters for the coast of Brazil (*Principal Navigations*, 3-vol. ed., III, 717–26). Hakluyt includes a detailed rutter from the River Plate to the Strait (pp. 724–26). He observes that from the River Plate south there "is never a good harbour for great shipping." The mark for Rio de Camarones is "seeing many white spots upon the water, and they are small shrimp" (*camarones*). He adds, "When thou hast sight of this land, it is good for thee to keepe from it a good bredth off." He compares Cabo Vírgenes to Cape St. Vincent, and urges sailors to beware of summer's southwest winds "which blow right in; and they put a man from his tackle, & make him to loose his voyage."

Mixup at and Passage of the Strait. Uriarte in Markham, p. 90, and J. T. Medina, *Documentos Inéditos Para la Historia de Chile*, III, 347–49. Since foul odors from the hold were taken for granted in those days (see my *Northern Voyages*, pp. 134–35), the stench in *Victoria* must have been of unsurpassed strength, owing to Loaysa's failure to have his ship "rummaged" at Santa Cruz. The official *Derrotero de la Costa de Chile* (5th ed., Santiago, 1968), Vol. IV, the Chilean sailing directions to the Strait, which I first perused on board *Orompello* in February 1972, are superior to and more detailed for the Strait than those of the British Admiralty or the United States.

Santiago's adventures. Markham (pp. 102–7) translates these from Navarrete.

Loaysa's and Elcano's deaths. Medina, *Colección de Documentos Inéditos . . . Chile*, II, 94–107, followed by an account of the heirs' efforts in 1533 to make Charles V pay up. Markham, pp. 50, 102–7.

Saavedra's Rescue Voyage. Ione S. Wright has written two excellent accounts: "First American Voyage Across the Pacific," *Geographical Review*, XXIX (1939), 478–82; and (more extended), "Voyages of Saavedra Cerón 1527–29," University of Miami *Hispanic-American Studies* No. 11 (1951). Sources (especially the account of one Vicente de Nápoles) are mostly in Navarrete, *Colección*, V; some are translated in the Miami article. Would that there were more North American researchers on Southern Voyages like Miss Wright!

The lengthy instructions of Cortés to Urdaneta are dated 27 May 1527 (translation in I. S. Wright's appendix). His main objectives are to find Loaysa, and Cabot! At Cebu he is to ransom any living survivors of the massacre of May 1521. He is to capture the Portuguese fort at Ternate. Most amusing are his instructions about translating the Latin letters of introduction to Oriental sultans and rajahs. In every port he is to hire a learned Jew to put them into the local language or into Arabic; if no Jew is available, his black "prisoner" from Calicut (how did that man ever get to Mexico?) might act as interpreter. Saavedra must find out all about the culture of spices, and attempt to bring home clove trees in pots, with a slave to care for them, so that cloves may be grown in Mexico. (Cf. Captain Bligh's famous mission for breadfruit.) The instructions also include routine prohibitions of blasphemy and gambling, and of women.

Line of Demarcation, and Treaty of Saragossa, 1529. Markham, *Early Spanish Voyages to the Strait*, p. 14n. Text in Navarrete, IV, 389–406; text and translation in Frances G. Davenport, *European Treaties Bearing on the History of the United States . . . to 1648* (Washington, 1917), pp. 146–98.

Villalobos, Legazpi, and Urdaneta's return voyage. Mitchell's *Urdaneta* and William Lytle Schurz, *The Manila Galleon* (New York, 1939) cover these well. The latter book, for depth of research and skill in presentation, is one of the best works on maritime history. Puerto la Navidad, at about 19° N, unhealthy, and much farther from Mexico City than Acapulco (lat. 15°51′N), was later abandoned, and the name has disappeared from the map.

✳ XXI ✳

Bermuda, Florida, and the Gulf

1505-1543

Discovery of Bermuda

What should we do but sing his Praise
That led us through the watry Maze,
Unto an isle so long unknown,
And yet far kinder than our own?

Thus wrote the English poet Andrew Marvell in his *Bermudas*, about
1653. So here we bring in the discovery and early history of that en-
chanting island or islands lying only six hundred miles from the coast
of Virginia. No far-roving American Indian nor any other human
being had been there prior to the visit of a Spaniard named Juan
Bermúdez in 1505. Somebody had to discover it shortly, because
Bermuda lay close aboard the best sailing route from Mexico and the
West Indies to Spain. After the conquest of Mexico and the formation of treasure fleets this route became standard: last call at the
Havana, catch the Gulf Stream to help push north off the coast of
Florida, steer off shore when safely past the Bahamas, and, as soon
as you enter the zone of westerlies, square away for the Azores, be-
tween 37° and 40° N.

Oviedo, in his *Historia General y Natural* (written about 1535)
gives Bermuda's latitude nearly correctly at 33° N but offers the bad

advice to mariners to approach within a lombard's shot and anchor in eight fathom. That would be all right on the southeast coast between Paget and Castle Harbor, but on the rest of the periphery, which a homeward-bound ship would usually approach, it might be fatal, and often was; this island group is more closely fringed with wrecks than any other part of the New World except the Carolina Outer Banks, and is proud of it. The island government sports a wrecked ship on its coat of arms, and the Bermuda Press publishes a map of the group fringed with wrecks. Moreover, the approach from the south, sometimes called the Bermuda Triangle (Puerto Rico–Miami–Bermuda) is notorious for sudden, severe squalls which to this day cause ships to founder with all hands. Yet Bermuda itself has a peculiar charm and restfulness.

Juan Bermúdez of Palos, captain of ship *La Garça* or *Garza*, discovered Bermuda in 1505, and early writers often called the island *Garza* after his ship, which was then on her homeward passage from a provisioning voyage to Hispaniola. Oviedo called there in her with Bermúdez on a second voyage in 1515, and they left ashore a dozen pigs and sows which happily multiplied, to the profit of later castaways. Even before that, "La Bermuda" appears—much too far east—on the map in the first edition of Peter Martyr's *Decades* (1511).

This writer (who in his salad days once piloted a sailing yacht into St. George's Harbor, Bermuda, after nightfall) is amazed that anyone managed to find his way through the intricate reefs and coral heads without navigational aids. Yet many Spaniards and Englishmen did, despite the bad reputation of the Bermudas for storms; they are in the zone where two different wind systems frequently clash. I suspect that most of those who called for fresh water (rare before catchments were built) or live swine (a-plenty but hard to catch), hove-to or even anchored off the southeast shore and sent in a boat to one of the gleaming sand beaches which are now such a delight to tourists. At any rate, it is on the south shore that Spanish Rock is located, a coral outcrop on which is an inscription now mostly effaced by weather: "R † 1543." We have no clue to the carver's identity.

One Fernando Camelo of St. Michael's in the Azores received a royal grant to settle there in 1527, but despite the promise of no taxes he did nothing. Two years later, Diego Ribero placed Bermuda fairly accurately on his world map. On the strength of a rumor that

Bermudian shellfish bore pearls, royal consent to exploit them was requested by one Pedro de Aspide in 1587, but he did not get it. Captain Diego Ramírez, whose homeward-bound galleon grounded at Bermuda in 1603 but floated off and anchored in Great Sound, spent twenty-two days ashore and wrote a fascinating description of the island group. Spain, however, left it alone and Bermuda acquired such a reputation for sudden, violent storms that navigators were content to take one look and then sheer off. It also acquired the reputation of harboring devils; a reflection, probably, of the eerie cries of the almost-extinct cahow bird.

Flagship *Sea Venture* of the Gates-Somers colonizing expedition to Virginia encountered "the taile of the West Indian horocane" on 24 July 1609, "the cloudes gathering thicke upon us, and the windes singing, and whistling most unusually, which made us to cast off our Pinnace towing the same untill then asterne, a dreadfull storme and hideous began to blow from out the North-east, which swelling, and roaring as it were by fits, some houres with more violence then others, at length did beate all light from heaven; which like an hell of darkenesse turned blacke upon us." In a sinking condition, with only a "Hollocke, or halfe forecourse" set,* it took eight men to steer her by the whipstaff. The ship labored so that she "spued out her Okam" (shed her caulking), took five, even ten feet of water in the hold; a great sea pooped her and "covered our Shippe from stearne to stemme, like a garment or a vast cloude." This went on from Tuesday to Friday, the people without sleep or food, casks of beer and fresh water not to be got at in the hold, "fire we could keepe none in the Cooke-roome to dresse any meate." On Friday morning Sir George Somers "cried Land." They fortunately were near a good lee (probably Church Bay near Gibbs Hill light), ran her on the beach, and got all 150 of the ship's company ashore safely. They ascertained it to be "the dangerous and dreaded Iland . . . of the Bermuda . . . feared and avoyded of all sea travellers alive, above any other place in the world. Yet it pleased our mercifull God, to make even this hideous and hated place, both the place of our safetie, and meanes of our deliverance."

They found the islands devoid of human kind, but rich in edible

---

* Hullocke—New English Dictionary: A small part of a mizzen or other small sail let out in a gale to keep the ship's head to the sea.

fauna and flora—"victtualls fytt for such Eaters as the English are," as William Strachey wrote; even coconut palms. They built two thirty-tun pinnaces of Bermudian cedar, departed within a year, and reached Virginia safely in May 1610.

This shipwreck and deliverance mark the beginning of the history of the English colony of "Bermuda, or the Somers Islands," and it also provided most of the maritime material for Shakespeare's *Tempest*. The English changed the name officially to Somers Islands, but seamen had been calling it Bermuda for so long that they refused to give it up.

Ponce de León's Quest

Juan Ponce de León has become one of the most popular figures in the history of American discovery, largely owing to his romantic quest for a Fountain of Youth. In Puerto Rico and Florida especially, his name seldom escapes the tourist's eye, on hotels and motels, streets and boulevards, beer parlors and the like. He deserves a better fate.

He was born in Tervás de San Campos, province of Valladolid, in 1474 to a noble family. His father, Luis Ponce de León, married a cousin, Doña Francesca, the daughter of Don Rodrigo Ponce de León (one of the heroes of the reconquest of Moorish Spain), and to this maternal grandfather our Juan bore a marked resemblance in physique and character. Both were red-haired, strong, active, and aggressive in warfare.

Very little is known about Juan's early life except that he was page to D. Pedro Nuñez de Guzmán, an important person at court, and fought as a youth against the Moors under Ferdinand and Isabella. At the age of nineteen he shipped to the New World as a gentleman volunteer in Columbus's Second Voyage of 1493. That fleet, as we have seen, called at Añasco Bay on the western coast of Puerto Rico. Ponce de León may then have noted the rich soil of the Añasco valley and the attractive rounded hills—the limestone *mogotes* which from a height look like enormous waves of the sea—and decided that one day he would try to make it his share of the Conquest.

What Ponce de León's relations were with Columbus we know not, but in Hispaniola, under the Admiral's successor Ovando, he helped materially and with ruthless brutality (says Las Casas) to conquer the native kingdom of Higuey. As a reward, Ovando appointed him governor of that province. Essentially a restless man, the report of a native of Borinquen that his island was rich in gold—with a big nugget to prove it—sent him hot-foot to Puerto Rico with one hundred soldiers and oral permission from Ovando to conquer it if he could. Ponce could and did. He landed at Añasco Bay on Midsummer Day 1506, subjugated within a year the Taino of the western half of Puerto Rico, and established a fortified capital a short distance up the Añasco, which he named Villa de San Germán. According to Oviedo, this was done without too much fighting because the mother of the local cacique, Aguaybana, a wise old lady, persuaded her son to submit to the inevitable; and the Taino were quiet for several years. In 1511, however, there occurred a general rising of Puerto Rican natives (probably the fault of one of Ponce's captains, Cristóbal de Sotomayor), and before this rebellion was quenched there was plenty of battling. A feature of this war was a dog named Becerillo, which Oviedo described as "of red pelt and black eyes, medium sized and not bad looking." He could distinguish by smell between a friendly and an enemy Indian, and his presence with the Spanish army was worth fifty men; but the Caribs got him in the end. Balboa acquired Bercerillo's pup Leoncillo, which served him equally well crossing the Isthmus.

The crown confirmed Ponce's conquest by appointing him governor in 1509, and in three years' time he not only held in his own hands practically every office in the government, but grew rich "on the labors, blood and sufferings of his subjects," says Las Casas, referring to the gold extorted from the Indians after the war was over. In 1512 he was replaced as governor by D. Diego Colón (the Discoverer's son) as a result of the latter's claim to make all top appointments in the Indies. The king then showed his favor to Ponce by giving him a grant to discover new lands, in preference to the Adelantado Bartholomew Colón, the Admiral's brother.

Next year Ponce de León commenced his search for a new land where there was said to be a Fountain of Youth whose waters rejuvenated old men and restored their virility. Oviedo makes it clear that Ponce wanted a cure for *el enflaquecimiento del sexo*, the debility of sex. At the age of thirty-nine he could hardly have needed this cure himself; but plenty of older conquistadors, lacking in the New

The Fountain of Youth. Woodcut by Hans Sebald Beham, early sixteenth century. Courtesy of Corcoran Art Gallery.

World the traditional aphrodisiacs such as unicorns' horns, could well profit by it.

There were two independent Fountain of Youth myths, one American and one Eurasian. As related by Peter Martyr, there existed on an island north of Cuba named Boiuca or Bimini, "a spring of running water of such marvellous virtue, that the water therof being drunk, perhaps with some diet, makes old men young again." "It was said, moreover, that on a neighboring shore might be found a river gifted with the same beneficent property." Herrera, who repeated the story in his *Historia General* (1601), insisted that native caciques paid regular visits to this fountain (as their Spanish successors used to do to Virginia Hot Springs and Saratoga), and that one old man with barely strength enough to endure the journey was so completely restored as to resume "all manly exercises . . . take a new wife and beget more children." Herrera states that the would-be native patrons from the Greater Antilles had searched every "river, brook, lagoon or pool" along the Florida coast for their hopefully rejuvenating drink and bath. Ponce de León probably picked this version up in Hispaniola; but as a well-educated Spanish nobleman he must also have heard the parallel Eurasian myth, a familiar feature in Renaissance painting. There, the Fountain of Youth is always connected with profane, gallant, and erotic love. The search for it in Florida is an episode in man's pathetic attempts to escape the inevitable consequences of old age, and to postpone death. Naturally it came to the New World in the mental baggage of the conquistadors, but only Ponce de León seems to have made its quest the object of a voyage.

It must be emphasized that the Fountain of Youth was a profane, not a religious myth, and Ponce de León bowed to it by naming the land where he expected to locate it, after a layman's paraphrase of the day. Bless him for that! One tires of the repetitious Spanish names: so many Trinidads, Santa Marias, Espíritu Santo's, Santa Fe's, Concepcións, and the like; we welcome *Pascua Florida*, the Floral Passover.

Subsequent to his displacement as governor of Puerto Rico, Ponce de León sailed back to Spain at the King's invitation. Ferdinand was evidently impressed by his appearance and personality—and Ferdinand was not easily impressed. At any rate, the King in February 1512 gave him an *asiento* to discover and conquer the "Island of Bimini."

We, too, would like to know more of the personality that impressed the King. Juan de Castellanos in Elegy VI of his mid-century *Elegias de Varones Ilustres de Indias*, as translated by Muna Lee, tells us:

> Courteous and kind he was, ruddy of face,
> Of his band the leader and the friend;
> In every gesture strong and full of grace,
> Hard tasks begun, he carried to the end.
> In danger his was ever foremost place,
> And his a doughty valor nought could bend.
> Enemy he was of those of gifts the wooers,
> And he was dearly hated by evil-doers.

Oviedo tells us that Ponce was a great fighter, always foremost in battle, "being a man spirited, sagacious and diligent in all warlike matters"; and again, "a hidalgo and a man of elegant and high thoughts," and an "honorable gentleman and noble person, who worked to good purpose in the conquest and pacification of Hispaniola in the Higuey war, and also was the first to populate and pacify the Island of St. John." Las Casas considered Ponce to be one of the most ruthless of the conquistadors toward the natives; this may be an exaggeration, but it seems significant that he never managed to conciliate any native inhabitants of Florida.

On 3 March 1513 Ponce de León set sail from the "Port of San Germán," meaning doubtless Añasco Bay, since San Germán itself lay a short distance up-river. His task organization follows:

SANTIAGO, caravel; Diego Bermúdez (brother to the discoverer of Bermuda), master. Antón de Alaminos, chief pilot. This man had been with Columbus on his Second Voyage (not his First as is frequently stated) and became so famous a pilot under Ponce as to be employed by Cortés to pilot a ship carrying a large amount of gold from Mexico to Charles V. Probably more immediately helpful to Ponce were two Indian pilots who knew the Bahamas.

SANTA MARIA DE CONSOLACIÓN; Captain: Juan Bono de Quexo.

SAN CRISTÓBAL, bergantina; she arrived from Spain too late to take part in the voyage to Bimini, but another bergantina of the same name which normally maintained shuttle service between Hispaniola and Puerto Rico was used in her place. All except this substitute were owned personally by Ponce de León, purchased for him in Spain out of his wealth acquired in Puerto Rico.

Besides the seamen, each caravel carried a number of *gente de tierra*, landsmen; of which some no doubt were soldiers, but not all; in *Santiago*, for instance, sailed Francisco de Ortega, his wife Beatriz Jiménez, and Juana Jiménez, probably her sister. It seems odd that these girls should have gone on a quest for male rejuvenation, and they are the first women to be recorded as having shipped on any short Caribbean voyage. *Santiago*'s roll includes "Jorge Negro," doubtless a black, among the gromets or ship's boys.

Ponce chose the Mona Passage route, then steered northwest and north, skirted the Caicos and Turks Island group, and on 14 March called at Guanahaní, Columbus's San Salvador. (This statement, in Herrera, is one of the most important and conclusive in locating Columbus's first American landfall.) Tarrying there or at the nearby Cat Island a few days to cleanse a ship's weedy bottom, Ponce took his departure to the northwestward. On Easter Sunday, 27 March, he passed on the port hand an island which must have been Ciguateo (Eleuthera), if not Great Abaco. Maintaining the same WNW course, the fleet "on 2 April when the water was growing shoal, came to in nine fathom, a league from the land, which was in 30°08′. They ran along the coast seeking harbor, and at night anchored near the shore in eight fathoms' water. Believing that land to be an island, they named it *La Florida*, because it appeared very delightful, having many and fresh groves, and it was all level, and also because they discover'd it at the season, which the Spaniards call *Pascua Florida*. Ponce . . . went ashore to discover and take possession." Thus writes Herrera.

If Captain Peters's estimate in E. W. Lawson's *First Landing Place* (1946) is correct, and you deduct one degree—the same mistake that Alaminos made at San Salvador—from 30°08′, you almost get latitude 29°05′, that of a little inlet near Daytona Beach, fifty miles south of St. Augustine, which has been named for Ponce de León. The people went ashore next day, Low Sunday, 3 April, still in the Easter season. The banks of the inlet were blooming and burgeoning with wild flowers and plants that sent delicious odors out to the ships. *Pascua Florida*, was then a common Spanish name for the Day of Resurrection, a profane version of which Ponce was seeking.

I find no evidence in Herrera or elsewhere that Ponce tried to sail north from his Florida landfall, or that he ever visited the site of St. Augustine. No prudent sailor wanting to return to Puerto Rico would have done so, on account of the force of the Gulf Stream. That extraordinary current's full force—five to six knots—Ponce first felt the next week.

Herrera says that on 8 April the fleet "sailed again the same way," i.e. north, but meeting a counter-current along the edge of the land, Ponce turned south, where he met a head current so strong that it drove them back, although they had "a fair wind." This was the Gulf Stream, which always runs south to north. The two larger vessels anchored, but the force of the stream strained their cables; the bergantina sought sea room and was lost sight of for two days, "tho' the day was bright and the weather fair." This discovery of the great Stream rivals in importance the discovery of Florida; in fact, Florida was originally valued as a base from which to protect valuable cargoes shooting north through the Strait of Florida with this mighty booster.

At a place where he saw native *bohios*, Ponce went ashore in his longboat, which an Indian welcoming committee tried to seize; Ponce

	70°		65°		60°	

CARIBBEAN SEA AND EASTERN GULF OF MEXICO
1500 — 1542
Scale of Nautical Miles
0   100   200   300   400

30°

A T L A N T I C

O C E A N

25°

BAHAMA

SAN SALVADOR
ISLANDS
ONG I.
CROOKED I.
ACKLINS
CAICOS
INAGUA
Turks Is.
Baracoa
C. Maisi
TORTUGA
Isabela
Pto. Plata
ndward
Passage

Course of
Ponce de León
1513

HISPANIOLA
Jacmel
Santo
Domingo
Tiburón
Beata I.
Alta Vela I.

C. Engaña
Mona passage

PUERTO
RICO
San Juan
San Germán

Virgin Is.

Sombrero
St. Martin
Saba
St. Kitts
Nevis
LEEWARD
ISLANDS
GUADALUPE
I. des Saintes
DOMINICA

Barbuda
Antigua
Montserrat
Deseada
Mariagalante

20°

15°

C A R I B   B E A N   S E A

MATININO
St. Lucia
WINDWARD
ISLANDS
St. Vincent
Barbados
Grenadines
Grenada

Bahia Honda
CAUCHIETE
Aruba
Gigantes (Curaçao)
Bonaire
C. de la Vela
Guaira Pen.
G. of
Venezuela
Paraguana Pen.
Los Roques
PEARL   COAST
Margarita
Cubagua I.
Bocas del Dragón
Tobago
Sta.
arta
18,947 ft.
Sa. Nevada
de Santa Marta
Coro
Curiana
Little Venice
(Caracas)
L. Maracaibo
Cumana
G. of Paria
TRINIDAD
Boca del Sierpe
Delta of
the Orinoco

10°

lena R.
V E N E Z U E L A
Orinoco R.
OMBIA

70°   65°   60°

scuffled with them, reserving his fire power until one Christian had been stunned by a blow on the head; then he let go, but little damage was suffered by the natives. Next day they sailed to a river where they took on wood and water and awaited the errant bergantina. This river they named Santa Cruz; Aurelio Tió identifies it as Jupiter Inlet, at latitude 26°57′ N.

In any case, Ponce de León passed the future Daytona Beach, rounded the prominent Cape Canaveral, passed the sites of Palm Beach, Fort Lauderdale, and Miami, going ashore wherever he saw signs of a native village to inquire about the rejuvenating fountain. Even with the aid of favoring northerly winds and cautiously using the counter-current close to shore, it took him one month to reach what he called the Cape of Florida, giving it the name of *Cabo de los Corrientes*, or Cape Currents, "because they are stronger there than the wind," and anchored off an Indian village named Abaioa. Here the people showed fight and killed a Spaniard; Ponce's men filled water casks, cut fire-wood, and retired. At another village, which Aurelio Tió believes to have been on the site of Key Biscayne, he had no trouble, and found a spring of sweet water, but drinking deep draughts of it did his men no good. They would have preferred a cask of sound Spanish wine! Now, hugging the chain of Florida Keys (which Ponce named *Los Mártires* "because the high rocks at a distance look like men that are suffering"), and passing the site of Key West, they careened *San Cristóbal* somewhere on the Marquesas Keys' lagoon. Here, for a change, Ponce did not send a landing party ashore but the natives came out to him and "laid hold of the cable" of one ship to tow it away; that, of course, was not to be tolerated, and Ponce sent his long-boat ashore, whose crew "took four women and broke two old canoes."

On 3 June they turned north into the Gulf of Mexico. A north-to-northeast rhumb took the fleet at least to the mouth of the Caloosa-hatchee River, or nearby Charlotte Harbor. Both afford snug protection from all winds, and enough room to make sail quickly and get away if the going got rough with the Indians. Relations here at first were friendly; an Indian appeared who spoke Spanish, interpreted for Ponce, and joined his fleet as local pilot and interpreter. As usual, the Spaniards outstayed their welcome, and the local cacique, named Calos or Calusa, tried to capture their ships. His attack on 11 June was mounted in eighty canoes full of archers with shields, from behind which they shot arrows barbed with fish spines, while others tried to cut the Spanish anchor cables.

Ponce must now have decided that his Pascua Florida, for all its beauty and amenity, was not the site of the Fountain of Youth; no Indian had ever heard of it. So, on 14 June 1513 he started his return voyage. He first called at the Dry Tortugas, where in one night his men captured 160 turtles, 14 seal, 7000 pelican, and other wild fowl. On Friday the 24th they took off, steering *Sudueste, quarta de Oueste*—SW by W—says Herrera. Why did Ponce choose this course instead of the obvious one, with the five-knot Gulf Stream to help him back to the Bahamas? We simply do not know, but guess that the captured Indian pilot, a native of Hispaniola, persuaded Ponce to take the direct route south of Cuba, on the pretense of thereby locating the elusive Fountain.

The southwesterly course from the Dry Tortugas took the fleet across the Yucatan Channel, sailing large before a brisk trade wind. On Sunday, 26 June 1513, they made land, sailed along it for two days, and went ashore. "Most of them took it for Cuba," wrote Herrera, but evidently it was something very different—a spot on the Yucatan Peninsula between Cabo Catoche and Progresso, the modern port of Mérida. Having found a harbor, they went ashore to mend their sails. Ponce named this island (as he supposed it to be), *Beimini*, obviously another spelling of Bimini, invoking the Fountain of Youth. Although once more he missed finding any rejuvenating waters, he acquired subsequent fame as the discoverer of the great Empire of Mexico, to which Yucatan belonged. Juan de Grijalba, hitherto credited with the discovery and taking possession of Yucatan, came five years later. And Grijalba's pilot was Antón de Alaminos.

Instead of sailing back to Puerto Rico south of Cuba, a route which would have been frustrating with its light airs and baffling currents, the fleet, departing the newly named Bimini on 6 August, backtracked around the western cape of Cuba (San Antonio), plunged into the Gulf Stream, and on 18 August made a Bahamian island which we identify as Eleuthera. There he ordered Alaminos to peel off in *San Cristóbal* and comb the Bahamas for the Fountain. Ponce de León now

Florida Keys discovered by Ponce de León.

had no Spanish pilot, but he handled the other two vessels well in foul weather. The bergantina foundered or ran too firmly aground to be got off, but all her men were rescued. Flagship *Santiago* reached Puerto Rico on 10 October 1513, and Alaminos turned up some four months later, having been rescued by a ship of Diego Miruelo.

Ponce sailed for Spain early in 1514, reported at the court on this voyage, and after presenting the King with 5000 gold pesos from Puerto Rico, received a royal grant "to colonize the island of Beniny and the island of Florida which you discovered by Our command." The next few years were not spent in "gloomy inactivity" in Puerto Rico as one modern historian has written; far from it. First, at the King's orders, he headed an expedition to one of the Leeward Islands, probably

Guadeloupe, in caravel *La Barbola* of 90 tuns' burthen, with two smaller vessels. The objective was to destroy the main source of Carib raids.

Aurelio Tió, searching notarial records, found evidence for Ponce's having sailed into the Gulf of Mexico and discovered the harbor of San Juan de Ulua,* where Cortés landed in 1519 and which, after he had conquered Mexico in 1521, became its main port of entry. This could have been a diversion by Ponce in *La Barbola*, wishing to pursue his earlier discovery of Yucatan. But the evidence is unconvincing. It consists of *pleitos* (depositions) taken down by the Audiencia of Guatemala in 1608 in a process initiated by a royal official named Perafán de Rivera, a descendant of Ponce's youngest daughter Maria, Señora Gaspar Troche. Rivera, who wanted a grant, testified that his ancestor had been "discoverer of Nueva España, Guatemala and Honduras." Since no early historian such as Oviedo, Las Casas, or Herrera mentions a voyage by Ponce de León to San Juan de Ulua, I suspect that the Ponce descendants, after fourscore years had elapsed, confused it with the Córdoba and Grijalba voyages of 1517–18 along the Gulf of Mexico, both of which were piloted by Alaminos.

The Córdoba expedition of two ships and a bergantina, carrying 110 soldiers under Francisco Hernández de Córdoba, was authorized by D. Diego Velásquez, the independent governor of Cuba who had conquered that Pearl of the Antilles in 1511. The main objective was to kidnap Indian slaves to replenish the already depleted labor force of Cuba. Bernal Díaz del Castillo, who had been at Darien with Pedrárias and would be the companion and chronicler of Cortés, was on board. Sailing from the Havana on 8 February 1517, four days later "they doubled Cape San Antonio, holding on their course to the westward" because pilot Alaminos said that the First Admiral "had always inclin'd that way, when he sailed with him, being a boy." The fleet, beaten back by a storm, took 21 days to reach Cabo Catoche, Yucatan, where the Spaniards had a fight with the natives. A fortnight later they reached the site of Campeche; more trouble with the natives. Six days more took them to a place they called Patouchan (now Champotón). Here they had a really big battle—over fifty Spaniards were killed, five more drowned, and Córdoba wounded by no fewer than twelve ar-

---

* Not Vera Cruz harbor where the fortress of that name was later built, but a place 20 miles northward along the coast.

rows. In only four days they reached Florida, had another fight, and Alaminos was wounded. Thence to the Martyrs (the Florida Keys) and back to Havana.

The account that Córdoba and his survivors gave of the wealth of Yucatan, the stone temples, and the gold objects, so excited the greed of D. Diego Velásquez that next year, 1518, he organized a fleet of three ships and a bergantina to pursue discovery further along the Mexican coast. To this command he appointed his twenty-eight-year-old nephew Juan de Grijalba, whom Herrera calls "a genteel young man . . . and well mannered, being a gentleman of the town of Cuellar." Antón de Alaminos again shipped as chief pilot; Pedro de Alvarado, later one of the principal lieutenants of Cortés, commanded one of the ships. Grijalba's expedition sailed from Santiago de Cuba 8 April 1518. Before making for Mexico they rounded Cape San Antonio northward in order to relieve the Spanish settlers at Matanzas who were being hard pressed by neighboring natives. After topping off with cassava bread and live swine, they again doubled Cape San Antonio where (as Herrera faithfully records) "they all voluntarily cut off their hair, thinking they should have little leisure to comb it"—a hint for modern sailors! Thrown off course, they discovered the Island of Cozumel, where they marveled at a Mayan temple, and Grijalba picked up as mistress an Indian girl whose canoe had been blown off course when fishing. At Champotón (Córdoba's Patouchan) the natives again showed fight, and Grijalba had some front teeth knocked out by an arrow. Proceeding along the coast, they entered the Tabasco River (later renamed the Grijalba), and as a result of their reconnaissance Cortés next year effected a landing at Punta de Palmares. Here, Grijalba was able peacefully to exchange compliments and presents with the local cacique.

The fleet continued along the Mexican coast, noted the island in Vera Cruz Bay still called Sacrificios, which the Aztecs used for their human sacrifices, and passed the site of San Juan de Ulua to a point north of the Pánuco River, enjoying good trade everywhere west of Yucatan. Alaminos now persuaded Grijalba that enough is enough, and the fleet returned to Matanzas in October 1518.

Everything was now set for the mighty effort of Cortés. Grijalba did not go with him but took service under Pedrárias on the Isthmus and was killed a few years later when raiding Nicaragua with Hurtado.

It is time to conclude with Ponce de León. Several years earlier he had removed his seat of government from the inconvenient San Germán to Caparra, a few miles south of the *Puerto Rico de San Juan* that he had discovered on the north coast; and before setting forth again, he reluctantly ordered that the capital be shifted to that harbor and that a town be built—the now famous and opulent San Juan de Puerto Rico.

Ponce's second and last voyage to Florida began on 15 February 1521. By that time he had given up the Fountain of Youth legend as false. He intended (as his latest *asiento* permitted) to plant a colony and, apparently, live on trading with the Indians. He sailed from the future Puerto Rican metropolis San Juan with several vessels carrying two hundred men and fifty horses, well provided with seeds, roots, rattoons, and "all manner of domestic animals useful for the service of man." We know nothing about his route—Herrera does not even mention this voyage or where he tried to pitch his colony, which from other sources we know to have been on Sanibel Island at the mouth of the Caloosahatchee River, not far from the present Fort Myers. Ponce brought with him a number of missionary priests to convert the Indians, but they had no success whatsoever. The Florida natives, says Oviedo, "were rough and very savage and bellicose and ferocious and indomitable and not accustomed to peace." The fact that Ponce always had trouble with the natives of Florida, whilst later-coming Spaniards and Frenchmen who did not visit the same places, found them friendly, strongly suggests that he was responsible; that he belonged to the "treat 'em rough" school, like Alonso de Ojeda. For instance, a pilot named Diego Miruelo, on a trading cruise from Cuba in 1516, ran up the Florida west coast and discovered a bay, probably Pensacola, which on early maps bore his name. He found the Indians friendly and exchanged his trading truck for silver and gold.

However that may be, these wicked Indians who preferred their own way of life to anything Europe had to offer, strongly resisted the Spaniards' landing, and in the brawl Ponce received an arrow wound that festered. His men sailed him to the nearest Cuba port, which happened to be Havana, and did their poor best to relieve him. But, beyond their care, he died in July 1521 at the age of forty-seven. Later in the century his remains were translated to San Juan de Puerto Rico where they still rest. From the altar of the Dominican church they were removed to the Cathedral of San Juan in 1908.

Juan Ponce de León is the most elusive of the early conquistadors. We know where he went and what he did, but of his personality, only the generalities which have been quoted early in the chapter. I hope, however, that I have said enough to convince my reader that he was no doddering old fellow looking for a cheap cure for impotence, but a young, valiant and enterprising conquistador to whose career his romantic search for the Fountain of Youth imparts a certain glamor. Although he never found the fabled Fountain, he discovered Florida and gave it a singularly beautiful name; and he was the first to report the mighty strength of the Gulf Stream, which became of vast value for Spanish fleets returning to Spain. The place he named Bimini in 1513 was Yucatan, where probably no European except shipwrecked sailors had been before. One wishes that he had survived his wound to found a real colony in Florida, for his brief career as governor of Puerto Rico was little short of brilliant.

Pilot Antón de Alaminos is the forgotten man of these Florida and Gulf voyages. From him Ponce de León learned to navigate. Under his pilotage no vessel came to grief in waters that are full of navigational hazards. Were it left me to select figures from our early history to honor with statue or tablet (which God forbid!), I would nominate Antón de Alaminos who, coming to the New World as a boy with Columbus, later piloted Ponce de León, Grijalba, and Cortés to Florida, New Spain, and "beyond the Mexique Bay."

Narváez and Cabeza de Vaca

The reader will have observed that the voyages related in this chapter, unlike those "minor voyages" of Chapter IX which started in Spain, were mounted in the West Indies at Puerto Rico, Santo Domingo, or Cuba; and now at Jamaica.

Antón de Alaminos, now Spain's No. 1 pilot for the Caribbean, could not rest until he had penetrated the Mexique Bay and satisfied himself that there was no passage thence to Balboa's *Mar del Sur*. As Don Diego Velásquez, governor of Cuba, did not care to venture a third voyage, Alaminos approached Don Francisco de Garay. This hidalgo had come to the Indies with Columbus in 1493, cast covetous eyes on Jamaica, and was named by D. Diego Colón his lieutenant for the government of that beautiful island. Although he had already grown rich by exploiting the natives at Nueva Sevilla, this gentleman eagerly embraced the opportunity to acquire more gold and glory. Having plenty of money and being on good terms with Bishop Fonseca, Garay easily obtained permission to equip a fleet of three or four vessels at his own expense, as well as an appointment as "Adelantado and Governor of the Provinces bordering on the River of SS. Pedro and Paulo" in Mexico.

Under the command of Alonso Álvarez de Pineda, they put to sea toward the end of 1518, with Alaminos as chief pilot. Their first landing took place somewhere on the lower west coast of Florida, where the natives gave them the same treatment they had handed out to Ponce de León. Pineda had enough force to land, but wisely retired and sailed west around the Gulf as far as the Rio Pánuco, where Cortés would presently found the town of Tampico. En route they sailed by the mouths of the Mississippi, noted the vast volume of water pouring into the Gulf, and managed to sail upstream for some twenty miles. Thus, Pineda was the original European discoverer of the Father of Waters. He named it after the Holy Spirit because the season was Pentecost.

Pineda and company had to fight their way around the shores of the future Texas; and at a place called Chila, near the mouth of the Pánuco, they were heavily defeated. Many, including Pineda himself, were killed, flayed, and eaten, and their skins hung in Aztec temples as trophies. The natives even managed to burn all Pineda's fleet but one lucky ship, commanded by Diego de Camargo. She arrived at Vera Cruz in very bad shape, all her crew "ill and very yellow and with swollen bellies." Painfully and slowly those wretched survivors were carried to Segura de la Frontera where Cortés happened to be, and were "treated with much consideration" by the great conquistador. Garay having sent out two more ships in the hope of succoring Pineda, these too turned up and their hearty crews were welcomed into Cortés's army. His soldiers nicknamed the crew of one "the strong backs," and those of the second, who were equipped with thick quilted cotton armor, "the pack saddles." But Camargo's sick men were called "the verdigris bellies, for they were the color of death."

Nevertheless, Pineda had accomplished something; he (and not De Soto or La Salle) discovered the Mississippi River, named it after the Holy Spirit, and spent forty days anchored inside one of the Passes, careening his ships and trading with the natives. These were adorned with gold ornaments, uniformly friendly, and well disposed toward conversion. In his short sail up this mighty river, he counted no fewer than forty Indian villages. And Pineda, who was the first to sail completely around the western shores of the Gulf, reported that there was no possibility of a strait in these parts. His employer Garay took all the credit and obtained a grant for the territory discovered by Pineda, giving it the name *Amichel*. That name soon disappeared, as did Pineda's name for the Father of Waters.

Another expedition to Florida, one which followed the east coast northward, was that of the licentiate Ayllón, justice of the Supreme Court of Hispaniola, in 1523. This unsuccessful expedition has already been related in my volume on the Northern Voyages (pages 332–37).

The next sea voyage of any consequence to these parts, one famous mostly for its misfortunes, was that of Pánfilo Narváez, which began in 1527. This hidalgo, the most incompetent of all who sailed for Spain in this era, had been one of the earliest settlers of Jamaica. He commanded a company of volunteers from that island to help Diego Velásquez to conquer Cuba. Later Velásquez sent him to capture and supersede Hernando Cortés, whom the Governor of Cuba thought to be getting too big for his boots. Cortés, on the contrary, persuaded Narváez to join him. Despite this fruitless effort, he received permission from Charles V to conquer and colonize a wide segment of the Gulf of Mexico between the Rio de Palmas * and Florida, which was still virgin territory from the Spanish point of view. His fleet of five ships, carrying six hundred persons and all proper materials to build a fort and start a colony, departed Sanlúcar de Barrameda 17 June 1527. Narváez gave himself the resounding, self-created title "Governor of Florida, Rio de Palmas, and the River Espiritu Santo"— the Mississippi. Of the 260 men that landed with him in Florida, only four survived; these were Cabeza de Vaca of the long march, Captains of Infantry Alonso del Castillo and Andrés Dorantes, and Dorantes's black slave who had been christened Esteban.

The first and the last of these became famous. Cabeza de Vaca was

---

* Hodge, in *Spanish Explorers* (1907), p. 14*n* (see Notes at end of Chapter), identifies this Rio de Palmas as the Rio Santander which empties into the Gulf about 80 miles north of the Pánuco. It is now called the Soto la Marina.

the adopted name of Álvar Núñez de Vera, grandson of Pedro de Vera, conqueror of the Grand Canary, and son of Teresa Cabeza de Vaca. She owed her bovine name to the exploit of an ancestor in the early thirteenth century who set up a cow's skull to guide a Christian army through a pass, thus enabling them to defeat the Moors. The family were natives of the sherry city, Xeres de Frontera, where our hero was born, probably in or around 1480. We know nought of his life prior to 1527, except that he was a well-educated gentleman and had never visited the New World. He was a tall, brawny man with a bright red beard, and as tough as any Castilian of his age. His account of the Narváez voyages and its foot-slogging outcome reflects a humble and compassionate nature and a singularly tolerant and understanding attitude toward the Indians. Esteban, whom Cabeza de Vaca always refers to by the affectionate diminutive *Estebancito*—"Little Steve"—was a big "blackamoor" from Morocco, undoubtedly the first African the natives of Florida and Texas had ever seen. We can well imagine the big, brawny, red-haired Cabeza de Vaca and the tall black man impressing the natives as beings from another world; but we know nothing of the personalities of the two captains of infantry, except that they were loyal to their leader.

However, I am anticipating.

The Narváez expedition, five ships lifting six hundred sailors, soldiers, and colonists, sailed from Sanlúcar 17 June 1527. Nothing worth mentioning happened until after it reached Santo Domingo, where it tarried forty-five days and Narváez acquired another vessel and a number of horses, but lost some 140 men who jumped ship. More horses were picked up at Trinidad in Cuba, whither the Captain General sent two ships from Cabo de Cruz. A hurricane blew up while they were at Trinidad and both ships were lost with fifty men and twenty horses. The survivors, those who luckily were on shore when the tempest struck in, stayed there until 5 November 1527, when Narváez arrived with the other four ships and decided to spend the winter.

On or about 22 February 1527 the fleet made a fresh start, with four ships and a bergantina, lifting four hundred men and eighty horses. Narváez had engaged a pilot who claimed to know exactly where the Rio de Palmas was situated, but instead took them, after several storms, to the west coast of Florida, anchoring at a place which the historians locate either at St. Clement's Point near the site of St. Petersburg, on

Tampa Bay or Charlotte Harbor, or at the mouth of the Caloosahatchee River near Fort Myers. Narváez landed on 1 May and pompously took possession for Spain. He then made the fatuous decision to send his ships away to look for a good harbor to the westward, and with 260 men on foot and forty mounted, to travel by land.

In the meantime, he tangled with the local Timucuan cacique, Hirrihigua by name, who resisted his advance. Narváez overcame him, but by way of warning (for Narváez was both cruel and stupid) had the cacique's nose cut off and cast his mother to his fierce dogs to be torn apart and eaten. This march was miserable enough, but nothing to what came later. The cavalcade pressed through a forest of tall trees until 25 June, when it came in sight of the chief town of the Apalachee tribe, from whom the Appalachian Mountains are named. It was at or near the site of Tallahassee, Florida; probably on the banks of Micco-sukee Lake. Here there was plenty of maize and other food, and the company stayed twenty-five days; a good part of the time under attack since Narváez had imprudently detained a cacique as hostage. These Apalachee were the most expert bowmen that Europeans encountered anywhere—far more expert than the Iroquois or Algonkin. Their bows were of oak, six feet long, so strong that no Spaniard could bend them, and their amazingly accurate archers wounded and killed Christians through joints in their steel armor. And the natives skipped about so nimbly while shooting that they could seldom be hit by a crossbow bolt or arquebus bullet.

After nine days' travel from the Apalachee's capital, frequently beset by hostile natives, the Spaniards reached a place that they called Aute on the Gulf near the modern St. Marks, Florida. Narváez, having had enough, sent a reconnoitering expedition to the coast (in Apalachee Bay) hoping to find his ships; but no ships were there.

Cabeza de Vaca found out, years later, what had happened to them. Narváez had left four ships at his original landing place under command of one Caravallo, with orders to proceed directly to the Rio Pánuco in Mexico and meet him there. (In spite of Pineda's voyage, Narváez seems to have been under the delusion that Pánuco was just around the corner from Florida.) One ship was "lost in the breakers" at the start, but the other three sailed off. Among the hundred souls on board were a few wives of the men who had gone ashore with Narváez; on the instigation of one who predicted that the entire landing party would perish, the ladies all "married, or became the concubines of those who remained on board the ships." Thus happily provided with that which most mariners lacked, Caravallo's ships, with one other that came from Cuba to look for Narváez, spent nearly a year searching for his landing party along the Gulf shore, then sailed to Mexico and were discharged. Had they put back into St. Marks Bay in September 1528, they would have found the landing party, saved over 200 lives, and deprived us of Cabeza de Vaca's fascinating story.

In their bad fix the only thing Narváez's men to do seemed to be to build boats which, with good luck, might carry them all to Mexico. Not a single man of the lot was a shipbuilder, and only one a carpenter; they had no materials for sails or rigging, no tools but their personal knives, and no food but their own horses. Yet somehow they managed. Bellows were made out of deerskins and hollowed logs, so a forge could be set up; nails, axes and saws were fashioned from spurs, stirrups, and crossbow iron; a Greek member of the crew knew how to make resin from pine trees; stuff for lines and caulking was twisted from palm fiber and horsehair, water bottles fashioned from the flayed-off skins of horses' legs; masts and oars were cut from the local pine, and sails sewn together from the men's shirts. For food, one horse was sacrificed every three days, and from the Indians (who attacked them intermittently) they acquired a store of maize by force. Every man worked so well that between 4 and 20 September 1528, five boats were finished, each about 33 feet long. Two days later the last horse was eaten and all survivors embarked to the number of 245, with 47 to 48 men in each boat. When loaded, each gunwale was less than a foot above the ocean, but later they contrived to make wash-boards. The place on St. Marks Bay they named Bahia de Caballos in honor of the horses which, so far, had saved their lives.

It took them thirty days or more to reach Pensacola Bay, their first real shelter. There the natives apparently were friendly but treacherous, attacking the Christians by night and wounding many. Cabeza de Vaca broke up a lot of their canoes in the morning, both to obtain fuel and to prevent pursuit. Another attack was beaten off in Mobile Bay, and on the last day of October they crossed the mouth of the Mississippi safely. Like Pinzón at the Amazon, they knew that they were off a mighty river because they could drink the water alongside.

It would be tedious to give every detail of this crazy voyage. One by one the boats disappeared, or were wrecked on shores where their crews fell prey to starvation or native hostility. Cabeza de Vaca's craft capsized near shore on 8 November when all but five of his crew were sick; but the shock revived them and, once ashore, they managed to light a fire and parch corn. Friendly Indians replenished their food supply, and they put to sea once more. Next day their boat capsized in heavy seas, several more men were drowned, and the survivors lost all their clothes and possessions. The same thing happened to Dorantes and Castillo, in another boat. The one in which Narváez sailed, he insisted on staying on board at night with one of his pages. Since this boat was moored only with a stone killick, she slipped out to sea one blowy night and was never heard of again.

On this shore, as the Indians seemed fairly friendly, Cabeza de Vaca and his fellow survivors stayed from November 1528 until May 1529. The place, which he called *Malhado* ("Bad Luck") Island, is doubtfully identified as Galveston Island, Texas. Some eighty men got ashore from the other boats wrecked there, but only fifteen were alive in the spring. "We survivors," wrote their indomitable leader, "escaped naked as we were born, with the loss of all we had, . . . and our bodies were so emaciated . . . that we looked like pictures of death."

In order to survive, Cabeza de Vaca, Dorantes, Esteban, and Castillo acquired, willy-nilly, a reputation as medicine men. The natives, regarding all four as visitors from another world, forced that role upon them. "Our method," wrote the leader, "was to bless the sick, breathing on them, and recite a Pater Noster and an Ave Maria, praying with all earnestness to God our Lord that He would give health and influence them to make us some good return." All four, including Esteban, became practitioners.

Since his Malhado Island hosts were gatherers of nuts, roots, and shellfish, living literally from hand to mouth, Cabeza de Vaca, to get more food, established friendly relations with a nearby mainland tribe, the Charucco. With them he lived until 1533. Although practicing their alleged cures, Cabeza de Vaca and the other three survivors were practically slaves to their hosts, required to do the hard labor of the camp such as carrying water and cutting and hauling firewood. The natives thought nothing of going three or four days without food; but, wrote Cabeza de Vaca, "They are a merry race, considering the hunger they suffer. . . . To them the happiest part of the year is the season of eating prickly pears; they have hunger then no longer, pass all the time in dancing and eating, day and night." Later he mentions seeing herds of wild buffalo, but does not seem to have been much impressed, and certainly enjoyed no buffalo steaks; these natives killed them only for their pelts. Catching and killing a deer was a big community operation, seldom performed. Our medicine men were often given slices of venison by grateful patients; but, as Cabeza de Vaca tells us, they had to gobble it up raw, or someone not so grateful would snatch it away and broil it for himself.

Finally, the four survivors of the Narváez expedition decided, literally, to walk for their lives. All had become medicine men of great repute, and that is what saved them. From September 1533, picture them, still "naked as their mothers bore them," walking barefoot from one village to another over the parched Texas plains; the massive, red-haired Cabeza de Vaca in the lead, followed by big black Esteban, Captain Dorantes his legal master, and Captain Castillo. And usually, behind but accompanying them, came hundreds of natives of the last village who joyfully informed those of the next one, which might be several days' marches away, that the peerless quartet were mighty healers. "No one whom we treated," and they often were numbered by the hundred, "but told us he was left well." Each native escort plundered the poor huts of the new hosts; but this did not seem to be resented, as the hosts promised themselves to steal it all back shortly, with interest.

"Throughout all this country," wrote Cabeza de Vaca, "we went naked, and . . . twice a year we cast our skins like serpents." The heavy loads of wood they had to bear for their hosts produced "sores on breasts and shoulders. . . . In these labors my only solace and relief was in thinking of the sufferings of my Redeemer Jesus Christ, and in the blood He shed for me, in considering how much greater must have been the torment He sustained." Yet, despite his sufferings, Cabeza de Vaca really liked the Indians. At one village the people had nothing to give the four "physicians" but leaves and the green fruit of the prickly pear. Yet, says he, "They did this with kindness and good will, and were happy to be without anything to eat, that they might have food to give us." And again, "These people see and hear better, and have keener senses than any other in the world. They are great in hunger, thirst and cold, as if they were made for the endurance of these more than other men, by habit and nature."

After crossing a "wide and deep river" (probably the Colorado below the site of Austin, Texas) the four men shaped their course west, "frequently accompanied by three or four thousand people." They crossed the Pecos River and were guided "through more than fifty leagues of desert, over rough mountains," in which they "suffered much from hunger." Now in Mexican territory, they encountered Indians who grew beans, maize, and pumpkins, wove cotton, and gave them cotton "shawls" partly to cover their nakedness.

In Cabeza de Vaca's narrative there is no mention of sex, or even whether the Indian girls were pretty. As alguacil, marshal of the fleet, he had police authority and may have been able to force his three companions to "lay off." As we shall see when we come to his next voyage, he was a chaste and virtuous, almost ascetic, man. Or it may be that he and his crew were so underfed as to have no sexual appetite. Most of the Indians they encountered lived the life of Hobbes's, not Rousseau's, state of nature. "Poor, nasty and brutish." They sowed not, neither did they reap, but ate what raw nature offered; in the walnut season they all ate nothing but walnuts; in the prickly pear season they ate prickly pear; and in between they picked up toads and snakes, or trapped a few fish in the streams, or just starved.

In northern Mexico the four men found that the natives had fled to the mountains for fear of slave-hunting Spaniards. "The sight was one of infinite pain to us; a land very fertile and beautiful, abounding in springs and streams, the villages deserted and burned, the people thin and weak, all fleeing or in concealment." Then somewhere on the Rio Sonora, Cabeza de Vaca grasped the hand of a fellow Spaniard, thus completing for the first time the circuit of the Gulf country by land. He encountered a slave-catching party of Mexican Spaniards under one Diego de Alcaraz. This nobleman had the indecency to propose not only to enslave those Indians following the "healers" but to scoop up another lot of six hundred fugitives who, at Cabeza de Vaca's request, had brought in maize to relieve the Spaniards from starvation! "We had many high words" on this subject, wrote the intrepid traveler, and Alcaraz even tried to suborn the Indians' loyalty by claiming that the four companions were "persons of mean condition." Finally, Alcaraz passed on the four wanderers to the city of Compostella where the local governor gave them clothes and beds, but "we could not wear any for some time, nor could we sleep anywhere but on the ground." Then on to Mexico City, where they arrived on 25 July 1536, almost eight years from the time their boats were destroyed.

Cabeza de Vaca soon decided to return to Spain. After an eventful and tempestuous voyage from Vera Cruz, he arrived at Lisbon on 10 August 1537. Alonso del Castillo and Andrés Dorantes went with him. Castillo returned to Mexico and became a rich man, as did Dorantes. When Fray Marcos, the precursor of Coronado, organized an expedition to find the fabulous Seven Cities of Cíbola in 1539, he obtained the services of Estébancito as guide and interpreter. The friars did not like him much, both because he "knew it all" and because, as they went along, he accumulated a harem of Indian girls—perhaps as compensation for opportunities missed on the long walk. So they sent him and his women ahead. The rulers of the Zuñi, in the first of the Seven Cities which he reached, had never seen a black man before; they suspected him of being a spy for enemies coming to destroy them, and put him to death.

As for Cabeza de Vaca, he could not rest after publishing in 1542 his *Relación* of the great trans-Texas walk. Within a few years we find him walking across Brazil, but with a larger and more distinguished retinue.

Hernando de Soto

Although I have warned my readers that they must not expect me to guide them on even longer inland explorations than Cabeza de Vaca's, namely, those of De Soto and Coronado, I feel bound at least to get De Soto under way. Coronado jumped off from Compostella in northern Mexico as soon as he heard from Fray Marcos, and at that point we shall have to leave him.

Hernando de Soto was the son of a gentleman of Xeres de los Caballeros, not the sherry headquarters of Andalusia but a small place further north, in the mountains. Having made a small fortune (180,000 cruzados) helping Pizarro to conquer Peru, he came to Seville where Charles V was holding court, and lived like a great prince. While he was still there, Cabeza de Vaca returned from Mexico and set everyone agog by his tales of Florida. De Soto decided that there, in the interior of the future Gulf states, lay his future field of action; he would establish a great vice-royalty of Florida to rival those of Mexico and Peru. He obtained on very favorable terms a grant from Charles V, to whom he had lent a considerable amount of his Peruvian loot. The Emperor appointed him governor of Cuba and Adelantado of Florida, with the promise of a noble title for any new territory he might discover.

De Soto purchased and equipped seven ships out of his own funds, appointed the captains and officers, and selected numerous gentlemen volunteers. The fleet sailed from Sanlúcar in April 1538, reached Gomera in the Canaries (Columbus's departure point in 1492) on Easter Sunday, stayed eight days topping off with provisions, and made a leisurely passage of forty-two days to Cuba, arriving at Santiago on Whitsunday. Thence he dispatched the ships around Cape San Antonio to the Havana—which took them another forty days; while he with favored members of his staff and 150 mounted men marched across Cuba with great pomp and circumstance. At Havana, De Soto tarried almost a year and beefed up his fleet to five ships, two caravels, and ten bergantinas floating 570 men and 223 horses. His flagship, *San Cristóbal,* was registered as 800 *tonelados; Magdalena* was "no smaller," *La Concepción,* captained by Luis de Moscoso de Alvarado, was of 500 tuns, and there were two more "large vessels," two caravels, and a bergantina. These were barely enough for so many men and horses.

De Soto took the good precaution to send a ship under a trusted captain, Juan de Añasco, to reconnoiter the west coast of Florida for a good harbor. That he did; and the Adelantado, making his landfall there on Whitsunday, 25 May 1539, named it after the Holy Spirit. On Whitmonday they entered the harbor, now identified as "the enlarged section of the Caloosahatchee River, where it ends at Beautiful Island above East Fort Myers." Here a treasure trove in human shape was acquired: a Spaniard named Ortiz, sole survivor of a ship sent from Cuba by the widow of Pánfilo de Narváez to search for him. All shipmates of Ortiz had been killed by the local Indians, he only being saved by the intercession of a cacique's wife and no fewer than three daughters, a whole family of Pocahontases. He joined De Soto and proved most valuable as interpreter, but did not survive the long journey.

The Adelantado, as Shea * wrote, "had been trained in a bad school,"

* See notes at end of Chapter.

that of Pizzaro; "he had no respect for the lives or rights of the Indians." Even his contemporary Oviedo accused him of killing natives just for sport. With 570 men and 223 horses he could afford to be rough and tough, and that he was on his four years' march. Even to the lady cacique of Cofachiqui (Silver Bluff on the Savannah River), who welcomed him with a superb necklace of baroque pearls, he acted with unpardonable cruelty.

De Soto's tactics were to enter an Indian village, seize the cacique and others as hostages, demand and receive provisions for man and beast, and after a tense rest, proceed to the next town with the captive cacique and hostages. These were allowed to go home when the second town capitulated. This usually worked, but sometimes it did not, and De Soto's men had several close shaves when an unusually brave tribe attacked *en masse*. De Soto's group of Spaniards had the same admiration for the long-bow tactics of the Indians they met as did the Narváez party. The best way they found to deal with those nimble and straight-shooting enemies was to charge them on horseback, and, at close quarters cut them down with pike or broadsword. The Indians feared those razor-edged Toledo points and blades far more than they dreaded the infantry weapons of crossbow and arquebus.

From the lady cacique's capital near the site of Augusta, Georgia, De Soto marched west to the Blue Ridge, southwest almost to Mobile Bay, and spent a second winter in the Yazoo delta. At the Chickasaw Bluffs below Memphis, he built four barges, each holding sixty to seventy men and five or six horses, and crossed the Mississippi. This happened about two years after his landing in Florida. A third winter they passed at the junction of the Arkansas and Canadian rivers in what is now Oklahoma. Returning to the Mississippi, De Soto caught a fever at the mouth of the Red River and died on 21 May 1542. His heavily weighted remains were sunk in the river. Luis Moscoso, who succeeded him as adelantado, led an incursion to the upper Brazos, and spent a fourth winter (1542–43) at the mouth of the Arkansas. There he built a fleet of bergantinas, sailed down the Mississippi, crossed the Gulf in fifty-two days, and arrived at Rio Pánuco in Mexico on 10 September 1543. The number of survivors was 311.

Although one cannot but admire De Soto's organizing ability, stubborn pride and ruthless courage which more than once saved his force from annihilation, one must admit that his Greater Florida expedition was wasted effort. The amount of gold that he extorted was not enough to tempt a second expedition; and although Cabeza de Vaca's experiences did lead, via Coronado and Oñate, to the founding of the frontier province of New Mexico, De Soto's expedition led to no colonizing effort, much less to a viceroyalty like those of Mexico and Peru. Final honors go to the red men who fought valiantly for their hearths and homes against these cruel invaders. They at least gained a respite of centuries before white men seized their lands and removed the survivors to Oklahoma.

Thus, in forty years from Ponce de León's sighting of Florida's east coast, the Gulf of Mexico and the hinterland had been explored and the possibility of finding an inter-oceanic strait in that region at last removed. Not so in South America, to which we now return. There the Spanish and Portuguese efforts to implement Solis's, Coelho's, and Magellan's voyages resulted in the founding of two empires—Brazil and La Plata.

Bibliography and Notes

BERMUDA

Henry C. Wilkinson, *The Adventurers of Bermuda* (London, 1958), is much the best modern history, with (p. 29) a list of 16th-century maps. He also reproduces the interesting story of Henry May's five months' stay there in 1593–94 with other castaways from James Lancaster's *Edward Bonaventure*. J. H. Lefroy, *Memorials of Discovery and Early Settlement of the Bermudas* (2 vols., 1877–79), contains the best collection of documents. R. Barreiro-Meiro, *Las Islas Bermudas y Juan Bermúdez* (Madrid, 1970), reproduces the Peter Martyr map and relates everything that is known about Juan Bermúdez. The same map may also be found in Arthur J. Weise, *The Discoverers of America* (1884), p. 221. A man testifying in the *Pleitos Colombinos* (1964 ed., VIII, 273) in 1535 deposed that he knew "Juan Vermudes, he who discovered La Vermuda." The classic Gabriel Archer account of Sir Thomas Gates's "Wracke on Bermuda" is in *Purchas His Pilgrimes* (MacLehose ed., XIX, 1906, chapter vi); Oviedo reference is to 1851 edition, I, 38. Correct co-ördinates for Gibbs Hill Light are latitude 32°15′ N, longitude 64°50′ W. The group is often called "The Bermudas," because in addition to the four almost continuous big islands there are hundreds of little ones and breaking cays.

Bermuda Triangle. Among mysterious disappearances are U.S.S. *Cyclops*, a U.S. Navy collier that vanished in 1918; five Navy torpedo bombers lost after a weird radio exchange with their base in 1945; an Air Force tanker plane that vanished in 1962; and, in 1963, a fishing boat, two Air Force tanker jets, and the merchant ship *Marine Sulphur Queen*. Story in *Sea Secrets*, XVI, No. 4 (July 1973), p. 3, referring to Vincent H. Gaddis, *Invisible Horizons, True Mysteries of the Sea* (Philadelphia, 1965).

For the English re-discovery of *1609*, William Strachey, *The Historie of Travell into Virginia Britania* (1612), Hakluyt Society ed. (2nd. ser., CIII, 1953), p. 90, is important.

FLORIDA AND PONCE DE LEÓN

We now come to a fresh set of sources. The books and pamphlets on the history of Florida, which have proliferated since the 400th anniversary of Ponce in 1913, are, I regret to say, a pretty sad lot, and the only ones I find worth mentioning are the monographs by Lawson, Florence Fritz, and Rolfe F. Schell.

Local historians seem to have embraced the myth that John Cabot discovered Florida in 1497–98, which started with the tall tales of Sebastian Cabot (Woodbury Lowery, *Spanish Settlements within . . . the United States 1513–1561* (New York, 1901), p. 43). This long-since discarded fable was hotted up again by D. O. True in *Imago Mundi*, XI (1954), 73–84. In my *Northern Voyages* will be found evidence that the 1497 voyage was confined to Newfoundland and adjacent waters; and absolutely nothing is known of Cabot's fate on the 1498 voyage. The alleged map evidence is imaginary. Since Cabot was looking for a Northwest Passage to the Indies, it is incredible that he should have sought it around Jacksonville or Key Biscayne. In Chapter XII above, I discussed the possibility of the mysterious coast on the 1502 Cantino map representing the voyage of some unknown discoverer.

The latest and most thorough studies of Ponce de León's life and voyages are all in Spanish and by my esteemed friend Aurelio Tió, a civil engineer of Santurce, Puerto Rico. Many of the documents are printed in his *Nuevas Fuentes Para la Historia de Puerto Rico* (San Germán, P.R., and Barcelona, 1961), and the voyages are intensively studied in his "Historia del descubrimiento de la Florida y Beimeni o Yucatan," in Academia Puertorriqueña de la Historia *Boletín*, II, No. 8 (1972). Ponce's pedigree is in *Nuevas Fuentes*, pp. 518–19 and 532–47. Our man was never granted a special coat of arms by the Sovereigns, but inherited one of numerous quarterings from his ancestors. The Instituto de Cultura Puertorriqueña published in 1967 a new edition of Juan de Castellanos (1522–1607), *Elegias de Varones Ilustres*, Elegia VI, which includes Ponce de León, with English translation by Señora Muna Lee of stanzas 46–48 pertaining to him.

Although every history and reference book states that our Ponce was born in 1460, they are wrong by 14 years. At an inquest in Seville on 28 September 1514, he swore that he was 40 years old. Academia Puertorriqueña *Boletín*, I, No. 2 (125–39).

In my opinion, the two best secondary histories in English on the Discovery of Florida are still John G. Shea's chapter "Ancient Florida" in Justin Winsor, *Narrative and Critical History of America*, II (1886), 231–98, and Woodbury Lowery, *Spanish Settlements within . . . the United States 1513–1561*. John Gilmary Shea (1824–92) was the foremost American Roman Catholic historian of the 19th century; and Lowery, a prominent member of the galaxy of North American Spanish scholars (Prescott, Ticknor, etc.) which, alas, appears to be almost extinct. Lowery, whose dates are 1853–1906, graduated from Harvard in 1875, became first a chemist and then a lawyer in New York. Owing largely to the circumstance of his sister's marrying the Duke of Arcos, ambassador of Spain to Mexico, he was persuaded to cultivate the largely untilled field of early Florida; and thus spent the rest of his life, very successfully. His scholarship was impeccable (every statement annotated); his style, unfortunately, is rather dull. The sequel to the above-mentioned volume, *Spanish Settlements within . . . the United States, Florida, 1562–74* (1905), covers the era of Franco-Spanish conflicts that I do not, and is a good offset to Parkman's brilliant but very pro-French *Pioneers of France in the New World* (2nd ed., 1885).

The primary source for Ponce's 1513 voyage was written at least 80 years later by the Spanish official historian Antonio de Herrera in his *Historia General de los Hechos de los Castellanos* (Madrid, 1601), dec. I, lib. 9, p. 302; and Herrera writes as if he had access to an original journal. My references are to the English translation by John Stevens (London, 1740).

Ponce in Puerto Rico. Aurelio Tió, *Nuevas Fuentes*, pp. 17–18, 27. On pp. 431, 434, is a list of Spanish arms lost in the conquest of Puerto Rico, for which Ponce's heirs sought compensation in 1587. They included 9-foot lances, arquebuses, fowling pieces, crossbows, and corselets. In *Fundación de San Germán* (San Juan, 1956), Tió establishes the date 1506. As we have seen (Chapter X), the crown had already appointed Vicente Yáñez Pinzón governor of Puerto Rico in 1505, but this appointment lapsed for lack of performance. The story of the dogs is in Oviedo (1851 ed.), I, 483.

The Fountain of Youth. Quotations from Peter Martyr in *De Orbe Novo*, 2nd dec., book x; Leonardo Olschki's translation. In Peter's already mentioned West Indies map of 1511, *isla de beimeni* lies directly north of Cuba at approximately the site of Andros. On the Freducci map (see below) it lies directly north of Matanzas. Francis Parkman, *Pioneers of France*, 2nd ed., chap. i, adds, for him, a rather naughty footnote; the story was "suggested, it is said, by the beauty of the native women, which none could resist, and which kindled the fires of youth in the reins of age." Further light on the beckoning fountain is thrown by Leonardo Olschki, "Ponce de León's Fountain of Youth, History of a Geographic Myth," *Hispanic American Historical Review*, XXI (1941), 361–85. The Eurasian myth is traceable to the *Letter of Prester John* (1165) and the fountain of *Le Roman d'Alexandre*, in whose waters fifty-six aged companions of Alexander the Great recovered the visage and vigor of youth.

Task Organization for Florida, found by Aurelio Tió in an obscure ships' register, is printed as Appendix I to his history in the Academia *Boletín*, II, No. 8 (1972), 141–43.

Ponce's first voyage to Florida. Edward W. Lawson, *The First Landing Place of Juan Ponce de León . . . in the Year 1513* (privately printed) is the most detailed account, up to the landfall. Lawson is a master mariner who knows the Florida waters and can expertly apply Herrera's courses. From the first landing place I follow Tió's reconstructed log of the voyage in the Academia *Boletín*, II, No. 8 (1972).

The Freducci map of 1514–15 is in the State Archives of Florence. The best reproduction to date is by Eugenio Casenova, *La Carta Nautica di Conte Ottomanno Freducci* (Firenze, 1894), Publication No. 21 of the Istituto di Studi Superiori.

Ponce de León at Guanahaní. Aurelio Tió in the Academia *Boletín* No. 5, pp. 37, 103, 154–79, goes at length into the significance of this visit in identifying Columbus's landfall of 1492. Herrera gives the latitude of San Salvador as 25°04′; actually it lies between 23°55′ and 24°10′. Captain Peters, who did the desk navigating for Lawson's *First Landing Place*, figured out that Pilot Alaminos had an obsolete edition of the Alphonsine Tables of Declination, which threw his calculations about one degree too far north, and so applied the same error to other latitudes reported by Herrera. I confess myself rather skeptical of this kind of figuring. L. D. Scisco in American Geographical Society *Bulletin*, XLV (Oct. 1913), 721–35, identifies the Bahamian islands. Useful, too, is Scisco's "Ponce de Leon's Patents for Colonization," in American Catholic Historical Society *Records*, XXIII, No. 4 (Dec. 1912), 208.

In the city of St. Augustine today there is an establishment that sells "water from Ponce's Fountain of Youth," at one dollar for a small glass. Myth or no myth, hundreds of thousands of elderly North Americans have moved to Florida in recent years to prolong their lives in that balmy climate.

Cape Florida has finally disappeared from the map, but the name appears on almost every one through the 19th century, located on Key Biscayne just south of Miami, at about lat. 25°40′ N. Even Bartholomew's *Oxford Advanced Atlas* (1936) placed it right on Miami Beach. Crossing Biscayne Bay from here, the coast makes a slight bend west of south, which is accentuated when one reaches the Florida Keys. Herrera's latitude for Cape Florida (II, 35), 18°15′, is a misprint for 28°15′.

Earlier historians assumed that the second landing of Ponce took place in Cuba; Tió has evidence in *Boletín*, II (1972), 81–82, which proves it to have been Yucatan. Part of the corroborative evidence is a petition of 1519 or 1520 to Diego Colón, the second admiral, referring to an island apart from Cuba "now called Ulloa Yucatan, formerly called Bimini among Christians"; and again, "las partes de Bimini." The petitioner, unnamed, not improbably one of Ponce's surviving relatives, was trying to prevent D. Diego from giving Yucatan to Cortés, on the ground that it had been discovered years before. This is in Duquesa de Alba, *Autógrafos de Colón*, (Madrid, 1892), p. 71. The name Bimini in the 19th century was given to a Bahamian island that is sufficiently near the Florida coast to serve one-day gamblers.

There is no record of any European except shipwrecked sailors having seen Mexico prior to Ponce's descent on that June day of 1513. Official recognition of Ponce de León as European discoverer of Mexico came in 1972, with the laureation of Aurelio Tió by the University of Mexico and learned academies.

Ponce's Carib expedition. Aurelio Tió, in the above-mentioned *Boletin*, II (1972), 149–53, prints a list of his formidable armament and ample sea stores for this expedition, and all that is known about the caravel. Ponce bought her from Bono de Quexo, captain of *Santa Maria de Consolación*, in 1513. Whether Ponce did manage to catch and punish the Caribs is unknown.

Ponce at San Juan de Ulua? See Tío in same *Boletín*, II, 258–64, and in his *Nuevas Fuentes*, pp. 110–16, and Document No. 5 with notes (pp. 344–411). It is true, as my obliging friend James Byrne pointed out to me, that the deposition of an octogenarian named Juan Griego is dated 37 years earlier than Rivera's (*Nuevas Fuentes*, p. 361 and notes, pp. 375–76), but all Griego says is that Ponce de León, whom he had known in Puerto Rico, had discovered *Nueva España*, meaning Yucatan.

Voyages of Córdoba and Grijalba. Two North American historians, eighty years apart: Edward Channing in Justin Winsor, *Narrative and Critical History of America*, II (1886), 203–4, 214–16, and Carl O. Sauer, *The Early Spanish Main* (Berkeley, 1966), pp. 212–17, have written brief accounts of these short voyages, based on the same sources, of which Channing gives a list. Herrera, II, 111–14, is responsible for the interesting remark about Columbus. Alaminos must have accompanied Columbus on his voyage of discovery in 1494 along the south coast of Cuba, and remembered how eager the Admiral had been to sail westward, and his regret at being forced to turn back.

Punta de Palmares. Commodore Matthew C. Perry landed there in 1847; see Morison, *Old Bruin* (Boston, 1967), p. 233.

Ponce de León's last voyage. Depositions of old men who had heard Alaminos tell about Ponce's death are in the Academia *Boletín*, II, 260–61. See also No. 5, pp. 180–213.

The Oviedo reference is in his *Historia General y Natural*, 1851 ed., III, 622 (lib. xxxvi, cap. i).

Miruelo's voyage. Justin Winsor, *Narrative and Critical History of America*, II, 236, quoting Herrera and Oviedo. Modern historians too readily assume that if discoverers met hostility from the natives, some European must have been there earlier. That by no means follows. Some, like Ojeda, alienated Indians who had never seen a white man, by a rough attitude and unreasonable demands; some natives initiated hostilities.

Ponce's epitaph, as recorded by the early Spanish historian Barcia, is

> Mole sub hac fortis Requiescunt ossa LEONIS
> Qui vivit factis Nomina magna suis

> Beneath this structure rest the bones of a Lion
> Who performed deeds mightier than his name.

And Oviedo, in his *Historia General y Natural* (1851 ed.), III, 621, said, *é cómo era hidalgo de gentíles é altos pensamientos*—"he was a nobleman of elegant and high thoughts."

Las Casas, who disliked Ponce for his brutality toward the Indians, admitted (*Historia de Las Indias*, 1927 ed., II, 450) that to him we owe the name Florida, "by which we now designate all the land and seacoast which commence at the great cape [of Florida] which he discovered, up to the Codfish Country, not to say the Labrador." Thus, Florida in the Spanish empire corresponded to the original Virginia, meaning everything Spanish on the North American continent east and north of Mexico. When the English settled Jamestown, Spain regarded them as intruders in Florida.

At Florence, Archivio di Stati, I examined the nautical chart by Ottomanno Freducci, the earliest known map to have the name Florida. Date is conjectural; I should say, shortly after 1515. It is in two halves, pasted together (like the La Cosa map), so there is no sense comparing his Florida latitudes with those of European. *I. Florida* is the northernmost name on the peninsula. It is followed by *Rio de Canoas* (scene of the fight?) and other names, not easily identifiable, as well as the *tortugas* and *martires*. *Beiminj* is a squarish island just west of *abaco*. These names are repeated on several later maps, such as the anonymous Turin and the 1529 Ribero. Freducci's map includes a not inaccurate depiction of *la bermuda*, with the names *monte peloso* (Gibbs Hill?), *quira suceron*, and *mira come vos* ("watch out!"). Yucatan and the bulge of Brazil are also on this map, which is reproduced and discussed in *Publicazioni* del Reale Istituto di Studi Superiori No. 4 (Florence, 1894). For the wrecks off Florida, see Robert F. Marx, *The Lure of Sunken Treasure* (New York, 1973).

What we now need is an historically minded yachtsman who, Herrera in hand, will follow Ponce's route from San Juan on the 1513 voyage, and study the shores of Florida to ascertain exactly where he called.

PINEDA AND EARLY GULF CARTOGRAPHY

John G. Shea's, "Ancient Florida" in Winsor, *Narrative and Critical History of America*, II, 237–42, 284, and Arthur J. Weise, *Discoveries of America to 1525* (New York, 1884), chapter viii, pp. 275–78. Both are based on Bernal Díaz's *Historia Verdadera*, of which I have used the excellent Alfred P. Maudslay translation, edited by Genaro García (New York, 1950).

This is the Mexican part of Sir Alfred's classic five-volume edition of Bernal Díaz published by the Hakluyt Society, 1908–16. Garay's *asiento* is on pp. 147–53, with outline map of Pineda's discoveries. Winsor's own chapter on "Early Cartography of the Gulf of Mexico and Adjacent Parts" in his *Narrative and Critical History*, II, 217–30, has never been surpassed.

Death of Pineda is in Maudslay's *Bernal Díaz*, II (Hakluyt Society, London, 1910), 282–83.

NARVÁEZ AND CABEZA DE VACA

Here the main source is *La Relación que Dio Alvar Nuñez Cabeça de Vaca de lo Acaescido en las Indias en la Armada Donde Iva por Governador Panphilo de Narváez* (Zamora, 1542). This classic of adventure and exploration is often referred to as his *Naufragios*, the title of the second edition. The earliest translation (more a paraphrase than a translation) is in *Purchas His Pilgrimes* (1613 ed., Part IV, lib. viii), but the best and most available is by Buckingham Smith, one of the first generation of North American Spanish scholars.* This is the translation used in Frederick W. Hodge and Theodore H. Lewis (eds.), *Spanish Explorers in the Southern United States, 1528–1543* of the *Original Narratives* series (New York, 1907, and many later editions). Hodge, a leading authority on the American Indian (author of the standard *Handbook of American Indians North of Mexico*, 2 vols., Washington, 1907–10) contributes valuable notes on the tribes encountered by Cabeza de Vaca. Another good translation, by Fanny Bandelier, edited by her husband Adolph F. A. Bandelier (1840–1914), a great authority on the Indians of this region, was published in the *Trail Makers* series in 1905.

Morris Bishop, *The Odyssey of Cabeza de Vaca* (New York, 1933) is not only the most scholarly and readable life of our hero, but one of the best biographies of any Spanish conquistador. Maps representing widely different attempts to chart the long walk are here (p. 32) and in Woodbury Lowery's *Spanish Settlements . . . 1513–1561* (p. 481).

Location of Narváez's landing. On Sebastian Cabot's world map of 1544 an unmistakable Apalachee Bay is labeled, "[Aqui] desembarco Panfilo de Narvaez," and Sebastian may have had this direct from Cabeza de Vaca in Seville; but I think he confused the landing place with the site of Narváez's boat-building. Florence Fritz, *Unknown Florida* (Coral Gables, 1963), convinces me that the landing took place near Fort Myers. Also, the beautiful

* Born in Georgia in 1810, son of a U. S. consul to Mexico, Buckingham Smith graduated from Trinity College, Hartford, and the Harvard Law School, practiced law at St. Augustine, served as secretary of legation in Mexico and Spain 1850–58, where (like Washington Irving and others) he became interested in early Spanish-American history. His translation of Cabeza de Vaca was privately printed (Washington, 1851); the second and revised edition appeared in 1871, the year of his death.

1542 map of the French cartographer Testu, reproduced in Cummings, Skelton, and Quinn, *Discovery of America,* shows a "baie de Narvaez" at about that distance up the west coast. The dog episode is from Fritz, p. 14; originally (I guess) from an edition of Garcilaso de la Vega that I have not seen. Lowery, *Spanish Settlements . . . 1513–1561,* p. 134, states that this cruel practice became such an integral part of Christian tactics that they invented a new name for it, *aperrear,* and the editor of the 1851 Oviedo (IV, 593) defines it as "echar á perros, para que devoren y maten la presa: costumbre que los españoles introdujeron en la conquista."

Cabeza de Vaca gives the length of each boat as 22 *cubitos;* a cubit was the forearm's length, varying in different countries from 17 to 22 inches.

Identity of Malhado Island is discussed in Hodge, *Spanish Explorers,* pp. 57–58, and in Morris Bishop, chap. vi.

Death of Esteban. Best account is in Woodbury Lowery, pp. 278–82, including the Zuñi tradition as taken down by Frank H. Cushing about four centuries after it happened. From this it appears that the black angered the Zuñi by brandishing a decorated gourd-rattle, which to them was an emblem of sovereignty.

HERNANDO DE SOTO

The principal account of this conquistador's expedition is that of his companion, the anonymous *fidalgo de Elvas,* a Portuguese gentleman of Elvas, first published at Évora, 1557. Of many translations, that by Buckingham Smith, first published in 1866, is conveniently found in *Spanish Explorers in the Southern United States, 1528–1543,* Hodge and Lewis (eds.), pp. 133–272; other references on pp. 130–32. Second in importance is Garcilaso de la Vega, *The Florida of the Inca,* translated by J. G. and J. J. Varner (Austin, 1951). This famous Inca historian was the son of a Spanish conquistador of Peru named Sebastian Garcilaso de la Vega and of Chimpa Ocllo, a niece of Huáscar Capac, last Inca emperor but one. Born at Cuzco in 1539 and brought up as a Christian, he remained intensely proud of his Inca heritage. In 1560 he went to Spain, served in the army, learned Latin and Italian, and read and wrote voluminously. At Lisbon in 1605 his *Florida del Inca* was printed, and in 1609–16 appeared his *Commentarios Reales del Peru,* a most valuable history of his country. The *Florida* is based largely on oral testimony of De Soto's survivors. He died in 1616 in Cordova and was buried in the cathedral. For bibliography, see Winsor, *Narrative and Critical History,* II (1886), 290, 575. The chapter by John Gilmary Shea (1824–1892) in Winsor, II, 245–56, remains, in my opinion, the best short account of the De Soto Expedition.

R. F. Schell, *De Soto Didn't Land at Tampa* (Fort Myers, 1968), is an admirable and exceptional bit of Florida research, as the author not only reads Spanish but has sailed all along the west coast in small boats. Would there were more like it! All earlier and "standard" books state that De Soto landed in Tampa Bay.

The sufferings of Ortiz under Hirrihigua, that cacique's revenge for the cruelty of Narváez, are related at length in *The Florida of the Inca* (Varners' translation), chaps. ii–iv. By the time of De Soto's arrival, another had succeeded Hirrihigua. For the lady cacique see chap. xi, and index under Cofachiqui.

✳ XXII ✳

Sebastian Cabot Goes to Sea

1526-1530

From Sanlúcar to Santa Catarina

Our old friend Sebastian Cabot, son of John the discoverer, now joins the conquerors. He commanded a voyage to "The Moluccas and Oriental China" which got no farther than the River Plate. This expedition was fraught with bad luck, incompetence, and disaster; but for Spain it accomplished what Jacques Cartier's did for France, opening up a water route to the heart of a continent.

Originally intended to be the third Spanish armada to the Pacific, the expedition had been talked about for a year before Loaysa set sail. Certain foreign merchants resident in Seville, including the enterprising Englishman Robert Thorne, were behind it. Encouraged by the enormous profits from *Victoria*'s cargo of cloves, they intended to procure a load of spice by the Magellan route before competition became too brisk. In September 1524 the Council of the Indies (says Peter Martyr) authorized *Sebastianus Cabotus Baccalorum repertor* (Sebastian Cabot the discoverer of Codfish Land) to head the expedition.

Sebastian, now at least forty-two years old, enjoyed an important and lucrative position in the Spanish government. In 1518, three years after the death of Juan de Solis, he had been appointed the third *piloto mayor* with the duty of instructing and licensing pilots for

537

overseas voyages, and preparing a *padrón real* or standard chart. This position paid him the handsome salary of 125,000 maravedis a year ($875 in gold), more than twice what Juan de Solis took in. Deducted from each pilot general's salary was a pension of 10,000 maravedis for the benefit of Vespucci's widow; Solis paid this regularly, but Sebastian tried to evade it.

Although Cabot enjoyed the favor of Charles V and other distinguished men, he lived uneasily. For several years he had been secretly negotiating with the Venetian Republic to enter her service, promising to restore the Queen of the Adriatic to her medieval supremacy by some new and shorter route to the Orient—probably the Northeast Passage which later occupied his attention in England. These negotiations had fallen through, but Sebastian was eager to leave his profitable post at Seville and go a-seafaring. Why? Were the Spaniards beginning to see through his prevarications, as the livery companies of London had already done? Several reputable people who testified at Cabot's lawsuits in Seville doubted whether he had ever before crossed the ocean. Diogo Garcia, the Portuguese pilot of Juan de Solis's fleet in 1515, once declared that Cabot "was no sailor nor did he know navigation"; but he can hardly have served as piloto mayor for almost a decade without knowing something of the sea; and Garcia, as we shall see, was Cabot's competitor. Had he run out of tall tales of the frozen north and, jealous perhaps of Pigafetta's success as a raconteur, become eager to pick up some fresh ones? Or was it simply a case of sea fever, or ambition to prove himself as a navigator and discoverer?

Savvy Sebastian had no sooner obtained his new command than he began working on the Emperor to enlarge it. The agreement between him and Charles V, dated 4 March 1525, declares the objectives to be China, Japan, and the biblical Tarshish and Ophir, reputed sources of King Solomon's fortune. One of these documents adds, "but return to Spain by a more rapid route than that taken by the *Victoria*." He could hardly have taken a slower one!

The Cabot fleet sailed from Seville 3 April 1526. Here are the ships and the most important people, as put together by historian José Toribio Medina from many sources.

Captain General: SEBASTIAN CABOT

SANTA MARIA DE LA CONCEPCIÓN, ship of 150 toneles (tuns)

Captain General: Sebastian Cabot. Captain and second in command: Martín Méndez. Master: Antón de Grajeda. Treasurer: Fernando Calderón. Flag pilot: Miguel de Rodas. Twenty other officers and petty officers, 12 mariners, 7 gromets, and 4 pages.

SANTA MARIA DE L'ESPINAR, ship

Captain: Rodrigo Caro. *Contador:* Miguel de Valdés. *Veedor* *: Alonso de Santa Cruz. Pilot: Enrique Patimer (or Latimer), English. Eight more officers and petty officers, 11 mariners, 4 gromets.

LA TRINIDAD, ship

Captain: Francisco de Rojas. Treasurer: Gonzalo Núñez de Balboa. *Veedor:* Álvaro Núñez de Balboa (both brothers to the discoverer of the Pacific). Pilot: Pero Fernández, who had been with Solis. Fourteen other officers and petty officers, 4 mariners, 6 gromets.

SAN GABRIEL, caravel of 35 to 40 tuns. Owned by Miguel Rifos. Captain: Hernando de Esquivel. Often confused with one of the bergantinas, which Cabot built in the course of the voyage.

Several members of Cabot's afterguard were people of consequence. Martín Méndez, the flag captain, and Miguel de Rodas (of Rhodes) were *Victoria* survivors who had been ennobled by Charles V and allowed to use a paraphrase of Elcano's crest and motto. Alonso de Santa Cruz, only twenty years old when he sailed, was the son of a Sevillian alcalde who contributed to the expenses. He rose to be chief cosmographer of the Casa de Contratación, and wrote the now famous *Islario*. The total number of crew members was two hundred "more or less," according to Cabot himself. An appreciable number were foreigners. Genoese sailors and Venetians were represented. Cristóbal de Jaén signed on as flagship cook, the earliest instance I have found of a mariner so designated. Sebastian Cabot, used to high living, probably refused to sail with the prospect of eating nothing but the dubious efforts of gromets who had been arbitrarily told off to "cook, damn

* *Veedor*—accountant and inspector.

Sebastian Cabot as seen by Venice in the early eighteenth century. Note his alleged Northern Voyages on the map, and Southern Voyage on the globe. Giaconelli photo. Courtesy Ducal Palace, Venice.

your eyes, and if we don't eat good you will be well flogged!" One hopes that Cristóbal lived up to his expectations, but fears that he did not, which might help to explain the Captain General's irascibility.

Spanish distrust of their own people as gunners, which we noted on the Magellan expedition, appears again here. The chief of ordnance, Lucas Corbe, was a Spaniard, but the other six gunners were Dutch, Flemish, Corsican, Savoyard, and Scots (two named Ramua of "Medyoenburque"—Edinburgh). Besides the two English passengers Thorne and Barlow and Pilot Patimer, there were three English mariners, David and "Cochy" of Essex, and Tom Terman (Storman?) of "Norofox" (Norfolk). A German gentleman, Casimir of Nuremberg, who quarreled with Cabot during the voyage, later became a conquistador in Venezuela, and is celebrated in the *Elegias de Varones Ilustres de Indias* of Juan de Castellanos. Nicolás de Nápoles, a Neapolitan and a particular favorite of Cabot's, made several later voyages to the Indies.

Other cronies of the Captain General were Francisco César of Cordova and Alonso Bueno of Seville, gentlemen volunteers whom Cabot made his personal guard. César never betrayed the confidence placed in him and subsequently made a creditable record under Pedro de Heredia, founder of Cartagena de las Indias. Castellanos called him, "Y César en el nombre y en el hecho"—Caesar both in name and deed. Alonso Bueno, however, turned out to be a rascal, whose misconduct caused Cabot to denounce him as *enemigo capital* after his return to Spain. Juan Cazagurri, flag carpenter, was Greek, and there were two Greek mariners, one of whom was accused (falsely, judged Medina) of trying to kill Cabot by dropping a heavy block on his head from a mast—the classic "accident" method of getting rid of an unpopular ship's officer. Jorge Gomes, a Portuguese who had been to Pernambuco before, acted as interpreter, and became a right-hand man to Cabot in his journeys up the Paraná River.

Most of those whose ages are known were twenty-five to thirty years old when the armada sailed. A few were older. Juan Baptista Ginovés, mariner in *Santa Maria de l'Espinar*, forty-seven, was the oldest man in the fleet. None of Cabot's men can be identified as black. The fleet returned with over sixty enslaved American natives, purchased for iron junk and other trifles. Those who survived the voyage were sold in the Seville or Cadiz slave mart.

Owing to the different aims of the *armadores* (investors) and the crown, dissension was endemic in the Cabot expedition. Some ships had two *veedors,* one for the Emperor and one for the merchants; on board *Trinidad,* for instance, a Genoese named Octavio de Brine served as *veedor por los armadores;* no wonder, since he and one other *armador* had contributed 610,760 maravedis to the outfitting. Particularly venomous were the relations between Cabot and the captains of two principal ships, Méndez and Rojas, who represented the outfitters and (as Cabot probably knew) tried to have him deposed before the fleet sailed. Later they bitterly opposed Cabot's limitation of objective to the River Plate. There was also a personal incompatibility; Rojas, as Medina says, was "frank, expansive, impetuous, but easily moved to repentance"; whilst Cabot was distinguished for "crafty reserve, deep and implacable hatreds, an inveterate love of money, and unscrupulousness in following his objectives."

Thus, the Cabot fleet was no band of brothers when it sailed from Sanlúcar de Barrameda on Easter Tuesday, 3 April 1526, after waiting three weeks for a fair wind. It had a swift passage of only seven days to Palma Island in the Western Canaries, on the direct sailing route from Spain to central Africa and Brazil. At Palma, where they remained seventeen days to take on supplies, Cabot learned from a garrulous priest that Rojas had confessed to him that he, Méndez, and others had sworn in Seville to stand by each other under all circumstances. Cabot brooded over this, imagined that there was a conspiracy to murder him; and upon arriving at Recife had both Rojas and Méndez put in irons and confined to the brig. After examining witnesses, the Captain General apparently decided there was nothing to this story, released both men, and even invited Rojas to dine with him in the flag cabin. But he continued to nourish suspicion.

Before leaving Spain, Cabot had been instructed by the King to inform his captains as to their course across the Atlantic, probably to avoid the trouble that Magellan had had with Cartagena and Mendoza. Both Méndez and Rojas asked him for the course, but he refused; and, after passing the Cape Verde Islands, to his officers' consternation he ordered their course to be south-southwest. Perhaps he intended thus to avoid Magellan's alleged error in sailing too far south before crossing the Atlantic Narrows. But Cabot made a worse mistake, as the south-southwest course took the fleet past the island Fernão de

Santa Catarina Island. "The Sisters," the three islets on the right, are where Sebastian Cabot first anchored. The underwater reef where his flagship struck runs fom the little island, center, almost to the big island, Santa Catarina, on left. M. Obregón photo.

Noronha and to the Brazilian coast so near to Cape San Roque that it fell in with head winds and currents. As piloto mayor, Cabot should have known better than to get into this trap. In a letter to his father Luis Ramírez, Cabot's faithful page, wrote: "We sailed all the month of May, sometimes with fair winds and other times with foul, . . . and many squalls off the coast of Guinea. . . . Calms delayed us a few days during which we suffered much travail from thirst because our rations were scanty; and it pleased God to give us fair weather when we crossed the equator, continuing our course until 3 June when we sighted land." The veteran pilots recognized it as Cabo Santo Agostinho on the bulge of Brazil a few miles south of Recife. Cabot did not wish to stop, for fear of trouble with the Portuguese, but as he had hit Brazil in the season of south winds,* the fleet was carried the wrong

---

* On the coast of Brazil, says Manoel de Figueyredo in his *Hydrographia* of 1608, the winds blow SE, ESE, and SSE March to August; rest of the year, NE and ENE. And so today.

Potosí and the Silver Cerro. Courtesy *Américas* Magazine.

way by wind and current for many miles. He then decided to chance it and, invited by a Portuguese who came out in a canoe, put into Recife, the harbor of Pernambuco. Fortunately the Portuguese garrison there, engaged in cutting logwood, and numbering only thirty men, were friendly and helpful, enabling the Spanish fleet to obtain plenty of fresh provisions, with the aid of Tupi Indians. Ramírez reported these natives to be "kind and good humored"; but he describes in disgusting detail their habit of fattening up war captives to eat.

The fleet tarried at Recife until 29 September 1526 when, the wind having changed, they departed and sailed along the coast, putting in at several harbors. In mid-October they encountered a severe gale which cost the flagship her longboat and caused the men to begin knocking down their stern castles to gain buoyancy.

On 19 October the fleet anchored in a good spot between the three Irmãs (Sisters) Islands off the southeast end of big Santa Catarina Island,* which extends between latitudes 27°22′ and 27°50′ S. Cabot

* *Catalina* in Spanish, *Catarina* in Portuguese; as the island is in Brazil, it is Santa Catarina today.

so named it in honor of his wife, Doña Catalina Medrano. He chose to call there because the heavy growth of timber made it suitable for building a boat to replace the one he had lost. And here he met a succession of European beachcombers who filled him with tales of the silver country. Certain modern writers have imagined that Cabot had a secret understanding with the Emperor to concentrate on the River Plate. But Luis Ramírez tells of Cabot's gradual conversion to that objective, as more and more glorious tales of silver wealth came to his ears. Not only the Portuguese but Spanish survivors from the Solis and Loaysa expeditions spun him yarns of fabulous wealth in gold and silver up-river. They asserted broadly that Cabot's men could "freight their ships with gold and silver" in the River Plate. Alonso García, a Solis survivor, having obtained the confidence of the local Indians and the hang of their language, heard that somewhere up the Paraná River

Rio de la Plata, by Alonso de Santa Cruz, in *Die Karten von Amerika in dem Islario* (1908), Plate XIV. Courtesy John Carter Brown Library.

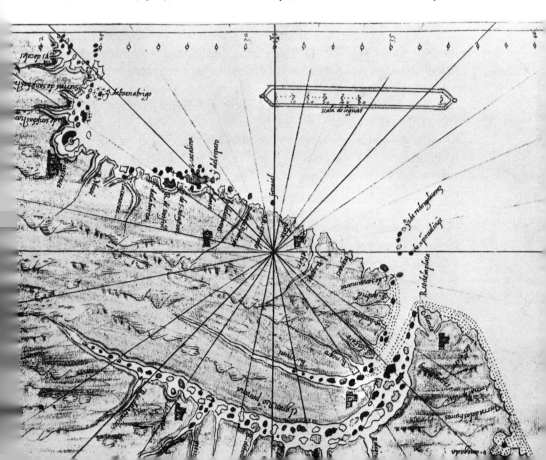

was a mountain of solid silver, ruled over by a monarch so covered and bedecked with plate as to be called *El Rey Blanco*. This silver-plated monarch balanced the more famous *El Dorado* of Nueva Granada, search for whom would lead Sir Walter Raleigh and many others to their doom. The Grand Inca, who always appeared in dazzling array, probably inspired the White King story, but the silver mountain did exist in the shape of the famous Cerro Rico of Potosí. Cabot was deeply impressed, but only reached his final decision after a serious accident.

That occurred on 28 October 1526 because two Loaysa survivors undertook to pilot the fleet around the south point of Santa Catarina Island into a protected harbor where they would be handy to a mountain covered with good ship timber. The entrance here is blocked by an underwater shoal, with a least depth of one fathom today, and a very narrow passage between it and the south point of Santa Catarina, now appropriately named *Ponta dos Náufragos*—of the Shipwrecked. The pilot made the natural mistake of steering through the center (as I confess to have done twice in a very similar unbuoyed passage in Maine waters). Cabot, alarmed by the decreasing depth, gave orders to anchor. Whether the master and pilot disobeyed or merely dragged their feet is disputed; but at any rate, while her men were still heaving the lead, *Santa Maria de la Concepción* struck, and struck hard. Cabot failed to order an anchor to be dropped from the stern where there was still plenty of water; and, as if panic-stricken, had a small boat lowered, saved himself first, and went on board *Espinar*. From a sailor's point of view, that was the unforgivable sin, quickly punished. With their commander away, the mariners directed their energies to stealing as many valuables as they could lay hands on, and saving themselves in the remaining boat. The proud flagship careened as the tide went out, rolled over, and became a total loss. And this, for Cabot, clinched the argument to concentrate on silver-hunting in the River Plate. He could hardly be expected to cross the Pacific without his largest and best ship. The rest of the fleet found a snug anchorage inside the big island, a spot they called *Porto dos Patos*. It is now called Rio Messiambú.*

Cabot's announcement to his officers of this change of objective was

* About 13 miles south of the present city of Florianópolis, as pretty as its name, situated on the narrows between Santa Catarina Island and the mainland.

Bergantina overtaking a felucca in the Mediterranean. From Henri Sbonski de Passebon, *Plan de plusieurs batimens de mer avec leurs proportions* (Marseilles, 1700). Courtesy Harvard College Library.

not well received. Several, led by Captain Caro of *Santa Maria de L'Espinar* (now flagship since the loss of the other *Santa Maria*) and Captain Rojas of *Trinidad*, objected so strenuously that the Captain General determined to get rid of them, alleging (when he returned to Spain) that Caro had been plotting a mutiny; but his charge against Rojas was ridiculously trivial. As captain of *Trinidad* Rojas had ordered the steward to serve a cup of wine to a sick and dying sailor. The steward refused, alleging that Cabot had commanded him to issue no extra rations unless authorized by himself. On this flimsy pretext the steward denounced Rojas to Cabot as soon as the diminished fleet lay safe in Porto dos Patos. The two captains, who were suffering from a fever, on Cabot's orders were pulled out of their bunks, and marooned on a nearby island inhabited only by Indians. There they were joined by Captain Méndez and at least six others whom Cabot regarded as fellow conspirators.

Fortunately, to be marooned on the coast of Brazil was not necessarily fatal, as in Patagonia. The Indians, instead of killing and eating the Spaniards, treated them well. Méndez fell sick and died, two were drowned; but Rojas and one or two others managed to escape by boat to the Portuguese factory at São Vicente near the site of Santos. There they built a ship, sailed home, and arrived at Seville in time to give vigorous testimony against Cabot.

Justified or not, Cabot's punishments and maroonings put an unholy fear of him into the hearts of his men, one that did not diminish when he hanged three more on the Paraná River for attempted mutiny and stealing food from the Indians. And he certainly made everyone work. Around the mouth of the Rio Messiambu and the southern end of the big island, where the expedition spent three months, there was plenty of food; and the Indians (not quite so naked as those of Recife) were friendly. Although the place proved to be unhealthy and several men died, Cabot's crews built a *galeota*, which he named *Santa Catalina*.

Up the Paraná and Home

Cabot's command now consisted of *Santa Maria de L'Espinar* (Fernando Calderón), *Trinidad* (one of the Balboas), *San Gabriel* (Esquivel), and the new galeota. Departing Santa Catarina 15 February 1527, the fleet reached Solis's Cabo Santa Maria (now Punta del Este, Uruguay), at the entrance to the River Plate estuary, on the 21st. Here they ran into foul weather, and after being tossed back and forth across the estuary, put in at a harbor on the Uruguayan shore which Cabot named *San Lázaro* because he entered on the fifth Sunday of Lent, 7 April 1527.* Hard by he discovered a short river that he called *San Salvador*, a name which he later applied to the harbor originally named after Lazarus. Here they picked up Francisco del Puerto, a Solis survivor who turned out to be a knowledgeable river pilot.

Leaving a small garrison and his two larger vessels at San Lázaro under command of the wrecked flagship master Grajeda, Cabot on 8 May pushed off on his own in the caravel *San Gabriel*, accompanied by the newly built galeota *Santa Catalina*. He wished to explore the Paraná, the great river that rises in the highlands of Brazil around

---

* The most likely sites are the mouth of the San Juan River, the modern city of Carmelo, and Punta Gorda, Uruguay.

Confluence of Paraná and Paraguay rivers. M. Obregón photo.

latitude 18° S and, after receiving the waters of the Paraguay and hundreds of lesser rivers, empties into the River Plate just above Buenos Aires. The lower reaches of the Paraná, on a modern map, are as intricate as the wing pattern of a monarch butterfly, but Cabot had a good pilot. With Del Puerto at the con, the two vessels ascended the Paraná for about 174 nautical miles to its confluence with the Carcaraña River, near latitude 33° S. There, in June, they built a wooden fort. Cabot named it *Sancti Spiritus* because he reached the spot on 19 May, the day of Pentecost. There he met, and apparently won over, a great concourse of Guaraní Indians, who provided his men with food and advice as to how to reach the White King.

After a delay of seven months, consolidating his position at Sancti Spiritus (as he fondly hoped), building a bergantina, and accumulating provisions, Cabot on 23 December 1527 resumed his up-river exploration in *Santa Catalina*. The newly built bergantina came along too, and a garrison of thirty men was left at the fort.

Here I shall attempt to describe a bergantina, although information on this type is remarkably scarce. It was the Spanish and Portuguese counterpart to the French *galion* and the English pinnace, a small craft not more than forty feet overall, with one or two masts and a bank of oars. She could be brought across "knocked-down" (in pieces) in a ship's hold, and easily assembled on any coast where there was suitable ship timber for planking. She may be classified with the galleys. In that family of ships the biggest in order were the *galeota* (often Englished as galliot), the *fusta*, and the *bergantina*. Galeotas had fourteen to twenty benches with one oar and rower to a bench; Cabot proved that they too could be built on the shores of the New World. The word *fusta* was used by the discoverers for a big dugout canoe or for a native galley type in the Moluccas. Finally came the bergantina. She had 8 to 16 benches with one or two oarsmen to each bench, one or two pole masts with lateen sails, a small superstructure (lower than the galeota's) for the captain and other officers, and a single deck. With a broad beam, she drew very little water, probably no more than eighteen inches. Light draft, together with the oar power, made the bergantina and her elder sister the galeota suitable for river work, like the old stern-wheelers on the Mississippi. We also hear, on other voyages, of the *fragata*, which was smaller than the bergantina and never spread more than one sail. All these types originated in the Mediterranean.

Now began a new experience for the Spaniards in river navigation. On their right were the open plains of Entre Rios, the modern Argentinian state between the Paraná and Uruguay rivers; on their left, the swampy plains of Santa Fe. Cabot was opening one of the great axes of penetration of South America, just as Jacques Cartier would shortly do for North America on the St. Lawrence. And the Guaraní that they encountered, wearing brilliant head-dresses of macaw feathers (and not much else), proved to be more timid than hostile.

For weeks he thrust upstream, to about latitude 27°30' S, where the Paraná makes an abrupt right angle, the upper branch becoming the boundary between the future republics of Paraguay, the Argentine, and Brazil. Here the Paraguay River enters the Paraná after flowing south from the back country of Matto Grosso, Brazil. About forty miles above this junction, they passed the mouth of the Bermejo (Vermilion) River, red from the soil of the Chaco, which would have given them a short cut to the silver-lined Andes, but they neglected this opportunity as the Indians warned them that the current was too swift. Sebastian probably did not attempt to navigate the Pilcomayo River, which might have led him to a pass in the Andes near Potosí,

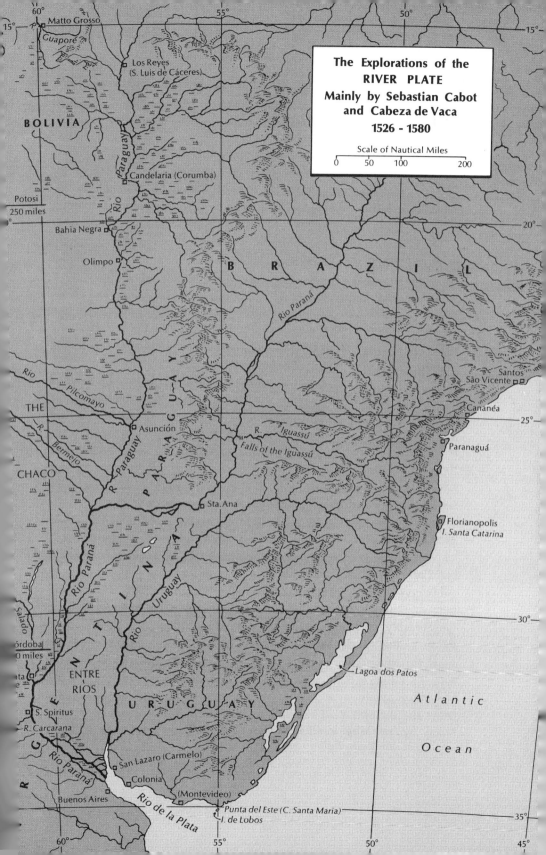

The Explorations of the
RIVER PLATE
Mainly by Sebastian Cabot
and Cabeza de Vaca
1526 - 1580

Scale of Nautical Miles

0   50   100   200

since it has a disconcerting habit of going underground and then reappearing. Exactly how far Cabot sailed and rowed up the Paraguay is a matter of controversy—probably no further than Asunción. And then he tried the upper Paraná.

These river voyages were slow, boring, and exhausting. The Paraná and Paraguay rivers are broad and deep enough, reminding one of the Mississippi at St. Paul, or of the middle Rhine; steamships like the modern *Presidente Stroessner*, of four-foot six-inch minimum draught, can get up to Corumbá at about 19° S. Characteristic of this river route is the vast number of islands. They are indicated on all the old maps, including Cabot's of 1544, and many created confusing eddies and currents.

Cabot's men escaped the ocean's constant menace, but they were always in danger of flushing hostile Indians. It was pleasant enough sailing upstream when the river currents were slack and the wind blew from the south or west, but difficult to make progress against a strong current and a head wind, even by bringing all the sweeps into action. In such situations Cabot and his sulky but obedient crew either towed or kedged the vessels. Where the river banks were open and not marshy, a tow-rope was broken out from bergantina or galeota, and a gang of sailors pulled each one along, making their own tow path. If the banks were forested, they had to kedge. The vessel anchored, the crew rowed a long line ahead in their skiff and secured it to a tree. The anchor was then weighed and the bergantina pulled ahead by the entire crew hauling on the line. Having reached the tree, she anchored again and repeated the painful process. No doubt the crews growled and grumbled at this slow and sweaty work, and one Francisco de Lepe tried to take possession of the galeota to turn back; but Cabot had him seized, tried for mutiny, and hanged.

Hunger made river navigation difficult to bear. There was nothing but water to drink. Issued daily rations fell to three ounces of flour (presumably corn meal), then to one ounce, then to nothing. Every evening each vessel tied up to one of the innumerable islands while the crew scattered through the forest looking for a palm tree with a soft top, or edible herbs which Del Puerto had learned about from the Indians. Anyone who caught a snake was considered lucky. Sometimes the men were in the last stages of exhaustion when they were saved by reaching a village where the Indians were friendly and

Engraving of feast at Buona Esperanza, the former Sancti Spiritus, in Ulrich Schmidel, *Viaje al Rio de la Plata.* Courtesy John Carter Brown Library.

traded corn, manioc, and game for gewgaws. At a place which Cabot named *Santa Ana* * on the Paraná, fifty miles or more above its junction with the Paraguay, all hands were regaled by an Indian cacique named Yazarón with maize, cassava, and fish a-plenty. From Santa Ana, where he remained until 28 March 1528, Cabot sent the bergantina further upstream on a silver-seeking expedition that required thirty days, but she found nothing significant, and a battle with the Agaces tribe cost her crew several lives. Luis Ramírez reveals that the Spaniards acted arbitrarily and cruelly to Indians who refused them food, and it is no wonder that they had to pay for this in the end.

Cabot was at Santa Ana when a rival appeared down-river—Diego

---

* By Medina identified as Itati; but Ramírez says it was 15 to 20 leagues above the Paraná-Paraguay confluence, and so must have been nearer Itá Ibaté. Col. Laguarda Trías identifies it as a place now called Yahapé, 192.7 nautical miles from the junction. I doubt whether they went that far.

García of Moguer, commanding ship *Nuestra Señora del Rosario*. She had been fitted out by merchants of Seville, with the intention of doing exactly what Cabot had decided to do, instead of making a voyage to Malacca. García was furious to hear that the Venetian had got ahead of him. The two exchanged coldly polite notes: García to Cabot: "Your honor should leave this river, for mine is the conquest." Cabot to García: "Your grace should not go further up the river, for I discovered it and it is a year and a half since I took possession. . . . I require you to get out of this river." They finally agreed to co-öperate, and actually made a joint voyage up the Paraná; but it is a matter of conjecture how far north they sailed. As long as both men were within La Plata, the situation was tense, and García, when he reached home, accused Cabot of having stripped the sails from his vessel, and of committing other high crimes and misdemeanors.

In the summer of 1528 Cabot sent caravel *San Gabriel* home under the command of Fernando Calderón. She carried glowing accounts of the wealth of the as yet undiscovered silver country, with a few enticing samples of the precious metal, and urgent demands for food and reinforcements. Early in November she arrived at Seville. Charles V ordered relief to be sent, but before his orders could be carried out, Cabot himself came home.

It would be tedious to try to follow all the comings and goings of Cabot and his men on the Paraná and its tributaries. Everywhere they encountered Indians who had little to offer in the way of food, even if friendly enough to trade. At one spot, in April 1528, the crews had a stand-up battle with natives and lost twenty-eight men. Over a year later, Cabot sailed upstream with two newly constructed bergantinas, one commanded by Francisco César, to make a fresh search for *El Rey Blanco*. Cabot went off in one direction and César in another; neither met the silver-plated king, but César picked up a tall tale of an imperial city, a Peruvian Saguenay or Norumbega, somewhere upstream. Thus began the legend of *La Ciudad de los Césares*, which long fascinated the Argentinians.

In the absence of Cabot and César, Indians attacked Sancti Spiritus in the late summer or early fall of 1529, killed the commander, and almost wiped out the garrison. Others attacked the garrison at San Lázaro but were repulsed. Cabot learned about the successful attack from

Spaniards who escaped upstream in a *bergantina*. Returning immediately to Sancti Spiritus, he found thirty corpses hideously sliced and mutilated. A captured Indian explained that his fellows had been sampling their flesh, hoping to find some tidbits less salty than other Spanish meat they had tasted.

Mounting the river again, Cabot and his men, suffering from famine, were attacked by Indians whenever they ventured forth to fish or dig edible roots; more than twenty were killed. Cabot called a council of surviving officers in October 1529 to decide whether or not to return to Spain. They voted unanimously to do just that, and in early November embarked for home in *Espinar*.

Ship *Trinidad*, accompanied by García's *Nuestra Señora del Rosario*, started home under command of a *contador* named Montoyer, but ran aground on an island near Punta del Este and became a total loss. Cabot, in passing, saw smoke signals, probably from survivors, but refused to stop. He continued the voyage in *Espinar*, after sending a gang of men to kill seals on islands in the estuary, such as Isla de Lobos.

Cabot took it easy on his homeward passage, calling at various places along the coast of Brazil, spending two months at the site of São Vicente to buy provisions and slaves—and to deny the marooned Rojas the means to get himself home. Rojas had cleverly built there a small vessel to go home in, but lacked nails and pitch; his former Captain General meanly denied him both. Somehow, however, he got home. *Espinar* sailed from São Vicente 28 March 1530 and made Seville in July with only twenty-five Christians on board, and at least twice that number of Indian slaves.

What did Cabot bring home as a result of his explorations? He encountered no *Rey Blanco*, but his quest for silver was far from fruitless. To Spain he brought a certain amount of gold and silver objects from Peru, obtained from the up-river Indians, and the slaves acquired in Brazil. He did not compile a good map of the La Plata estuary; his own world map of 1544 depicts that region most inaccurately. But he had opened one of the two leading axes of penetration into South America, showing later comers what to expect; and the information that Alonso de Santa Cruz acquired under his command came out in his informative *Islario* of 1541.

The Portuguese had already been impressed with the possibility of a silver strike. D. João III in 1531 sent a fleet of five sail under Martim Afonso de Sousa to establish a colony in or near the River Plate. It was he who founded a *feitoria* and a sugar plantation, the first in Brazil, at São Vicente, near the site of Santos, where Cabot called on his way home. Before that call, Sousa had sent one Martim Garcia to probe the interior. He joined a party of migrating Indians, which took him as far as Paraguay or even Bolivia, but on his return overland was killed by natives near the famous falls of the Iguassú River, which he was probably the first European to see. That concluded Portugal's best effort to extend her empire south and west to encompass the basin of the River Plate.

Sebastian Cabot, upon arrival home, enjoyed the usual official reception to Spanish explorers, a sojourn in jail. But not for long. Released on bail, he defended himself ably in suits brought by the widows Rojas and Méndez and several others, alleging cruelty, mismanagement, and criminal abuse of his authority. Found guilty of all charges, he was sentenced to four years' banishment in Morocco and assessed some 100,000 maravedis in costs and fines. Sounds grim, does it not? But you could always count on Sebastian's landing on his feet. His friend the Emperor, absent in Germany when these sentences were pronounced, returned to Spain, gave Cabot a hearing, and was so favorably impressed by his glowing account of the riches of La Plata that he remitted every fine, canceled every sentence including the exile, and even restored the old boy to his lucrative office of piloto mayor! Sebastian then had the nerve to ask Charles V to give him command of another fleet to go to the Moluccas; but the king-emperor refused to go that far.

Truly, Cabot had a personality that charmed all the great men he knew, but irritated or infuriated subordinates. Among the early European discoverers and explorers he was the last man under whom one would have cared to serve, even though his conversation would have enlivened many tedious hours at sea.

For sixteen years from 1532, when his office was restored, we may picture Sebastian keeping bankers' hours in his chief pilot's office in the Alcazar adjoining the Casa de Contratación. There, in the painting by Alejo Fernandez, "The Virgin Protector of the Navigators" (also called "Our Lady of the Fair Wind"), she looks down benignly on a fleet of ships and a group of merchant-navigators, one of whom may be Sebas-

Nuestra Señora del Buen Aire (Our Lady of the Fair Wind), in the restored original hall of the Casa de Contratación, Seville. Serrano photo.

tion.* Besides performing his regular duties to the King's taste, Cabot compiled his famous world map of 1544, which fixed for a generation an inaccurate topography of the River Plate, the only part of America that he really knew; and he also wrote a useless treatise on finding longitude from compass variation. He must have gathered a fresh collection of anecdotes to replace those of the frozen north. Yet one suspects that his social life in Seville had become less pleasant owing to the many enemies he had made on the southern voyage. His Spanish wife Doña

* I would guess second from the right. The painting, after many vicissitudes, is now (1974) in its proper place in the restored hall of the Casa de Contratación, in the Alcazar of Seville.

Catalina, after fiercely supporting him in the lawsuits, died in 1547 following the death of their only child, a daughter. Thus it is not surprising that Sebastian decided to return to England in 1548.

The historian Oviedo, who talked with Alonso de Santa Cruz and other survivors of the expedition, wrote a judicious summary of Cabot. He was "a good person and dextrous in his office of cosmographer . . . but it is one thing to command and govern people and another to mark with a quadrant or astrolabe." In one of the many lawsuit against Cabot, Juan de Junco, an officer of *Espinar*, testified that Cabot was unsuited to command men, to which Sebastian retorted that Junco was a thief who stole a parrot and an Indian girl (both, apparently, equally valuable) from his cabin! Yet we must admit that this Captain General showed courage and resourcefulness in his Paraná River explorations, that he suffered the same privations as his loyal seamen, and that he was the first to open up an important route to the center of South America. Charles V did well to reward him for his exploits rather than to let the old man be punished for his misdeeds, which after all were no worse than those of many other discoverers.

Sancti Spiritus did not hold out until the next Spanish expedition came up the Paraná. The garrison commander, deciding that the place was untenable, transferred all survivors in his one remaining bergantina to a Brazilian port called Iuga, about seventy-five miles from São Vicente. Martim Afonso de Sousa who (as we have just seen) had founded a *feitoria* at São Vicente, attacked the Spaniards, and they, after beating off the Portuguese, retired to a more defensible site on Santa Catarina Island. Sancti Spiritus, destroyed by the local Indians, was later rebuilt by Cabeza de Vaca and officially named *Buena Esperanza*. But the rank and file of Spaniards long called it *La Torre de Gaboto*, and the village on or near its site is now named Puerto Gaboto after the brave, if unreliable, old Venetian.

Bibliography and Notes

SEBASTIAN CABOT

Assuming that Sebastian was fifteen when his father made the voyage of 1497, he would now be forty-two or forty-three.

José Toribio Medina, *El Veneciano Sebastián Caboto al Servicio de España* (2 vols., Santiago, 1898), comprises not only a detailed biography of Cabot in Spain and of his last days in England, but biographies of his shipmates, and it prints every known document on the voyage. It is, in fact, so comprehensive that few have dared to write another account of the old boy's La Plata adventure. One who has, my friend and benefactor Col. Laguarda Trías, kindly read my first draft and obliged me with numerous corrections and suggestions. His account of Sebastian will come out in Max Justo Guedes's forthcoming Brazilian Naval History.

In English there are several biographies, of which the best is Henry Harrisse, *John Cabot . . . and Sebastian His Son* (London, 1896), although Harrisse did not use all Medina's documents and is somewhat careless with his facts. James A. Williamson, *Voyages of the Cabots* (London, 1929), chapter xiii, tends to the apologetic. The standard Italian biography is that by Francesco Tarducci, of which there is an English translation by Henry F. Brownson (Detroit, 1893). None of these writers attempted to follow Cabot's course on this voyage. Diogo Garcia's devastating opinion of Cabot is quoted by Teixeira da Mota in Royal Society of Edinburgh *Proceedings*, LXXIII B (1972), 59–67.

The sources are copious though fragmentary. There exists no official journal, map, or narrative of the voyage. The nearest is the letter of Luis Ramírez to his father, which is very important because (1) this common sailor served as a page or servant to Cabot, who remained his hero throughout: a useful offset to Medina who leaned heavily on the anti-Cabot testimony of the lawsuits; and (2) because he alone describes the severe conditions and sufferings of river navigation. The handiest text is in Medina, I, 442–47, and a good critical edition by the Rev. Guillermo Furlong S.J. is in *Revista* de la Sociedad Amigos de la Arqueología, VII (Montevideo, 1933), 169–228. For further bibliography, see Harrisse, p. 407 and Medina, I, 457.

Cabot's objectives are controversial. Medina and Harrisse thought they were not changed before the fleet reached Brazil; Williamson guessed that the shift to the River Plate resulted from a secret understanding between Sebastian and Charles V, as suggested by the Emperor's tolerance of Cabot's failure to go farther, and his attitude toward him after the voyage ended. I agree with Medina. All documents on the voyage, before it began, describe it as "a voyage to Tarshish and Ophir and Oriental China" (Medina, I, 421–26), adding sometimes (Medina, II, 89) that these were to be regarded as "continuation of the Spicery at our Islands of Maluco." As Ramírez tells the story, Cabot became more and more intrigued with the tales of silver told by the beachcombers, and the loss of his biggest ship at Santa Catarina clinched the argument for the River Plate. Also, Cortés expected Saavedra to contact Cabot's fleet in the Pacific. Cf. Columbus's change of plans after he lost *Santa Maria*.

Task organization. Medina, I, 105–8, has a more complete one than Harrisse (p. 192); and also has a chapter (xviii) arranged as an alphabetical dictionary of "Los Compañeros de Caboto," giving every detail he could find about them. Tulia Piñeros, *Navegantes y Maestres de Bergantinas en el Rio de la Plata, Siglo XVI* (Buenos Aires, 1962), found nothing more, nor have I; gleaning after Medina is highly unprofitable! Harrisse's list includes two English friends of Robert Thorne; a pilot of *Espinar* named Latimer (Patimer) who came from Colchester, and Roger Barlow (whom Herrera calls "Rigiel Barloque"), a merchant of Seville who contributed substantially to the financing of the expedition (Medina, I, 226). The total number of men on board the four vessels is variously estimated between 200 and 250.

Porto dos Patos is not the modern Lagoa dos Patos but the little harbor, now Rio Messiambu, behind the southern tip of Santa Catarina Island. Commander Guedes (ed.), *O Quatri Partitu de Alonso de Chaves* (Rio de Janeiro, 1971).

The investments. Medina, I, 84–85, 228–29, and 481–98, where all "big campaign contributions" are displayed. Brine's was the biggest. A merchant named Catano, who stayed ashore, gave half a million; Rifos, who sailed, contributed 401,250; and Roger Barlow, 206,250 maravedis. This, we are told elsewhere, was about six-tenths of the total cost; the king provided the rest. Probably nobody got a penny back.

Atlantic crossing. Ramírez says they called at Palma Island, one of the outer Canaries. Manoel de Figueyredo's *Hydrographia* of 1608 (Beinecke Library, Yale) directs ships from the Peninsula bound for Brazil to leave Palma Island 10 to 12 leagues to port.

Loss of the flagship. Cf. Juan de La Cosa's desertion of Columbus's *Santa Maria* when she struck on Christmas Eve 1492. Harrisse gives all the evidence about the loss at Santa Catarina on pp. 234–38; and Medina, who calls Cabot's action "shameful" (I, 146), prints all the post-mortem evidence.

Bergantinas. I owe it to Mr. Naish of the Greenwich Maritime Museum that after searching far and wide I found all available information in Auguste Jal, *Archéologie navale* (Paris, 1840), pp. 318–19 (with picture) and 454–57, and his *Glossaire nautique* (Paris, 1847), p. 286. Howard Chapelle believes that the Spaniards brought out readymade keel, stem and stern pieces, sails, cordage, perhaps even frames, and planked and masted the bergantina wherever they found proper wood. Thanks also to Señor José-Maria Martínez-Hidalgo, director of the Museo Marítimo of Barcelona, who sent me all the information that he could find. In order not to confuse the reader with a wholly different type—the *brigantine*, a two-masted sailing vessel developed in the late 17th and early 18th century—I consistently refer to those used by the Spanish discoverers as bergantinas. Later derivatives are described in Rafel Monleon's *Maritime Dictionary*, a manuscript in the Museo Naval, Madrid.

Riverian explorations. Capitán de Navío Laurio H. Destéfani, chief of the Argentine navy's historical section, directed me to several recent accounts: Teniente de Navío Marcos A. Savón, *Descubrimientos y Exploraciones* (Buenos Aires, 1929), chap. vi, Ernesto J. Fitte, *Hambre y Disnudeces en la Conquista del Rio de la Plata* (Buenos Aires, 1963).

J. C. Chaves, *Descubrimiento . . . Paraguay*, p. 64. Groussac's monograph (see Notes to Chapter XXIII below), p. xliii. García, says José Maria Rosa, was the first Spaniard to call the Rio Solís, *Rio de la Plata. Historia Argentina*, I (Buenos Aires, 1968), 93–94. Chaves, on p. 63, note 124, discusses the question of how far Cabot went upstream, and what was meant by the *Rio de la Traición* in Alonso de Santa Cruz.

Loss of Trinidad. Deposition of her sailor Pedro de Niza in Medina, II, 198–200, doc. 146.

Martim Afonso de Sousa's expedition is related by Jordão de Freitas in great detail, with documents, in *História da Colonização Portuguesa do Brasil* (Porto, 1921–24), III, 96–164.

Sebastian Cabot's world map of 1544 (see *Northern Voyages*, p. 196) is astonishingly inaccurate on the La Plata basin. He does not even put down Sancti Spiritus, and Santa Ana is on the wrong river. There are many tributaries of the Paraná whose names have disappeared. Either his memory was bad or he wished to deceive. And the map of his shipmate Alonso de Santa Cruz in the *Islario* is not much better.

Appendix to Chapter XXII
THE STORY OF LUCIA DE HURTADO

After Cabot's departure, Sancti Spiritus, under Captain Nuño de Lara, became the scene of a tragic love drama. Mangora, cacique of the Timbú tribe, conceived an unholy passion for Lucia de Hurtado, the young and beautiful wife of a captain in the garrison. As the Timbú came and went with no security measures, Lucia was unable to avoid the lustful gaze and lecherous proposals of the cacique, but treated both with disdain. Mangora then decided to rape her, and almost did; but his warriors, who stormed their way into Sancti Spiritus when the garrison was temporarily depleted, were no match for the Spaniards. In a fierce night battle Captain Nuño de Lara killed Mangora and then himself fell dead from an arrow wound. But that was not the end of it. Mangora's brother Seripo, who inherited the cacique's appetite with his diadem, carried off Lucia for himself. Captain Hurtado pursued; Seripo released her on condition that she no longer live with her husband; but an Indian spy surprised them in each other's arms, and by the cacique's orders they were killed by burning alive.

This story cannot be traced beyond Rui Díaz de Guzmán, *La Argentina* (1612). Enrique de Gandía, in his edition of this famous epic, states that the story is pure romance, and Medina agrees. There were no women in the Cabot expedition, and there is no record of any Hurtado at Sancti Spiritus.

* XXIII *

The Conquest of the River Plate

1534-1580

Pedro de Mendoza's Expedition

If you suppose that the unsatisfactory and controversial results of Cabot's expedition would have put a stopper on La Plata exploration for a generation, you do not know the sixteenth-century Spaniard. Apparently, everyone who returned home in *Trinidad* or *Santa Maria de l'Espinar* insisted that the banks of the Paraná were lined with silver ore; if they had brought none home, Indian hostility and Cabot's incompetence were responsible. Charles V, during an unusually long stay of two years in Spain, appears to have reviewed the several attempts to explore and exploit the La Plata basin, and decided it was time for action; if he did not scoop up the River of Silver for Spain, the Portuguese would. So in 1534 the Emperor set up a grand colonizing expedition; and by selecting a wealthy member of the nobility to command it, Don Pedro de Mendoza, he avoided investing in it himself.

One cannot help but gasp at the energy of imperial Spain. Besides the Mendoza fleet, in this same year 1534 the king-emperor dispatched the Alcazaba expedition to sail through the Strait of Magellan to Chile, and a convoy of twelve sail, each ship of 300 to 400 tuns' burthen, carrying 450 Spaniards and 200 black slaves, to reinforce the Christians in Peru. And, apart from these, 86 merchant ships of 100 to 200 tuns' burthen cleared Seville for the West Indies, and thirty-four returned. Yet Charles V was not idle in Europe. He had taken over the responsibility of chastising the Turks, and was preparing a formidable armada, commanded by the Genoese admiral Andrea Doria, to capture Tunis.

The Mendoza were one of the first families of Spain. Don Pedro was cousin to the viceroys of Mexico and Peru, younger son to an ambassador, younger brother to another ambassador to Rome, and to Diego Hurtado de Mendoza, cardinal archbishop of Seville; another Diego and a cousin, Jorge de Mendoza, accompanied his fleet. As proof of the value Charles V and the bankers attached to the River Plate, Mendoza's armada of eleven ships and from one to two thousand men was the largest and most powerful that Spain had sent to the New World for many years. It lacked neither social eminence nor financial backing. Don Pedro, connected by marriage with everyone who was anyone in Spain including the leading bankers, attracted capital and noblemen to support and man his expedition. Unfortunately, during the notorious sack of Rome he had contracted *el morbo gallico*, (in plain speech, syphilis), which debilitated him and finally brought about his death upon the great waters.

Charles V empowered Mendoza to conquer and colonize the River Plate (with 200 leagues of the southern coast of Chile thrown in) for a salary of 2000 ducats a year, plus the same amount "toward his expenses," and the title of Adelantado. He was also bound to search for a new water route between Atlantic and Pacific, to treat the Indians well, and to take out eight priests or friars to convert them. He was encouraged to admit women so that his colony would endure, and was authorized to buy two hundred black slaves in the Cape de Verdes, half of them women, so that the Spanish ladies would have no domestic problems, nor would their husbands be forced to do manual labor. The atmosphere of Mendoza's expedition resembled that of Sieur de Roberval's to Canada in 1542; it was one of gay, adventurous young lords and ladies hoping to make a fortune in a pleasant climate among friendly natives.

Vignette of Ulrich Schmidel riding a llama. From his *Viaje al Rio de la Plata* (1599). Courtesy John Carter Brown Library.

Unlike Roberval, Mendoza laid out some 40,000 ducats of his own money, and for the balance borrowed from several Flemish and German merchant-banker houses which had been lending money to Charles V for years. These were the Fuggers and the Welzers, each of whom contributed a ship, completely outfitted and manned by Germans; the Welzers' ship was commanded by their factor Heinrich Paine. One of the Fuggers' mercenaries, Ulrich Schmidel, or Schmidt, of Bavaria, became self-appointed chronicler of the expedition. Eleven great ships assembled at Seville. On deck they carried a hundred head of horse-kind as well as cattle and swine; stowed below were the tools of husbandry and everything that Spanish experience had indicated to be needed for a successful colony. The fleet made a brave show, but one thing it lacked was know-how. Fernández de Oviedo, who saw it sail from Seville in August 1534, said that "without doubt 'twas a company which would have made a good show in Caesar's

army, or in all parts of the world." * Many of the leaders were "gentlemen and persons of honor; as I can testify, as when I saw them at
Seville I found some that I knew." Evidently it was a strange experience to find "someone you knew" embarking for the New World!
He watched their departure with grief, guessing that few would ever
return; and only about 150 out of the estimated 2000 who embarked,
did return. *La Magdalena* was the name of the flagship, but I have been
unable to find any task organization.

At the Island of Palma in the Canaries the fleet put in for replenishment. Columbus, one remembers, had begun the practice of topping
off at these islands where fresh provisions and livestock were cheap;
but Mendoza tarried four whole weeks. This unusually long stay gave
his cousin Jorge de Mendoza the opportunity to contract a delicious
liaison with the fair daughter of a local burgher. Jorge could not bear
the idea of parting from her, nor she from him; so at midnight before
sailing day he and twelve boon companions helped her elope from her
father's house, complete with maid, clothes, jewels, and money. The
lovers might have founded a First Family of Buenos Aires but for an
unfortunate shift of the wind which blew the fleet back into the
same harbor. There, when Captain Paine went ashore in his gig, he was
taken prisoner in retaliation for the elopement, and his ship fired on by
the fort. Peace was concluded on the basis of Jorge and damsel going
ashore to live as man and wife. Such was the unromantic conclusion
of this affair.

After a five-day call at Santiago in the Cape de Verdes, the fleet
crossed the Atlantic Narrows. The passage took two months, indicating
that the pilots did not succeed in avoiding doldrums. They made landfall on an island off the Brazilian coast—probably one of those near
Bahia—and proceeded to Rio de Janeiro where they tarried a fortnight. Here Pedro de Mendoza, "always melancholy, weak and ill,"
says Schmidel, caused one of his noble shipmates, Juan de Osorio, to
be executed without trial on the strength of mere gossip that he intended mutiny. Osorio "was treated wrongly," wrote the German,
"for he was a pious, fair dealing and valiant warrior."

Rounding Cabo Santa Maria (now Punta del Este), Mendoza in
La Magdalena picked up the rest of his fleet at San Gabriel Island

* Oviedo, *Historia General y Natural* (1852 ed.), II, 181–82.

Cape Frio, guide to Rio de Janeiro.

(facing Colonia, Uruguay), crossed the River Plate, and (2 February 1536) on the banks of a little tributary, the Rio Chuelo, landed several hundred men and seventy-two surviving horses and mares. Don Pedro named the place *Puerto de Santa Maria del Buen Aire*. He chose well; this settlement, after many vicissitudes, grew to the great city of Buenos Aires, with three million population, fourth largest in Latin America.*

The beginnings of "B.A." were not propitious. Respecting relations with the nearby Indians, a branch of the Quirandí, the usual thing happened. For the first fortnight they shared with the Spaniards their scanty victuals of fish and game and then grew tired of feeding freeloaders. Pedro de Mendoza sent three hundred foot and thirty armed

---

* Mexico, D. F., 7,000,000; São Paulo, 6,339,000; Rio de Janeiro, 4,500,000; Buenos Aires, 2,972,000 (Associated Press *Almanac*, 1974). The name is traditionally due to Sancho del Campo, first Spaniard ashore, exclaiming, "Que buenos aires son los de este sitio!"

horsemen under his brother Diego to "teach the Indians a lesson," but they taught him one; these River Plate natives were no Peruvians to fall flat by the thousands before a platoon of mounted conquistadores, and feared no horses because they had the proper weapon to bring down a quadruped. They killed Don Diego, about two hundred more Spaniards, twenty-five horses, chased the survivors back to Buenos Aires, and besieged the garrison there behind its mud fort. In this fight the Spaniards first felt the force of the South American Indians' great weapon, the *bolas,* which Schmidel described as two stone balls connected by a cord, which they threw around the legs of a horse, forcing it to fall. The besieged held out until all available rats, mice, and snakes had been eaten and cannibalism had been resorted to. On St. John's Day, 24 June 1535, the natives attacked the fort. It held out, but when noses were counted after the enemy retired, only 560 Christians were yet alive, and four great ships of the fleet had been burned in the harbor.

In the meantime Juan de Ayolas, one of Don Pedro's noble companions, had sailed up the Paraná River and founded a fort which he named *Corpus Christi.* Mendoza went with him. They had four bergantinas and three smaller craft which, in Schmidel's German, are called *pat* and *podell,** and altogether carried several hundred men. At the site of Cabot's Sancti Spiritus the Adelantado founded *Nuestra Señora de Buena Esperanza.* There the survivors remained for four years, hunting for gold and silver deposits. Long before that, Pedro de Mendoza, "full of infirmities," gave up and sailed down-river to Buenos Aires. En route, four of his boats were attacked by Indians and more than thirty Spanish lives were lost in beating them off.

Mendoza, still sick, sent two of his lieutenants north to look for Ayolas in 1537, but did not wait for them to return. In view of his personal disability and the difficulty of finding food at Buenos Aires, he decided, toward the end of April, to go home. Naming Juan de Ayolas Captain General, and leaving 250 men at the future Argentine capital, he took *Magdalena* and another surviving ship and sailed for Spain on 20 April 1537. Three months later, when his ship was within sight of Terceira, Don Pedro died at sea.

---

* *Podell* may be Schmidel's rendering of *paddeln,* canoe; *pat* or *pod* has eluded me and all other translators. I shall not claim that the Maine-coast *pod* or *pea-pod* had reached the River Plate!

Pedro de Mendoza was a good soldier; but, harassed by a wasting disease, he could not be an effective colonial founder. The net result of his pompous expedition was meager, whether expressed in terms of colonists or horses, but it was enough to encourage further attempts at conquest and colonization.

Ayolas proceeded up the Paraguay River for hundreds of miles past the site of Asunción to about latitude 19° S,* a place which he named *Nuestra Señora de la Candelaria,* since it was Candlemas Day, 2 February 1537. There, at last, he found Indians who had plenty of silver from the mines of Peru and were willing to trade. Schmidel described this expedition, in which he participated. Every few days the Christians encountered a new tribe of the Guaraní group. Some lived only on game and fish; others had gardens of maize, manioc, potatoes, yams, and other edible plants. If the natives came forth bearing gifts, they were spared; if they showed fight, they were slaughtered and driven from their settlement which (even if they merely fled in fear) was plundered and burned. Schmidel seems to have been mostly interested in the women, as he always states whether or not they wore a flap over their privities. On this trip, says he, the rank and file, who had been forbidden to trade with the Indians, secretly obtained by barter nearly 200 ducats' worth of silver and cotton mantles. The official take for the government must have been far greater.

On the way down-river, Ayolas and many of his party were ambushed and killed by supposedly friendly Indians. This (according to one account) was the fault of Domingo de Irala whom Ayolas left behind with orders to rendezvous with him at Candelaria. Instead, he slipped down-river to Asunción in the bergantinas which Ayolas was counting on for transport. Others deny this, but that Ayolas was killed is certain.

On one of these expeditions, Captain Juan de Salazar de Espinosa chose a spot that the natives called Lambaré, situated some 150 miles up the Paraguay River from its junction with the Paraná, and there began a fort on 15 August 1537. This was the feast of the Assumption of the

* The late Hon. Efraim Cardozo, senator of the Republic and an expert on his country's history, who discussed the site of Candelaria with me at Asunción, identified it as that of modern Corumbá, in the Matto Grosso opposite the Laguna Careras-Bolivia. But he admitted that it might have been at any one of three high-and-dry spots on the river bank further south: Bahia Negra, Olimpo, or San Lázaro.

Virgin, whence the name Asunción. After the death of Ayolas, the Spaniards already there elected Domingo de Irala their governor, as Charles V had given them permission to do. This settlement turned out beautifully for the Spaniards, as the Guaraní Indians in the neighborhood of Asunción were friendly, providing plenty of food and scores of pretty, accommodating girls. Every man acquired a harem, and Governor Irala married all seven daughters (the eldest aged 18) of the principal cacique. No wonder that an early Argentinian writer called Asunción "Mohammed's Paradise." Irala assumed command of the entire colony on 31 July 1539, and two years later decided to remove the miserable remnant of Buenos Aires thither. Thus, by the middle of 1541 the only traces of Spain in the future city of nearly three million souls were abandoned houses around whose ruins grazed the horses left behind by Mendoza. Their descendants were broken in by the local Indians, who became expert bareback riders like the Sioux and Comanche of the North American West.

Cabeza de Vaca

Charles V took considerable interest in the future of La Plata. Although these years were difficult for him in European politics, he did not leave little far-off colonies to wither on the vine, as had happened and would happen to many others, north and south. Twice he sent reinforcements to Buenos Aires. And, even before the displaced Spaniards from the future Argentine metropolis had completed their toilsome journey to Asunción, a new adelantado appointed by the Emperor appeared, like a figure of magic, out of the forest. This was none other than tough old Álvar Núñez Cabeza de Vaca, already well known for his overland journey on foot across Texas to Mexico.* He had already reached his sixtieth year, an advanced age for a man to penetrate the wilderness of South America; but Álvar Núñez proved that he could take it. Disliking inactivity at Seville, he snapped at the Emperor's offer to be adelantado and governor of La Plata.

The Emperor could not have chosen a better man. If Sebastian Cabot was the Jacques Cartier of La Plata, Cabeza de Vaca was its Samuel de Champlain, comparable to the Father of New France for endurance, austerity, and humanity; and for all his accomplishments he received

* See above, Chapter XXI.

La relacion y comentarios del gouernador Aluar nuñez cabeça de vaca, de lo acaecido en las dos jornadas que hizo a las Jndias.

Con priuilegio.

E sta tassada por los señores del consejo en O chica y cinco mrs

Title page of Cabeza de Vaca's, *Relación y Comentarios* (1555). Courtesy John Carter Brown Library.

even less appreciation from Charles V than Champlain did from Louis XIII. Among his little prejudices he hated lawyers, and his contract with the king provided that none of that kidney be allowed in his province; that did him no harm, as no men of law cared to emigrate. Again like Champlain, ascetic in his personal life, Cabeza de Vaca disapproved of promiscuity; incorruptible himself, he loathed the graft and extortion that he found rife in Asunción. As we shall see, his attempts to enforce virtue and honesty led to his ruin.

Cabeza de Vaca sailed from Cadiz 2 November 1540 with two ships: a big one of 350 tuns' burthen which they called *La Capitana*, the flagship, and one unnamed, of 150 tuns. Together with a caravel which the

Adelantado picked up in the Canaries, they carried 400 men and 46 horses. *La Capitana,* although a new vessel, leaked badly and had to be repaired at Santiago, Cape de Verdes, where the Portuguese authorities were now friendly and co-öperative. While she was being patched up under the direction of her master, whom Cabeza de Vaca calls "the best diver in Spain" for detecting leaks, the horses were turned loose to browse. He considered it "a great marvel" that he lost not one man during the fleet's twenty-five days at Santiago, which had a bad reputation for unhealthiness, especially in the winter. The place had grown rich, he says, on the African slave trade.

Exactly where this little fleet hit the coast of Brazil he does not say; but he tells an amusing story about his landfall. One of the sailors had taken on board at Cadiz or Santiago a pet rooster, hoping to enjoy his crowing; but, like the canary birds one buys hopefully in the Canary Islands, Chanticleer never gave throat during the crossing. Then, in the darkness before dawn as they were closing the land, suddenly the cock crew. This aroused all hands, who found they were drifting toward sharp rocks, and were able to anchor just in time to save the ship and go ashore to get water. The rooster continued to "give us his music every night" as they sailed along the Brazilian coast to Cananéia, at latitude 25° S, and to the Island of Santa Catarina where Sebastian Cabot had lost his flagship. The fleet arrived there 29 March 1541, almost five months out from Spain. Once more I call the reader's attention to the length of these southern voyages. Cabeza de Vaca's crew were down to their last barrel of water when the miraculous cockcrow saved them.

The Adelantado promptly took possession for Spain. He had no special orders about his route to Asunción, but after talking with refugees from Buenos Aires who informed him of the sad plight of that settlement, he decided to avoid the long river route. Having figured out that Santa Catarina and Asunción were not far apart in latitude, it occurred to Cabeza de Vaca that an overland route might prove the quickest way from the ocean to the new northern capital. And it might also inaugurate a short way to the silver mines of Peru. For, by the early 1540s, ambitious conquerors of Peru were moving south, colonizing the central valley of Chile and the Bolivian *Puna* or bleak region, fighting the Araucanians; and four years after Cabeza de Vaca reached Santa Catarina, they discovered the fabulous silver mountain of Potosí.

Iguassú Falls

First the Adelantado sent a trusted shipmate, with a hundred Spaniards and Indian guides, to reconnoiter the overland route. It took them
three months and a half. Cabeza de Vaca then reconnoitered the first
part of it himself, and decided it was practicable. So, leaving 152 men
at Santa Catarina under the command of his nephew Estopiñán Pedro
Cabeza de Vaca, and sending his flagship to Buenos Aires, he formed
a cavalcade of 250 soldiers and the 26 horses which had survived the
ocean voyage. They set forth on 2 November 1541. This cross-country
journey was very arduous. The Indian guides did not take the Spaniards along the valley of the Iguassú, because there were no settlements
on its banks from which to procure provisions, but roundabout through
the mountains. The Adelantado and other officers had to walk, since
the horses were needed to transport food, trading truck, and equipment, or to give the sick a lift.

During the first month, the party progressed by cutting paths
through the forest. They had to build as many as eighteen bridges in
one day to get the sumpter horses across small rivers. Whenever the
food seemed about to give out, the Spaniards had the good luck to run
into a new settlement of friendly Guaraní who provided all they
wanted. These Indians were deathly afraid of the Spaniards' horses, begging the Adelantado "to tell the horses not to be angry with them." To

appease these strange beasts, the Indiains would set game and fish before them, and were puzzled by their refusing it. This recalls the story of the black horse of Cortés, *El Morzillo*. Left behind on an island in a lake, he was adored as a god by the local Indians, but starved to death because they tried to feed him on what they liked to eat themselves.

Just as provisions were again giving out, the party tumbled into a land of friendly Indians on the banks of the Rio Iguassú; these provided not only food but dugout canoes. It was the end of January 1542. Cabeza de Vaca took possession of the region for his imperial master and named it *La Vera* after his grandfather, a Canary Islands conquistador. Here he broke out his astrolabe and figured the latitude at $25°30'$ S, very nearly correct. This terrain, today a prosperous region of soybean culture, was then heavily wooded, and the men sometimes found it easier to swim their horses than to plunge through the forest. The Spaniards were attended by hordes of natives, who responded to Cabeza de Vaca's good usage and his severe punishment of any Spaniard who took anything without payment or otherwise wronged them. That is probably why he was so disliked by Schmidel and other rank-and-file, who regarded Indians as fit only to serve them for free, and to be killed if they demurred.

Presently they came upon the spectacular falls of the Iguassú, eight

The Rio Vermelho enters the Paraná. M. Obregón photo.

miles above the place where that river joins the Paraná. These falls must have amazed the Spaniards, for there was nothing even approaching them for extent and beauty in Europe; but nobody recorded anything about them except the difficulty of getting by. Warned that the people about the falls were hostile and had killed the Portuguese Martim Garcia who (years earlier) has been sent from São Vicente to reconnoiter,[*] Cabeza de Vaca cannily divided his forces. He and eighty men paddled as near as they dared to the falls, then carried their heavy dugouts around the cascades while the rest of the party followed the portage with the horses. At the foot of the falls they were confronted by a multitude of Indians in martial array, but the sight of mounted men threw them into confusion. The tactful Adelantado spoke to them gently through interpreters and distributed gifts. This appeased the natives, and, without opposition or disturbance, the Christians made an eight-mile portage parallel to the swift gorge of the Iguassú to where it flows into the big Paraná. There today the boundaries of Argentina, Brazil, and Paraguay converge.

At the Paraná the Spaniards made rafts by building decks of hewn wood over pairs of dugouts, and thus transported baggage and horses across the river into what is now Paraguayan territory. It all sounds like an early Canadian canoe journey of which, naturally, Cabeza de Vaca had no knowledge; but he conducted it without losing a single horse, and only one man, who fell overboard and was drowned in the big river. Cabeza de Vaca remarks that the Paraná here was a long crossbow shot wide, very deep, and rapid. The actual width, six-tenths of a statute mile, is an interesting measure of crossbow range.

Asunción still lay some 190 miles distant, a difficult march over a cordillera, even with Indian guides. Cabeza de Vaca now sent thirty sick men with fifty arquebusiers and bowmen by dugout and raft down the Paraná and up the Paraguay to Asunción. He himself pressed cross-country with most of his men, and everywhere was greeted cheerfully by the natives. They marched into Asunción in triumph on 11 March 1542. He had been four months and nine days en route. Cunninghame Graham, after studying all overland marches by conquistadores, called Cabeza de Vaca's "unparalleled," because, though fraught with hardship, it was accomplished without a fight and with minimal loss. This

* See Chapter XXII, above.

leader proved himself to be not only courageous but humane; but he never understood creole politics, and that was his undoing.

Cabeza de Vaca's vision of an eastern entrance and outlet for Asunción was first vindicated in 1554–55 when Cipriano de Goës drove seven cows and a bull along his route to Asunción—the first domestic cattle from Spain to arrive south of the Line. Four more centuries passed; in 1965 a bridge was thrown over the Paraná a short distance above Cabeza de Vaca's crossing, and a hard-surface road built cross-country to the Brazilian port of Paranaguá. This place, about 125 miles north of Florianópolis, admits deep-draft vessels to an ample harbor, which the prettily-named town on Santa Catarina Island does not. Nowadays one can see fleets of trucks roaring back and forth where Cabeza de Vaca and his men toiled on foot and horseback.

After arriving at Asunción and taking over command from an unwilling and sulky Irala, Cabeza de Vaca got in wrong with *los viejos*, the old-comers, by declaring it illegal to enslave Indians and by trying to correct all manner of abuses. The two friars at Asunción were alienated by the abolition of what they called their "nunnery" of native girls. In cahoots with Irala, they decided to return to Spain, lay their grievances before the government, and have Cabeza de Vaca recalled. Unfortunately they tried to take some thirty-five "nuns" with them. Owing to their flogging the girls (who loudly protested against practicing their alleged religious rites cross-country and cross-ocean), the parents protested. The Adelantado rounded up both friars and girls, clapped the clerics into jail, and sent the "nuns" home.

Cabeza de Vaca now had to subdue two tribes, the Guaicurú and the Agaces, who had been causing trouble to the town and to nearby friendly Indians. In the meantime he superintended the building of no fewer than ten bergantinas from native timber. Then, leaving Juan de Salazar de Espinosa as lieutenant governor at Asunción, Cabeza de Vaca led a formidable expedition up-river toward Peru. Four hundred Spanish and German arquebusiers and crossbow men, a thousand or more friendly Indians, ten vessels, and 120 canoes comprised this army. The flotilla, stretching a mile along the Paraguay River, made a brave sight, especially when the lanterns were lighted. They started 8 September 1543, rowed, sailed, towed, and kedged hundreds of miles through marshy country, and on 12 October reached the place named Candelaria by Ayolas six years earlier. (This was probably the site of Corumbá at about latitude 18°45′ S.) It took them almost another month to reach a place on the upper Paraguay which had already been discovered by Irala on a reconnaissance and named *Puerto de Los Reyes*, since he arrived there on the Epiphany of 1542. It was probably at the site of São Luiz de Cáceres. Here the river became too shoal even for the bergantinas, but they got through by the crew's jumping overboard and pushing. At Los Reyes, Cabeza de Vaca took possession for Charles V, raised a cross, built a little church, and left the two guilty friars (whom he had taken along to keep them out of trouble) to convert the natives. He and his soldiers and horses were tortured by the bites of vampire bats, and the natives had to contend with enormous ants and sting-rays. They were also bothered by crickets eating the straw roofs of their huts, but tame geese took care of them. It became a morning rite to let the geese into the huts and shake the crickets down to the floor, where the geese gobbled them up.

From Candelaria (if we are right that it was at the modern Corumbá) a road now leads northwesterly across the Bolivian Chaco to the silver country. The Spaniards may have heard about this from the Indians, but they dared not try it for want of provisions. Los Reyes would have been nearer; today a road starts at São Luiz de Cáceres for Matto Grosso, Brazil, on the upper waters of the Rio Guaporé, a tributary of the Rio Madeira which flows into the mighty Amazon.

At Los Reyes, Cabeza de Vaca interrogated a Guaraní who had been part of the marauding party joined, years before, by the unfortunate Martim Garcia, the Portuguese killed near the falls of the Iguassú. This Indian insisted that they were very close to the silver country. So, leaving a garrison at Los Reyes to guard the bergantinas, Cabeza de Vaca struck westward on foot on 26 November 1543 with three hundred soldiers, seven hundred Indian allies, and ten horsemen. They marched for eight days westward into the forest. There, said his Indian guides, Christians would be met after a journey of sixteen more days. He had really reached Upper Peru. But provisions ran out, and, encountering no natives to furnish food, he had to march back to Los Reyes. There he found the garrison on the point of starving, and the Indians turned hostile. The reason for their change of attitude is curious: A roving band of defeated Guaycuró, bent on revenge, had surrounded, attacked, and killed a crew of Spaniards who were on the

Reception of Ribera by the Xarayes. From De Bry, *Collectiones . . . Indiam Orientalem*. Courtesy Hispanic Society of America.

river bank towing a lone bergantina; the victors reported to the natives at Los Reyes that the Spaniards had "soft heads" (they were not wearing helmets) and need not be feared.

The Adelantado now sent Captain Gonzalo de Mendoza in search of provisions, and Captain Hernando de Ribera to the land of the Xarayes Indians in bergantina *Golondrino* with fifty-two Christians and six hundred Indian archers, who presumably walked. Mendoza had to drive Indians from a village and plunder it to get food. Ribera and his men, after a delightful reception at the Xarayes' capital upstream, returned to Los Reyes on 20 January 1544, still hungry. They brought nothing but tall tales from the Indians of big towns further west where there was plenty of silver and gold, and where the women fought like Amazons. The Xarayes were giving an exaggerated account of the Inca empire of Peru.

The Spaniards and their allies now fell on evil days at Los Reyes. Indians attacked and killed almost sixty of the party, floods prevented further exploration, the Adelantado and others came down with fever, and "there were so many mosquitoes of various kinds that we could neither sleep nor rest day and night." So Cabeza de Vaca decided to return. Highly disapproving as "an offense against God" the licentiousness of his people, he made them return to their families about a hundred girls whom they had acquired. This respect for Christian morality led to his ruin. The men, very willing to continue offending God in that pleasant manner, were furious, talked against their Adelantado all the way downstream, and became easy prey to rebels at Asunción. There they arrived 8 April 1544, mostly weak, sick, and starving.

A few days later Irala raised a rebellion at Asunción, deposed Cabeza de Vaca in the name of "Liberty," and looted all his property. And that finished him. The Adelantado had made the fatal error of trying to reform Irala's regime by stopping the leading men from plundering friendly Indians and the poorer Spaniards, and by jailing principal offenders. He had led a successful expedition over six hundred miles north of Asunción to Upper Peru without alienating more than one Indian tribe. But that was nothing to Irala and his merry men. They were satisfied with "Mohammed's Paradise" and would not suffer being ordered to the contrary by their austere and incorruptible Adelantado. Yet it must be admitted that they, not the puritanical Cabeza de Vaca, were riding a wave of history. In Paraguay, unions between Spaniards and Indians have been the rule rather than the exception; and nowadays 90 per cent of the republic's population speak Guaraní as a second language.

And how was Cabeza de Vaca rewarded for his three notable exploits—traversing wildest Texas to Sonora, crossing pathless Brazil to Asunción, and sailing up uncharted waterways to Upper Peru? You have probably guessed it, reader—jail! Ten months with ill usage in a prison cell at Asunción; hustled on board a bergantina, sick and in irons; a three months' ocean voyage to the Azores in this inadequate craft, chained to a ring-bolt and fed on bread and water. There his captors—not wishing him to die on their hands—transferred him to a ship bound for Lisbon; and this gave rise to a fresh accusation (like the one against Columbus in 1493) that he intended to sell out to Portugal. Instead, he proceeded to Seville early in 1546, where he was condemned, largely on trumped-up charges by Irala and his partisans. That earned him six more years in prison, followed by a sentence of exile to Oran. Although Cabeza de Vaca enjoyed but little of the imperial favor that let off Sebastian Cabot, Charles V revoked his banishment in 1551 and four years later made him a beggarly grant of 12,000 maravedis. He died in poverty and obscurity at Seville in 1556 or 1557.

When Cabeza de Vaca was demoted, Schmidel still had eight years more of Mohammed's Paradise. In mid-1552 he received a letter from the Fuggers' agent in Seville ordering him to come home. That he did in style, as an engraving in his book indicates. Attended by twenty Indian bearers and sundry pet parrots, mounted on his favorite saddle llama, Schmidel and his party embarked in two big dugouts in December 1552. From the Paraná, where other returning Spaniards joined, they walked or rode cross-country to São Vicente, Brazil. There they embarked in a Portuguese vessel which was loading sugar and logwood for a German firm in Lisbon, on Midsummer's Day 1553. After one call at another Brazilian port, this vessel took four months to reach Terceira in the Azores, and two weeks more to make Lisbon. Schmidel made his way thence by land to Cadiz, where he embarked in a newly-built Dutch hulk, one of a fleet of twenty-five bound for Antwerp. All his Indian bearers had died, but the parrots survived. The Dutch fleet plunged into the worst winter weather in twenty years; between New Year's Day and Epiphany of 1554, eight ships were wrecked on the coast of England and all hands lost. Schmidel's hulk, however, reached Cowes in safety, and Antwerp on 26 January 1554. There his narrative ends. We may be certain that he brought home enough silver to live well in his native Bavaria, and that he was still alive when the first edition of his *Wahrhafftige Beschreibunge* came out in 1567. It became one of the most popular travel books of the century.

Most of Cabeza de Vaca's oppressors came to a bad end, but the Emperor confirmed Irala as adelantado, and he continued to rule Asunción until his death in 1556. Although a very unsavory character, he did take up the task of northern exploration beyond Los Reyes, and one of his captains, Nufrio de Chaves, is said actually to have reached Lima. But it was Cabeza de Vaca who had done nine-tenths of the work, opening communications between La Plata and Peru.

As a geographical exploit this was memorable; unfortunately the

Council of the Indies in Seville insisted on this very difficult trail becoming a major trade route. With typical bureaucratic ineptitude the Council tried to deny Buenos Aires her shorter ocean route from Spain and force the entire La Plata region to trade with Spain via the Paraná, Peru, and the Isthmus of Panama.

Álvar Núñez Cabeza de Vaca stands out as a truly noble and humane character. Nowhere in the lurid history of the Conquest does one find such integrity and devotion to Christian principles in the face of envy, malice, treachery, cruelty, lechery, and plain greed, as at early Asunción. The entire story, as related by the early chroniclers, only part of which I have told here, makes one sick at heart. Yet good eventually came out of evil. Asunción lived down her foulness and iniquity and became one of the most charming and law-abiding capitals in Spanish. America.

Juan de Garay

Passing over the many tiresome intrigues among Spaniards in La Plata, and the founding of Tucumán by García Hurtado de Mendoza, governor of Chile (1565), we may conclude this chapter on a happier note with the attractive figure of Juan de Garay, second founder of Buenos Aires. After reaching Lima in the retinue of a new viceroy of Peru, he moved to Asunción in 1568, and a few years later received a commission to plant a new settlement near the mouth of the La Plata estuary. Garay himself wrote that he received this appointment "because of the warmth with which I declared that we should *open gates* into that region." With nine other Spaniards and seventy-five young creoles he founded the Argentinian city of Santa Fe on 15 November 1573. This lies about two-thirds of the way downstream from Asunción to salt water, but it was not enough for Garay. Seven years later he began to rebuild Buenos Aires on a site a few miles east of Mendoza's pioneer fort. On 11 June 1580 the ceremonies of refounding the future metropolis were held on board caravel *San Cristóbal* at the hands of Garay and his companions.

Far more important in the colonial era than Buenos Aires was Potosí, the silver city in what is now Bolivia, founded in 1545 at an altitude of almost 13,000 feet above sea level. There the *cerro rico*, a conical mountain containing some of the world's richest silver ore, rises

2400 feet above the plateau and 16,000 feet above sea level. Here is the reality behind the legend of *El Rey Blanco*. Charles V conferred on Postosí the title of *villa imperial*, and a coat of arms featuring the mountain. The output was enormously valuable, and although the silver could legally be exported only through west coast ports like Arica and Panama, a good deal slipped southward illegally by mule train.

By 1608, when a French traveler named Acarette du Biscay visited Buenos Aires, the best route thence north to Potosí lay west of the Paraná, by bridle path. Acarette undertook the journey with three horses, three mules, and an Indian guide, and it took him sixty-three days. The country as far as Córdoba was well settled, that beyond, less so; but there were enough *estancias* where the proprietors raised cattle, horse kind, and corn for Potosí, and where a traveler could spend the night. He found the reputed seat of *El Rey Blanco* a prosperous city, the *cerro* being worked over by 2200 slaves, many of them blacks provided by Genoese slave traders. Acarette states that General Pereyra, the royal governor, was able to give his daughter a dowry of 2,300,000 pesos d'oro, equal to as many dollars. But Buenos Aires shared very little of this wealth. To grow and prosper, the future metropolis of the River Plate had to wait until Spanish efforts to channel her trade the wrong way came to an end, two centuries later. For, until 1778, in the vast area covered by the modern Argentine Republic, the economy was topsy-turvy. Imagine, if you will, France conquering New Netherland in the following century and then requiring Montreal and Quebec to route all their commerce via Lake Champlain, the Hudson, and New York City. That will give you some idea of what it meant to creoles in Santa Fe, in Colonia (across the estuary in Uruguay), and Buenos Aires to be forced to obtain all their legal imports and send out all legal exports via Panama. Imports had to come by an ocean voyage that took weeks, a pack train across the Isthmus, another voyage to a Peruvian port, a two-month journey by pack train to the head of navigation of the Paraná, and fifteen hundred miles of river.

At this point we must leave La Plata, since her history from mid-century has little to do with voyages. This region needs an historian with the genius of Prescott to weave together the disparate and confusing facts about its early years and produce a work comparable to *The Conquest of Peru*. Fewer spectacular events there are than in Prescott's epic, but the story of these many voyages up the Paraná and its tributaries, the laborious sailing and rowing of bergantinas for a thousand miles against the current, and on many occasions having to endure starvation and fight natives, is worthy to record in enduring prose. So, with apologies for my poor effort, here's to the future historian of the Conquest of La Plata!

Bibliography and Notes

EXPLORATION OF THE LA PLATA BASIN

For this subject we have one work in English, R. B. Cunninghame Graham, *The Conquest of the River Plate* (London, 1924), slapdash and uncritical. Cunninghame Graham, half Scot, half Spanish creole, married to a Chilean poetess, and in succession man of action, M.P., novelist, and historian, is best remembered for his *Conquest of New Granada* (Boston, 1922). He had lived in the lower River Plate region as a young man, and well describes the pampas, but did not know the upper Paraná.

Enrique de Gandía, *Historia de la Conquista del Río de la Plata y del Paraguay. Los Gobiernos de Don Pedro de Mendoza, Alvar Nuñez y Domingo de Irala 1535–1556* (Buenos Aires, 1932), is a scholarly and comprehensive history of this subject. Gandía, born in 1906, is a native of Buenos Aires and author of several monographs covering this area. For a shorter, illustrated history, Julio César Chaves, *Descubrimiento y Conquista del Río de la Plata y el Paraguay* (Asunción, 1968), is recommended.

Of Argentine illustrated popular histories, the only one (to my knowledge) to have been translated into English is Ricardo Levene, *A History of Argentina* (W. S. Robertson trans., Chapel Hill, 1937). Vicente de Sierra, *Historia de la Argentina* (Buenos Aires, 1956), libro ii, pp. 152–285, is the best illustrated of these general histories. Others which better cover the era of exploration are: José Maria Rosa, *Historia Argentina*, I (Buenos Aires, 1968); Roberto Levillier (ed.), *Historia Argentina* (Buenos Aires, 1968; Vol. I includes a chapter on "Descubrimientos Marítimos 1500–1516" by the learned editor); Laurio H. Destéfani's chapter in *Temas de Historia Marítima Argentina* (Buenos Aires, 1970) relates the struggles of Buenos Aires to prosper despite Spanish regulations to conduct all trade via Peru. Not until 1778 were this city and Montevideo accorded the privilege of trading directly with 15 Spanish and 25 American ports. In the meantime, they did pretty well through contraband trade.

MENDOZA EXPEDITION

Paul Groussac, "La Expedición de Mendoza," in Republica Argentina *Anales de la Biblioteca*, VIII (1912), ix–clxxviii, is an excellent account, followed by over 300 pages of documents. All Argentine histories mentioned above have chapters on Mendoza; R. B. Merriman's *Rise of the Spanish Empire* (New York, 1925), III, has the best in English. Huguette and Pierre Chaunu, *Séville et l'Atlantique*, II, 245, has some useful references and in the same volume we find what was going on elsewhere. Long ago the Hakluyt Society came to our assistance with an excellent set of translations well annotated by an Argentinian authority: Luis L. Domingues, *The Conquest of the River Plate 1535–1555* (London, 1891), including the Ulrich Schmidel Narrative, the Commentaries of Cabeza de Vaca, and the Narrative of Captain Hernando de Ribera. Schmidel's *Wahrhafftige Beschreibunge* first appeared in 1567 in Sebastian Franck's collection of voyages. There is an early English translation in which he is called "Hulderike Schnitel" in *Purchas His Pilgrimes* of 1625 (MacLehose ed. Vol. XVII, 1907). A copy of the 1599 edition, illustrated, is in the John Carter Brown Library. Ulrich Schmidel, a typical German mercenary, was one of a contingent of 80 men "armed with arquebuses and muskets." His book was probably ghost-written for his German banker employers, the evidence being the phonetic spelling of proper names, e.g. Mendoza is rendered *Manchossa;* bergantinas, *parchkadienes* (p. 10); La Fortaleza de Nuestra Señora de l'Asunción, *Vardellesse Noster Signora Desumsion*, etc. Judged by his book, Schmidel was an unpleasant character, and I do not hesitate to give Cabeza de Vaca the palm for verity when the two conflict, as they often do. Bibliography of Schmidel in Catalogue of the *Exposición Histórica del Rio de la Plata* (Buenos Aires, 1964), pp. 23–27.

CABEZA DE VACA

The Domingues volume of the Hakluyt Society (see above, under Mendoza) has a good English translation of the original (Valladolid, 1555) edition of his *Relación y Comentarios del Governador Álvar Núñez Cabeca de Vaca*, the second half of which honest Álvar Núñez admits to have been written by Pedro Hernandez, his scribe. The best modern edition, edited by M. Serrano y Sanz, is entitled *Relación de los Naufragios y Comentarios* (2 vols., with supplementary sources, Madrid, 1906). This is not to be confused with the *Relación* of his Texas journey (Zamora, 1542; see notes to Chapter XXI, above).

Cabeza de Vaca's furthest north. There is a curious reluctance on the part of South American historians to locate Los Reyes. Bishop, *The Odyssey of Cabeza de Vaca*, p. 228, quoting Gandía, *Historia*, places it on Lagoa Guaiba which, with Lagoa Uberaba, forms a spectacles-shaped body of water at about latitude 17°45′ S. Without having been there, I judge that this section of the upper Paraguay was too marshy for a European settlement, and that Los Reyes was pitched higher up, at the side of Descalvado, or of São Luiz de Cáceres, which the modern map of Brazil makes the head of navigation. No historian, to my knowledge, has located the Xarayes' capital, the

Spaniards' furthest north for many years by the river route, but it cannot have been beyond latitude 14° S, where the Rio Paraguay rises in the Sierra dos Parecis.

See the Argentine histories mentioned at the beginning of this chapter's Notes. The Hon. Martínez Montero of Uruguay, taking his text from Garay's *puertos abiertos* has written a fascinating pamphlet, *Les Portes de la terre* (Paris, n.d.), pointing out the importance of Garay for the later history of this region.

Potosí. The classic account, Arzáns de Orsúa, *Historia de la Villa Imperial de Potosí*, has been edited by Lewis Hanke and Gunnar Mendoza (3 vols., Providence, R.I., 1963-65); and Hanke's *Imperial City of Potosí* (The Hague, 1956), is the best in English. Although the Indians knew about the *cerro*, they never exploited it, but the Spaniards began digging as soon as they discovered it in 1545. Potosí quickly became a boom town (120,000 inhabitants in 1590), more populous than Seville, and, like mining boom towns in North America, a "sink of iniquity" with luxury, gambling, and prostitution. The accession of Philip II in 1556 was celebrated by a 24-day fiesta that cost millions of pesos. Francisco de Toledo, viceroy of Peru, took a great interest in Potosí and sponsored a new mercury process for extracting the silver from the ore more efficiently, as well as creating a series of artificial lakes to power the grinding mills with water. The quicksilver had to be imported from Spain, and in the Chaunus' *Séville et l'Atlantique*, VIII (1959), 1124-33, we find the record of one ship taking out 1500 quintal (hundredweights) of it to Puerto Bello. Imagine manhandling that across the Isthmus, reloading it at Panama, discharging it at Arica, and then taking it on muleback to Potosí! In the Silver City, mining and other heavy labor was done by Indian serfs and black slaves from Africa, most of whom died like flies in the cold and rarefied atmosphere.

By 1555 the River Plate, no longer considered a frontier province, had entered into the system of the *carrera de Indias*, the controlled trade and navigation with Spain.

✷ XXIV ✷

France and Portugal in Brazil

1504-1568

French Interlopers

The ports of Normandy, especially Rouen, Dieppe, Fécamp, and Honfleur, early became rivals to England and Portugal in American exploration and trade. Since Dieppe and Rouen were textile centers, the discovery of Brazilian logwood particularly appealed to them for making dyes. Earlier all dyewoods had to be imported at great cost from India.

We do not know exactly when the French learned about this new source for the valuable wood. Probably it was on the controversial voyage of the ship *L'Espoir*, organized by one Binot Palmier de Gonneville, a native of that little town. He with two companions happend to be in Lisbon when Vaco da Gama's fleet, laden with spices, lay anchored off Restelo upon its return from India. They decided to muscle into that valuable trade themselves. For France never admitted the exclusive right of Spain and Portugal to divide the non-European world. Accordingly, Gonneville and his friends hired as pilots two Portuguese who had been on the Gama voyage, took into their consortium several wealthy bourgeois of Honfleur, equipped and provisioned for two years a locally built 120-tun ship named *L'Espoir*, and merrily set sail from Honfleur for the Cape of Good Hope on Midsummer Day, 24 June 1503.

Brazilian coast south of Salvador. M. Obregón photo.

It is impossible to trace *L'Espoir*'s voyage with any precision; the sources are so diverse and corrupt. Off the African coast she encountered a succession of storms, succeeded by flat calms. Apparently the same thing happened to her as to Cabral; while en route to the Cape of Good Hope, she raised land at the mouth of the Rio São Francisco do Sul in Brazil on 5 January 1504. There friendly Indians soon caused the Norman sailors to forget their East Indian objective. The local cacique, Arosca, not only traded willingly but gave a hostage to fortune. He let one of his sons, Essomericq by name, return to France with Gonneville to become a proper Christian and learn all about ordnance; and it is expressly stated that he did this in order to master his tribe's local enemies. Smart old Arosca! He had perceived the unnatural alliance between Christianity and gunpowder.

After a stay of six months with Arosca's people—a long time to remain on friendly terms but the French were good at that—*L'Espoir* sailed from Brazil on 3 July 1504, expecting to return home by the quickest route. But storms delayed her, provisions ran low, and scurvy broke out. At the first land sighted, about 10 October, the natives were hostile; so she quickly departed and sailed north "300 leagues" from Arosca-land, where she found a suitable harbor with friendly Indians. This may have been at or near Bahia. There she replenished supplies, loaded a profitable cargo of logwood, and made her third departure, for home.

Eight days out, *L'Espoir* passed a wooded island, probably Fernão de Noronha. She made Fayal (Azores) safely, but her tribulations were not yet over. A storm forced her into an Irish port. Next, off the Channel Islands, pirates attacked, captured, and scuttled her, and only twenty-eight of the French crew, including Captain Gonneville and the cacique's son, survived.

Essomericq, after a proper conversion, married Gonneville's daughter, and their progeny interested themselves in the problem of locating where Gonneville had been; the debate continued for centuries. "Terre de Gonneville" was spotted on maps all over the world. In 1867 Pierre Margry (the same French historian who became an uneasy friend of Francis Parkman) declared, on the basis of a newly discovered manuscript, that the Arosca country was in Brazil. And nobody now disagrees. The latest authority, Professor Bennichen, assigns it to the region around the mouth of the Rio São Francisco do Sul.

Although Gonneville lost his logwood to pirates, the Dieppois did not take long to go after that valuable product themselves. Jean Ango the wealthy shipowner, of whom we found plenty to say in *Northern Voyages*, smelled a profitable trade. Just how many Norman ships subsequent to *L'Espoir* anchored off the Brazilian coastline long enough to cut a load of logwood and make off, we shall never know. But there were so many of them that around 1527 D. João III ordered a former Frenchman in his service, Cristóvão Jacques, to sweep the Brazilian coast with a naval squadron and destroy every French ship or shore establishment that he encountered. He captured three ships being loaded at Bahia, and had three hundred survivors hanged or buried alive to their shoulders, and then used for target practice by his arquebusiers. Jacques continued this police operation all the way to Cape Frio, or even beyond.

The king of France, François-premier, protested through diplomatic channels, but that did no good. Verrazzano was on his way to cut logwood when the Caribs killed and ate him in the West Indies. Jean Ango decided to take revenge into his own hands. Armed with a French letter of marque, he operated against Portuguese ships off Europe or wherever his mariners could find them, and so continued until 1531, when he accepted a bribe of some 60,000 francs from Portugal to desist. Philippe Chabot, Admiral of France, also accepted a Portuguese *douceur,* and in return clapped an embargo on French departures for Brazil or the Guinea coast.

Before this prohibition was decreed, a French consortium organized by Bertrand d'Orneson de Saint-Blancard, general of the royal galleys in the Mediterranean, had set up a French factory on Brazilian soil, his principal patron being Jean Dupéret, a citizen of Lyons. Their expedition was mounted at Marseilles in ship *La Pèlerine*—"The Lady Pilgrim." Sailing in 1531 under Dupéret's command, with 120 men on board, an excellent site was chosen and named Isle Saint-Alexis; it is still called Ilha de Santo Aleixo, situated near Pernambuco (Recife), at latitude 8°37′ S. Here the Frenchmen built a fort and a warehouse for logwood, and after laboring a few months sailed for Marseilles with a valuable cargo: 300 quintal of cotton worth 3000 ducats, 500 quintal of logwood worth 4000 ducats, 3000 "leopard skins," 600 parrots "already knowing our language," and 300 monkeys worth 6 ducats each. (What fun to have been a small boy in those days at Lisbon, Marseilles, or Dieppe when a ship from Brazil came in, and you could view the wild life on board and perhaps persuade your parents to buy you a pet!) But this ship and cargo never did get home. Off Malaga, *La Pèlerine* was captured and looted by a Portuguese squadron, and D. João III decided to wipe out the intrusive French factory. In December of that year, a Portuguese fleet of three vessels under Pero Lopes de Sousa laid siege to Saint-Alexis and forced the garrison to capitulate. Although the Portuguese promised to spare every Frenchman's life, the commander and twenty others were hanged, two of the plumpest soldiers were delivered to the nearby Indians for lunch and dinner, and the rest were imprisoned for two years in Portugal. Only eleven men survived. And that was the end of this French colony.

Whilst there is no reason to believe that this rude action prevented French corsairs from attacking Portuguese ships, or nipping in and out

’k Heb voglen tee goed aapen ’k Brand om bij jou te slapen
J’ai oiseaux animaux Accouchons comme il faut

Te Amsterd: by A. Allard in de beurs straat in Pr.

Oost Indise Bootsgezel MATELOT retenu des INDES.

Home Is the Sailor, engraving by A. Allard, *c.*1700. Courtesy Maritiem
Museum "Prins Hendrik," Rotterdam.

of a Brazilian harbor to cut logwood, many years elapsed before a fresh
attempt was made to plant a French base on Brazilian territory.

La France Antarctique

In 1541, during the siege of Malta by Charles V, the knight who most
distinguished himself on the Christian side was one Nicolas Durand.
Born in 1510 at Provins (a little town some 80 kilometers southeast of

589

Paris) to a haute bourgeoisie family, he assumed the title of Chevalier de Villegagnon (a nearby village where he owned a bit of land), and so signed his letters. He attended the University of Paris at the same time as John Calvin and became a scholar and linguist who wrote two accounts in Latin of the siege of Malta; and, in addition, lived the life of a man of action. An able and accomplished mariner, "commanding in presence, eloquent and persuasive in discourse," as Parkman wrote, "his sleepless intellect was matched with a spirit as restless, vain, unstable, and ambitious as it was enterprising."

After the siege of Malta he became secretary to François-premier's ambassador to Venice, and later Henri II named him commander of war galleys. As such he took charge, successfully, of a romantic enterprise of 1548, evading an English fleet in wartime to pick up the child Marie Stuart (later Mary Queen of Scots) at Dumbarton Castle near the mouth of the Clyde and bring her to France to marry the Dauphin.

At this time there was an uneasy balance in France between Protestants and Catholics, between the spirit of Calvin and the authority of the Pope. Villegagnon espoused *la religion prétendue réformée,* as the Calvinists or Huguenots were generally called by their adversaries when they wished to be polite, as they seldom did. Villegagnon, having become a Calvinist, conceived the scheme of establishing a French colony in the very navel of the Brazilian coast. He sold it to his Catholic king, who had created him Vice-Admiral of Brittany for his many maritime services, as a means for France to share in the riches of the New World. At the same time, to Calvin at Geneva and to Admiral Coligny, a Protestant high in the affairs of state, he promoted the idea that this colony could be a Protestant refuge, an asylum for Huguenots in the event that they were worsted in the civil wars that were constantly breaking out in France.

Officially a royal expedition, only in part was it financed by the crown. Three ships of 200 tuns' burthen each (names unknown) were equipped, and 600 men sailed, probably as many Catholics as Protestants. There were peasants, mingled with young, restless, and poor noblemen and jail-birds who would do anything to be free, and a considerable number of hired artisans such as masons, carpenters, tailors, tanners, and *vignerons.* The seamen were largely Norman and Breton.

They sailed from Dieppe 14 August 1555, after a false start. A voyage to Brazil at that time of year was no longer considered risky, as attested to by the fact that the insurance premium on cargoes from Rouen to Brazil was only 18 per cent, about the same as to Italian ports. Villegagnon's ships were both staunch and well found. At Tenerife they exchanged cannon shots with the Spanish garrison. Following the African coast too far, they were batted back and forth between two continents until 31 October, when they made landfall somewhere under the bulge of Brazil. Coasting along, they called at Cape Frio 6 November. There the local Indians offered Villegagnon a shoulder and leg of a Portuguese captive, all ready to grill; he not only declined the gift but gave them a lecture against cannibalism and ransomed two live Portuguese awaiting their turn to be slaughtered.

On 10 November 1555, the fleet entered the breathtaking harbor of Rio de Janeiro, already called Guanabara Bay. An island named Governador (so close to the international airport that travelers by air may easily look it over) was chosen by Villegagnon for his colony, which he later named *La France Antarctique*.* The Indians, apparently pleased to see so many Europeans who were not Portuguese, brought them manioc and other food, and taught the French to smoke tobacco, which they called *petun;* the word reached Canada. Villegagnon, like Cabeza de Vaca, performed faith cures, which rid the Indians of a big epidemic. He had the interior explored, and many valuable woods were discovered. Prospects were rosy. They did not remain so long.

"Le Général," as the people called Villegagnon, gave evidence of his recently acquired Calvinism by vigorously attempting to curb the natural impulses of his more youthful colonists. "Marry or perish" were the alternatives offered to casual liaisons with the native girls; mixed marriages were encouraged. But the lash and the pillory were prescribed for the slightest offense. An odd edict of the Governor forced all colonists to wear a semi-monastic costume, unsuitable for that climate. A plot against the General, discovered by two Scots (of whom there were many among the Calvinists), was cruelly crushed.

Two ships returned to France with logwood and curiosities early in 1556. Three ships (*Petite Ramberge, Grande Ramberge,* and *Rosée*), with reinforcements to the number of 184 men, five young girls and

---

* Also used in the title of André Thevet's book, *Les Singularités de la France antarctique* (1551), which includes the story of this colony. In northern European nations it was usual to call everything below the Tropic of Capricorn, antarctic; but Thevet stretched the term to include Florida.

their matron, arrived 7 March 1557. Great was the rejoicing over everything but the food. Just as the Pilgrim Fathers of Plymouth regretted that they had nought to offer newcomers but lobsters and a cup of spring water, so La France Antarctique could produce nothing for a "welcome to Brazil" feast but corn meal, dried fish, and rain water.

The *Ramberges* and *Rosée* brought to La France Antarctique something supposedly more precious than supplies: a group of Protestant parsons trained at Geneva. Villegagnon had asked for them. One, named Jean de Léry (whom we have already quoted on Crossing the Line), wrote the story of the voyage.

As later in Acadia and Canada, so in Brazil, French Protestants and Catholics seemed incapable of living together in peace. Both sides engaged in endless disputes; the superb mountains around Guanabara Bay echoed to screaming debates on such trivial subjects as "Is it lawful to make the sacramental bread of corn meal?" The dogmatic stiffness of the ministers from Geneva infuriated Villegagnon to the point of committing murder; and as he arrogated to himself all governmental powers, he had three reverends thrown into the sea and forced two to live on the mainland among the Indians. These took passage on a vessel returning with logwood to France. Their voyage home resembled Magellan's for hardship. Sailors and passengers alike ate rats and the horn windows of their lanterns; even chewed logwood. Landing at length in Brittany, they suffered the supreme indignity, a sealed letter of introduction from Villegagnon himself to the first magistrate they might encounter, denouncing them as heretics, deserving death by fire.

It must not be assumed that nothing but quasi-religious disputations happened at La France Antarctique. The colony was well managed for production. Villegagnon deserves credit for this because his humane policy toward the local Indians won their loyalty; and, what was more important, their co-operation in cutting logwood inland and stacking it on shore for export. The colony, in fact, was so successful that some of the French began to think of expanding southward to include the Portuguese factory at São Vicente, and perhaps everything up to Rio de Uruguay or the River Plate. Why not a far-southern New France as well as Canada? It was of course a mistake to try to enforce sexual continence in a French colony, but Villegagnon as a Knight of Malta had taken vows of chastity and thought he could enforce it in Brazil. One wonders whether he had heard about Cabeza de Vaca's experiences at Asunción.

In the meantime, Villegagnon openly declared a renewed attachment to the Catholic faith, and warned all heretics present to follow suit or keep silent. Then, in 1559, alleging no particular reason, he took refuge in flight. Leaving his nephew Bois-le-Comte in charge of La France Antarctique, he returned to France itself.

He arrived in good time. Although his friend Henri II was dead, Marie Stuart, the little girl whom he had rescued, had become queen of France. He joined her party of the Guises, wrote tracts against Calvinists (who replied vigorously in pamphlets against the "renegade"), and took a somewhat peripheral part in palace politics. He received the comfortable appointment of ambassador from the Order of St. John of Jerusalem (Malta) to the court of France, and became a gentleman of the King's Chamber. The years passed pleasantly. On 29 January 1572, in his sixty-second year, he died. Seven months later, Admiral Coligny and many other old friends fell victim to the St. Bartholomew's Day massacre in the streets of Paris.

In the meantime, La France Antarctique had ceased to be. Portugal, unwilling to tolerate this enclave in her territory which irritated her (as, recently, Portuguese Goa irritated India), sent a strong force overseas against the French colony in 1560, and all members of the garrison not slain sought asylum among the natives.

That was not too bad for them. For one trait of Villegagnon that everyone praised, friend or foe, was his humanity to the natives. Mem de Sá, head of one of the Portuguese captaincies in Brazil, wrote to his court of Villegagnon, "He does not treat the natives as do the Portuguese; he is liberal with them to excess and observes strict justice. If one of his people commits a wrong [on the Indians] he is immediately hanged; thus he is feared by them but adored by the natives. He has taught them the use of arms, and as the tribe with which he is allied is very numerous and one of the bravest, he could become very redoubtable." And some fifty Indians volunteered to go home with him to France. But for his defects of character, especially his arbitrariness and religious conceit, Villegagnon might have become the Champlain of a New France in South America, a Gallic wedge in Brazil. His enemies called him, maliciously, "Le Roi d'Amérique" and accused him of aiming at a viceroyalty like those of Mexico and Peru.

This was the last attempt of France to found a settlement in Brazil. Yet, but a few years after the fall of Antarctic France, Admiral Coligny and the Huguenots tried again. Jean Ribaut on 1 May 1562 planted a colony on what he called the *Rivière de Mai*, the St. John River, Florida. This situation, next to and even within sight of the Spanish treasure fleets booming along home in the Gulf Stream, could not be brooked by Spain. But the oft-told tale of the ruthless wiping out of this French colony by Menéndez de Avilés is beyond our scope. At the end of the century there were plenty of French interloping voyages to Brazil, but no attempt to plant a colony.

The tradition, or theory, that the French, of all European nations, knew best how to treat the natives of America is certainly sustained by the Indian relations of Villegagnon and lesser interlopers. Hans Staden, the German castaway who walked almost the entire length of Brazil, recorded that he always talked French or something that sounded like French to the Indians, in order to avoid being eaten. He records one cacique saying in effect, "Damn it, whenever I select a particularly plump and juicy European for my dinner, he claims to be French and I have to go hungry!"

Bibliography and Notes

The French in Brazil. Most historians virtually ignore this subject, of which the most comprehensive accounts are in Ch.-André Julien, *Les Voyages de découverte et les premiers établissements* (Paris, 1948), and Eugène Guérin, *Ango et ses pilotes* (Paris, 1900). Both are used to good purpose in the best English account: Regina Johnson Tomlinson, *The Struggle for Brazil: Portugal and "the French Interlopers"* (New York, 1970). The best coverage of this subject, however, will be in the Brazilian Naval History now (1974) in preparation under the editorship of my friend Captain Max Justo Guedes. He generously sent to me, well in advance of publication, the chapters of this work on "França Antártica" by Professor Philippe Bennichen of the Sorbonne. These will render obsolete all other accounts including the leading monograph on La France Antarctique,—Arthur Heulhard's *Villegagnon, roi d'Amérique* (Paris, 1897), a sumptuously illustrated quarto. Heulhard argued that Villegagnon was no Calvinist when he arrived in Brazil, that he did not intend his colony to be a Protestant refuge, and that Admiral Coligny forced the Genevan missionaries on it. This is hard to believe, as letters are extant from Villegagnon to Calvin, asking for help. And Heulhard is defective on the economic side. It is high time for some competent scholar interested in voyages as well as theology (rare combination!) to write a new biography of Durand de Villegagnon.

Francis Parkman's chapter on Villegagnon in his *Pioneers of France* is not one of his best efforts; but he did use two of the leading contemporary sources: André Thevet, *Les Singularités de la France antarctique* (Paris,

1551, see my *Northern Voyages*, p. 451), and Jean de Léry, *Histoire d'un voyage fait en la terre du Brésil* (Paris, 1578). Paul Gaffarel published a modern edition in two volumes in 1870.

Ramberge. My old French dictionary calls this an English type. The *New English Dictionary* describes it as a "long, narrow and swift war vessel," and refers us to Du Bellay, *Mémoires*, X (1545).

☀ XXV ☀

Back to the Strait

1534-1558

Simon de Alcazaba's Expedition

Charles V never lost interest in the Strait of Magellan. In 1534, before he knew of the death of Loaysa and Elcano, the Emperor contracted with a Portuguese exile and prominent member of his court, Simon de Alcazaba Sotomayor, to sail through the Strait with two ships named *Madre de Dios* and *San Pedro* and explore the still unknown coast of Chile between Cabo Pilar and Callao. His object was to open up a southern all-water route to Peru. Sailing from Sanlúcar 21 September 1534, only a month later than Mendoza, Alcazaba arrived at Rio Gallego, Patagonia, on 17 January 1535, in time to profit by the Antarctic summer; but then his luck ran out. After penetrating the Strait for some 80 miles, Alcazaba suffered the indignity of being driven out to sea by a westerly gale. His water supply fell so low that he could only keep his livestock alive by issuing them wine, which they probably relished no better than the French cattle liked Cartier's cider off Newfoundland. But for pickled penguin meat, all hands would have starved to death.

Returning from the high seas and passing Cabo Vírgenes, Alcazaba managed to reach the First Narrows. There his men, already surly and discontented, were further discouraged by finding an inscription under a cross left by Loaysa, stating that he had been forced to winter there for over nine months! Weather turned so foul and frigid that the crew mutinied and forced their captain to turn back and put in at an unidentified place on the coast of Patagonia which they named *Puerto de los Lobos*. Thence the crews insisted on returning to Spain. Off shore they "discovered some islands in the sea, where there were a vast quantity of animals called sea wolves, although they looked more like lions." Ruiz-Guiñazú believes that these islands were the Falklands. Possibly; but more probably they were the Pingoïn group nearer the continent.

Alcazaba, whom J. G. Kohl calls "a somewhat corpulent and helpless man," was killed during the mutiny. The other officers then got the upper hand, hanged some of the mutineers, and marooned the rest. From Puerto de los Lobos they organized a land exploration with the object of finding gold and seeing the Pacific Ocean, but returned empty-handed, and with no other view than that of the Andean mountain wall. The loyal mariners, under Captains Rodrigo de Isla and Rodrigo Martínez, now decided to sail to Mexico. *Madre de Dios* foundered with all hands in a storm off Brazil. *San Pedro*, her complement reduced to 20 men, finally reached Santo Domingo. There these pitiful survivors were tried for mutiny, condemned, and hanged. Thus Alcazaba's expedition suffered the melancholy distinction of total and complete annihilation, more by act of man than act of God.

The Bishop of Plasencia's Expedition

The appearance of Loaysa's pinnace at the Isthmus of Tehuantepec may well have suggested to the viceroy of Mexico that the Strait of Magellan might be put to good use as part of an oceanic route from Spain to the west coast of South America. Hernando Cortés, to be sure, had established shipyards at Tehuantepec and elsewhere on that coast, but so much of the equipment had to be carried by Indian bearer or mule train across Mexico that it was difficult to cope with the growing passenger and freight traffic required by the conquest of Peru.

Antonio de Mendoza, viceroy of Mexico, took the initiative. He put up his brother-in-law the Most Reverend Gutiérrez de Varga Carvajal, bishop of Plasencia, to equipping a fleet of three vessels at his own expense to inaugurate the trade route Spain—Strait of Magellan—Chile and Peru. Plasencia is one of the most picturesque towns in the mountainous Estremadura, and the bishop belonged to a leading family; but it was an odd place from which to organize a fleet. During the absence of Charles V in Genoa, the bishop received a *capitulación* (what the English would have called a patent or contract) from the regent, dated 6 November 1536, allowing him to "conquer and people" the shores of the Pacific from Peru to the Strait.

Unfortunately we know very little about this expedition, which brought more important results than Loaysa's pretentious armada. It comprised three ships whose names are not even recorded. Two must have been fairly big, as each carried 150 soldiers as well as crew and would-be colonists. The Comendador Francisco de la Ribera sailed as Captain General, and two near relations of the bishop, Alonso and Francisco de Camargo, were captains—a neat little family affair. (For this reason, the bishop's fleet is often referred to as the Camargo Expedition.) It took them almost three years after obtaining the imperial permission to take off from Seville, in August 1539.

According to the fragment of one ship's journal that has been preserved, they first made land at a harbor of Patagonia. This seems incredible; they must earlier have touched at one or more Brazilian ports. They passed Rio Santa Cruz on 12 January 1540, anchored off Cabo Vírgenes, and there suffered the usual experience of being blown out to sea by a westerly gale. Re-entering on the 20th, "Number 1," the biggest ship, drove ashore two days later; she and Captain General Ribera were lost, but most of the crew survived. They were taken on board what, for want of a name, is referred to as the "Third Ship." The "Second Ship" (*La Incognita* as the Argentine historians call her for convenience), with a Camargo in command, wintered in Tierra del Fuego and eventually returned to Spain. She did not scuttle and run like her predecessors, but made a wide sweep to the southward, and Argentine historians like to believe that she passed through the Strait of Le Maire and even looked into Beagle Channel; but this is mere conjecture. *La Incognita* awaited the next Antarctic summer, sailed for home 30 December 1541, and arrived safely. On her way back, according to Admiral Basílico's researches, she discovered "eight or more islands" which Argentine historians believe to have been *Las Islas Malvinas*, the Falkland Islands. Maybe; but, as we have seen, there are plenty of other claimants.

Two survivors later deposed that after the loss of Ribera's "Number 1," Captain Sebastián de Argüello, 150 soldiers, 38 adventurers, mariners, gunners and gromets, three married women, and all the arms, munitions, and provisions were saved and placed on board "Third Ship." Either Sebastián de Argüello or Alonso de Camargo took command of her and sailed through the Strait of Magellan and up the west coast of Chile, which Governor Valdivia had recently explored and occupied. She touched at Valparaiso and reached the port of Quilca, near Arequipa, in a pitiful condition. This must have been late in 1540 or early in 1541. As the first vessel (not counting little *Santiago*) to reach a west coast port, she and her people were made much of locally.

It is ironical that the first vessel in the history of American discovery to be made into a museum, like U.S.S. *Constitution* and H.M.S. *Victory*, was this episcopal ship whose name is not even known, and the name of whose captain is a matter of controversy. For, according to an early Chilean historian who absorbed much local tradition, "Third Ship" sailed from Quilca to Callao, where the people had her hauled out to be preserved as a memorial, and set up her mainmast in front of the viceregal palace at Lima. There it lasted many years, serving the honorable purpose of displaying the banners of Spain and of the Church. The Peruvians soon discovered what we have all learned, that it is monstrously expensive to preserve a wooden ship ashore. "Third Ship" disintegrated long before her mainmast became too rotten even to display flags.

Alonso de Camargo, who sailed in "Third Ship" even if he did not command her, remained in Peru and took part in the Peruvian expedition which discovered the mines of Potosí, Bolivia, in 1545 or thereabouts. The fabulous *cerro* or mountain of silver ore at Potosí became the cynosure which drew Spaniards up from the River Plate to Peru, ignoring the all-ocean route that Magellan had discovered.

Although the bishop's "Third Ship" proved that the Magellan route was practicable between Spain and the west coast, and the increasing coastal population of Mexico, Peru, and Chile made an all-sea substitute for the Panama route more and more desirable, her only effect was to exaggerate the navigational difficulties of the Magellan Strait. Consequently, both Spanish and colonial authorities concentrated on improving the land passage over the Isthmus of Panama, and west coast harbors. It remained for Francis Drake, thirty-eight years later, really to open the Strait by force.

At the same time, the imperial government frowned on any rival strait being opened by any other power. In 1541 Jacques Cartier's preparations for his third voyage to Canada aroused almost hysterical efforts in Spain to stop him, or at least to ascertain his objectives; the English ambassador in Paris even warned Henry VIII that Cartier's orders were "to seeke the trayde of spicerey by a shorter waye than the portingallez doth use." That was indeed the main objective of Frobisher's and Davis's voyages. Ironical, is it not, that so much effort was expended on finding a northern strait between Atlantic and Pacific, when Magellan's was available?

Yet it is not surprising that mariners and rulers alike found the great Strait highly disappointing. At least six expeditions had tried to get through, with about seventeen vessels, twelve of which had been cast away in or near the eastern entrance; and Elcano's *Victoria* still held the unique distinction of passing through and returning home. Of these vessels' crews, not one man in five ever saw his native land again; probably well over a thousand had perished. Strange and sinister rumors sprang up and spread through European seaports. "They said" that a vessel entering the Strait from the Atlantic could seldom find good enough holding ground to ride out the violent westerlies and avoid dragging ashore or being blown out to sea. And were a ship lucky enough to round Cape Froward, she would find the Strait blocked by a rocky island torn from its place by the awful wind and waves and hurled into the channel, stopping all vessels from reaching the Pacific.

Ulloa, Hojea, and Ladrillero

In the meantime the long arms of Spain were stretching in both directions from the Isthmus of Panama along the shores of the Pacific. Right arm pushed up the Mexican coast along Baja (Lower) and Alta (Upper) California; left arm pushed along the coasts of the future republics of Colombia, Ecuador, Peru, and Chile, to the Strait. We shall deal with California later, but now tell how the left arm closed the great gap between Darien and the Strait of Magellan.

The Spanish colonists showed remarkable energy and enterprise in building vessels on the west coast. Vasco Núñez de Balboa began it, constructing four bergantinas at the mouth of the Rio de Balsas on the Gulf of San Miguel. Boating Indian slaves from Nicaragua to Old

Panama (founded 1519) proved a great stimulus to shipbuilding, since the nature of the terrain forbade the captives' being marched by land. This traffic was organized by Pedrárias Dávila, and as early as 1533, fifteen to twenty country-built ships were engaged in it. Vessels were built where there were superior resources of ship timber, mast trees, pitch, and native *pita* fiber capable of being twisted into ships' cordage. Hernando Cortés showed great interest in shipbuilding; it was in *La Florida,* built at Zacatula, that Saavedra sailed across the Pacific to help Loaysa. After the conquest of Peru, repair facilities were established at Callao, and later in the century Guayaquil became an important ship-building center. Considering that all hardware and sails * had to be hauled or carried across the Isthmus (Vera Cruz to Zacatula, or via Lake Nicaragua to Realejo, or Nombre de Dios to Old Panama), it is amazing how many big merchant ships were built on the Pacific coast. The 700-tun *Santa Ana* captured by Cavendish in 1587 was Realejo-built, but long before that there were enough west coast vessels to float Pizarro's troops to the conquest of Peru (1531–35) and to bring in Spanish colonists. By 1540 a basic pattern of Mexico-Peru trade had been established, which lasted for a century and a half. Passengers and all kinds of consumer goods were sailed south. Vast quantities of silver went north, especially after the discovery of the mercury process by Enrique Garcés had unlocked the lower grades of ore; and, by the second half of the century, the "wealth of Peru" had become proverbial throughout Europe. A good indication is this table of royal revenues in silver pesos or "pieces of eight," from different parts of the Spanish-American Empire, in 1557.**

The astonishing Peruvian item, roughly equivalent to a million dollars, proves that a lot of money was being made out of this west coast

---

* It became the custom for Spanish ships bound to Panama or Mexico to bring out a fresh suit of sails and sell their worn ones to be carried across to a ship-building center on the Pacific.

** Ramón Carande, *Carlos V y Sus Banqueros* II (1965), 553.

MEXICO (New Spain, New Galicia, and Yucatan)	217,225
Central America (Guatemala, Honduras, Nicaragua)	38,740
Spanish Main, including Cartagena	22,592
Popayán (Colombia)	19,365
West Indies (Cuba, Puerto Rico, Hispaniola)	50,133
PERU	622,784
	970,839

trade, but it had notable disadvantages. The winds were so light and variable between April and September that the passage to Panama required four to six weeks, and the southward one, to Peru, seven to eight *months*.* Authorities complained that it often took longer to sail from Mexico to Peru than from Mexico to Manila! So, what with the heavy cost of shipbuilding on the west coast, the time consumption, and the enormous markup of consumer goods from Spain, the viceroys of Mexico and Peru had every incentive to open up the Strait of Magellan and establish an all-sea route between Atlantic and Pacific. These attempts, of which one (Ladrillero's) brilliantly succeeded, yet mysteriously were muffled and ignored, are an integral chapter of the European discovery of America.

Pedro de Valdivia, the first governor general of Chile (then subordinate to the viceroy of Peru) was the earliest explorer to push south by sea. He reached latitude 40° S, where, later, the town of Valdivia was named for him, then returned to Valparaiso which he had founded in 1536. Both places lay so far south that the route thither from Spain via the Isthmus of Panama became insufferably long; hence Valdivia determined to open the Strait of Magellan from the west. In 1553, after two more Chilean towns had been founded, La Concepción and La Imperial, Valdivia sent Captain Francisco de Ulloa with two ships to enter the Strait of Magellan from the Pacific end. The captain of his second ship was Cortés Hojea, who later played the same role under Ladrillero. Ulloa passed Cabo Pilar and found no giant rock-stopper blocking the Strait; but before even reaching Cape Froward, he turned back, owing to "the bad state of his vessels, scarcity of provisions, and hostility of the natives." Upon his return he found that Governor Valdivia had been killed in the Araucanian war, and that nothing more could then be done; but Ulloa at least proved a west-east passage of the Strait to be possible.

The next governor general of Chile, Don García Hurtado de Mendoza, son of the very magnificent Don Andrés Hurtado de Mendoza, viceroy of Peru 1556–60, received a royal command dated 29 May 1555 to go through with the west-east project. At the end of 1557 he placed Juan Fernández Ladrillero, a native of Moguer sixty or more years old

* Woodrow Borah, *Early Colonial Trade* . . . (Berkeley, 1954), pp. 29–30. During the rest of the year, the passage from Huatulco to Manta (seaport of Puerto Viejo, Ecuador) took but two to three months.

Vaz Dourado's map of Patagonia, 1568, from the atlas he executed that year at Goa. This earliest dated work of this Portuguese cartographer is in the Palacio Liria, Madrid. The late Duke of Alba, D. Luís (d.1972), kindly gave me permission to study and use it. Described by Armando Cortesão.

and veteran of no fewer than eleven round voyages from Spain to the West Indies, in command of three little country-built vessels, with the mission to discover, explore and take formal possession of all the country from Valdivia south, and through the Strait of Magellan. Ladrillero had come to the governor's notice by commanding the ships that escorted him to Chile in 1556 and showing his skill by sailing him safely through a "furious tempest."

Here is the modest task organization:

Ship *San Luis,* 50 tuns, Captain Ladrillero; pilot, Hernando Gallego, the same who in 1567 accompanied Mendaña on the expedition which discovered the Solomon Islands.

Ship *San Sebastián,* 50 tuns, Captain Cortés Hojea; * pilot, Pedro Gallego (Hernando's brother); *escribano* (scribe or secretary), Miguel de Goicueta.

Bergantina *San Salvador,* captain not known.

Total complement: 60 men.

The three vessels sortied from Concepción, Chile, 17 November 1557, before a favoring northerly wind. With main courses furled they made a port that they called *Nuestra Señora de la Valle,* since they had prayed Our Lady for survival. Very early in the voyage—9 December—the ships separated in a storm and never found each other again. Hojea in *San Sebastián,* with the bergantina, spent several months exploring the deep, mountain-walled sounds (in Chile called *canales*) that extend from Valdivia south, and which make the modern steamer trip from Puerto Montt to Cabo Pilar one of the most beautiful in the world. The Indians they encountered had the same culture as the Tierra del Fuegians; Goicueta, who wrote the narrative, noted that the pointed ends and graceful sheer of their sealskin canoes reminded him of a new moon four days old. Sarmiento de Gamboa thought that he had been the first to explore this watery maze, but he was second to Hojea.

An amusing byproduct of this leg of the voyage was a Portuguese invasion scare at Valdivia. Indians, passing the word north after sighting Ladrillero's three small vessels, blew it up to a fleet of seven or eight big ships. The authorities at Valdivia jumped to the conclusion that this must be a Portuguese fleet which had sneaked through the

* Also spelled Hogea, Ogea, and Hojeda. Nothing is known about him except that he had been with Ulloa.

Strait to set up a colony on Spanish territory. Don García, "with that Catalonian arrogance so common among captains of that century," wrote to the king boasting that he could take care not only of a Portuguese invasion but of a French one. Fortunately both fleets proved to be imaginary.

Hojea, after spending some time at a harbor around latitude 51° S that he named *Puerto Roberto*—probably the modern Canal Ignacio on Isla Hanover—made a lengthy exploration of the labyrinth of sounds to the eastward. He even entered one at the very base of the Andes which he named *Última Esperanza*, Last Hope; it bears the same name today.

Returning to the ocean, on the day after Christmas 1557 Hojea sortied from a harbor that he calls "Campaña, on rocky headland Horcado" (probably Canal Guadalupe on Isla Hanover) to search for the mouth of the Strait of Magellan. *San Sebastián* was quickly blown back again, and for nineteen days suffered such foul, blowy weather that the mariners "could neither rest nor sleep day or night, keeping watch over the cables and stoppers which we secured to the mainmast, . . . commending ourselves to God and promising to make pilgrimages, as is usual in time of peril." God heard them on the nineteenth day "and gave us a day of fair weather with clear light and warm sun in which we dried our clothes and cables." What memories that simple statement brings to old salts! Rain, rain, rain; no chance to get warm or to cook food; followed by a genuine dry-out and feast which made one feel it could never happen again. But it always did.

On 12 January 1558, *San Sebastián* and *San Salvador* sortied from Campaña and made six leagues to a harbor that Hojea named *San Victoriano*. Here they suffered another big blow, evidently a strong williwaw; one cable parted, and they were in imminent peril of losing the others and their lives. Captain Hojea made his voice heard above the howling of the wind, begging the men to prepare for death, and *"los mas bistos marineros"*—the toughest sailors—"spent the entire night saying litanies and other prayers." Thoughtfully, in order to save the souls of the Indian serfs on board, they managed to baptize the lot at the height of the storm.

Next day the wind dropped and they made another port "like a river, at the foot of a high sierra," where they were perfectly protected, and obtained fresh water and wood. Here they lost a second anchor and part of a cable. That they could ill afford, and *San Sebastián* had but one left. The captain now made his men a little speech, stating that although their ship had reached the latitude where the entrance of the Strait should have been, he could not locate it; and, having lost two anchors and consumed most of the victuals, with no prospect of finding any more in this barren country, and that only *San Luis* had on board the tools necessary to effect repairs, he thought they had better turn back. These words were received with joy and relief. So, on 31 January 1558, *San Sebastián* and bergantina *San Salvador* turned back without even finding Cabo Pilar.

Many more miseries were endured on the return passage to Valdivia. When they approached the Chiloé Archipelago, Hojea and his men received relief from friendly natives ashore with whom the Indians on board could communicate. *San Sebastián* was in such a sorry shape that they cannibalized her to build a new bergantina, launched on 25 July 1558. There was no anchor for her, and no boat; the new vessel had to sail with neither ground tackle nor tender. But she sailed all survivors to Valdivia, arriving 1 October. What became of bergantina *San Salvador* we are not told; she too must have been broken up or abandoned.

Exactly where Ladrillero's flagship *San Luis* separated from Hojea's two vessels on 9 December 1557 he does not say; but his own account indicates that he explored even more *canales* and sounds than Hojea did. The Chilean historian Barros regards this part of the voyage as Ladrillero's great contribution to geography: "He reconnoitered this region with the skill of an experienced geographer. Reading his *roteiro*, with a good modern chart, one can follow his itinerary step by step. His hydrography, his general description of the lands visited, the courses, the compass directions of the cordilleras and mountains, the aspect of the level parts, the climatic conditions, the animals that the explorers saw, and the clothes of the natives, were recorded with an exactitude rare among explorers of the sixteenth century. The practical surveys of three centuries later have confirmed the exactness of the geographical notes of this old pilot."

In January 1558, which he spent in this exploration, Ladrillero enjoyed fair weather and north winds. After calling at the modern Estrecho Nelson (which Ladrillero named Bahia de San Lázaro), *San Luis*

Parts of the Strait that Ladrillero saw. James F. Nields photos.

sailed well outside the dangerous reefs and islets (now named after Sir John Narborough) and passed the western entrance of the Strait of Magellan. The Captain gives the correct landmarks and his latitude was only 15 miles out; but he did not enter, owing doubtless to the late season. Instead, he explored a considerable distance to the southward, beyond Desolation Island and the dangerous Apostles Rocks off it; and at latitude 54° S entered Canal Santa Barbara which has a direct connection with the Strait of Magellan. Although he did not find this outer coast of the Fuegian islands (as later did Narborough) "horrible . . . like the ruins of a world destroyed by terrific earthquakes," he admitted that it "looks ill to the eyes." The Indians he found comely and well built, well nourished on seal, shellfish, and various raw foods; and he admired their canoes of beech bark sewed with whale or other animal sinews. Ladrillero holed up in a harbor—still unidentified— which he named *Nuestra Señora de los Remedios,* from 22 March to 22 July 1558. It puzzles his Chilean editor, as it does me, why so bold a navigator as Ladrillero should choose to tarry in this unlikely spot, and to postpone entering the Strait of Magellan to the Antarctic winter (June, July, and August) with its chill temperature and scanty daylight.

Exactly what day Ladrillero's *San Luis* entered the Strait he tells us not; probably near the end of July 1558. He mentions the islands later named after Carlos III and Stuart princes, and gives useful compass directions for the channel. He explored several "all mountainous" dead-end canals. He passed the island later named by Drake after Queen Elizabeth I of England, calling it Gonzalo de Borja—possibly a ship-mate. A promontory which he called Juan Mazia later received from Sir John Narborough the sporty name of his ship *Sweepstakes,* and Punta Sweepstakes is still on the map. Landing at the Punta de San Gregorio, Ladrillero took formal possession of everything he had explored, in the name of his king and Viceroy Hurtado de Mendoza, and of his son Don García, governor of Chile. Hence the name Bahía Posesión, the only name given by Ladrillero that is on modern charts.

After what he had seen on the west coast. Ladrillero was astonished to find the shores of the Strait, in its eastern half, low and grassy. He arrived at Cabo Vírgenes 9 August 1558 in the midst of a very cold and snowy Antarctic winter. Here again he encountered natives and found them *soberbia*—a proud and arrogant people—but the women had coarse faces. Like every other European, Ladrillero was astonished to find these Indians going practically naked in the winter. He makes out the Strait to be one hundred leagues long—which, supposing he used the same league as Columbus and Magellan did, measuring 3.18 nautical miles, was only six and a half miles short of the actual distance cape to cape. Fish and edible products of the land he found hard to procure.

On 9 August 1558, without tarrying a day, Ladrillero turned *San Luis* back from *la Mar del Norte*, as he calls the Atlantic. In midwinter he must have suffered from blustery northwest winds, but he does not mention them. Nor does he mention anchoring anywhere prior to Woods Bay, which he calls *Puerto de las Tortas* ("Pie Bay"). This the modern Chilean coast pilot recommends as a good harbor of refuge because the mountains protect it from the prevailing winds. The island later named after King Charles of England Ladrillero calls *San Juan*. He noted the dangerous mingling of the waters where Canal Jerónimo empties into the main Strait, forming whirlpools which at certain moments of each tide are dangerous to small sailing vessels.

Noting several openings to canals, Ladrillero observed that the Strait narrows to the length of a crossbow shot, which (as we have seen with Cabeza de Vaca) was over half a mile.* The next harbor westward, unnamed on the modern chart, he called *Puerto de la Traición* (Treason) because, when his ship's prow was moored to the shore, the natives attacked with spears and stones. All were driven off by arquebus fire. *San Luis* hastily made sail, and, after investigating the bay now called Beaufort and passing Cabo Parker, closed Cabo Deseado. He noted its "two little peaks tall and slender and black," the pillars which caused it to be renamed Cabo Pilar. Unfortunately Ladrillero did not note the date, so we cannot compare his passage of the Strait with those of his predecessors and successors; but his Chilean editor does not think that he got out before early March 1559.

From that point *San Luis* had a tempestuous passage back to Valdivia.

Ladrillero advised everyone who wished to follow him, to leave

---

* The Strait is nowhere less than one nautical mile wide; but the mountains seem to close in as you sail through, so that it seems much narrower.

Valdivia in September and enter the Strait in October. Vessels should stand well off shore down to latitude 51° S (that of the Campaña harbor), where there are facilities for careening; or else continue to Bahia de San Lázaro (Nelson Strait). Then crawl down, as it were, to the Strait's entrance. But if you try to sail all the way off shore to the latitude of Cabo Deseado, you are likely to get into trouble when you haul in to the land, "first, owing to the cloudy weather and obscurity which the north wind brings, and second, owing to the archipelago around the mouth, which extends four leagues seaward." He means the Grupo Narborough, the Evangelistas, and the Apostles Rocks; the warning is well worth heeding. Once inside the Strait, all you have to do is to stick to the middle "and invoke the aid of God and His blessed Mother" to keep out of trouble. He holds out the hope that, with prevailing north to northwest winds, one could sail through to the Atlantic in six or seven days—no exaggeration. The best time, he says, to enter the Strait from the Atlantic for a westward passage is in summer, from December through February, "since the weather is more mild," and you have more south and southeast winds. In winter the days are much shorter, and you have frost and snow; thus in the month of July you will have only six and one-half hours of daylight, and the storms endure eight, ten, and twelve days. "So it seems to me that, to make a good passage, you should leave the ocean between March and the end of September." October to February, he concludes, are the best months to enter the Strait from Spain; and March and April to enter it from the Pacific. The modern sailing directions bear him out.

"The Strait is the most noble channel in this region," concludes Ladrillero, a noble captain who deserved better treatment than he has had from contemporaries or from posterity. Part of the reason was the myth of the big rock stopper in the Strait, which Hojea was unable to deny because he never sailed far enough to investigate. Ulloa, to be sure, had entered, but only went partway through. Unfortunately, Ercilla embalmed the myth in his *La Araucana*:

> The secret of this passage, once discovered,
> Since from our people has been ever hidden;
> Perchance a thunderbolt from high heaven,
> Perchance some islet forcibly ripped up
> And hurled by tempest seas and monstrous winds,
> Hath stopped its mouth, and choked it for all time.
>
> (Part I, canto i)

This was written in Chile between 1555 and 1558, when the author left for Spain where *La Araucana* was printed; may he not have written this stanza between Hojea's return and Ladrillero's? And, like other poets, thought his verses too good to rewrite? So Ladrillero got no credit from the poet for having twice traversed the Strait without finding any rock-stopper, and Ercilla's poetical rendering of the myth spread farther than the master mariner's matter-of-fact *derrotero*. Modern Chilean historians have suggested that Philip II (who succeeded to the throne of Spain in 1556) deliberately suppressed accounts of Ladrillero's voyage because it made out the passage of the Strait to be too easy, and he wanted the myth to deter foreigners and others from trying it. Nobody is known to have tried the Strait for twenty years after Ladrillero, and the first who did was Francis Drake who, we may say, "busted it wide open."

Ladrillero received neither royal reward nor recognition. In his day it was customary for viceregal and provincial governments to draw up an *Información de méritos y servicios* of faithful servants of the crown. In the 22-page one relating to Don García Hurtado de Mendoza, dated May 1561, Merit No. 49 is his sending the Ladrillero expedition to explore the Strait of Magellan. Therein "said don García well served His Majesty, since navigating said Strait will be a great accommodation to this country, and make it possible for Spanish ships to come here *and sell things much cheaper*." But Ladrillero's name is never mentioned, nor did he get a separate statement of merits, as did many petty judges, mayors, and soldiers.

In my opinion, the phrase "sell things much cheaper" is the key to this neglect. A vested interest had been built up in the Isthmus of Panama and west coast shipyards for carrying merchandise to and from Spain, and those who profited by it wanted to keep prices high.

Juan Fernández Ladrillero, despite his age, came to terms with the Patagonian climate and natives better than any other explorer of his century. One likes to imagine him, gray of hair and beard, on the quarterdeck of his little *San Luis*, conning her through the Strait, keeping one eye out for snow squalls and williwaws, and the other on the leadsman in the chains. It is time that this forgotten man in the history of South American discovery be recognized for what he was, a great mariner and a devoted servant to his king and viceroy, neither of whom honored him.

All that we know of his later life is that he continued "navigating in American waters," and by 1574 was living in Colima, Mexico, where, on 13 December, he made a deposition which gives us some leading facts of his life. The circumstances were these: the Spanish ambassador at the Court of St. James's informed Philip II that the English were preparing an expedition under Sir Richard Grenville to sail through to the Pacific by the Northwest Passage, the "Strait of Anian." The Council of the Indies wished the viceroy of Mexico to collect information about this mythical passage. Ladrillero, who described himself as "more than sixty years of age" (actually about seventy-five), declared that he had been an officer in the expedition of Francisco de Bolaños in 1540–41, to explore the west coast north of Mexico. This expedition, to his disappointment, was turned back by foul weather and dismasting before discovering any Strait of Anian. He believed that the Strait opened up from the head of the Gulf of California, because Bolaños had on board a letter from Charles V saying that he had information about it from a Portuguese gentleman who had passed through it. Also, an English shipmate of Ladrillero's declared that he had entered said Strait "on a voyage from England after codfish." Ladrillero considered it "certain and true that there is such a strait, and that it can be navigated; and *although he is old and weary, if His Majesty orders it he will endeavor to discover it*."

There's Ladrillero for you! Some seventy-five years old, wearied by his many labors at sea, longing to be left at peace to cultivate his Mexican garden, yet he would set forth again at his sovereign's command. But why, in this long deposition, did he not mention the Strait of Magellan? He must have been ordered to keep his mouth shut on that subject.

This deposition of the loyal old mariner is the last we hear of Juan Fernández Ladrillero. We do not even know where or when he died. May God rest his soul!

Bibliography and Notes

Alcazaba's expedition. The sordid details of the Simon de Alcazaba expedition seem to have fascinated Oviedo, who devotes a whole *libro* to it in his *Historia General y Natural* (1852 ed., II, 155–66). Herrera's briefer account in his dec. V, lib. viii, chap. v, is quoted in French translation in

Henry Feuilleret, *Le Détroit de Magellan* (Tours, 1881), pp. 161-64. This chapter is left out of the 1740 English translation of Herrera. The fullest modern secondary account that has come to my notice is J. G. Kohl's in his *Geschichte . . . zur Magellan's-Strasse* (Berlin, 1877), pp. 56-62. Considering that the survivors were executed, and that all our knowledge comes from their statements under torture, it is not surprising that there is no agreement as to exactly what happened. Oviedo's account and Herrera's differ widely, and my efforts to get at the truth are but an approximation.

The Bishop of Plasencia's expedition. Richard Ford's famous old *Handbook for Travellers in Spain*, II (London, 1855), 494-95, has a vivid description of Plasencia at a time when the Carvajal were still the leading family. Markham, *Early Spanish Voyages*, pp. 161-68, translates the anonymous log of the bishop's "Second Ship." Some of the older books, notably Feuilleret, *Le Détroit de Magellan*, p. 157, erroneously give the command of the bishop's fleet to one Quirós. Vice Admiral Ernesto Basílico, *La Armada del Obispo de Plasencia y el Descubrimiento de las Malvinas* (Buenos Aires, 1967), contains all available information about this voyage, and useful maps. Father Diego de Rosales, *Historia General del Reyno de Chile* (Valparaiso, 1847), tells the story of the "Third Ship" ashore.

West coast shipbuilding. Well covered in an admirable monograph by Woodrow Borah, *Early Colonial Trade and Navigation between Mexico and Peru* (Ibero-Americana No. 38, Berkeley, 1954), and D. R. Radell and J. R. Parsons, "Realejo . . . in Nicaragua," *Hispanic-American Historical Review*, LII (1971), 295-312. Diego García de Palacio, *Instrucción Náutica* (Mexico, 1587; facsimile ed., Madrid, 1955), has detailed description of design, masting, and rigging of a 400-tun ship, but nothing on bergantinas.

Ulloa's attempt. "Reseña historica," in *Derrotero de la Costa de Chile*, IV, 45. Herrera briefly mentions Ulloa's voyage in dec. V, book viii, chap. ii (1740 English translation, VI, 320). Diego Barros Arana, *Historia Jeneral de Chile* (Santiago, 1884), I, 417-18, discusses whether this was the same Ulloa who figures in the early exploration of California, and decides that he was not. Dates for founding Chilean towns are from J. G. Kohl, *Geschichte . . . zur Magellan's-Strasse*, p. 68.

The Voyage of Ladrillero. To this day the best accounts are those in the *Anuarios Hidrográficos de Chile: Año 1879*, pp. 482-520, and *Año VI (1880)*, pp. 453-525. The 1879 *Anuario* reproduces textually the account of Hojea's voyage in *San Sebastián* by Miguel de Goicueta, his scribe. It is very involved; even the Chilean editor, who knew his coast well, admits (p. 491, n. 50) that it is "difficult to interpret the document, as much by the uncertainty of latitudes, as by the vagueness of the descriptions, the courses cited, and the distances." So I have done a good deal of skipping. The 1880 *Anuario* reproduces Ladrillero's own account, and is heavily annotated. It is to be hoped that one of Chile's clever young naval officers will straighten out Hojea's course for us, and that the Hakluyt Society will publish an English translation of both his narrative and Ladrillero's, with map. The only history of Chile that pays much attention to Hojea and Ladrillero is Barros, *Historia Jeneral*, II, 195–207. Barros has a long bibliographical note on Ladrillero, showing that the early historians of Chile and South America studiously ignored him. Herrera in dec. V, lib. x, chap. 7 (1615) devotes but a few lines to him. Juan B. Múñoz in 1782 was the first Spanish historian to attempt to do him justice. Francisco A. Encina's 20-volume *Historia de Chile* (Santiago, 1940–52) devotes but four pages to Ladrillero (I, 542–45), and they from Barros. Crescente Errázuriz, *Don García Hurtado de Mendoza* (Santiago, 1914), devotes a chapter to Ladrillero.

Referring to the *Anuario* for 1880, pp. 454–55, it is certain that the explorer was born at Moguer in the last decade of the fifteenth century, went to sea at an early age, and after making eleven round voyages to the West Indies, received a pilot's license in 1535 from Sebastian Cabot. He was pilot in the fleet that brought Don Antonio de Mendoza to Mexico as viceroy, and in the New World he remained. In 1537–38 we find him sailing out of Old Panama and taking latitudes of various west coast capes and ports. In 1539–40 he commanded three ships and two bergantinas in which, for the Adelantado Pascual de Andagoya, he discovered the Bahia de la Cruz and helped to found the town of Buenaventura, Colombia (Oviedo, lib. xliv, chap. iii or iii). Also in 1539, he commanded one of Hernando Cortés's ships, *San Lázaro*, on a commercial voyage from Tehuantepec to Panama, carrying a cargo of flour, biscuit, sugar, and wooden shields for Indian allies (Borah, p. 17). After taking part in several local intrigues, he left for Quito in 1545 and then moved to Lima. For several years he lived retired on his encomienda in Chuquiago.

The "Catalonian arrogance" and summary of Ladrillero are in Barros, *Historia Jeneral*, II, 158.

Nuestra Señora de los Remedios. Ladrillero says (1880 *Anuario*, p. 488, note 110) that it lay around latitude 53°30′ S. The editors discuss the location on pp. 491–92, note 118. They identify it with a canal "not yet surveyed"; probably the one named Sea Shell after a North American schooner that took refuge there in 1871. J. C. Beaglehole, in the Hakluyt Society edition of the *Journals of Captain James Cook*, p. 588n, states that some of this coast had not yet (1961) been thoroughly surveyed and that "the Admiralty charts of southwestern Tierra del Fuego still depend, in the main, on the *Beagle*'s surveys in 1830–4." This reminds me of World War II, when one of the better charts of Tarawa Atoll issued to the U.S. Fifth Fleet in 1943 was that made by Lieutenant Charles Wilkes in 1841.

Puerto de las Tortas, and other names. *Derrotero de la Costa de Chile*, IV (1968), 265. Ladrillero's *Tortas* is identified in 1880 *Anuario*, p. 506, n. 507. One difficulty in straightening out Magellanic toponymy is that voyages through the Strait were so far apart that every fresh navigator made up his own names and ignored (if indeed he even knew) those of his predecessor. The only earlier names used by Ladrillero are Magellan's for the two ends of the Strait.

Ercilla and the Strait. J. T. Medina's "Viaje de Ercilla al Estrecho de Magellanes," *Revista Chilena de Historia y Geografía*, VI (1913), 343–95, takes Ercilla no nearer the Strait than the Island of Chiloé, but argues that in the course of this journey he picked up his misinformation. Alexander von Humboldt was the first to suggest that Ercilla wrote this between Hojea's return and Ladrillero's, as Barros observes in *Historia Jeneral*, II, 206. Walter Owen, in his bilingual edition of *La Araucana* (Buenos Aires, 1945), p. xvii, states that Ercilla did not leave Peru for Spain until 1562.

Don García's *Información* is printed in *Colección de Documentos Inéditos Para la Historia de Chile*, 2nd ser., VI (Santiago, 1963), p. 19. The "ridiculous story" is in Captain James Burney, *Chronological History of the Discoveries in the South Sea* (London, 1803), I, 248–49. Burney got it from Cristóbal Suárez de Figueroa's 17th-century *Hechos de don García Hurtado de Mendoza, Cuatro Marqués de Cañete,* beginning of lib. iii. Figueroa added that all three survivors were "so disfigured as to be unrecognizable." I suspect that this wild yarn was circulated to discourage anyone else from using the Strait.

Ladrillero's deposition of 1574 is translated in Henry R. Wagner, *Spanish Voyages to the Northwest Coast of America* (San Francisco, 1929), pp. 66–71. But both Errázuriz and my esteemed correspondent Dr. Ricardo Donoso believe this to have been written by a different Ladrillero.

Minor west coast voyages. "Around the year 1570," says Kohl (*Geschichte*, p. 70, referring to Navarrete, IV, pp. xiii and 220), "a pair of famous Chilean navigators, Juan Fernández and . . . Fernando Gallego, after more exploring in the Pacific came into the neighborhood of Patagonia. Gallego lost his life around 49° S. On many Spanish and other maps one finds on this point the legend, '*aqui se perdio Fernando Gallego.*'" Kohl continues (p. 71), "Juan Fernández made discoveries on a voyage from Lima to Valparaiso, which he made in 1572, and on which he, encountering south winds along the coast, sailed westward, discovering the Juan Fernández Islands which were named after him."

SIR JOHN NARBOROUGH, 1640–1688

This man has been mentioned so many times that I owe the reader a note on him. An officer in the Royal Navy, he was selected by the Admiralty to command a voyage of discovery in 1669 in H.M.S. *Sweepstakes* of 300 tons, with 36 guns and a crew of 80. On 25 March 1670 he took possession of Port Desire on the Patagonian coast for Charles II, but the merry monarch did nothing to follow that up. Narborough, unlike Magellan, enjoyed his long stay in Patagonia. On 22 October he reached Cabo Vírgenes. *Sweepstakes* appears from her captain's narrative to have encountered no trouble getting through the Strait; and he applied many names that have stuck, including Wood Bay (named after his first mate), Cordes, Fortescue, Cape Quod, Cape Pillar, Charles and the other Stuart princes' islands; and, in the Pacific, Narborough Island after himself. He described the Indians

THE EUROPEAN DISCOVERY OF AMERICA

and the "brave green woods," caused herbs and grass to be "plucked up . . . for salletting . . . which relished pretty well," and estimated the length of the Strait to be 348 nautical miles—not too bad. After commanding the English flagship in the Battle of Solebay, he was promoted admiral of the red, and knighted. Sir John died of yellow fever on active duty in the Caribbean. His *Account of the Late Voyages . . . Towards the Strait of Magellan* was first published in 1695; it may also be found in John Callendar (ed.), *Terra Australis Cognita* (Edinburgh, 1766), Vol. II. The manuscript is in the Bodleian Library.

✳ XXVI ✳

California Before Drake

Cortés Discovers California

In 1510 there appeared in Seville the first edition of what became a popular romance of chivalry, *Las Sergas del Virtuoso Cavallero Esplandian.** A mythical Eastern emperor, defending Constantinople against the Turks, is succored by an army of Amazons led by their queen, whose kingdom is an island called California. It is located "on the right hand of the Indies" close to the terrestrial paradise, and the queen's subjects are all black women "of strong and hardy bodies." Their weapons were made of gold; they tamed wild beasts, and for riding harnessed them with gold-studded tackle; and they built ships which carried them halfway around the world to Constantinople, which they helped the emperor, Esplandian, to deliver from the infidels.

This is the sort of story that would appeal to a conquistador, and Cortés seems to have been the first to apply the romantic name of this black Amazon kingdom to a peninsula of the New World that he discovered. At least so says the reliable historian Herrera. And, on what

---

* "Exploits of the virtuous cavalier Esplandian," title from the 1525 edition in the Harvard College Library; the reference to California is on p. xcv *verso*. García Rodríguez Montalvo was the author.

Esplandian.

Las fergas del virtuofo cauallero eſplādian hijo de amadis de gaula.

Las Sergas del Virtuoso Cavallero Esplandian (Roma 1525), title page. Courtesy Harvard College Library.

is probably the earliest surviving map made in America, the Castillo of 1541, *California* is found on the southern end of the Lower California peninsula, up against La Paz the provincial capital.* It is not, to be sure, on the map that Cortés himself made, or caused to be made, on his own northern voyage; but perhaps that was the result of disappointment with the country.

Cortés, whose energy and alacrity in setting up shipyards and buildings vessels on the Pacific coast we have already observed, began

* This map was first engraved for the *Historia de Nueva España* (Mexico, 1770) by Francisco A. Lorenzana. He says he got it from Cortés's estate, and that the original was inscribed, "Domingo del Castillo piloto me fecit en Mexico, año MDXLI."

618

planning to explore that coast himself, northward, as early as the autumn of 1522 when he heard of Elcano's *Victoria* returning from the great voyage of circumnavigation. He asked for an *asiento* lasting six years, to explore the Pacific coast northward for 400 leagues or more; to be made governor of all he might discover, keep 10 per cent of precious metals and other valuable products brought from the new land, and other privileges. This was not granted at that time, but Cortés was determined to get it, and did. In anticipation, he set up a shipyard at Zacatula near the mouth of the Balsas River and a short distance north of Acapulco. And in 1523 one of his coast-hopping captains brought back from Colima a story about an "Island of Women"—that persistent tale which made its American debut with Columbus, and now crops up here. Cortés, being no saint, must have pricked up his ears and thought of adding a few "black Amazons" to his harem.

In the meantime, the Emperor, bitten by the urge to "search for a strait"—that of Magellan being too far away—had ordered the great conquistador to go find it. West coast shipbuilding being in its primitive stage, before cross-Mexico portage routes had been established, the fleet that Cortés built here was not ready until 1527, when by the Em-

Page xcv of *Sergas de Esplandian*. Where *California* is first mentioned.
Courtesy Harvard College Library.

Ⱦyſtoꝛia ꝺe

na Ꞓalafia en fauoꝛ ꝺeloſ turcoſ al puerto ꝺe conſtantinopla llego.

ⱿⱿiero agoꝛa q̃ ſepayſ vna coſa la mas eſtraña que nunca poꝛ eſ crituraːni en memoꝛia ꝺe gente ningun caſo ballar ſe pudo poꝛ ꝺõꝺe el ꝺia ſiguiente fue la ciu-ꝺaꝺ en pũto ꝺe ſer perdidaːꞇ como ꝺe allı ꝺõ ꝺe le vino el peligro; le vino la ſalud . Ѕabeꝺ q̃ ala ꝺieſtra mano ꝺelaſ yndiaſ ouo vna yſla llamada Ꞓalifoꝛnia mucho llegaꝺa ala parte ꝺel parayſo terrenal laqual fue poblaꝺa ꝺ̃ mu gereſ negraſ ſin q̃ algũ varõ entre ellaſ ouie ſſeːq̃ caſi como laſ amaꝫonaſ era ſu eſtilo ꝺe biuirːeſtaſ erã ꝺe valieteſ cuerpoſ y eſfoꝛça-ꝺoſ y ardieteſ coꝛaçoneſːꞇ ꝺe grandeſ fuer-çaſ. Ꞡa ynſola en ſi la mas fuerte ꝺe riſcoſ ꞇ

enla yſla entraſſe: luego poꝛ ellos era muerto ꞇ comiꝺoː ꞇ a vn que fartoſ eſtuuieſſen no ꝺe xauan poꝛeſſo ꝺelos tomarːꞇ alçar loſ arriba bolanꝺo poꝛ el ayreːꞇ quanꝺo ſe enojauan ꝺe los traer ꝺexauan loſ caer ꝺonꝺe luego eran muertoſ . Pueſ al tiempo que aq̃lloſ grã-ꝺeſ bombꝛeſ ꝺelos paganoſ partieron con aquellaſ tan granꝺeſ flotaſ como la byſto-ria voſ ba contaꝺoːreynaua en aquella yſla ca lifoꝛnia vna reyna muy grãꝺe ꝺe cuerpo muy bermoſa para entre ellaſ en floꝛeciente eꝺaꝺ/ ꝺeſſcoſa en ſu penſamiento ꝺe acabar grãꝺeſ coſaſ/ valiente en eſfuerço ꞇ arꝺiꝺ ꝺel ſu bꝛa-uo coꝛaçon mas que otra ninguna ꝺelaſ que antes ꝺella aquel ſeñoꝛio manꝺaron . Ɛ oye-ꝺo ꝺeꝫir como toda la mayoꝛ parte ꝺel mũꝺo ſe mouia en aquel viaje cõtra los cbꝛiſtianos

peror's orders it was diverted to the Far East under Saavedra Cerón, to succor Loaysa.*

The great conquistador, having returned to Spain to press for his northward grant, easily got it from the Emperor, who as an additional honor admitted him to the higher nobility with the imposing title of Marqués del Valle de Oaxaca, the Mexican valley where the biggest of his vast estates, with thousands of Indian slaves, was located. Returning to Mexico in 1530, the newly created Marqués bought two vessels on the stocks at Zacatula, appointed Diego Hurtado de Mendoza to the command, and in May of 1532 sent them off to California from Acapulco.

Unfortunately the hated rival of Cortés, Nuño de Guzmán, had marched by land up the Mexican west coast, both in search of gold and of the elusive black Amazons, and founded the town of Culiacan at the eastern entrance to the Gulf of California. Hurtado was ordered to by-pass Guzmán and take possession for Cortés. Guzmán retaliated by closing his port to Hurtado, who pushed north and disappeared.

Even before this bad news had been confirmed, Cortés himself went to Tehuantepec on the like-named gulf and personally oversaw the construction of two new vessels, *San Lázaro* and *Concepción*. They sailed in October 1533, and enjoyed consistently foul weather and ill luck. *Concepción*, in distress, put in at a port held by Guzmán and was seized by him; *San Lázaro* survived a mutiny but sailed at least halfway up the west coast of Lower California and returned to Acapulco. But even this second failure did not stop Cortés. He promptly acquired and armed two more vessels and a bergantina, collected a small army, and marched northwest a good thousand miles to rendezvous with his fleet at the little port of Chiametla, where *Concepción* had been seized by Guzmán. That character now found it convenient to be absent. Cortés went on board his flagship, crossed the mouth of the Gulf, sighted the coast of Baja California on 1 May 1535, passed Isla Ceralbo on the port hand, entered the Bahia de La Paz, landed (3 May), and took possession for Charles V, under the name *Terra de Santa Cruz*. This is *the* discovery of California, although it was but a small part of the Lower California peninsula. He left three place names which have not survived—two little islands off the coast called Saints Philip and James (since it was on their feast day that he discovered them), and

* See above, Chapter XX.

Perlas. All three are seen on his map, here reproduced.

Nothing valuable was found; no gold, no silver, no black Amazons; but Cortés in the bergantina ranged the opposite shore of the Gulf from Cabo Corrientes up to about the Estero de Agiabampo, and mapped it.

Before he was ready to leave the lands of his new discovery, Cortés heard that the Emperor had appointed Antonio de Mendoza the first viceroy of Nueva España (Mexico). Rightly anticipating a clash between the new civil head and himself, the Captain General, he hastened back to Mexico City, leaving his officer Francisco de Ulloa in charge of his camp at Santa Cruz, which he hoped to expand into a colony, or at least a presidio.

At this juncture Cabeza de Vaca arrived at Mexico City after his long trek, with startling stories of the Seven Cities of Cibola. These, as we have seen, sparked off the Coronado expedition and provided a fresh motive for pushing north along the west coast. For, if the rumored wealth of the Seven Cities were but partly true, a left wing of the exploration by sea would be desirable, especially if the English or French managed to find the fabled Strait of Anian and came booming down from the north.

Francisco de Ulloa's Voyage

Viceroy Mendoza, unwilling to let Cortés acquire more fame than he already had, issued a proclamation on 25 July 1535 forbidding anyone to go to sea without his license. But Cortés was too quick for him. Francisco de Ulloa (whose earlier life is still obscure) had just returned from Baja California, where Cortés had left him in charge of his camp near the site of La Paz. He had well served the Marqués, who placed him in command of three of his own ships, and he got them out to sea on 8 July. Mendoza, frustrated, managed to seize one of the Ulloa fleet which put in for provisions at a west coast port; Cortés appeared before the high court of Mexico to demand permission to replace it, but was refused. So after fruitless litigation at Mexico City, the great conquistador returned to Spain toward the last of 1539, and embarked on another series of suits and petitions that occupied him the rest of his life.

Ulloa had under his command three ships, flagship *Santa Águeda*, *Trinidad*, and *Santo Tomás*—all built on the west coast. Sailing 8 July from Acapulco, they soon ran into trouble. In a storm on 27 August *Santo Tomás* became separated from her consorts and, after one futile call at Acapulco, where she got nothing but abuse from the viceroy's men, turned south and anchored off the bar at Tehuantepec. While waiting for a good chance to enter the port, a norther blew up (it was now November) and she had to cut her cable and run for it, leaving anchor and boat behind. With no other anchor (they were in short supply on the west coast owing to the necessity of manhandling every one across Mexico), she was really in a fix, but finally moored beside another vessel in the little port of Guatulco. There, as a final indignity, two viceregal officers bustled on board, imprisoned the captain, and impounded his sails, tiller, and oars. Cortés finally forced the Viceroy to return them, but too late for this voyage.

Ulloa's two bigger ships made a sort of whistle-stop voyage around the Gulf of California, which they named *El Mar Vermejo*, the Vermilion Sea, owing to the reddish discharge from the Colorado River, Ulloa rowed a few miles up this great river in his longboat. He did not admire the shores of the Gulf, calling them "Very poor . . . mountains or bare rock, without trees or green except *cardon*" (the giant cactus). He called at Cortés's attempted settlement of Santa Cruz near the site of La Paz and found all the construction destroyed, then rounded Cape San Lucas, southern extremity of Lower California, and in January 1540 reached Isla de Cedros, a pretty island marked by a grove of cedars. After ineffectual attempts, owing to head winds, at making further progress northward, he gave up, and on 5 April sent *Santa Águeda* back to Mexico with an account of his progress, or lack of it; Ulloa in *Trinidad* made another attempt northwestward. This time he probably got up to latitude 32° or 33° by July, when he turned back and reached Acapulco safely. Ulloa's report of Baja California, which he called *Terra de Santa Cruz*, was most unflattering. The groups of islands, of which the one of Cedars was most prominent, were "as ugly and sterile and of as wretched aspect as the lands south of it." Scanty rainfall made the cactus-studded semi-desert shores of the Vermilion Sea repulsive to Spaniards.

No Spanish voyage of discovery was ever known to start without an *escribano*, a notary public, on board, to record official acts and, if

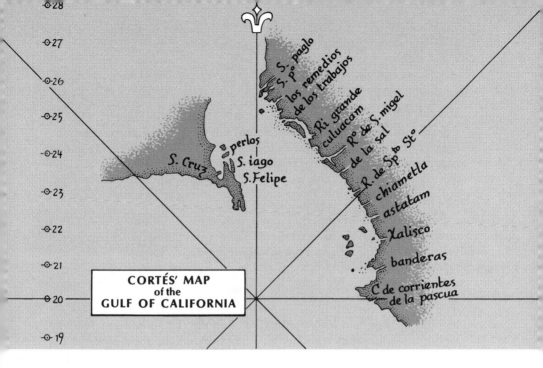

CORTÉS' MAP
of the
GULF OF CALIFORNIA

necessary, adjudicate shipboard disputes. One Francisco Preciado, who performed that function for Ulloa, left us a brief narration of the voyage, in which he records the act of taking possession at seven different places. So, as we have frequently mentioned such acts in this book, we welcome this opportunity to see how it was done. On 28 September 1539, here was the procedure at the top of the Gulf of California near Punta San Carlos:

> The very magnificent Señor Francisco de Ulloa, governor's lieutenant and commanding this fleet for the very illustrious Señor Marqués del Valle de Oaxaca, . . . took possession for the Marqués in the name of the Emperor our master, King of Castile, actually and in reality placing his hand upon his sword and saying that if any person disputed it, he was ready to defend it; cutting trees with his sword, pulling up grass, moving stones from one place to another . . . and taking water from the sea and throwing it upon the land, all in token of said possession. [Followed by signatures of the principal witnesses.]

We need an historically minded yachtsman to skirt the Vermilion Sea and sail up the outer coast of the California peninsula as far as San Diego. Wagner thinks that Ulloa got that far in *Trinidad* before turning back, but in my opinion he went no farther than Cape Engaño at latitude 30° N. At least he saw a bit of the Golden State when, being rowed up the mouth of the Colorado River, he sighted mountains afar off. He was less impressed by them than by a multitude of sea-lions (100,000 at least!) at the river mouth, which caused him to name the head of the Gulf, *El Puerto de los Lobos*. Ulloa returned to Acapulco some time that summer, and slipped back into obscurity. He received no more sea commands, because he was Cortés's man, and Cortés was now nearing his end in Spain.

The Marqués, having paid the entire cost of Ulloa's voyage, was now living at his estate near Seville, and deeply engaged in litigation in defense of his rights. Cortés was too great a popular hero to be clapped into jail, like other Spanish discoverers; but the court snubbed him, and the Emperor at length refused to receive him. It was then, if ever, that occurred his famous confrontation with Charles V. After waiting over a year for an interview, one day he shouldered his way through the imperial guard to the coach in which the Emperor was traveling, mounted its high step, and when Charles exclaimed, "Who is this importunate fellow?" replied, in effect, "I am the man who conquered more provinces for Your Highness than you had cities at your accession." At the age of sixty-three Cortés died at his estate near Seville on 2 December 1547, still a very rich man but neglected, and his only heir a bastard by his Indian mistress.

By any standard, Cortés was the greatest of the conquistadors, and among them his activities as a sea lord on the west coast were outstanding. López de Gómara, the sixteenth-century historian, stated that Cortés spent 200,000 ducats on these discoveries "according to the account he rendered to Charles V," and got almost nothing back; but "nobody spent his money in similar enterprises with so much spirit."

Cabrillo's Voyage

Antonio de Mendoza, viceroy of Mexico, and his kinsman Hurtado de Mendoza took advantage of Cortés's absence in Spain to set on foot a few voyages of their own. Of those rather inconsequential expeditions, we may briefly mention that of Francisco de Bolaños in 1541. He commanded at least three ships, one named *San Gabriel*. According to the 1574 deposition of Juan Fernandez de Ladrillero, the Strait of Magellan explorer who accompanied Bolaños, and a few other bits

Juan Rodriguez Cabrillo, Point Loma. Courtesy National Park Service.

of evidence, all they did was to sail up the Vermilion Sea to the mouth of the Colorado River, which Ladrillero felt certain was the western entrance of the fabled Strait of Anian. There two of the three ships lost some of their masts in a northwest storm and were forced to turn back after making temporary repairs. The only actual fruit of this voyage was Bolaños's giving the name *Puerto de California* to a small bay or harbor near Cabo San Lucas, the tip-end of the California

37

36.

35.

34

33,

32

31.

3o:

29

28.

27

26.

25.

24.

23.

22.

21.

2o.

19.

18

17.

16.

15.

Rio de buena Guia p.ᵗᵃ

Braza de Mⁱⁿᵃ Jⁱᵃⁿᵃ p.ᵗᵃ

Braza de Sanguꜳ p.ᵗᵃ

Sierra p.ᵗᵃ

Sᵗᵃ Catarina.

Sierra de las

Punta del Moro p.ᵗᵃ

Cabo la +

Estero Ondo p.ᵗᵃ

P.ᵗᵃ de buena Esperanza.

Ancon de Sᵗᵃ Maria

P.ᵗᵃ de Sᵗᵃ Maria

Algunas Islas Desiertas p.ᵗᵃ

Punta Raxadas p.ᵗᵃ

P.ᵗᵃ de Sᵗᵃ Clara p.ᵗᵃ

P.ᵗᵃ de S. Elena

P.ᵗᵃ de Lena

Albᵃ p.ᵗᵃ

b.ᵃ de Islas Fregoᵃˢ

El Aguada p.ᵗᵃ

P.ᵗᵃ de los Donoˢ

El Ancornado.

P.ᵗᵃ de Sᵗ punto p.ᵗᵃ

Ancorado del Roxᵗᵒ

b.ᵃ de los Puertos

Braza de Puertᵒ p.ᵗᵃ

Rio de Sᵗᵃ Fran.ᵗᵃ

S.ᵗᵃ Bermeja

b.ᵃ de Santiago.

b.ᵃ de las Fuerzᵃˢ p.

Rio de Nᵗᵃ Sᵃ P. S

Braza dᵉ

P.ᵗᵃ de

Paungꜳ

C. del

Trauron

C.ᵗᵃ del

p. Jadra

p.

p.ᵗᵃ

Cᵃ del Engaño

P.ᵗᵃ del Chamara

S. Estevan

S.ᵗᵃ Roperio

Bahia

los Tusones

R.ᵗᵃ de Perlas

P.ᵗᵃ de Perlamueˢ

Bahia p.ᵗᵃ

R.ᵗᵃ de

Caguaˢ

R.ᵗᵃ de

Cinaloa

Quivira

R.ᵗᵃ de

Culiacan

p.ᵗᵃ de la Alameda

p.ᵗᵃ p.ᵗᵃ

Ahomada p.ᵗᵃ

p.ᵗᵃ de la Sal

P.ᵗᵃ de la Trinidad

P.ᵗᵃ de la Sadra

p.ᵗᵃ de S. Sebaˢ

S.ᵗᵃ p.ᵗᵃ

MAR

DE EL

S U

Sᵗ Thomaˢ

Este Mapa esta sacado de el Original que para
Ciudad, que entorzes o por Relaciones se creio cierta i
Golfo de Californias pone dos Rios el uno le llama de Bue
el Gila que incorporados en una Madr

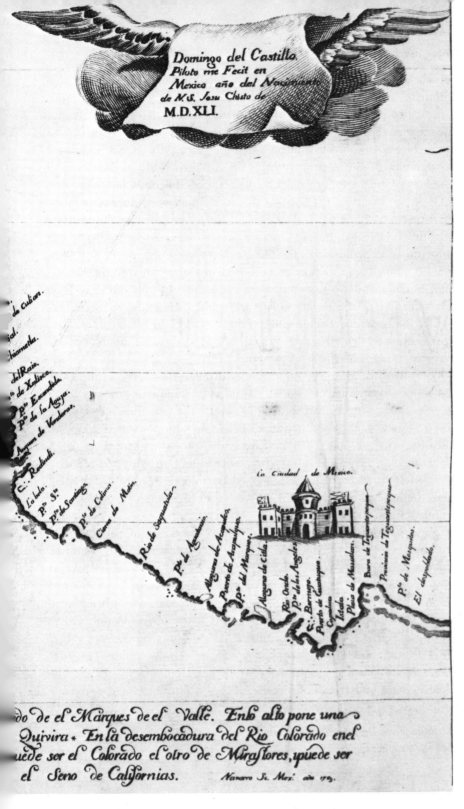

Castillo's map of lower California (1541). From Lorenzana, *Historia de Nueva España* (1770). Courtesy Harvard College Library.

peninsula. Since Herrera, writing at the turn of the century, is our sole authority for Cortés having actually applied this name from the famous romance to a place north of Mexico, it is possible that he was wrong; and, that Bolaños was the man who first actually bestowed this name of the black Amazons' island on a definite place. We have a significant cartographical confirmation of this on the map made in Mexico and dated 1541, by Domingo del Castillo, one of Bolaños's pilots.

Of Juan Rodríguez Cabrillo, the next and most important west coast discoverer, we have plenty of information. Born João Rodrigues Cabrilho in Portugal, he had come to Mexico in 1520 as a soldier in the unfortunate expedition of Pánfilo de Narváez. Fortunately for himself, he jumped ship in time to take part in Cortés's march on Mexico City, as commander of a company of crossbow men. He did so well on that occasion, and later in Guatemala under Alvarado, as to be rewarded with several encomiendas, which made him a man of wealth. This, however, was his first sea command, conferred upon him by Viceroy Mendoza, who paid the bills.

The object of the expedition seems to have been exploration pure and simple, including, of course, the hope of discovering new sources of gold and silver, or a seaport in "Quivira," the fabled country of the Seven Cities. Cabrillo's flagship, a sizable ship, was named *San Salvador*, and the other, *Victoria* by name, was a small open vessel, a *bergantina* or *fragata*. Both were country-built in Mexico. His flag pilot, an Italian Levantine, was named Bartolomé Ferrer. They sailed from the little port of Navidad on the west coast on 27 June 1542, and rounded Cabo Corrientes next day.

"Sunday, July 2 they sighted California," says the official *Relación*, "and on the following Monday, the 3rd, they anchored at the Point of California." This was probably Point Palmas, the easternmost part of Cape San Lucas. Cabrillo sailed boldly up the west coast, named Magdalena and other bays, called at the Isle of Cedars and other points, noted the dangerous rocks that he named *Habre Ojo* (Watch Out!) and are now the Abrejos at latitude 26°45'. Passing, on 27 September, the Coronado Islands in latitude 32°24', which he called *Las Islas Desiertas*, he crossed the present international boundary between the Golden State and Baja California, and eased into a "closed and very good harbor." This Cabrillo named *San Miguel*—it is now San Diego.*

---

* Cabrillo gives the latitude 34°20'; Bowditch as 32°43'! Like Ulloa's, Cabrillo's latitudes are almost always too high by one degree or more.

What Cabrillo avoided: surf on the Big Sur.

From the Indians they received news of Coronado's party in the interior, and they rode out safely a heavy storm.

Departing this site of San Diego on 3 October 1542, they sailed close along the coast, and on the 7th sighted the first two of the Santa Barbara Channel Islands now named San Clemente and Santa Catalina. At San Clemente (not to be confused with the magnificent presidential retreat on the mainland) the Indians were friendly and the women very free. That pleasant situation lasted throughout the Santa Barbara Channel, where Cabrillo noted the names of 25 Chumasu Indian villages on the shore. Passing the site of Santa Barbara, they found a "cape like a galley" and so named it *Cabo Galera* at latitude 36° N; this has been identified as Point Concepción at latitude 34°27′. They called at San Miguel Island and spent several days, sailed seaward to avoid an onshore wind, and on All Saints' Eve beat to windward to reach the mouth of a river that the Indians had told them about. A heavy wind forced them to strip down to bare poles, and they took refuge under Cape Galera. Here the Indians were very helpful and so friendly as to spend nights on board the Spanish ships.

Other storms followed, and off the Big Sur "so great was the swell of the ocean that it was terrifying to see" (it still is!) "and the coast was bold and the mountains very high." Like everyone else for two more centuries, Cabrillo missed the Golden Gate, and on 16 November anchored in a great bay which he named *Los Pinos;* it is generally identified as Drake's Bay where Francis Drake spent five weeks some thirty-seven years later, and took possession for England, unaware that in 1542 Cabrillo had done the same for Spain.

Somewhere a little north of Bodega Bay, Cabrillo turned back, owing to stormy weather, again missed the Golden Gate and the Farallons, made San Miguel, westernmost of the Santa Barbara Channel Islands on 23 November, and decided to winter there. And there on 3 January 1543 Cabrillo died as a result of breaking his arm near the shoulder in a fall. The accident had happened on his first call going north; throughout all the tempestuous weather, this tough soldier turned mariner must have been nursing an infected upper arm. There can be no doubt of his ability at sea. Being caught on a lee shore off Big Sur and having to claw off may not have been as bad as Columbus's situation in *Niña* off Sintra in 1493, but it is something any sailor can admire.

Just before his death Cabrillo appointed the Levantine pilot Bartolomé Ferrer (or Ferrelo) his successor in command, and charged him to continue the exploration of the Alta California coast. Accordingly, Ferrer weighed on 19 January 1543, and his two ships were buffeted about the Santa Barbara Channel, taking refuge under the lee of one island after another for a full month. They then started north again, reaching what Cabrillo had named Cabo Pinos on 25 February. On the last day of that month Ferrer shot the sun and found the latitude to be 43° N. Deducting the usual error of navigators along that coast in the sixteenth century, this may well have been 41°30′, the latitude of Klamath, California. In any case, his was the furthest north of any European navigator on the west coast prior to Drake.

Here Ferrer's ships were forced to scud northeast before a howling gale, seas breaking right over them, "with great fear and travail," the seamen making vows to Our Lady of Guadalupe. At 3:00 p.m. on 28 February, weather very thick but signs of land ahead, the men had given themselves up for lost when "the Mother of God succored them, by the grace of her Son," suddenly whipping the wind around to north. Under bare poles they scudded with mere scraps of sail set, to the southeast and east-southeast. When they encountered a big wave from the previous southerly storm, they thrust right through, and so were swept fore and aft. This went on for three days, "with a sea so high that they became crazed, and if God and His blessed Mother had not miraculously saved them they could not have escaped." On 5 March they found themselves back at San Miguel Island, but the sea was breaking across the entrance to the harbor where the normal depth was fifteen fathom! In the lee of San Salvador Island they found shelter, but lost sight of *Victoria* and gave her up for lost as she was not fully decked; she turned up, however, at the Isla de Cedros, having strained the mercy of the heavenly host even more severely than in the case of *San Salvador*. That ship, aground on a shoal, the sailors begged Our Lady to float off, promising to make a pilgrimage to one of her shrines *en carne* (in their shirts). That had worked for Columbus's sailors in the Azores, and it worked here. *San Salvador* and *Victoria* anchored at Navidad 14 April 1543, and their crews promptly formed a penitential procession *en carne* to the little chapel.

The Spanish naval officer and historian Navarrete, who sailed along this same coast in the *Sutil* in the late eighteenth century, admired Cabrillo's "courage and intrepidity," which, he warned, could no longer be appreciated, at a time "when the navigator is fairly dazzled by the assistance furnished him through the wonderful progress of the arts and sciences." And he was writing in the early nineteenth century. Certainly nobody but a sailing fisherman or yachtsman today can appreciate what Cabrillo and Ferrer and their men went through, slugging their way up to north of Cape Mendocino and back.

Cabrillo as we have seen died en route; what became of Ferrer we know not, and as their voyage brought home neither silver nor gold, it was soon forgotten. No Spaniard is known to have sailed along Alta California until after Francis Drake showed the way, more than thirty-five years later.

Bibliography and Notes

The all-embracing, comprehensive book on this subject is Henry R. Wagner, *Spanish Voyages to the Northwest Coast of America in the Sixteenth Century* (San Francisco, 1929, 571 pp.). Wagner, a San Francisco businessman, became the No. 1 scholar on early California voyages. This book contains author's narrative, the principal original narratives in facsimile and extensive notes, and reproductions of charts, and is well indexed.

Early maps. Cortés's, reproduced in Justin Winsor, *Narrative and Critical History of America*, II, 442. Toponymy in Henry Harrisse, *North America*, pp. 611–12. John Leighy, *California*.

Name California. Winsor, II, 442–44.

Ulloa's Voyage. His own narrative, written at the Isla de Cedros 5 April 1540, translated and reprinted in Wagner, pp. 15–50, together with parts of notary Preciado's report. Wagner's notes are on pp. 304–12. For Ulloa's ships, Wagner, p. 12 and 304, n. 4, quoting Preciado, who gives the ships' measurements in the Italian *botta*. Frederick C. Lane, *Venetian Ships* (Baltimore, 1934), pp. 246–48, concludes that the Venetian *botta* was either .7 or .75 of a *tonelada*. Using the latter factor, Ulloa's flagship (240 *botta*) would have been 187 *toneladas;* Trinidad, 70 *botta*, 50 *toneladas*, and Santo Tomás 40 *botta*, 30 *toneladas*. I suspect these figures of being too high; the last-named had a crew of but three or four.

For the taking possession. Wagner, p. 47. Palencia locates this act "in the Ancón de San Andrés and mar Bermejo . . . in latitude 33°30'." But the Gulf does not extend north of 32°; another instance of the pilots of those west coast voyages almost always calculating their latitudes a degree or two further north than was accurate.

For discussion of his return, see Wagner, pp. 13–14.

Cortés and Charles V. R. B. Merriman wrote that although no printed version of this story appears earlier than that of Voltaire, he believes it to be true, as do other historians. Gómara's estimate, in *Historia de las Indias y Conquista de México* (1552; Vedia ed., 1852), p. 428, is quoted in Wagner, p. 417.

Bolaños's voyage in the Gulf of California. Wagner, pages 63–71 and 314–19, contain all the facts known about it, including a translation of Ladrillero's deposition which we noticed in an earlier chapter. On the Castillo map the important toponymy of the Lower California peninsula is *Pto. de Santiago* (western tip of Cape San Lucas), *Pto. de Sta. Cruz* (on east side), CALIFORNIA (on the land), *Pto. de Reparo* (on Isla Cedros), and *C. de Engaño*, furthest north. Wagner (p. 332) identifies this as Punta Baja at latitude 29°56', just south of the town of Rosario.

Cabrillo's voyage. Wagner, pp. 72–93 and 318–23, 330–33, 417–31. Also, Herbert E. Bolton (ed.), *Spanish Explorations in the Southwest* (*Original Narratives* series, 1916 and later dates), pp. 13–39. Visconde de Lagôa, *João Rodrigues Cabrilho* (Lisbon, 1958) and *Cabrillo's Log 1542–1543*, a summary by Juan Páez, translated by J. R. Moriarity and Mary Keistman, a separate from *The Western Explorer*, V (San Diego, 1968).

The *Relación* of the Cabrillo voyage was written by Juan Páez de Castro, official chronicler of the Indies, about 1555. Buckingham Smith brought it to light in 1857 from the Seville Archives. Bolton's translation, the best so far, is in his *Spanish Explorations in the Southwest* (see above). Wagner's is on his pp. 79–93, with notes, on pp. 219–21, and facsimile at pp. 450–53.

The Portuguese community at San Diego, perhaps to help efface the unflattering image of them in John Steinbeck's *Tortilla Flat* (1935), caused to be erected a heroic statue of Cabrillo on Point Loma, which he probably discovered. Unfortunately they have backed him by a finely carved *padrão*, of the type that Portuguese discoverers set up in Africa to nail down the king's claim to territory.

Navidad or *Natividad* had disappeared from the map of Mexico. Bolton states it to have been latitude 19°13′ N, 20 miles WNW from Manzanillo. This was the principal west coast shipyard until major operations north of Panama were shifted to Acapulco.

* XXVII *

Drake's Voyage of Circumnavigation

1577-1579

From Plymouth to Puerto San Julián

The World Encompassed by Sir Francis Drake is the title of a proud narrative of this first English circumnavigation, by the Rev. Francis Fletcher. It began mainly as a privateering voyage, a campaign in the yet undeclared war between England and Spain; but Drake also made two new discoveries—islands south of Tierra del Fuego, and part of the west coast of North America. Although he definitely did not discover Cape Horn—Le Maire and Schouten did that in 1616—Drake made a new furthest south: Henderson Island at latitude 53°35' S, which lies only about sixty miles northwesterly from the true Cape Horn. And the first New England was Drake's Nova Albion on the coast of California.

Francis Drake, born in Devonshire about 1541, was the son of an ardently Protestant chaplain to the royal dockyard of Chatham. His first sea experience came with John Lovell's and John Hawkins's slave-trading voyages to the West Indies. He commanded the fifty-tun *Judith* of Hawkins's "third and troublesome voyage" of 1568, and in her escaped from the treacherous attack of the Spaniards at San Juan de Ulua. This seems to have given him an inextinguishable lust for revenge. Many times, in his great voyage, he told Spanish prisoners that he was merely getting back a "bit of his own" from that defeat. He first expended his rage against Spain in 1571, by a raid on the Isthmus of Panama in the twenty-five-tun pinnace *Swan*. Next year he commanded both her and the 70-tun *Pasco* belonging to John Hawkins. At isolated Port Pheasant (now Puerto Escocés) near the Gulf of Darien, he assembled three knocked-down pinnaces and captured Nombre de Dios on the Isthmus in a brilliant amphibious operation. But he failed to carry off the stacked-up bars of silver, owing to the combination of a bad wound and a torrential downpour. Learning that no more treasure would move across the Isthmus for many months, Drake raided Cartagena and Santa Marta and captured several coastal ships. Near the end of January 1573, informed by Cimaroons (runaway slaves who looked on the English as liberators), Drake with his lieutenant John Oxenham, eighteen Englishmen and twenty blacks, marched across the Isthmus and captured a mule train. It yielded only victuals; but the two leaders, climbing a tall tree near Old Panama, sighted both the town and the Pacific Ocean, and made a vow that some day they would sail those waters. Again, in alliance with Guillaume le Testu, Drake waylaid a treasure train. He captured rich booty but his French ally was killed.

John Oxenham, with a hundred-tun ship, two knocked-down pinnaces, and fifty men, tried to capture the Isthmus of Panama in 1576. After the local Spaniards under Gabriel de Loarte captured most of his shipping, Oxenham with amazing energy built a forty-five-foot pinnace at the head of navigation of the Rio Chucunaque, which flows into the Pacific, and rowed her to the Pearl Islands in the Gulf of Panama. There he spent a month, capturing a number of Spanish ships; but the unexpected energy and good tactics of Loarte captured his party and most of them were hanged.

Long before Oxenham's fate was known in England, Drake had embarked on the enterprise that led him around the world. It was a southern counterpart to the Northwest Passage idea which Michael Lok, Martin Frobisher, and the Company of Cathay had been promoting. England should enter the Pacific by the Strait of Magellan, sail to latitude 40° or 50° N, seek out the Northwest Passage at its western terminus, and find a good location for an English colony somewhere on the west coast of America. That is what the careful historian James A. Williamson infers to have been the main object of Drake's famous

Sir Francis Drake. Portrait by unknown artist, 1581. Courtesy National Portrait Gallery, London.

voyage. Others deem it to have been nothing more than an exalted privateering expedition against Spain, using the west coast as a new and untouched source of plunder. In my opinion, Drake was an opportunist. His first object was to reach the Pacific; but what he would do when he got there would depend on wind, weather, luck, and circumstances.

A syndicate comprising the Earl of Leicester, Sir Francis Walsingham, Sir Christopher Hatton, the Earl of Lincoln (then Lord High Admiral), Sir William Winter and his brother George, both high officials in the Royal Navy, and John Hawkins the navy treasurer, was formed to finance this voyage. Drake himself put in £1000, presumably prize money, for he had no inherited wealth. All this must have been done with Queen Elizabeth's knowledge and her tacit or ambiguous consent; one can well imagine her saying, with a toothy grin, "Go forward, and God bless ye; but fail not lest I disavow the lot o' ye!" In the summer of 1577 this syndicate issued instructions to Drake to pass through the Strait of Magellan and explore the continental coast beyond, from latitude 42° S to 30° S, "as not being under the obedience of any Christian prince." He should prospect for mineral wealth, spy out places fit for vending English goods, and return by the way he came. The 50°–30° bracket obviously meant Chile and possibly Peru, since the English did not know how far south the Spanish had settled. But everyone agrees that there was a secret, unavowed motive for the expedition, to spoil the Spaniard in a region full of treasure, where he felt completely safe from enemies. The leader himself revealed that the Queen had said to him, "Drake! So it is that I would gladly be revenged on the King of Spain for divers injuries that I have received!" And he had on board some sort of royal commission which made him a privateer, not a pirate.

The task organization, vessels which assembled at Plymouth during the summer of 1577, was as follows:

CAPTAIN GENERAL: FRANCIS DRAKE
Captain of men-at-arms, Thomas Doughty

Ship PELICAN (later renamed GOLDEN HIND), the "Admirall" (flagship); 100–120 tuns, 16 to 18 guns on two decks; Drake captain

Ship ELIZABETH, "vice-admirall," 80 tuns, 16 guns, John Winter captain

Bark MARYGOLD, 30 tuns, 16 guns, John Thomas captain

Flyboat SWAN, acting as storeship, 50 tuns, 5 guns, John Chester captain

Pinnace BENEDICT, 12 tuns, 1 gun

Pinnace CHRISTOPHER, 15 tuns, Thomas Moore captain

Elizabeth and *Benedict* belonged to John Winter, *Christopher* to Drake himself. *Pelican* (*Golden Hind*) has been more intensely studied than any other historic ship between Columbus's *Santa Maria*

and the Pilgrim Fathers' *Mayflower*. A fairly new vessel, built in France, she was owned by the Hawkinses, who had probably bought her from a Huguenot sea-rover. She was a fine, stout vessel, double-sheathed with a layer of tarred horsehair between the two skins to foil teredos. Her gun ports could be closed and caulked tight and the guns stowed below. She usually towed her longboat. Even so, with up to eighty men on board, her main deck must have been uncomfortably crowded. Drake, anticipating a long voyage, had a forge and black-smith's shop fitted up somewhere—probably under the forecastle—and by helping himself from Spanish prizes and shore raids, he kept well supplied with dry provisions, wine, cordage, sails, and all manner of sea stores. After his great voyage the Queen ordered *Golden Hind* to be preserved ashore at Deptford, but the house planned to cover her was never built and she rotted away. From the plans of this projected house, Gregory Robinson infers that she was 90 feet long, 19 feet beam, with a depth of hold of 9 feet 6 inches. The Spanish captives on board *Golden Hind* were greatly impressed by her and invariably over-estimated her burthen by 100 to 500 tuns.

Among the important gentlemen volunteers were John Doughty (half-brother to Thomas), two Hawkinses, Drake's youngest brother Thomas, and his cousin John. The total complement, including sailors, soldiers, and volunteers, amounted to something between 150 and 164, of which fourteen were boys. Almost all were English or Irish, except that Drake had a "black moore" named Diego, who was mortally wounded in the raid on Valparaiso.

After the usual delays in provisioning and getting to sea, this fleet made a fair start from Plymouth on 13 December 1577. An earlier at-tempt ran into a gale in which *Pelican* was forced to cut away her mainmast and *Marygold* drove ashore but successfully floated. On Christmas Day 1577, Drake put in at the island of Mogador on the outer Barbary Coast south of Safi. There he set up one of the prefabri-cated pinnaces carried in a ship's hold, and for the first time disclosed to his company their true objectives. Alexandria had earlier been the "official" destination. On the way to Cape Blanco they took several Spanish or Portuguese prizes, and at the Cape the fleet was "washed and trimmed." A forty-tun Spanish fisherman of a type called a *canter* or *caunter* was exchanged with her owner for *Benedict* and given that pinnace's name. And here they first sighted the Southern Cross. The

The *Golden Hind*. From Gregory Robinson, *The Elizabethan Ship* (1956), illustration by P. A. Jobson. Courtesy Longman Group Ltd.

native inhabitants of Mogador gave them no trouble, but Master Fletcher regarded the "Arabs" as the most filthy and degraded people he ever encountered; they performed all bodily functions, copulation included, in full view of a crowd containing English sailors.

Before the end of January 1578, the fleet called at Maio and Santiago in the Cape de Verdes, where Fletcher gratified his Protestant prejudices by throwing down a cross erected by the Portuguese, and regaled himself on delicious coconut and grapes. At Santiago they easily captured a Portuguese ship from Oporto, named *Maria*, "laden with singuler wines, sacks & Canaryes with woolens and Linen Clothes, silkes and velveets & many other good commodityes which stood us in that stead that shee was the life of our voyage, the neck of which otherwise had been broken for the shortnes of our provisions." Drake exchanged her for the second newly assembled pinnace and sent the Portuguese crew home in pinnace *Christopher* with "a Butte of wine, and some victuals and their wearing clothes." *Maria* he placed under the command of Thomas Doughty, and that was a mistake. Doughty misbehaved; and when Drake, to keep an eye on his old friend, made him master of flag-ship *Pelican*, he threw his weight around to such ill purpose that Drake "disgraded" him and sent him on board flyboat *Swan*.

At volcanic Fogo, Drake dismissed all Portuguese taken prisoner except pilot Nuno da Silva (called Silvester by the English), who volunteered to pilot the fleet in Brazil, which he did well and became very intimate with his commander.

The fleet, now reduced to six sail, dropped Fogo in the dark of the moon on 2 February, crossed the Line on the 17th, and approached the Brazilian coast at the latitude of Porto Alegre (30° S) on 5 April; but before they could work up the lagoon into the harbor a severe gale blew them out to sea. They finally anchored off Punta del Este, Uruguay. Francis Fletcher the chaplain and chronicler observed that they lost sight of Polaris at one degree north of the Equator and picked up the Guards of the South Celestial Pole one degree south of that. He made the same observation about shipboard lice as had Columbus: from England to the Tropic of Capricorn the vessel grew lousier and lousier; then of a sudden the lice "all dyed and consumed away of themselves."

Proceeding from Punta del Este to El Rincon roadstead, in the lee of a rocky island, they remained until 20 April, briefly explored the lower River Plate, and put out to sea on the 25th, with a full moon. Drake, having the latest Spanish maps of South America, sailed south, aiming at Cabo Tres Puntas which they sighted 12 May. Here the Captain General almost lost his life exploring in a ship's boat. For two weeks they lay at anchor in Port Desire, and on 20 June reached Puerto San Julián.

The parallel between Drake's voyage and Magellan's, more than half a century earlier, cannot have escaped the reader. The only landmark

Beagle Channel.

What Drake saw.

False Cape Horn.

that Drake could see upon entering San Julián was a gibbet, which they assumed to be the one on which Quesada and Mendoza had been hanged; but could that sinister tree have survived fifty-eight winters?

At the previous port of call, Drake's men made their first acquaintance with naked, painted Patagonians, who did some friendly trading for "toyes and trifles," and revealed the name of their god "Settaboth" —Pigafetta's Setebos. Here, however, they had a serious brawl. Drake went ashore with six men including master gunner Oliver. This fellow, shooting with bow and arrow to amuse or impress the natives, broke his bowstring; the Indians "tooke present advantage, and charging his bowe clapt an arrow into the body of him and through his Lunges." The Captain General acted promptly. Picking up Oliver's arquebus, heavily charging it "with a bullet and haile shot," he dispatched the beginner of the quarrel, tearing out his guts. "His cry was so hideous and horrible a roare, as if ten bulls had joyned together in roaring." That panicked the Patagonians who (says *The World Encompassed*) were "nothing so monstrous or giant as they were reported" by Pigafetta, and no taller than a tall Englishman, but most repulsive to the view.

"This bloody Tragedie being ended, another more grevious ensueth," observes the reverend chronicler. He meant the trial and execution of Master Doughty for mutiny. Doughty had been Drake's companion in arms in Ireland and a true friend, or so he thought. Fletcher could not explain why so Christian a gentleman, "a sweet Orator, a pregnant Philosopher, a good gift for the Greeke tongue and a Reasonable tast of Hebrew, . . . and in Ireland an aproved Soldier and not behind many in the Study of the Law," should have acted as he did. The court-martial brought out the fact—or hearsay—that he conducted among the mariners in every ship that he commanded a sort of whispering campaign against Drake. Certain modern writers believe in a deep, dark plot of Doughty as stooge for Lord Treasurer Burghley, to usurp command of the fleet and take it home, in order to avoid offending Spain. In my opinion clashing personalities were the main cause. On these long Southern voyages the "top brass" got on each other's nerves, so that vague suspicion and idle gossip became magnified into mutiny and treason, and Drake by fair means or foul acquired such an antipathy to Doughty that he had to go. One remembers Magellan's executions at this very spot, and others by Mendoza and Sebastian Cabot further north.

The court, over forty in number, comprising all officers and gentlemen volunteers of the fleet, met on an island inside Puerto San Julián. So many proofs, both oral and written, were produced of Doughty's disloyalty that he broke down and confessed "that he conspired, not onely the overthrow of the action, but of the principall actor also . . . a deare and true friend," and admitted that he deserved to die. The court rendered the verdict "that it would be unsafe to let him live." Drake, apparently devastated by these revelations, sentenced Doughty to death, giving him the choice of three methods: execution then and there, marooning, or being sent to England "to answer his deed before the Lords of her Majesties Cowncell." Doughty chose immediate execution, desiring only the favor that he and Drake might receive communion together, "and that he might not die other than a gentleman's death."

There followed one of those pious and pathetic scenes that the Elizabethans loved—mutual forgiveness, dinner with the Captain General, last communion, Doughty "preparing at once his necke for the axe, and his spirit for heaven," head severed from body by an executioner of his choice. They buried him on the "Bloody Island" under the old gibbet, the grave marked by "a great grinding stone," carved with his name "in Latin, that it might the better be understood by all that should come after us." Next day all hands heard Master Fletcher preach a hortatory sermon, followed by holy communion and psalm singing. And—indicating that even in those days men liked grim souvenirs—the flag cooper made tankards of the gibbet for any sailor who wanted one.

Doughty's execution did not end grumblings and mutterings among the men, for Puerto San Julián, as Magellan had found, is no snug winter harbor. So Drake decided to risk a winter passage of the Strait rather than wait six months for summer. Before leaving, he preached a sermon ashore. This was the famous discourse in which he laid down the rules of discipline which should govern any hazardous undertaking: equal sharing of hardship and labor, no privilege of rank save that of an officer in the expedition, entire subordination to the commander. He chided the mariners for unruliness, but more weightily reproved the gentlemen for "stomaching daintiness in face of toil. . . . I must have

Psalms sung on board *Golden Hind*. From *The Whole Booke of Psalmes Collected into English by Thomas Sternhold and John Hopkins* (London: John Daye, 1578), p. 73. Courtesy Harvard College Library.

the gentleman to haul and draw with the mariner and the mariner with the gentleman. What! let us show ourselves all to be of a company, and let us not give occasion to the enemy to rejoice at our decay and over-throw. I would know him that would refuse to set his hand to a rope, but know there is not any such here." He then dismissed each and every officer from his post; and after another ringing appeal for all to rise to the occasion, reinstated them "as servants of the Queen under her General Francis Drake, to sail against the Spaniard at his sole command."

Sunday, 17 August 1578, the fleet, now reduced to three ships (*Pelican, Elizabeth,* and *Marygold*) and two pinnaces (*Swan* having been abandoned as unseaworthy), departed San Julián with a fair north wind and moon two days short of full. On the 20th they sighted Cabo Vírgenes, which the pilot recognized as the èntrance to the Strait. It reminded Fletcher of Cape St. Vincent. Drake, always observing great occasions with ceremony, ordered a time-honored naval salute, striking topsails "upon the bunt" as "homage to our soveraigne lady the Queenes majesty"; and each ship held a service of thanksgiving to God for having brought them so far in safety. As a special accent, Drake proclaimed with sound of trumpet that flagship *Pelican* would henceforth be called *Golden Hind*. He chose this name because a golden hind *trippant* was the crest of his principal supporter at court, Sir Christopher Hatton. Ordinarily, renaming a ship in the course of a voyage would have been considered unlucky and caused grumbling among the sailors. So, why did Drake do it? Possibly Doughty had been part-owner of the ship; probably Drake regarded "the pelican, whose bill can hold more than his belly can," as a bird unworthy to be the eponym of an important ship.

"These things thus accomplished, wee joyfully entered the Streight with hope of Good Success." It was 21 August 1578.

Through the Strait to Furthest South

And good success they had. Magellan the pioneer took thirty-seven days to get through; Cavendish took forty-nine, and Richard Hawkins in 1593, forty-six days. Drake's ships did the 363 miles in only sixteen days, including calls to take on water and kill penguins. Pilot Silva records that the wind blew steadily from between northeast and east-northeast, which accounted for their speed, but the *Famous Voyage* account in Hakluyt declares: "we had the wind often against us, so that some of the fleet recouering a Cape or point of land, others should be forced to turne backe agayne, and to come to an anker where they could." It was still Antarctic winter, the mountains were snow-covered, and the beech forests "seeme to stoope with the burden of the weather." Hakluyt's narrator describes the "monstrous and wonderfull" mountains, rising tier after tier, "reaching themselves above their fellowes so high, that between them did appeare three regions of cloudes." We marveled at the same effect in 1972.

On 24 August 1578, having passed through the two Narrows, "We fell [in] with three Ilands, bearing triangle-wise one from another; one of them was very faire and large and of a fruitfull soile, upon which, being next unto us and the weather very calme, our Generall with his gentlemen and certaine of his mariners, then landed, taking possession thereof in her Majesties name, and to her use, and called the same *Elizabeth* Iland."

Drake certainly had nerve to claim this land for the Queen, seeing that Magellan's and several other Spanish fleets had passed it long before he did; but, surprisingly, the name he gave to the largest of the three islands has survived in Spanish translation: Isla Isabel. The other two, mere rocks (now named Santa Marta and Santa Magdalena) were "exceeding useful," as covered by helpless birds "which the Welch men named Pengwin." "In the space of one day we killed no less than 3000," wrote Fletcher. "They are a very good and wholesome victuall." Maybe so for a time, when properly pickled; but penguin meat quickly cloys and goes putrid. Nuno da Silva the Portuguese pilot agreed that their flavor was good, not fishy, and that the lightest of them weighed ten pounds.

From Elizabeth Island the fleet sailed south, rounded Cape Froward and then steered northwest, following Magellan's course and often beating to windward. Fletcher left a very vivid picture of a williwaw: "Two or three of these winds would com togeather & meet . . . in one body whose forces . . . did so violently fall into the sea whirleing, or as the Spanyard sayth with a Tornado, that they would peirse into the verry bowells of the sea & make it swell upwards on every syde. . . . Besides this the sea is so deep in all this passage that, upon life and death, there is no coming to Anker." Nuno da Silva, on the contrary, recorded, on the south side, "many small bays or coves in which one could . . . safely anchor." This they obviously did. Master Fletcher tells us that the Antarctic beech branches made natural arbors where flourished herbs and "simples" such as wild celery, thyme, marjoram, scurvy grass, and "other strange plants." At this juncture, "nearly all" the flagship's crew were down with scurvy, but Drake had the juice squeezed from some of the herbs, and, administering it in wine, cured all but two men, who died. Drake had a big beech tree cut down and a section of the trunk placed in the *Golden Hind*'s hold; good evidence, observed pilot Silva, that he never intended to return that way.

Having worked through Paso Inglés, Paso Tortuoso, and Paso

Largo, "We had such a shutting up to the Northwards, and such large and open fretes toward the South, that it was doubtfull which way wee should passe." The same thing had happened to Magellan. Drake brought his fleet to anchor under an island (probably Providence or Beaufort), and had himself rowed to check the entrance to the Pacific. At that time the fleet received a visit from friendly Fuegians in a beech-bark canoe with a high bow and stern, so well framed and proportioned that the English thought it must have been built "for the pleasure of some great and noble personage, yea, of some Prince"—but the poor Fuegians had no prince. They were "of a meane stature" compared with the Patagonians, "gentile & familiar to strangers, heavily painted and almost naked." Nomads, they lived in skin wigwams and slept on the hard ground. "The women," wrote Fletcher, "weare chaines of white shells upon their armes & som about their Necks whereof they seem to be verry proud. They are well spedd [equipped] for Bellyes, Brests & Buttocks, but nothing in Comparison with the Giant women" of Patagonia.

On 6 September, under a new moon, the fleet passed Cabo Pilar and "entered into the South Sea or *Mare del Zur*." There Drake's luck changed. The Pacific (Fletcher said it should better have been named the Furious) Ocean was in one of her ugly moods. Drake intended now to sail north toward the Line, to get away from "the nipping cold, under so cruell and frowning a winter," but the ships could make no headway against the north wind and heavy seas. For an entire month, to 7 October, the three vessels * were batted about and driven south, even down to latitude 57° S says Fletcher; Nuno da Silva's log agrees that they made land at latitude 57° and anchored for an hour in forty fathom. It is anyone's guess where that was. One night, during the second watch, *Marygold*, with Captain Thomas, Master Bright, and twenty-eight men, disappeared; last seen "spooming" away from the flagship toward the iron-bound Chilean coast. She probably sought to raise Cabo Pilar and take refuge within the Strait. Fletcher guessed that they "were swallowed up with horrible & unmercifull waves or rather Mountains of the sea"; for he and another man on watch in the *Golden Hind* "did heare their feareful cryes"; but Drake long hoped that the *Marygold* had survived and would rejoin him.

Prayers coming from the *Hind* finally were heeded. At the end of

* The two pinnaces appear to have been abandoned.

this terrible month, sun, moon, and stars came out, the wind moderated, the tempestuous seas were stilled, and she began crawling north again. In the last week of October she sighted land, and anchored off what Drake believed to be "the uttmost Iland of *terra incognita*, to the Southward of America." He gave it no name, but called the group to which it belonged, "the Elizabeth Isles."

This island, identified by Wagner (and by myself in 1972) as Henderson Island at longitude 69°05′ W, latitudes 55°32′ to 55°37.5′ S, had never yet been seen by a European. Drake was certain that he had attained "the uttermost Cape or hedland . . . without which there is no maine nor Iland to be seene to the Southwards, but that the Atlanticke Ocean and the South Sea, meete in a most large and free scope." No Antarctic continent, my masters. "The West Occidental [the Western Ocean] and the South Sea are but one!" But it took

Drake's furthest south, Henderson Island, 55°35′ S. Saunderson Island in foreground. Courtesy of the photographer Bill Ray.

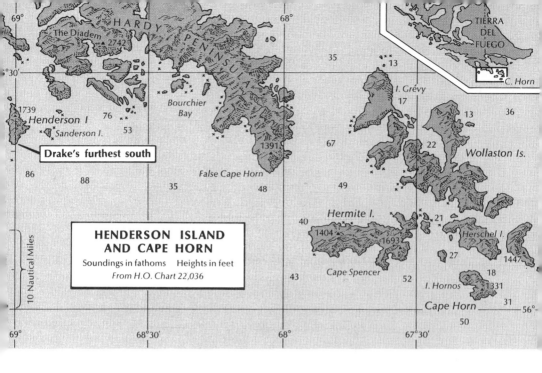

HENDERSON ISLAND
AND CAPE HORN
Soundings in fathoms   Heights in feet
From H.O. Chart 22,036

cartographers about a century to get over depicting a great land mass extrapolated from Tierra del Fuego and circling the earth. Australia represents all that remains of this geographical myth.

Cape Horn, the southernmost land of any consequence until you hit the Palmer Peninsula of the real Antarctic, lies some sixty miles southeast of Henderson Island, on latitude 55°59′ S. The International Oceanographic Conference of London in 1919 fixed the meridian of Cape Horn as the boundary between Atlantic and Pacific. But Drake had proved the two great oceans to be one, and opened the way for Schouten and Le Maire's discovery of Cape Horn in 1616.

Golden Hind anchored off Henderson Island on 24 October 1578 and tarried until a new moon rose on 1 November. Master Fletcher went ashore with the Captain General, walked down the grassy slopes, found them thick with delicious wild currants, and on its southernmost point set up a stone and carved thereupon the date and the Queen's name. Drake later told Hawkins that he "grovelled"—threw himself on his belly—at the uttermost tip of this cape and stretched out his arms as far as he could toward the South Pole, so he could boast that no man had been so near it as himself. So typical of Drake—always something of the big boy in him.

The Buccaneering Phase

Of the gallant fleet of six that sailed from Plymouth in December 1577 there now (1 November 1578) remained but one, the *Golden Hind*. *Elizabeth*, the second largest ship, had parted company in early October without Drake's permission and sailed back to England through the Strait. For over three centuries this was assumed to be a plain case of desertion by Captain Winter, like that of Gómez from Magellan; but Winter's tale excuses if not justifies his action. During the foul weather he had ducked back into the Strait as a refuge and there anchored. Drake, he averred, had told him, when they last exchanged words during a lull in the storm, that he intended to give up bucking violent north and west winds, to re-thread the Strait and make for the Moluccas via the Cape of Good Hope. So Winter tarried for a month, lighting signal fires at night; then, assuming that Drake had been cast away, he put his Cape of Good Hope plan to *Elizabeth*'s crew. To a man they protested that they had had enough, and rejected it. Captain Winter gave in and sailed for England, arriving in June 1579 after calling at Belle Isle on the French coast, where he did his best to blacken Drake's name.

Weather exerted an overriding influence on the boldest mariners in days of sail. Drake, having made furthest south, and the winds having turned fair, decided to sail *Golden Hind* north along the coasts of Chile and Peru and see what he could pick up.

And plenty did he pick up! In the previous thirty years Spain, as we have seen, had extended her empire along the west coast as far as Valdivia, Chile, on latitude 40° S. Most of the settlements were very small, with fewer men-at-arms than Drake had on board *Golden Hind*, thus easily captured and sacked. Spain employed a considerable fleet of coast-built merchantmen to carry silver and other treasures from the ports of Bolivia, and from Callao, port of Lima, to Old Panama. *Golden Hind* played wolf among sheep to this merchant fleet, for none were armed with cannon, never expecting to encounter anything bigger than an Indian balsa raft in the Pacific. The Englishmen embarked on this adventure in the spirit of schoolboy pranksters; even Master Fletcher the preacher enjoyed the fun. Finding a Spaniard ashore asleep beside thirteen barrels of silver, a flock of sheep, and "much *charqui*," * they "freed him of his charge" but left him screaming with rage and resentment. At another point, encountering a hidalgo driving a train of llamas loaded with silver, "we could not indure to see a gentleman Spaniard turned carrier . . . therefore we offered our own service and became drivers." Capturing a vessel laden with linen, "we thought [it] might stand us in some stead and therefore tooke it with us."

At Mocha Island near Valdivia they encountered tough resistance from the local Indians, who with arrows "thick as gnatts in the sonn" attacked the party when watering. Not one Englishman escaped having two or more arrows stuck into him; two men were killed outright; and two more, cut off from the boat, were killed and eaten most horribly—the barbarians cutting "gubblets" of their flesh, tossing them in the air, catching them while dancing, and devouring them "like doggs." The rest of the crew wanted to take revenge by cannonfire, but Drake refused, saying that the cruel Spaniards made the Indians act that way, and there were too many on hand (an estimated 2000) for one ship to punish.

Drake's tactics were to surprise, capture, and sack a Spanish settlement with all shipping in the harbor, and when he had looted everything valuable, turn ships and sailors loose, but with no sails to enable them to pursue him. Whilst Drake always remained a hero to his countrymen, he was usually denounced by Spanish and other Catholic writers as a cruel, ruthless, and unprincipled pirate. But since the publication of documents from Spanish archives by the Hakluyt Society in 1914, this view has become untenable; for his Spanish prisoners uniformly praised *El Draque* for humanity and generosity; nor did he ever kill anyone in cold blood. His men, rushing ashore, desecrated churches, stole sacred vessels, and destroyed statues, paintings, and crucifixes; but they did not rape or kill. Incidentally, Drake spoke Spanish well enough to converse with his prisoners.

Entering the great harbor of Valparaiso, the Englishmen were invited on board a small Spanish vessel whose crew, assuming that they too were Spaniards, beat a drum in welcome, invited them on board, and broke out "a Buttizo of wine of Chile." The guests' nationality was given away by their tough red-haired boatswain Tom Moone, who had been with Drake on his West Indies voyages and hated the dons. He

* Jerked beef, which the English learned to eat in Spanish America.

not only struck a Spaniard but aggravated the offense by crying to him, *abaxo perro,* "Down dog!" The English boarding party then clapped the Spanish sailors under hatches and joined their friends in "rifling" the town. Since Valparaiso then contained barely nine houses, they confined their ravages to the church, "the spoyle whereof our Generall gave to M. Fletcher his minister," and a warehouse which yielded several pipes of wine. The English sailors so relished the "buttizo" that they became patrons of Chilean wine and carried away so much of it from various ships and ports that it never gave out until mid-Pacific, if then.

At Quillóta and Coquimbo it was much the same story. At Valdivia they captured the ship that had been Mendaña's *Capitana* on his voyage of discovery to the Solomon Islands, with 24,000 *pesos d'oro,** and took her along with a genial cargo of 1700 jars of wine captured ashore. Nuno da Silva tells us they had to heave overboard six pipes of tar to make room for the wine. Who wouldn't? Drake landed at Bahia Saleda (latitude 27°55′ S) on 20 December and tarried a whole month to assemble the last of his knocked-down pinnaces; it speaks ill for Chilean communications that this delay did not alert the entire west coast. Arica, on the present border between Chile and Peru, port for Potosí and other silver mines, he reached on 7 February 1579, moon at first quarter. Loot from two vessels riding there yielded "about forty bars" of silver, a chest of pieces of eight, and "some wine." Passing Punta Chala ("Chawley" to Fletcher), Drake captured a ship from which he learned that a rich haul was awaiting him in Callao, seaport of Lima, the "City of Kings" and capital of the Peruvian viceroyalty.

Golden Hind sailed by the south channel, unheralded and unseen, into Callao harbor. There the men plundered a dozen or more ships "aboard whom we made somewhat bold to bid ourselves welcome," says Fletcher, and looted 1500 "barres of plate," a chestful of silver reals, and a quantity of linen and silk. This alerted the authorities at Lima, and the Viceroy himself, mounted and in armor, led two hundred men to the waterfront to repel invaders. Too late! It was 14 February, and *Golden Hind* had already slipped out to sea, towed by her longboat in the early morning calm, to pursue *Nuestra Señora de la Concepción,* a

* Sarmiento *dixit* (Nuttall, *New Light on Drake,* p. 60), but the Spanish official report from Callao (*ibid.,* p. 92) says 1,400,000 pesos! This ship Drake later destroyed (p. 169).

treasure-laden ship headed for Panama. Drake offered a gold chain to whoever first sighted her, and his fifteen-year-old cousin John Drake won it. The attempt of the viceroy of Peru, D. Francisco de Toledo, to pursue, in two hastily armed vessels, was a complete flop. His ships were so clumsily handled as to get becalmed near shore while Drake went zooming along in a fresh breeze. But (wrote Sarmiento de Gamboa), "the most imperative reason for returning seemed to be that many of the gentlemen were very seasick and in no condition to stand, much less to fight." These weak-stomached defenders of Peru were all severely punished on their return. This was typical of the many bumbling attempts of the Spanish authorities, owing largely to confused orders and bad seamanship, to catch Drake. He showed them all a clean pair of heels; but in truth, as one Spanish witness wrote to the king, "in this South Sea there is no vessel or vessels that can harm him, for they are small in size and their crews are inexperienced."

Drake's target on this occasion was the famous vessel generally known by her Spanish nickname *Cacafuego,* which nice North American and English writers have translated "Spitfire"; it really means "Shitfire." The name is not only indecent but inappropriate, as she mounted no heavy ordnance. Her master, San Juan de Antón, suspecting no harm, allowed *Golden Hind* to sail alongside and grapple. Antón turned out to be a Basque who had lived in Southampton and spoke English well. According to his report, Drake's men shouted, "We're English, strike sail! . . . If not, look out for you will be sent to the bottom!" He answered, "What England is this? Come on board and strike the sails yourselves!" A bosun's whistle shrilled, a trumpet sounded, and a volley crashed out from Drake's arquebuses. This was followed by crossbow bolts and chain shot which severed the Spaniard's mizzen mast. Drake's new pinnace laid aboard her on the larboard side, and "about 40" archers scrambled up the channels and took possession of the ship. Antón was hustled on board *Golden Hind* and into the flag cabin where Drake, in the act of removing his armor, greeted him thus: "Have patience, such is the usage of war." Next day, 2 March 1579, Drake breakfasted on board *Cacafuego* and left orders with his own steward to prepare meals for the Spanish captain as if for himself.

It took three days for the English pinnace to transfer to *Golden Hind* all the plunder, which amounted (says San Juan de Antón) to 447,000 pesos in specie, equivalent to about half a million dollars in gold; and two other Spaniards present deposed that it was "more than 360,000 pesos." At the end of this process an impudent Spanish pilot's boy remarked that his ship should no longer be called *Cacafuego* but *Cacaplata*—the English thought this to be a wonderful witticism. Before releasing the Spanish captain and his ship, Drake gave to every member of her crew, clothing, knives, weapons, and a fistful of pesos; a merchant passenger received fans and mirrors "for his lady," and to Captain Antón a German-made musket, six hundred pounds of iron, a barrel of powder, a gilt corselet, a silver-gilt bowl inscribed "Francisqus Draques," a safe-conduct in case he met the two missing English ships, and a plea to the viceroy of Peru to spare the lives of John Oxenham and the Englishmen captured with him. One touch of gallantry that particularly appealed to the Spaniards was Drake's allowing one of his prizes to keep her royal ensign flying, saying, "Leave the arms of King Philip where they are, for he is the best king in the world."

No wonder Antón and his crew parted from Drake in good humor, regarding him a very proper *caballero*. But the viceroy of Peru paid no attention to his plea for mercy to Oxenham and his men. All were executed in 1580. Drake himself always showed mercy to captives. A black slave seized at Arica, unhappy at sea, begged to be allowed to return to his master; Drake said, "Go, with God's blessing," and let Antón take him ashore.

On his way to catch *Cacafuego*, Drake captured a vessel "laden with ropes and tackles for ships," and a golden crucifix "with goodly great Emerauds set in it." These were probably the same emeralds that he later set in a new crown for his Queen.

Drake now turned north, to evade certain pursuit, and anchored behind Caño Island off the coast of Costa Rica. Sighting a vessel sailing in the offing, Drake sent out his pinnace to capture it, which was easily done. This fifteen-tun *fragata,* belonging to one Rodrigo Tello, carried a cargo of silver and sarsaparilla, but more important were two professional pilots who were about to take the annual Acapulco galleon to the Philippines. Drake impounded all their Pacific charts and tried to bribe or threaten one of them, Alonso Sánchez Colchero by name, to pilot him across the Pacific. For refusing, he was threatened with the noose but let off with no hurt, and a gift of fifty pesos for his wife. Drake, however, kept the charts.

After graving *Golden Hind* rather ineffectively on a beach near Caño Island, and with Tello's *fragata* as prize, Drake continued northward. On 2 April 1579 his calculated latitude was 13°20′ N. Next day he surprised and captured a small vessel upon which a Spanish nobleman, Dr. Francisco de Zárate, a cousin to the Duke of Medina Sidonia, had embarked as passenger. Zárate has left us an impressive picture of Drake's style and courtesy. He dined with the Captain General in the flag cabin, and tells in his narrative that Drake gave him food from his own plate and told him "not to grieve, that my life and property were safe." Next day being Sunday, *Golden Hind* dressed ship. Drake "decked himself very finely," went on board the prize and took four chests of Chinese porcelain and several packs of linen and fine silks, and a gold falcon with an emerald in its breast which belonged to Don Francisco, giving him in return a silver brazier. Zárate describes Drake as a man about thirty-five years old, short in stature, and bearded, "one of the greatest mariners that exist, both as a celestial navigator and in knowledge of command. . . . He treats his men with affection, and they treat him with respect." One prisoner reported that "all his men trembled before him" and bowed low, hats in hand, whenever they passed him on deck; but several whom Don Francisco questioned, declared that they "adored" him. Nine or ten young gentlemen volunteers, and pilot Nuno da Silva, dined in the Captain General's mess, where they were served "on silver dishes with gold borders and gilded garlands within which are his arms"; and the fiddlers played both at dinner and supper. Most important, from a legal point of view, Drake displayed his *provisiones*, his commission from the Queen, and other legal documents.

Drake now calculated that the entire west coast of South America would be alerted, and armed ships buzzing like angry hornets whose nest has been disturbed. So there was no question of returning home the way he came. His last call in settled Spanish America was at Guatalco, Mexico, mainly to obtain water and provisions for a long voyage, but also to top off with more silver. His men captured an entire court of justice from judge to black prisoners, haled them on board ship, and forced the judge to write a letter to the town fathers permitting the English to water there. After so doing, they "ransaked the town," completely cleaning out from the church the communion plate, vestments, holy images, even the bell. Tom Moone, Drake's red-haired and pock-marked boatswain, acquired "a chaine of gold and some other jewells, which we intreated a gentleman Spaniard to leave behinde him, as he was flying out of the towne." The gentleman probably did not think it so funny. When Drake regaled two leading citizens with wine in his flag cabin, one complained that the town had nothing to eat, all Indians having fled to the woods; so Drake sent ashore, to help keep the population alive, two bags of flour, two jars of wine, one of oil, and two sugar-loaves. He kept the black prisoners but later released them, together with a wench belonging to Zárate, on a Pacific island.

At Guatulco, Drake released Don Francisco and Nuno da Silva, who had served him well as pilot but knew nothing of the waters to come. Once ashore, Nuno wrote interesting reports of his experience with Drake, together with a lively description of him: "Francis Drake is a man aged 38. He may be two years more or less. He is short in stature, thickset and very robust. He has a fine countenance, ruddy of complexion, and a fair beard. He has the mark of an arrow wound in his right cheek which is not apparent if one looks not with special care. In one leg he has a ball of an arquebus which was shot at him in the Indies. . . . He had seated at his table the captain, pilot and doctor. He also read the psalms and preached. . . . He carries a book in which he enters his log, and paints birds, trees and sea-lions. He is an adept in painting and carries along a boy [John Drake] a relative of his, who is a great painter. When they both shut themselves up in his cabin they were always painting." (All these sketches and paintings, alas, have perished.) Nuno also had a high opinion of Drake as a mariner.

This straightforward account of Nuno's got him into trouble with the Mexican branch of the Spanish Inquisition, which accused him of having complacently attended Drake's shipboard Protestant services where psalms were sung. The singing of translated psalms, the only hymns used in the Anglican church for centuries, appears to have been particularly irritating at that time to Catholics. Nuno defended himself by saying that he "attended" no regular service but could not help hearing the English heretics bellowing their unauthorized psalms. The Inquisition sentenced him to perpetual exile from the Indies. But he did escape the torch if not the rack, and is even said to have visited England before he died. In any case, the Admiralty restored to him the value of the merchandise on board his ship, when Drake captured it in the Cape de Verdes.

Sailing from Guatulco under the paschal moon on Maundy Thursday, 16 April 1579, *Golden Hind* struck out into the Pacific "to get a winde," finally caught the northwest trades, and, sailing close-hauled, on 5 June made land somewhere in the present state of Oregon.

Before leaving Mexico for the north, Drake destroyed the three biggest prizes he had taken, keeping only Tello's fragata for a tender. One of those he relinquished with regret because of her speed on the wind; when sailing in company with *Golden Hind*, Drake had to order her to tow anchors wrapped in old sails, so she would not thrust ahead of him. Colchero and the other pilot whom Drake set free reported to the viceroy that he would undoubtedly make the coast of Alta California, "because the season for navigation to China is now past . . . and the winds are contrary." *Golden Hind*, already leaking from the strain of her heavy cargo, badly needed a good careening, graving, and caulking.

Bibliography and Notes

SOURCES

The earliest account of Drake's voyage to be printed is "The Famous Voyage" in Hakluyt's *Voyages*, 1589 edition. Hakluyt threw in a signature on the subject when the book was already in press; it follows II, 643. The Hakluyt Society's reproduction of this edition (see my *Northern Voyages*, p. 579) is the one I refer to as *The Famous Voyage*.

The "Anonymous Narrative" manuscript in the British Museum. Text printed in Wagner's Drake biography (below), pp. 264–65, and discussed on pp. 243–44. A deposition by a participant not over-friendly to Drake but made shortly after his return, and has the ring of authority.

John Drake depositions of 1581–87. By Drake's young cousin, who was with him on the voyage, when later a Spanish prisoner. Text and discussion in Zelia Nuttall, *New Light on Drake* (Hakluyt Society, London, 1914), pp. 18–56 and Wagner, pp. 236–37 and 328–44.

The famous tract *The World Encompassed by Sir Francis Drake Carefully Collected Out of the Notes of Master Francis Fletcher* (London, 1628). Probably written by John Drake, from Fletcher's notes. The best modern edition is that of the Argonaut Press (London, 1926), edited by N. M. Penzer, together with Fletcher's Notes (often more detailed than the finished product), and sundry other documents. (Nobody should miss sailor Cooke's anti-Drake narrative at pp. 142–68.) A facsimile edition, with introduction by A. L. Rowse, and Schouten's Cape Horn voyage as supplement, was published by World Publishing Company of Cleveland, Ohio, in 1966. Rowse believes that Fletcher himself wrote it some years prior to the publication.

John Hampden, ed., *Francis Drake Privateer* (London, 1972), is a handy compilation of the sources.

Spanish Narratives. Those of Sarmiento de Gamboa, and of various dons captured by Drake, are in Zelia Nuttall, *New Light on Drake*. "Aunt Zelia," as she was known to a generation of North American students in Mexico whom she counseled and entertained, did extensive research in Mexican and Spanish archives, and came up with some very important material such as Nuno da Silva's accounts (pp. 242–319). Although her ideas about Drake verge on the bizarre, she did not deserve Wagner's attack in his autobiography, *Bullion to Books*, p. 267 (see below).

SECONDARY

Henry R. Wagner, *Sir Francis Drake's Voyage Around the World, Its Aims and Achievements* (San Francisco, 1926), is still the best book on this voyage. Wagner (1862–1957), a California businessman and collector, studied all known sources and investigated many localities; and his corpus of documents is comprehensive. Unfortunately, his reproductions of maps, whether ancient or modern, are mostly illegible. Written before the "Plate of Brass" (see below) was discovered, Wagner's book is supplemented by an 18-page pamphlet printed in 1970 for the Zamorano Club of Los Angeles: *Drake on the Pacific Coast. Henry R. Wagner. With an Introduction and Notes by Ruth Frey Axe*, his research assistant. This gives Wagner's emphatic opinion against the Plate and the San Francisco Bay hypothesis. The same Club printed his autobiography, *Bullion to Books*, but therein he says nothing about the Plate and little about Drake.

A number of California gentlemen interested in Drake in 1954 incorporated themselves as The Drake Navigators' Guild, with Fleet Admiral Chester W. Nimitz USN as honorary chairman. Over the years they have done meticulous research on Drake in California and issued a number of valuable publications, of which the most comprehensive is Raymond Aker, *Report of Findings Relating to Identification of Sir Francis Drake's Encampment at Point Reyes National Seashore* (461 pp. mimeographed and illustrated, Point Reyes [1970]). It is to be hoped that this will be printed, together with the riposte by the Bodega Bay proponents, Robert F. Heizer, John H. Kemble, and Andrew Rolls, *Analysis of Raymond Aker's Report* (mimeographed, Point Reyes, 1970).

Two more important monographs, Robert W. Allen and Robert W. Parkinson, *Identification of the Nova Albion Conie*, and *Examination of the Botanical References . . . at Nova Albion*, both illustrated, were published by the Guild in 1971.

Hans P. Kraus (ed), *Sir Francis Drake, a Pictorial Biography*, with an historical introduction by David W. Waters and Richard Boulind (Amsterdam, 1970). Immoderately priced at $80.00, this is a useful corpus of illustrations, and reproduces in facsimile the Hakluyt account of 1589.

Earlier biographies and articles of some value are:

Edward Everett Hale's chapter and Justin Winsor's notes in the latter's *Narrative and Critical History*, III (1884), 59-84.

Sir Julian Corbett, *Drake and the Tudor Navy* (2 vols., London, 1889) and *Sir Francis Drake* (London and New York, 1890) cover his entire career, but are unsatisfactory on this voyage. James A. Williamson, *The Age of Drake* (London, 1938), gives the background of Drake's voyage and has a good account of it.

Winter's account was discovered by Professor E. G. R. Taylor in the Public Records Office and printed in *Mariner's Mirror*, XVI (April 1930), as part of her article "More Light on Drake: 1577-80," pp. 134-51.

DETAILED NOTES

Drake's objectives. Williamson, chap. ix. He and E. G. R. Taylor argued that Drake's orders to explore between latitudes 52° and 30° S meant the imaginary Australian continent running around the world, which cartographers had extrapolated from Magellan's Tierra del Fuego. Williamson, pp. 168-70, quoting E. G. R. Taylor in *Geographical Journal*, LXXV (Jan. 1930), 46-47, "The Missing Draft Project of Drake's Voyage of 1577-80," her *Tudor Geography 1485-1583* (1930), pp. 113-19, and her "John Dee, Drake and the Straits of Anian" in *Mariner's Mirror*, XV (1929), 125-30. Williamson writes "To assume that Drake was ordered to treat as unoccupied territory the greater part of . . . Chile including . . . Valparaiso and Santiago assumes a remarkable ignorance on the part of the promoters. . . ."; but "that ignorance is just possible." To me, to assume that a northerly exploration from 52° S to 30° S would apply to a continent running east-west is even less comprehensible.

Task organization. World Encompassed (Argonaut Press ed., London, 1926), p. xxv. It is very difficult to keep track of Drake's smaller vessels, even more so of the prizes he took, and I do not claim absolute accuracy.

Pelican-Golden Hind. Gregory Robinson, *Elizabethan Ships* (London, 1956), pp. 4-12, and "Evidence about the *Golden Hind*" in *Mariner's Mirror*, XXXV (1949), 56-65. Also, R. Morton Nance, "The Little Ship of the Ashmolean" in same, XXIV (1938), 95-100, and articles by F. C. Prideaux Naish in same, XXXIV (1948), 42-45, and XXXVI (1950), 129-33. Zelia Nuttall, pp. 424-28, has compiled a list of 97 men and boys who were with the fleet when it sailed, but only 51 went round the world with him. At the time of writing, a so-called replica of *Golden Hind* is being built at Appledore for show purposes. Probably the best model of her is the one at Buckland Abbey, Devonshire.

Course to Brazil. Fletcher's Notes (*World Encompassed*, p. 102) say:

"We set our course for the southerly part of Brazil," and sailed 34 days "without sight of land." This was evidently in March, after sighting Fernão de Noronha, for which Nuno da Silva (in Nuttall, p. 277) is our authority. Contemporary authorities contradict each other on Drake's dates in Atlantic ports. See Nuttall, pp. 272–81, with the others in footnotes.

The Patagonians. Fletcher's Notes, in *World Encompassed,* pp. 118–21, are detailed and interesting on the manners and customs of the Patagonians, "whose feet are like shovells," and "hands like shoulders of Mutton"; the women's breasts "reach to their Navells and their bellyes . . . like woole sacks hang to their knees . . . and under their chinns a bagg reaching to their breasts."

Doughty's execution. Fletcher and others thought it was all wrong. See especially John Cooke's narrative in *World Encompassed,* pp. 142–68, followed by Doughty's speech on board *Pelican.*

The Hakluyt reference is *Principall Navigations,* II, 643D (1965 reprint of 1589 ed.). Nuno, however (Nuttall, p. 315), says that they entered 24 August after waiting three days for an ENE wind. This would reduce the length of Drake's transit to only 14 days—hardly credible.

Drake's furthest south. Wagner, p. 34. Fletcher (*World Encompassed,* pp. 34, 135) says that it lay between latitudes 55° and 56° S; Nuno da Silva (Nuttall, p. 285), that it was in 57° S. From Henderson Island no land can be seen to the southward except Isla Ildefonso on an exceptionally clear day, and the sea there is usually covered with mist. The story of his "grovelling" Drake told to Sir Richard Hawkins, who relates it in his *Observations on His Voyage into the South Seas, 1593* (Hakluyt Society ed., London, 1847), p. 142. Few will believe Sir Julian Corbett's contention that this island was Cape Horn; but the statement that Drake discovered Cape Horn is still found in English text and reference books. Thomas Kitchin's *New Map of the Southern Parts of America* (London, 1772) shows an archipelago named "Drake's Islands" west of Cape Horn and south of Cabo Pilar.

Drake's shipboard services. Prisoners whom Drake later released describe these services in their depositions for the Mexican Inquisition. Before both dinner and supper, Drake uncovered, knelt, and "chanted in a low voice" from a very large book in English, and his table-mates made responses. Sometimes the "viols" gave a concert which lasted an hour. From the second prisoner's report it is evident that Drake had with him a copy of Foxe's *Book of Martyrs.* (Nuttall, p. 325–26, 336, 355–56).

Carder's adventures. In what would seem to have been a singular lapse in seamanship, Drake, shortly after passing Cabo Pilar, cast off Peter Carder and seven other seamen in "an open pinnasse or shallop of five tuns," telling them to stand by. What happened to them is told in *Purchas His Pilgrimes,* XVI (MacLehose ed., 1906), 136:

> The Relation of Peter Carder of Saint Verian in Cornwall
> . . . which went with Sir Francis in his Voyage about the

World . . . who with seven others in an open Pinnasse or Shallop of five tuns, with eight Oares, was separated from his Generall by foule weather in the South Sea, in October, An. 1578, who returning by the Straites of Magellan toward Brazill, were all cast away, save this one only afore named, who came into England nine yeares after miraculously, having escaped many strange dangers, as well among divers Savages as Christians.

After *Elizabeth* had disappeared, 8 October 1578, Drake caused Carder and eight other seamen to man his "small pinnasse or shallop" * and ordered her to stand by. That night she lost sight of the flagship and, after searching for her for 14 days, food and water being exhausted, she stood into the Strait and the men fed on shellfish and penguin. They sailed through the Strait successfully, and called at San Julián and other Patagonian ports to replenish food. On the north coast of the River Plate, six men landed to seek food in the woods. They were attacked by natives and four men were killed. The two survivors, Carder and William Pitcher of London, took refuge on an island off shore (probably Lobos). There the pinnace broke up in a gale. After almost dying of thirst, they got ashore, each pushing a plank; but Pitcher died of overdrinking at the first stream of sweet water, leaving Carder sole survivor. He ingratiated himself with the Brazilian natives and escaped being eaten, although he saw plenty of cannibalism going on, and walked all the way to Salvador da Bahia. At the factory there he was befriended and employed for two years by a Portuguese who finally gave him a boat to escape to Pernambuco. There he took passage on a "hulke" which took him to Pico in the Azores where the hulk was captured by an English man-of-war, which took him to Chichester. In November 1586, more than eight years since he had parted from *Golden Hind*, Peter was presented to the Queen. She listened to his story and tipped him 22 angels, about £11 sterling. Good old Bess!

The Cacafuego capture. Pedro Sarmiento de Gamboa, who headed the squadron sent by the Viceroy to catch Drake, wrote an excellent account of it which is translated in Nuttall, pp. 56–88.

Caño Island (on few modern maps) lies a short distance north of Golfo Dulce at latitude 8°45′ N. Behind the island is a fairly good harbor, which after Drake's visit was called Puerto Inglés. Since the 19th century it has been called Costa Rica Bay. Sarmiento (Nuttall, p. 83) said that Drake was there 20–25 March. One of the Spanish depositions says that the beach was no good for careening; but another witness said that Drake careened and caulked *Golden Hind* in a small bay after landing the silver and ordnance; yet she continued to leak, and then he could find no suitable beach. Witness

*Probably one of the prizes taken in the Atlantic, of which we have lost track, or *Golden Hind*'s longboat which would ordinarily have been towed. Perhaps the latter, as Peter says they had neither compass nor chart on board.

says there were then 86 men on board, including 2 blacks and 3 boys. Drake allowed the Spaniards to "tell their beads," and said, if they didn't like his "Lutheran" worship, to go to the other end of the ship, "which they did." Nuttall, pp. 185–88, 192.

Alzata y Ramírez, *Mapa . . . de la América Septentrional* (1780), places Guatulco at lat. 15°20′ N, just east of the Gulf of Tehuantepec. In Drake's time it was a principal port of embarkation for Peru and Honduras (Nuttall, p. 353n), but it has disappeared from the modern map.

✳ XXVIII ✳

Drake in California

1579

Nova Albion

Everyone, including Drake, with whom the Spanish prisoners talked on board *Golden Hind*, reported that he intended to sail home around the world. Nuno da Silva, however, felt confident that he was going north first. Did Drake change his mind, or had he always intended to seek the fabled Strait of Anian, the Northwest Passage which attracted so much misguided effort by his English contemporaries? We simply do not know. It has been surmised that he picked up from the Spanish pilot, his unwilling captive, the timetable of the Manila galleons, which always cleared Acapulco by 27 March, and that he considered mid-April too late for fair winds on a Pacific crossing. Hardly credible; weather reports of the Manila ships were not so accurate as to deter a navigator like Drake who had successfully threaded the Strait of Magellan in winter. Or he may have felt that the fifty days' supply of water that he took on board at Guatulco was not enough for a trans-Pacific voyage. Or he may have decided he must find a safe place to repair *Golden Hind*, whose heavy cargo of silver had started a number of leaks. Actually this leg of the voyage, to somewhere in Alta California on 5 June 1579, took almost exactly fifty days; a very neat calculation, or merely Drake's usual good luck.

Golden Hind and the Tello pinnace made a wide sweep into the Pacific and then headed for the west coast, close-hauled on the port tack. The mariners at sea were "grievously pinched" with "extreme and nipping cold," says *The Famous Voyage*, "complained of the extremitie thereof, and the further we went, the more colde increased upon us." Hence Drake started his sheets "to seeke the land." The wind veered northward on 5 June 1579, when Drake's ships "were forced by contrary windes to runne in with the Shoare, which we then first descried, and to cast anchor in a bad bay, the best roads we could for the present meete with." This bay spoken of so disparagingly was probably the little cove just south of Cape Arago on the coast of Oregon at latitude 43°20′ N. There the two vessels were subjected to "extreme gusts and flawes" and these were succeeded by "most vile, thicke, and stinking fogges." "In this place was no abiding for us," wrote Fletcher; the only direction in which anyone wanted to go was south. And that is what Drake did. He abandoned his search for the Strait of Anian—if that had ever been his intention.

In June they coasted south for a good five degrees, always with moonlight, saw snow-covered mountains of the Coast Range in the distance, and suffered from more "nipping cold." Master Fletcher, anticipating criticism from "chamber champions," men "who lye on their feather beds till they go to sea," and whose teeth chatter when drinking "a cup of cold Sack and sugar by the fire," became indignant over slug-abed criticism of this southerly turn, as are we. California weather is not all golden sunshine and gentle rain; there were ten days of frost and snow at Oakland in the winter of 1972–73, and why should Fletcher have reported foul weather had it been fair? The cold cannot possibly have been anything like what northern discoverers such as Frobisher and Davis had endured, but the temperature did drop to the point where the lines froze; and by comparison with the equatorial heat they had been through, and lacking winter clothing, the men doubtless were very uncomfortable. So were the crew of the famous Captain Cook on this same coast almost two centuries later.

More astonishing to us (and repugnant to west coast tourist bureaus) is Master Fletcher's statement that the face of the earth all along the west coast appeared "unhandsome and deformed . . . shewing trees without leaves, and the ground without greenes in those moneths of June and July." But that may be explained by drought, or normal

Cape Arago and South Cove. Robert W. Allen photo.

midsummer parching. We in May 1973 found the coast beautifully green.

Since Drake's shipmates seldom if ever recorded their impressions of scenery, we cannot scold them for not alluding to the beauty of the California coast that they followed so assiduously. Rolling hills come right down to the shore and, as often as not, break off as cliffs. Trees are scarce except in sheltered valleys, as the prevalent west and north-west winds will not let them grow tall. Surf continually roars upon the shore, and even today sea birds are plentiful; we plowed through vast sheets of tiny paddling phalaropes dipping for plankton, and there was hardly a moment when gulls, terns, cormorants, and many others were not crossing our bows in flight. The water is chilled summer and winter by a southward flowing current, into which the cold Japan current feeds. Partly because this makes bad sea bathing, but mostly because Californians have foresightedly made this shore into state parks or reservations, the coast that Drake examined has escaped "development." One can gaze on a Drake's Bay almost as untouched by humans as when the "Generall" passed that way.

From the 43° landfall (state two out of the three original narratives) *Golden Hind* coasted south in search of a comfortable harbor and found it at 38° N. (The third narrative says 38°15'.) Here they put in on 17 June 1579 and tarried until 23 July; and 38° N is the exact latitude of Point Reyes, some thirty-six miles north of the Golden Gate.

Before examining the question of where Drake spent those five weeks in June and July 1579, let us relate what happened there. The most important thing, after graving the *Golden Hind,* was the friendly attitude of the natives, Indians known as the Coast Miwok tribe who lived from about Cape Mendocino to San Francisco Bay. When Drake careened his flagship on a beach so that her leak could be got at, he built a fortified camp ashore. This drew a multitude of Indians armed with bows and arrows; for like other natives of America, they instinctively resented foreigners who gave the impression of having come to stay. Drake was expert enough at the universal sign language to allay their suspicions, especially after he had distributed liberal gifts of cloth, shirts, and "other things. "

These Miwok were great talkers, delivering lengthy orations in a language that no Englishman could make head or tail of, and relentless singers and dancers after their fashion. The men went completely naked; and the women, who wore miniskirts of bulrushes, had a curious habit which has puzzled later ethnologists, of lacerating cheeks and torsos with their fingernails until the blood flowed in torrents, and, as further self-punishment, casting themselves on rough ground or briars. The English sources say nothing of sexual relations between the two races, but it is difficult to believe that they did not occur, considering the long time that Drake's men had been at sea.* These natives amiably augmented the Englishmen's rations during their five weeks' stay, mostly with broiled fish and a root that they called *petáh*. This was the bulb of a wild lily that they ground into meal and ate, and they also made bread of acorns; but they had no corn or manioc to offer, and it puzzles one how Drake managed to provision his ship for the long

---

* It may be significant that in the numerous Spanish reports of Drake's incursions on the west coast, his men were never accused of raping, or even molesting the Indian girls.

voyage ahead. Presumably his men shot and cured the small rodents that they called "conies." This has been identified recently as *Thomomys bottae bottae*, the Bötta Pocket Gopher, although some authorities still assert that it was the common ground squirrel. Maybe they cured fish on shore, as in Newfoundland. But where could they have obtained salt?

One of the earlier yelling and lacerating orgies by native visitors was broken up by Drake's calling on Preacher Fletcher to conduct divine service, complete with psalm-singing. The Indians then stopped their clamor to listen, stare, and occasionally shout. "Yea, they tooke such pleasure in our singing of Psalmes, that whensoever they resorted to us, their first request was commonly this, *Gnaáh*, by which they intreated that we would sing." The historian J. Franklin Jameson once sagely observed that *gnaáh* proved that all Englishmen, and not only the Puritans, sang psalms through their noses!

On one occasion, at least, the native visitors brought their chief, distinguished by several necklaces of local shells, a mantle of gopher skins, a wood "septer or royall mace," and a knitted cap in which feathers were stuck, as a crown. He greeted Drake with the title of *Hyó*, "set a rustic crown on his head, inriched his necke with all their chains," and laid on a special song and dance. What the natives meant by all this is anyone's guess, but Drake chose to regard it as a feudal ceremony in which these humble creatures placed themselves under the protection of Queen Elizabeth. Consquently, shortly before his July departure, Drake named the country *Nova Albion*, "for two causes; the one in respect of the white bancks and cliffes, which lie toward the sea; the other, that it might have some affinity, even in name also, with our own country, which was sometime so called." (Albion was the Greek name for England.) He then "set up a monument of our being there . . . a plate of brasse, fast nailed to a great and firme post; whereon is engraven" the Queen's name, the date, and the fact of the king and people freely acknowledging her sovereignty, the Queen being represented by a silver sixpence with her effigy, and "our Generall" by his name. So says Fletcher; more about this Plate anon. But the white cliffs are right there on Drake's Bay, outside the Estero, and they bear a striking resemblance to those on the English Channel.

After *Golden Hind* had been graved, repaired, and floated, Drake "with his gentleman and many of his company, made a journey up

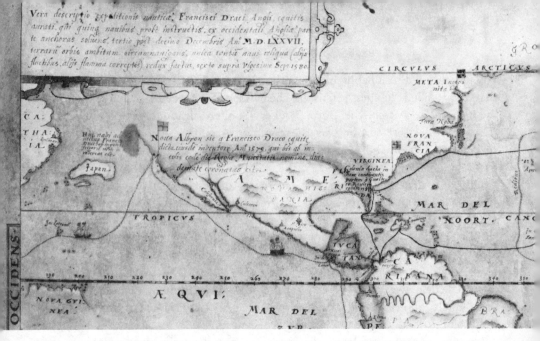

CIRCVLVS ARCTICVS

META Incog
nita

Tara Noba

NOVA
FRAN
CIA

CA:
THA:
IA.

Hæc nobis ad
. . . Prouc
. . . . .
Japan:

Noua Albion sic a Francisco Draco equite
dicta, eiusde inuentore Anō 1579, qui hic ab in-
colis coēs diē Regia Maiestatis nomine, dia . . .
demisse coronatus est . . .

VIRGINEA
Colonia deducta in
hanc continentis
. . . Galli . . .
. . . ensis

A   M   E
R   I   C
ANIA

NOVA GVI
NEA

TROPICVS

Cæliforn . .
Culiucan
Acapulco

IVCA
TAN

CA
RIBANA

MAR   DEL
NOORT   CANC

Æ   Q   VI:

MAR   DEL
ZVR.

BRA

OCCIDENS

190   200   210   220   230   240   250   260   270   280   290   300   310   320   330   340   350

The Mellon-Drake map, 1517. In Mr. and Mrs. Paul Mellon's Collection,
Upperville, Va. Photo Courtesy Robert H. Power.

into the land." The inland parts they found "farre different from the
shoare, a goodly country, and fruitfull soyle, stored with many bless-
ings fit for the use of man" such as great herds of deer. It is indeed a
beautiful rolling country, reminding one of the downs along the English Channel. Those who do not know this region may wonder why
this inland excursion did not reveal San Francisco Bay to Drake and
his merry men. The answer is simple: a day's walk along the valley as
far as Olema at the head of Tomales Bay is screened from San Francisco Bay by high ridges and Mount Tamalpais of 2600 feet altitude.

Drake's men never wore out their welcome. As the Indians observed
preparations for departure, "so did the sorrowes and miseries of this
people" seem to increase; more lacerations by the women, more
"wofull complaints and moanes, . . . refusing all comfort." Which
certainly indicates that those Englishmen had behaved with singular
kindness and patience, and suggests that if only the Northwest Passage
had opened up, Nova Albion might have become an earlier New
England with a more salubrious climate and better race relations.

Tello's pinnace was abandoned, probably because Drake no longer had enough men to work her as well as *Golden Hind*. The flagship left California with between fifty and sixty men on board.

"The 23 of July," says Fletcher, the Indians "tooke a sorrowfull farewell of us, but being loath to leave us, they presently ranne to the top of the hills to keepe us in their sight as long as they could, making fires before and behind, and on each side of them." Drake never returned, nor did any other Englishman for centuries.

Now, in which bay did *Golden Hind* spend those five golden weeks?

The Good Bay of Nova Albion

Numerous scholars and amateurs from California and elsewhere have attempted to answer this question. Each selects his bay and despises any other solution. And, after my short coastal reconnaissance, I have become as positive as any!

If we accept the contemporary statements that the bay lay on or around latitude 38° N, the choice boils down to Bodega Bay at 38°20′ N, Drake's Bay at 38°00′ N, and San Francisco Bay, entering by the Golden Gate at 37°49′ N.

Data available in the three contemporary accounts are as follows:

1. Drake hit the coast at or around latitude 43° N (Cape Arago) on 5 June, sailed southward looking for a suitable harbor to careen and repair *Golden Hind*, and found it between 38° and 38°30′ N on 17 June. These latitudes we must accept, for Drake and his pilots knew perfectly well how to take accurate sights ashore, and they had five weeks in which to find fair days and clear nights to shoot the sun and Polaris.

2. Fogs were common, and lasted for days on end; but the grass was still brown and the weather chilly.

3. "White bancks and cliffes which lie toward the sea" were seen, reminding Drake of the familiar south-coast cliffs in old England, and suggesting the name *Nova Albion*.

4. Fish, clams, mussels, and pocket gophers were abundant, and the natives ground meal out of a lily root.

5. Jodocus Hondius's map of about 1589–90 has an inset of *Portus Novae Albionis*. Everybody thinks this fits "his" bay neatly; and ingenious attempts have been made to identify it as Bodega Harbor, the Estero of Drake's Bay, and the part of San Francisco Bay where the

DRAKE IN CALIFORNIA
17 June - 23 July 1579

Track of USCG Cutters "Harris Point" and "Chico Point"
7-9 May 1973
with John Gordon, S. E. Morison and Emily Beck

Soundings in fathoms   Heights in feet
All modern navigational aids omitted

38°20'

40'   30'   20'   122°10'

38°10'

SAN
PABLO
BAY

38°N

Site of 1936 plate
"discovery" by Shinn

San Rafael ☐ ×

Pt. San Pedro

Point
St. Quentin

RICHMOND

le Pt.

Steep
Cliffs

nas Pt.   Duxbury Pt.

Mt. Tamalpais
2571

California Pt.

where
n Gate
d not
een

Bolinas
Bay

× 6
4 × ×
9

Bold and broken

1028

Tiburon

Angel I.

BERKELEY

7

14

11

5

FOUR FATHOM BANK

9

Pt. Bonita

Pt. Diablo

S   A   N

37°50'

OAKLAND

6

GOLDEN GATE

33

Fort Pt.

Alcatraz I.

Yerba
Buena I.

5

Pt.
Lobos

SAN
FRANCISCO
920

F   R   A   N   C   I   S   C   O

22

14   8

6

Point where Golden Gate
was no longer visible

7

13

10 fathom curve

San Bruno Mt.
1315

7

B   A   Y

37°40'

29

40'   30'   Pt. San Pedro   20'   122°10'

Hilly   Country

N
E
S

Brass Plate was last picked up. I cannot see any resemblance to any of them. It looks a bit like Trinidad Bay up north, but that was no place to careen a ship safely, and the three contemporary authorities state that the bay was at 38°30' or 38° N.

Rounding Cape Mendocino at latitude 40°26.5', the next good harbor you reach is Bodega Bay, latitude 38°20' N, one of the favorites. Bodega Head is a fist-like, conspicuous headland, altitude 228 feet. Passing it, sailing south, you find a narrow inlet with (nowadays) a dredged depth of seven feet at the entrance, leading into Bodega Harbor, home port for several hundred salmon-fishing boats. The neighboring country resembles the downs along the English Channel, but no more so than the country around Drake's Bay.

The absence of white cliffs is the principal reason for rejecting Bodega Bay as Drake's. The outer shores of the Tamales Peninsula are indeed bold, and the cliffs are of a pale gray color flecked with yellow, which might by a stretch of the imagination be called white; but they certainly do not resemble those of the south coast of old England. As for the long but shoal Tamales Bay running thirteen miles southeasterly from Bodega Bay, no careful seaman would have let his ship be trapped in that pocket.

Eighteen to twenty miles to the southward of Bodega Head, and right on latitude 38° N, is Point Reyes, protecting what is now officially called Drake's Bay. When we visited it in May 1973, we found the shores to be almost as wild and devoid of human touch as four centuries ago. The first thing that strikes one here are conspicuous white cliffs, highest on the coast, and closely resembling the group called the Seven Sisters of Beachy Head on the English Channel. In the northern bight of Drake's Bay there opens a shallow estuary now officially named Drake's Estero. Its mouth is now closed by a bar of sand and silt, but in the U. S. Coast Guard chart of 1860 it could be entered by a channel with least depth of eight feet, and there are records of coastal schooners using it as a refuge early in the twentieth century. The anchorage in the outer Bay is hard and bad,* but the Estero, with a good mud and sand bottom, is ample in extent and would have offered Drake a perfect shelter to careen and repair the

---

* In March 1973 the German training ship *Deutschland*, 4400 tons, anchored here hoping to clean up in preparation for an official visit to San Francisco, but found it too rough to launch a boat, and dragged her anchors.

Ketch *Little Revenge* rounding Point Reyes. Courtesy Drake Navigators Guild.

leaks in *Golden Hind*. George Davidson, professor of geodesy and astronomy at Berkeley, made a special study of Drake's California in the 1880's, and decided that he landed there, which led to both state and nation officially naming it Drake's Bay and Drake's Estero. I see no reason to disagree.

The subsequent history of Drake's Bay is interesting. Sixteen years after Drake's voyage, Sebastián Rodríguez Cermeño, in command of the Spanish ship *San Agustín*, examined this coast on his way from Manila to Mexico. *San Agustín* was cast away in November 1595 in this same bay, which her captain named San Francisco. In his narrative Cermeño reports three fathom of water on the bar to the Estero. He heard nothing about Drake from the Indians, who were still friendly, and saw nothing to suggest that anyone had been there before. He explored the Estero, which he valued largely for its supply of fresh

Ketch *Little Revenge* and the "white cliffs of Albion" in Drake's Bay. Courtesy Drake Navigators Guild.

water. Before he got around to bringing *San Agustín* inside, an onshore wind drove her on the beach and he never got her off. Some old ship timbers which are still in Drake's Bay may be hers. Cermeño then caused a pinnace (which he called a *luncha*) to be assembled on the spot, and in her sailed to Mexico, arriving 31 January 1596 at Acapulco with some eighty people on board. His name San Francisco has led to much confusion, but everyone now agrees that Cermeño's bay was the one now named Drake's.

The next important Spanish voyage thither was that of Sebastian Vizcaíno in January, 1603, Although first to chart the Farallons, Vizcaíno never sighted the Golden Gate, which was so named by John C. Frémont in 1849. The annual Manila galleons returning to Acapulco passed along this coast, within sight of the shore, for two hundred years, without ever seeing the Golden Gate. San Francisco Bay was finally discovered in 1769 by an overland expedition led by Gaspar de Portolá, the first Spanish governor of Alta California; and the first ship known to have entered it is Juan Manuel de Ayala's *San Carlos* in 1755.

No mariner who knows the California coast will find this surprising. The lay of the land is such that one can sail almost up to the Golden Gate without realizing that there is an opening; headlands and the Berkeley-Oakland hills look like a continuous land mass. On a clear May day in 1973 we could not see the Golden Gate when eight miles away, at the outer buoy to the dredged ship channel. Approaching it from the north, as Drake might have done had he clung to the coast

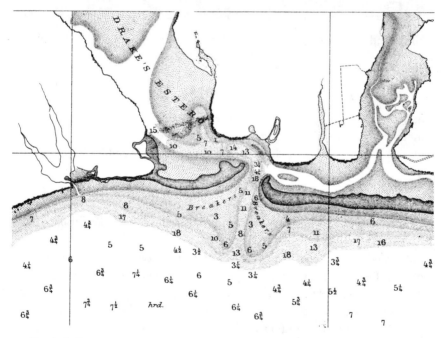

Drake's Estero, Drake's Bay. From U. S. Coast Guard Chart of 1860.

Nineteenth-century square-rigger entering Golden Gate. Courtesy Gabriel Moulin Studios.

before sighting the Farallons, one cannot see the Golden Gate three miles away. And that Drake could have entered this gorgeous bay, one of the world's finest, without describing it, is incredible. In the great gold rush of the 1850's it was not infrequent for sailing ships coming from Cape Horn to miss the Golden Gate and pile up on a rocky shore nearby. Innumerable cases of the sort could be cited; almost any seaman with experience of this coast will think it preposterous that Drake could have seen this entrance.

Nevertheless, there are many advocates for San Francisco Bay having been Drake's bay. Edward Everett Hale in Justin Winsor's *Narrative and Critical History*, predicted that "it will not be long, probably, before the question is decided," and "does not hesitate" to give the palm to San Francisco Bay. Too bad Dr. Hale could not have lived another fifty years, when he would have found the dispute blown sky-high and the site thrown into San Francisco's lap by the discovery of the now famous "Drake Plate of Brass."

My conclusion, and that of my shipmates on our brief examination of the Marin County coast, is that Drake's Bay is correctly so named; that here he spent five weeks, repaired *Golden Hind*, sang psalms for the Indians, and marched up country. The white cliffs like those of Albion "on the side of the sea" (from the Estero) were for us the determining factor. If Drake or any of his men had climbed Mount Tamalpais, they would have seen the magnificent panorama of San Francisco Bay and probably sailed in to investigate it; but Englishmen in those days did not climb a mountain for fun.

The Plate of Brass—or Was It Lead?

The World Encompassed states that Drake caused a plate of brass to be engraved with a record of his taking possession, and nailed it to a post, together with an English sixpence bearing Queen Elizabeth's effigy. *The Famous Voyage* in Hakluyt says substantially the same thing, without stating the metal of the plate. The *Anonymous Narrative*, however, says that in this "harborow where he grounded his ship to trim her, while they were graving of their ship . . . in this place Drake set up a greate post and nayled there on a sixpence which the contraye people woorshipped as if it had bin god [space] also he nayled upon this post a plate of lead and scratched therein the Queenes name."

So, brass or lead? Lead is the more probable, because every seagoing ship in that era carried sheet lead for covering leaks, keckling (wrapping) cables to prevent their chafing in a hawse-hole, and a variety of uses. Brass, on the other hand, was then little used on ships, and it would have been unusual to find a sheet of this size among the *Golden Hind*'s sea stores or in her shipboard forge.

For many years, Professor Herbert E. Bolton of the University of California at Berkeley, lecturing to his classes on early west coast history, quoted *The World Encompassed* story about the brass plate, and begged his students to keep their eyes open; and if it were found, bring it to him. Anyone with a knowledge of undergraduate humor would regard that as an invitation to a student "rag" or "gag."

In the summer of 1936 a man named Beryle Shinn picked up a tarnished brass plate "on a pile of rocks on the brow of a hill on the north shore of Corte Madera Inlet, in Marin County, overlooking the waters of San Francisco Bay," near San Quentin. He tossed it into the trunk of his car, thinking it might do for repairs; but in February 1937, a neighbor who had been a pupil of Professor Bolton, and who helped Shinn to cleanse it, noticed the name "Francis Drake." He then took it to Bolton, who promptly pronounced it genuine, as did Mr. Allen L. Chickering, president of the California Historical Society. Shinn played coy about selling the plate, but finally accepted $3500 as an "award," and the plate is now prominently displayed near the entrance to the Bancroft Library, Berkeley. Here is the inscription:

BEE IT KNOWNE VNTO ALL MEN BY THESE PRESENTS

IVNE 17 1579

BY THE GRACE OF GOD AND IN THE NAME OF HERR

MAIESTY QVEEN ELIZABETH OF ENGLAND AND HERR

SVCCESSORS FOREVER I TAKE POSSESSION OF THIS

KINGDOME WHOSE KING AND PEOPLE FREELY RESIGNE

THEIR RIGHT AND TITLE IN THE WHOLE LAND VNTO HERR

MAIESTIES KEEPEING NOW NAMED BY ME AN TO BEE

KNOWNE VNTO ALL MEN AS NOVA ALBION.

FRANCIS DRAKE

At the lower right corner is a jagged hole through which, presumably, the bemused Indians could see the effigy of their new queen on a silver sixpence.*

The place where Shinn found the plate has ever since been a leading argument of the proponents of San Francisco as having been Drake's

---

* Here, for comparison, is exactly what Fletcher wrote in *The World Encompassed* (Penzer ed., p. 62; facsimile ed., p. 80): "Before we went from thence, our Generall caused to be set vp a monument of our being there, as also of her maiesties and successors right and title to that kingdome; namely, a plate of brasse, fast nailed to a great and firme post; whereon is engrauen her graces name, and the day and yeare of our arriuall there, and of the free giuing vp of the prouince and kingdome, both by the king and people, into her maiesties hands: together with her highnesse picture and armes, in a piece of sixpence currant English monie, shewing itselfe by a hole made of purpose through the plate; vnderneath was likewise engrauen the name of our Generall, etc."

bay. But it is difficult to see what the Plate contributes to this argument. For, during the early publicity about this "discovery," a chauffeur named William Caldeira alleged that he had picked up the Plate in 1933 on a roadside about two and a half miles from the shore of Drake's Bay, washed it enough to see the word "Drake" but (since his employer was not interested) discarded it as useless about half a mile from the place where Shinn found it. Nobody seems to have reflected that a heavy object like a brass plate, after the post to which it was attached had rotted, would in the course of over 350 years have buried itself in the ground and been completely overgrown by turf; so if Caldeira found it on the surface, someone must have dug it up, or forged it, and placed it there. Shinn does indeed describe the position of his find as "embedded in the ground with a rock partly overlaying it"; but it could not have been deeply embedded since he saw a corner of it sticking out, and the rock was small enough for him to pick up and roll down the hill. Thus the claim of sundry writers that the Plate had been right there waiting, for 350 years, to be discovered, cannot be sustained:

Experts disagree as to whether or not the brass is contemporary with Drake. Analysis by Colin J. Fink of Columbia University and George R. Harrison of Massachusetts Institute of Technology, declared it to be hundreds of years old. But Henry R. Wagner, a practising metallurgist before he shifted to the less exact field of history, declared that, judging from its zinc content, this particular piece of brass could not have been more than sixty or seventy years old. And Professor Calley of Princeton, who also analyzed it, states that the zinc content was much too great for it to have been Elizabethan. A faker could have picked it up in an old junk shop.

Apart from provenance, the contents condemn the Plate as a fraud. No such odd lettering, especially the capital B which resembles a four-paned window, can be found in the British Isles. Mr. Reginald Haselden, curator of manuscripts at the Huntington Library at the time of the discovery, declared it to be a forgery. Experts in the British Museum pronounced it an undoubted fake; no such letter forms for the M and N exist in Elizabethan graffiti or manuscripts. The language, too, is wrong for the era. "By the Grace of God" should have come after "Elizabeth" and before "of England," as anyone with

Drake's or Fletcher's education would have known.* Among other spellings, *herr*, used twice, is also suspect. The *New English Dictionary*, V, 228, gives over twenty different spellings to this possessive of the pronoun *she*, but not one of them is *herr*. I am reminded of the remark of an eminent philologist at Copenhagen with whom I discussed alleged runic inscriptions in America: "If you dig up an alleged Greek vase sitting on a telephone directory, there is no need to argue further." Since the letters and language of the Drake Plate are not of the period, there is no sense quibbling about the age of the brass or who picked it up and where.

In my opinion, the Plate is a hoax perpetrated by some collegiate joker who knew little about Drake except what he had heard from Dr. Bolton and read in one of the modern editions of *The World Encompassed*. He naturally chose that text to be blown up for the inscription, tried to give it a "quaint" look by odd lettering and spelling, then dropped it at a place where it was likely to be picked up. "Drake's Plate of Brass" is as successful a hoax as the Piltdown Man or the Kensington Rune Stone.

Voyage Home

On 24 July 1579, the day after *Golden Hind* left her anchorage, she sighted the Farallon Islands and "called them the Islands of St. James," as it was the vigil of that saint's feast. They landed on the Southeast Farallon, the biggest, whose 350-foot hill, from a distance, looks like a miniature Rock of Gibraltar. Here Drake topped off his provisions with sea-lion meat and the eggs and flesh of numerous wild fowl which nest there. This seems an odd thing to do at the beginning of a long voyage; but maybe the native provisions obtained at Drake's bay were deemed insufficient.

Golden Hind made a westerly passage of sixty-five or sixty-six days without sighting land. Her first call was on 30 September at a group of islands where the natives were great thieves and pestered the English sailors by hurling stones at them from outrigger dugouts. One remembers Magellan's experience at Guam in the Ladrones; but Fletcher gives the latitude as "about" 8° N, which won't do for Guam, latitude

* For instance, the grant to Adrian Gilbert in 1583 begins, "Elizabeth, by the Grace of God, of England, France and Ireland Queene."

My Drake Reconnaissance. The Morison Team: Emily Beck; Lt. Roger
Piquet, USN; Lt. Commander John Gordon, USNR.

The Southeast Farallon.

13° N. It was probably an island of the Pelew or Palau group. From this Isle of Thieves, *Golden Hind* sailed along the south coast of Mindanao and then took off for the fabulous Ternate, where the ships of Magellan and Loaysa had tarried after the death of their captain general. Drake found Ternate to be much the same as Elcano had reported it sixty years earlier. The rajah, Babù by name, sent out to check the strange ship and, having ascertained that she was neither Spanish nor Portuguese, invited her into port, sending four big canoes to tow her in during a calm. Babù was enchanted to open trade with a rival to the monopolizing Portuguese. He flew into a rage when Drake declined to pay heavy export duty on six tons of cloves that he bought, but the Captain appeased him with valuable gifts and discussed the possibility of setting up an English factory at Ternate.

Drake spent but four or five days at Ternate, departing 6 November 1579. *Golden Hind* again needed a complete bottom-cleansing and rummaging, so Drake sought out an uninhabited island to do it.* He found one, which the men called Crab Island because it was full of big king crabs, "One whereof was sufficient for hungrie stomachs at a dinner." Drake stayed there twenty-six days, "a wonderful refreshing to our wearied bodies." Upon departing, he left behind two blacks he had picked up somewhere in the eastern seas, "and likewise the negro wench Maria, being gotten with childe in the ship." Maria had been a slave to Francisco Zárate and as she had been on board about eight months, Fletcher's statement is probably correct. Drake's purpose in leaving these three on the isle of the king crabs, says the *Anonymous Narrative*, was to start a settlement. What became of the marooned blacks we know not.

Departing Crab Island 12 December, *Golden Hind* followed the east coast of Celebes, blown by the northeast monsoon. On the night of 8 or 9 January 1580, Drake almost lost his ship and his voyage. *Golden Hind* ran on a shelving reef off shore. To get her off, he jettisoned several big bronze cannon, half his precious cargo of Ternate cloves, and even some sacks of flour and beans; but nothing could move her. Then Preacher Fletcher tried prayer and administered holy communion to

---

*Heaving down and graving left a ship and her company as defenseless as a lobster changing its shell; that is why captains from Columbus down, if unable to do it in a friendly civilized port, had to seek out a lonely spot. Drake's place is identified by Wagner as one of the small islands in the Banggai archipelago.

every member of the crew, which now numbered but fifty-eight. That seems to have done the trick. The wind changed, and by setting all sail, the ship slid off into deep water and resumed her voyage, undamaged. The poor parson, instead of being thanked for invoking divine aid, was disgraced for remarking, when things looked very bad, that this accident was divine punishment for the execution of Doughty. Drake, incensed, played God himself, excommunicated the minister from the Church of England, and condemned him to wear about his arm a paper declaring, "FRANCIS FLETCHER YE FALSEST KNAVE THAT LIVETH." But Drake seldom stayed angry long, and within a few days Fletcher was again leading shipboard prayers and preaching sermons.

Golden Hind, following much the same course as Elcano's *Victoria* sixty years earlier, called frequently and with no trouble at Moslem-held islands for provisions, Drake even signing treaties with the local rajahs. At Tjilatjap, Java, "as many as nine kings came and entered the vessel," and were much pleased with the music and the banquets that the Englishmen gave them. From there, she crossed the Indian Ocean, rounded the Cape of Good Hope about 18 June 1580, and, avoiding the islands under Spanish or Portuguese sovereignty, called at a river mouth in Sierra Leone to replenish water (which was down to half a pint a day for three men), and provisions. It is obvious that Drake had learned from Pigafetta's narrative, a copy of which he had on board, the urgent necessity of keeping his crew well fed. Sailing from Sierra Leone 24 July, *Golden Hind* avoided the usual route of Portuguese East Indiamen returning home, and sailed into Plymouth on 26 September 1580, the day of full moon. It was three years less eleven weeks since the day she left England.

The first question Drake is said to have asked ashore was about the health of his Queen. For he sensed that had she died, he might be repudiated as an unauthorized pirate. His second request was to straighten out his calendar; for, like Elcano, he had lost a day sailing west and could not make out why.

By any standards, this was a great and memorable voyage, even though it came sixty years later than Magellan's and brought meager results in actual discovery. Drake had shown consummate seamanship throughout. He had kept most of his men alive, well fed, and healthy. Despite one non-stop run of sixty-three days in the Atlantic, two of fifty and sixty-eight days in the Pacific, and a third of at least seven weeks' duration in the Indian Ocean and South Atlantic, they suffered very little from illness. Only seventeen men, including those killed in brawls with Indians or Spaniards, lost their lives during the voyage. That is a remarkably good record for the sixteenth century, or indeed for the next two centuries. Moreover, he took good care of his ship, heaving her down often enough to keep her bottom clean and tight. For his countrymen he opened a new seaway to wealth and glory in the East Indies. The proposed English "factory" at Ternate was never set up; but after a few years, both English and Dutch were plucking the feathers of Portugal in the Far East.

Golden Hind brought home more valuable plunder than any ship of any nation, prior to Cavendish's prize *Santa Ana*. Exactly how much, historians have been unable to figure out because there was a great deal of smuggling bars of silver ashore at night. She sailed to London in November 1580 and unloaded considerable bar silver at the Tower. Drake had already delivered some of it to a royal treasury official, who stowed it in Saltash Castle at Plymouth, and he sent a few horse-loads of silver and gold to Sion House, Richmond, where the Queen was staying, as a harbinger of plenty to come.

Bernardo de Mendoza, the Spanish ambassador to England, made every effort to persuade Elizabeth to repudiate Drake and return his booty to Spain. Characteristically, she stalled him along for months, not being ready for a complete breach with Spain, and in the meantime secretly ordered £10,000 of the spoil, lying in the Tower, to be delivered to Drake personally. Wagner estimated the total value of his booty in gold, silver, and precious stones at 950,000 *pesos d'oro*, equivalent to £332,000 in the currency of the day; contemporary rumor, which Treasurer Tremayne vainly tried to verify by interrogating leading members of the crew, put it at £1,500,000. A good part went to the government; but the "undertakers" who paid for fitting out the fleet at an estimated cost of £4000, were said to have received 1000 per cent on their investment.

Drake enjoyed the Queen's personal favor to a high degree, and he presented her with a diamond cross and a new crown made of Peruvian silver and emeralds. At her orders he was knighted on 4 April 1581 on the deck of his flagship at Deptford. That marked her defiance to Spain, and the beginning of Philip II's organization of the "invincible armada" to conquer England and depose Elizabeth. Drake bought Buckland Abbey in his ancestral county of Devon, where he set himself up as a country gentleman. His first wife (Mary Newman) having died in 1583, he married, two years later, Elizabeth Sydenham. They left no children; but Drake's heir, his brother Thomas, is ancestor to the present Drake family.

Sir Francis never ceased to work for further humiliation of Spain, and of his activities after 1581 we have written briefly in *Northern Voyages*. He took a leading part in the defeat of the Spanish Armada, and sailed to the West Indies on his last cruise against the dons in 1595. The following year he died of yellow fever on board his flagship off Nombre de Dios, Panama, and was buried at sea.

During his lifetime and ever since, Drake became a folk hero to the English, in a class with King Alfred and Lord Nelson; and rightly so. He loved God, loved England and hated her enemies, loved the sea, loved fighting, loved fame and fortune. The late Alfred Noyes wrote an epic on Drake in twelve books, and tells in his poem "The Admiral's Ghost" of the Devonshire tradition that Nelson was one of them. Another legend of the gallant captain is told in "Drake's Drum," Sir Henry Newbolt's poem:—

> Drake he's in his hammock an' a thousand mile away,
>   (Capten, art tha sleepin' there below?),
> Slung atween the round shot in Nombre Dios Bay,
>   An' dreamin' arl the time o' Plymouth Hoe.
> Yarnder lumes the Island, yarnder lie the ships,
>   Wi' sailor lads a-dancin' heel-an'-toe,
> An' the shore-lights flashin', an' the night-tide dashin',
>   He sees et arl so plainly as he saw et long ago.
> Drake he was a Devon man, an' ruled the Devon seas,
>   (Capten, art tha sleepin' there below?),
> Rovin' tho' his death fell, he went wi' heart at ease,
>   An' dreamin' arl the time o' Plymouth Hoe.
> "Take my drum to England, hang et by the shore,
>   Strike et when your powder's runnin' low;
> IF THE DONS SIGHT DEVON, I'LL QUIT THE PORT O' HEAVEN,
>   AN' DRUM THEM UP THE CHANNEL AS WE DRUMMED THEM LONG AGO."

Bibliography and Notes

DRAKE'S ANCHORAGE

George Davidson, *Identification of Sir Francis Drake's Anchorage on the Coast of California* (San Francisco, 1890), with old maps well reproduced, and plenty of personal observation. He favored the 43° N landfall and Drake's Bay.*

Alexander G. McAdie, "Nova Albion, 1579," American Antiquarian Society *Proceedings*, n.s., XXVIII (1918), 18–98. McAdie, an eminent meteorologist, made many trips by sail and steam along the west coast with Drake's course in mind. He argues for the 43° landfall; thinks Drake could never have made latitude 38° in 12 days from latitude 48° N. He mistook dense white fog in the hills for snow, as did Captain Cook, and tourists still do. But the only really white cliffs are on Drake's Bay. Sailing thence to the Southeast Farallon, he could not possibly have seen the Golden Gate. McAdie tried many times to sight it from a few miles out but never could, though he knew where the opening was; Mount Tamalpais and the hills about San Francisco Bay "blend into one skyline," and in the summer months the entrance is usually blanketed by fog, which prevents one's seeing the Golden Gate until right on top of it (p. 195 and note 5). McAdie recorded the fog at Point Reyes between 13 June and 23 July for five successive years and found 97 days of fog and 98 of no fog. Davidson did this in 1859 and found fog over Point Reyes for 39 consecutive days and nights (p. 197). Fletcher says that Drake's crew for 14 consecutive days and nights could not take sights of sun or star. That would never fit upper San Francisco Bay.

Cape Arago is the conclusion of Mr. Raymond Aker of the Drake Navigators' Guild, after exhaustive research into winds, currents, early sources, and secondary accounts, in which I concur. *The World Encompassed* and John Drake's statement that *Golden Hind* made landfall at lat. 48° N, south of Cape Flattery and the entrance to the Juan de Fuca Strait, must be a mistake.

Trinidad Harbor on lat. 41°03′ N, identified by Wagner (p. 154) as *Portus Novae Albionis*, is not a real harbor but a high cape which affords protection from the northwest wind only. Drake may well have called there, sent a boat ashore and looked around; but what he wanted was a harbor protected from the wind, and a beach where he could safely careen *Golden Hind*. No mariner in his senses, especially one so experienced as Drake, would have done this on an exposed beach like that of Trinidad Bay.

F. W. Howay (ed.), *The Journal of Captain James Colnett Aboard the Argonaut* (Champlain Society *Publications*, Montreal, 1940), p. 174.

Commander John Gordon, who acompanied me on my search for the authentic bay, on his sail from Japan to California in 1952, made landfall on 15 July at Point Reyes light. Becalmed next morning off the Duxbury Reef bell buoy, the Golden Gate 8.5 miles to the southeast, was invisible; nor could he see it until he rounded Bonita Point.

"Drake's Drum" is from Sir Henry Newbolt, *Poems New and Old* (London, 1933), reprinted by permission of John Murray, Ltd.

* Also, his *Methods and Results. Voyages of Discovery . . . on the Northwest Coast of America, 1539–1603* (Washington, 1887).

Trinidad Head and harbor. Courtesy Drake Navigators Guild.

THE PLATE OF BRASS

The subject has become so emotional as to lead to exaggeration and misrepresentation. The favorite argument of the pros is the close resemblance of the Plate's language to that of *The World Encompassed*. To me this proves the contrary: the faker had access to one of the several editions of this book and based his plate inscription on it.

The phony orthography has never, to my knowledge, been ventilated in print, but the Huntington Library has furnished me with a typed article "Some Further Notes on Drake's Plate of Brass," written by Captain R. B. Haselden after he had submitted photographs of it to authorities at the British Museum, and to Professor Vincent T. Harlow of Oxford; as well as the replies of Harlow and Professor Earle R. Calley of the Frick Chemical Laboratory, Princeton University. "Nobody has been able to produce any examples of the curious m's and n's which appear on the Plate. The British Museum authorities state that they cannot parallel these letters with any Elizabethan writing, inscription, or printing." Or, for that matter, the capital B like a four-paned window. The style, too, is wrong for the period; the date should have been put at the end, not the beginning. The first line, beginning, "Bee it knowne," was evidently an afterthought: "It is unbelievable that Drake or any of the gentlemen of his party would have allowed a proclamation of such great importance to be so crudely

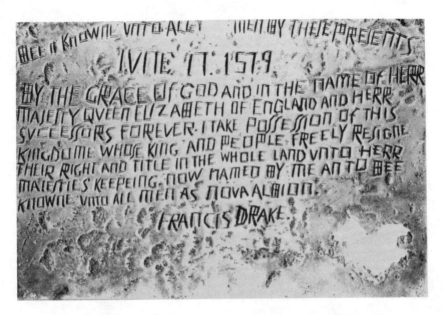

The Plate of Brass. Courtesy Bancroft Library.

worded," said Harlow. And I agree with Wagner's opinion at the time of ahe Shinn "discovery," that the Drake Plate is a complete and clumsy hoax.

California Historical Society Special Publications No. 13, *Drake's Plate of Brass* (1937), with articles by Bolton and Waters, excerpts from the three contemporary narratives, and bibliography; No. 14 (1938), *Drake's Plate of Brass Authenticated*, Report by Colin G. Fink et al.; No. 25 (1953): *The Plate of Brass*, combining Nos. 13 and 14, with an account of exploration of 16th-century Indian mounds in Drake's Bay by Clement W. Meighan and Robert F. Heizer (pp. 78–81). They turned up artifacts that must have come from Cermeño's *San Agustín*, wrecked there in 1595, but nothing that can be connected with Drake. Greenbrae on San Francisco Bay, where Shinn picked up the Plate, has also been thoroughly excavated, with negative results.

Fink and Polushkin in *The Plate of Brass*, pp. 51–52, report that certain letters have been distorted by being gouged with a sharp tool. At the left of FRANCIS DRAKE is an almost obliterated C or G. Re-examining the Plate in May 1973, I concluded that the faker started to scratch CAPTAIN or GENERAL, but gave it up.

Robert H. Power, "A Case for San Francisco Bay," California Historical Society *Quarterly*, LII (Summer, 1973), pp. 100–28, puts this case very persuasively. He argues that the Hondius map's *Portus Novae Albionis* fits the upper bay perfectly. In "The Significance of Francis Drake's Discovery of San Francisco Bay in 1579," as yet unpublished, Mr. Power links Gilbert's western voyage of 1583 to Drake's Nova Albion, using Parmenius's Latin poem (see my *Northern Voyages*, pp. 572, 580) as evidence. Both, he argues, were part of an imperial plan to link up the two coasts into a northern viceroyalty to stop the Spaniards' advance.* See also Fleet Admiral Chester W. Nimitz USN, *Drake's Cove*, (California Academy of Sciences, n.d.), well illustrated; and Walter A. Starr, "Drake Landed in San Francisco Bay," California Historical Society *Quarterly* XLI (1962), No. 3. On the natives, Robert F. Heizer and William W. Elmendorf, "Drake's California Anchorage in Light of the Indian Language Spoken There," *Pacific Historical Review*, XI (1942), 213–17.

Francis P. Farquhar, "Sir Francis Drake and the Plate of Brass" (paper dictated August 1971), argues cogently that Drake needed a place to grave his ship where she would not be seen by a passing Spaniard. Granted, but wouldn't the Estero have served?

THE CERMEÑO EXPEDITION

Raymond Aker, *The Cermeño Expedition at Drake's Bay, 1595*. A Research Report of the Drake Navigators' Guild (mimeographed, 1965, and well ilustrated), is a fine example of honest and thorough research. Cermeño was probably a Portuguese who had been captured on the Manila galleon *Santa Ana* in 1587, but released and restored to his former service. His ship *San Agustín* sailed from Manila 5 July 1595, hit the California coast at Latitude 43° N in late October, and anchored in Drake's Bay 6 November.

* Mr. Power's thesis is supported by the world map in the Paul Mellon collection at Upperville, Virginia, dated conjecturally 1587, part of which we have reproduced.

✳ XXIX ✳

The Voyages of
Sarmiento de Gamboa

1571-1589

Pedro Sarmiento de Gamboa

Pedro Sarmiento de Gamboa, possibly the most talented and versatile Spanish navigator of the sixteenth century, achieved fame not only as mariner but as poet, historian, and antiquary. Born in Galicia about 1532, he was brought up in the house of his parents at Pontevedra. After serving a term in the Spanish army, he sought his fortune in the Indies and settled in Peru before he was twenty-one. Somehow he acquired enough education to enable him, much later, to carry on a two-hour conversation in Latin with Queen Elizabeth I. During the seven years that he held a minor office in the viceregal government at Lima, Pedro studied the history and antiquities of the Incas. In fact he learned too much for his health; the Inquisition in Peru persecuted him for years on various frivolous pretexts, and he had to appeal to the Pope to escape banishment.

Pedro's maritime career began in 1567, when he sailed as flag captain in Álvaro de Mendaña's famous voyage which discovered the Solomon Islands, and named Guadalcanal. When Don Francisco de Toledo became viceroy of Peru in 1569, Sarmiento became one of his favorites; and when *Golden Hind* arrived at Callao in 1579, he took part in the unsuccessful pursuit of the Englishmen. Upon his return to Callao the

Viceroy decided to fit out an expedition for two objects: to catch Drake if he returned the way he came, and to explore not only the Strait of Magellan but the neighboring coasts of Chile, in search of localities suitable for placing garrisons to prevent future irruptions by the English or others. To the command of this expedition he appointed Pedro Sarmiento de Gamboa, whom he regarded as the most expert seaman and loyal subject in Peru.

The Viceroy purchased two ships then at Callao, named the larger (the *capitana* or flagship), *Nuestra Señora de Esperanza;* and the smaller (the *almiranta*),* *San Francisco.* Neither was a big ship. Sarmiento sailed as Captain General and captain of *Nuestra Señora;* with him were six officers, including a "venerable person," the Franciscan Antonio Guadranibo, and two pilots, Antón Pablos and Hernando Alonso. His total complement numbered fifty-four. *San Francisco,* commanded by Juan de Villalobos, carried five officers and 49 men; thus the fleet complement numbered 108, not counting blacks and Indian servants. One or the other carried a small knocked-down bergantina in her hold. Each ship mounted two pieces of artillery, and in the arms racks were forty arquebuses, numerous pikes, and other small arms. He carried materials for making *escaupiles,* the quilted jackets which had replaced steel armor as a more efficient defense against arrows.

Sarmiento's little squadron sailed from the Isla San Lorenzo off Callao on 12 October 1579 and steered south in search of "El Draque," who by that date was somewhere in the North Pacific. Shortly they discovered that the bow planking of the flagship had not been caulked, thus admitting a dangerous amount of water. They were forced to put in at Pisco to make repairs, especially in the bows where the Callao shipwrights had cheated, and Sarmiento signed on a caulker who (as he informs us) received "a wage and a half," 37 pesos a month. More provisions were purchased there by Sarmiento, including 200 jars of the local wine, half to each ship, at 4½ pesos per jar; and wine is one thing that never gave out on his voyage. Sailing from Pisco 21 October 1579, the two ships enjoyed fresh and fair winds for several days. The Captain General issued the usual instructions for the *almiranta* to report to him every evening, and to follow his flag signals by day and his

* Whilst the English then called a flagship "The Admirall," Spain reserved *almiranta* for the second in command.

lanterns by night. But Juan de Villalobos, captain of *San Francisco*, early showed insubordination, and Sarmiento rightly anticipated that he was seeking an excuse to cut and run back to Peru, as had happened to Ladrillero and others.

Sarmiento was a careful and accurate navigator who with his two pilots "took the sun" with his astrolabe every fair day, and the Southern Cross every clear night, to keep track of his latitude. He observed that many mistakes were made by pilots' not shooting the sun at its full meridian altitude, and recommended that "you should wait with astrolabe in hand, until, by looking through the sights, you see it is passing the zenith." He decried the current practice in Spain of fiddling with the compass needles so that North on the card would be true north, well observing that owing to regional differences in variation, this did more harm than good.

After a long stretch of fair wind—the fleet in one day making sixty-two leagues—there blew up a northerly gale in which they scudded under half-lowered courses, with topmasts housed, and preventer backstays rigged to the masts. Suddenly the wind changed to South, and it grew very chilly. On 17 November 1579 they sighted two capes: Cabos Primero and Tres Puntas, and between them a wide opening which he named after the Holy Trinity. It is still El Golfo Trinidad. Sarmiento decided to enter, partly as a refuge from the sea, partly in hope of finding a sheltered back passage to the Strait of Magellan, some three degrees to the southward.

Sarmiento's exploration of the inland waterways of southern Chile, was not unique; we have seen Ladrillero and Hojea doing it twelve years earlier. But Sarmiento's was the most thorough, lasting from 18 November 1579 to mid-January 1580. The first good port he named Nuestra Señora del Rosario; and another nearby, where they almost dragged ashore, Puerto Peligroso—but the sailors called it *Cacho-diablo*, "devil's smack." Sarmiento left *San Francisco* at Rosario and took his flagship on the intricate course shown on our chart.

His technique was to find a good anchorage for *Esperanza*, then shove off in the longboat with both pilots and fourteen men to row or fight if need be, carrying provisions for a week; but they were often away ten days or more. His object was to spy out a channel; for a view ahead he climbed a mountain when the weather was clear.

The crew, spending nights ashore in the cold rain, suffered hunger and thirst and underwent numerous hairbreadth escapes, for which the Captain General never failed to thank the Heavenly Host both by prayer and chant. On 22 November he staged an unusually elaborate taking-possession, singing both *Te Deum Laudamus* and the ancient hymn *Vexilla Regis;* and he erected numerous small crosses as he went along. Unique (so far as I have observed) among Spanish master mariners, he frequently gives credit and sympathy to his subordinates and to the common sailors, viz:

"The poor fellows arrived wet and tired with rowing, and without the means of changing their clothes"; "with great strength of arm the good and valiant sailors stemmed the current and doubled a cape which a galley would have found it hard work to get around." "Antón Pablos worked like a very good pilot, and a very careful and vigilant man, without resting day or night; besides the hard work there was the wet and the great cold, from which the sailors suffered very much, and it almost came to a point where they would succumb. But God showed us His favor, and made them stout men and true, and hard workers, attending to what the pilot ordered with alacrity."

A glance at our map will tell more of what Sarmiento explored than any amount of description. His first boat journey took him on 8 December, the feast of Our Lady's conception, into a broad channel which he appropriately called Canal de Concepción, and the name has endured. This took him to a good harbor that he named Puerto Bermejo, apparently from the reddish rocks. Sarmiento made a full report of the fauna and flora, similar to those of the Strait, and including the Steamboat Duck and the Antarctic Evergreen Beech.

On his third boat voyage, in mid-December, Sarmiento continued past Puerto Bermejo to a rock that he named *Roca Partida,** at the mouth of the Canal de Concepción. On one of his southward boat journeys, through the channel since named after him, he observed on the port hand a crest of snowy mountains, an offshoot of the Andes; they too are now called Sarmiento.

San Francisco, having moved south to Puerto Bermejo for her bergantina-building operation, was encountered again on Christmas Eve 1579, and the crews of both ships kept the Feast of the Nativity to-

* I cannot find this on a modern chart.

What Sarmiento saw: Bahia Tuesday and islet; Bahia Wodsworth; Glacier descending to Strait.

gether. Sarmiento here ascertained that Villalobos had been deliberately squandering provisions in order to have an excuse to return to Chile.

After a long and interesting colloquy with the pilots as to whether it was worth while to search more inner passages in the hope of finding the Strait, Sarmiento wisely decided to make for it by the open sea. They were now at latitude 50°30′ S, and he knew that Cabo Pilar was at about 53° S. Their final search for the Strait began on 21 January 1580 when flagship *Nuestra Señora de Esperanza*, almiranta *San Francisco*, and the newly built bergantina, departed Puerto Bermejo. The bergantina must have been very small, since she was manned by one pilot and seven men, and the flagship could tow her. The following night a furious wind made up from the northwest as they were passing Cape Santiago. The people in the bergantina were having such a hard time keeping afloat that next morning Sarmiento hove-to the flagship, using his capstan to haul the small craft alongside; and as it was too rough to keep her in that position, he made all the crew of the little vessel jump overboard and be rescued by grabbing lines thrown to them. Only one man was lost in this operation. The next day was frightfully blowy and rough, and only pilot Pablos's skillful handling kept her from going on the rocks. On the third day, when they were less than three leagues from a visible shore, the wind suddenly ceased, and the swell set her horribly near the coast. Then, just in time, a fair, light, offshore wind sprang up and saved them. This must have been somewhere on the west shore of the big island now called Hanover. They passed Cabo Santa Lucía, which Sarmiento had named on one of his boat voyages.

On 30 January 1580 Sarmiento rounded Cabo Pilar and five miles within the Strait found a little bight open to the north which he entered, anchored in fifteen fathom, and named Bahia de Gracia; it is called Bahia Tuesday on the modern chart. Here, for a change, the holding ground of white clay held so well that they had trouble breaking out their anchor.

Through the Strait and to Spain

In the meantime, Villalobos in *San Francisco* had carried out his secret plan and deserted. He seems to have returned safely to Peru.

The bergantina having been cast adrift, Sarmiento now had only his flagship and her longboat. He made an interesting traverse of the Strait, which he tried to have renamed Madre de Dios as a tribute to the Virgin Mother who had saved him; but Philip II would not allow it. Our captain seems to have had little or no information from earlier traverses, and he repeated no name already given to the Strait except Magellan's Cabo Vírgenes. But a number of his own new names have endured.

A few miles up-Strait from his first anchorage he entered what is probably now Bahia Wodsworth * on 2 February 1580, Candlemas Day, and so named it Candelaria. Here he met his first natives, who were cautious but friendly, and told him by signs of ships by "bearded people like us," who had called there the previous year—obviously Drake's. In return for the usual trading truck they gave Sarmiento some hemstitched strips of cloth which the Englishmen had given to them.

In a strong blow two strands of two anchor cables parted, and *Nuestra Señora* had to ride to a small hawser with strands only as thick as one's thumb. This so discouraged the pilots and the men that they urged Sarmiento to turn back, but he resolutely pressed on. They

---

* Wodsworth is described in the Chilean *Derrotero,* IV, 116, as "one of the best anchorages in the western Strait."

Pacific side of Desolation Island with its four points and Twelve Apostles Rocks. James F. Nields photo.

Scenery at Pacific end of Strait. James F. Nields photos.

was rewarded by the Antarctic summer bringing warm weather, even "as hot as Spain in July." After noting the native name Xaultegua Bay (which is still on the map) on the port hand, they cleared Desolation Island on 8 February and passed inside Carlos III Island, frequently pausing to set up crosses and climb mountains for the view ahead. On an island which Narborough later named after a Stuart prince they saw a high mountain "which the old narratives call the Bell of Roldán." That was Magellan's gunner who climbed a mountain from which the South Sea was visible; but this identification with Roldán must have been wrong, for one cannot sight the Pacific from so far to the eastward. Sarmiento rounded Cape Froward, naming it *Santa Agueda*, and a point which he named, and is still called, *Santa Ana*. This marked the harbor where in 1584 he pitched his second colony, Rey Don Felipe. At the river here, which he named San Juan, he performed an unusually detailed act of possession, depositing in a bottle a paper listing every man on board ship—12 officers, 12 soldiers, and 20 sailors besides "negroes, mulattos and Indian servants." No later navigator is reported to have found any of Sarmiento's many crosses and other records so elaborately prepared and carefully deposited.

Here the character of the Strait changed, and Sarmiento made the sage observation that the grassland would make good sheep pasture. At one point his men had a scuffle with some Patagonian "giants" and managed to kidnap one. This man survived the voyage to Spain and was presented to Philip II.

Passing the site of Punta Arenas and Drake's Elizabeth Island, *Nuestra Señora* threaded the Second Narrows and rounded Cabo San Gregorio, so named by Sarmiento. On the nearby shore they had a scuffle with natives armed with bows and arrows, one of which "struck the General between the eyes" but did him so little harm as to confirm Pigafetta's statement that there was not much power in Patagonian archery. Next, passing through the First Narrows, they entered the Bay of the Eleven Thousand Virgins, a name bestowed by Magellan. After a narrow escape from running aground, in which Sarmiento revealed that his ship drew eighteen feet, they rounded Cabo Vírgines twenty-four days from entering the Strait at Cabo Pilar. The weather was fair and the light wind westerly, but they passed an anxious night until well clear of the land. "The Pilots, Antón Pablos and Hernando Alonso," wrote Sarmiento, "did nothing but sound all night; at dawn their hands, and those of the sailors who assisted them, were quite benumbed from heaving and hauling in the lead out of the cold water." This is one of the many human touches which endear Sarmiento to sailors, most of whom have experienced the same thing prior to the invention of the echo-sounder. When one enters the Strait from the Atlantic, warned Sarmiento, "The approach should be made very carefully, and one should not go near the land on the starboard hand," i.e. the north side, "without the lead always in the chains, and with every precaution." Excellent advice!

The rest of the voyage, to Spain, was far from uneventful. On 31 March 1580, Sarmiento made himself a cross-staff to ascertain his longitude by measuring the angular distance between a full moon and the rising sun, and found his ship to be 18 degrees west of the meridian of Seville. This is the earliest recorded instance of taking "lunars" at sea, excepting Vespucci's phony one; unfortunately we cannot correct it, since we know not his real position. He also made latitude observations at night of the Southern Cross, evidently having on board a Portuguese *Regimento* for that constellation.

Sarmiento had earlier taken part in a longitude computation at Lima in 1578 by timing an eclipse and comparing it with the almanac's calculated time of it at Seville. The result: 4 hours 56 minutes or 74 degrees was about three degrees too far west. This, however, was a great improvement over earlier efforts at Jamaica and Mexico City. Columbus made an error of 39°37′, and the Mexican savants in 1541 were about 25°30′ off.*

In the first week of April, *Nuestra Señora* made Ascension Island in mid-Atlantic. Sarmiento went ashore, noted graves of shipwrecked Portuguese sailors, and his men caught turtles and a quantity of fish which they salted down. Here he made another longitude observation which placed Ascension Island only three degrees west of the meridian of Cadiz; but 8°06′ is the correct difference.

Departing Ascension on 11 April, he sighted the coast of Sierra Leone on the 28th but did not stop, owing to that region's already bad reputation for engendering fevers. Even so, several men suffered fevers and scurvy when they entered the great heat of the equatorial calms. After a smart brush with a French pirate ship which never got close enough to board, *Nuestra Señora de Esperanza* entered Santiago, Cape

* See my *Admiral of the Ocean Sea*, I, 243; II, 406.

de Verdes, on 23 May 1580. There the men were well received, in spite of disgust at their filthy and ragged clothes. They performed their pilgrimage vows, took in water and provisions, and caulked and graved their ship. Sarmiento continued his course northward and made Terceira in the Azores on 18 July. Joining some ships returning from Mexico, he sailed from the Azores on 3 August and made landfall six leagues north of Cape St. Vincent on the 15th. On 19 August 1580 they arrived Sanlúcar de Barrameda.

So ended one of the most interesting voyages of the sixteenth century, but not, as we shall see, one of the more productive.

Return Passage under Flores

On Sarmiento's strong recommendation, Philip II decided to fortify and colonize the Strait of Magellan, and to that end organized a formidable expedition. He appointed Sarmiento governor and captain general of the Strait, but over him placed D. Diego Flores de Valdés, knight of the Order of Santiago, as captain general. The fleet included three vessels belonging to the new governor of Chile, D. Alonso de Sotomayor. His Majesty's galleas *San Crístoval* served as flagship, and the king lent him four other vessels described as fragatas. Sarmiento's *Nuestra Señora de Esperanza* (with Antón Pablos as chief pilot) went along, and sixteen chartered ships (names unknown), some of which Sarmiento reported to be old, rotten and unseaworthy. Complaining of this to D. Diego Flores, the captain general replied, in effect, "What do you care? you do not have to sail in one of them." "A nice reply!" snorted Sarmiento.

He went to Portugal to order plans for the Strait forts from a famous engineer located there, and was helped by the third Duke of Alba, of Netherlands fame. The historian Herrera reports that Alba opposed the entire scheme; he knew too well how vulnerable fortresses were. Sarmiento had full charge of engaging pilots and other officers and found them hard to recruit, as neither gold nor other things of value could be expected on a colonizing venture. When their patriotism and loyalty were appealed to, said Sarmiento, the "bad characters," were wont to reply, *Ni el Rey da vida ni sana heridas*—"The King neither gives life nor cures wounds." He complained, in his *Concise Narrative* of this voyage, that Flores did everything possible to thwart him, even refusing to take most of his baggage on board Sarmiento also spent many hours at the Casa de Contratación in Seville, examining, correcting, and copying charts (they then had on file those of Magellan, Ladrillero, and others, long since destroyed), and himself drafted twenty-three new charts and a new *padrón real*. The ships were amply provided with astrolabes, cross-staffs, needles, and other navigational instruments. And, to construct forts at the Strait, Sarmiento recruited 111 masons, carpenters, gunners, and blacksmiths at ten ducats a month. To accommodate so many people, the second or orlop deck on each big ship must have been fitted with tiers of bunks. Probably several hundred mariners, settlers and soldiers, not counting Sotomayor's people, embarked at Sanlúcar de Barrameda on 25 September 1581. Nothing is known of how these wretched people were recruited.

Their number quickly diminished. A few days out, ship *San Esteban de Arriola* and six other vessels foundered in a storm and over seventy people were drowned. A few substitutes were then enlisted at Cadiz, making 233 civilians and ten friars who finally embarked. Of these, thirty were wives, and twenty-six, children.

The fleet's stay at Cadiz, until 9 December 1581, was fraught with insubordination, peculation, and even worse experiences than Columbus or any other master mariner had suffered from the "land sharks." Flores even tried to leave Sarmiento on the beach, and he had to charter a local bergantina to catch up with the flagship. Next, the fleet spent a month at Santiago, Cape Verdes (where more than fifty people jumped ship), and thence crossed the Atlantic Narrows to Rio de Janeiro where they arrived 24 March 1582, after burying upward of 150 bodies at sea. At Rio they wintered, and more died. Sarmiento had a prefabricated house built for the prospective colony, but many of the stores destined for the settlers "down to needles and thread" were sold by the ships' officers. Some ship captains even sold their entire cargoes destined for the colony, in order to load logwood for sale in Spain; and one vessel became so strained by this heavy cargo that she foundered on the next leg of the voyage. All vessels except those of the navy, which were sheathed with lead, became riddled with teredos. And so this wretched expedition continued. Don Alonso de Sotomayor, the governor of Chile, wisely decided he had better break off, land somewhere on the River Plate, and go overland to Chile, which he did,

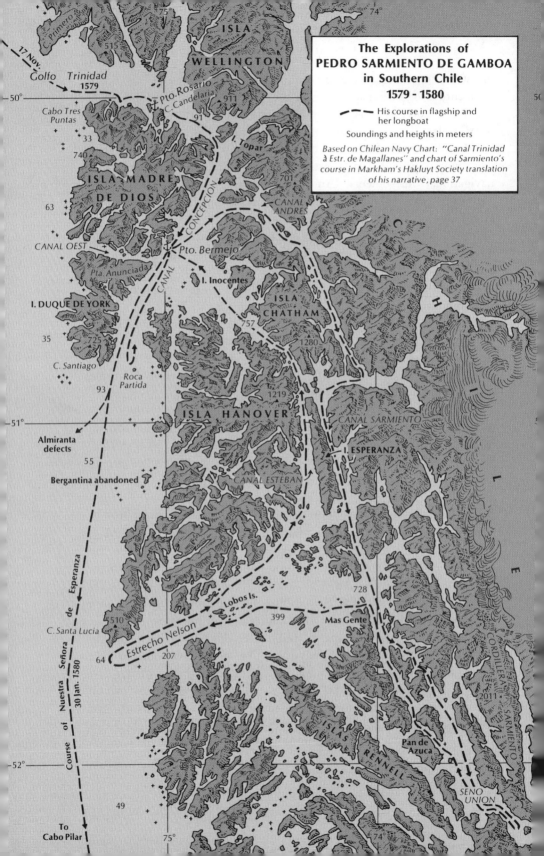

The Explorations of
PEDRO SARMIENTO DE GAMBOA
in Southern Chile
1579 - 1580

– – – His course in flagship and
her longboat

Soundings and heights in meters

*Based on Chilean Navy Chart: "Canal Trinidad
à Estr. de Magallanes" and chart of Sarmiento's
course in Markham's Hakluyt Society translation
of his narrative, page 37*

17 Nov.
Golfo Trinidad
1579

75°

74°

ISLA
WELLINGTON

C. Primero

515

50°

Cabo Tres
Puntas

Pto. Rosario
C. Candelaria

911

91

33

740

63

ISLA MADRE
DE DIOS

CANAL OEST

Pto. Bermejo

Pta. Anunciada

I. DUQUE DE YORK

I. Inocentes

CANAL

CONCEPCION

Topar

701

CANAL
ANDRES

ISLA
CHATHAM

757

1280

35

725

C. Santiago

93

Roca
Partida

1219

ISLA HANOVER

CANAL SARMIENTO

51°

Almiranta
defects

55

Bergantina abandoned

CANAL ESTEBAN

I. ESPERANZA

728

Esperanza

Lobos Is.

Mas Gente

510

de

399

C. Santa Lucia

Señora

64

Estrecho Nelson

207

Pan de
Azuca

Nuestra

CORDILLERA

30 Jan. 1580

SARMIENTO

ISLAS

2011

of

RENNELL

52°

Course

49

SENO
UNION

To
Cabo Pilar

75°

74°

taking the three ships lifting his soldiers, and landing his men some-where near Buenos Aires.

Sarmiento's spicy details of his altercations with Don Diego Flores, and of the latter's incompetence, dishonesty, and cowardice, need not detain us further. Suffice it to say that Flores, who consistently sneered at the plans for the Strait and sought any excuse not to go there, refused to go further than São Vicente. He kept some of the best ships with him. On his way home, Flores called at Parnaíba in northern Brazil (latitude 3° S) where his big galleas easily sank five French ships which were surreptitiously loading logwood. That exploit gave him such merit at court that all Sarmiento's complaints were ignored and Flores received command of a squadron in the famous Armada of 1588. There his conduct was so disgraceful as to be the subject of a court-martial, which condemned him to a year's imprisonment in the castle of Burgos.

Sarmiento, now relieved of Don Diego's presence, departed Rio de Janeiro 2 December 1583 with the only five vessels—two big ones and three fragatas—remaining to him. Favored by fair winds and fine weather, they arrived at Cape Virgins on 1 February 1584, the height of the Antarctic summer. Nevertheless they suffered the common experience of being blown off shore. Returning four days later, they anchored "under the low land of Cape Virgins, 14 leagues from the Narrows." This measurement makes no sense, but the place must have been either on the north coast of Bahia Posesión or of Bahia San Felipe, next bay west. Sarmiento staged a taking-possession, complete with *Te Deum* and *Vexilla Regis*. Whatever place it was, Sarmiento could not have chosen a worse site for a colony. Both bays were full of foul ground, and subject to terrific gales from the west; we have already seen how Loaysa's ships, and others, dragged ashore here. Sarmiento probably never knew that Nuno da Silva (Drake's pilot), had recommended the grassy south shore of the First Narrows as a proper site for a fort; but anyway it was good advice.

On his first day in the doomed locality, Sarmiento disembarked three hundred persons, pitched tents, and found five springs of good water a mile inland; this place he selected for the site of his first fort and colony, calling it *Nombre de Jesus*. He laid out his plan for a town, set up his prefabricated building as a storehouse, and searched for native wild provisions without success. *Trinidad* was grounded at high water to get out her flour and other stores for the colony, but the grounding was done so clumsily that this ship became a total loss. The people dragged ordnance up from the shore for defense, and an initial attack by natives was easily repulsed. Diego de Ribera secretly departed with the three fragatas, fearing lest Sarmiento unload some of their sea stores for the colony.

Sarmiento, having already cast his eye on a favorable spot for a second colony during his last voyage, now sent ship *Maria* to locate the place and start felling trees, while he followed by land. This seems an odd arrangement, but it made sense; the bay by Nombre de Jesus was too dangerous an anchorage to risk *Maria* there a day longer.

So, on 4 March 1584, Sarmiento set forth with one hundred soldiers, carrying eight days' rations (which most of them consumed in two days) and escorted by sundry dogs, sheep, and a flock of goats from Brazil that he wanted for breeding purposes. Natives encountered en route were friendly and performed the arrow-swallowing trick that had so bemused Magellan's men sixty-four years earlier; but there was one brisk scuffle in which several Spaniards were wounded and one killed, by arrows. By 20 March, after having marched some 220 miles (circling the bays and arms of the Strait and over trackless mountains, with compass always in hand), they came down to the Strait near the site of Punta Arenas, and marched along the shore to within a few miles of Cabo Santa Ana, the agreed rendezvous with ship *Maria*. There the soldiers, dog-tired, hungry, with many sick from eating a poisonous berry, collapsed, declaring they could go no farther. Providentially, at that very juncture a boat appeared from the *Maria*. She had already anchored in the selected harbor, now Puerto Hambre. On 25 March, Sarmiento took formal possession, naming the place *Rey Don Felipe* after Philip II, started building a church and erecting a storehouse, laying out the town around a plaza, and constructing huts of evergreen beechwood. This site was not too bad; President Bulnes of Chile endorsed Sarmiento's choice in 1834 by choosing it for the first permanent garrison and settlement on the Strait. There was a snug little harbor, fields which sloped down to the shore, plenty of small fish (Magellan's *sardinas*), shellfish, wild fowl, and deer. Every prospect pleased until winter set in with a bang. It snowed continually for fifteen days, and then Sarmiento sailed away, planning to return with supplies to make up for those spoiled or stolen by his own people in Brazil. He never did.

From the Strait to Spain

Sarmiento embarked in the *Maria* on 25 May 1584, and next day anchored off his other settlement, Nombre de Jesus. Before he could communicate with the people ashore, a furious gale sprang up, *Maria's* one cable parted, and she was driven seaward in horribly cold weather. Unable to beat back against the wind, she continued to São Vicente, Brazil. There she had to be run aground for want of an anchor, but they got her off.

To the adventures of Pedro Sarmiento de Gamboa there is no end. He bought a new anchor at São Vicente, made a new cable from the bark of trees, and proceeded to Pernambuco (Recife), arriving 15 September 1584; then turned back to Bahia (Salvador), looking for a ship in which to send supplies to the Strait settlers. But at Bahia he lost faithful *Maria*. She dragged ashore and dashed to pieces while the crew took to the boats, and he with his black slave and a priest got ashore on a couple of boards. The local authorities furnished him with another vessel, and in her, charged with fresh supplies, he happily started for the Strait in January 1585. A furious gale from the west and southwest caught her off the River Plate. She ran before it for fifty-one days (so he says) to Rio, the men arriving "nearly naked and barefoot." After repairing the ship and quelling a mutiny, Sarmiento decided the best thing to do was to go home and organize a genuine relief expedition. He departed Bahia 22 June 1586, already two years after leaving his settlers.

On 11 August, in the Azores, his new ship was captured and the captain taken prisoner by two English privateers belonging to Sir Walter Raleigh. Unfortunately for us, Sarmiento threw overboard most of his papers, including a "large book in color" with pictures of the Strait and Chile.

In England, arriving in August 1586, Sarmiento was turned over to Raleigh, made friends with him, and otherwise fared well, even being presented to Queen Elizabeth. He "conversed with her in Latin for more than two hours and a half, in which language she is proficient."

She graciously gave him a passport to proceed home to Spain, but that concluding part of his journey took over three years. In December 1586, passing through France where the wars of religion were raging, he was captured, asleep at an inn, by a company of Protestant arquebusiers. They held him prisoner for ransom, very nastily and uncomfortably, in the Château de Marsan. Philip II eventually paid the ransom demanded by the heretics (four horses and 6000 ducats) and Sarmiento entered Spain at about the end of 1589.

The Captain reached Spain a broken old man. He had not forgotten his colonists; but his repeated petitions to the king to send them relief or rescue fell on deaf ears. In part he took refuge in literature. Enrique Garcés, the scientist-poet who invented the mercury process for silver ore and translated Petrarch and the *Lusiads*, became his friend, and Sarmiento translated for him several Italian sonnets into Castilian. He was employed by the Council of the Indies to censor the Eulogies of Illustrious Men by Juan de Castellanos, and a severe censor he was, throwing out some five thousand lines of this long and turgid poem.

There is some mystery about Sarmiento's end. According to one version, he went out to the Philippines, commanded an unsuccessful attempt to capture Tidore, and was still alive at Manila in 1608. Another, that he sailed for the Indies as second in command of a fleet under one Apallúa, which foundered at sea in 1592. And a third, that he died of old age at Seville, among his friends. Let us hope that this version is correct.

Pedro Sarmiento de Gamboa, in addition to his literary gifts, proved to be an expert and courageous soldier, mariner, and navigator. He knew the secret of command, humoring his men as far as the state of things thus allowed, winning their confidence; and he was notably equipped with that indomitable perseverance which deserves, though it does not always win, success. The one thing he could not cope with was being placed under the orders of a tricky, incompetent courtier who was also a ruffian and a coward; as if Magellan had been made subordinate to Cartagena. Under this impossible handicap he did all that he could to fortify the Strait, and it was not his fault that the garrisons were left to perish. A sincere Christian, he attributed all his escapes from marine disaster to the Heavenly Host, and his loyalty to the king never wavered. No more truehearted, loyal, and brave man ever sailed the far-off seas. One can imagine him, on numerous occasions, heartening his sailors with the prospect that if God saved them this time, well and good; but if they died like men they would receive a heavenly award.

Bibliography and Notes

Sarmiento's own *Narrative* of his first voyage, *Viage al Estrecho de Magallanes . . . en los Años de 1579 y 1580,* was printed at Madrid in 1768. This, together with his *Relación* of 1583, the *Concise Narration* of his second voyage, and other documents, was translated and edited as *Narratives of the Voyages of Pedro Sarmiento de Gamboa to the Straits of Magellan* by Sir Clements Markham for the Hakluyt Society in 1895 (Vol. XCI). This is "Don Clemente's" finest work—translation, maps, and annotations are all superb. Ernecé Editores of Buenos Aires brought out in 1950 an excellent compilation in two volumes: *Pedro Sarmiento de Gamboa, Viajes al Estrecho de Magallanes.* The best biography in English is Stephen Clissold, *Conquistador* (London, 1954).

The caulker's high wage. Markham, p. 25. On page 312 Sarmiento reveals that everyone got a bonus for serving in the Pacific, and pilots' salaries were doubled.

The big day's run. Markham, p. 31, last line. If he was using the same league as Columbus did, this means 196 nautical miles and an average speed of 8 knots. Markham in one of his footnotes states that Sarmiento's league measured 4 nautical miles; this would have given him an average speed of over 13 knots, which is impossible. A better indication is Sarmiento's later statement that the length of the Strait was 110 leagues. As Brown's *Almanac* gives the length as 311 or 334 nautical miles, depending on whether you start from Cabo Pilar or the Evangelistas, it would seem, assuming that by this time Sarmiento was a good dead-reckoner, that his league measured about 3 nautical miles.

The galleas. This is the first time we have encountered this type; it was a big ship of several hundred tuns, and one of the capital ships of the Spanish navy. The entire task organization will be found in Markham, xxix, notes, p. 2.

Casualties. These are the figures given by Sarmiento in Markham, pp. 223–25. Please do not blame Don Clemente or me if they don't add up!

Nombre de Jesus. I was told when visiting the Strait in 1972 that digging had revealed the site at the head of Bahia Felipe.

Puerto Hambre, as the place has been called since the visit of Cavendish (see Chapter XXX), is now a favorite excursion point from Punta Arenas, as the road goes no further and the view of the Strait is superb. When we were there in February 1972, the original Rey Don Felipe was being excavated, and the outlines of the church and other buildings bear out Sarmiento's description. R. Ortiz Troncaso, "Excavación arqueológica de la iglesia . . . del Rey D. Felipe," *Anales* del Instituto de la Patagonia, I, No. 1 (1970), 5–14.

Jokes are so rare on these voyages that I am tempted to report one told by Raleigh in his *History of the World* (1628 ed., p. 490). Sir Walter asked Sarmiento a question about an unnamed island on a map of the Magellan Strait. "He told me merrily that it was to be called 'Painters Wives Island,' saying that whilst the fellow drew that Map his wife, sitting by, desired him to put in one countrey for her, that she, in imagination, might have an island of her owne."

✳ XXX ✳

The Voyages of Thomas Cavendish

1586-1593

The "Admirable and Prosperous Voyage"

In 1560, when Queen Elizabeth had been on her throne two years, there was born to a country gentleman named William Cavendish,* at his house in Suffolk, a boy destined to be a famous circumnavigator. The family was fairly affluent (his mother being Mary, sister to Lord Wentworth), and the boy's younger sister Anne became a lady-in-waiting to the Queen. At the age of fifteen Thomas went up to Cambridge, matriculated at Corpus Christi College, and remained two years. What he read we do not know, but he never learned to spell; gentlemen, however, were not supposd to spell correctly in those days. It may be assumed that in Cambridge he met George Clifford, later Lord Cumberland, who (as we have seen in *Northern Voyages*) was deeply concerned in maritime affairs.

Having gone down, Thomas, as an attractive youth with money of his own, found no trouble getting on in London court society while he read law at one of the Inns of Court. Important people like Walsingham, the Careys, Sidneys, and Pembrokes befriended him, and under their patronage he stood twice and successfully for election to the

---

* Then pronounced *Cawndish,* and often written Candish. Thomas signed his name Caundysh or Caundyssh.

World map showing Cavendish's route and portrait. From *Journal du voyage de Guill. Schouten dans les Indes* (Paris, 1618). Courtesy Harvard College Library.

House of Commons. There he met Walter Raleigh, lobbying to have his grant to Virginia confirmed, and Raleigh was so attracted to the young man as to send him on his first Virginia voyage. Cavendish commanded his own fifty-tun bark *Elizabeth;* and Raleigh also appointed him high marshal—corresponding to the Spanish *alguacil*—of the fleet. Although his family planned a legal career for young Thomas, this voyage to Virginia gave him an unquenchable love of sea adventure which lead to glory and death.

Only three months after his return from Virginia, early in 1586, we find him building a new ship for himself, the *Desire* of 120 to 140 tuns, and buying two smaller ones, *Content* (60 tuns) and *Hugh Gallant* (40 tuns). The total complement was 123 men and boys.

The war with Spain was very much on, and Cavendish's main object was to emulate Drake, make captures in the South Sea, and return home around the world. He sailed from Plymouth 21 July 1586. The Captain General was twenty-six years old, several officers were as young or younger, and they prosecuted this "admirable and prosperous voyage" as Francis Pretty called it, with high spirits. A Portuguese seaman whom Cavendish picked up in the Philippines reported that the Captain was "slight of stature" and looked no more than twenty-two years old; and he described his heretical daily shipboard prayers, very like those held by Drake. They prayed and sang hymns (i.e. metrical psalms) sitting down; but attendance was voluntary.

The first lark took place at Sierra Leone, where "the Generall sent some of his company on shore, and there . . . played and daunced all the forenoone among the Negroes." That did not prevent their having a scuffle in which an Englishman named William Pickman was killed by a poisoned arrow, "which wrought so that night, that hee was marveilously swollen and all his belly and privie parts were as blacke as ynke, and the next morning he died."

On 10 September the fleet departed the Cape Verde Islands, crossed the Atlantic Narrows without mishap, and on 31 October, beyond Cape Frio, sighted "a great mountaine which had an high round knoppe on the top of it" (Rio's famous Sugar Loaf). Prudently they put in at an unfrequented harbor behind Ilha São Sebastião (the site of Vitória), at latitude 23°43′ S. There they remained for over three weeks, replenishing wood and water and building a ten-tun pinnace. On 17 December, sailing along the Patagonian coast, they

Rey D. Felipe (Puerto Hambre), the cove.

Fort Bulnes. View up Strait.

entered a fair harbor which Cavendish named Port Desire after his flagship; this was Magellan's *Puerto de los Trabajos* (of Travails), but the happier name, *Puerto Deseado* in Spanish, stuck. Here the men marveled at the multitude of big "seales" (elephant seals) "of a wonderful great big nose . . . and monstrous of shape," and killed many of their young, which they found to be "marveilous good meate, and being boyled or rosted, are hardly to be knowenn from lambe or mutton." Nearby, when seeking fresh water, they had a brief scrap with giant Patagonians, "As wilde as ever was a bucke or any other wilde beast." The Englishmen measured a footprint and found it to be eighteen inches long—size 28 to us. Magellan was right about the big-feet! After killing and salting down a multitude of penguin, they continued southward and passed into the Strait of Magellan on 6 January 1587.

Next day, according to Francis Pretty's account, on the shore just east of the First Narrows they picked up a Spaniard named Tomé Hernández, "who was there was 23 Spaniards more, which were all that remained of 400," of the Sarmiento settlement Nombre de Jesus, "all the rest being dead with famine." This man, whom Cavendish took on board, jumped ship at Peru, and over thirty years later made a deposition which tells almost all we know of the fate of this miserable colony; and of Rey Don Felipe too, as Tomé had visited them. Here is his story:

Two months after Sarmiento sailed away, the Nombre de Jesus settlers made their way by land to Rey Don Felipe, where the commander, Andrés de Viedma, was by no means pleased with this increase of population. After a year had elapsed with no word from Sarmiento, and, hunger increasing, the colonists built two boats in which 45 men and 5 women embarked for the first settlement. They did not make it; one boat struck a rock and was lost; Viedma and 22 others in the second boat returned to Rey Don Felipe, after coldly ordering the wrecked boat's survivors (5 women and 31 men) "to scatter and try to live on the shellfish they could pick up along the beach." Only 3 women and 15 men survived that winter; "All the rest had died of hunger and sickness." Viedma sent for these survivors next summer, when they expressed the wish to return by land to Nombre de Jesus; and they were walking along the shore east of Cabo San Gregorio when they sighted Cavendish's four vessels breezing in.

Beech tree on site of Rey D. Felipe Fort.

Head of the harbor, Rey D. Felipe.

The Pacific end of the Strait. Desolation Island and Twelve Apostles Rocks.

Cabo Pilar. James F. Nields photo.

Tuesday Cove. James F. Nields photo.

Cavendish sent a boat ashore. Tomé and two other soldiers met it and were invited to come on board. Tomé did so, but the other two were ordered by Cavendish to pick up the remaining 12 men and 3 women and tell them to join. While these two men were about their mission, Cavendish unaccountably changed his mind and, without any change of weather to excuse him, made sail, leaving all 17 people to starve. He then called at the southern settlement, Rey Don Felipe, and there found only 21 men and 2 women still alive, out of the original 300 to 400 who had been landed by Sarmiento. Their stores spent, and none of their planted seeds having produced anything edible, "they dyed like dogges in their houses and in their clothes," recorded Francis Pretty; and as the living were too weak to bury their dead, the place became so "wonderfully taynted with the smell and the savour of the dead" that the survivors scattered along the shore, living on shellfish, roots, leaves, "and sometimes a foule." Pretty declares that they refused Cavendish's offer to take them on board, as he was going the wrong way; they were determined somehow to get to the River Plate. None ever did.

"Our Generall named this town Port Famine," wrote Pretty, and it is known by the Spanish equivalent, Puerto Hambre, to this day. The ship *Delight* of Bristol found a lone survivor there in January 1590. He was taken on board but did not survive the voyage home.

The sad, short existence of these two imperial outposts illustrates the principle of which we have seen sundry examples in Virginia, Canada, and elsewhere; even in Norse Greenland. No European colony in an "undeveloped" region could sustain itself without relief and communication with home. Sarmiento did his best to bring relief; but both Philip II, and the viceregal government in Peru which initiated this whole business, chose to forget about Nombre de Jesus and Rey Don Felipe, and let their people die miserably. Sarmiento, of course, should have followed Nuno da Silva's advice and established his garrison on or near the First Narrows, where mounted ordnance could have prevented enemy ships' entering the Strait. Yet, even had he done so, the people would have been doomed to die from neglect.

Cavendish made a successful traverse of the Strait; he named Cape Froward and perhaps also Caleta Gallant after his smaller vessel, *Hugh Gallant*. After a seven weeks' passage, he debouched from the Strait on 24 February 1587.

The Big Prize, and Circumnavigation

The voyage from Cabo Pilar to Baja California consumed over eight months, filled with incidents that we must pass by—captures of Spanish ships, towns sacked and burned, and ambuscades by Spaniards and Indians. The Englishmen were highly impressed by the herds of cattle and horses which had been established at various points of the west coast. Cavendish took over one prize ship and renamed her *George;* she, with *Desire* and *Content*, were successfully careened and graved in the Gulf of Guayaquil; *Hugh Gallant*, which did not stand up well, was scrapped. Guatalco, the little west coast port where Drake had called, was looted, and all eight houses burned. From a captured pilot, a Marseillais who hated Spaniards, Cavendish obtained valuable information about the movements of the galleons returning to Mexico from Manila, and on 14 October stationed himself off Cape San Lucas at the tip of Lower California to await one expected shortly.

On 4 November 1587 the big galleon *Santa Ana* (600 tuns) came lumbering along. Taken by surprise, with all her heavy ordnance in the hold, she was the underdog in this fight with *Desire* and *Content*. She repelled the Englishmen's first attempt to board, with small arms and a "sort of great stones which they threw upon our heads." After that repulse, Cavendish changed his tactics and pounded *Santa Ana* with heavy guns for five or six hours. Her captain then displayed a white flag, struck all sails, and came on board *Desire* to surrender. Crew and passengers were landed at San Lucas Bay, provided with food and small arms, and the ship was stripped. She yielded more plunder even than Drake's *Cacafuego:* 122,000 gold pesos, each worth eight shillings, a quantity of pearls, and all manner of Chinese silks and damasks. The royal treasurer at Manila estimated that the whole represented an investment of a million pesos, worth double in Europe. Her very size and wealth were an embarrassment to Cavendish, for he could not spare the men from *Desire* and *Content* (*George* having disappeared) to sail so big a ship. So, taking all the most valuable articles on board (and they weighed 50 tons), he set her afire and abandoned her. Under the leadership of Sebastián Vizcaíno (later in the century a noted California explorer), the 190 people left on the beach extinguished the flames and managed to work *Santa Ana* into Acapulco.

Interesting passengers taken on board Cavendish's flagship were two Japanese young men, a Portuguese who had been in China, and *Santa Ana*'s Spanish pilot. This man amiably piloted *Desire* as far as the Philippines, where Cavendish had him hanged from the yardarm for trying to communicate with Manila. *Desire* made Guam in forty-five days from California, on 3 January 1588. *Content* disappeared on this leg of the voyage; no trace of her was ever found. Touching at north-eastern Samar on the 14th, the now solitary *Desire* passed through narrow San Bernardino Strait into the Sibuyan Sea, then sailed south to Panay. This foray into Philippine waters was great fun for the English, and irritating as well as mortifying to the Spanish authorities; Bishop Salazar of the Philippines complained in a letter to Philip II that "an English youth of about 22 years, with a wretched little vessel of about 100 tuns, 40 to 50 companions" raided his villa on an island, boasted of the damage he had wrought, and went away laughing. But Cavendish did miss a great opportunity to destroy a new Manila galleon on the stocks; the builders' gang drove away his landing party.

Cavendish returned to England around the world; and like Drake obtained sufficient provisions as he went along to keep his men fairly well and happy. *Desire* sailed on 16 March 1588, from a port in Java where the General had been conversing with a friendly rajah. She made the coast of Africa in two months, called at St. Helena, and suffered her last storm in the chops of the Channel, losing most of her threadbare sails. But on 9 September 1588 she managed to work into Plymouth, whence she had departed two years and a month earlier. Her captain was still only twenty-eight years old.

It was a merry time to be in England, full of enthusiasm over the defeat of the Spanish Armada, to which Cavendish's exploit seemed a jubilant footnote. The prize goods, said to have been worth £125,000, were mostly unloaded at Plymouth; but Cavendish retained plenty to make a great show in the Thames. His men were fitted with new uniforms of silk damask and the officers wore gold chains; even the sails were of blue damask. *Desire* fired a full salvo in salute to the Queen when she anchored off Greenwich, and Her Majesty attended a banquet in her honor in the great cabin, hung with cloth of gold. There she made some witty remarks about the enemy. "Their ships loaded with gold and silver from the Indies come hither after all."

The Second and Fatal Voyage

Cavendish promptly began consuming his prize money in what a contemporary described as "the pursuit of gallantry and court life." But he did not blow it all in. Largely with his own means he prepared for a second voyage to the Indies. The object now was to bypass the Philippines and open direct trade between England and China. The sample of rich Chinese wares that he had seen in the *Santa Ana*, the stories he picked up from her former passengers, and the map of China that he acquired in the Philippines, convinced him that here, not in the frozen north, lay England's way to wealth. And, when we contemplate the history of British India, we must admit that the young man was right.

At the start of his Second Voyage, this was Cavendish's task organization:

GALLEON LEICESTER, former privateer ship of 400 tuns. Cavendish, captain and "Generall."

ROEBUCK, former privateer ship of 240 tuns, 20 guns, 100 men. John Cooke, captain.

DESIRE, ship of 120 tuns, the same as on his first voyage. Randolph Cotton, captain.

DAINTY, bark of about 60 tuns. John Davis, captain and part owner with Adrian Gilbert.

THE BLACK PINNACE (we know not her real name) of anywhere from 20 to 40 tuns. She was always called by this name because, all swathed in mourning black, she had brought the body of Sir Philip Sidney from Ireland to England. She was much too big to have been carried knocked down in a vessel's hold and set ashore, like the Spanish bergantinas or those carried by Frobisher and Davis on the Northern Voyages. The *Black Pinnace* had three masts, two of them square-rigged, and sailed on her own bottom. After signal service to the fleet, she was lost with all hands in the Pacific.

David Quinn figures that Cavendish was out of pocket some £ 12,700 for ships, guns, provisions for a year, and advance wages for

The Black Pinnace. From *Procession at the Obsequies of Sir Philip Sidney* (1587).

a twelvemonth. If he gave that much advance pay, he was unusually generous. The total complement was about 350 men.

On Midsummer Day 1591, Cavendish received a royal license allowing him to undertake a sea voyage with no objective other than to "doe service to us and our Realm." Finally, on 26 August, he in *Galleon Leicester,* with *Roebuck* and *Desire, Dainty* and the big pinnace, departed Plymouth. Their ocean crossing was very slow, for Cavendish's Portuguese pilot (whom he later hanged) steered them into the equatorial calms where they were stuck for twenty-seven days. On 27 November they entered the Brazilian bay of Salvador—not the big Bahia at latitude 13° S but a little place ten degrees further south, near Cape Frio. The men were ravenous for fresh food, and Cavendish decided to satisfy their craving, as well as his own for loot, by sacking the brisk new town of Santos. The fleet tarried there a month, but something went wrong on the reprovisioning, as the ships were very inadequately supplied when they departed on 22 January 1592, after burning down São Vicente.

Here Cavendish's troubles began, and they became not only numerous but often unnecessary. The fleet suffered a terrible pampero off the River Plate estuary, losing several boats and a new twenty-tun pinnace just built at Santos. They reunited at Port Desire in mid-March. The crew of *Galleon Leicester* became so "abject mynded and mutanus" that Cavendish shifted his flag to his old ship *Desire*, but later returned to the big and relatively comfortable galleon.

The fleet entered the Strait of Magellan 8 April 1592, with winter already closing in. Beyond Cape Froward, unable to make way against the wind, they anchored in "a small coove" from 21 April to 15 May, where "Many of our men died with cursed famine, and miserable cold, not having wherewith to cover their bodies, nor to fill their bellies, but living by muskles, water, and weeds of the sea, with a small relief of the ships store in meale sometimes." One sailor even had his frozen nose drop off when he tried to blow it with his fingers. Sails and lines were rotting, and victuals so very short, that Cavendish accepted the plea of his officers to return to Brazil and refit. First, however, he set eight sick men from the *Galleon* on shore to die, another instance of this young man's singular inhumanity. The ships, "beaten out of the Straighte with a most monstrous storme at WSW," kept together until 20 May, off Port Desire, when they parted, taking opposite tacks in the night, and never rejoined. John Davis's *Dainty* went one way with the *Black Pinnace*, and the *Galleon* and *Roebuck* another. Davis put in at Port Desire, and we shall hear more of him presently.

Arriving before São Vicente, Cavendish encouraged his now almost starving men to raid local plantations for food. The Portuguese settlers, who did not appreciate this attention from the men who had burned their town, attacked an English shore party and wiped it out. *Roebuck*, in a worse state even than the *Galleon*, rejoined here. After other mishaps and losing more men, Cavendish expressed a desire to return to the Strait; but his crew absolutely refused to consider it. He then compromised by sailing for the Island of St. Helena at latitude 16° S, but missed it by at least eighteen leagues. Turning north to look for Ascension Island, he missed that too. This, to Cavendish, was the last straw. He made his will and wrote his own version of the voyage for the eyes of his cousin Tristram Gorgas; then he lay down and died. Where he was buried at sea, and on what date we do not know; it must have been around 20–25 May 1592. He was only thirty-one or thirty-two years old.

What really was the matter with this man? He had been disintegrating since his fleet crossed the Atlantic, showing bad judgment, blowing hot and cold, flying into rages (he hanged a pilot for giving bad advice), imagining plots, blaming everyone but himself. He had evidently become, emotionally, a sick man; and one naturally wonders whether there were not some physical disability too. Possibly a gnawing cancer, or the disease which killed Pedro de Mendoza at sea. But there is no evidence of anything of the sort, and no shipmate of his who wrote about the voyage could put his finger on the cause of his captain's death.

Galleon Leicester was alone at the time. She and *Roebuck* returned to England, we know not when. John Davis in *Dainty*, with the *Black Pinnace*, spent two months in Port Desire refitting and salting down seal and penguin meat, and then made for the Strait. En route, on 14 August 1592, they were "driven in among certain Isles never before discovered"—the Falklands, establishing England's claim to this group. Four days later they passed Cape Virgins, and when near the Pacific end of the Strait, anchored and waited, hoping that Cavendish would show up; but the winter cold forced Davis to get under way for the Pacific. Boisterous north winds blew his ships back twice into the Strait, and on a third attempt, in early October, *Black Pinnace* disappeared, lost with all hands. Finally Davis had to renounce the Pacific, and *Dainty* dashed back into the Strait.

John Jane, who was on board, has a fine description of *Dainty* weathering Cape Deseado (Cabo Pilar) by the skin of her teeth. The master declared that, with the wind turned north, they could not double it. Captain Davis replied: "Either we must double it, or before noon we must die; therefore loose your sails, and let us put it to Gods mercy. The master being a man of good spirit resolutely made quicke dispatch and set sails. Our sailes had not bene half an houre aboord, but the footrope of our foresaile brake, so that nothing held but the oylet holes. The seas continually brake over the ships poope, and flew into the sailes with such violence, that we still expected the tearing of our sayles, or oversetting of the ship, and withall to our utter discomfort, wee pereceived that wee fell still more and more to leeward, so that wee could not double the cape." They came so close to an outlying rock as to receive backwash, "wind and Seas raging beyond measure." Tentatively the master veered a little main sheet; and whether it was that or a current, "or by the wonderfull power of God, . . . the ship quickened her way, and shot past that rocke," and doubled the point

Berehaven Harbor, Ireland. Courtesy Bord Failte, Dublin.

of Cabo Pilar with but a ship's length to spare. Once around, they furled all sails, and under bare poles "spooned before the sea," three men at the helm. In six hours' time they were 25 leagues within the Strait, says Jane; if he was a good estimater of distance, this means an average speed of at least 12½ knots.

Dainty passed Cape Virgins on 27 October, and on the 30th reached Port Desire, staying almost two months to pickle penguin meat and make a dish of "scurvy grasse" and penguin eggs fried in train-oil, which relieved incipient scurvy. At Port Desire, Patagonians attacked a shore party and killed nine men, and on Ilha Grande, Brazil, they lost twenty more. Only twenty-seven out of seventy-six who sailed from Plymouth, were now left on board. The penguin (they had 14,000 carcases on board) not only became putrid but bred swarms of maggots which devoured everything; food, clothes, boots, wood, "only yron excepted," wrote Jane. This plague of maggots was followed by a "monstrous disease" of swelling, of which eleven more men died "in most lothsome and furious paine"; and of the sixteen remaining alive, only Captain Davis and four men were strong enough to work the ship. Finally, having no anchor left, and with sails in tatters, on 11 June 1593 they ran *Dainty* ashore in Berehaven, a tiny port on Bantry Bay, Ireland. This was not far from Dursey Head whence the early navigators liked to take their departure for the New World.

"Cavendish's last voyage was not one of the great achievements of the Elizabethan seamen," is the conclusion of David B. Quinn. A notable understatement! On his first voyage Cavendish enjoyed unusually good luck, and it turned out to be a great lark as well as very profitable. But on his second voyage everything went wrong. He was poorly served by his Plymouth victuallers; the "twelve months' provisions" were not nearly enough, and he did not have the gumption to stock up in Brazil to prevent his men's falling back on seal, penguin, and seaweed in the Strait. Missing two such lofty and conspicuous islands as Ascension and St. Helen, even though he had no pilot at the time (having hanged his last one), gives him poor marks as a navigator. He was indecisive, cruel at times, inhuman and unable by temperament to exercise control over a fleet. Yet Thomas Cavendish seemed qualified after commanding a ship on a round voyage to Virginia and another around the world; and his idea of England's opening a traffic with China independent of Spain and Portugal was sound. But there was a screw loose somewhere in Cavendish. And the survivors of his second voyage, barely one out of three who originally embarked, had nothing to show for all their hard work and suffering.

Bibliography and Notes

David B. Quinn of the University of Liverpool has edited for the Society of the History of Discoveries a volume entitled *The Last Voyage of Thomas Cavendish*. It will be brought out by the Chicago University Press, probably before mine sees the light, but the editor graciously allowed me to see a copy prior to publication. This book is built around a hitherto unknown manuscript on Cavendish's last voyage, in the Paul Mellon Collection, but Quinn's introduction gives a racy acount of both voyages, and an immense amount of additional information.

The principal sources for "the admirable and prosperous" first voyage are Francis Pretty's account with Thomas Fuller's and other Notes in Hakluyt's *Voyages* (MacLehose ed., 1904), XI, 290–381, and *Purchas His Pilgrimes* (MacLehose ed.), II, 149–87. For the second and last voyage, John Jane's account in Hakluyt, XI, 339–416. For further bibliography, consult Professor Quinn's forthcoming *Last Voyage*.

The Tomé Hernández story may be found in the Markham volume on Sarmiento (see notes to Chapter XXIX), pp. 352–75. The *Delight* story is in Hakluyt, XI, 381–89.

William L. Schurz's *Manila Galleon* (1939 ed.), pp. 305–9, gives a spirited account of the *Santa Ana* capture; for reference to Spanish sources see Quinn's note 20 to Introduction.

The Black Pinnace. This famous vessel, the only one of her class to be depicted, is from *The Procession at the Obsequies of Sir Philip Sidney Knight* (London, 1587), here reproduced from Hakluyt, XI, 400. She is shown with a long waistcloth decorated by coats of arms, and stretched from stem to stern, and numerous banners. Cavendish probably gave her taller spars and more sail area when she joined his fleet.

In the Biblioteca Nazionale, Florence, in November 1973 I was allowed a brief glance at what David Quinn believes to have been Cavendish's own map, signed, "B. H.," and dated 1588, immediately after his first voyage. The Patagonian coast and the Strait are drawn in the vacant space behind Brazil. Toponymy: Puerto Desire, "A Pond of Fresh Water," Port St. Julian, Rio de Gallegos, A Low Beach, Cape Santa Maria, "A Great Indraft" at Useless Bay, Puerto Famine, C. Froward, C. Sta. Vitoria (Pilar). The Chilean coast up to about Valdivia is left completely blank, but on the back country of Brazil is written, "Silver Country."

John Davis. A. H. Markham, *Voyages and Works of John Davis* (1880), and my *Northern Voyages*, pp. 583–616. Respecting *Dainty*'s tough time weathering Cabo Pilar, a yachtsman asked me, "Why didn't Davis bring her about and take a long tack off shore?" Well, me lad, bringing one of those old ships about in a heavy sea required a lot of headway, for which she had no room. It was nothing like a "ready, about!" at Larchmont or Cowes. Tacking, or even wearing under *Dainty*'s conditions, would have been suicide.

✳ XXXI ✳

The Discovery of Cape Horn

1598-1616

Enter the Dutch

We cannot conclude this volume without a few words about the Dutch later entering the game; and, before they had been at it many years, making the highly important discovery of the Strait of Le Maire and Cape Horn.

The seventeenth century opened, as we have seen, without any nation but Spain and Portugal having placed a single permanent colony on American soil. But others would soon catch up. English Virginia began in 1607 with Jamestown, and New France as a colony dates from the following year with Champlain's founding of Quebec. Henry Hudson's voyage up the great river that bears his name, in 1609, and the founding of Dutch trading posts at Albany and Manhattan in 1613–14, mark the entry of the Seven United Provinces of the Netherlands into American colonial rivalry. About the same time there began long Dutch voyages to South America and the Far East.

The ultimate reason for these was the character and seafaring experience of the Dutch. By 1600 they were already noted for clean, taut ships, and for economy in operation: more blocks and tackle, shortening of the main and topsail yards, and cutting sails into smaller units, saved many men and much money. Dutch seapower, formerly

Dutch caricature of navigating, 1602. Courtesy Maritiem Museum "Prins Hendrik," Rotterdam.

confined to northern Europe, now bubbled over and spread world-wide as a result of their War of Independence from Spain. The revolt of the Netherlands began in 1568, and the ensuing war to suppress it lasted for many, many years; but the essential factor that drove the Dutch seamen from the narrow seas into blue water was the spice trade. While Portugal held a virtual monopoly of spices, she allowed the Dutch merchant marine to distribute them from Lisbon throughout northern Europe, but when Philip II of Spain usurped (or should we say inherited?) the throne of Portugal in 1580, he forbade that practice. So, Dutch sea-dogs and merchants being what they were, they decided to go after spices themselves. To that end they started voyages to the Far East, incidentally picking up bits of the far-flung Portuguese empire such as Ternate and Tidore.

First, apparently, to try Magellan's route to wealth and glory, was the Sebold de Weert expedition, a fleet of five ships from Amsterdam. "*Hope*, admirall of 250 tuns," and four more (*Charity*, vice admiral, 160 tuns, *Faith*, 160 tuns, *Fidelity*, 100 tuns, and *Good News*, 75 tuns). Commanded at first by one Jacques Mahu and subsequently by Sebold de Weert and with an English pilot,* this fleet made a voyage marked by many mishaps to Sierra Leone, across the Atlantic, through the Strait of Magellan, and back, in 1598–99.

A less pretentious voyage beginning in 1598 went farther. This, from the name of its captain general, is called the Oliver de Noort voyage. It consisted of ships *Maurice* and *Concord* of Rotterdam, *Henry Frederike*, and *Hope* (not the same as De Weert's *Hope*). For flag pilot they had a man named Melis who had been around the world with Cavendish. Sailing from Amsterdam 2 July 1598, they had a fight with the Portuguese at Ilha Príncipe in the Gulf of Guinea in which pilot Melis was killed, took their departure from Annobon on New Year's Day 1599, and made their Brazilian landfall at Cabo São Tomé, latitude 22° S, on 5 February. Sailing south, with winter approaching and scurvy making its appearance, the captain general made the odd decision to seek St. Helena for provisions, but missed it; he then made Ascension Island and "knocked downe many Fowles." Back at southern Brazil, they "found little but Herbes, and two trees of sower Plumbes, which cured the sicke in fifteen dayes." Here they burned *Concord*, now leaky beyond repair, and left "two Malefactors to their forlorne fortunes"—i.e. marooned the poor devils.

At Port Desire, Patagonia, De Noort careened his three ships and loaded penguin in September; but his shore party, ambushed by "Savages of admirable stature, painted unto terrour," lost three men. On 4 November *Maurice*, *Henry*, and *Hope* were off Cape Virgins, but their efforts to enter the Strait were thwarted by "tempestuous Windes, Raine, Hailes, Snowes, Sicknesse and Contention," and "these sensible crosses were accompanied with losses of Anchors, Cables, and . . . time." Inside at last on 25 November, they kidnapped six little Patagonian children from their mothers' arms, after killing their fathers, and on the 29th viewed the deserted and depressing site of Rey Don Felipe—Cavendish's Port Famine. Beyond Cape Froward

* William Adams, subsequently the pioneer Englishman in Japan.

they encountered De Weert's fleet sadly sailing home after having lost thirty-eight men and spending five futile months in or about the Strait.

As De Noort supplies a completely new set of names, he is difficult to follow through the Strait. At a place that he called Goose Bay, the Vice Admiral, name not given, was cruelly condemned by the Admiral's Council of War to be marooned where "Famine, or wilde beasts, or wilder men must needs make an end of his mutinous unquiet life." Not until February 1600, more than two months after their entrance, did they pass Cabo Pilar "into the South sea, with thanks to the Almighty for that happy success. . . . Their company was now an hundred fortie seven."

De Noort followed very closely Cavendish's tactics and course, sacking Spanish west coast towns, capturing ships, and in general making a nuisance of himself. On 5 May 1600 he took off from Cocos Island, Gulf of Panama, for the Ladrones, en route casting overboard a recently acquired Spanish pilot "for ill demeanures." The rest of this circumnavigation, following the routes of Elcano and Cavendish, we will pass over; they rounded the Cape of Good Hope in May of 1601, sighted the "Sorlings," (Scilly Islands) 19 August, and on the 26th, three years and a month after their departure, anchored at Amsterdam.

De Noort's was the fourth circumnavigation. It served to acquaint Dutch merchants with the riches of the Far East, and to stimulate their successful attempts to carve out pieces of the Portuguese empire for their own.

Schouten and Le Maire

The fifth circumnavigation was also Dutch, by Georges Spilbergen, in 1614–17. His fleet the *Aeolus, Lucifer, Huntsman,* and three more, sailed from the Texel 8 August 1614, passed through the Strait of Magellan in April 1615, in dead of winter, sacked towns and captured prizes along the west coast of South America, and returned around the world, calling at the Spice Islands already conquered by their countrymen.

In the seventeen years since De Noort's return, the Dutch position among maritime nations had vastly improved. A twelve-year truce with Spain, concluded in 1609, enabled Dutch pioneers to thrust into all parts of the world. In the north, the colony of New Netherland was founded. At Leyden the English Pilgrim Fathers decided to pull up stakes, and were discussing where to go; they rejected the Guianas in favor of Northern Virginia (New England), owing to the unpleasant eating habits of the South American Indians that they read about in Dutch books and saw depicted by De Bry. The Seven United Provinces of the Netherlands now spawned a galaxy of scholars, scientists, painters, and sculptors. Amsterdam became the chief money market of Europe. The United East India Company, chartered in 1602 to exploit the Far East, prohibited all who were not members from passing the Cape of Good Hope or sailing through the Strait of Magellan. This prohibition prompted Isaak Le Maire, a merchant of Amsterdam, and Willem Cornelison Schouten of Hoorn, a master mariner who had thrice visited the East Indies, to seek an alternate route, largely at their own expense. That is how Cape Horn happened to be discovered, and named, at this time.

Hoorn, a charming old town right on the Isselmer (the former Zuyder Zee), also furnished the two ships for this expedition: a "great ship called the *Unitie* of 360 tunnes," of which Schouten was master * and chief pilot, and Jacob Le Maire, Isaak's brother, supercargo. She carried 65 men, 19 cannon, plenty of muskets, a sailing pinnace, and a rowing pinnace. Of the "lesser ship" called the *Hoorne* of 110 tuns, "whereof John Cornelison Schouten [Willem's brother] was master," carried 22 men and mounted "eight great Pieces." Note the small total complement of eighty-seven for both ships; this would not have been enough for one Spanish or Portuguese ship of the burthen of *Unitie*. She was very heavily constructed and planked with "two thicke Plankes of greene [wood] and one of Oken wood." Other nations, too, were trying experiments to baffle the teredo. Henri IV of France, ordering a fleet of thirty large vessels to be constructed for his Compagnie des Indes, prescribed that they not only be double-planked but have a layer of German felt (which was said to make teredos sick) between the two sheathings, and cover everything below the waterline with brass plates.

---

* The English and Dutch at this time adopted the practice that still prevails in their merchant navies, of calling commanders of merchantment *Master*, reserving *Captain* for a military commander.

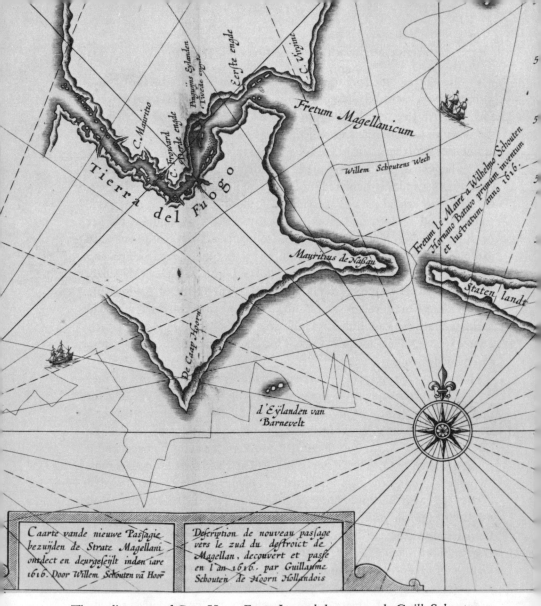

The earliest map of Cape Horn. From *Journal du voyage de Guill. Schouten dans les Indes* (Paris, 1618). Courtesy Harvard College Library.

On 14 June 1615 they sailed from the Texel. Rations were set at "a Can * of Beere a day, foure pound of Bisket, and halfe a pound of Butter (besides sweet Suet) a weeke, and five Cheeses for the whole Voyage." No Hollander could sail without cheese! They followed what seems to have been the favorite Dutch route, sailing from the Cape Verde Islands along the coast of Guinea. At Sierra Leone they loaded 750 ripe lemons which they dried. These probably explain the absence of scurvy on this voyage.

Schouten and Le Maire did not take the quickest route to cross the Atlantic Narrows. On 4 September they departed Sierra Leone, and two months later sighted Ascension Island but did not call, finding their compasses to vary 12 degrees easterly. This variation increased to 17 degrees on 21 November, day of new moon, when they thought they were nearing Brazil; but they skipped Brazil and made land as planned, on 7 December, at Port Desire. That Patagonian harbor seems to have had a lot of traffic at this era—no wonder Sir John Narborough wished to seize it for England! There they "tooke great muscles and other fish," including sixteen-inch smelt, and made the usual raid on the seemingly inexhaustible penguin island. There *Unitie* had a narrow escape, dragging ashore under the cliffs and falling on her beam ends at low water; but they floated her free with slight damage, thanks to the triple planking. Unfortunately a few days later *Hoorne* was lost by fire, owing to the men's carelessness in graving her.

On 24 January 1616, sailing far beyond Cape Virgins, at latitude calculated as 54°46' S, *Unitie* sighted an opening and sailed through, seeing penguins innumerable "and thousands of Whales, so that we were forced to looke well about us, and to winde and turne to shunne the Whales." This strait they named Le Maire, and the big island on the port hand, Staten Island after the States General, the governing body of the United Provinces.** There also they saw plenty of albatross, which they called "great Sea-mewes, bigger of body than Swannes, their wings beeing spread abroad, each of them above a fathome long." Sailing southwest, on 29 January 1616, *Unitie* passed a "high hilly land, covered over with snow, ending with a sharpe point, which we called Cape Horne." And that it still is. From their map and this text it is evident that the channel between Cape Horn and Tierra del

* Not a modern beer can but a small mug, containing about half a pint.
** They found the latitude to be 57°48'; it is actually 55°50'.

Fuego was shrouded in fog, so the Dutch discoverers never knew that it was an island.

Two more degrees south they sailed, until on 12 February Schouten calculated that they were west of the Strait of Magellan, and the master issued to all hands three cups of wine to celebrate.

Schouten did well to accent the discovery of Cape Horn, because for ocean-borne commerce it was the most important discovery since that of the Strait of Magellan. His statement that his mariners had there "endured much trouble, miserie and disease" was a harbinger of what old "Cape Stiff" would mean to sailors. But I must refer my readers to Alan Villiers's and Richard Hough's books to learn the history of ships battling their way around it. Equally to Schouten's credit is the fact that eighty-five "sound men" out of eighty-seven were still alive when they reached Java. One of the two or three who died was Jacob Le Maire.

To pursue *Unitie* further would be an anticlimax. She sighted the Juan Fernández Islands, picked up Puka Puka, the first of Magellan's *islas infortunatas*, discovered a number of other mid-Pacific islands, visited the Spice Islands, and had no trouble until she reached Bantam, Java. This had become an important factory of the Dutch East India Company and was ruled by the Very Magnificent Jan Pieterzoon Coen. Although he too was a Hoorn man, he refused to listen to any explanation of how Schouten got there by a new route, and on 2 November 1616 he confiscated ship and cargo. The officers and men were repatriated in two Dutch ships and reached home 7 July 1617. "And so performed our Voyage in two years, and eighteene dayes."

Thus, Schouten barely escaped jail, the usual reward for discoverers of America, and we are glad to relate that he found justice in Dutch courts. He sued Governor Coen for damages and recovered the value of *Unitie*, the first European ship to sail through the Strait of Le Maire and around Cape Horn into the great South Sea.

Here, reader, I beg to take leave. We have traversed together the first century and a quarter of European discovery of America—an era that we might call the Epiphany to Columbus's Nativity. During this stretch of 125 years, the New World gradually revealed its borders, and even part of its vast interior, to a series of magi, the robust explorers and mariners of five nations. By 1616, when Schouten and

Cape Horn, taken from *Wander Bird*, by her master Captain Warwick Tompkins, December 1936. She was the last American vessel to round the Horn under sail alone. Courtesy of Captain Warwick Tompkins.

Le Maire rounded Cape Horn, the entire hemisphere from Baffin Bay south and around to the Oregon coast had been visited by these new Gentiles; and no West European any longer doubted that this was indeed a New World separated from Asia by the mighty Pacific.

What a pageant! Columbus on his First Voyage pierced the ages-old ocean barrier between the Old World and the New; a voyage that can never be duplicated for vitality and interest. Then John Cabot broke the ice in Newfoundland where the Portuguese, French, and English created codfish empires. In the South, a multitude of sailor pioneers—Ojeda, Bastidas, La Cosa, Niño, the Guerras, Balboa—closed the gaps between Columbus's discoveries; Ponce de León discovered Florida; Ayllon, Gómez, and Verrazzano swept up the coast between

Florida and Newfoundland, Pinzón and Cabral inaugurated the six-teenth century by discovering Brazil, and Coelho with Vespucci as self-appointed navigator explored the long Brazilian coast.

Magellan, starting in 1519, made the greatest sailing voyage of all time by discovering and threading the "strait that shall forever bear his name" and crossing the Pacific, only to throw away his life in the Philippines, leaving Elcano to complete the planned circumnavigation with eighteen survivors. Several Portuguese navigators and Sebastian Cabot explored the River Plate, a watery network penetrating the Southern Continent, where the Spaniards had to construct shoal-draft bergantinas and contend with famine and hostile natives as well as shoals and rapids. Cabeza de Vaca, after walking across Texas, traversed Brazil on foot to reach the Paraná and the Paraguay, but never found the fabled Rey Blanco; and, after vainly trying to enforce Puritan morals in Asunción, ended in a Spanish jail. Equally amazing are the early maritime exploits of Spaniards on the west coast, especially those of Ladrillero and Sarmiento de Gamboa who explored the intricate sounds of southern Chile and threaded the great Strait from west to east.

Francis Drake, after a record passage through the Strait of Magel-lan and making a new furthest south, erupted into what sailors still called the South Sea, and continued home around the world. Cavendish made a brisk circumnavigation, but succumbed on his next voyage. With him sailed John Davis who had already made a record furthest north at Hope Sanderson, Greenland (latitude 72°46′ N), and now at-tained latitude 54° S at the Strait of Magellan, returning to Ireland with so few men surviving that his ship *Dainty* had to drift into harbor. His experiences were little more severe than those of most mariners on these voyages; not one in four of those who gaily set forth from Europe ever returned home. But so robust and persistent were the mariners in this century of their Epiphany that they laid the founda-tions of four great empires—French and English in the north, Spanish and Portuguese in the south. Thus, the new century opened on a note of expectation which was fully realized with the founding of new colonies, the intensive development of Mexico, Peru, and the Antilles, the discovery of Australia, New Zealand, and myriad Pacific islands, and the opening of trading relations with China and Japan. Camoëns's proud claim for Portugal we may extend to each of her rival nations:

Dominions in AMERICA she has;
And, were there more *Worlds*, Thither she would pass.*

All this with no other motive power than sail and oar.

Santa Maria, Niña, Trinidad, Victoria, Concepción, Golden Hind, Dainty, Unitie, and fifty more, we salute you and the shipwrights who built and rigged you. Slow, clumsy, crowded, and like as not ill found, you carried our pioneer mariners to the ends of the earth centuries before men learned to wring power from the earth's stored minerals.

Let us not forget that this century was also an Epiphany in the religious sense; the main conception and aim of Columbus, to carry the Word of God and knowledge of His Son to the far corners of the globe, became a fact: Christ had been made manifest to a new race of Gentiles. By 1615 the Christian Mass was being celebrated in hundreds of churches from the St. Lawrence through the Antilles to the River Plate, and along the west coast from Valdivia to Lower California. To the people of this New World, pagans expecting short and brutish lives, void of hope for any future, had come the Christian vision of a merciful God and a glorious Heaven. And from the decks of ships traversing the two great oceans and exploring the distant verges of the earth, prayers arose like clouds of incense to the Holy Trinity and to Mary, Queen of the Sea.

Thus, having accomplished my purpose to tell the story of every important voyage of American discovery from Columbus through Schouten, I say farewell to my readers young and old, wishing them, in the words of Captain John Smith, "a flown sheate, a faire winde and a boune voyage" to wheresoever they may wish to sail.

Bibliography and Notes

Original narratives, in translation, of all voyages covered by this chapter, were published by Hakluyt's successor Samuel Purchas in *Purchas His Pilgrimes* (1625, MacLehose ed., II (1905), 187–284.

The Schouten narrative was first published at Amsterdam in 1618 as *Journal ofte Beschryvinghe van de wonderlicke reyse ghedaen door Willem Cornelisz Schouten van Hoorne, in de Jaren 1615, 1616, en 1617 . . .* , by Willem Jansz, and Jansz also brought out a French translation, *Journal ou Description du merveilleux voyage de Guilliaume Schouten*, the same year.

* *Lusiads*, VII, 14, Richard Fanshawe translation.

And another, *Journal ou Relation exacte du voyage . . . dans les Indes par un nouveau destroit*, came out in Paris (chez M. Gobert) in 1618. Madrid, next year, brought out a Spanish translation, *Relación diaria del viage de Iacobo Demayre y Guillalmo Cornelis Schouten;* and there is a Latin translation, too, *Novi Freti a parte Meridionali freti Magallanici* (Amsterdam, 1619). The English translation by William Philip, *The Relation of a Wonderfull Voiage made by William Cornelison Schouten of Horne, Shewing how South from the Straights of Magelan in Terra Del-fuogo; he found and discovered a newe passage through the great South Sea*, printed in London, 1619, was reprinted in *Purchas His Pilgrimes*, MacLehose ed., II (1905), 232–84, as *The Sixth Circum-Navigation, by William Cornelison Schouten of Horne;* also as an appendix to the facsimile edition of Fletcher's *World Encompassed by Sir Francis Drake* (Cleveland, 1966; this facsimile is accompanied by an historical introduction by A. L. Rowse).

The reference to Henri IV's double-planked fleet is in Charles de La Roncière, *Histoire de la marine française*, IV (Paris, 1910), 272. I doubt whether these orders were ever carried out.

The Alan J. Villiers books that I particularly recommend are *By Way of Cape Horn* and *The War with Cape Horn* (New York, 1971). Richard Hough's is *The Blind Horn's Hate* (New York, 1971). But I still think that the best narrative of a beat around Cape Horn without benefit of auxiliary, radio, or any modern gadget, is that of my old friend and shipmate Warwick M. Tompkins, *Fifty South to Fifty South, the Story of a Voyage West Around Cape Horn in the Schooner Wander Bird* (New York, 1938).

The eminent Portuguese historian Armando Cortesão, with whom I have had a good-natured controversy over the alleged "policy of secrecy" for some thirty-five years, sent to me, after I had gone to press, his latest book *The Mystery of Vasco de Gama* (Coimbra, 1973), which gives the last word on secret voyages, and much more.

List of Illustrations

Maps

Drawn by Vaughn Gray

743

Index